Letters to His Son, Complete

Earl of Philip Dormer Stanhope Chesterfield

SPECIAL INTRODUCTION

The proud Lord Chesterfield would have turned in his grave had he known that he was to go down to posterity as a teacher and preacher of the gospel of not grace, but—"the graces, the graces, the graces." Natural gifts, social status, open opportunities, and his ambition, all conspired to destine him for high statesmanship. If anything was lacking in his qualifications, he had the pluck and good sense to work hard and persistently until the deficiency was made up. Something remained lacking, and not all his consummate mastery of arts could conceal that conspicuous want,—the want of heart.

Teacher and preacher he assuredly is, and long will be, yet no thanks are his due from a posterity of the common people whom he so sublimely despised. His pious mission was not to raise the level of the multitude, but to lift a single individual upon a pedestal so high that his lowly origin should not betray itself. That individual was his, Lord Chesterfield's, illegitimate son, whose inferior blood should be given the true blue hue by concentrating upon him all the externals of aristocratic education.

Never had pupil so devoted, persistent, lavish, and brilliant a guide, philosopher, and friend, for the parental relation was shrewdly merged in these. Never were devotion and uphill struggle against doubts of success more bitterly repaid. Philip Stanhope was born in 1732, when his father was thirty-eight. He absorbed readily enough the solids of the ideal education supplied him, but, by perversity of fate, he cared not a fig for "the graces, the graces, the graces," which his father so wisely deemed by far the superior qualities to be cultivated by the budding courtier and statesman. A few years of minor services to his country were rendered, though Chesterfield was breaking his substitute for a heart because his son could not or would not play the superfine gentleman—on the paternal model, and then came the news of his death, when only thirty-six. What was a still greater shock to the lordly father, now deaf, gouty, fretful, and at outs with the world, his informant reported that she had been secretly married for several years to Young Hopeful, and was left penniless with two boys. Lord Chesterfield was above all things a practical philosopher, as hard and as exquisitely rounded and polished as a granite column. He accepted the vanishing of his lifelong dream with the admirable stolidity of a fatalist, and in those last days of his radically artificial life he disclosed a welcome tenderness, a touch of the divine, none the less so for being common duty, shown in the few brief letters to his son's widow and to "our boys." This, and his enviable gift of being able to view the downs as well as the ups of life in the consoling humorous light, must modify the sterner judgment so easily passed upon his characteristic inculcation, if not practice, of heartlessness.

The thirteenth-century mother church in the town from which Lord Chesterfield's title came has a peculiar steeple, graceful in its lines, but it points askew, from whatever quarter it is seen. The writer of these Letters, which he never dreamed would be published, is the best self-portrayed Gentleman in literature. In everything he was naturally a stylist, perfected by assiduous art, yet the graceful steeple is somehow warped out of the beauty of the perpendicular. His ideal Gentleman is the frigid product of a rigid mechanical drill, with the mien of a posture master, the skin-deep graciousness of a French Marechal, the calculating adventurer who cuts unpretentious worthies to toady to society magnates, who affects the supercilious air of a shallow dandy and cherishes the heart of a frog. True, he repeatedly insists on the obligation of truthfulness in all things, and of, honor in dealing with the world. His Gentleman may; nay, he must, sail with the stream, gamble in moderation if it is the fashion, must stoop to wear ridiculous clothes and ornaments if they are the mode, though despising his weakness all to himself, and no true Gentleman could afford to keep out of the little gallantries which so effectively advertised him as a man of spirit sad charm. Those repeated injunctions of honor are to be the rule, subject to these exceptions, which transcend the common proprieties when the subject is the rising young gentleman of the period and his goal social success. If an undercurrent of shady morality is traceable in this Chesterfieldian philosophy it must, of course, be explained away by the less perfect moral standard of his period as compared with that of our day. Whether this holds strictly true of men may be open to discussion, but his lordship's worldly instructions as to the utility of women as stepping-stones to favor in high places are equally at variance with the principles he so impressively inculcates and with modern conceptions of social honor. The externals of good breeding cannot be over-estimated, if honestly come by, nor is it necessary to examine too deeply into the prime motives of those who urge them upon a generation in whose eyes matter is more important than manner. Superficial refinement is better than none, but the Chesterfield pulpit cannot afford to shirk the duty of proclaiming loud and far that the only courtesy worthy of respect is that 'politesse de coeur,' the politeness of the heart, which finds expression in consideration for others as the ruling principle of conduct. This militates to some extent against the assumption of fine airs without the backing of fine behavior, and if it tends to discourage the effort to use others for selfish ends, it nevertheless pays better in the long run.

Chesterfield's frankness in so many confessions of sharp practice almost merits his canonization as a minor saint of society. Dr. Johnson has indeed placed him on a Simeon Stylites pillar, an immortality of penance from which no good member of the writers' guild is likely to pray his deliverance. He commends the fine art and high science of dissimulation with the gusto of an apostle and the authority of an expert. Dissimulate, but do not simulate, disguise your real sentiments, but do not falsify them. Go through the world with your eyes and ears open and mouth mostly shut. When new or stale gossip is brought to you, never let on that you know it already, nor that it really interests you. The reading of these Letters is better than hearing the average comedy, in which the wit of a single sentence of Chesterfield suffices to carry an act. His man-of-the-world philosophy is as old as the Proverbs of Solomon, but will always be fresh and true, and enjoyable at any age, thanks to his pithy expression, his unfailing common sense, his sparkling wit and charming humor. This latter gift shows in the seeming lapses from his rigid rule requiring absolute elegance of expression at all times, when an unexpected coarseness, in some provincial colloquialism, crops out with picturesque force. The beau ideal of superfineness occasionally enjoys the bliss of harking back to mother English.

Above all the defects that can be charged against the Letters, there rises the substantial merit of an honest effort to exalt the gentle in woman and man—above the merely genteel. "He that is gentil doeth gentil deeds," runs the mediaeval saying which marks the distinction between the genuine and the sham in behavior. A later age had it thus: "Handsome is as handsome does," and in this larger sense we have agreed to accept the motto of William of Wykeham, which declares that "Manners maketh Man."

OLIVER H. G. LEIGH

1746-1747

LETTER I

EARL OF PHILIP DORMER STANHOPE CHESTERFIELD

BATH, October 9, O. S. 1746

DEAR BOY: Your distresses in your journey from Heidelberg to Schaffhausen, your lying upon straw, your black bread, and your broken 'berline,' are proper seasonings for the greater fatigues and distresses which you must expect in the course of your travels; and, if one had a mind to moralize, one might call them the samples of the accidents, rubs, and difficulties, which every man meets with in his journey through life. In this journey, the understanding is the 'voiture' that must carry you through; and in proportion as that is stronger or weaker, more or less in repair, your journey will be better or worse; though at best you will now and then find some bad roads, and some bad inns. Take care, therefore, to keep that necessary 'voiture' in perfect good repair; examine, improve, and strengthen it every day: it is in the power, and ought to be the care, of every man to do it; he that neglects it, deserves to feel, and certainly will feel, the fatal effects of that negligence.

'A propos' of negligence: I must say something to you upon that subject. You know I have often told you, that my affection for you was not a weak, womanish one; and, far from blinding me, it makes me but more quick-sighted as to your faults; those it is not only my right, but my duty to tell you of; and it is your duty and your interest to correct them. In the strict scrutiny which I have made into you, I have (thank God) hitherto not discovered any vice of the heart, or any peculiar weakness of the head: but I have discovered laziness, inattention, and indifference; faults which are only pardonable in old men, who, in the decline of life, when health and spirits fail, have a kind of claim to that sort of tranquillity. But a young man should be ambitious to shine, and excel; alert, active, and indefatigable in the means of doing it; and, like Caesar, 'Nil actum reputans, si quid superesset agendum.' You seem to want that 'vivida vis animi,' which spurs and excites most young men to please, to shine, to excel. Without the desire and the pains necessary to be considerable, depend upon it, you never can be so; as, without the desire and attention necessary to please, you never can please. 'Nullum numen abest, si sit prudentia,' is unquestionably true, with regard to everything except poetry; and I am very sure that any man of common understanding may, by proper culture, care, attention, and labor, make himself whatever he pleases, except a good poet. Your destination is the great and busy world; your immediate object is the affairs, the interests, and the history, the constitutions, the customs, and the manners of the several parts of Europe. In this, any man of common sense may, by common application, be sure to excel. Ancient and modern history are, by attention, easily attainable. Geography and chronology the same, none of them requiring any uncommon share of genius or invention. Speaking and Writing, clearly, correctly, and with ease and grace, are certainly to be acquired, by reading the best authors with care, and by attention to the best living models. These are the qualifications more particularly necessary for you, in your department, which you may be possessed of, if you please; and which, I tell you fairly, I shall be very angry at you, if you are not; because, as you have the means in your hands, it will be your own fault only.

If care and application are necessary to the acquiring of those qualifications, without which you can never be considerable, nor make a figure in the world, they are not less necessary with regard to the lesser accomplishments, which are requisite to make you agreeable and pleasing in society. In truth, whatever is worth doing at all, is worth doing well; and nothing can be done well without attention: I therefore carry the necessity of attention down to the lowest things, even to dancing and dress. Custom has made dancing sometimes necessary for a young man; therefore mind it while you learn it that you may learn to do it well, and not be ridiculous, though in a ridiculous act. Dress is of the same nature; you must dress; therefore attend to it; not in order to rival or to excel a fop in it, but in order to avoid singularity, and consequently ridicule. Take great care always to be dressed like the reasonable people of your own age, in the place where you are; whose dress is never spoken of one way or another, as either too negligent or too much studied.

What is commonly called an absent man, is commonly either a very weak, or a very affected man; but be he which he will, he is, I am sure, a very disagreeable man in company. He fails in all the common offices of civility; he seems not to know those people to-day, whom yesterday he appeared to live in intimacy with. He takes no part in the general conversation; but, on the contrary, breaks into it from time to time, with some start of his own, as if he waked from a dream. This (as I said before) is a sure indication, either of a mind so weak that it is not able to bear above one object at a time; or so affected, that it would be supposed to be wholly engrossed by, and directed to, some very great and important objects. Sir Isaac Newton, Mr. Locke, and (it may be) five or six more, since the creation of the world, may have had a right to absence, from that intense thought which the things they were investigating required. But if a young man, and a man of the world, who has no such avocations to plead, will claim and exercise that right of absence in company, his pretended right should, in my mind, be turned into an involuntary absence, by his perpetual exclusion out of company. However frivolous a company may be, still, while you are among them, do not show them, by your inattention, that you think them so; but rather take their tone, and conform in some degree to their weakness, instead of manifesting your contempt for them. There is nothing that people bear more impatiently, or forgive less, than contempt; and an injury is much sooner forgotten than an insult. If, therefore, you would rather please than offend, rather be well than ill spoken of, rather be loved than hated; remember to have that constant attention about you which flatters every man's little vanity; and the want of which, by mortifying his pride, never fails to excite his resentment, or at least his ill will. For instance, most people (I might say all people) have their weaknesses; they have their aversions and their likings, to such or such things; so that, if you were to laugh at a man for his aversion to a cat, or cheese (which are common antipathies), or, by inattention and negligence, to let them come in his way, where you could prevent it, he would, in the first case, think himself insulted, and, in the second, slighted, and would remember both. Whereas your care to procure for him what he likes, and to remove from him what he hates, shows him that he is at least an object of your attention; flatters his vanity, and makes him possibly more your friend, than a more important service would have done. With regard to women, attentions still below these are necessary, and, by the custom of the world, in some measure due, according to the laws of good-breeding.

My long and frequent letters, which I send you, in great doubt of their success, put me in mind of certain papers, which you have very lately, and I formerly, sent up to kites, along the string, which we called messengers; some of them the wind used to blow away, others were torn by the string, and but few of them got up and stuck to the kite. But I will content myself now, as I did then, if some of my present messengers do but stick to you. Adieu!

LETTER II

DEAR BOY: You are by this time (I suppose) quite settled and at home at Lausanne; therefore pray let me know how you pass your time there, and what your studies, your amusements, and your acquaintances are. I take it for granted, that you inform yourself daily of the nature of the government and constitution of the Thirteen Cantons; and as I am ignorant of them myself, must apply to you for information. I know the names, but I do not know the nature of some of the most considerable offices there; such as the Avoyers, the Seizeniers, the Banderets, and the Gros Sautier. I desire, therefore, that you will let me know what is the particular business, department, or province of these several magistrates. But as I imagine that there may be some, though, I believe, no essential difference, in the governments of the several Cantons, I would not give you the trouble of informing yourself of each of them; but confine my inquiries, as you may your informations, to the Canton you reside in, that of Berne, which I take to be the principal one. I am not sure whether the Pays de Vaud, where you are, being a conquered country, and taken from the Dukes of Savoy, in the year 1536, has the same share in the government of the Canton, as the German part of it has. Pray inform yourself and me about it.

I have this moment received yours from Berne, of the 2d October, N. S. and also one from Mr. Harte, of the same date, under Mr. Burnaby's cover. I find by the latter, and indeed I thought so before, that some of your letters and some of Mr. Harte's have not reached me. Wherefore, for the future, I desire, that both he and you will direct your letters for me, to be left ches Monsieur Wolters, Agent de S. M. Britanique, a Rotterdam, who will take care to send them to me safe. The reason why you have not received letters either from me or from Grevenkop was that we directed them to Lausanne, where we thought you long ago: and we thought it to no purpose to direct to you upon your ROUTE, where it was little likely that our letters would meet with you. But you have, since your arrival at Lausanne, I believe, found letters enough from me; and it may be more than you have read, at least with attention.

I am glad that you like Switzerland so well; and am impatient to hear how other matters go, after your settlement at Lausanne. God bless you!

LETTER III

LONDON, December 2, O.S. 1746.

DEAR BOY: I have not, in my present situation,—[His Lordship was, in the year 1746, appointed one of his Majesty's secretaries of state.]—time to write to you, either so much or so often as I used, while I was in a place of much more leisure and profit; but my affection for you must not be judged of by the number of my letters; and, though the one lessens, the other, I assure you, does not.

I have just now received your letter of the 25th past, N. S., and, by the former post, one from Mr. Harte; with both which I am very well pleased: with Mr. Harte's, for the good account which he gives me of you; with yours, for the good account which you gave me of what I desired to be informed of. Pray continue to give me further information of the form of government of the country you are now in; which I hope you will know most minutely before you leave it. The inequality of the town of Lausanne seems to be very convenient in this cold weather; because going up hill and down will keep you warm. You say there is a good deal of good company; pray, are you got into it? Have you made acquaintances, and with whom? Let me know some of their names. Do you learn German yet, to read, write, and speak it?

Yesterday, I saw a letter from Monsieur Bochat to a friend of mine; which gave me the greatest pleasure that I have felt this great while; because it gives so very good an account of you. Among other things which Monsieur Bochat says to your advantage, he mentions the tender uneasiness and concern that you showed during my illness, for which (though I will say that you owe it to me) I am obliged to you: sentiments of gratitude not being universal, nor even common. As your affection for me can only proceed from your experience and conviction of my fondness for you (for to talk of natural affection is talking nonsense), the only return I desire is, what it is chiefly your interest to make me; I mean your invariable practice of virtue, and your indefatigable pursuit of knowledge. Adieu! and be persuaded that I shall love you extremely, while you deserve it; but not one moment longer.

LETTER IV

LONDON, December 9, O. S. 1746.

DEAR BOY: Though I have very little time, and though I write by this post to Mr. Harte, yet I cannot send a packet to Lausanne without a word or two to yourself. I thank you for your letter of congratulation which you wrote me, notwithstanding the pain it gave you. The accident that caused the pain was, I presume, owing to that degree of giddiness, of which I have sometimes taken the liberty to speak to you. The post I am now in, though the object of most people's views and desires, was in some degree inflicted upon me; and a certain concurrence of circumstances obliged me to engage in it. But I feel that to go through with it requires more strength of body and mind than I have: were you three or four years older; you should share in my trouble, and I would have taken you into my office; but I hope you will employ these three or four years so well as to make yourself capable of being of use to me, if I should continue in it so long. The reading, writing, and speaking the modern languages correctly; the knowledge of the laws of nations, and the particular constitution of the empire; of history, geography, and chronology, are absolutely necessary to this business, for which I have always intended you. With these qualifications you may very possibly be my successor, though not my immediate one.

I hope you employ your whole time, which few people do; and that you put every moment to, profit of some kind or other. I call company, walking, riding, etc., employing one's time, and, upon proper occasions, very usefully; but what I cannot forgive in anybody is sauntering, and doing nothing at all, with a thing so precious as time, and so irrecoverable when lost.

Are you acquainted with any ladies at Lausanne? and do you behave yourself with politeness enough to make them desire your company?

I must finish: God bless you!

LETTER V

LONDON, February 24, O. S. 1747

SIR: In order that we may, reciprocally, keep up our French, which, for want of practice, we might forget; you will permit me to have the honor of assuring you of my respects in that language: and be so good to answer me in the same. Not that I am apprehensive of your forgetting to speak French: since it is probable that two-thirds of our daily prattle is in that language; and because, if you leave off writing French, you may perhaps neglect that grammatical purity, and accurate orthography, which, in other languages, you excel in; and really, even in French, it is better to write well than ill. However, as this is a language very proper for sprightly, gay subjects, I shall conform to that, and reserve those which are serious for English. I shall not therefore mention to you, at present, your Greek or Latin, your study of the Law of Nature, or the Law of Nations, the Rights of People, or of Individuals; but rather discuss the subject of your Amusements and Pleasures; for, to say the truth, one must have some. May I be permitted to inquire of what nature yours are? Do they consist in little commercial play at cards in good company? are they little agreeable suppers, at which cheerfulness and decency are united? or, do you pay court to some fair one, who requires such attentions as may be of use in contributing to polish you? Make me your confidant upon this subject; you shall not find a severe censor: on the contrary, I wish to obtain the employment of minister to your pleasures: I will point them out, and even contribute to them.

Many young people adopt pleasures, for which they have not the least taste, only because they are called by that name. They often mistake so totally, as to imagine that debauchery is pleasure. You must allow that drunkenness, which is equally destructive to body and mind, is a fine pleasure. Gaming, that draws you into a thousand scrapes, leaves you penniless, and gives you the air and manners of an outrageous madman, is another most exquisite pleasure; is it not? As to running after women, the consequences of that vice are only the loss of one's nose, the total destruction of health, and, not unfrequently, the being run through the body.

These, you see, are all trifles; yet this is the catalogue of pleasures of most of those young people, who never reflecting themselves, adopt, indiscriminately, what others choose to call by the seducing name of pleasure. I am thoroughly persuaded you will not fall into such errors; and that, in the choice of your amusements, you will be directed by reason, and a discerning taste. The true pleasures of a gentleman are those of the table, but within the bound of moderation; good company, that is to say, people of merit; moderate play, which amuses, without any interested views; and sprightly gallant conversations with women of fashion and sense.

These are the real pleasures of a gentleman; which occasion neither sickness, shame, nor repentance. Whatever exceeds them, becomes low vice, brutal passion, debauchery, and insanity of, mind; all of which, far from giving satisfaction, bring on dishonor and disgrace. Adieu.

LETTER VI

LONDON, March 6, O. S. 1747

DEAR BOY: Whatever you do, will always affect me, very sensibly, one way or another; and I am now most agreeably affected, by two letters, which I have lately seen from Lausanne, upon your subject; the one from Madame St. Germain, the other from Monsieur Pampigny: they both give so good an account of you, that I thought myself obliged, in justice both to them and, to you, to let you know it. Those who deserve a good character, ought to have the satisfaction of knowing that they have it, both as a reward and as an encouragement. They write, that you are not only 'decrotte,' but tolerably well-bred; and that the English crust of awkward bashfulness, shyness, and roughness (of which, by the bye, you had your share) is pretty well rubbed off. I am most heartily glad of it; for, as I have often told you, those lesser talents, of an engaging, insinuating manner, an easy good-breeding, a genteel behavior and address, are of infinitely more advantage than they are generally thought to be, especially here in England. Virtue and learning, like gold, have their intrinsic value but if they are not polished, they certainly lose a great deal of their luster; and even polished brass will pass upon more people than rough gold. What a number of sins does the cheerful, easy good-breeding of the French frequently cover? Many of them want common sense, many more common learning; but in general, they make up so much by their manner, for those defects, that frequently they pass undiscovered: I have often said, and do think, that a Frenchman, who, with a fund of virtue, learning and good sense, has the manners and good-breeding of his country, is the perfection of human nature. This perfection you may, if you please, and I hope you will, arrive at. You know what virtue is: you may have it if you will; it is in every man's power; and miserable is the man who has it not. Good sense God has given you. Learning you already possess enough of, to have, in a reasonable time, all that a man need have. With this, you are thrown out early into the world, where it will be your own fault if you do not acquire all, the other accomplishments necessary to complete and adorn your character. You will do well to make your compliments to Madame St. Germain and Monsieur Pampigny; and tell them, how sensible you are of their partiality to you, in the advantageous testimonies which, you are informed, they have given of you here.

Adieu. Continue to deserve such testimonies; and then you will not only deserve, but enjoy my truest affection.

LETTER VII

LONDON, March 27, O. S. 1747.

DEAR BOY: Pleasure is the rock which most young people split upon: they launch out with crowded sails in quest of it, but without a compass to direct their course, or reason sufficient to steer the vessel; for want of which, pain and shame, instead of pleasure, are the returns of their voyage. Do not think that I mean to snarl at pleasure, like a Stoic, or to preach against it, like a parson; no, I mean to point it out, and recommend it to you, like an Epicurean: I wish you a great deal; and my only view is to hinder you from mistaking it.

The character which most young men first aim at, is that of a man of pleasure; but they generally take it upon trust; and instead of consulting their own taste and inclinations, they blindly adopt whatever those with whom they chiefly converse, are pleased to call by the name of pleasure; and a man of pleasure in the vulgar acceptation of that phrase, means only, a beastly drunkard, an abandoned whoremaster, and a profligate swearer and curser. As it may be of use to you, I am not unwilling, though at the same time ashamed to own, that the vices of my youth proceeded much more from my silly resolution of being, what I heard called a man of pleasure, than from my own inclinations. I always naturally hated drinking; and yet I have often drunk; with disgust at the time, attended by great sickness the next day, only because I then considered drinking as a necessary qualification for a fine gentleman, and a man of pleasure.

The same as to gaming. I did not want money, and consequently had no occasion to play for it; but I thought play another necessary ingredient in the composition of a man of pleasure, and accordingly I plunged into it without desire, at first; sacrificed a thousand real pleasures to it; and made myself solidly uneasy by it, for thirty the best years of my life.

I was even absurd enough, for a little while, to swear, by way of adorning and completing the shining character which I affected; but this folly I soon laid aside, upon finding berth the guilt and the indecency of it.

Thus seduced by fashion, and blindly adopting nominal pleasures, I lost real ones; and my fortune impaired, and my constitution shattered, are, I must confess, the just punishment of my errors.

Take warning then by them: choose your pleasures for yourself, and do not let them be imposed upon you. Follow nature and not fashion: weigh the present enjoyment of your pleasures against the necessary consequences of them, and then let your own common sense determine your choice.

Were I to begin the world again, with the experience which I now have of it, I would lead a life of real, not of imaginary pleasures. I would enjoy the pleasures of the table, and of wine; but stop short of the pains inseparably annexed to an excess of either. I would not, at twenty years, be a preaching missionary of abstemiousness and sobriety; and I should let other people do as they would, without formally and sententiously rebuking them for it; but I would be most firmly resolved not to destroy my own faculties and constitution; in complaisance to those who have no regard to their own. I would play to give me pleasure, but not to give me pain; that is, I would play for trifles, in mixed companies, to amuse myself, and conform to custom; but I would take care not to venture for sums; which, if I won, I should not be the better for; but, if I lost, should be under a difficulty to pay: and when paid, would oblige me to retrench in several other articles. Not to mention the quarrels which deep play commonly occasions.

I would pass some of my time in reading, and the rest in the company of people of sense and learning, and chiefly those above me; and I would frequent the mixed companies of men and women of fashion, which, though often frivolous, yet they unbend and refresh the mind, not uselessly, because they certainly polish and soften the manners.

These would be my pleasures and amusements, if I were to live the last thirty years over again; they are rational ones; and, moreover, I will tell you, they are really the fashionable ones; for the others are not, in truth, the pleasures of what I call people of fashion, but of those who only call themselves so. Does good company care to have a man reeling drunk among them? Or to see another tearing his hair, and blaspheming, for having lost, at play, more than he is able to pay? Or a whoremaster with half a nose, and crippled by coarse and infamous debauchery? No; those who practice, and much more those who brag of them, make no part of good company; and are most unwillingly, if ever, admitted into it. A real man of fashion and pleasures observes decency: at least neither borrows nor affects vices: and if he unfortunately has any, he gratifies them with choice, delicacy, and secrecy.

I have not mentioned the pleasures of the mind (which are the solid and permanent ones); because they do not come under the head of what people commonly call pleasures; which they seem to confine to the senses. The pleasure of virtue, of charity, and of learning is true and lasting pleasure; with which I hope you will be well and long acquainted. Adieu!

LETTER VIII

LONDON, April 3, O. S. 1747

DEAR BOY: If I am rightly informed, I am now writing to a fine gentleman, in a scarlet coat laced with gold, a brocade waistcoat, and all other suitable ornaments. The natural partiality of every author for his own works makes me very glad to hear that Mr. Harte has thought this last edition of mine worth so fine a binding; and, as he has bound it in red, and gilt it upon the back, I hope he will take care that it shall be LETTERED too. A showish binding attracts the eyes, and engages the attention of everybody; but with this difference, that women, and men who are like women, mind the binding more than the book; whereas men of sense and learning immediately examine the inside; and if they find that it does not answer the finery on the outside, they throw it by with the greater indignation and contempt. I hope that, when this edition of my works shall be opened and read, the best judges will find connection, consistency, solidity, and spirit in it. Mr. Harte may 'recensere' and 'emendare,' as much as he pleases; but it will be to little purpose, if you do not cooperate with him. The work will be imperfect.

I thank you for your last information of our success in the Mediterranean, and you say very rightly that a secretary of state ought to be well informed. I hope, therefore, you will take care that I shall. You are near the busy scene in Italy; and I doubt not but that, by frequently looking at the map, you have all that theatre of the war very perfect in your mind.

I like your account of the salt works; which shows that you gave some attention while you were seeing them. But notwithstanding that, by your account, the Swiss salt is (I dare say) very good, yet I am apt to suspect that it falls a little short of the true Attic salt in which there was a peculiar quickness and delicacy. That same Attic salt seasoned almost all Greece, except Boeotia, and a great deal of it was exported afterward to Rome, where it was counterfeited by a composition called Urbanity, which in some time was brought to very near the perfection of the original Attic salt. The more you are powdered with these two kinds of salt, the better you will keep, and the more you will be relished.

Adieu! My compliments to Mr. Harte and Mr. Eliot.

LETTER IX

LONDON, April 14, O. S. 1747.

DEAR BOY: If you feel half the pleasure from the consciousness of doing well, that I do from the informations I have lately received in your favor from Mr. Harte, I shall have little occasion to exhort or admonish you any more to do what your own satisfaction and self love will sufficiently prompt you to. Mr. Harte tells me that you attend, that you apply to your studies; and that beginning to understand, you begin to taste them. This pleasure will increase, and keep pace with your attention; so that the balance will be greatly to your advantage. You may remember, that I have always earnestly recommended to you, to do what you are about, be that what it will; and to do nothing else at the same time. Do not imagine that I mean by this, that you should attend to and plod at your book all day long; far from it; I mean that you should have your pleasures too; and that you should attend to them for the time; as much as to your studies; and, if you do not attend equally to both, you will neither have improvement nor satisfaction from either. A man is fit for neither business nor pleasure, who either cannot, or does not, command and direct his attention to the present object, and, in some degree, banish for that time all other objects from his thoughts. If at a ball, a supper, or a party of pleasure, a man were to be solving, in his own mind, a problem in Euclid, he would be a very bad companion, and make a very poor figure in that company; or if, in studying a problem in his closet, he were to think of a minuet, I am apt to believe that he would make a very poor mathematician. There is time enough for everything, in the course of the day, if you do but one thing at once; but there is not time enough in the year, if you will do two things at a time. The Pensionary de Witt, who was torn to pieces in the year 1672, did the whole business of the Republic, and yet had time left to go to assemblies in the evening, and sup in company. Being asked how he could possibly find time to go through so much business, and yet amuse himself in the evenings as he did, he answered, there was nothing so easy; for that it was only doing one thing at a time, and never putting off anything till to-morrow that could be done to-day. This steady and undissipated attention to one object is a sure mark of a superior genius; as hurry, bustle, and agitation are the never-failing symptoms of a weak and frivolous mind. When you read Horace, attend to the justness of his thoughts, the happiness of his diction, and the beauty of his poetry; and do not think of Puffendorf de Homine el Cive; and, when you are reading Puffendorf, do not think of Madame de St. Germain; nor of Puffendorf, when you are talking to Madame de St. Germain.

Mr. Harte informs me, that he has reimbursed you of part of your losses in Germany; and I consent to his reimbursing you of the whole, now that I know you deserve it. I shall grudge you nothing, nor shall you want anything that you desire, provided you deserve it; so that you see, it is in your own power to have whatever you please.

There is a little book which you read here with Monsieur Codere entitled, 'Maniere de bien penser dans les Ouvrages d'Esprit,' written by Pyre Bonhours. I wish you would read this book again at your leisure hours, for it will not only divert you, but likewise form your taste, and give you a just manner of thinking. Adieu!

LETTER X

LONDON, June 30, O. S. 1747

DEAR BOY: I was extremely pleased with the account which you gave me in your last, of the civilities that you received in your Swiss progress; and I have written, by this post, to Mr. Burnaby, and to the 'Avoyer,' to thank them for their parts. If the attention you met with pleased you, as I dare say it did, you will, I hope, draw this general conclusion from it, that attention and civility please all those to whom they are paid; and that you will please others in proportion as you are attentive and civil to them.

Bishop Burnet has wrote his travels through Switzerland; and Mr. Stanyan, from a long residence there, has written the best account, yet extant, of the Thirteen Cantons; but those books will be read no more, I presume, after you shall have published your account of that country. I hope you will favor me with one of the first copies. To be serious; though I do not desire that you should immediately turn author, and oblige the world with your travels; yet, wherever you go, I would have you as curious and inquisitive as if you did intend to write them. I do not mean that you should give yourself so much trouble, to know the number of houses, inhabitants, signposts, and tombstones, of every town that you go through; but that you should inform yourself, as well as your stay will permit you, whether the town is free, or to whom it belongs, or in what manner: whether it has any peculiar privileges or customs; what trade or manufactures; and such other particulars as people of sense desire to know. And there would be no manner of harm if you were to take memorandums of such things in a paper book to help your memory. The only way of knowing all these things is to keep the best company, who can best inform you of them. I am just now called away; so good night.

LETTER XI

LONDON, July 20, O. S. 1747

DEAR BOY: In your Mamma's letter, which goes here inclosed, you will find one from my sister, to thank you for the Arquebusade water which you sent her; and which she takes very kindly. She would not show me her letter to you; but told me that it contained good wishes and good advice; and, as I know she will show your letter in answer to hers, I send you here inclosed the draught of the letter which I would have you write to her. I hope you will not be offended at my offering you my assistance upon this occasion; because, I presume, that as yet, you are not much used to write to ladies. 'A propos' of letter-writing, the best models that you can form yourself upon are, Cicero, Cardinal d'Ossat, Madame Sevigne, and Comte Bussy Rebutin. Cicero's Epistles to Atticus, and to his familiar friends, are the best examples that you can imitate, in the friendly and the familiar style. The simplicity and the clearness of Cardinal d'Ossat's letters show how letters of business ought to be written; no affected turns, no attempts at wit, obscure or perplex his matter; which is always plainly and clearly stated, as business always should be. For gay and amusing letters, for 'enjouement and badinage,' there are none that equal Comte Bussy's and Madame Sevigne's. They are so natural, that they seem to be the extempore conversations of two people of wit, rather, than letters which are commonly studied, though they ought not to be so. I would advise you to let that book be one in your itinerant library; it will both amuse and inform you.

I have not time to add any more now; so good night.

LETTER XII

LONDON, July 30, O. S. 1747

DEAR BOY: It is now four posts since I have received any letter, either from you or from Mr. Harte. I impute this to the rapidity of your travels through Switzerland; which I suppose are by this time finished.

You will have found by my late letters, both to you and Mr. Harte, that you are to be at Leipsig by next Michaelmas; where you will be lodged in the house of Professor Mascow, and boarded in the neighborhood of it, with some young men of fashion. The professor will read you lectures upon 'Grotius de Jure Belli et Pacis,' the 'Institutes of Justinian' and the 'Jus Publicum Imperii;' which I expect that you shall not only hear, but attend to, and retain. I also expect that you make yourself perfectly master of the German language; which you may very soon do there, if you please. I give you fair warning, that at Leipsig I shall have an hundred invisible spies about you; and shall be exactly informed of everything that you do, and of almost everything that you say. I hope that, in consequence of those minute informations, I may be able to say of you, what Velleius Paterculus says of Scipio; that in his whole life, 'nihil non laudandum aut dixit, aut fecit, aut sensit.' There is a great deal of good company in Leipsig, which I would have you frequent in the evenings, when the studies of the day are over. There is likewise a kind of court kept there, by a Duchess Dowager of Courland; at which you should get introduced. The King of Poland and his Court go likewise to the fair at Leipsig twice a year; and I shall write to Sir Charles Williams, the king's minister there, to have you presented, and introduced into good company. But I must remind you, at the same time, that it will be to a very little purpose for you to frequent good company, if you do not conform to, and learn their manners; if you are not attentive to please, and well bred, with the easiness of a man of fashion. As you must attend to your manners, so you must not neglect your person; but take care to be very clean, well dressed, and genteel; to have no disagreeable attitudes, nor awkward tricks; which many people use themselves to, and then cannot leave them off. Do you take care to keep your teeth very clean, by washing them constantly every morning, and after every meal? This is very necessary, both to preserve your teeth a great while, and to save you a great deal of pain. Mine have plagued me long, and are now falling out, merely from want of care when I was your age. Do you dress well, and not too well? Do you consider your air and manner of presenting yourself enough, and not too much? Neither negligent nor stiff? All these things deserve a degree of care, a second-rate attention; they give an additional lustre to real merit. My Lord Bacon says, that a pleasing figure is a perpetual letter of recommendation. It is certainly an agreeable forerunner of merit, and smoothes the way for it.

Remember that I shall see you at Hanover next summer, and shall expect perfection; which if I do not meet with, or at least something very near it, you and I shall, not be very well together. I shall dissect and analyze you with a microscope; so that I shall discover the least speck or blemish. This is fair warning; therefore take your measures accordingly. Yours.

LETTER XIII

LONDON, August 21, O. S. 1747.

DEAR BOY: I reckon that this letter has but a bare chance of finding you at Lausanne; but I was resolved to risk it, as it is the last that I shall write to you till you are settled at Leipsig. I sent you by the last post, under cover to Mr. Harte, a letter of recommendation to one of the first people at Munich; which you will take care to present to him in the politest manner; he will certainly have you presented to the electoral family; and I hope you will go through that ceremony with great respect, good breeding, and ease. As this is the first court that ever you will have been at, take care to inform yourself if there be any particular, customs or forms to be observed, that you may not commit any mistake. At Vienna men always make courtesies, instead of bows, to the emperor; in France nobody bows at all to the king, nor kisses his hand; but in Spain and England, bows are made, and hands are kissed. Thus every court has some peculiarity or other, of which those who go to them ought previously to inform themselves, to avoid blunders and awkwardnesses.

I have not time to say any more now, than to wish you good journey to Leipsig; and great attention, both there and in going there. Adieu.

LETTER XIV

LONDON, September 21, O. S. 1747

DEAR BOY: I received, by the last post, your letter of the 8th, N. S., and I do not wonder that you are surprised at the credulity and superstition of the Papists at Einsiedlen, and at their absurd stories of their chapel. But remember, at the same time, that errors and mistakes, however gross, in matters of opinion, if they are sincere, are to be pitied, but not punished nor laughed at. The blindness of the understanding is as much to be pitied as the blindness of the eye; and there is neither jest nor guilt in a man's losing his way in either case. Charity bids us set him right if we can, by arguments and persuasions; but charity, at the same time, forbids, either to punish or ridicule his misfortune. Every man's reason is, and must be, his guide; and I may as well expect that every man should be of my size and complexion, as that he should reason just as I do. Every man seeks for truth; but God only knows who has found it. It is, therefore, as unjust to persecute, as it is absurd to ridicule, people for those several opinions, which they cannot help entertaining upon the conviction of their reason. It is the man who tells, or who acts a lie, that is guilty, and not he who honestly and sincerely believes the lie. I really know nothing more criminal, more mean, and more ridiculous than lying. It is the production either of malice, cowardice, or vanity; and generally misses of its aim in every one of these views; for lies are always detected sooner or later. If I tell a malicious lie, in order to affect any man's fortune or character, I may indeed injure him for some time; but I shall be sure to be the greatest sufferer myself at last; for as soon as ever I am detected (and detected I most certainly shall be), I am blasted for the infamous attempt; and whatever is said afterward, to the disadvantage of that person, however true, passes for calumny. If I lie, or equivocate (for it is the same thing), in order to excuse myself for something that I have said or done, and to avoid the danger and the shame that I apprehend from it, I discover at once my fear as well as my falsehood; and only increase, instead of avoiding, the danger and the shame; I show myself to be the lowest and the meanest of mankind, and am sure to be always treated as such. Fear, instead of avoiding, invites danger; for concealed cowards will insult known ones. If one has had the misfortune to be in the wrong, there is something noble in frankly owning it; it is the only way of atoning for it, and the only way of being forgiven. Equivocating, evading, shuffling, in order to remove a present danger or inconveniency, is something so mean, and betrays so much fear, that whoever practices them always deserves to be, and often will be kicked. There is another sort of lies, inoffensive enough in themselves, but wonderfully ridiculous; I mean those lies which a mistaken vanity suggests, that defeat the very end for which they are calculated, and terminate in the humiliation and confusion of their author, who is sure to be detected. These are chiefly narrative and historical lies, all intended to do infinite honor to their author. He is always the hero of his own romances; he has been in dangers from which nobody but himself ever escaped; he has seen with his own eyes, whatever other people have heard or read of: he has had more 'bonnes fortunes' than ever he knew women; and has ridden more miles post in one day, than ever courier went in two. He is soon discovered, and as soon becomes the object of universal contempt and ridicule. Remember, then, as long as you live, that nothing but strict truth can carry you through the world, with either your conscience or your honor unwounded. It is not only your duty, but your interest; as a proof of which you may always observe, that the greatest fools are the greatest liars. For my own part, I judge of every man's truth by his degree of understanding.

This letter will, I suppose, find you at Leipsig; where I expect and require from you attention and accuracy, in both which you have hitherto been very deficient. Remember that I shall see you in the summer; shall examine you most narrowly; and will never forget nor forgive those faults, which it has been in your own power to prevent or cure; and be assured that I have many eyes upon you at Leipsig, besides Mr. Harte's.
Adieu!

LETTER XV

LONDON, October 2, O. S. 1747

DEAR BOY: By your letter of the 18th past, N. S., I find that you are a tolerably good landscape painter, and can present the several views of Switzerland to the curious. I am very glad of it, as it is a proof of some attention; but I hope you will be as good a portrait painter, which is a much more noble science. By portraits, you will easily judge, that I do not mean the outlines and the coloring of the human figure; but the inside of the heart and mind of man. This science requires more attention, observation, and penetration, than the other; as indeed it is infinitely more useful. Search, therefore, with the greatest care, into the characters of those whom you converse with; endeavor to discover their predominant passions, their prevailing weaknesses, their vanities, their follies, and their humors, with all the right and wrong, wise and silly springs of human actions, which make such inconsistent and whimsical beings of us rational creatures. A moderate share of penetration, with great attention, will infallibly make these necessary discoveries. This is the true knowledge of the world; and the world is a country which nobody ever yet knew by description; one must travel through it one's self to be acquainted with it. The scholar, who in the dust of his closet talks or writes of the world, knows no more of it, than that orator did of war, who judiciously endeavored to instruct Hannibal in it. Courts and camps are the only places to learn the world in. There alone all kinds of characters resort, and human nature is seen in all the various shapes and modes, which education, custom, and habit give it; whereas, in all other places, one local mode generally prevails, and producing a seeming though not a real sameness of character. For example, one general mode distinguishes an university, another a trading town, a third a seaport town, and so on; whereas, at a capital, where the Prince or the Supreme Power resides, some of all these various modes are to be seen and seen in action too, exerting their utmost skill in pursuit of their several objects. Human nature is the same all over the world; but its operations are so varied by education and habit, that one must see it in all its dresses in order to be intimately acquainted with it. The passion of ambition, for instance, is the same in a courtier, a soldier, or an ecclesiastic; but, from their different educations and habits, they will take very different methods to gratify it. Civility, which is a disposition to accommodate and oblige others, is essentially the same in every country; but good-breeding, as it is called, which is the manner of exerting that disposition, is different in almost every country, and merely local; and every man of sense imitates and conforms to that local good-breeding of the place which he is at. A conformity and flexibility of manners is necessary in the course of the world; that is, with regard to all things which are not wrong in themselves. The 'versatile ingenium' is the most useful of all. It can turn itself instantly from one object to another, assuming the proper manner for each. It can be serious with the grave, cheerful with the gay, and trifling with the frivolous. Endeavor by all means, to acquire this talent, for it is a very great one.

As I hardly know anything more useful, than to see, from time to time, pictures of one's self drawn by different hands, I send you here a sketch of yourself, drawn at Lausanne, while you were there, and sent over here by a person who little thought that it would ever fall into my hands: and indeed it was by the greatest accident in the world that it did.

LETTER XVI

LONDON, October 9, O. S. 1747.

DEAR BOY: People of your age have, commonly, an unguarded frankness about them; which makes them the easy prey and bubbles of the artful and the experienced; they look upon every knave or fool, who tells them that he is their friend, to be really so; and pay that profession of simulated friendship, with an indiscreet and unbounded confidence, always to their loss, often to their ruin. Beware, therefore, now that you are coming into the world, of these preferred friendships. Receive them with great civility, but with great incredulity too; and pay them with compliments, but not with confidence. Do not let your vanity and self-love make you suppose that people become your friends at first sight, or even upon a short acquaintance. Real friendship is a slow grower and never thrives unless engrafted upon a stock of known and reciprocal merit. There is another kind of nominal friendship among young people, which is warm for the time, but by good luck, of short duration. This friendship is hastily produced, by their being accidentally thrown together, and pursuing the course of riot and debauchery. A fine friendship, truly; and well cemented by drunkenness and lewdness. It should rather be called a conspiracy against morals and good manners, and be punished as such by the civil magistrate. However, they have the impudence and folly to call this confederacy a friendship. They lend one another money, for bad purposes; they engage in quarrels, offensive and defensive for their accomplices; they tell one another all they know, and often more too, when, of a sudden, some accident disperses them, and they think no more of each other, unless it be to betray and laugh, at their imprudent confidence. Remember to make a great difference between companions and friends; for a very complaisant and agreeable companion may, and often does, prove a very improper and a very dangerous friend. People will, in a great degree, and not without reason, form their opinion of you, upon that which they have of your friends; and there is a Spanish proverb, which says very justly, TELL ME WHO YOU LIVE WITH AND I WILL TELL YOU WHO YOU ARE. One may fairly suppose, that the man who makes a knave or a fool his friend, has something very bad to do or to conceal. But, at the same time that you carefully decline the friendship of knaves and fools, if it can be called friendship, there is no occasion to make either of them your enemies, wantonly and unprovoked; for they are numerous bodies: and I, would rather choose a secure neutrality, than alliance, or war with either of them. You may be a declared enemy to their vices and follies, without being marked out by them as a personal one. Their enmity is the next dangerous thing to their friendship. Have a real reserve with almost everybody; and have a seeming reserve with almost nobody; for it is very disagreeable to seem reserved, and very dangerous not to be so. Few people find the true medium; many are ridiculously mysterious and reserved upon trifles; and many imprudently communicative of all they know.

The next thing to the choice of your friends, is the choice of your company. Endeavor, as much as you can, to keep company with people above you: there you rise, as much as you sink with people below you; for (as I have mentioned before) you are whatever the company you keep is. Do not mistake, when I say company above you, and think that I mean with regard to, their birth: that is the least consideration; but I mean with regard to their merit, and the light in which the world considers them.

There are two sorts of good company; one, which is called the beau monde, and consists of the people who have the lead in courts, and in the gay parts of life; the other consists of those who are distinguished by some peculiar merit, or who excel in some particular and valuable art or science. For my own part, I used to think myself in company as, much above me, when I was with Mr. Addison and Mr. Pope, as if I had been with all the princes in Europe. What I mean by low company, which should by all means be avoided, is the company of those, who, absolutely insignificant and contemptible in themselves, think they are honored by being in your company; and who flatter every vice and every folly you have, in order to engage you to converse with them. The pride of being the first of the company is but too common; but it is very silly, and very prejudicial. Nothing in the world lets down a character quicker than that wrong turn.

You may possibly ask me, whether a man has it always in his power to get the best company? and how? I say, Yes, he has, by deserving it; providing he is but in circumstances which enable him to appear upon the footing of a gentleman. Merit and good-breeding will make their way everywhere. Knowledge will introduce him, and good-breeding will endear him to the best companies: for, as I have often told you, politeness and good-breeding are absolutely necessary to adorn any, or all other good qualities or talents. Without them, no knowledge, no perfection whatever, is seen in its best light. The scholar, without good-breeding, is a pedant; the philosopher, a cynic; the soldier, a brute; and every man disagreeable.

I long to hear, from my several correspondents at Leipsig, of your arrival there, and what impression you make on them at first; for I have Arguses, with an hundred eyes each, who will watch you narrowly, and relate to me faithfully. My accounts will certainly be true; it depends upon you, entirely, of what kind they shall be. Adieu.

LETTER XVII

LONDON, October 16, O. S. 1747

DEAR BOY: The art of pleasing is a very necessary one to possess; but a very difficult one to acquire. It can hardly be reduced to rules; and your own good sense and observation will teach you more of it than I can. Do as you would be done by, is the surest method that I know of pleasing. Observe carefully what pleases you in others, and probably the same thing in you will please others. If you are pleased with the complaisance and attention of others to your humors, your tastes, or your weaknesses, depend upon it the same complaisance and attention, on your part to theirs, will equally please them. Take the tone of the company that you are in, and do not pretend to give it; be serious, gay, or even trifling, as you find the present humor of the company; this is an attention due from every individual to the majority. Do not tell stories in company; there is nothing more tedious and disagreeable; if by chance you know a very short story, and exceedingly applicable to the present subject of conversation, tell it in as few words as possible; and even then, throw out that you do not love to tell stories; but that the shortness of it tempted you. Of all things, banish the egotism out of your conversation, and never think of entertaining people with your own personal concerns, or private, affairs; though they are interesting to you, they are tedious and impertinent to everybody else; besides that, one cannot keep one's own private affairs too secret. Whatever you think your own excellencies may be, do not affectedly display them in company; nor labor, as many people do, to give that turn to the conversation, which may supply you with an opportunity of exhibiting them. If they are real, they will infallibly be discovered, without your pointing them out yourself, and with much more advantage. Never maintain an argument with heat and clamor, though you think or know yourself to be in the right: but give your opinion modestly and coolly, which is the only way to convince; and, if that does not do, try to change the conversation, by saying, with good humor, "We shall hardly convince one another, nor is it necessary that we should, so let us talk of something else."

Remember that there is a local propriety to be observed in all companies; and that what is extremely proper in one company, may be, and often is, highly improper in another.

The jokes, the 'bonmots,' the little adventures, which may do very well in one company, will seem flat and tedious, when related in another. The particular characters, the habits, the cant of one company, may give merit to a word, or a gesture, which would have none at all if divested of those accidental circumstances. Here people very commonly err; and fond of something that has entertained them in one company, and in certain circumstances, repeat it with emphasis in another, where it is either insipid, or, it may be, offensive, by being ill-timed or misplaced. Nay, they often do it with this silly preamble; "I will tell you an excellent thing"; or, "I will tell you the best thing in the world." This raises expectations, which, when absolutely disappointed, make the relater of this excellent thing look, very deservedly, like a fool.

If you would particularly gain the affection and friendship of particular people, whether men or women, endeavor to find out the predominant excellency, if they have one, and their prevailing weakness, which everybody has; and do justice to the one, and something more than justice to the other. Men have various objects in which they may excel, or at least would be thought to excel; and, though they love to hear justice done to them, where they know that they excel, yet they are most and best flattered upon those points where they wish to excel, and yet are doubtful whether they do or not. As, for example, Cardinal Richelieu, who was undoubtedly the ablest statesman of his time, or perhaps of any other, had the idle vanity of being thought the best poet too; he envied the great Corneille his reputation, and ordered a criticism to be written upon the "Cid." Those, therefore, who flattered skillfully, said little to him of his abilities in state affairs, or at least but 'en passant,' and as it might naturally occur. But the incense which they gave him, the smoke of which they knew would turn his head in their favor, was as a 'bel esprit' and a poet. Why? Because he was sure of one excellency, and distrustful as to the other. You will easily discover every man's prevailing vanity, by observing his favorite topic of conversation; for every man talks most of what he has most a mind to be thought to excel in. Touch him but there, and you touch him to the quick. The late Sir Robert Walpole (who was certainly an able man) was little open to flattery upon that head; for he was in no doubt himself about it; but his prevailing weakness was, to be thought to have a polite and happy turn to gallantry; of which he had undoubtedly less than any man living: it was his favorite and frequent subject of conversation: which proved, to those who had any penetration, that it was his prevailing weakness. And they applied to it with success.

Women have, in general, but one object, which is their beauty; upon which, scarce any flattery is too gross for them to swallow. Nature has hardly formed a woman ugly enough to be insensible to flattery upon her person; if her face is so shocking, that she must in some degree, be conscious of it, her figure and her air, she trusts, make ample amends for it. If her figure is deformed, her face, she thinks, counterbalances it. If they are both bad, she comforts herself that she has graces; a certain manner; a 'je ne sais quoi,' still more engaging than beauty. This truth is evident, from the studied and elaborate dress of the ugliest women in the world. An undoubted, uncontested, conscious beauty, is of all women, the least sensible of flattery upon that head; she knows that it is her due, and is therefore obliged to nobody for giving it her. She must be flattered upon her understanding; which, though she may possibly not doubt of herself, yet she suspects that men may distrust.

Do not mistake me, and think that I mean to recommend to you abject and criminal flattery: no; flatter nobody's vices or crimes: on the contrary, abhor and discourage them. But there is no living in the world without a complaisant indulgence for people's weaknesses, and innocent, though ridiculous vanities. If a man has a mind to be thought wiser, and a woman handsomer than they really are, their error is a comfortable one to themselves, and an innocent one with regard to other people; and I would rather make them my friends, by indulging them in it, than my enemies, by endeavoring (and that to no purpose) to undeceive them.

There are little attentions likewise, which are infinitely engaging, and which sensibly affect that degree of pride and self-love, which is inseparable from human nature; as they are unquestionable proofs of the regard and consideration which we have for the person to whom we pay them. As, for example, to observe the little habits, the likings, the antipathies, and the tastes of those whom we would gain; and then take care to provide them with the one, and to secure them from the other; giving them, genteelly, to understand, that you had observed that they liked such a dish, or such a room; for which reason you had prepared it: or, on the contrary, that having observed they had an aversion to such a dish, a dislike to such a person, etc., you had taken care to avoid presenting them. Such attention to such trifles flatters self-love much more than greater things, as it makes people think themselves almost the only objects of your thoughts and care.

These are some of the arcana necessary for your initiation in the great society of the world. I wish I had known them better at your age; I have paid the price of three-and-fifty years for them, and shall not grudge it, if you reap the advantage. Adieu.

LETTERS TO HIS SON, COMPLETE

LETTER XVIII

LONDON, October 30, O. S. 1747

DEAR BOY: I am very well pleased with your 'Itinerarium,' which you sent me from Ratisbon. It shows me that you observe and inquire as you go, which is the true end of traveling. Those who travel heedlessly from place to place, observing only their distance from each other, and attending only to their accommodation at the inn at night, set out fools, and will certainly return so. Those who only mind the raree-shows of the places which they go through, such as steeples, clocks, town-houses, etc., get so little by their travels, that they might as well stay at home. But those who observe, and inquire into the situations, the strength, the weakness, the trade, the manufactures, the government, and constitution of every place they go to; who frequent the best companies, and attend to their several manners and characters; those alone travel with advantage; and as they set out wise, return wiser.

I would advise you always to get the shortest description or history of every place where you make any stay; and such a book, however imperfect, will still suggest to you matter for inquiry; upon which you may get better informations from the people of the place. For example; while you are at Leipsig, get some short account (and to be sure there are many such) of the present state of the town, with regard to its magistrates, its police, its privileges, etc., and then inform yourself more minutely upon all those heads in, conversation with the most intelligent people. Do the same thing afterward with regard to the Electorate of Saxony: you will find a short history of it in Puffendorf's Introduction, which will give you a general idea of it, and point out to you the proper objects of a more minute inquiry. In short, be curious, attentive, inquisitive, as to everything; listlessness and indolence are always blameable, but, at your age, they are unpardonable. Consider how precious, and how important for all the rest of your life, are your moments for these next three or four years; and do not lose one of them. Do not think I mean that you should study all day long; I am far from advising or desiring it: but I desire that you would be doing something or other all day long; and not neglect half hours and quarters of hours, which, at the year's end, amount to a great sum. For instance, there are many short intervals during the day, between studies and pleasures: instead of sitting idle and yawning, in those intervals, take up any book, though ever so trifling a one, even down to a jest-book; it is still better than doing nothing.

Nor do I call pleasures idleness, or time lost, provided they are the pleasures of a rational being; on the contrary, a certain portion of your time, employed in those pleasures, is very usefully employed. Such are public spectacles, assemblies of good company, cheerful suppers, and even balls; but then, these require attention, or else your time is quite lost.

There are a great many people, who think themselves employed all day, and who, if they were to cast up their accounts at night, would find that they had done just nothing. They have read two or three hours mechanically, without attending to what they read, and consequently without either retaining it, or reasoning upon it. From thence they saunter into company, without taking any part in it, and without observing the characters of the persons, or the subjects of the conversation; but are either thinking of some trifle, foreign to the present purpose, or often not thinking at all; which silly and idle suspension of thought they would dignify with the name of ABSENCE and DISTRACTION. They go afterward, it may be, to the play, where they gape at the company and the lights; but without minding the very thing they went to, the play.

Pray do you be as attentive to your pleasures as to your studies. In the latter, observe and reflect upon all you read; and, in the former, be watchful and attentive to all that you see and hear; and never have it to say, as a thousand fools do, of things that were said and done before their faces, that, truly, they did not mind them, because they were thinking of something else. Why were they thinking of something else? and if they were, why did they come there? The truth is, that the fools were thinking of nothing. Remember the 'hoc age,' do what you are about, be what it will; it is either worth doing well, or not at all. Wherever you are, have (as the low vulgar expression is) your ears and your eyes about you. Listen to everything that is said, and see everything that is done. Observe the looks and countenances of those who speak, which is often a surer way of discovering the truth than from what they say. But then keep all those observations to yourself, for your own private use, and rarely communicate them to others. Observe, without being thought an observer, for otherwise people will be upon their guard before you.

Consider seriously, and follow carefully, I beseech you, my dear child, the advice which from time to time I have given, and shall continue to give you; it is at once the result of my long experience, and the effect of my tenderness for you. I can have no interest in it but yours. You are not yet capable of wishing yourself half so well as I wish you; follow therefore, for a time at least, implicitly, advice which you cannot suspect, though possibly you may not yet see the particular advantages of it; but you will one day feel them. Adieu.

LETTER XIX

LONDON, November 6, O. S. 1747

DEAR BOY: Three mails are now due from Holland, so that I have no letter from you to acknowledge; I write to you, therefore, now, as usual, by way of flapper, to put you in mind of yourself. Doctor Swift, in his account of the island of Laputa, describes some philosophers there who were so wrapped up and absorbed in their abstruse speculations, that they would have forgotten all the common and necessary duties of life, if they had not been reminded of them by persons who flapped them, whenever they observed them continue too long in any of those learned trances. I do not indeed suspect you of being absorbed in abstruse speculations; but, with great submission to you, may I not suspect that levity, inattention, and too little thinking, require a flapper, as well as too deep thinking? If my letters should happen to get to you when you are sitting by the fire and doing nothing, or when you are gaping at the window, may they not be very proper flaps, to put you in mind that you might employ your time much better? I knew once a very covetous, sordid fellow, who used frequently to say, "Take care of the pence; for the pounds will take care of themselves." This was a just and sensible reflection in a miser. I recommend to you to take care of the minutes; for hours will take care of themselves. I am very sure, that many people lose two or three hours every day, by not taking care of the minutes. Never think any portion of time whatsoever too short to be employed; something or other may always be done in it.

While you are in Germany, let all your historical studies be relative to Germany; not only the general history of the empire as a collective body; but the respective electorates, principalities, and towns; and also the genealogy of the most considerable families. A genealogy is no trifle in Germany; and they would rather prove their two-and-thirty quarters, than two-and-thirty cardinal virtues, if there were so many. They are not of Ulysses' opinion, who says very truly,

——Genus et proavos, et qua non fecimus ipsi; Vix ea nostra voco.

Good night.

LETTER XX

LONDON, November 24, O. S. 1747

DEAR BOY: As often as I write to you (and that you know is pretty often), so often I am in doubt whether it is to any purpose, and whether it is not labor and paper lost. This entirely depends upon the degree of reason and reflection which you are master of, or think proper to exert. If you give yourself time to think, and have sense enough to think right, two reflections must necessarily occur to you; the one is, that I have a great deal of experience, and that you have none: the other is, that I am the only man living who cannot have, directly or indirectly, any interest concerning you, but your own. From which two undeniable principles, the obvious and necessary conclusion is, that you ought, for your own sake, to attend to and follow my advice.

If, by the application which I recommend to you, you acquire great knowledge, you alone are the gainer; I pay for it. If you should deserve either a good or a bad character, mine will be exactly what it is now, and will neither be the better in the first case, nor worse in the latter. You alone will be the gainer or the loser.

Whatever your pleasures may be, I neither can nor shall envy you them, as old people are sometimes suspected by young people to do; and I shall only lament, if they should prove such as are unbecoming a man of honor, or below a man of sense. But you will be the real sufferer, if they are such. As therefore, it is plain that I can have no other motive than that of affection in whatever I say to you, you ought to look upon me as your best, and, for some years to come, your only friend.

True friendship requires certain proportions of age and manners, and can never subsist where they are extremely different, except in the relations of parent and child, where affection on one side, and regard on the other, make up the difference. The friendship which you may contract with people of your own age may be sincere, may be warm; but must be, for some time, reciprocally unprofitable, as there can be no experience on either side. The young leading the young, is like the blind leading the blind; (they will both fall into the ditch.) The only sure guide is, he who has often gone the road which you want to go. Let me be that guide; who have gone all roads, and who can consequently point out to you the best. If you ask me why I went any of the bad roads myself, I will answer you very truly, That it was for want of a good guide: ill example invited me one way, and a good guide was wanting to show me a better. But if anybody, capable of advising me, had taken the same pains with me, which I have taken, and will continue to take with you, I should have avoided many follies and inconveniences, which undirected youth run me into. My father was neither desirous nor able to advise me; which is what, I hope, you cannot say of yours. You see that I make use, only of the word advice; because I would much rather have the assent of your reason to my advice, than the submission of your will to my authority. This, I persuade myself, will happen, from that degree of sense which I think you have; and therefore I will go on advising, and with hopes of success.

You are now settled for some time at Leipsig; the principal object of your stay there is the knowledge of books and sciences; which if you do not, by attention and application, make yourself master of while you are there, you will be ignorant of them all the rest of your life; and, take my word for it, a life of ignorance is not only a very contemptible, but a very tiresome one. Redouble your attention, then, to Mr. Harte, in your private studies of the 'Literae Humaniores,' especially Greek. State your difficulties, whenever you have any; and do not suppress them, either from mistaken shame, lazy indifference, or in order to have done the sooner. Do the same when you are at lectures with Professor Mascow, or any other professor; let nothing pass till you are sure that you understand it thoroughly; and accustom yourself to write down the capital points of what you learn. When you have thus usefully employed your mornings, you may, with a safe conscience, divert yourself in the evenings, and make those evenings very useful too, by passing them in good company, and, by observation and attention, learning as much of the world as Leipsig can teach you. You will observe and imitate the manners of the people of the best fashion there; not that they are (it may be) the best manners in the world; but because they are the best manners of the place where you are, to which a man of sense always conforms. The nature of things (as I have often told you) is always and everywhere the same; but the modes of them vary more or less, in every country; and an easy and genteel conformity to them, or rather the assuming of them at proper times, and in proper places, is what particularly constitutes a man of the world, and a well-bred man.

Here is advice enough, I think, and too much, it may be, you will think, for one letter; if you follow it, you will get knowledge, character, and pleasure by it; if you do not, I only lose 'operam et oleum,' which, in all events, I do not grudge you.

I send you, by a person who sets out this day for Leipsig, a small packet from your Mamma, containing some valuable things which you left behind, to which I have added, by way of new-year's gift, a very pretty tooth-pick case; and, by the way, pray take great care of your teeth, and keep them extremely clean. I have likewise sent you the Greek roots, lately translated into English from the French of the Port Royal. Inform yourself what the Port Royal is. To conclude with a quibble: I hope you will not only feed upon these Greek roots, but likewise digest them perfectly. Adieu.

LETTER XXI

LONDON, December 15, O. S. 1747

DEAR Boy: There is nothing which I more wish that you should know, and which fewer people do know, than the true use and value of time. It is in everybody's mouth; but in few people's practice. Every fool, who slatterns away his whole time in nothings, utters, however, some trite commonplace sentence, of which there are millions, to prove, at once, the value and the fleetness of time. The sun-dials, likewise all over Europe, have some ingenious inscription to that effect; so that nobody squanders away their time, without hearing and seeing, daily, how necessary it is to employ it well, and how irrecoverable it is if lost. But all these admonitions are useless, where there is not a fund of good sense and reason to suggest them, rather than receive them. By the manner in which you now tell me that you employ your time, I flatter myself that you have that fund; that is the fund which will make you rich indeed. I do not, therefore, mean to give you a critical essay upon the use and abuse of time; but I will only give you some hints with regard to the use of one particular period of that long time which, I hope, you have before you; I mean, the next two years. Remember, then, that whatever knowledge you do not solidly lay the foundation of before you are eighteen, you will never be the master of while you breathe. Knowledge is a comfortable and necessary retreat and shelter for us in an advanced age; and if we do not plant it while young, it will give us no shade when we grow old. I neither require nor expect from you great application to books, after you are once thrown out into the great world. I know it is impossible; and it may even, in some cases, be improper; this, therefore, is your time, and your only time, for unwearied and uninterrupted application. If you should sometimes think it a little laborious, consider that labor is the unavoidable fatigue of a necessary journey. The more hours a day you travel, the sooner you will be at your journey's end. The sooner you are qualified for your liberty, the sooner you shall have it; and your manumission will entirely depend upon the manner in which you employ the intermediate time. I think I offer you a very good bargain, when I promise you, upon my word, that if you will do everything that I would have you do, till you are eighteen, I will do everything that you would have me do ever afterward.

I knew a gentleman, who was so good a manager of his time, that he would not even lose that small portion of it, which the calls of nature obliged him to pass in the necessary-house; but gradually went through all the Latin poets, in those moments. He bought, for example, a common edition of Horace, of which he tore off gradually a couple of pages, carried them with him to that necessary place, read them first, and then sent them down as a sacrifice to Cloacina: this was so much time fairly gained; and I recommend you to follow his example. It is better than only doing what you cannot help doing at those moments; and it will made any book, which you shall read in that manner, very present in your mind. Books of science, and of a grave sort, must be read with continuity; but there are very many, and even very useful ones, which may be read with advantage by snatches, and unconnectedly; such are all the good Latin poets, except Virgil in his "AEneid": and such are most of the modern poets, in which you will find many pieces worth reading, that will not take up above seven or eight minutes. Bayle's, Moreri's, and other dictionaries, are proper books to take and shut up for the little intervals of (otherwise) idle time, that everybody has in the course of the day, between either their studies or their pleasures. Good night.

LETTER XXII

LONDON, December 18, O. S. 1747.

DEAR Boy: As two mails are now due from Holland,

I have no letters of yours, or Mr. Harte's to acknowledge; so that this letter is the effect of that 'scribendi cacoethes,' which my fears, my hopes, and my doubts, concerning you give me. When I have wrote you a very long letter upon any subject, it is no sooner gone, but I think I have omitted something in it, which might be of use to you; and then I prepare the supplement for the next post: or else some new subject occurs to me, upon which I fancy I can give you some informations, or point out some rules which may be advantageous to you. This sets me to writing again, though God knows whether to any purpose or not; a few years more can only ascertain that. But, whatever my success may be, my anxiety and my care can only be the effects of that tender affection which I have for you; and which you cannot represent to yourself greater than it really is. But do not mistake the nature of that affection, and think it of a kind that you may with impunity abuse. It is not natural affection, there being in reality no such thing; for, if there were, some inward sentiment must necessarily and reciprocally discover the parent to the child, and the child to the parent, without any exterior indications, knowledge, or acquaintance whatsoever; which never happened since the creation of the world, whatever poets, romance, and novel writers, and such sentiment-mongers, may be pleased to say to the contrary. Neither is my affection for you that of a mother, of which the only, or at least the chief objects, are health and life: I wish you them both most heartily; but, at the same time, I confess they are by no means my principal care.

My object is to have you fit to live; which, if you are not, I do not desire that you should live at all. My affection for you then is, and only will be, proportioned to your merit; which is the only affection that one rational being ought to have for another. Hitherto I have discovered nothing wrong in your heart, or your head: on the contrary I think I see sense in the one, and sentiments in the other. This persuasion is the only motive of my present affection; which will either increase or diminish, according to your merit or demerit. If you have the knowledge, the honor, and probity, which you may have, the marks and warmth of my affection shall amply reward them; but if you have them not, my aversion and indignation will rise in the same proportion; and, in that case, remember, that I am under no further obligation, than to give you the necessary means of subsisting. If ever we quarrel, do not expect or depend upon any weakness in my nature, for a reconciliation, as children frequently do, and often meet with, from silly parents; I have no such weakness about me: and, as I will never quarrel with you but upon some essential point; if once we quarrel, I will never forgive. But I hope and believe, that this declaration (for it is no threat) will prove unnecessary. You are no stranger to the principles of virtue; and, surely, whoever knows virtue must love it. As for knowledge, you have already enough of it, to engage you to acquire more. The ignorant only, either despise it, or think that they have enough: those who have the most are always the most desirous to have more, and know that the most they can have is, alas! but too little.

Reconsider, from time to time, and retain the friendly advice which I send you. The advantage will be all your own.

LETTER XXIII

LONDON, December 29, O. S. 1747

DEAR BOY: I have received two letters from you of the 17th and 22d, N. S., by the last of which I find that some of mine to you must have miscarried; for I have never been above two posts without writing to you or to Mr. Harte, and even very long letters. I have also received a letter from Mr. Harte, which gives me great satisfaction: it is full of your praises; and he answers for you, that, in two years more, you will deserve your manumission, and be fit to go into the world, upon a footing that will do you honor, and give me pleasure.

I thank you for your offer of the new edition of 'Adamus Adami,' but I do not want it, having a good edition of it at present. When you have read that, you will do well to follow it with Pere Bougeant's 'Histoire du Traite de Munster,' in two volumes quarto; which contains many important anecdotes concerning that famous treaty, that are not in Adamus Adami.

You tell me that your lectures upon the 'Jus Publicum' will be ended at Easter; but then I hope that Monsieur Mascow will begin them again; for I would not have you discontinue that study one day while you are at Leipsig. I suppose that Monsieur Mascow will likewise give you lectures upon the 'Instrumentum Pacis,' and upon the capitulations of the late emperors. Your German will go on of course; and I take it for granted that your stay at Leipsig will make you a perfect master of that language, both as to speaking and writing; for remember, that knowing any language imperfectly, is very little better than not knowing it at all: people being as unwilling to speak in a language which they do not possess thoroughly, as others are to hear them. Your thoughts are cramped, and appear to great disadvantage, in any language of which you are not perfect master. Let modern history share part of your time, and that always accompanied with the maps of the places in question; geography and history are very imperfect separately, and, to be useful, must be joined.

Go to the Duchess of Courland's as often as she and your leisure will permit. The company of women of fashion will improve your manners, though not your understanding; and that complaisance and politeness, which are so useful in men's company, can only be acquired in women's.

Remember always, what I have told you a thousand times, that all the talents in the world will want all their lustre, and some part of their use too, if they are not adorned with that easy good-breeding, that engaging manner, and those graces, which seduce and prepossess people in your favor at first sight. A proper care of your person is by no means to be neglected; always extremely clean; upon proper occasions fine. Your carriage genteel, and your motions graceful. Take particular care of your manner and address, when you present yourself in company. Let them be respectful without meanness, easy without too much familiarity, genteel without affectation, and insinuating without any seeming art or design.

You need not send me any more extracts of the German constitution; which, by the course of your present studies, I know you must soon be acquainted with; but I would now rather that your letters should be a sort of journal of your own life. As, for instance, what company you keep, what new acquaintances you make, what your pleasures are; with your own reflections upon the whole: likewise what Greek and Latin books you read and understand. Adieu!

EARL OF PHILIP DORMER STANHOPE CHESTERFIELD

1748

LETTER XXIV

January 2, O. S. 1748.

DEAR BOY: I am edified with the allotment of your time at Leipsig; which is so well employed from morning till night, that a fool would say you had none left for yourself; whereas, I am sure you have sense enough to know, that such a right use of your time is having it all to yourself; nay, it is even more, for it is laying it out to immense interest, which, in a very few years, will amount to a prodigious capital.

Though twelve of your fourteen 'Commensaux' may not be the liveliest people in the world, and may want (as I easily conceive that they do) 'le ton de la bonne campagnie, et les graces', which I wish you, yet pray take care not to express any contempt, or throw out any ridicule; which I can assure you, is not more contrary to good manners than to good sense: but endeavor rather to get all the good you can out of them; and something or other is to be got out of everybody. They will, at least, improve you in the German language; and, as they come from different countries, you may put them upon subjects, concerning which they must necessarily be able to give you some useful informations, let them be ever so dull or disagreeable in general: they will know something, at least, of the laws, customs, government, and considerable families of their respective countries; all which are better known than not, and consequently worth inquiring into. There is hardly any body good for every thing, and there is scarcely any body who is absolutely good for nothing. A good chemist will extract some spirit or other out of every substance; and a man of parts will, by his dexterity and management, elicit something worth knowing out of every being he converses with.

As you have been introduced to the Duchess of Courland, pray go there as often as ever your more necessary occupations will allow you. I am told she is extremely well bred, and has parts. Now, though I would not recommend to you, to go into women's company in search of solid knowledge, or judgment, yet it has its use in other respects; for it certainly polishes the manners, and gives 'une certaine tournure', which is very necessary in the course of the world; and which Englishmen have generally less of than any people in the world.

I cannot say that your suppers are luxurious, but you must own they are solid; and a quart of soup, and two pounds of potatoes, will enable you to pass the night without great impatience for your breakfast next morning. One part of your supper (the potatoes) is the constant diet of my old friends and countrymen,— [Lord Chesterfield, from the time he was appointed Lord-lieutenant of Ireland, 1775, used always to call the Irish his countrymen.]—the Irish, who are the healthiest and the strongest bodies of men that I know in Europe.

As I believe that many of my letters to you and to Mr. Harte have miscarried, as well as some of yours and his to me; particularly one of his from Leipsig, to which he refers in a subsequent one, and which I never received; I would have you, for the future, acknowledge the dates of all the letters which either of you shall receive from me; and I will do the same on my part.

That which I received by the last mail, from you, was of the 25th November, N. S.; the mail before that brought me yours, of which I have forgot the date, but which inclosed one to Lady Chesterfield: she will answer it soon, and, in the mean time, thanks you for it.

My disorder was only a very great cold, of which I am entirely recovered. You shall not complain for want of accounts from Mr. Grevenkop, who will frequently write you whatever passes here, in the German language and character; which will improve you in both. Adieu.

LETTER XXV

LONDON, January 15, O. S. 1748.

DEAR BOY: I willingly accept the new-year's gift which you promise me for next year; and the more valuable you make it, the more thankful I shall be. That depends entirely upon you; and therefore I hope to be presented, every year, with a new edition of you, more correct than the former, and considerably enlarged and amended.

Since you do not care to be an assessor of the imperial chamber, and that you desire an establishment in England; what do you think of being Greek Professor at one of our universities? It is a very pretty sinecure, and requires very little knowledge (much less than, I hope, you have already) of that language. If you do not approve of this, I am at a loss to know what else to propose to you; and therefore desire that you will inform me what sort of destination you propose for yourself; for it is now time to fix it, and to take our measures accordingly. Mr. Harte tells me that you set up for a—————; if so, I presume it is in the view of succeeding me in my office;—[A secretary of state.]—which I will very willingly resign to you, whenever you shall call upon me for it. But, if you intend to be the—————, or the—————, there are some trifling circumstances upon which you should previously take your resolution. The first of which is, to be fit for it: and then, in order to be so, make yourself master of ancient and, modern history, and languages. To know perfectly the constitution, and form of government of every nation; the growth and the decline of ancient and modern empires; and to trace out and reflect upon the causes of both. To know the strength, the riches, and the commerce of every country. These little things, trifling as they may seem, are yet very necessary for a politician to know; and which therefore, I presume, you will condescend to apply yourself to. There are some additional qualifications necessary, in the practical part of business, which may deserve some consideration in your leisure moments; such as, an absolute command of your temper, so as not to be provoked to passion, upon any account; patience, to hear frivolous, impertinent, and unreasonable applications; with address enough to refuse, without offending, or, by your manner of granting, to double the obligation; dexterity enough to conceal a truth without telling a lie; sagacity enough to read other people's countenances; and serenity enough not to let them discover anything by yours; a seeming frankness with a real reserve. These are the rudiments of a politician; the world must be your grammar.

Three mails are now due from Holland; so that I have no letters from you to acknowledge. I therefore conclude with recommending myself to your favor and protection when you succeed. Yours.

LETTER XXVI

LONDON, January 29, O. S. 1748.

DEAR BOY: I find, by Mr. Harte's last letter, that many of my letters to you and him, have been frozen up on their way to Leipsig; the thaw has, I suppose, by this time, set them at liberty to pursue their journey to you, and you will receive a glut of them at once. Hudibras alludes, in this verse,

"Like words congealed in northern air,"

to a vulgar notion, that in Greenland words were frozen in their utterance; and that upon a thaw, a very mixed conversation was heard in the air, of all those words set at liberty. This conversation was, I presume, too various and extensive to be much attended to: and may not that be the case of half a dozen of my long letters, when you receive them all at once? I think that I can, eventually, answer that question, thus: If you consider my letters in their true light, as conveying to you the advice of a friend, who sincerely wishes your happiness, and desires to promote your pleasure, you will both read and attend to them; but, if you consider them in their opposite, and very false light, as the dictates of a morose and sermonizing father, I am sure they will be not only unattended to, but unread. Which is the case, you can best tell me. Advice is seldom welcome; and those who want it the most always like it the least. I hope that your want of experience, of which you must be conscious, will convince you, that you want advice; and that your good sense will incline you to follow it.

Tell me how you pass your leisure hours at Leipsig; I know you have not many; and I have too good an opinion of you to think, that, at this age, you would desire more. Have you assemblies, or public spectacles? and of what kind are they? Whatever they are, see them all; seeing everything, is the only way not to admire anything too much.

If you ever take up little tale-books, to amuse you by snatches, I will recommend two French books, which I have already mentioned; they will entertain you, and not without some use to your mind and your manners. One is, 'La Maniere de bien penser dans les Ouvrages d'Esprit', written by Pere Bouhours; I believe you read it once in England, with Monsieur Coderc; but I think that you will do well to read it again, as I know of no book that will form your taste better. The other is, 'L'Art de plaire dans la Conversation', by the Abbe de Bellegarde, and is by no means useless, though I will not pretend to say, that the art of pleasing can be reduced to a receipt; if it could, I am sure that receipt would be worth purchasing at any price. Good sense, and good nature, are the principal ingredients; and your own observation, and the good advice of others, must give the right color and taste to it. Adieu! I shall always love you as you shall deserve.

LETTER XXVII

LONDON, February 9, O. S. 1748.

DEAR BOY: You will receive this letter, not from a Secretary of State but from a private man; for whom, at his time of life, quiet was as fit, and as necessary, as labor and activity are for you at your age, and for many years yet to come. I resigned the seals, last Saturday, to the King; who parted with me most graciously, and (I may add, for he said so himself) with regret. As I retire from hurry to quiet, and to enjoy, at my ease, the comforts of private and social life, you will easily imagine that I have no thoughts of opposition, or meddling with business. 'Otium cum dignitate' is my object. The former I now enjoy; and I hope that my conduct and character entitle me to some share of the latter. In short, I am now happy: and I found that I could not be so in my former public situation.

As I like your correspondence better than that of all the kings, princes, and ministers, in Europe, I shall now have leisure to carry it on more regularly. My letters to you will be written, I am sure, by me, and, I hope, read by you, with pleasure; which, I believe, seldom happens, reciprocally, to letters written from and to a secretary's office.

Do not apprehend that my retirement from business may be a hindrance to your advancement in it, at a proper time: on the contrary, it will promote it; for, having nothing to ask for myself, I shall have the better title to ask for you. But you have still a surer way than this of rising, and which is wholly in your own power. Make yourself necessary; which, with your natural parts, you may, by application, do. We are in general, in England, ignorant of foreign affairs: and of the interests, views, pretensions, and policy of other courts. That part of knowledge never enters into our thoughts, nor makes part of our education; for which reason, we have fewer proper subjects for foreign commissions, than any other country in Europe; and, when foreign affairs happen to be debated in Parliament, it is incredible with how much ignorance. The harvest of foreign affairs being then so great, and the laborers so few, if you make yourself master of them, you will make yourself necessary; first as a foreign, and then as a domestic minister for that department.

I am extremely well pleased with the account which you give me of the allotment of your time. Do but go on so, for two years longer, and I will ask no more of you. Your labors will be their own reward; but if you desire any other, that I can add, you may depend upon it.

I am glad that you perceive the indecency and turpitude of those of your 'Commensaux', who disgrace and foul themselves with dirty w——s and scoundrel gamesters. And the light in which, I am sure, you see all reasonable and decent people consider them, will be a good warning to you. Adieu.

LETTER XXVIII

LONDON, February 13, O. S. 1748

DEAR BOY: your last letter gave me a very satisfactory account of your manner of employing your time at Leipsig. Go on so but for two years more, and, I promise you, that you will outgo all the people of your age and time. I thank you for your explanation of the 'Schriftsassen', and 'Amptsassen'; and pray let me know the meaning of the 'Landsassen'. I am very willing that you should take a Saxon servant, who speaks nothing but German, which will be a sure way of keeping up your German, after you leave Germany. But then, I would neither have that man, nor him whom you have already, put out of livery; which makes them both impertinent and useless. I am sure, that as soon as you shall have taken the other servant, your present man will press extremely to be out of livery, and valet de chambre; which is as much as to say, that he will curl your hair and shave you, but not condescend to do anything else. I therefore advise you, never to have a servant out of livery; and, though you may not always think proper to carry the servant who dresses you abroad in the rain and dirt, behind a coach or before a chair, yet keep it in your power to do so, if you please, by keeping him in livery.

I have seen Monsieur and Madame Flemming, who gave me a very good account of you, and of your manners, which to tell you the plain truth, were what I doubted of the most. She told me, that you were easy, and not ashamed: which is a great deal for an Englishman at your age.

I set out for Bath to-morrow, for a month; only to be better than well, and enjoy, in, quiet, the liberty which I have acquired by the resignation of the seals. You shall hear from me more at large from thence; and now good night to you.

LETTER XXIX

BATH, February 18, O. S. 1748.

DEAR BOY: The first use that I made of my liberty was to come here, where I arrived yesterday. My health, though not fundamentally bad yet, for want of proper attention of late, wanted some repairs, which these waters never fail giving it. I shall drink them a month, and return to London, there to enjoy the comforts of social life, instead of groaning under the load of business. I have given the description of the life that I propose to lead for the future, in this motto, which I have put up in the frize of my library in my new house:—

Nunc veterum libris, nunc somno, et inertibus horis

LETTERS TO HIS SON, COMPLETE

Ducere sollicitae jucunda oblivia vitas.

I must observe to you upon this occasion, that the uninterrupted satisfaction which I expect to find in that library, will be chiefly owing to my having employed some part of my life well at your age. I wish I had employed it better, and my satisfaction would now be complete; but, however, I planted while young, that degree of knowledge which is now my refuge and my shelter. Make your plantations still more extensive; they will more than pay you for your trouble. I do not regret the time that I passed in pleasures; they were seasonable; they were the pleasures of youth, and I enjoyed them while young. If I had not, I should probably have overvalued them now, as we are very apt to do what we do not know; but, knowing them as I do, I know their real value, and how much they are generally overrated. Nor do I regret the time that I have passed in business, for the same reason; those who see only the outside of it, imagine it has hidden charms, which they pant after; and nothing but acquaintance can undeceive them. I, who have been behind the scenes, both of pleasure and business, and have seen all the springs and pullies of those decorations which astonish and dazzle the audience, retire, not only without regret, but with contentment and satisfaction. But what I do, and ever shall regret, is the time which, while young, I lost in mere idleness, and in doing nothing. This is the common effect of the inconsideracy of youth, against which I beg you will be most carefully upon your guard. The value of moments, when cast up, is immense, if well employed; if thrown away, their loss is irrecoverable. Every moment may be put to some use, and that with much more pleasure, than if unemployed. Do not imagine, that by the employment of time, I mean an uninterrupted application to serious studies. No; pleasures are, at proper times, both as necessary and as useful; they fashion and form you for the world; they teach you characters, and show you the human heart in its unguarded minutes. But then remember to make that use of them. I have known many people, from laziness of mind, go through both pleasure and business with equal inattention; neither enjoying the one, nor doing the other; thinking themselves men of pleasure, because they were mingled with those who were, and men of business, because they had business to do, though they did not do it. Whatever you do, do it to the purpose; do it thoroughly, not superficially. 'Approfondissez': go to the bottom of things. Any thing half done or half known, is, in my mind, neither done nor known at all. Nay worse, it often misleads. There is hardly any place or any company, where you may not gain knowledge, if you please; almost everybody knows some one thing, and is glad to talk upon that one thing. Seek and you will find, in this world as well as in the next. See everything; inquire into everything; and you may excuse your curiosity, and the questions you ask which otherwise might be thought impertinent, by your manner of asking them; for most things depend a great deal upon the manner. As, for example, I AM AFRAID THAT I AM VERY TROUBLESOME WITH MY QUESTIONS; BUT NOBODY CAN INFORM ME SO WELL AS YOU; or something of that kind.

Now that you are in a Lutheran country, go to their churches, and observe the manner of their public worship; attend to their ceremonies, and inquire the meaning and intention of everyone of them. And, as you will soon understand German well enough, attend to their sermons, and observe their manner of preaching. Inform yourself of their church government: whether it resides in the sovereign, or in consistories and synods. Whence arises the maintenance of their clergy; whether from tithes, as in England, or from voluntary contributions, or from pensions from the state. Do the same thing when you are in Roman Catholic countries; go to their churches, see all their ceremonies: ask the meaning of them, get the terms explained to you. As, for instance, Prime, Tierce, Sexte, Nones, Matins, Angelus, High Mass, Vespers, Complines, etc. Inform yourself of their several religious orders, their founders, their rules, their vows, their habits, their revenues, etc. But, when you frequent places of public worship, as I would have you go to all the different ones you meet with, remember, that however erroneous, they are none of them objects of laughter and ridicule. Honest error is to be pitied, not ridiculed. The object of all the public worships in the world is the same; it is that great eternal Being who created everything. The different manners of worship are by no means subjects of ridicule. Each sect thinks its own is the best; and I know no infallible judge in this world, to decide which is the best. Make the same inquiries, wherever you are, concerning the revenues, the military establishment, the trade, the commerce, and the police of every country. And you would do well to keep a blank paper book, which the Germans call an ALBUM; and there, instead of desiring, as they do, every fool they meet with to scribble something, write down all these things as soon as they come to your knowledge from good authorities.

I had almost forgotten one thing, which I would recommend as an object for your curiosity and information, that is, the administration of justice; which, as it is always carried on in open court, you may, and I would have you, go and see it with attention and inquiry.

I have now but one anxiety left, which is concerning you. I would have you be, what I know nobody is—perfect. As that is impossible, I would have you as near perfection as possible. I know nobody in a fairer way toward it than yourself, if you please. Never were so much pains taken for anybody's education as for yours; and never had anybody those opportunities of knowledge and improvement which you, have had, and still have, I hope, I wish, I doubt, and fear alternately. This only I am sure of, that you will prove either the greatest pain or the greatest pleasure of, Yours.

LETTER XXX

BATH, February 22, O. S. 1748.

DEAR Boy: Every excellency, and every virtue, has its kindred vice or weakness; and if carried beyond certain bounds, sinks into one or the other. Generosity often runs into profusion, economy into avarice, courage into rashness, caution into timidity, and so on:—insomuch that, I believe, there is more judgment required, for the proper conduct of our virtues, than for avoiding their opposite vices. Vice, in its true light, is so deformed, that it shocks us at first sight, and would hardly ever seduce us, if it did not, at first, wear the mask of some virtue. But virtue is, in itself, so beautiful, that it charms us at first sight; engages us more and more upon further acquaintance; and, as with other beauties, we think excess impossible; it is here that judgment is necessary, to moderate and direct the effects of an excellent cause. I shall apply this reasoning, at present, not to any particular virtue, but to an excellency, which, for want of judgment, is often the cause of ridiculous and blamable effects; I mean, great learning; which, if not accompanied with sound judgment, frequently carries us into error, pride, and pedantry. As, I hope, you will possess that excellency in its utmost extent, and yet without its too common failings, the hints, which my experience can suggest, may probably not be useless to you.

Some learned men, proud of their knowledge, only speak to decide, and give judgment without appeal; the consequence of which is, that mankind, provoked by the insult, and injured by the oppression, revolt; and, in order to shake off the tyranny, even call the lawful authority in question. The more you know, the modester you should be: and (by the bye) that modesty is the surest way of gratifying your vanity. Even where you are sure, seem rather doubtful; represent, but do not pronounce, and, if you would convince others, seem open to conviction yourself.

Others, to show their learning, or often from the prejudices of a school education, where they hear of nothing else, are always talking of the ancients, as something more than men, and of the moderns, as something less. They are never without a classic or two in their pockets; they stick to the old good sense; they read none of the modern trash; and will show you, plainly, that no improvement has been made, in any one art or science, these last seventeen hundred years. I would by no means have you disown your acquaintance with the ancients: but still less would I have you brag of an exclusive intimacy with them. Speak of the moderns without contempt, and of the ancients without idolatry; judge them all by their merits, but not by their ages; and if you happen to have an Elzevir classic in your pocket neither show it nor mention it.

Some great scholars, most absurdly, draw all their maxims, both for public and private life, from what they call parallel cases in the ancient authors; without considering, that, in the first place, there never were, since the creation of the world, two cases exactly parallel; and, in the next place, that there never was a case stated, or even known, by any historian, with every one of its circumstances; which, however, ought to be known, in order to be reasoned from. Reason upon the case itself, and the several circumstances that attend it, and act accordingly; but not from the authority of ancient poets, or historians. Take into your consideration, if you please, cases seemingly analogous; but take them as helps only, not as guides. We are really so prejudiced by our education, that, as the ancients deified their heroes, we deify their madmen; of which, with all due regard for antiquity, I take Leonidas and Curtius to have been two distinguished ones. And yet a solid pedant would, in a speech in parliament, relative to a tax of two pence in the pound upon some community or other, quote those two heroes, as examples of what we ought to do and suffer for our country. I have known these absurdities carried so far by people of injudicious learning, that I should not be surprised, if some of them were to propose, while we are at war with the Gauls, that a number of geese should be kept in the Tower, upon account of the infinite advantage which Rome received IN A PARALLEL CASE, from a certain number of geese in the Capitol. This way of reasoning, and this way of speaking, will always form a poor politician, and a puerile declaimer.

There is another species of learned men, who, though less dogmatical and supercilious, are not less impertinent. These are the communicative and shining pedants, who adorn their conversation, even with women, by happy quotations of Greek and Latin; and who have contracted such a familiarity with the Greek and Roman authors, that they, call them by certain names or epithets denoting intimacy. As OLD Homer; that SLY ROGUE Horace; MARO, instead of Virgil; and Naso, Instead of Ovid. These are often imitated by coxcombs, who have no learning at all; but who have got some names and some scraps of ancient authors by heart, which they improperly and impertinently retail in all companies, in hopes of passing for scholars. If, therefore, you would avoid the accusation of pedantry on one hand, or the suspicion of ignorance on the other, abstain from learned ostentation. Speak the language of the company that you are in; speak it purely, and unlarded with any other. Never seem wiser, nor more learned, than the people you are with. Wear your learning, like your watch, in a private pocket: and do not pull it out and strike it; merely to show that you have one. If you are asked what o'clock it is, tell it; but do not proclaim it hourly and unasked, like the watchman.

Upon the whole, remember that learning (I mean Greek and Roman learning) is a most useful and necessary ornament, which it is shameful not to be master of; but, at the same time most carefully avoid those errors and abuses which I have mentioned, and which too often attend it. Remember, too, that great modern knowledge is still more necessary than ancient; and that you had better know perfectly the present, than the old state of Europe; though I would have you well acquainted with both.

I have this moment received your letter of the 17th, N. S. Though, I confess, there is no great variety in your present manner of life, yet materials can never be wanting for a letter; you see, you hear, or you read something new every day; a short account of which, with your own reflections thereupon, will make out a letter very well. But, since you desire a subject, pray send me an account of the Lutheran establishment in Germany; their religious tenets, their church government, the maintenance, authority, and titles of their clergy.

'Vittorio Siri', complete, is a very scarce and very dear book here; but I do not want it. If your own library grows too voluminous, you will not know what to do with it, when you leave Leipsig. Your best way will be, when you go away from thence, to send to England, by Hamburg, all the books that you do not absolutely want.

Yours.

LETTER XXXI

BATH, March 1, O. S. 1748.

DEAR BOY: By Mr. Harte's letter to Mr. Grevenkop, of the 21st February, N. S., I find that you had been a great while without receiving any letters from me; but by this time, I daresay you think you have received enough, and possibly more than you have read; for I am not only a frequent, but a prolix correspondent.

Mr. Harte says, in that letter, that he looks upon Professor Mascow to be one of the ablest men in Europe, in treaty and political knowledge. I am extremely glad of it; for that is what I would have you particularly apply to, and make yourself perfect master of. The treaty part you must chiefly acquire by reading the treaties themselves, and the histories and memoirs relative to them; not but that inquiries and conversations upon those treaties will help you greatly, and imprint them better in your mind. In this course of reading, do not perplex yourself, at first, by the multitude of insignificant treaties which are to be found in the Corps Diplomatique; but stick to the material ones, which altered the state of Europe, and made a new arrangement among the great powers; such as the treaties of Munster, Nimeguen, Ryswick, and Utrecht.

But there is one part of political knowledge, which is only to be had by inquiry and conversation; that is, the present state of every power in Europe, with regard to the three important points, of strength, revenue, and commerce. You will, therefore, do well, while you are in Germany, to inform yourself carefully of the military force, the revenues, and the commerce of every prince and state of the empire; and to write down those informations in a little book, for that particular purpose. To give you a specimen of what I mean:—

THE ELECTORATE OF HANOVER

The revenue is about L500,000 a year.

The military establishment, in time of war, may be about 25,000 men;

but that is the utmost.

The trade is chiefly linens, exported from Stade.

There are coarse woolen manufactures for home-consumption.

The mines of Hartz produce about L100,000 in silver, annually.

Such informations you may very easily get, by proper inquiries, of every state in Germany if you will but prefer useful to frivolous conversations.

There are many princes in Germany, who keep very few or no troops, unless upon the approach of danger, or for the sake of profit, by letting them out for subsidies, to great powers: In that case, you will inform yourself what number of troops they could raise, either for their own defense, or furnish to other powers for subsidies.

There is very little trouble, and an infinite use, in acquiring of this knowledge. It seems to me even to be a more entertaining subject to talk upon, than 'la pluie et le beau tens'.

Though I am sensible that these things cannot be known with the utmost exactness, at least by you yet, you may, however, get so near the truth, that the difference will be very immaterial.

Pray let me know if the Roman Catholic worship is tolerated in Saxony, anywhere but at Court; and if public mass-houses are allowed anywhere else in the electorate. Are the regular Romish clergy allowed; and have they any convents?

Are there any military orders in Saxony, and what? Is the White Eagle a Saxon or a Polish order? Upon what occasion, and when was it founded? What number of knights?

Adieu! God bless you; and may you turn out what I wish!

LETTER XXXII

EARL OF PHILIP DORMER STANHOPE CHESTERFIELD

BATH, March 9, O. S. 1748.

DEAR BOY: I must from time to time, remind you of what I have often recommended to you, and of what you cannot attend to too much; SACRIFICE TO THE GRACES. The different effects of the same things, said or done, when accompanied or abandoned by them, is almost inconceivable. They prepare the way to the heart; and the heart has such an influence over the understanding, that it is worth while to engage it in our interest. It is the whole of women, who are guided by nothing else: and it has so much to say, even with men, and the ablest men too, that it commonly triumphs in every struggle with the understanding. Monsieur de Rochefoucault, in his "Maxims," says, that 'l'esprit est souvent la dupe du coeur.' If he had said, instead of 'souvent, tresque toujours', I fear he would have been nearer the truth. This being the case, aim at the heart. Intrinsic merit alone will not do; it will gain you the general esteem of all; but not the particular affection, that is, the heart of any. To engage the affections of any particular person, you must, over and above your general merit, have some particular merit to that person by services done, or offered; by expressions of regard and esteem; by complaisance, attentions, etc., for him. And the graceful manner of doing all these things opens the way to the heart, and facilitates, or rather insures, their effects. From your own observation, reflect what a disagreeable impression an awkward address, a slovenly figure, an ungraceful manner of speaking, whether stuttering, muttering, monotony, or drawling, an unattentive behavior, etc., make upon you, at first sight, in a stranger, and how they prejudice you against him, though for aught you know, he may have great intrinsic sense and merit. And reflect, on the other hand, how much the opposites of all these things prepossess you, at first sight, in favor of those who enjoy them. You wish to find all good qualities in them, and are in some degree disappointed if you do not. A thousand little things, not separately to be defined, conspire to form these graces, this je ne sais quoi, that always please. A pretty person, genteel motions, a proper degree of dress, an harmonious voice, something open and cheerful in the countenance, but without laughing; a distinct and properly varied manner of speaking: All these things, and many others, are necessary ingredients in the composition of the pleasing je ne sais quoi, which everybody feels, though nobody can describe. Observe carefully, then, what displeases or pleases you in others, and be persuaded, that in general; the same things will please or displease them in you. Having mentioned laughing, I must particularly warn you against it: and I could heartily wish, that you may often be seen to smile, but never heard to laugh while you live. Frequent and loud laughter is the characteristic of folly and in manners; it is the manner in which the mob express their silly joy at silly things; and they call it being merry. In my mind, there is nothing so illiberal, and so ill-bred, as audible laughter. True wit, or sense, never yet made anybody laugh; they are above it: They please the mind, and give a cheerfulness to the countenance. But it is low buffoonery, or silly accidents, that always excite laughter; and that is what people of sense and breeding should show themselves above. A man's going to sit down, in the supposition that he has a chair behind him, and falling down upon his breech for want of one, sets a whole company a laughing, when all the wit in the world would not do it; a plain proof, in my mind, how low and unbecoming a thing laughter is: not to mention the disagreeable noise that it makes, and the shocking distortion of the face that it occasions. Laughter is easily restrained, by a very little reflection; but as it is generally connected with the idea of gaiety, people do not enough attend to its absurdity. I am neither of a melancholy nor a cynical disposition, and am as willing and as apt to be pleased as anybody; but I am sure that, since I have had the full use of my reason, nobody has ever heard me laugh. Many people, at first, from awkwardness and 'mauvaise honte', have got a very disagreeable and silly trick of laughing whenever they speak; and I know a man of very good parts, Mr. Waller, who cannot say the commonest thing without laughing; which makes those, who do not know him, take him at first for a natural fool. This, and many other very disagreeable habits, are owing to mauvaise honte at their first setting out in the world. They are ashamed in company, and so disconcerted, that they do not know what they do, and try a thousand tricks to keep themselves in countenance; which tricks afterward grow habitual to them. Some put their fingers in their nose, others scratch their heads, others twirl their hats; in short, every awkward, ill-bred body has his trick. But the frequency does not justify the thing, and all these vulgar habits and awkwardnesses, though not criminal indeed, are most carefully to be guarded against, as they are great bars in the way of the art of pleasing. Remember, that to please is almost to prevail, or at least a necessary previous step to it. You, who have your fortune to make, should more particularly study this art. You had not, I must tell you, when you left England, 'les manieres prevenantes'; and I must confess they are not very common in England; but I hope that your good sense will make you acquire them abroad. If you desire to make yourself considerable in the world (as, if you have any spirit, you do), it must be entirely your own doing; for I may very possibly be out of the world at the time you come into it. Your own rank and fortune will not assist you; your merit and your manners can alone raise you to figure and fortune. I have laid the foundations of them, by the education which I have given you; but you must build the superstructure yourself.

I must now apply to you for some informations, which I dare say you can, and which I desire you will give me.

Can the Elector of Saxony put any of his subjects to death for high treason, without bringing them first to their trial in some public court of justice?

Can he, by his own authority, confine any subject in prison as long as he pleases, without trial?

Can he banish any subject out of his dominions by his own authority?

Can he lay any tax whatsoever upon his subjects, without the consent of the states of Saxony? and what are those states? how are they elected? what orders do they consist of? Do the clergy make part of them? and when, and how often do they meet?

If two subjects of the elector's are at law, for an estate situated in the electorate, in what court must this suit be tried? and will the decision of that court be final, or does there lie an appeal to the imperial chamber at Wetzlaer?

What do you call the two chief courts, or two chief magistrates, of civil and criminal justice?

What is the common revenue of the electorate, one year with another?

What number of troops does the elector now maintain? and what is the greatest number that the electorate is able to maintain?

I do not expect to have all these questions answered at once; but you will answer them, in proportion as you get the necessary and authentic informations.

You are, you see, my German oracle; and I consult you with so much faith, that you need not, like the oracles of old, return ambiguous answers; especially as you have this advantage over them, too, that I only consult you about past end present, but not about what is to come.

I wish you a good Easter-fair at Leipsig. See, with attention all the shops, drolls, tumblers, rope-dancers, and 'hoc genus omne': but inform yourself more particularly of the several parts of trade there. Adieu.

LETTER XXXIII

LONDON, March 25, O. S. 1748.

DEAR BOY: I am in great joy at the written and the verbal accounts which I have received lately of you.

The former, from Mr. Harte; the latter, from Mr. Trevanion, who is arrived here: they conspire to convince me that you employ your time well at Leipsig. I am glad to find you consult your own interest and your own pleasure so much; for the knowledge which you will acquire in these two years is equally necessary for both. I am likewise particularly pleased to find that you turn yourself to that sort of knowledge which is more peculiarly necessary for your destination: for Mr. Harte tells me you have read, with attention, Caillieres, Pequet, and Richelieu's "Letters." The "Memoirs" of the Cardinal de Retz will both entertain and instruct you; they relate to a very interesting period of the French history, the ministry of Cardinal Mazarin, during the minority of Lewis XIV. The characters of all the considerable people of that time are drawn, in a short, strong, and masterly manner; and the political reflections, which are most of them printed in italics, are the justest that ever I met with: they are not the labored reflections of a systematical closet politician, who, without the least experience of business, sits at home and writes maxims; but they are the reflections which a great and able man formed from long experience and practice in great business. They are true conclusions, drawn from facts, not from speculations.

As modern history is particularly your business, I will give you some rules to direct your study of it. It begins, properly with Charlemagne, in the year 800. But as, in those times of ignorance, the priests and monks were almost the only people that could or did write, we have scarcely any histories of those times but such as they have been pleased to give us, which are compounds of ignorance, superstition, and party zeal. So that a general notion of what is rather supposed, than really known to be, the history of the five or six following centuries, seems to be sufficient; and much time would be but ill employed in a minute attention to those legends. But reserve your utmost care, and most diligent inquiries, from the fifteenth century, and downward. Then learning began to revive, and credible histories to be written; Europe began to take the form, which, to some degree, it still retains: at least the foundations of the present great powers of Europe were then laid. Lewis the Eleventh made France, in truth, a monarchy, or, as he used to say himself, 'la mit hors de Page'. Before his time, there were independent provinces in France, as the Duchy of Brittany, etc., whose princes tore it to pieces, and kept it in constant domestic confusion. Lewis the Eleventh reduced all these petty states, by fraud, force, or marriage; for he scrupled no means to obtain his ends.

About that time, Ferdinand King of Aragon, and Isabella his wife, Queen of Castile, united the whole Spanish monarchy, and drove the Moors out of Spain, who had till then kept position of Granada. About that time, too, the house of Austria laid the great foundations of its subsequent power; first, by the marriage of Maximilian with the heiress of Burgundy; and then, by the marriage of his son Philip, Archduke of Austria, with Jane, the daughter of Isabella, Queen of Spain, and heiress of that whole kingdom, and of the West Indies. By the first of these marriages, the house of Austria acquired the seventeen provinces, and by the latter, Spain and America; all which centered in the person of Charles the Fifth, son of the above-mentioned Archduke Philip, the son of Maximilian. It was upon account of these two marriages, that the following Latin distich was made:

LETTERS TO HIS SON, COMPLETE

Bella gerant alii, Tu felix Austria nube;

Nam qua, Mars aliis; dat tibi regna Venus.

This immense power, which the Emperor Charles the Fifth found himself possessed of, gave him a desire for universal power (for people never desire all till they have gotten a great deal), and alarmed France; this sowed the seeds of that jealousy and enmity, which have flourished ever since between those two great powers. Afterward the House of Austria was weakened by the division made by Charles the Fifth of his dominions, between his son, Philip the Second of Spain, and his brother Ferdinand; and has ever since been dwindling to the weak condition in which it now is. This is a most interesting part of the history of Europe, of which it is absolutely necessary that you should be exactly and minutely informed.

There are in the history of most countries, certain very remarkable eras, which deserve more particular inquiry and attention than the common run of history. Such is the revolt of the Seventeen Provinces, in the reign of Philip the Second of Spain, which ended in forming the present republic of the Seven United Provinces, whose independency was first allowed by Spain at the treaty of Munster. Such was the extraordinary revolution of Portugal, in the year 1640, in favor of the present House of Braganza. Such is the famous revolution of Sweden, when Christian the Second of Denmark, who was also king of Sweden, was driven out by Gustavus Vasa. And such also is that memorable era in Denmark, of 1660; when the states of that kingdom made a voluntary surrender of all their rights and liberties to the Crown, and changed that free state into the most absolute monarchy now in Europe. The Acta Regis, upon that occasion, are worth your perusing. These remarkable periods of modern history deserve your particular attention, and most of them have been treated singly by good historians, which are worth your reading. The revolutions of Sweden, and of Portugal, are most admirably well written by L'Abbe de Vertot; they are short, and will not take twelve hours' reading. There is another book which very well deserves your looking into, but not worth your buying at present, because it is not portable; if you can borrow or hire it, you should; and that is, 'L' Histoire des Traits de Paix, in two volumes, folio, which make part of the 'Corps Diplomatique'. You will there find a short and clear history, and the substance of every treaty made in Europe, during the last century, from the treaty of Vervins. Three parts in four of this book are not worth your reading, as they relate to treaties of very little importance; but if you select the most considerable ones, read them with attention, and take some notes, it will be of great use to you. Attend chiefly to those in which the great powers of Europe are the parties; such as the treaty of the Pyrenees, between France and Spain; the treaties of Nimeguen and Ryswick; but, above all, the treaty of Munster should be most circumstantially and minutely known to you, as almost every treaty made since has some reference to it. For this, Pere Bougeant is the best book you can read, as it takes in the thirty years' war, which preceded that treaty. The treaty itself, which is made a perpetual law of the empire, comes in the course of your lectures upon the 'Jus Publicum Imperii'.

In order to furnish you with materials for a letter, and at the same time to inform both you and myself of what it is right that we should know, pray answer me the following questions:

How many companies are there in the Saxon regiments of foot? How many men in each company?

How many troops in the regiments of horse and dragoons; and how many men in each?

What number of commissioned and non-commissioned officers in a company of foot, or in a troop of horse or dragoons? N. B. Noncommissioned officers are all those below ensigns and cornets.

What is the daily pay of a Saxon foot soldier, dragoon, and trooper?

What are the several ranks of the 'Etat Major-general'? N. B. The Etat Major-general is everything above colonel. The Austrians have no brigadiers, and the French have no major-generals in their Etat Major. What have the Saxons? Adieu!

LETTER XXXIV

LONDON, March 27, O. S. 1748.

DEAR BOY: This little packet will be delivered to you by one Monsieur Duval, who is going to the fair at Leipsig. He is a jeweler, originally of Geneva, but who has been settled here these eight or ten years, and a very sensible fellow: pray do be very civil to him.

As I advised you, some time ago, to inform yourself of the civil and military establishments of as many of the kingdoms and states of Europe, as you should either be in yourself, or be able to get authentic accounts of, I send you here a little book, in which, upon the article of Hanover, I have pointed out the short method of putting down these informations, by way of helping your memory. The book being lettered, you can immediately turn to whatever article you want; and, by adding interleaves to each letter, may extend your minutes to what particulars you please. You may get such books made anywhere; and appropriate each, if you please, to a particular object. I have myself found great utility in this method. If I had known what to have sent you by this opportunity I would have done it. The French say, 'Que les petits presens entretiennent l'amite et que les grande l'augmentent'; but I could not recollect that you wanted anything, or at least anything that you cannot get as well at Leipsig as here. Do but continue to deserve, and, I assure you, that you shall never want anything I can give.

Do not apprehend that my being out of employment may be any prejudice to you. Many things will happen before you can be fit for business; and when you are fit, whatever my situation may be, it will always be in my power to help you in your first steps; afterward you must help yourself by your own abilities. Make yourself necessary, and, instead of soliciting, you will be solicited. The thorough knowledge of foreign affairs, the interests, the views, and the manners of the several courts in Europe, are not the common growth of this country. It is in your power to acquire them; you have all the means. Adieu! Yours.

LETTER XXXV

LONDON, April 1, O. S. 1748.

DEAR BOY: I have not received any letter, either from you or from Mr. Harte, these three posts, which I impute wholly to accidents between this place and Leipsig; and they are distant enough to admit of many. I always take it for granted that you are well, when I do not hear to the contrary; besides, as I have often told you, I am much more anxious about your doing well, than about your being well; and, when you do not write, I will suppose that you are doing something more useful. Your health will continue, while your temperance continues; and at your age nature takes sufficient care of the body, provided she is left to herself, and that intemperance on one hand, or medicines on the other, do not break in upon her. But it is by no means so with the mind, which, at your age particularly, requires great and constant care, and some physic. Every quarter of an hour, well or ill employed, will do it essential and lasting good or harm. It requires also a great deal of exercise, to bring it to a state of health and vigor. Observe the difference there is between minds cultivated, and minds uncultivated, and you will, I am sure, think that you cannot take too much pains, nor employ too much of your time in the culture of your own. A drayman is probably born with as good organs as Milton, Locke, or Newton; but, by culture, they are as much more above him as he is above his horse. Sometimes, indeed, extraordinary geniuses have broken out by the force of nature, without the assistance of education; but those instances are too rare for anybody to trust to; and even they would make a much greater figure, if they had the advantage of education into the bargain. If Shakespeare's genius had been cultivated, those beauties, which we so justly admire in him, would have been undisgraced by those extravagancies, and that nonsense, with which they are frequently accompanied. People are, in general, what they are made, by education and company, from fifteen to five-and-twenty; consider well, therefore, the importance of your next eight or nine years; your whole depends upon them. I will tell you sincerely, my hopes and my fears concerning you. I think you will be a good scholar; and that you will acquire a considerable stock of knowledge of various kinds; but I fear that you neglect what are called little, though, in truth, they are very material things; I mean, a gentleness of manners, an engaging address, and an insinuating behavior; they are real and solid advantages, and none but those who do not know the world, treat them as trifles. I am told that you speak very quick, and not distinctly; this is a most ungraceful and disagreeable trick, which you know I have told you of a thousand times; pray attend carefully to the correction of it. An agreeable and, distinct manner of speaking adds greatly to the matter; and I have known many a very good speech unregarded, upon account of the disagreeable manner in which it has been delivered, and many an indifferent one applauded, from the contrary reason. Adieu!

LETTER XXXVI

LONDON, April 15, O. S. 1748

DEAR BOY: Though I have no letters from you to acknowledge since my last to you, I will not let three posts go from hence without a letter from me. My affection always prompts me to write to you; and I am encouraged to do it, by the hopes that my letters are not quite useless. You will probably receive this in the midst of the diversions of Leipsig fair; at which, Mr. Harte tells me, that you are to shine in fine clothes, among fine folks. I am very glad of it, as it is time that you should begin to be formed to the manners of the world in higher life. Courts are the best schools for that sort of learning. You are beginning now with the outside of a court; and there is not a more gaudy one than that of Saxony. Attend to it, and make your observations upon the turn and manners of it, that you may hereafter compare it with other courts which you will see; And, though you are not yet able to be informed, or to judge of the political conduct and maxims of that court, yet you may remark the forms, the ceremonies, and the exterior state of it. At least see everything that you can see, and know everything that you can know of it, by asking questions. See likewise everything at the fair, from operas and plays, down to the Savoyard's raree-shows.

Everything is worth seeing once; and the more one sees, the less one either wonders or admires.

Make my compliments to Mr. Harte, and tell him that I have just now received his letter, for which I thank him. I am called away, and my letter is therefore very much shortened. Adieu.

I am impatient to receive your answers to the many questions that I have asked you.

LETTER XXXVII

LONDON, April 26, O. S. 1748.

DEAR BOY: I am extremely pleased with your continuation of the history of the Reformation; which is one of those important eras that deserves your utmost attention, and of which you cannot be too minutely informed. You have, doubtless, considered the causes of that great event, and observed that disappointment and resentment had a much greater share in it, than a religious zeal or an abhorrence of the errors and abuses of popery.

Luther, an Augustine monk, enraged that his order, and consequently himself, had not the exclusive privilege of selling indulgences, but that the Dominicans were let into a share of that profitable but infamous trade, turns reformer, and exclaims against the abuses, the corruption, and the idolatry, of the church of Rome; which were certainly gross enough for him to have seen long before, but which he had at least acquiesced in, till what he called the rights, that is, the profit, of his order came to be touched. It is true, the church of Rome furnished him ample matter for complaint and reformation, and he laid hold of it ably.

This seems to me the true cause of that great and necessary, work; but whatever the cause was, the effect was good; and the Reformation spread itself by its own truth and fitness; was conscientiously received by great numbers in Germany, and other countries; and was soon afterward mixed up with the politics of princes; and, as it always happens in religious disputes, became the specious covering of injustice and ambition.

Under the pretense of crushing heresy, as it was called, the House of Austria meant to extend and establish its power in the empire; as, on the other hand, many Protestant princes, under the pretense of extirpating idolatry, or at least of securing toleration, meant only to enlarge their own dominions or privileges. These views respectively, among the chiefs on both sides, much more than true religious motives, continued what were called the religious wars in Germany, almost uninterruptedly, till the affairs of the two religions were finally settled by the treaty of Munster.

Were most historical events traced up to their true causes, I fear we should not find them much more noble or disinterested than Luther's disappointed avarice; and therefore I look with some contempt upon those refining and sagacious historians, who ascribe all, even the most common events, to some deep political cause; whereas mankind is made up of inconsistencies, and no man acts invariably up to his predominant character. The wisest man sometimes acts weakly, and the weakest sometimes wisely. Our jarring passions, our variable humors, nay, our greater or lesser degree of health and spirits, produce such contradictions in our conduct, that, I believe, those are the oftenest mistaken, who ascribe our actions to the most seemingly obvious motives; and I am convinced, that a light supper, a good night's sleep, and a fine morning, have sometimes made a hero of the same man, who, by an indigestion, a restless night, and rainy morning, would, have proved a coward. Our best conjectures, therefore, as to the true springs of actions, are but very uncertain; and the actions themselves are all that we must pretend to know from history. That Caesar was murdered by twenty-three conspirators, I make no doubt: but I very much doubt that their love of liberty, and of their country, was their sole, or even principal motive; and I dare say that, if the truth were known, we should find that many other motives at least concurred, even in the great Brutus himself; such as pride, envy, personal pique, and disappointment. Nay, I cannot help carrying my Pyrrhonism still further, and extending it often to historical facts themselves, at least to most of the circumstances with which they are related; and every day's experience confirms me in this historical incredulity. Do we ever hear the most recent fact related exactly in the same way, by the several people who were at the same time eyewitnesses of it? No. One mistakes, another misrepresents, and others warp it a little to their own, turn of mind, or private views. A man who has been concerned in a transaction will not write it fairly; and a man who has not, cannot. But notwithstanding all this uncertainty, history is not the less necessary to be known, as the best histories are taken for granted, and are the frequent subjects both of conversation and writing. Though I am convinced that Caesar's ghost never appeared to Brutus, yet I should be much ashamed to be ignorant of that fact, as related by the historians of those times. Thus the Pagan theology is universally received as matter for writing and conversation, though believed now by nobody; and we talk of Jupiter, Mars, Apollo, etc., as gods, though we know, that if they ever existed at all, it was only as mere mortal men. This historical Pyrrhonism, then, proves nothing against the study and knowledge of history; which, of all other studies, is the most necessary for a man who is to live in the world. It only points out to us, not to be too decisive and peremptory; and to be cautious how we draw inferences for our own practice from remote facts, partially or ignorantly related; of which we can, at best, but imperfectly guess, and certainly not know the real motives. The testimonies of ancient history must necessarily be weaker than those of modern, as all testimony grows weaker and weaker, as it is more and more remote from us. I would therefore advise you to study ancient history, in general, as other people, do; that is, not to be ignorant of any or those facts which are universally received, upon the faith of the best historians; and whether true or false, you have them as other people have them. But modern history, I mean particularly that of the last three centuries, is what I would have you apply to with the greatest attention and exactness. There the probability of coming at the truth is much greater, as the testimonies are much more recent; besides, anecdotes, memoirs, and original letters, often come to the aid of modern history. The best memoirs that I know of are those of Cardinal de Retz, which I have once before recommended to you; and which I advise you to read more than once, with attention. There are many political maxims in these memoirs, most of which are printed in italics; pray attend to, and remember them. I never read them but my own experience confirms the truth of them. Many of them seem trifling to people who are not used to business; but those who are, feel the truth of them.

It is time to put an end to this long rambling letter; in which if any one thing can be of use to you, it will more than pay the trouble I have taken to write it. Adieu! Yours.

LETTER XXXVIII

LONDON, May 10, O. S. 1748.

DEAR BOY: I reckon that this letter will find you just returned from Dresden, where you have made your first court caravanne. What inclination for courts this taste of them may have given you, I cannot tell; but this I think myself sure of, from your good sense, that in leaving Dresden, you have left dissipation too; and have resumed at Leipsig that application which, if you like courts, can alone enable you to make a good figure at them. A mere courtier, without parts or knowledge, is the most frivolous and contemptible of all beings; as, on the other hand, a man of parts and knowledge, who acquires the easy and noble manners of a court, is the most perfect. It is a trite, commonplace observation, that courts are the seats of falsehood and dissimulation. That, like many, I might say most, commonplace observations, is false. Falsehood and dissimulation are certainly to be found at courts; but where are they not to be found? Cottages have them, as well as courts; only with worse manners. A couple of neighboring farmers in a village will contrive and practice as many tricks, to over-reach each other at the next market, or to supplant each other in the favor, of the squire, as any two courtiers can do to supplant each other in the favor of their prince.

Whatever poets may write, or fools believe, of rural innocence and truth, and of the perfidy of courts, this is most undoubtedly true that shepherds and ministers are both men; their nature and passions the same, the modes of them only different.

Having mentioned commonplace observations, I will particularly caution you against either using, believing, or approving them. They are the common topics of witlings and coxcombs; those, who really have wit, have the utmost contempt for them, and scorn even to laugh at the pert things that those would-be wits say upon such subjects.

Religion is one of their favorite topics; it is all priest-craft; and an invention contrived and carried on by priests of all religions, for their own power and profit; from this absurd and false principle flow the commonplace, insipid jokes, and insults upon the clergy. With these people, every priest, of every religion, is either a public or a concealed unbeliever, drunkard, and whoremaster; whereas, I conceive, that priests are extremely like other men, and neither the better nor the worse for wearing a gown or a surplice: but if they are different from other people, probably it is rather on the side of religion and morality, or, at least, decency, from their education and manner of life.

Another common topic for false wit, and cool raillery, is matrimony. Every man and his wife hate each other cordially, whatever they may pretend, in public, to the contrary. The husband certainly wishes his wife at the devil, and the wife certainly cuckolds her husband. Whereas, I presume, that men and their wives neither love nor hate each other the more, upon account of the form of matrimony which has been said over them. The cohabitation, indeed, which is the consequence of matrimony, makes them either love or hate more, accordingly as they respectively deserve it; but that would be exactly the same between any man and woman who lived together without being married.

These and many other commonplace reflections upon nations or professions in general (which are at least as often false as true), are the poor refuge of people who have neither wit nor invention of their own, but endeavor to shine in company by second-hand finery. I always put these pert jackanapes out of countenance, by looking extremely grave, when they expect that I should laugh at their pleasantries; and by saying WELL, AND SO, as if they had not done, and that the sting were still to come. This disconcerts them, as they have no resources in themselves, and have but one set of jokes to live upon. Men of parts are not reduced to these shifts, and have the utmost contempt for them, they find proper subjects enough for either useful or lively conversations; they can be witty without satire or commonplace, and serious without being dull. The frequentation of courts checks this petulancy of manners; the good-breeding and circumspection which are necessary, and only to be learned there, correct those pertnesses. I do not doubt but that you are improved in your manners by the short visit which you have made at Dresden; and the other courts, which I intend that you shall be better acquainted with, will gradually smooth you up to the highest polish. In courts, a versatility of genius and softness of manners are absolutely necessary; which some people mistake for abject flattery, and having no opinion of one's own; whereas it is only the decent and genteel manner of maintaining your own opinion, and possibly of bringing other people to it. The manner of doing things is often more important than the things themselves; and the very same thing may become either pleasing or offensive, by the manner of saying or doing it. 'Materiam superabat opus', is often said of works of sculpture; where though the materials were valuable, as silver, gold, etc., the workmanship was still more so. This holds true, applied to manners; which adorn whatever knowledge or parts people may have; and even make a greater impression upon nine in ten of mankind, than the intrinsic value of the materials. On the other hand, remember, that what Horace says of good writing is justly applicable to those who would make a good figure in courts, and distinguish themselves in the shining parts of life; 'Sapere est principium et fons'. A man who, without a good fund of knowledge and parts, adopts a court life, makes the most ridiculous figure imaginable. He is a machine, little superior to the court clock; and, as this points out the hours, he points out the frivolous employment of them. He is, at most, a comment upon the clock; and according to the hours that it strikes, tells you now it is levee, now dinner, now supper time, etc. The end which I propose by your education, and which (IF YOU PLEASE) I shall certainly attain, is to unite in you all the knowledge of a scholar with the manners of a courtier; and to join, what is seldom joined by any of my countrymen, books and the world. They are commonly twenty years old before they have spoken to anybody above their schoolmaster, and the fellows of their college. If they happen to have learning, it is only Greek and Latin, but not one word of modern history, or modern languages. Thus prepared, they go abroad, as they call it; but, in truth, they stay at home all that while; for being very awkward, confoundedly ashamed, and not speaking the languages, they go into no foreign company, at least none good; but dine and sup with one another only at the tavern. Such examples, I am sure, you will not imitate, but even carefully avoid. You will always take care to keep the best company in the place where you are, which is the only use of traveling: and (by the way) the pleasures of a gentleman are only to be found in the best company; for that not which low company, most falsely and impudently, call pleasure, is only the sensuality of a swine.

I ask hard and uninterrupted study from you but one year more; after that, you shall have every day more and more time for your amusements. A few hours each day will then be sufficient for application, and the others cannot be better employed than in the pleasures of good company. Adieu.

LETTER XXXIX

LONDON, May 31, O. S. 1748.

DEAR BOY: I received yesterday your letter of the 16th, N. S., and have, in consequence of it, written this day to Sir Charles Williams, to thank him for all the civilities he has shown you. Your first setting out at court has, I find, been very favorable; and his Polish Majesty has distinguished you. I hope you received that mark of distinction with respect and with steadiness, which is the proper behavior of a man of fashion. People of a low, obscure education cannot stand the rays of greatness; they are frightened out of their wits when kings and great men speak to them; they are awkward, ashamed, and do not know what nor how to answer; whereas, 'les honnetes gens' are not dazzled by superior rank: they know, and pay all the respect that is due to it; but they do it without being disconcerted; and can converse just as easily with a king as with any one of his subjects. That is the great advantage of being introduced young into good company, and being used early to converse with one's superiors. How many men have I seen here, who, after having had the full benefit of an English education, first at school, and then at the university, when they have been presented to the king, did not know whether they stood upon their heads or their heels! If the king spoke to them, they were annihilated; they trembled, endeavored to put their hands in their pockets, and missed them; let their hats fall, and were ashamed to take them up; and in short, put themselves in every attitude but the right, that is, the easy and natural one. The characteristic of a well-bred man, is to converse with his inferiors without insolence, and with his superiors with respect and ease. He talks to kings without concern; he trifles with women of the first condition with familiarity, gayety, but respect; and converses with his equals, whether he is acquainted with them or not, upon general common topics, that are not, however, quite frivolous, without the least concern of mind or awkwardness of body: neither of which can appear to advantage, but when they are perfectly easy.

The tea-things, which Sir Charles Williams has given you, I would have you make a present of to your Mamma, and send them to her by Duval when he returns. You owe her not only duty, but likewise great obligations for her care and tenderness; and, consequently, cannot take too many opportunities of showing your gratitude.

I am impatient to receive your account of Dresden, and likewise your answers to the many questions that I asked you.

Adieu for this time, and God bless you!

LETTER XL

LETTERS TO HIS SON, COMPLETE

LONDON, May 27, O. S. 1748.

DEAR BOY: This and the two next years make so important a period of your life, that I cannot help repeating to you my exhortations, my commands, and (what I hope will be still more prevailing with you than either) my earnest entreaties, to employ them well. Every moment that you now lose, is so much character and advantage lost; as, on the other hand, every moment that you now employ usefully, is so much time wisely laid out, at most prodigious interest. These two years must lay the foundations of all the knowledge that you will ever have; you may build upon them afterward as much as you please, but it will be too late to lay any new ones. Let me beg of you, therefore, to grudge no labor nor pains to acquire, in time, that stock of knowledge, without which you never can rise, but must make a very insignificant figure in the world. Consider your own situation; you have not the advantage of rank or fortune to bear you up; I shall, very probably, be out of the world before you can properly be said to be in it. What then will you have to rely on but your own merit? That alone must raise you, and that alone will raise you, if you have but enough of it. I have often heard and read of oppressed and unrewarded merit, but I have oftener (I might say always) seen great merit make its way, and meet with its reward, to a certain degree at least, in spite of all difficulties. By merit, I mean the moral virtues, knowledge, and manners; as to the moral virtues, I say nothing to you; they speak best for themselves, nor can I suspect that they want any recommendation with you; I will therefore only assure you, that without them you will be most unhappy.

As to knowledge, I have often told you, and I am persuaded you are thoroughly convinced, how absolutely necessary it is to you, whatever your destination may be. But as knowledge has a most extensive meaning, and as the life of man is not long enough to acquire, nor his mind capable of entertaining and digesting, all parts of knowledge, I will point out those to which you should particularly apply, and which, by application, you may make yourself perfect master of. Classical knowledge, that is, Greek and Latin, is absolutely necessary for everybody; because everybody has agreed to think and to call it so. And the word ILLITERATE, in its common acceptation, means a man who is ignorant of those two languages. You are by this time, I hope, pretty near master of both, so that a small part of the day dedicated to them, for two years more, will make you perfect in that study. Rhetoric, logic, a little geometry, and a general notion of astronomy, must, in their turns, have their hours too; not that I desire you should be deep in any one of these; but it is fit you should know something of them all. The knowledge more particularly useful and necessary for you, considering your destination, consists of modern languages, modern history, chronology, and geography, the laws of nations, and the 'jus publicum Imperii'. You must absolutely speak all the modern Languages, as purely and correctly as the natives of the respective countries: for whoever does not speak a language perfectly and easily, will never appear to advantage in conversation, nor treat with others in it upon equal terms. As for French, you have it very well already; and must necessarily, from the universal usage of that language, know it better and better every day: so that I am in no pain about that: German, I suppose, you know pretty well by this time, and will be quite master of it before you leave Leipsig: at least, I am sure you may. Italian and Spanish will come in their turns, and, indeed, they are both so easy, to one who knows Latin and French, that neither of them will cost you much time or trouble. Modern history, by which I mean particularly the history of the last three centuries, should be the object of your greatest and constant attention, especially those parts of it which relate more immediately to the great powers of Europe. This study you will carefully connect with chronology and geography; that is, you will remark and retain the dates of every important event; and always read with the map by you, in which you will constantly look for every place mentioned: this is the only way of retaining geography; for, though it is soon learned by the lump, yet, when only so learned, it is still sooner forgot.

Manners, though the last, and it may be the least ingredient of real merit, are, however, very far from being useless in its composition; they adorn, and give an additional force and luster to both virtue and knowledge. They prepare and smooth the way for the progress of both; and are, I fear, with the bulk of mankind, more engaging than either. Remember, then, the infinite advantage of manners; cultivate and improve your own to the utmost good sense will suggest the great rules to you, good company will do the rest. Thus you see how much you have to do; and how little time to do it in: for when you are thrown out into the world, as in a couple of years you must be, the unavoidable dissipation of company, and the necessary avocations of some kind of business or other, will leave you no time to undertake new branches of knowledge: you may, indeed, by a prudent allotment of your time, reserve some to complete and finish the building; but you will never find enough to lay new foundations. I have such an opinion of your understanding, that I am convinced you are sensible of these truths; and that, however hard and laborious your present uninterrupted application may seem to you, you will rather increase than lessen it. For God's sake, my dear boy, do not squander away one moment of your time, for every moment may be now most usefully employed. Your future fortune, character, and figure in the world, entirely depend upon your use or abuse of the two next years. If you do but employ them well, what may you not reasonably expect to be, in time? And if you do not, what may I not reasonably fear you will be? You are the only one I ever knew, of this country, whose education was, from the beginning, calculated for the department of foreign affairs; in consequence of which, if you will invariably pursue, and diligently qualify yourself for that object, you may make yourself absolutely necessary to the government, and, after having received orders as a minister abroad, send orders, in your turn, as Secretary of State at home. Most of our ministers abroad have taken up that department occasionally, without having ever thought of foreign affairs before; many of them, without speaking any one foreign language; and all of them without manners which are absolutely necessary toward being well received, and making a figure at foreign courts. They do the business accordingly, that is, very ill: they never get into the secrets of these courts, for want of insinuation and address: they do not guess at their views, for want of knowing their interests: and, at last, finding themselves very unfit for, soon grow weary of their commissions, and are impatient to return home, where they are but too justly laid aside and neglected. Every moment's conversation may, if you please, be of use to you; in this view, every public event, which is the common topic of conversation, gives you an opportunity of getting some information. For example, the preliminaries of peace, lately concluded at Aix-la-Chapelle, will be the common subject of most conversations; in which you will take care to ask the proper questions: as, what is the meaning of the Assiento contract for negroes, between England and Spain; what the annual ship; when stipulated; upon what account suspended, etc. You will likewise inform yourself about Guastalla, now given to Don Philip, together with Parma and Placentia; who they belonged to before; what claim or pretensions Don Philip had to them; what they are worth; in short, everything concerning them. The cessions made by the Queen of Hungary to the King of Sardinia, are, by these preliminaries, confirmed and secured to him: you will inquire, therefore, what they are, and what they are worth. This is the kind of knowledge which you should be most thoroughly master of, and in which conversation will help you almost as much as books: but both are best. There are histories of every considerable treaty, from that of Westphalia to that of Utrecht, inclusively; all which I would advise you to read. Pore Bougeant's, of the treaty of Westphalia, is an excellent one; those of Nimeguen, Ryswick, and Utrecht, are not so well written; but are, however, very useful. 'L'Histoire des Traites de Paix', in two volumes, folio, which I recommended to you some time ago, is a book that you should often consult, when you hear mention made of any treaty concluded in the seventeenth century.

Upon the whole, if you have a mind to be considerable, and to shine hereafter, you must labor hard now. No quickness of parts, no vivacity, will do long, or go far, without a solid fund of knowledge; and that fund of knowledge will amply repay all the pains that you can take in acquiring it. Reflect seriously, within yourself, upon all this, and ask yourself whether I can have any view, but your interest, in all that I recommend to you. It is the result of my experience, and flows from that tenderness and affection with which, while you deserve them, I shall be, Yours.

Make my compliments to Mr. Harte, and tell him that I have received his letter of the 24th, N. S.

LETTERS TO HIS SON, COMPLETE

LETTER XLI

LONDON, May 31, O. S. 1748

DEAR BOY: I have received, with great satisfaction, your letter of the 28th N. S., from Dresden: it finishes your short but clear account of the Reformation which is one of those interesting periods of modern history, that can not be too much studied nor too minutely known by you. There are many great events in history, which, when once they are over, leave things in the situation in which they found them. As, for instance, the late war; which, excepting the establishment in Italy for Don Philip, leave things pretty much in state quo; a mutual restitution of all acquisitions being stipulated by the preliminaries of the peace. Such events undoubtedly deserve your notice, but yet not so minutely as those, which are not only important in themselves, but equally (or it may be more) important by their consequences too: of this latter sort were the progress of the Christian religion in Europe; the Invasion of the Goths; the division of the Roman empire into Western and Eastern; the establishment and rapid progress of Mahometanism; and, lastly, the Reformation; all which events produced the greatest changes in the affairs of Europe, and to one or other of which, the present situation of all the parts of it is to be traced up.

Next to these, are those events which more immediately effect particular states and kingdoms, and which are reckoned entirely local, though their influence may, and indeed very often does, indirectly, extend itself further, such as civil wars and revolutions, from which a total change in the form of government frequently flows. The civil wars in England, in the reign of King Charles I., produced an entire change of the government here, from a limited monarchy to a commonwealth, at first, and afterward to absolute power, usurped by Cromwell, under the pretense of protection, and the title of Protector.

The Revolution in 1688, instead of changing, preserved one form of government; which King James II. intended to subvert, and establish absolute power in the Crown.

These are the two great epochs in our English history, which I recommend to your particular attention.

The league formed by the House of Guise, and fomented by the artifices of Spain, is a most material part of the history of France. The foundation of it was laid in the reign of Henry II., but the superstructure was carried on through the successive reigns of Francis II., Charles IX. and Henry III., till at last it was crushed, partly, by the arms, but more by the apostasy of Henry IV.

In Germany, great events have been frequent, by which the imperial dignity has always either gotten or lost; and so it they have affected the constitution of the empire. The House of Austria kept that dignity to itself for near two hundred years, during which time it was always attempting extend its power, by encroaching upon the rights and privileges of the other states of the empire; till at the end of the bellum tricennale, the treaty of Munster, of which France is guarantee, fixed the respective claims.

Italy has been constantly torn to pieces, from the time of the Goths, by the Popes and the Anti-popes, severally supported by other great powers of Europe, more as their interests than as their religion led them; by the pretensions also of France, and the House of Austria, upon Naples, Sicily, and the Milanese; not to mention the various lesser causes of squabbles there, for the little states, such as Ferrara, Parma, Montserrat, etc.

The Popes, till lately, have always taken a considerable part, and had great influence in the affairs of Europe; their excommunications, bulls, and indulgences, stood instead of armies in the time of ignorance and bigotry; but now that mankind is better informed, the spiritual authority of the Pope is not only less regarded, but even despised by the Catholic princes themselves; and his Holiness is actually little more than Bishop of Rome, with large temporalities, which he is not likely to keep longer than till the other greater powers in Italy shall find their conveniency in taking them from him. Among the modern Popes, Leo the Tenth, Alexander the Sixth, and Sextus Quintus, deserve your particular notice; the first, among other things, for his own learning and taste, and for his encouragement of the reviving arts and sciences in Italy. Under his protection, the Greek and Latin classics were most excellently translated into Italian; painting flourished and arrived at its perfection; and sculpture came so near the ancients, that the works of his time, both in marble and bronze, are now called Antico-Moderno.

Alexander the Sixth, together with his natural son Caesar Borgia, was famous for his wickedness, in which he, and his son too, surpassed all imagination. Their lives are well worth your reading. They were poisoned themselves by the poisoned wine which they had prepared for others; the father died of it, but Caesar recovered.

Sixtus the Fifth was the son of a swineherd, and raised himself to the popedom by his abilities: he was a great knave, but an able and singular one.

Here is history enough for to-day: you shall have some more soon. Adieu.

LETTER XLII

LONDON, June 21, O. S. 1748.

DEAR BOY: Your very bad enunciation runs so much in my head, and gives me such real concern, that it will be the subject of this, and, I believe, of many more letters. I congratulate both you and myself, that, was informed of it (as I hope) in time to prevent it: and shall ever think myself, as hereafter you will, I am sure think yourself, infinitely obliged to Sir Charles Williams for informing me of it. Good God! if this ungraceful and disagreeable manner of speaking had, either by your negligence or mine, become habitual to you, as in a couple of years more it would have been, what a figure would you have made in company, or in a public assembly? Who would have liked you in the one or attended you; in the other? Read what Cicero and Quintilian say of enunciation, and see what a stress they lay upon the gracefulness of it; nay, Cicero goes further, and even maintains, that a good figure is necessary for an orator; and particularly that he must not be vastus, that is, overgrown and clumsy. He shows by it that he knew mankind well, and knew the powers of an agreeable figure and a graceful, manner. Men, as well as women, are much oftener led by their hearts than by their understandings. The way to the heart is through the senses; please their eyes and their ears and the work is half done. I have frequently known a man's fortune decided for ever by his first address. If it is pleasing, people are hurried involuntarily into a persuasion that he has a merit, which possibly he has not; as, on the other hand, if it is ungraceful, they are immediately prejudiced against him, and unwilling to allow him the merit which it may be he has. Nor is this sentiment so unjust and unreasonable as at first it may seem; for if a man has parts, he must know of what infinite consequence it is to him to have a graceful manner of speaking, and a genteel and pleasing address; he will cultivate and improve them to the utmost. Your figure is a good one; you have no natural defect in the organs of speech; your address may be engaging, and your manner of speaking graceful, if you will; so that if you are not so, neither I nor the world can ascribe it to anything but your want of parts. What is the constant and just observation as to all actors upon the stage? Is it not, that those who have the best sense, always speak the best, though they may happen not to have the best voices? They will speak plainly, distinctly, and with the proper emphasis, be their voices ever so bad. Had Roscius spoken QUICK, THICK, and UNGRACEFULLY, I will answer for it, that Cicero would not have thought him worth the oration which he made in his favor. Words were given us to communicate our ideas by: and there must be something inconceivably absurd in uttering them in such a manner as that either people cannot understand them, or will not desire to understand them. I tell you, truly and sincerely, that I shall judge of your parts by your speaking gracefully or ungracefully. If you have parts, you will never be at rest till you have brought yourself to a habit of speaking most gracefully; for I aver, that it is in your power —You will desire Mr. Harte, that you may read aloud to him every day; and that he will interrupt and correct you every time that you read too fast, do not observe the proper stops, or lay a wrong emphasis. You will take care to open your teeth when you speak; to articulate every word distinctly; and to beg of Mr. Harte, Mr. Eliot, or whomsoever you speak to, to remind and stop you, if you ever fall into the rapid and unintelligible mutter. You will even read aloud to yourself, and time your utterance to your own ear; and read at first much slower than you need to do, in order to correct yourself of that shameful trick of speaking faster than you ought. In short, if you think right, you will make it your business; your study, and your pleasure to speak well. Therefore, what I have said in this, and in my last, is more than sufficient, if you have sense; and ten times more would not be sufficient, if you have not; so here I rest it.

Next to graceful speaking, a genteel carriage, and a graceful manner of presenting yourself, are extremely necessary, for they are extremely engaging: and carelessness in these points is much more unpardonable in a young fellow than affectation. It shows an offensive indifference about pleasing. I am told by one here, who has seen you lately, that you are awkward in your motions, and negligent of your person: I am sorry for both; and so will you be, when it will be too late, if you continue so some time longer. Awkwardness of carriage is very alienating; and a total negligence of dress and air is an impertinent insult upon custom and fashion. You remember Mr.———very well, I am sure, and you must consequently remember his, extreme awkwardness: which, I can assure you, has been a great clog to his parts and merit, that have, with much difficulty, but barely counterbalanced it at last. Many, to whom I have formerly commended him, have answered me, that they were sure he could not have parts, because he was so awkward: so much are people, as I observed to you before, taken by the eye. Women have great influence as to a man's fashionable character; and an awkward man will never have their votes; which, by the way, are very numerous, and much oftener counted than weighed. You should therefore give some attention to your dress, and the gracefulness of your motions. I believe, indeed, that you have no perfect model for either at Leipsig, to form yourself upon; but, however, do not get a habit of neglecting either; and attend properly to both, when you go to courts, where they are very necessary, and where you will have good masters and good models for both. Your exercises of riding, fencing, and dancing, will civilize and fashion your body and your limbs, and give you, if you will but take it, 'l'air d'un honnete homme'.

I will now conclude with suggesting one reflection to you; which is, that you should be sensible of your good fortune, in having one who interests himself enough in you, to inquire into your faults, in order to inform you of them. Nobody but myself would be so solicitous, either to know or correct them; so that you might consequently be ignorant of them yourself; for our own self-love draws a thick veil between us and our faults. But when you hear yours from me, you may be sure that you hear them from one who for your sake only desires to correct them; from one whom you cannot suspect of any, partiality but in your favor; and from one who heartily wishes that his care of you, as a father, may, in a little time, render every care unnecessary but that of a friend. Adieu.

P. S. I condole with you for the untimely and violent death of the tuneful Matzel.

LETTER XLIII

LONDON, July 1, O. S. 1748.

DEAR Boy: I am extremely well pleased with the course of studies which Mr. Harte informs me you are now in, and with the degree of application which he assures me you have to them. It is your interest to do so, as the advantage will be all your own. My affection for you makes me both wish and endeavor that you may turn out well; and, according as you do turn out, I shall either be proud or ashamed of you. But as to mere interest, in the common acceptation of that word, it would be mine that you should turn out ill; for you may depend upon it, that whatever you have from me shall be most exactly proportioned to your desert. Deserve a great deal, and you shall have a great deal; deserve a little, and you shall have but a little; and be good for nothing at all, and, I assure you, you shall have nothing at all.

Solid knowledge, as I have often told you, is the first and great foundation of your future fortune and character; for I never mention to you the two much greater points of Religion and Morality, because I cannot possibly suspect you as to either of them. This solid knowledge you are in a fair way of acquiring; you may, if you please; and I will add, that nobody ever had the means of acquiring it more in their power than you have. But remember, that manners must adorn knowledge, and smooth its way through the world. Like a great rough diamond, it may do very well in a closet by way of curiosity, and also for its intrinsic value; but it will never be worn or shine if it is not polished. It is upon this article, I confess, that I suspect you the most, which makes me recur to it so often; for I fear that you are apt to show too little attention to everybody, and too much contempt to many. Be convinced, that there are no persons so insignificant and inconsiderable, but may, some time or other, have it in their power to be of use to you; which they certainly will not, if you have once shown them contempt. Wrongs are often forgiven; but contempt never is. Our pride remembers it forever. It implies a discovery of weaknesses, which we are much more careful to conceal than crimes. Many a man will confess his crimes to a common friend, but I never knew a man who would tell his silly weaknesses to his most intimate one—as many a friend will tell us our faults without reserve, who will not so much as hint at our follies; that discovery is too mortifying to our self-love, either to tell another, or to be told of one's self. You must, therefore, never expect to hear of your weaknesses, or your follies, from anybody but me; those I will take pains to discover, and whenever I do, shall tell you of them.

Next to manners are exterior graces of person and address, which adorn manners, as manners adorn knowledge. To say that they please, engage, and charm, as they most indisputably do, is saying that one should do everything possible to acquire them. The graceful manner of speaking is, particularly, what I shall always holloa in your ears, as Hotspur holloaed MORTIMER to Henry IV., and, like him too, I have aimed to have a starling taught to say, SPEAK DISTINCTLY AND GRACEFULLY, and send him you, to replace your loss of the unfortunate Matzel, who, by the way, I am told, spoke his language very distinctly and gracefully.

As by this time you must be able to write German tolerably well, I desire that you will not fail to write a German letter, in the German character, once every fortnight, to Mr. Grevenkop: which will make it more familiar to you, and enable me to judge how you improve in it.

Do not forget to answer me the questions, which I asked you a great while ago, in relation to the constitution of Saxony; and also the meaning of the words 'Landsassii and Amptsassii'.

I hope you do not forget to inquire into the affairs of trade and commerce, nor to get the best accounts you can of the commodities and manufactures, exports and imports of the several countries where you may be, and their gross value.

I would likewise have you attend to the respective coins, gold, silver, copper, etc., and their value, compared with our coin's; for which purpose I would advise you to put up, in a separate piece of paper, one piece of every kind, wherever you shall be, writing upon it the name and the value. Such a collection will be curious enough in itself; and that sort of knowledge will be very useful to you in your way of business, where the different value of money often comes in question.

I am doing to Cheltenham to-morrow, less for my health; which is pretty good, than for the dissipation and amusement of the journey. I shall stay about a fortnight.

L'Abbe Mably's 'Droit de l'Europe', which Mr. Harte is so kind as to send me, is worth your reading. Adieu.

LETTER XLIV.

CHELTENHAM, July 6, O. S. 1748.

DEAR BOY: Your school-fellow, Lord Pulteney,—[Only child of the Right Hon. William Pulteney, Earl of Bath. He died before his father.]—set out last week for Holland, and will, I believe, be at Leipsig soon after this letter: you will take care to be extremely civil to him, and to do him any service that you can while you stay there; let him know that I wrote to you to do so. As being older, he should know more than you; in that case, take pains to get up to him; but if he does not, take care not to let him feel his inferiority. He will find it out of himself without your endeavors; and that cannot be helped: but nothing is more insulting, more mortifying and less forgiven, than avowedly to take pains to make a man feel a mortifying inferiority in knowledge, rank, fortune, etc. In the two last articles, it is unjust, they not being in his power: and in the first it is both ill-bred and ill-natured. Good-breeding, and good-nature, do incline us rather to raise and help people up to ourselves, than to mortify and depress them, and, in truth, our own private interest concurs in it, as it is making ourselves so many friends, instead of so many enemies. The constant practice of what the French call 'les Attentions', is a most necessary ingredient in the art of pleasing; they flatter the self-love of those to whom they are shown; they engage, they captivate, more than things of much greater importance.

The duties of social life every man is obliged to discharge; but these attentions are voluntary acts, the free-will offerings of good-breeding and good nature; they are received, remembered, and returned as such. Women, particularly, have a right to them; and any omission in that respect is downright ill-breeding.

Do you employ your whole time in the most useful manner? I do not mean, do you study all day long? nor do I require it. But I mean, do you make the most of the respective allotments of your time? While you study, is it with attention? When you divert yourself, is it with spirit? Your diversions may, if you please, employ some part of your time very usefully. It depends entirely upon the nature of them. If they are futile and frivolous it is time worse than lost, for they will give you an habit of futility. All gaming, field-sports, and such sort of amusements, where neither the understanding nor the senses have the least share, I look upon as frivolous, and as the resources of little minds, who either do not think, or do not love to think. But the pleasures of a man of parts either flatter the senses or improve the mind; I hope at least, that there is not one minute of the day in which you do nothing at all. Inaction at your age is unpardonable.

Tell me what Greek and Latin books you can now read with ease. Can you open Demosthenes at a venture, and understand him? Can you get through an "Oration" of Cicero, or a "Satire" of Horace, without difficulty? What German books do you read, to make yourself master of that language? And what French books do you read for your amusement? Pray give me a particular and true account of all this; for I am not indifferent as to any one thing that relates to you. As, for example, I hope you take great care to keep your whole person, particularly your mouth, very clean; common decency requires it, besides that great cleanliness is very conducive to health. But if you do not keep your mouth excessively clean, by washing it carefully every morning, and after every meal, it will not only be apt to smell, which is very disgusting and indecent, but your teeth will decay and ache, which is both a great loss and a great pain. A spruceness of dress is also very proper and becoming at your age; as the negligence of it implies an indifference about pleasing, which does not become a young fellow. To do whatever you do at all to the utmost perfection, ought to be your aim at this time of your life; if you can reach perfection, so much the better; but at least, by attempting it, you will get much nearer than if you never attempted it at all.

Adieu! SPEAK GRACEFULLY AND DISTINCTLY if you intend to converse ever with, Yours.

P. S. As I was making up my letter, I received yours of the 6th, O. S. I like your dissertation upon Preliminary Articles and Truces. Your definitions of both are true. Those are matters which I would have you be master of; they belong to your future department, But remember too, that they are matters upon which you will much oftener have occasion to speak than to write; and that, consequently, it is full as necessary to speak gracefully and distinctly upon them as to write clearly and elegantly. I find no authority among the ancients, nor indeed among the moderns, for indistinct and unintelligible utterance. The Oracles indeed meant to be obscure; but then it was by the ambiguity of the expression, and not by the inarticulation of the words. For if people had not thought, at least, they understood them, they would neither have frequented nor presented them as they did. There was likewise among the ancients, and is still among the moderns, a sort of people called Ventriloqui, who speak from their bellies, on make the voice seem to come from some other part of the room than that where they are. But these Ventriloqui speak very distinctly and intelligibly. The only thing, then, that I can find like a precedent for your way of speaking (and I would willingly help you to one if I could) is the modern art 'de persifler', practiced with great success by the 'Petits maitres' at Paris. This noble art consists in picking out some grave, serious man, who neither understands nor expects, raillery, and talking to him very quick, and inarticulate sounds; while the man, who thinks that he did not hear well; or attend sufficiently, says, 'Monsieur? or 'Plait-il'? a hundred times; which affords matter of much mirth to those ingenious gentlemen. Whether you would follow, this precedent, I submit to you.

Have you carried no English or French comedies of tragedies with you to Leipsig? If you have, I insist upon your reciting some passages of them every day to Mr. Harte in the most distinct and graceful manner, as if you were acting them upon a stage.

The first part of my letter is more than an answer to your questions concerning Lord Pulteney.

LETTER XLV

LONDON, July, 20, O. S. 1748

DEAR BOY: There are two sorts of understandings; one of which hinders a man from ever being considerable, and the other commonly makes him ridiculous; I mean the lazy mind, and the trifling, frivolous mind: Yours, I hope, is neither. The lazy mind will not take the trouble of going to the bottom of anything; but, discouraged by the first difficulties (and everything worth knowing or having is attained with some), stops short, contents, itself with easy, and consequently superficial knowledge, and prefers a great degree of ignorance to a small degree of trouble. These people either think, or represent most things as impossible; whereas, few things are so to industry and activity. But difficulties seem to them, impossibilities, or at least they pretend to think them so—by way of excuse for their laziness. An hour's attention to the same subject is too laborious for them; they take everything in the light in which it first presents itself; never consider, it in all its different views; and, in short, never think it through. The consequence of this is that when they come to speak upon these subjects, before people who have considered them with attention; they only discover their own ignorance and laziness, and lay themselves open to answers that put them in confusion. Do not then be discouraged by the first difficulties, but 'contra audentior ito'; and resolve to go to the bottom of all those things which every gentleman ought to know well. Those arts or sciences which are peculiar to certain professions, need not be deeply known by those who are not intended for those professions. As, for instance; fortification and navigation; of both which, a superficial and general knowledge, such as the common course of conversation, with a very little inquiry on your part, will give you, is sufficient. Though, by the way, a little more knowledge of fortification may be of some use to you; as the events of war, in sieges, make many of the terms, of that science occur frequently in common conversation; and one would be sorry to say, like the Marquis de Mascarille in Moliere's 'Precieuses Ridicules', when he hears of 'une demie lune, Ma foi! c'etoit bien une lune toute entiere'. But those things which every gentleman, independently of profession, should know, he ought to know well, and dive into all the depth of them. Such are languages, history, and geography ancient and modern, philosophy, rational logic; rhetoric; and, for you particularly, the constitutions and the civil and military state of every country in Europe: This, I confess; is a pretty large circle of knowledge, attended with some difficulties, and requiring some trouble; which, however; an active and industrious mind will overcome; and be amply repaid. The trifling and frivolous mind is always busied, but to little purpose; it takes little objects for great ones, and throws away upon trifles that time and attention which only important things deserve. Knick-knacks; butterflies; shells, insects, etc., are the subjects of their most serious researches. They contemplate the dress, not the characters of the company they keep. They attend more to the decorations of a play than the sense of it; and to the ceremonies of a court more than to its politics. Such an employment of time is an absolute loss of it. You have now, at most, three years to employ either well or ill; for, as I have often told you, you will be all your life what you shall be three years hence. For God's sake then reflect. Will you throw this time away either in laziness, or in trifles? Or will you not rather employ every moment of it in a manner that must so soon reward you with so much pleasure, figure, and character? I cannot, I will not doubt of your choice. Read only useful books; and never quit a subject till you are thoroughly master of it, but read and inquire on till then. When you are in company, bring the conversation to some useful subject, but 'a portee' of that company. Points of history, matters of literature, the customs of particular countries, the several orders of knighthood, as Teutonic, Maltese, etc., are surely better subjects of conversation, than the weather, dress, or fiddle-faddle stories, that carry no information along with them. The characters of kings and great men are only to be learned in conversation; for they are never fairly written during their lives. This, therefore, is an entertaining and instructive subject of conversation, and will likewise give you an opportunity of observing how very differently characters are given, from the different passions and views of those who give them. Never be ashamed nor afraid of asking questions: for if they lead to information, and if you accompany them with some excuse, you will never be reckoned an impertinent or rude questioner. All those things, in the common course of life, depend entirely upon the manner; and, in that respect, the vulgar saying is true, 'That one man can better steal a horse, than another look over the hedge.' There are few things that may not be said, in some manner or other; either in a seeming confidence, or a genteel irony, or introduced with wit; and one great part of the knowledge of the world consists in knowing when and where to make use of these different manners. The graces of the person, the countenance, and the way of speaking, contribute so much to this, that I am convinced, the very same thing, said by a genteel person in an engaging way, and GRACEFULLY and distinctly spoken, would please, which would shock, if MUTTERED out by an awkward figure, with a sullen, serious countenance. The poets always represent Venus as attended by the three Graces, to intimate that even beauty will not do without: I think they should have given Minerva three also; for without them, I am sure learning is very unattractive. Invoke them, then, DISTINCTLY, to accompany all your words and motions. Adieu.

P. S. Since I wrote what goes before, I have received your letter, OF NO DATE, with the inclosed state of the Prussian forces: of which, I hope, you have kept a copy; this you should lay in a 'portefeuille', and add to it all the military establishments that you can get of other states and kingdoms: the Saxon establishment you may, doubtless, easily find. By the way, do not forget to send me answers to the questions which I sent you some time ago, concerning both the civil and the ecclesiastical affairs of Saxony.

Do not mistake me, and think I only mean that you should speak elegantly with regard to style, and the purity of language; but I mean, that you should deliver and pronounce what you say gracefully and distinctly; for which purpose I will have you frequently read very loud, to Mr. Harte, recite parts of orations, and speak passages of plays; for, without a graceful and pleasing enunciation, all your elegancy of style, in speaking, is not worth one farthing.

I am very glad that Mr. Lyttelton approves of my new house, and particularly of my CANONICAL—[James Brydges, duke of Chandos, built a most magnificent and elegant house at CANNONS, about eight miles from London. It was superbly furnished with fine pictures, statues, etc., which, after his death, were sold, by auction. Lord Chesterfield purchased the hall-pillars, the floor; and staircase with double flights; which are now in Chesterfield House, London.]—pillars. My bust of Cicero is a very fine one, and well preserved; it will have the best place in my library, unless at your return you bring me over as good a modern head of your own, which I should like still better. I can tell you, that I shall examine it as attentively as ever antiquary did an old one.

Make my compliments to Mr. Harte, at whose recovery I rejoice.

LETTER XLVI

LONDON, August 2, O. S. 1748.

DEAR BOY: Duval the jeweler, is arrived, and was with me three or four days ago. You will easily imagine that I asked him a few questions concerning you; and I will give you the satisfaction of knowing that, upon the whole, I was very well pleased with the account he gave me. But, though he seemed to be much in your interest, yet he fairly owned to me that your utterance was rapid, thick, and ungraceful. I can add nothing to what I have already said upon this subject; but I can and do repeat the absolute necessity of speaking distinctly and gracefully, or else of not speaking at all, and having recourse to signs. He tells me that you are pretty fat for one of your age: this you should attend to in a proper way; for if, while very young; you should grow fat, it would be troublesome, unwholesome, and ungraceful; you should therefore, when you have time, take very strong exercise, and in your diet avoid fattening things. All malt liquors fatten, or at least bloat; and I hope you do not deal much in them. I look upon wine and water to be, in every respect; much wholesomer.

Duval says there is a great deal of very good company at Madame Valentin's and at another lady's, I think one Madame Ponce's, at Leipsig. Do you ever go to either of those houses, at leisure times? It would not, in my mind, be amiss if you did, and would give you a habit of ATTENTIONS; they are a tribute which all women expect; and which all men, who would be well received by them; must pay. And, whatever the mind may be, manners at least are certainly improved by the company of women of fashion.

I have formerly told you, that you should inform yourself of the several orders, whether military or religious, of the respective countries where you may be. The Teutonic Order is the great Order of Germany, of which I send you inclosed a short account. It may serve to suggest questions to you for more particular inquiries as to the present state of it, of which you ought to be minutely informed. The knights, at present, make vows, of which they observe none, except it be that of not marrying; and their only object now is, to arrive, by seniority, at the Commanderies in their respective provinces; which are, many of them, very lucrative. The Order of Malta is, by a very few years, prior to the Teutonic, and owes its foundation to the same causes. These' knights were first called Knights Hospitaliers of St. John of Jerusalem, then Knights of Rhodes; and in the year 1530, Knights of Malta, the Emperor Charles V. having granted them that island, upon condition of their defending his island of Sicily against the Turks, which they effectually did. L'Abbe de Vertot has written the history of Malta, but it is the least valuable of all his works; and moreover, too long for you to read. But there is a short history, of all the military orders whatsoever, which I would advise you to get, as there is also of all the religious orders; both which are worth your having and consulting, whenever you meet with any of them in your way; as, you will very frequently in Catholic countries. For my own part, I find that I remember things much better, when I recur, to my books for them, upon some particular occasion, than by reading them 'tout de suite'. As, for example, if I were to read the history of all the military or religious orders, regularly one after another, the latter puts the former out of my head; but when I read the history of any one, upon account, of its having been the object of conversation or dispute, I remember it much better. It is the same in geography, where, looking for any particular place in the map, upon some particular account, fixes it in one's memory forever. I hope you have worn out your maps by frequent, use of that sort. Adieu.

A SHORT ACCOUNT OF THE TEUTONIC ORDER

In the ages of ignorance, which is always the mother of superstition, it was thought not only just, but meritorious, to propagate religion by fire and sword, and to take away the lives and properties of unbelievers. This enthusiasm produced the several crusades, in the 11th, 12th, and following centuries, the object of which was, to recover the Holy Land out of, the hands of the Infidels, who, by the way, were the lawful possessors.

Many honest enthusiasts engaged in those crusades, from a mistaken principle of religion, and from the pardons granted by the Popes for all the sins of those pious adventurers; but many more knaves adopted these holy wars, in hopes of conquest and plunder. After Godfrey of Bouillon, at the head of these knaves and fools, had taken Jerusalem, in the year 1099, Christians of various nations remained in that city; among the rest, one good honest German, that took particular care of his countrymen who came thither in pilgrimages. He built a house for their reception, and an hospital dedicated to the Virgin. This little establishment soon became a great one, by the enthusiasm of many considerable people who engaged in it, in order to drive the Saracens out of the Holy Land. This society then began to take its first form; and its members were called Marian Teutonic Knights. Marian, from their chapel sacred to the Virgin Mary; Teutonic, from the German, or Teuton, who was the author of it, and Knights from the wars which they were to carry on against the Infidels.

These knights behaved themselves so bravely, at first; that Duke Frederick of Swabia, who was general of the German army in the Holy Land, sent, in the year 1191, to the Emperor Henry VI. and Pope Celestine III. to desire that this brave and charitable fraternity might be incorporated into a regular order of knighthood; which was accordingly done, and rules and a particular habit were given them. Forty knights, all of noble families, were at first created by the King of Jerusalem and other princes then in the army. The first grand master of this order was Henry Wallpot, of a noble family upon the Rhine. This order soon began to operate in Europe; drove all the Pagans out of Prussia, and took possession of it. Soon after, they got Livonia and Courland, and invaded even Russia, where they introduced the Christian religion. In 1510, they elected Albert, Marquis of Bradenburg, for their grand master, who, turning Protestant, soon afterward took Prussia from the order, and kept it for himself, with the consent of Sigismund, King of Poland, of whom it was to hold. He then quitted his grand mastership and made himself hereditary Duke of that country, which is thence called Ducal Prussia. This order now consists of twelve provinces; viz., Alsatia, Austria, Coblentz, and Etsch, which are the four under the Prussian jurisdiction; Franconia, Hesse, Biessen, Westphalia, Lorraine, Thuringia, Saxony, and Utrecht, which eight are of the German jurisdiction. The Dutch now possess all that the order had in Utrecht. Every one of the provinces have their particular Commanderies; and the most ancient of these Commandeurs is called the Commandeur Provincial. These twelve Commandeurs are all subordinate to the Grand Master of Germany as their chief, and have the right of electing the grand master. The elector of Cologne is at present 'Grand Maitre'.

This order, founded by mistaken Christian zeal, upon the anti-Christian principles of violence and persecution, soon grew strong by the weakness and ignorance of the time; acquired unjustly great possessions, of which they justly lost the greatest part by their ambition and cruelty, which made them feared and hated by all their neighbors.

I have this moment received your letter of the 4th, N. S., and have only time to tell you that I can by no means agree to your cutting off your hair. I am very sure that your headaches cannot proceed from thence. And as for the pimples upon your head, they are only owing to the heat of the season, and consequently will not last long. But your own hair is, at your age, such an ornament, and a wig, however well made, such a disguise, that I will upon no account whatsoever have you cut off your hair. Nature did not give it to you for nothing, still less to cause you the headache. Mr. Eliot's hair grew so ill and bushy, that he was in the right to cut it off. But you have not the same reason.

LETTER XLVII

LONDON, August 23, O. S. 1748.

DEAR BOY: Your friend, Mr. Eliot, has dined with me twice since I returned here, and I can say with truth that while I had the seals, I never examined or sifted a state prisoner with so much care and curiosity as I did him. Nay, I did more; for, contrary to the laws of this country, I gave him in some manner, the QUESTION ordinary and extraordinary; and I have infinite pleasure in telling you that the rack which I put him to, did not extort from him one single word that was not such as I wished to hear of you. I heartily congratulate you upon such an advantageous testimony, from so creditable a witness. 'Laudati a laudato viro', is one of the greatest pleasures and honors a rational being can have; may you long continue to deserve it! Your aversion to drinking and your dislike to gaming, which Mr. Eliot assures me are both very strong, give me, the greatest joy imaginable, for your sake: as the former would ruin both your constitution and understanding, and the latter your fortune and character. Mr. Harte wrote me word some time ago, and Mr. Eliot confirms it now, that you employ your pin money in a very different manner, from that in which pin money is commonly lavished: not in gew-gaws and baubles, but in buying good and useful books. This is an excellent symptom, and gives me very good hopes. Go on thus, my dear boy, but for these next two years, and I ask no more. You must then make such a figure and such a fortune in the world as I wish you, and as I have taken all these pains to enable you to do. After that time I allow you to be as idle as ever you please; because I am sure that you will not then please to be so at all. The ignorant and the weak are only idle; but those who have once acquired a good stock of knowledge, always desire to increase it. Knowledge is like power in this respect, that those who have the most, are most desirous of having more. It does not clog, by possession, but increases desire; which is the case of very few pleasures.

Upon receiving this congratulatory letter, and reading your own praises, I am sure that it must naturally occur to you, how great a share of them you owe to Mr. Harte's care and attention; and, consequently, that your regard and affection for him must increase, if there be room for it, in proportion as you reap, which you do daily, the fruits of his labors.

I must not, however, conceal from you that there was one article in which your own witness, Mr. Eliot, faltered; for, upon my questioning him home as to your manner of speaking, he could not say that your utterance was either distinct or graceful. I have already said so much to you upon this point that I can add nothing. I will therefore only repeat this truth, which is, that if you will not speak distinctly and graceful, nobody will desire to hear you. I am glad to learn that Abbe Mably's 'Droit Public de l'Europe' makes a part of your evening amusements. It is a very useful book, and gives a clear deduction of the affairs of Europe, from the treaty of Munster to this time. Pray read it with attention, and with the proper maps; always recurring to them for the several countries or towns yielded, taken, or restored. Pyre Bougeant's third volume will give you the best idea of the treaty of Munster, and open to you the several views of the belligerent' and contracting parties, and there never were greater than at that time. The House of Austria, in the war immediately preceding that treaty, intended to make itself absolute in the empire, and to overthrow the rights of the respective states of it. The view of France was to weaken and dismember the House of Austria to such a degree, as that it should no longer be a counterbalance to that of Bourbon. Sweden wanted possessions on the continent of Germany, not only to supply the necessities of its own poor and barren country, but likewise to hold the balance in the empire between the House of Austria and the States. The House of Brandenburg wanted to aggrandize itself by pilfering in the fire; changed sides occasionally, and made a good bargain at last; for I think it got, at the peace, nine or ten bishoprics secularized. So that we may date, from the treaty of Munster, the decline of the House of Austria, the great power of the House of Bourbon, and the aggrandizement of that of Bradenburg: which, I am much mistaken, if it stops where it is now.

Make my compliments to Lord Pulteney, to whom I would have you be not only attentive, but useful, by setting him (in case he wants it) a good example of application and temperance. I begin to believe that, as I shall be proud of you, others will be proud too of imitating you: Those expectations of mine seem now so well grounded, that my disappointment, and consequently my anger, will be so much the greater if they fail; but as things stand now, I am most affectionately and tenderly, Yours.

LETTER XLVIII

LONDON, August 30, O. S. 1748

DEAR BOY: Your reflections upon the conduct of France, from the treaty of Munster to this time, are very just; and I am very glad to find, by them, that you not only read, but that you think and reflect upon what you read. Many great readers load their memories, without exercising their judgments; and make lumber-rooms of their heads instead of furnishing them usefully; facts are heaped upon facts without order or distinction, and may justly be said to compose that

'———-Rudis indigestaque moles

Quem dixere chaos'.

Go on, then, in the way of reading that you are in; take nothing for granted, upon the bare authority of the author; but weigh and consider, in your own mind, the probability of the facts and the justness of the reflections. Consult different authors upon the same facts, and form your opinion upon the greater or lesser degree of probability arising from the whole, which, in my mind, is the utmost stretch of historical faith; certainty (I fear) not being to be found. When a historian pretends to give you the causes and motives of events, compare those causes and motives with the characters and interests of the parties concerned, and judge for yourself whether they correspond or not. Consider whether you cannot assign others more probable; and in that examination, do not despise some very mean and trifling causes of the actions of great men; for so various and inconsistent is human nature, so strong and changeable are our passions, so fluctuating are our wills, and so much are our minds influenced by the accidents of our bodies that every man is more the man of the day, than a regular consequential character. The best have something bad, and something little; the worst have something good, and sometimes something great; for I do not believe what Velleius Paterculus (for the sake of saying a pretty thing) says of Scipio, 'Qui nihil non laudandum aut fecit, aut dixit, aut sensit'. As for the reflections of historians, with which they think it necessary to interlard their histories, or at least to conclude their chapters (and which, in the French histories, are always introduced with a 'tant il est vrai', and in the English, SO TRUE IT IS), do not adopt them implicitly upon the credit of the author, but analyze them yourself, and judge whether they are true or not.

But to return to the politics of France, from which I have digressed. You have certainly made one further reflection, of an advantage which France has, over and above its abilities in the cabinet and the skill of its negotiators, which is (if I may use the expression) its SOLENESS, continuity of riches and power within itself, and the nature of its government. Near twenty millions of people, and the ordinary revenue of above thirteen millions sterling a year, are at the absolute disposal of the Crown. This is what no other power in Europe can say; so that different powers must now unite to make a balance against France; which union, though formed upon the principle of their common interest, can never be so intimate as to compose a machine so compact and simple as that of one great kingdom, directed by one will, and moved by one interest. The Allied Powers (as we have constantly seen) have, besides the common and declared object of their alliance, some separate and concealed view to which they often sacrifice the general one; which makes them, either directly or indirectly, pull different ways. Thus, the design upon Toulon failed in the year 1706, only from the secret view of the House of Austria upon Naples: which made the Court of Vienna, notwithstanding the representations of the other allies to the contrary, send to Naples the 12,000 men that would have done the business at Toulon. In this last war too, the same causes had the same effects: the Queen of Hungary in secret thought of nothing but recovering of Silesia, and what she had lost in Italy; and, therefore, never sent half that quota which she promised, and we paid for, into Flanders; but left that country to the maritime powers to defend as they could. The King of Sardinia's real object was Savona and all the Riviera di Ponente; for which reason he concurred so lamely in the invasion of Provence, where the Queen of Hungary, likewise, did not send one-third of the force stipulated, engrossed as she was by her oblique views upon the plunder of Genoa, and the recovery of Naples. Insomuch that the expedition into Provence, which would have distressed France to the greatest degree, and have caused a great detachment from their army in Flanders, failed shamefully, for want of every one thing necessary for its success. Suppose, therefore, any four or five powers who, all together, shall be equal, or even a little superior, in riches and strength to that one power against which they are united; the advantage will still be greatly on the side of that single power, because it is but one. The power and riches of Charles V. were, in themselves, certainly superior to those of Frances I., and yet, upon the whole, he was not an overmatch for him. Charles V.'s dominions, great as they were, were scattered and remote from each other; their constitutions different; wherever he did not reside, disturbances arose; whereas the compactness of France made up the difference in the strength. This obvious reflection convinced me of the absurdity of the treaty of Hanover, in 1725, between France and England, to which the Dutch afterward acceded; for it was made upon the apprehensions, either real or pretended, that the marriage of Don Carlos with the eldest archduchess, now Queen of Hungary, was settled in the treaty of Vienna, of the same year, between Spain and the late Emperor Charles VI., which marriage, those consummate politicians said would revive in Europe the exorbitant power of Charles V. I am sure, I heartily wish it had; as, in that case, there had been, what there certainly is not now, one power in Europe to counterbalance that of France; and then the maritime powers would, in reality, have held the balance of Europe in their hands. Even supposing that the Austrian power would then have been an overmatch for that of France (which, by the way, is not clear), the weight of the maritime powers, then thrown into the scale of France, would infallibly have made the balance at least even. In which case too, the moderate efforts of the maritime powers on the side of France would have been sufficient; whereas now, they are obliged to exhaust and beggar themselves; and that too ineffectually, in hopes to support the shattered; beggared, and insufficient House of Austria.

This has been a long political dissertation; but I am informed that political subjects are your favorite ones; which I am glad of, considering your destination. You do well to get your materials all ready, before you begin your work. As you buy and (I am told) read books of this kind, I will point out two or three for your purchase and perusal; I am not sure that I have not mentioned them before, but that is no matter, if you have not got them. 'Memoires pour servir a l'Histoire du 17ieme Siecle', is a most useful book for you to recur to for all the facts and chronology of that country: it is in four volumes octavo, and very correct and exact. If I do not mistake, I have formerly recommended to you, 'Les Memoires du Cardinal de Retz'; however, if you have not yet read them, pray do, and with the attention which they deserve. You will there find the best account of a very interesting period of the minority of Lewis XIV. The characters are drawn short, but in a strong and masterly manner; and the political reflections are the only just and practical ones that I ever saw in print: they are well worth your transcribing. 'Le Commerce des Anciens, par Monsieur Huet. Eveque d'Avranche', in one little volume octavo, is worth your perusal, as commerce is a very considerable part of political knowledge. I need not, I am sure, suggest to you, when you read the course of commerce, either of the ancients or of the moderns, to follow it upon your map; for there is no other way of remembering geography correctly, but by looking perpetually in the map for the places one reads of, even though one knows before, pretty near, where they are.

Adieu! As all the accounts which I receive of you grow better and better, so I grow more and more affectionately, Yours.

LETTER XLIX

LONDON, September 5, O. S. 1748.

DEAR BOY: I have received yours, with the inclosed German letter to Mr. Gravenkop, which he assures me is extremely well written, considering the little time that you have applied yourself to that language. As you have now got over the most difficult part, pray go on diligently, and make yourself absolutely master of the rest. Whoever does not entirely possess a language, will never appear to advantage, or even equal to himself, either in speaking or writing it. His ideas are fettered, and seem imperfect or confused, if he is not master of all the words and phrases necessary to express them. I therefore desire, that you will not fail writing a German letter once every fortnight to Mr. Gravenkop; which will make the writing of that language familiar to you; and moreover, when you shall have left Germany and be arrived at Turin, I shall require you to write even to me in German; that you may not forget with ease what you have with difficulty learned. I likewise desire, that while you are in Germany, you will take all opportunities of conversing in German, which is the only way of knowing that, or any other language, accurately. You will also desire your German master to teach you the proper titles and superscriptions to be used to people of all ranks; which is a point so material, in Germany, that I have known many a letter returned unopened, because one title in twenty has been omitted in the direction.

St. Thomas's day now draws near, when you are to leave Saxony and go to Berlin; and I take it for granted, that if anything is yet wanting to complete your knowledge of the state of that electorate, you will not fail to procure it before you go away. I do not mean, as you will easily believe, the number of churches, parishes, or towns; but I mean the constitution, the revenues, the troops, and the trade of that electorate. A few questions, sensibly asked, of sensible people, will produce you the necessary informations; which I desire you will enter in your little book, Berlin will be entirely a new scene to you, and I look upon it, in a manner, as your first step into the great world; take care that step be not a false one, and that you do not stumble at the threshold. You will there be in more company than you have yet been; manners and attentions will therefore be more necessary. Pleasing in company is the only way of being pleased in it yourself. Sense and knowledge are the first and necessary foundations for pleasing in company; but they will by no means do alone, and they will never be perfectly welcome if they are not accompanied with manners and attentions. You will best acquire these by frequenting the companies of people of fashion; but then you must resolve to acquire them, in those companies, by proper care and observation; for I have known people, who, though they have frequented good company all their lifetime, have done it in so inattentive and unobserving a manner, as to be never the better for it, and to remain as disagreeable, as awkward, and as vulgar, as if they had never seen any person of fashion. When you go into good company (by good company is meant the people of the first fashion of the place) observe carefully their turn, their manners, their address; and conform your own to them. But this is not all neither; go deeper still; observe their characters, and pray, as far as you can, into both their hearts and their heads. Seek for their particular merit, their predominant passion, or their prevailing weakness; and you will then know what to bait your hook with to catch them. Man is a composition of so many, and such various ingredients, that it requires both time and care to analyze him: for though we have all the same ingredients in our general composition, as reason, will, passions, and appetites; yet the different proportions and combinations of them in each individual, produce that infinite variety of characters, which, in some particular or other, distinguishes every individual from another. Reason ought to direct the whole, but seldom does. And he who addresses himself singly to another man's reason, without endeavoring to engage his heart in his interest also, is no more likely to succeed, than a man who should apply only to a king's nominal minister, and neglect his favorite. I will recommend to your attentive perusal, now that you are going into the world, two books, which will let you as much into the characters of men, as books can do. I mean, 'Les Reflections Morales de Monsieur de la Rochefoucault, and Les Caracteres de la Bruyere': but remember, at the same time, that I only recommend them to you as the best general maps to assist you in your journey, and not as marking out every particular turning and winding that you will meet with. There your own sagacity and observation must come to their aid. La Rochefoucault, is, I know, blamed, but I think without reason, for deriving all our actions from the source of self-love. For my own part, I see a great deal of truth, and no harm at all, in that opinion. It is certain that we seek our own happiness in everything we do; and it is as certain, that we can only find it in doing well, and in conforming all our actions to the rule of right reason, which is the great law of nature. It is only a mistaken self-love that is a blamable motive, when we take the immediate and indiscriminate gratification of a passion, or appetite, for real happiness. But am I blamable if I do a good action, upon account of the happiness which that honest consciousness will give me? Surely not. On the contrary, that pleasing consciousness is a proof of my virtue. The reflection which is the most censured in Monsieur de la Rochefoucault's book as a very ill-natured one, is this, 'On trouve dans le malheur de son meilleur ami, quelque chose qui ne des plait pas'. And why not? Why may I not feel a very tender and real concern for the misfortune of my friend, and yet at the same time feel a pleasing consciousness at having discharged my duty to him, by comforting and assisting him to the utmost of my power in that misfortune? Give me but virtuous actions, and I will not quibble and chicane about the motives. And I will give anybody their choice of these two truths, which amount to the same thing: He who loves himself best is the honestest man; or, The honestest man loves himself best.

The characters of La Bruyere are pictures from the life; most of them finely drawn, and highly colored. Furnish your mind with them first, and when you meet with their likeness, as you will every day, they will strike you the more. You will compare every feature with the original; and both will reciprocally help you to discover the beauties and the blemishes.

As women are a considerable, or, at least a pretty numerous part of company; and as their suffrages go a great way toward establishing a man's character in the fashionable part of the world (which is of great importance to the fortune and figure he proposes to make in it), it is necessary to please them. I will therefore, upon this subject, let you into certain Arcana that will be very useful for you to know, but which you must, with the utmost care, conceal and never seem to know. Women, then, are only children of a larger growth; they have an entertaining tattle, and sometimes wit; but for solid reasoning, good sense, I never knew in my life one that had it, or who reasoned or acted consequentially for four-and-twenty hours together. Some little passion or humor always breaks upon their best resolutions. Their beauty neglected or controverted, their age increased, or their supposed understandings depreciated, instantly kindles their little passions, and overturns any system of consequential conduct, that in their most reasonable moments they might have been capable of forming. A man of sense only trifles with them, plays with them, humors and flatters them, as he does with a sprightly forward child; but he neither consults them about, nor trusts them with serious matters; though he often makes them believe that he does both; which is the thing in the world that they are proud of; for they love mightily to be dabbling in business (which by the way they always spoil); and being justly distrustful that men in general look upon them in a trifling light, they almost adore that man who talks more seriously to them, and who seems to consult and trust them; I say, who seems; for weak men really do, but wise ones only seem to do it. No flattery is either too high or too low for them. They will greedily swallow the highest, and gratefully accept of the lowest; and you may safely flatter any woman from her understanding down to the exquisite taste of her fan. Women who are either indisputably beautiful, or indisputably ugly, are best flattered, upon the score of their understandings; but those who are in a state of mediocrity, are best flattered upon their beauty, or at least their graces; for every woman who is not absolutely ugly thinks herself handsome; but not hearing often that she is so, is the more grateful and the more obliged to the few who tell her so; whereas a decided and conscious beauty looks upon every tribute paid to her beauty only as her due; but wants to shine, and to be considered on the side of her understanding; and a woman who is ugly enough to know that she is so, knows that she has nothing left for it but her understanding, which is consequently and probably (in more senses than one) her weak side. But these are secrets which you must keep inviolably, if you would not, like Orpheus, be torn to pieces by the whole sex; on the contrary, a man who thinks of living in the great world, must be gallant, polite, and attentive to please the women. They have, from the weakness of men, more or less influence in all courts; they absolutely stamp every man's character in the beau monde, and make it either current, or cry it down, and stop it in payments. It is, therefore; absolutely necessary to manage, please, and flatter them and never to discover the least marks of contempt, which is what they never forgive; but in this they are not singular, for it is the same with men; who will much sooner forgive an injustice than an insult. Every man is not ambitious, or courteous, or passionate; but every man has pride enough in his composition to feel and resent the least slight and contempt. Remember, therefore, most carefully to conceal your contempt, however just, wherever you would not make an implacable enemy. Men are much more unwilling to have their weaknesses and their imperfections known than their crimes; and if you hint to a man that you think him silly, ignorant, or even ill-bred, or awkward, he will hate you more and longer, than if you tell him plainly, that you think him a rogue. Never yield to that temptation, which to most young men is very strong; of exposing other people's weaknesses and infirmities, for the sake either of diverting the company, or showing your own superiority. You may get the laugh on your side by it for the present; but you will make enemies by it forever; and even those who laugh with you then, will, upon reflection, fear; and consequently hate you; besides that it is ill-natured, and a good heart desires rather to conceal than expose other people's weaknesses or misfortunes. If you have wit, use it to please, and not to hurt: you may shine, like the sun in the temperate zones, without scorching. Here it is wished for; under the Line it is dreaded.

These are some of the hints which my long experience in the great world enables me to give you; and which, if you attend to them, may prove useful to you in your journey through it. I wish it may be a prosperous one; at least, I am sure that it must be your own fault if it is not.

Make my compliments to Mr. Harte, who, I am very sorry to hear, is not well. I hope by this time he is recovered. Adieu!

LETTER L

LONDON, September 13, O. S. 1748.

DEAR BOY: I have more than once recommended to you the "Memoirs" of the Cardinal de Retz, and to attend particularly to the political reflections interspersed in that excellent work. I will now preach a little upon two or three of those texts.

In the disturbances at Paris, Monsieur de Beaufort, who was a very popular, though a very weak man, was the Cardinal's tool with the populace.

Proud of his popularity, he was always for assembling the people of Paris together, thinking that he made a great figure at the head of them. The Cardinal, who was factious enough, was wise enough at the same time to avoid gathering the people together, except when there was occasion, and when he had something particular for them to do. However, he could not always check Monsieur de Beaufort; who having assembled them once very unnecessarily, and without any determined object, they ran riot, would not be kept within bounds by their leaders, and did their cause a great deal of harm: upon which the Cardinal observes most judiciously, 'Que Monsieur de Beaufort me savoit pas, que qui assemble le peuple, l'emeut'. It is certain, that great numbers of people met together, animate each other, and will do something, either good or bad, but oftener bad; and the respective individuals, who were separately very quiet, when met together in numbers, grow tumultuous as a body, and ripe for any mischief that may be pointed out to them by the leaders; and, if their leaders have no business for them, they will find some for themselves. The demagogues, or leaders of popular factions, should therefore be very careful not to assemble the people unnecessarily, and without a settled and well-considered object. Besides that, by making those popular assemblies too frequent, they make them likewise too familiar, and consequently less respected by their enemies. Observe any meetings of people, and you will always find their eagerness and impetuosity rise or fall in proportion to their numbers: when the numbers are very great, all sense and reason seem to subside, and one sudden frenzy to seize on all, even the coolest of them.

Another very just observation of the Cardinal's is, That, the things which happen in our own times, and which we see ourselves, do not surprise us near so much as the things which we read of in times past, though not in the least more extraordinary; and adds, that he is persuaded that when Caligula made his horse a Consul, the people of Rome, at that time, were not greatly surprised at it, having necessarily been in some degree prepared for it, by an insensible gradation of extravagances from the same quarter. This is so true that we read every day, with astonishment, things which we see every day without surprise. We wonder at the intrepidity of a Leonidas, a Codrus, and a Curtius; and are not the least surprised to hear of a sea-captain, who has blown up his ship, his crew, and himself, that they might not fall into the hands of the enemies of his country. I cannot help reading of Porsenna and Regulus, with surprise and reverence, and yet I remember that I saw, without either, the execution of Shepherd,—[James Shepherd, a coach-painter's apprentice, was executed at Tyburn for high treason, March 17, 1718, in the reign of George I.]—a boy of eighteen years old, who intended to shoot the late king, and who would have been pardoned, if he would have expressed the least sorrow for his intended crime; but, on the contrary, he declared that if he was pardoned he would attempt it again; that he thought it a duty which he owed to his country, and that he died with pleasure for having endeavored to perform it. Reason equals Shepherd to Regulus; but prejudice, and the recency of the fact, make Shepherd a common malefactor and Regulus a hero.

Examine carefully, and reconsider all your notions of things; analyze them, and discover their component parts, and see if habit and prejudice are not the principal ones; weigh the matter upon which you are to form your opinion, in the equal and impartial scales of reason. It is not to be conceived how many people, capable of reasoning, if they would, live and die in a thousand errors, from laziness; they will rather adopt the prejudices of others, than give themselves the trouble of forming opinions of their own. They say things, at first, because other people have said them, and then they persist in them, because they have said them themselves.

The last observation that I shall now mention of the Cardinal's is, "That a secret is more easily kept by a good many people, than one commonly imagines." By this he means a secret of importance, among people interested in the keeping of it. And it is certain that people of business know the importance of secrecy, and will observe it, where they are concerned in the event. To go and tell any friend, wife, or mistress, any secret with which they have nothing to do, is discovering to them such an unretentive weakness, as must convince them that you will tell it to twenty others, and consequently that they may reveal it without the risk of being discovered. But a secret properly communicated only to those who are to be concerned in the thing in question, will probably be kept by them though they should be a good many. Little secrets are commonly told again, but great ones are generally kept. Adieu!

LETTER LI

LONDON, September 20, O. S. 1748.

DEAR BOY: I wait with impatience for your accurate history of the 'Chevaliers Forte Epees', which you promised me in your last, and which I take to be the forerunner of a larger work that you intend to give the public, containing a general account of all the religious and military orders of Europe. Seriously, you will do well to have a general notion of all those orders, ancient and modern; both as they are frequently the subjects of conversation, and as they are more or less interwoven with the histories of those times. Witness the Teutonic Order, which, as soon as it gained strength, began its unjust depredations in Germany, and acquired such considerable possessions there; and the Order of Malta also, which continues to this day its piracies upon the Infidels. Besides one can go into no company in Germany, without running against Monsieur le Chevalier, or Monsieur le Commandeur de l' Ordre Teutonique. It is the same in all the other parts of Europe with regard to the Order of Malta, where you never go into company without meeting two or three Chevaliers or Commandeurs, who talk of their 'Preuves', their 'Langues', their 'Caravanes', etc., of all which things I am sure you would not willingly be ignorant. On the other hand, I do not mean that you should have a profound and minute knowledge of these matters, which are of a nature that a general knowledge of them is fully sufficient. I would not recommend you to read Abbe Vertot's "History of the Order of Malta," in four quarto volumes; that would be employing a great deal of good time very ill. But I would have you know the foundations, the objects, the INSIGNIA, and the short general history of them all.

As for the ancient religious military orders, which were chiefly founded in the eleventh and twelfth centuries, such as Malta, the Teutonic, the Knights Templars, etc., the injustice and the wickedness of those establishments cannot, I am sure, have escaped your observation. Their pious object was, to take away by force other people's property, and to massacre the proprietors themselves if they refused to give up that property, and adopt the opinions of these invaders. What right or pretense had these confederated Christians of Europe to the Holy Land? Let them produce their grant of it in the Bible. Will they say, that the Saracens had possessed themselves of it by force, and that, consequently, they had the same right? Is it lawful then to steal goods because they were stolen before? Surely not. The truth is, that the wickedness of many, and the weakness of more, in those ages of ignorance and superstition, concurred to form those flagitious conspiracies against the lives and properties of unoffending people. The Pope sanctified the villany, and annexed the pardon of sins to the perpetration of it. This gave rise to the Crusaders, and carried such swarms of people from Europe to the conquests of the Holy Land. Peter the Hermit, an active and ambitious priest, by his indefatigable pains, was the immediate author of the first crusade; kings, princes, all professions and characters united, from different motives, in this great undertaking, as every sentiment, except true religion and morality, invited to it. The ambitious hoped for kingdoms; the greedy and the necessitous for plunder; and some were enthusiasts enough to hope for salvation, by the destruction of a considerable number of their fellow creatures, who had done them no injury. I cannot omit, upon this occasion, telling you that the Eastern emperors at Constantinople (who, as Christians, were obliged at least to seem to favor these expeditions), seeing the immense numbers of the 'Croisez', and fearing that the Western Empire might have some mind to the Eastern Empire too, if it succeeded against the Infidels, as 'l'appetit vient en mangeant'; these Eastern emperors, very honestly, poisoned the waters where the 'Croisez' were to pass, and so destroyed infinite numbers of them.

The later orders of knighthood, such as the Garter in England; the Elephant in Denmark; the Golden Fleece in

Burgundy; the St. Esprit, St. Michel, St. Louis, and St. Lazare, in France etc., are of a very different nature and were either the invitations to, or the rewards of, brave actions in fair war; and are now rather the decorations of the favor of the prince, than the proofs of the merit of the subject. However, they are worth your inquiries to a certain degree, and conversation will give you frequent opportunities for them. Wherever you are, I would advise you to inquire into the respective orders of that country, and to write down a short account of them. For example, while you are in Saxony, get an account of l'Aigle Blanc and of what other orders there may be, either Polish or Saxon; and, when you shall be at Berlin, inform yourself of three orders, l'Aigle Noir, la Generosite et le Vrai Merite, which are the only ones that I know of there. But whenever you meet with straggling ribands and stars, as you will with a thousand in Germany, do not fail to inquire what they are, and to take a minute of them in your memorandum book; for it is a sort of knowledge that costs little to acquire, and yet it is of some use. Young people have frequently an incuriousness about them, arising either from laziness, or a contempt of the object, which deprives them of several such little parts of knowledge, that they afterward wish they had acquired. If you will put conversation to profit, great knowledge may be gained by it; and is it not better (since it is full as easy) to turn it upon useful than upon useless subjects? People always talk best upon what they know most, and it is both pleasing them and improving one's self, to put them upon that subject. With people of a particular profession, or of a distinguished eminency in any branch of learning, one is not at a loss; but with those, whether men or women, who properly constitute what is called the beau monde, one must not choose deep subjects, nor hope to get any knowledge above that of orders, ranks, families, and court anecdotes; which are therefore the proper (and not altogether useless) subjects of that kind of conversation. Women, especially, are to be talked to as below men and above children. If you talk to them too deep, you only confound them, and lose your own labor; if you talk to them too frivolously, they perceive and resent the contempt. The proper tone for them is, what the French call the 'Entregent', and is, in truth, the polite jargon of good company. Thus, if you are a good chemist, you may extract something out of everything.

A propos of the beau monde, I must again and again recommend the Graces to you: There is no doing without them in that world; and, to make a good figure in that world, is a great step toward making one in the world of business, particularly that part of it for which you are destined. An ungraceful manner of speaking, awkward motions, and a disagreeable address, are great clogs to the ablest man of business, as the opposite qualifications are of infinite advantage to him. I am told there is a very good dancing-master at Leipsig. I would have you dance a minuet very well, not so much for the sake of the minuet itself (though that, if danced at all, ought to be danced, well), as that it will give you a habitual genteel carriage and manner of presenting yourself.

Since I am upon little things, I must mention another, which, though little enough in itself, yet as it occurs at, least once in every day, deserves some attention; I mean Carving. Do you use yourself to carve ADROITLY and genteelly, without hacking half an hour across a bone; without bespattering the company with the sauce; and without overturning the glasses into your neighbor's pockets? These awkwardnesses are extremely disagreeable; and, if often repeated, bring ridicule. They are very easily avoided by a little attention and use.

How trifling soever these things may seem, or really be in themselves, they are no longer so when above half the world thinks them otherwise. And, as I would have you 'omnibus ornatum—excellere rebus', I think nothing above or below my pointing out to you, or your excelling in. You have the means of doing it, and time before you to make use of them. Take my word for it, I ask nothing now but what you will, twenty years hence, most heartily wish that you had done. Attention to all these things, for the next two or three years, will save you infinite trouble and endless regrets hereafter. May you, in the whole course of your life, have no reason for any one just regret! Adieu.

Your Dresden china is arrived, and I have sent it to your Mamma.

LETTER LII

LONDON, September 27, O. S. 1748.

DEAR BOY: I have received your Latin "Lecture upon War," which though it is not exactly the same Latin that Caesar, Cicero, Horace, Virgil, and Ovid spoke, is, however, as good Latin as the erudite Germans speak or write. I have always observed that the most learned people, that is, those who have read the most Latin, write the worst; and that distinguishes the Latin of gentleman scholar from that of a pedant. A gentleman has, probably, read no other Latin than that of the Augustan age; and therefore can write no other, whereas the pedant has read much more bad Latin than good, and consequently writes so too. He looks upon the best classical books, as books for school-boys, and consequently below him; but pores over fragments of obscure authors, treasures up the obsolete words which he meets with there, and uses them upon all occasions to show his reading at the expense of his judgment. Plautus is his favorite author, not for the sake of the wit and the vis comica of his comedies, but upon account of the many obsolete words, and the cant of low characters, which are to be met with nowhere else. He will rather use 'olli' than 'illi', 'optume' than 'optima', and any bad word rather than any good one, provided he can but prove, that strictly speaking, it is Latin; that is, that it was written by a Roman. By this rule, I might now write to you in the language of Chaucer or Spenser, and assert that I wrote English, because it was English in their days; but I should be a most affected puppy if I did so, and you would not understand three words of my letter. All these, and such like affected peculiarities, are the characteristics of learned coxcombs and pedants, and are carefully avoided by all men of sense.

I dipped accidentally, the other day, into Pitiscus's preface to his "Lexicon," where I found a word that puzzled me, and which I did not remember ever to have met with before. It is the adverb 'praefiscine', which means, IN A GOOD HOUR; an expression which, by the superstition of it, appears to be low and vulgar. I looked for it: and at last I found that it is once or twice made use of in Plautus, upon the strength of which this learned pedant thrusts it into his preface. Whenever you write Latin, remember that every word or phrase which you make use of, but cannot find in Caesar, Cicero, Livy, Horace, Virgil; and Ovid, is bad, illiberal Latin, though it may have been written by a Roman.

I must now say something as to the matter of the "Lecture," in which I confess there is one doctrine laid down that surprises me: It is this, 'Quum vero hostis sit lenta citave morte omnia dira nobis minitans quocunque bellantibus negotium est; parum sane interfuerit quo modo eum obruere et interficere satagamus, si ferociam exuere cunctetur. Ergo veneno quoque uti fas est', etc., whereas I cannot conceive that the use of poison can, upon any account, come within the lawful means of self-defense. Force may, without doubt, be justly repelled by force, but not by treachery and fraud; for I do not call the stratagems of war, such as ambuscades, masked batteries, false attacks, etc., frauds or treachery: They are mutually to be expected and guarded against; but poisoned arrows, poisoned waters, or poison administered to your enemy (which can only be done by treachery), I have always heard, read, and thought, to be unlawful and infamous means of defense, be your danger ever so great: But 'si ferociam exuere cunctetur'; must I rather die than poison this enemy? Yes, certainly, much rather die than do a base or criminal action; nor can I be sure, beforehand, that this enemy may not, in the last moment, 'ferociam exuere'. But the public lawyers, now, seem to me rather to warp the law, in order to authorize, than to check, those unlawful proceedings of princes and states; which, by being become common, appear less criminal, though custom can never alter the nature of good and ill.

Pray let no quibbles of lawyers, no refinements of casuists, break into the plain notions of right and wrong, which every man's right reason and plain common sense suggest to him. To do as you would be done by, is the plain, sure, and undisputed rule of morality and justice. Stick to that; and be convinced that whatever breaks into it, in any degree, however speciously it may be turned, and however puzzling it may be to answer it, is, notwithstanding, false in itself, unjust, and criminal. I do not know a crime in the world, which is not by the casuists among the Jesuits (especially the twenty-four collected, I think, by Escobar) allowed, in some, or many cases, not to be criminal. The principles first laid down by them are often specious, the reasonings plausible, but the conclusion always a lie: for it is contrary, to that evident and undeniable rule of justice which I have mentioned above, of not doing to anyone what you would not have him do to you. But, however, these refined pieces of casuistry and sophistry, being very convenient and welcome to people's passions and appetites, they gladly accept the indulgence, without desiring to detect the fallacy or the reasoning: and indeed many, I might say most people, are not able to do it; which makes the publication of such quibblings and refinements the more pernicious. I am no skillful casuist nor subtle disputant; and yet I would undertake to justify and qualify the profession of a highwayman, step by step, and so plausibly, as to make many ignorant people embrace the profession, as an innocent, if not even a laudable one; and puzzle people of some degree of knowledge, to answer me point by point. I have seen a book, entitled 'Quidlibet ex Quolibet', or the art of making anything out of anything; which is not so difficult as it would seem, if once one quits certain plain truths, obvious in gross to every understanding, in order to run after the ingenious refinements of warm imaginations and speculative reasonings. Doctor Berkeley, Bishop of Cloyne, a very worthy, ingenious, and learned man, has written a book, to prove that there is no such thing as matter, and that nothing exists but in idea: that you and I only fancy ourselves eating, drinking, and sleeping; you at Leipsig, and I at London: that we think we have flesh and blood, legs, arms, etc., but that we are only spirit. His arguments are, strictly speaking, unanswerable; but yet I am so far from being convinced by them, that I am determined to go on to eat and drink, and walk and ride, in order to keep that MATTER, which I so mistakenly imagine my body at present to consist of, in as good plight as possible. Common sense (which, in truth, very uncommon) is the best sense I know of: abide by it, it will counsel you best. Read and hear, for your amusement, ingenious systems, nice questions subtilly agitated, with all the refinements that warm imaginations suggest; but consider them only as exercitations for the mind, and turn always to settle with common sense.

I stumbled, the other day, at a bookseller's, upon "Comte Gabalis," in two very little volumes, which I had formerly read. I read it over again, and with fresh astonishment. Most of the extravagances are taken from the Jewish Rabbins, who broached those wild notions, and delivered them in the unintelligible jargon which the Caballists and Rosicrucians deal in to this day. Their number is, I believe, much lessened, but there are still some; and I myself have known two; who studied and firmly believed in that mystical nonsense. What extravagancy is not man capable of entertaining, when once his shackled reason is led in triumph by fancy and prejudice! The ancient alchemists give very much into this stuff, by which they thought they should discover the philosopher's stone; and some of the most celebrated empirics employed it in the pursuit of the universal medicine. Paracelsus, a bold empiric and wild Caballist, asserted that he had discovered it, and called it his 'Alkahest'. Why or wherefore, God knows; only that those madmen call nothing by an intelligible name. You may easily get this book from The Hague: read it, for it will both divert and astonish you, and at the same time teach you 'nil admirari'; a very necessary lesson.

Your letters, except when upon a given subject, are exceedingly laconic, and neither answer my desires nor the purpose of letters; which should be familiar conversations, between absent friends. As I desire to live with you upon the footing of an intimate friend, and not of a parent, I could wish that your letters gave me more particular accounts of yourself, and of your lesser transactions. When you write to me, suppose yourself conversing freely with me by the fireside. In that case, you would naturally mention the incidents of the day; as where you had been, who you had seen, what you thought of them, etc. Do this in your letters: acquaint me sometimes with your studies, sometimes with your diversions; tell me of any new persons and characters that you meet with in company, and add your own observations upon them: in short, let me see more of you in your letters. How do you go on with Lord Pulteney, and how does he go on at Leipsig? Has he learning, has he parts, has he application? Is he good or ill-natured? In short, What is he? at least, what do you think him? You may tell me without reserve, for I promise you secrecy. You are now of an age that I am desirous to begin a confidential correspondence with you; and as I shall, on my part, write you very freely my opinion upon men and things, which I should often be very unwilling that anybody but you and Mr. Harte should see, so, on your part, if you write me without reserve, you may depend upon my inviolable secrecy. If you have ever looked into the "Letters" of Madame de Sevigne to her daughter, Madame de Grignan, you must have observed the ease, freedom, and friendship of that correspondence; and yet, I hope and I believe, that they did not love one another better than we do. Tell me what books you are now reading, either by way of study or amusement; how you pass your evenings when at home, and where you pass them when abroad. I know that you go sometimes to Madame Valentin's assembly; What do you do there? Do you play, or sup, or is it only 'la belle conversation?' Do you mind your dancing while your dancing-master is with you? As you will be often under the necessity of dancing a minuet, I would have you dance it very well. Remember, that the graceful motion of the arms, the giving your hand, and the putting on and pulling off your hat genteelly, are the material parts of a gentleman's dancing. But the greatest advantage of dancing well is, that it necessarily teaches you to present yourself, to sit, stand, and walk, genteelly; all of which are of real importance to a man of fashion.

I should wish that you were polished before you go to Berlin; where, as you will be in a great deal of good company, I would have you have the right manners for it. It is a very considerable article to have 'le ton de la bonne compagnie', in your destination particularly. The principal business of a foreign minister is, to get into the secrets, and to know all 'les allures' of the courts at which he resides; this he can never bring about but by such a pleasing address, such engaging manners, and such an insinuating behavior, as may make him sought for, and in some measure domestic, in the best company and the best families of the place. He will then, indeed, be well informed of all that passes, either by the confidences made him, or by the carelessness of people in his company, who are accustomed to look upon him as one of them, and consequently are not upon their guard before him. For a minister who only goes to the court he resides at, in form, to ask an audience of the prince or the minister upon his last instructions, puts them upon their guard, and will never know anything more than what they have a mind that he should know. Here women may be put to some use. A king's mistress, or a minister's wife or mistress, may give great and useful informations; and are very apt to do it, being proud to show that they have been trusted. But then, in this case, the height of that sort of address, which, strikes women, is requisite; I mean that easy politeness, genteel and graceful address, and that 'exterieur brilliant' which they cannot withstand. There is a sort of men so like women, that they are to be taken just in the same way; I mean those who are commonly called FINE MEN; who swarm at all courts; who have little reflection, and less knowledge; but, who by their good breeding, and 'train-tran' of the world, are admitted into all companies; and, by the imprudence or carelessness of their superiors, pick up secrets worth knowing, which are easily got out of them by proper address. Adieu.

LETTER LIII

BATH, October 12, O. S. 1748.

DEAR BOY: I came here three days ago upon account of a disorder in my stomach, which affected my head and gave me vertigo. I already find myself something better; and consequently do not doubt but that the course of these waters will set me quite right. But however and wherever I am, your welfare, your character, your knowledge, and your morals, employ my thoughts more than anything that can happen to me, or that I can fear or hope for myself. I am going off the stage, you are coming upon it; with me what has been, has been, and reflection now would come too late; with you everything is to come, even, in some manner, reflection itself; so that this is the very time when my reflections, the result of experience, may be of use to you, by supplying the want of yours. As soon as you leave Leipsig, you will gradually be going into the great world; where the first impressions that you shall give of yourself will be of great importance to you; but those which you shall receive will be decisive, for they always stick. To keep good company, especially at your first setting out, is the way to receive good impressions. If you ask me what I mean by good company, I will confess to you that it is pretty difficult to define; but I will endeavor to make you understand it as well as I can.

Good company is not what respective sets of company are pleased either to call or think themselves, but it is that company which all the people of the place call, and acknowledge to be, good company, notwithstanding some objections which they may form to some of the individuals who compose it. It consists chiefly (but by no means without exception) of people of considerable birth, rank, and character; for people of neither birth nor rank are frequently, and very justly admitted into it, if distinguished by any peculiar merit, or eminency in any liberal art or science. Nay, so motly a thing is good company, that many people, without birth, rank, or merit, intrude into it by their own forwardness, and others slide into it by the protection of some considerable person; and some even of indifferent characters and morals make part of it. But in the main, the good part preponderates, and people of infamous and blasted characters are never admitted. In this fashionable good company, the best manners and the best language of the place are most unquestionably to be learned; for they establish and give the tone to both, which are therefore called the language and manners of good company: there being no legal tribunal to ascertain either.

A company, consisting wholly of people of the first quality, cannot, for that reason, be called good company, in the common acceptation of the phrase, unless they are, into the bargain, the fashionable and accredited company of the place; for people of the very first quality can be as silly, as ill-bred, and as worthless, as people of the meanest degree. On the other hand, a company consisting entirely of people of very low condition, whatever their merit or parts may be, can never be called good company; and consequently should not be much frequented, though by no means despised.

A company wholly composed of men of learning, though greatly to be valued and respected, is not meant by the words GOOD COMPANY; they cannot have the easy manners and, 'tournure' of the world, as they do not live in it. If you can bear your part well in such a company, it is extremely right to be in it sometimes, and you will be but more esteemed in other companies, for having a place in that. But then do not let it engross you; for if you do, you will be only considered as one of the 'literati' by profession; which is not the way either, to shine, or rise in the world.

The company of professed wits and pests is extremely inviting to most young men; who if they have wit themselves, are pleased with it, and if they have none, are sillily proud of being one of it: but it should be frequented with moderation and judgment, and you should by no means give yourself up to it. A wit is a very unpopular denomination, as it carries terror along with it; and people in general are as much afraid of a live wit, in company, as a woman is of a gun, which she thinks may go off of itself, and do her a mischief. Their acquaintance is, however, worth seeking, and their company worth frequenting; but not exclusively of others, nor to such a degree as to be considered only as one of that particular set.

But the company, which of all others you should most carefully avoid, is that low company, which, in every sense of the word, is low indeed; low in rank, low in parts, low in manners, and low in merit. You will, perhaps, be surprised that I should think it necessary to warn you against such company, but yet I do not think it wholly, unnecessary, from the many instances which I have seen of men of sense and rank, discredited, verified, and undone, by keeping such company.

EARL OF PHILIP DORMER STANHOPE CHESTERFIELD

Vanity, that source of many of our follies, and of some of our crimes, has sunk many a man into company, in every light infinitely, below himself, for the sake of being the first man in it. There he dictates, is applauded, admired; and, for the sake of being the Coryphœus of that wretched chorus, disgraces and disqualifies himself soon for any better company. Depend upon it, you will sink or rise to the level of the company which you commonly keep: people will judge of you, and not unreasonably, by that. There is good sense in the Spanish saying, "Tell me whom you live with, and I will tell you who you are." Make it therefore your business, wherever you are, to get into that company which everybody in the place allows to be the best company next to their own; which is the best definition that I can give you of good company. But here, too, one caution is very necessary, for want of which many young men have been ruined, even in good company.

Good company (as I have before observed) is composed of a great variety of fashionable people, whose characters and morals are very different, though their manners are pretty much the same. When a young man, new in the world, first gets into that company, he very rightly determines to conform to, and imitate it. But then he too often, and fatally, mistakes the objects of his imitation. He has often heard that absurd term of genteel and fashionable vices. He there sees some people who shine, and who in general are admired and esteemed; and observes that these people are whoremasters, drunkards, or gamesters, upon which he adopts their vices, mistaking their defects for their perfections, and thinking that they owe their fashions and their luster to those genteel vices. Whereas it is exactly the reverse; for these people have acquired their reputation by their parts, their learning, their good-breeding, and other real accomplishments: and are only blemished and lowered, in the opinions of all reasonable people, and of their own, in time, by these genteel and fashionable vices. A whoremaster, in a flux, or without a nose, is a very genteel person, indeed, and well worthy of imitation. A drunkard, vomiting up at night the wine of the day, and stupefied by the headache all the next, is, doubtless, a fine model to copy from. And a gamester, tearing his hair, and blaspheming, for having lost more than he had in the world, is surely a most amiable character. No; these are alloys, and great ones too, which can never adorn any character, but will always debase the best. To prove this, suppose any man, without parts and some other good qualities, to be merely a whoremaster, a drunkard, or a gamester; how will he be looked upon by all sorts of people? Why, as a most contemptible and vicious animal. Therefore it is plain, that in these mixed characters, the good part only makes people forgive, but not approve, the bad.

I will hope and believe that you will have no vices; but if, unfortunately, you should have any, at least I beg of you to be content with your own, and to adopt no other body's.

The adoption of vice has, I am convinced, ruined ten times more young men than natural inclinations.

As I make no difficulty of confessing my past errors, where I think the confession may be of use to you, I will own that when I first went to the university, I drank and smoked, notwithstanding the aversion I had to wine and tobacco, only because I thought it genteel, and that it made me look like a man. When I went abroad, I first went to The Hague, where gaming was much in fashion, and where I observed that many people of shining rank and character gamed too. I was then young enough, and silly enough, to believe that gaming was one of their accomplishments; and, as I aimed at perfection, I adopted gaming as a necessary step to it. Thus I acquired by error the habit of a vice which, far from adorning my character, has, I am conscious, been a great blemish in it.

Imitate then, with discernment and judgment, the real perfections of the good company into which you may get; copy their politeness, their carriage, their address, and the easy and well-bred turn of their conversation; but remember that, let them shine ever so bright, their vices, if they have any, are so many spots which you would no more imitate, than you would make an artificial wart upon your face, because some very handsome man had the misfortune to have a natural one upon his: but, on the contrary, think how much handsomer he would have been without it.

Having thus confessed some of my 'egaremens', I will now show you a little of my right side. I always endeavored to get into the best company wherever I was, and commonly succeeded. There I pleased to some degree by showing a desire to please. I took care never to be absent or 'distrait'; but on the contrary, attended to everything that was said, done, or even looked, in company; I never failed in the minutest attentions and was never 'journalier'. These things, and not my 'egaremens', made me fashionable. Adieu! This letter is full long enough.

LETTER LIV

BATH, October 19, O. S. 1748.

DEAR BOY: Having in my last pointed out what sort of company you should keep, I will now give you some rules for your conduct in it; rules which my own experience and observation enable me to lay down, and communicate to you, with some degree of confidence. I have often given you hints of this kind before, but then it has been by snatches; I will now be more regular and methodical. I shall say nothing with regard to your bodily carriage and address, but leave them to the care of your dancing-master, and to your own attention to the best models; remember, however, that they are of consequence.

Talk often, but never long: in that case, if you do not please, at least you are sure not to tire your hearers. Pay your own reckoning, but do not treat the whole company; this being one of the very few cases in which people do not care to be treated, everyone being fully convinced that he has wherewithal to pay.

Tell stories very seldom, and absolutely never but where they are very apt and very short. Omit every circumstance that is not material, and beware of digressions. To have frequent recourse to narrative betrays great want of imagination.

Never hold anybody by the button or the hand, in order to be heard out; for, if people are not willing to hear you, you had much better hold your tongue than them.

Most long talkers single out some one unfortunate man in company (commonly him whom they observe to be the most silent, or their next neighbor) to whisper, or at least in a half voice, to convey a continuity of words to. This is excessively ill-bred, and in some degree a fraud; conversation-stock being a joint and common property. But, on the other hand, if one of these unmerciful talkers lays hold of you, hear him with patience (and at least seeming attention), if he is worth obliging; for nothing will oblige him more than a patient hearing, as nothing would hurt him more than either to leave him in the midst of his discourse, or to discover your impatience under your affliction.

Take, rather than give, the tone of the company you are in. If you have parts, you will show them, more or less, upon every subject; and if you have not, you had better talk sillily upon a subject of other people's than of your own choosing.

Avoid as much as you can, in mixed companies, argumentative, polemical conversations; which, though they should not, yet certainly do, indispose for a time the contending parties toward each other; and, if the controversy grows warm and noisy, endeavor to put an end to it by some genteel levity or joke. I quieted such a conversation-hubbub once, by representing to them that, though I was persuaded none there present would repeat, out of company, what passed in it, yet I could not answer for the discretion of the passengers in the street, who must necessarily hear all that was said.

Above all things, and upon all occasions, avoid speaking of yourself, if it be possible. Such is the natural pride and vanity of our hearts, that it perpetually breaks out, even in people of the best parts, in all the various modes and figures of the egotism.

Some, abruptly, speak advantageously of themselves, without either pretense or provocation. They are impudent. Others proceed more artfully, as they imagine; and forge accusations against themselves, complain of calumnies which they never heard, in order to justify themselves, by exhibiting a catalogue of their many virtues. They acknowledge it may, indeed, seem odd that they should talk in that manner of themselves; it is what they do not like, and what they never would have done; no; no tortures should ever have forced it from them, if they had, not been thus unjustly and monstrously accused. But, in these cases; justice is surely due to one's self, as well as to others; and when our character is attacked, we may say in our own justification, what otherwise we never would have said. This thin veil of Modesty drawn before Vanity, is much too transparent to conceal it, even from very moderate discernment.

Others go more modestly and more slyly still (as they think) to work; but in my mind still more ridiculously. They confess themselves (not without some degree of shame and confusion) into all the Cardinal Virtues, by first degrading them into weaknesses and then owning their misfortune in being made up of those weaknesses. They cannot see people suffer without sympathizing with, and endeavoring to help them. They cannot see people want, without relieving them, though truly their own circumstances cannot very well afford it. They cannot help speaking truth, though they know all the imprudence of it. In short, they know that, with all these weaknesses, they are not fit to live in the world, much less to thrive in it. But they are now too old to change, and must rub on as well as they can. This sounds too ridiculous and 'outre', almost, for the stage; and yet, take my word for it, you will frequently meet with it upon the common stage of the world. And here I will observe, by the bye, that you will often meet with characters in nature so extravagant, that a discreet dramatist would not venture to set them upon the stage in their true and high coloring.

This principle of vanity and pride is so strong in human nature that it descends even to the lowest objects; and one often sees people angling for praise, where, admitting all they say to be true (which, by the way, it seldom is), no just praise is to be caught. One man affirms that he has rode post an hundred miles in six hours; probably it is a lie: but supposing it to be true, what then? Why he is a very good post-boy, that is all. Another asserts, and probably not without oaths, that he has drunk six or eight bottles of wine at a sitting; out of charity, I will believe him a liar; for, if I do not, I must think him a beast.

Such, and a thousand more, are the follies and extravagances, which vanity draws people into, and which always defeat their own purpose; and as Waller says, upon another subject,—

> "Make the wretch the most despised,
>
> Where most he wishes to be prized."

The only sure way of avoiding these evils, is never to speak of yourself at all. But when, historically, you are obliged to mention yourself, take care not to drop one single word that can directly or indirectly be construed as fishing for applause. Be your character what it will, it will be known; and nobody will take it upon your own word. Never imagine that anything you can say yourself will varnish your defects, or add lustre to your perfections! but, on the contrary, it may, and nine times in ten, will, make the former more glaring and the latter obscure. If you are silent upon your own subject, neither envy, indignation, nor ridicule, will obstruct or allay the applause which you may really deserve; but if you publish your own panegyric upon any occasion, or in any shape whatsoever, and however artfully dressed or disguised, they will all conspire against you, and you will be disappointed of the very end you aim at.

Take care never to seem dark and mysterious; which is not only a very unamiable character, but a very suspicious one too; if you seem mysterious with others, they will be really so with you, and you will know nothing. The height of abilities is to have 'volto sciolto' and 'pensieri stretti'; that is, a frank, open, and ingenuous exterior, with a prudent interior; to be upon your own guard, and yet, by a seeming natural openness, to put people off theirs. Depend upon it nine in ten of every company you are in will avail themselves of every indiscreet and unguarded expression of yours, if they can turn it to their own advantage. A prudent reserve is therefore as necessary as a seeming openness is prudent. Always look people in the face when you speak to them: the not doing it is thought to imply conscious guilt; besides that you lose the advantage of serving by their countenances what impression your discourse makes upon them. In order to know people's real sentiments, I trust much more to my eyes than to my ears: for they can say whatever they have a mind I should hear; but they can seldom help looking, what they have no intention that I should know.

Neither retail nor receive scandal willingly; defamation of others may for the present gratify the malignity of the pride of our hearts; cool reflection will draw very disadvantageous conclusions from such a disposition; and in the case of scandal, as in that of robbery, the receiver is always thought, as bad as the thief.

Mimicry, which is the common and favorite amusement of little low minds, is in the utmost contempt with great ones. It is the lowest and most illiberal of all buffoonery. Pray, neither practice it yourself, nor applaud it in others. Besides that the person mimicked is insulted; and, as I have often observed to you before, an insult is never forgiven.

I need not (I believe) advise you to adapt your conversation to the people you are conversing with: for I suppose you would not, without this caution, have talked upon the same subject, and in the same manner, to a minister of state, a bishop, a philosopher, a captain, and a woman. A man of the world must, like the chameleon, be able to take every different hue; which is by no means a criminal or abject, but a necessary complaisance; for it relates only to manners and not to morals.

One word only as to swearing, and that, I hope and believe, is more than is necessary. You may sometimes hear some people in good company interlard their discourse with oaths, by way of embellishment, as they think, but you must observe, too, that those who do so are never those who contribute, in any degree, to give that company the denomination of good company. They are always subalterns, or people of low education; for that practice, besides that it has no one temptation to plead, is as silly and as illiberal as it is wicked.

Loud laughter is the mirth of the mob, who are only pleased with silly things; for true wit or good sense never excited a laugh since the creation of the world. A man of parts and fashion is therefore only seen to smile; but never heard to laugh.

But to conclude this long letter; all the above-mentioned rules, however carefully you may observe them, will lose half their effect, if unaccompanied by the Graces. Whatever you say, if you say it with a supercilious, cynical face, or an embarrassed countenance, or a silly, disconcerted grin, will be ill received. If, into the bargain, YOU MUTTER IT, OR UTTER IT INDISTINCTLY AND UNGRACEFULLY, it will be still worse received. If your air and address are vulgar, awkward, and gauche, you may be esteemed indeed, if you have great intrinsic merit; but you will never, please; and without pleasing you will rise but heavily. Venus, among the ancients, was synonymous with the Graces, who were always supposed to accompany her; and Horace tells us that even Youth and Mercury, the god of Arts and Eloquence, would not do without her:

'Parum comis sine to Juventas Mercuriusque.'

They are not inexorable Ladies, and may be had if properly, and diligently pursued. Adieu.

LETTER LV

BATH, October 29, O. S. 1748.

DEAR BOY: My anxiety for your success increases in proportion as the time approaches of your taking your part upon the great stage of the world. The audience will form their opinion of you upon your first appearance (making the proper allowance for your inexperience), and so far it will be final, that, though it may vary as to the degrees, it will never totally change. This consideration excites that restless attention with which I am constantly examining how I can best contribute to the perfection of that character, in which the least spot or blemish would give me more real concern, than I am now capable of feeling upon any other account whatsoever.

I have long since done mentioning your great religious and moral duties, because I could not make your understanding so bad a compliment as to suppose that you wanted, or could receive, any new instructions upon those two important points. Mr. Harte, I am sure, has not neglected them; and, besides, they are so obvious to common sense and reason, that commentators may (as they often do) perplex, but cannot make them clearer. My province, therefore, is to supply by my experience your hitherto inevitable inexperience in

LETTERS TO HIS SON, COMPLETE

the ways of the world. People at your age are in a state of natural ebriety; and want rails, and 'gardefous', wherever they go, to hinder them from breaking their necks. This drunkenness of youth is not only tolerated, but even pleases, if kept within certain bounds of discretion and decency. These bounds are the point which it is difficult for the drunken man himself to find out; and there it is that the experience of a friend may not only serve, but save him.

Carry with you, and welcome, into company all the gaiety and spirits, but as little of the giddiness, of youth as you can. The former will charm; but the latter will often, though innocently, implacably offend. Inform yourself of the characters and situations of the company, before you give way to what your imagination may prompt you to say. There are, in all companies, more wrong heads than right ones, and many more who deserve, than who like censure. Should you therefore expatiate in the praise of some virtue, which some in company notoriously want; or declaim against any vice, which others are notoriously infected with, your reflections, however general and unapplied, will, by being applicable, be thought personal and leveled at those people. This consideration points out to you, sufficiently, not to be suspicious and captious yourself, nor to suppose that things, because they may be, are therefore meant at you. The manners of well-bred people secure one from those indirect and mean attacks; but if, by chance, a flippant woman or a pert coxcomb lets off anything of that kind, it is much better not to seem to understand, than to reply to it.

Cautiously avoid talking of either your own or other people's domestic affairs. Yours are nothing to them but tedious; theirs are nothing to you. The subject is a tender one: and it is odds but that you touch somebody or other's sore place: for, in this case, there is no trusting to specious appearances; which may be, and often are, so contrary to the real situations of things, between men and their wives, parents and their children, seeming friends, etc., that, with the best intentions in the world, one often blunders disagreeably.

Remember that the wit, humor, and jokes, of most mixed companies are local. They thrive in that particular soil, but will not often bear transplanting. Every company is differently circumstanced, has its particular cant and jargon; which may give occasion to wit and mirth within that circle, but would seem flat and insipid in any other, and therefore will not bear repeating. Nothing makes a man look sillier than a pleasantry not relished or not understood; and if he meets with a profound silence when he expected a general applause, or, what is worse, if he is desired to explain the bon mot, his awkward and embarrassed situation is easier imagined' than described. 'A propos' of repeating; take great care never to repeat (I do not mean here the pleasantries) in one company what you hear in another. Things, seemingly indifferent, may, by circulation, have much graver consequences than you would imagine. Besides, there is a general tacit trust in conversation, by which a man is obliged not to report anything out of it, though he is not immediately enjoined to secrecy. A retailer of this kind is sure to draw himself into a thousand scrapes and discussions, and to be shyly and uncomfortably received wherever he goes.

You will find, in most good company, some people who only keep their place there by a contemptible title enough; these are what we call VERY GOOD-NATURED FELLOWS, and the French, 'bons diables'. The truth is, they are people without any parts or fancy, and who, having no will of their own, readily assent to, concur in, and applaud, whatever is said or done in the company; and adopt, with the same alacrity, the most virtuous or the most criminal, the wisest or the silliest scheme, that happens to be entertained by the majority of the company. This foolish, and often criminal complaisance flows from a foolish cause,—the want of any other merit. I hope that you will hold your place in company by a nobler tenure, and that you will hold it (you can bear a quibble, I believe, yet) 'in capite'. Have a will and an opinion of your own, and adhere to them steadily; but then do it with good humor, good-breeding, and (if you have it) with urbanity; for you have not yet heard enough either to preach or censure.

All other kinds of complaisance are not only blameless, but necessary in good company. Not to seem to perceive the little weaknesses, and the idle but innocent affectations of the company, but even to flatter them, in a certain manner, is not only very allowable, but, in truth, a sort of polite duty. They will be pleased with you, if you do; and will certainly not be reformed by you if you do not.

For instance: you will find, in every group of company, two principal figures, viz., the fine lady and the fine gentleman who absolutely give the law of wit, language, fashion, and taste, to the rest of that society. There is always a strict, and often for the time being, a tender alliance between these two figures. The lady looks upon her empire as founded upon the divine right of beauty (and full as good a divine right it is as any king, emperor, or pope, can pretend to); she requires, and commonly meets with, unlimited passive obedience. And why should she not meet with it? Her demands go no higher than to have her unquestioned preeminence in beauty, wit, and fashion, firmly established. Few sovereigns (by the way) are so reasonable. The fine gentleman's claims of right are, 'mutatis mutandis', the same; and though, indeed, he is not always a wit 'de jure', yet, as he is the wit 'de facto' of that company, he is entitled to a share of your allegiance, and everybody expects at least as much as they are entitled to, if not something more. Prudence bids you make your court to these joint sovereigns; and no duty, that I know of, forbids it. Rebellion here is exceedingly dangerous, and inevitably punished by banishment, and immediate forfeiture of all your wit, manners, taste, and fashion; as, on the other hand, a cheerful submission, not without some flattery, is sure to procure you a strong recommendation and most effectual pass, throughout all their, and probably the neighboring, dominions. With a moderate share of sagacity, you will, before you have been half an hour in their company, easily discover those two principal figures: both by the deference which you will observe the whole company pay them, and by that easy, careless, and serene air, which their consciousness of power gives them. As in this case, so in all others, aim always at the highest; get always into the highest company, and address yourself particularly to the highest in it. The search after the unattainable philosopher's stone has occasioned a thousand useful discoveries, which otherwise would never have been made.

What the French justly call 'les manieres nobles' are only to be acquired in the very best companies. They are the distinguishing characteristics of men of fashion: people of low education never wear them so close, but that some part or other of the original vulgarism appears. 'Les manieres nobles' equally forbid insolent contempt, or low envy and jealousy. Low people, in good circumstances, fine clothes, and equipages, will insolently show contempt for all those who cannot afford as fine clothes, as good an equipage, and who have not (as their term is) as much money in their pockets: on the other hand, they are gnawed with envy, and cannot help discovering it, of those who surpass them in any of these articles; which are far from being sure criterions of merit. They are likewise jealous of being slighted; and, consequently, suspicious and captious; they are eager and hot about trifles because trifles were, at first, their affairs of consequence. 'Les manieres nobles' imply exactly the reverse of all this. Study them early; you cannot make them too habitual and familiar to you.

Just as I had written what goes before, I received your letter of the 24th, N. S., but I have not received that which you mention for Mr. Harte. Yours is of the kind that I desire; for I want to see your private picture, drawn by yourself, at different sittings; for though, as it is drawn by yourself, I presume you will take the most advantageous likeness, yet I think that I have skill enough in that kind of painting to discover the true features, though ever so artfully colored, or thrown into skillful lights and shades.

By your account of the German play, which I do not know whether I should call tragedy or comedy, the only shining part of it (since I am in a way of quibbling) seems to have been the fox's tail. I presume, too, that the play has had the same fate with the squib, and has gone off no more. I remember a squib much better applied, when it was made the device of the colors of a French regiment of grenadiers; it was represented bursting, with this motto under it: 'Peream dum luceam'.

I like the description of your PIC-NIC; where I take it for granted, that your cards are only to break the formality of a circle, and your SYMPOSION intended more to promote conversation than drinking. Such an AMICABLE COLLISION, as Lord Shaftesbury very prettily calls it, rubs off and smooths those rough corners which mere nature has given to the smoothest of us. I hope some part, at least, of the conversation is in German. 'A propos': tell me do you speak that language correctly, and do you write it with ease? I have no doubt of your mastering the other modern languages, which are much easier, and occur much oftener; for which reason, I desire that you will apply most diligently to German, while you are in Germany, that you may speak and write that language most correctly.

I expect to meet Mr. Eliot in London, in about three weeks, after which you will soon see him at Leipsig. Adieu.

LETTER LVI

LONDON, November 18, O. S. 1748.

DEAR BOY: Whatever I see or whatever I hear, my first consideration is, whether it can in any way be useful to you. As a proof of this, I went accidentally the other day into a print-shop, where, among many others, I found one print from a famous design of Carlo Maratti, who died about thirty years ago, and was the last eminent painter in Europe: the subject is 'il Studio del Disegno'; or "The School of Drawing." An old man, supposed to be the master, points to his scholars, who are variously employed in perspective, geometry, and the observation of the statues of antiquity. With regard to perspective, of which there are some little specimens, he has wrote, 'Tanto che basti', that is, "As much as is sufficient"; with regard to geometry, 'Tanto che basti' again; with regard to the contemplation of the ancient statues, there is written, 'Non mai a bastanza',—"There never can be enough." But in the clouds, at the top of the piece, are represented the three Graces, with this just sentence written over them, 'Senza di noi ogni fatica e vana', that is, "Without us, all labor is vain." This everybody allows to be true in painting; but all people do not seem to consider, as I hope you will, that this truth is full as applicable to every other art or science; indeed to everything that is to be said or done. I will send you the print itself by Mr. Eliot, when he returns; and I will advise you to make the same use of it that the Roman Catholics say they do of the pictures and images of their saints, which is, only to remind them of those; for the adoration they disclaim. Nay, I will go further, as the transition from Popery to Paganism is short and easy, I will classically end poetically advise you to invoke, and sacrifice to them every day, and all the day. It must be owned, that the Graces do not seem to be natives of Great Britain; and, I doubt, the best of us here have more of rough than polished diamond.

Since barbarism drove them out of Greece and Rome, they seem to have taken refuge in France, where their temples are numerous, and their worship the established one. Examine yourself seriously, why such and such people please and engage you, more than such and such others, of equal merit; and you will always find that it is because the former have the Graces and the latter not. I have known many a woman with an exact shape, and a symmetrical assemblage of beautiful features, please nobody; while others, with very moderate shapes and features, have charmed everybody. Why? because Venus will not charm so much, without her attendant Graces, as they will without her. Among men, how often have I seen the most solid merit and knowledge neglected, unwelcome, or even rejected, for want of them! While flimsy parts, little knowledge, and less merit, introduced by the Graces, have been received, cherished, and admired. Even virtue, which is moral beauty, wants some of its charms if unaccompanied by them.

If you ask me how you shall acquire what neither you nor I can define or ascertain, I can only answer, BY OBSERVATION. Form yourself, with regard to others, upon what you feel pleases you in them. I can tell you the importance, the advantage, of having the Graces; but I cannot give them you: I heartily wish I could, and I certainly would; for I do not know a better present that I could make you. To show you that a very wise, philosophical, and retired man thinks upon that subject as I do, who have always lived in the world, I send you, by Mr. Eliot, the famous Mr. Locke's book upon education; in which you will end the stress that he lays upon the Graces, which he calls (and very truly) good-breeding. I have marked all the parts of that book that are worth your attention; for as he begins with the child, almost from its birth, the parts relative to its infancy would be useless to you. Germany is, still less than England, the seat of the Graces; however, you had as good not say so while you are there. But the place which you are going to, in a great degree, is; for I have known as many well-bred, pretty men come from Turin, as from any part of Europe. The late King Victor Amedee took great pains to form such of his subjects as were of any consideration, both to business and manners; the present king, I am told, follows his example: this, however, is certain, that in all courts and congresses, where there are various foreign ministers, those of the King of Sardinia are generally the ablest, the politest, and 'les plus delies'. You will therefore, at Turin, have very good models to form yourself upon: and remember, that with regard to the best models, as well as to the antique Greek statues in the print, 'non mai a bastanza'. Observe every word, look, and motion of those who are allowed to be the most accomplished persons there. Observe their natural and careless, but genteel air; their unembarrassed good-breeding; their unassuming, but yet unprostituted dignity. Mind their decent mirth, their discreet frankness, and that 'entregent' which, as much above the frivolous as below the important and the secret, is the proper medium for conversation in mixed companies. I will observe, by the bye, that the talent of that light 'entregent' is often of great use to a foreign minister; not only as it helps him to domesticate himself in many families, but also as it enables him to put by and parry some subjects of conversation, which might possibly lay him under difficulties both what to say and how to look.

Of all the men that ever I knew in my life (and I knew him extremely well), the late Duke of Marlborough possessed the graces in the highest degree, not to say engrossed them; and indeed he got the most by them; for I will venture (contrary to the custom of profound historians, who always assign deep causes for great events), to ascribe the better half of the Duke of Marlborough's greatness and riches to those graces. He was eminently illiterate; wrote bad English and spelled it still worse. He had no share of what is commonly called PARTS: that is, he had no brightness, nothing shining in his genius. He had most undoubtedly, an excellent good plain understanding with sound judgment. But these alone, would probably have raised him but something higher than they found him; which was page to King James the Second's queen. There the Graces protected and promoted him; for while he was an ensign of the Guards, the Duchess of Cleveland, then favorite mistress to King Charles the Second, struck by those very Graces, gave him five thousand pounds, with which he immediately bought an annuity for his life of five hundred pounds a year, of my grandfather Halifax; which was the foundation of his subsequent fortune. His figure was beautiful; but his manner was irresistible, by either man or woman. It was by this engaging, graceful manner, that he was enabled, during all his war, to connect the various and jarring powers of the Grand Alliance, and to carry them on to the main object of the war, notwithstanding their private and separate views, jealousies, and wrongheadednesses. Whatever court he went to (and he was often obliged to go himself to some resty and refractory ones), he as constantly prevailed, and brought them into his measures. The Pensionary Heinsius, a venerable old minister, grown gray in business, and who had governed the republic of the United Provinces for more than forty years, was absolutely governed by the Duke of Marlborough, as that republic feels to this day. He was always cool; and nobody ever observed the least variation in his countenance; he could refuse more gracefully than other people could grant; and those who went away from him the most dissatisfied as to the substance of their business, were yet personally charmed with him and, in some degree, comforted by his manner. With all his gentleness and gracefulness, no man living was more conscious of his situation, nor maintained his dignity better.

With the share of knowledge which you have already gotten, and with the much greater which I hope you will soon acquire, what may you not expect to arrive at, if you join all these graces to it? In your destination particularly, they are in truth half your business: for, if you once gain the affections as well as the esteem of the prince or minister of the court to which you are sent, I will answer for it, that will effectually do the business of the court that sent you; otherwise it is up-hill work. Do not mistake, and think that these graces which I so often and so earnestly recommend to you, should only accompany important transactions, and be worn only 'les jours de gala'; no, they should, if possible, accompany every, the least thing you do or say; for, if you neglect them in little things, they will leave you in great ones. I should, for instance, be extremely concerned to see you even drink a cup of coffee ungracefully, and slop yourself with it, by your awkward manner of holding it; nor should I like to see your coat buttoned, or your shoes buckled awry. But I should be outrageous, if I heard you mutter your words unintelligibly, stammer, in your speech, or hesitate, misplace, and mistake in your narrations; and I should run away from you with greater rapidity, if possible, than I should now run to embrace you, if I found you destitute of all those graces which I have set my heart upon their making you one day, 'omnibus ornatum excellere rebus'.

This subject is inexhaustible, as it extends to everything that is to be said or done: but I will leave it for the present, as this letter is already pretty long. Such is my desire, my anxiety for your perfection, that I never think I have said enough, though you may possibly think that I have said too much; and though, in truth, if your own good sense is not sufficient to direct you, in many of these plain points, all that I or anybody else can say will be insufficient. But where you are concerned, I am the insatiable man in Horace, who covets still a little corner more to complete the figure of his field. I dread every little corner that may deform mine, in which I would have (if possible) no one defect.

I this moment receive yours of the 17th, N. S., and cannot condole with you upon the secession of your German 'Commensaux'; who both by your and Mr. Harte's description, seem to be 'des gens d'une amiable absence'; and, if you can replace them by any other German conversation, you will be a gainer by the bargain. I cannot conceive, if you understand German well enough to read any German book, how the writing of the German character can be so difficult and tedious to you, the twenty-four letters being very soon learned; and I do not expect that you should write yet with the utmost purity and correctness, as to the language: what I meant by your writing once a fortnight to Grevenkop, was only to make the written character familiar to you. However, I will be content with one in three weeks or so.

I believe you are not likely to see Mr. Eliot again soon, he being still in Cornwall with his father; who, I hear, is not likely to recover. Adieu.

LETTER LVII

LONDON, November 29, O. S. 1748.

DEAR BOY: I delayed writing to you till I could give you some account of the motions of your friend Mr. Eliot; for whom I know you have, and very justly, the most friendly concern. His father and he came to town together, in a post-chaise a fortnight ago, the rest of the family remaining in Cornwall. His father, with difficulty, survived the journey, and died last Saturday was seven-night. Both concern and decency confined your friend, till two days ago, when I saw him; he has determined, and I think very prudently, to go abroad again; but how soon, it is yet impossible for him to know, as he must necessarily put his own private affairs in some order first; but I conjecture that he may possibly join you at Turin; sooner, to be sure, not. I am very sorry that you are likely to be so long without the company and the example of so valuable a friend; and therefore I hope that you will make it up to yourself, as well as you can at this distance, by remembering and following his example. Imitate that application of his, which has made him know all thoroughly, and to the bottom. He does not content himself with the surface of knowledge; but works in the mine for it, knowing that it lies deep. Pope says, very truly, in his "Essay on Criticism":—

A little learning is a dangerous thing;

Drink deep, or taste not the Pierian spring.

I shall send you by a ship that goes to Hamburg next week (and by which Hawkins sends Mr. Harte some things that he wrote for) all those which I propose sending you by Mr. Eliot, together with a very little box that I am desired to forward to Mr. Harte. There will be, likewise, two letters of recommendation for you to Monsieur Andrie and Comte Algarotti, at Berlin, which you will take care to deliver to them, as soon as you shall be rigged and fitted out to appear there. They will introduce you into the best company, and I depend upon your own good sense for your avoiding of bad. If you fall into bad and low company there, or anywhere else, you will be irrecoverably lost; whereas, if you keep good company, and company above yourself, your character and your fortune will be immovably fixed.

I have not time to-day, upon account of the meeting of the parliament, to make this letter of the usual length; and indeed, after the volumes that I have written to you, all I can add must be unnecessary. However, I shall probably, 'ex abundanti', return soon to my former prolixity; and you will receive more and more last words from, Yours.

LETTER LVIII

LONDON, December 6, O. S. 1748.

DEAR BOY: I am at present under very great concern for the loss of a most affectionate brother, with whom I had always lived in the closest friendship. My brother John died last Friday night, of a fit of the gout, which he had had for about a month in his hands and feet, and which fell at last upon his stomach and head. As he grew, toward the last, lethargic, his end was not painful to himself. At the distance which you are at from hence, you need not go into mourning upon this occasion, as the time of your mourning would be near over, before you could put it on.

By a ship which sails this week for Hamburg, I shall send you those things which I proposed to have sent you by Mr. Eliot, viz., a little box from your Mamma; a less box for Mr. Harte; Mr. Locke's book upon education; the print of Carlo Maratti, which I mentioned to you some time ago; and two letters of recommendation, one to Monsieur Andrie and the other to Comte Algarotti, at Berlin. Both those gentlemen will, I am sure, be as willing as they are able to introduce you into the best company; and I hope you will not (as many of your countrymen are apt to do) decline it. It is in the best companies only; that you can learn the best manners and that 'tournure', and those graces, which I have so often recommended to you, as the necessary means of making a figure in the world.

I am most extremely pleased with the account which Mr. Harte gives me of your progress in Greek, and of your having read Hesiod almost critically. Upon this subject I suggest but one thing to you, of many that I might suggest; which is, that you have now got over the difficulties of that language, and therefore it would be unpardonable not to persevere to your journey's end, now that all the rest of your way is down hill.

I am also very well pleased to hear that you have such a knowledge of, and taste for curious books and scarce and valuable tracts. This is a kind of knowledge which very well becomes a man of sound and solid learning, but which only exposes a man of slight and superficial reading; therefore, pray make the substance and matter of such books your first object, and their title-pages, indexes, letter, and binding, but your second. It is the characteristic of a man of parts and good judgment to know, and give that degree of attention that each object deserves. Whereas little minds mistake little objects for great ones, and lavish away upon the former that time and attention which only the latter deserve. To such mistakes we owe the numerous and frivolous tribes of insect-mongers, shell-mongers, and pursuers and driers of butterflies, etc. The strong mind distinguishes, not only between the useful and the useless, but likewise between the useful and the curious. He applies himself intensely to the former; he only amuses himself with the latter. Of this little sort of knowledge, which I have just hinted at, you will find at least as much as you need wish to know, in a superficial but pretty French book, entitled, 'Spectacle de la Nature'; which will amuse you while you read it, and give you a sufficient notion of the various parts of nature. I would advise you to read it, at leisure hours. But that part of nature, which Mr. Harte tells me you have begun to study with the Rector magnificus, is of much greater importance, and deserves much more attention; I mean astronomy. The vast and immense planetary system, the astonishing order and regularity of those innumerable worlds, will open a scene to you, which not only deserves your attention as a matter of curiosity, or rather astonishment; but still more, as it will give you greater, and consequently juster, ideas of that eternal and omnipotent Being, who contrived, made, and still preserves that universe, than all the contemplation of this, comparatively, very little orb, which we at present inhabit, could possibly give you. Upon this subject, Monsieur Fontenelle's 'Pluralite des Mondes', which you may read in two hours' time, will both inform and please you. God bless you! Yours.

LETTER LIX

LONDON, December 13, O. S. 1748.

DEAR BOY: The last four posts have brought me no letters, either from you or from Mr. Harte, at which I am uneasy; not as a mamma would be, but as a father should be: for I do not want your letters as bills of health; you are young, strong, and healthy, and I am, consequently, in no pain about that: moreover, were either you or Mr. Harte ill, the other would doubtless write me word of it. My impatience for yours or Mr.

Harte's letters arises from a very different cause, which is my desire to hear frequently of the state and progress of your mind. You are now at that critical period of life when every week ought to produce fruit or flowers answerable to your culture, which I am sure has not been neglected; and it is by your letters, and Mr. Harte's accounts of you, that, at this distance, I can only judge at your gradations to maturity; I desire, therefore, that one of you two will not fail to write to me once a week. The sameness of your present way of life, I easily conceive, would not make out a very interesting letter to an indifferent bystander; but so deeply concerned as I am in the game you are playing, even the least move is to me of importance, and helps me to judge of the final event.

As you will be leaving Leipsig pretty soon after you shall have received this letter, I here send you one inclosed to deliver to Mr. Mascow. It is to thank him for his attention and civility to you, during your stay with him: and I take it for granted, that you will not fail making him the proper compliments at parting; for the good name that we leave behind at one place often gets before us to another, and is of great use. As Mr. Mascow is much known and esteemed in the republic of letters, I think it would be of advantage to you, if you got letters of recommendation from him to some of the learned men at Berlin. Those testimonials give a lustre, which is not to be despised; for the most ignorant are forced to seem, at least, to pay a regard to learning, as the most wicked are to virtue. Such is their intrinsic worth.

Your friend Duval dined with me the other day, and complained most grievously that he had not heard from you above a year; I bid him abuse you for it himself; and advised him to do it in verse, which, if he was really angry, his indignation would enable him to do. He accordingly brought me, yesterday, the inclosed reproaches and challenge, which he desired me to transmit to you. As this is his first essay in English poetry, the inaccuracies in the rhymes and the numbers are very excusable. He insists, as you will find, upon being answered in verse; which I should imagine that you and Mr. HARTE, together, could bring about; as the late Lady Dorchester used to say, that she and Dr. Radcliffe, together, could cure a fever. This is however sure, that it now rests upon you; and no man can say what methods Duval may take, if you decline his challenge. I am sensible that you are under some disadvantages in this proffered combat. Your climate, at this time of the year especially, delights more in the wood fire, than in the poetic fire; and I conceive the Muses, if there are any at Leipsig, to be rather shivering than singing; nay, I question whether Apollo is even known there as god of Verse, or as god of Light: perhaps a little as god of Physic. These will be fair excuses, if your performance should fall something short; though I do not apprehend that it will.

While you have been at Leipsig, which is a place of study more than of pleasure or company, you have had all opportunities of pursuing your studies uninterruptedly; and have had, I believe, very few temptations to the contrary. But the case will be quite different at Berlin, where the splendor and dissipation of a court and the 'beau monde', will present themselves to you in gaudy shapes, attractive enough to all young people. Do not think, now, that like an old fellow, I am going to advise you to reject them, and shut yourself up in your closet: quite the contrary; I advise you to take your share, and enter into them with spirit and pleasure; but then I advise you, too, to allot your time so prudently, as that learning may keep pace with pleasures; there is full time, in the course of the day, for both, if you do but manage that time right and like a good economist. The whole morning, if diligently and attentively devoted to solid studies, will go a great way at the year's end; and the evenings spent in the pleasures of good company, will go as far in teaching you a knowledge, not much less necessary than the other, I mean the knowledge of the world. Between these two necessary studies, that of books in the morning, and that of the world in the evening, you see that you will not have one minute to squander or slattern away. Nobody ever lent themselves more than I did, when I was young, to the pleasures and dissipation of good company. I even did it too much. But then, I can assure you, that I always found time for serious studies; and, when I could find it no other way, I took it out of my sleep, for I resolved always to rise early in the morning, however late I went to bed at night; and this resolution I have kept so sacred, that, unless when I have been confined to my bed by illness, I have not, for more than forty years, ever been in bed at nine o'clock in the morning but commonly up before eight.

When you are at Berlin, remember to speak German as often as you can, in company; for everybody there will speak French to you, unless you let them know that you can speak German, which then they will choose to speak. Adieu.

LETTER LX

LONDON, December 20, O. S. 1748.

DEAR BOY: I received last Saturday by three mails, which came in at once, two letters from Mr. Harte, and yours of the 8th, N. S.

It was I who mistook your meaning, with regard to your German letters, and not you who expressed it ill. I thought it was the writing of the German character that took up so much of your time, and therefore I advised you, by the frequent writing of that character, to make it easy and familiar to you: But, since it is only the propriety and purity of the German language which make your writing it so tedious and laborious, I will tell you I shall not be nice upon that article; and did not expect that you should yet be master of all the idioms, delicacies, and peculiarities of that difficult language. That can only come by use, especially frequent speaking; therefore, when you shall be at Berlin, and afterward at Turin, where you will meet many Germans, pray take all opportunities of conversing in German, in order not only to keep what you have got of that language, but likewise to improve and perfect yourself in it. As to the characters, you form them very well, and as you yourself own, better than your English ones; but then let me ask you this question: Why do you not form your Roman characters better? for I maintain, that it is in every man's power to write what hand he pleases; and, consequently, that he ought to write a good one. You form, particularly, your 'ee' and your 'll' in zigzag, instead of making them straight, as thus, 'ee', 'll'; a fault very easily mended. You will not, I believe, be angry with this little criticism, when I tell you, that by all the accounts I have had of late from Mr. Harte and others, this is the only criticism that you give me occasion to make. Mr. Harte's last letter, of the 14th, N. S., particularly, makes me extremely happy, by assuring me that, in every respect, you do exceedingly well. I am not afraid, by what I now say, of making you too vain; because I do not think that a just consciousness and an honest pride of doing well, can be called vanity; for vanity is either the silly affectation of good qualities which one has not, or the sillier pride of what does not deserve commendation in itself. By Mr. Harte's account, you are got very near the goal of Greek and Latin; and therefore I cannot suppose that, as your sense increases, your endeavors and your speed will slacken in finishing the small remains of your course. Consider what lustre and 'eclat' it will give you, when you return here, to be allowed to be the best scholar, for a gentleman, in England; not to mention the real pleasure and solid comfort which such knowledge will give you throughout your whole life. Mr. Harte tells me another thing, which, I own, I did not expect: it is, that when you read aloud, or repeat parts of plays, you speak very properly and distinctly. This relieves me from great uneasiness, which I was under upon account of your former bad enunciation. Go on, and attend most diligently to this important article. It is, of all Graces (and they are all necessary), the most necessary one.

Comte Pertingue, who has been here about a fortnight, far from disavowing, confirms all that Mr. Harte has said to your advantage. He thinks that he shall be at Turin much about the time of your arrival there, and pleases himself with the hopes of being useful to you. Though, should you get there before him, he says that

Comte du Perron, with whom you are a favorite, will take that care. You see, by this one instance, and in the course of your life you will see by a million of instances, of what use a good reputation is, and how swift and advantageous a harbinger it is, wherever one goes. Upon this point, too, Mr. Harte does you justice, and tells me that you are desirous of praise from the praiseworthy. This is a right and generous ambition; and without which, I fear, few people would deserve praise.

But here let me, as an old stager upon the theatre of the world, suggest one consideration to you; which is, to extend your desire of praise a little beyond the strictly praiseworthy; or else you may be apt to discover too much contempt for at least three parts in five of the world, who will never forgive it you. In the mass of mankind, I fear, there is too great a majority of fools and, knaves; who, singly from their number, must to a certain degree be respected, though they are by no means respectable. And a man who will show every knave or fool that he thinks him such, will engage in a most ruinous war, against numbers much superior to those that he and his allies can bring into the field. Abhor a knave, and pity a fool in your heart; but let neither of them, unnecessarily, see that you do so. Some complaisance and attention to fools is prudent, and not mean; as a silent abhorrence of individual knaves is often necessary and not criminal.

As you will now soon part with Lord Pulteney, with whom, during your stay together at Leipsig, I suppose you have formed a connection, I imagine that you will continue it by letters, which I would advise you to do. They tell me that he is good-natured, and does not want parts; which are of themselves two good reasons for keeping it up; but there is also a third reason, which, in the course of the world, is not to be despised: His father cannot live long, and will leave him an immense fortune; which, in all events will make him of some consequence; and, if he has parts into the bargain, of very great consequence; so that his friendship, may be extremely well worth your cultivating, especially as it will not cost you above one letter in one month.

I do not know whether this letter will find you at Leipsig: at least, it is the last that I shall direct there. My next to either you or Mr. Harte will be directed to Berlin; but as I do not know to what house or street there, I suppose it will remain at the posthouse till you send for it. Upon your arrival at Berlin you will send me your particular direction; and also, pray be minute in your accounts of your reception there, by those whom I recommend you to, as well as by those to whom they present you. Remember, too, that you are going to a polite and literate court, where the Graces will best introduce you.

Adieu. God bless you, and may you continue to deserve my love, as much as you now enjoy it!

P. S. Lady Chesterfield bids me tell you, that she decides entirely in your favor against Mr. Grevenkop, and even against herself; for she does not think that she could, at this time, write either so good a character or so good German. Pray write her a German letter upon that subject, in which you may tell her, that, like the rest of the world, you approve of her judgment, because it is in your favor; and that you true Germans cannot allow Danes to be competent judges of your language, etc.

LETTERS TO HIS SON, COMPLETE

LETTER LXI

LONDON, December 30, O. S. 1748.

DEAR BOY: I direct this letter to Berlin, where, I suppose, it will either find you, or at least wait but a very little time for you. I cannot help being anxious for your success, at this your first appearance upon the great stage of the world; for, though the spectators are always candid enough to give great allowances, and to show great indulgence to a new actor; yet, from the first impressions which he makes upon them, they are apt to decide, in their own minds, at least, whether he will ever be a good one, or not. If he seems to understand what he says, by speaking it properly; if he is attentive to his part, instead of staring negligently about him; and if, upon the whole, he seems ambitious to please, they willingly pass over little awkwardnesses and inaccuracies, which they ascribe to a commendable modesty in a young and inexperienced actor. They pronounce that he will be a good one in time; and, by the encouragement which they give him, make him so the sooner. This, I hope, will be your case: you have sense enough to understand your part; a constant attention, and ambition to excel in it, with a careful observation of the best actors, will inevitably qualify you, if not for the first, at least for considerable parts.

Your dress (as insignificant a thing as dress is in itself) is now become an object worthy of some attention; for, I confess, I cannot help forming some opinion of a man's sense and character from his dress; and I believe most people do as well as myself. Any affectation whatsoever in dress implies, in my mind, a flaw in the understanding. Most of our young fellows here display some character or other by their dress; some affect the tremendous, and wear a great and fiercely cocked hat, an enormous sword, a short waistcoat and a black cravat; these I should be almost tempted to swear the peace against, in my own defense, if I were not convinced that they are but meek asses in lions' skins. Others go in brown frocks, leather breeches, great oaken cudgels in their hands, their hats uncocked, and their hair unpowdered; and imitate grooms, stage-coachmen, and country bumpkins so well in their outsides, that I do not make the least doubt of their resembling them equally in their insides. A man of sense carefully avoids any particular character in his dress; he is accurately clean for his own sake; but all the rest is for other people's. He dresses as well, and in the same manner, as the people of sense and fashion of the place where he is. If he dresses better, as he thinks, that is, more than they, he is a fop; if he dresses worse, he is unpardonably negligent. But, of the two, I would rather have a young fellow too much than too little dressed; the excess on that side will wear off, with a little age and reflection; but if he is negligent at twenty, he will be a sloven at forty, and stink at fifty years old. Dress yourself fine, where others are fine; and plain where others are plain; but take care always that your clothes are well made, and fit you, for otherwise they will give you a very awkward air. When you are once well dressed for the day think no more of it afterward; and, without any stiffness for fear of discomposing that dress, let all your motions be as easy and natural as if you had no clothes on at all. So much for dress, which I maintain to be a thing of consequence in the polite world.

As to manners, good-breeding, and the Graces, I have so often entertained you upon those important subjects, that I can add nothing to what I have formerly said. Your own good sense will suggest to you the substance of them; and observation, experience, and good company, the several modes of them. Your great vivacity, which I hear of from many people, will be no hindrance to your pleasing in good company: on the contrary, will be of use to you, if tempered by good-breeding and accompanied by the Graces. But then, I suppose your vivacity to be a vivacity of parts, and not a constitutional restlessness; for the most disagreeable composition that I know in the world, is that of strong animal spirits, with a cold genius. Such a fellow is troublesomely active, frivolously busy, foolishly lively; talks much with little meaning, and laughs more, with less reason whereas, in my opinion, a warm and lively genius with a cool constitution, is the perfection of human nature.

Do what you will at Berlin, provided you do but do something all day long. All that I desire of you is, that you will never slattern away one minute in idleness and in doing of nothing. When you are (not) in company, learn what either books, masters, or Mr. Harte, can teach you; and when you are in company, learn (what company can only teach you) the characters and manners of mankind. I really ask your pardon for giving you this advice; because, if you are a rational creature and thinking being, as I suppose, and verily believe you are, it must be unnecessary, and to a certain degree injurious. If I did not know by experience, that some men pass their whole time in doing nothing, I should not think it possible for any being, superior to Monsieur Descartes' automatons, to squander away, in absolute idleness, one single minute of that small portion of time which is allotted us in this world.

I have lately seen one Mr. Cranmer, a very sensible merchant, who told me that he had dined with you, and seen you often at Leipsig. And yesterday I saw an old footman of mine, whom I made a messenger, who told me that he had seen you last August. You will easily imagine, that I was not the less glad to see them because they had seen you; and I examined them both narrowly, in their respective departments; the former as to your mind, the latter, as to your body. Mr. Cranmer gave me great satisfaction, not only by what he told me of himself concerning you, but by what he was commissioned to tell me from Mr. Mascow. As he speaks German perfectly himself, I asked him how you spoke it; and he assured me very well for the time, and that a very little more practice would make you perfectly master of it. The messenger told me that you were much grown, and, to the best of his guess, within two inches as tall as I am; that you were plump, and looked healthy and strong; which was all that I could expect, or hope, from the sagacity of the person.

I send you, my dear child (and you will not doubt it), very sincerely, the wishes of the season. May you deserve a great number of happy New-years; and, if you deserve, may you have them. Many New-years, indeed, you may see, but happy ones you cannot see without deserving them. These, virtue, honor, and knowledge, alone can merit, alone can procure, 'Dii tibi dent annos, de te nam cetera sumes', was a pretty piece of poetical flattery, where it was said: I hope that, in time, it may be no flattery when said to you. But I assure you, that wherever I cannot apply the latter part of the line to you with truth, I shall neither say, think, or wish the former. Adieu!

1749

LETTER LXII

LONDON, January 10, O. S. 1749.

DEAR BOY: I have received your letter of the 31st December, N. S. Your thanks for my present, as you call it, exceed the value of the present; but the use, which you assure me that you will make of it, is the thanks which I desire to receive. Due attention to the inside of books, and due contempt for the outside, is the proper relation between a man of sense and his books.

LETTERS TO HIS SON, COMPLETE

Now that you are going a little more into the world; I will take this occasion to explain my intentions as to your future expenses, that you may know what you have to expect from me, and make your plan accordingly. I shall neither deny nor grudge you any money, that may be necessary for either your improvement or your pleasures: I mean the pleasures of a rational being. Under the head of improvement, I mean the best books, and the best masters, cost what they will; I also mean all the expense of lodgings, coach, dress; servants, etc., which, according to the several places where you may be, shall be respectively necessary to enable you to keep the best company. Under the head of rational pleasures, I comprehend, first, proper charities, to real and compassionate objects of it; secondly, proper presents to those to whom you are obliged, or whom you desire to oblige; thirdly, a conformity of expense to that of the company which you keep; as in public spectacles; your share of little entertainments; a few pistoles at games of mere commerce; and other incidental calls of good company. The only two articles which I will never supply, are the profusion of low riot, and the idle lavishness of negligence and laziness. A fool squanders away, without credit or advantage to himself, more than a man of sense spends with both. The latter employs his money as he does his time, and never spends a shilling of the one, nor a minute of the other, but in something that is either useful or rationally pleasing to himself or others. The former buys whatever he does not want, and does not pay for what he does want. He cannot withstand the charms of a toyshop; snuff-boxes, watches, heads of canes, etc., are his destruction. His servants and tradesmen conspire with his own indolence to cheat him; and, in a very little time, he is astonished, in the midst of all the ridiculous superfluities, to find himself in want of all the real comforts and necessaries of life. Without care and method, the largest fortune will not, and with them, almost the smallest will, supply all necessary expenses. As far as you can possibly, pay ready money for everything you buy and avoid bills. Pay that money, too, yourself, and not through the hands of any servant, who always either stipulates poundage, or requires a present for his good word, as they call it. Where you must have bills (as for meat and drink, clothes, etc.), pay them regularly every month, and with your own hand. Never, from a mistaken economy, buy a thing you do not want, because it is cheap; or from a silly pride, because it is dear. Keep an account in a book of all that you receive, and of all that you pay; for no man who knows what he receives and what he pays ever runs out. I do not mean that you should keep an account of the shillings and half-crowns which you may spend in chair-hire, operas, etc.: they are unworthy of the time, and of the ink that they would consume; leave such minutia to dull, penny-wise fellows; but remember, in economy, as well as in every other part of life, to have the proper attention to proper objects, and the proper contempt for little ones. A strong mind sees things in their true proportions; a weak one views them through a magnifying medium, which, like the microscope, makes an elephant of a flea: magnifies all little objects, but cannot receive great ones. I have known many a man pass for a miser, by saving a penny and wrangling for twopence, who was undoing himself at the same time by living above his income, and not attending to essential articles which were above his 'portee'. The sure characteristic of a sound and strong mind, is to find in everything those certain bounds, 'quos ultra citrave nequit consistere rectum'. These boundaries are marked out by a very fine line, which only good sense and attention can discover; it is much too fine for vulgar eyes. In manners, this line is good-breeding; beyond it, is troublesome ceremony; short of it, is unbecoming negligence and inattention. In morals, it divides ostentatious puritanism from criminal relaxation; in religion, superstition from impiety: and, in short, every virtue from its kindred vice or weakness. I think you have sense enough to discover the line; keep it always in your eye, and learn to walk upon it; rest upon Mr. Harte, and he will poise you till you are able to go alone. By the way, there are fewer people who walk well upon that line, than upon the slack rope; and therefore a good performer shines so much the more.

Your friend Comte Pertingue, who constantly inquires after you, has written to Comte Salmour, the Governor of the Academy at Turin, to prepare a room for you there immediately after the Ascension: and has recommended you to him in a manner which I hope you will give him no reason to repent or be ashamed of. As Comte Salmour's son, now residing at The Hague, is my particular acquaintance, I shall have regular and authentic accounts of all that you do at Turin.

During your stay at Berlin, I expect that you should inform yourself thoroughly of the present state of the civil, military, and ecclesiastical government of the King of Prussia's dominions; particularly of the military, which is upon a better footing in that country than in any other in Europe.

You will attend at the reviews, see the troops exercised, and inquire into the numbers of troops and companies in the respective regiments of horse, foot, and dragoons; the numbers and titles of the commissioned and non-commissioned officers in the several troops and companies; and also take care to learn the technical military terms in the German language; for though you are not to be a military man, yet these military matters are so frequently the subject of conversation, that you will look very awkwardly if you are ignorant of them. Moreover, they are commonly the objects of negotiation, and, as such, fall within your future profession. You must also inform yourself of the reformation which the King of Prussia has lately made in the law; by which he has both lessened the number, and shortened the duration of law-suits; a great work, and worthy of so great a prince! As he is indisputably the ablest prince in Europe, every part of his government deserves your most diligent inquiry, and your most serious attention. It must be owned that you set out well, as a young politician, by beginning at Berlin, and then going to Turin, where you will see the next ablest monarch to that of Prussia; so that, if you are capable of making political reflections, those two princes will furnish you with sufficient matter for them.

I would have you endeavor to get acquainted with Monsieur de Maupertuis, who is so eminently distinguished by all kinds of learning and merit, that one should be both sorry and ashamed of having been even a day in the same place with him, and not to have seen him. If you should have no other way of being introduced to him, I will send you a letter from hence. Monsieur Cagenoni, at Berlin, to whom I know you are recommended, is a very able man of business, thoroughly informed of every part of Europe; and his acquaintance, if you deserve and improve it as you should do, may be of great use to you.

Remember to take the best dancing-master at Berlin, more to teach you to sit, stand, and walk gracefully, than to dance finely. The Graces, the Graces; remember the Graces! Adieu!

LETTER LXIII

LONDON, January 24, O. S. 1749.

DEAR BOY: I have received your letter of the 12th, N. S., in which I was surprised to find no mention of your approaching journey to Berlin, which, according to the first plan, was to be on the 20th, N. S., and upon which supposition I have for some time directed my letters to you, and Mr. Harte, at Berlin. I should be glad that yours were more minute with regard to your motions and transactions; and I desire that, for the future, they may contain accounts of what and who you see and hear, in your several places of residence; for I interest myself as much in the company you keep, and the pleasures you take, as in the studies you pursue; and therefore, equally desire to be informed of them all. Another thing I desire, which is, that you will acknowledge my letters by their dates, that I may know which you do, and which you do not receive.

As you found your brain considerably affected by the cold, you were very prudent not to turn it to poetry in that situation; and not less judicious in declining the borrowed aid of a stove, whose fumigation, instead of inspiration, would at best have produced what Mr. Pope calls a souterkin of wit. I will show your letter to Duval, by way of justification for not answering his challenge; and I think he must allow the validity of it; for a frozen brain is as unfit to answer a challenge in poetry, as a blunt sword is for a single combat.

You may if you please, and therefore I flatter myself that you will, profit considerably by your stay at Berlin, in the article of manners and useful knowledge. Attention to what you will see and hear there, together with proper inquiries, and a little care and method in taking notes of what is more material, will procure you much useful knowledge. Many young people are so light, so dissipated, and so incurious, that they can hardly be said to see what they see, or hear what they hear: that is, they hear in so superficial and inattentive a manner, that they might as well not see nor hear at all. For instance, if they see a public building, as a college, an hospital, an arsenal, etc., they content themselves with the first 'coup d'oeil', and neither take the time nor the trouble of informing themselves of the material parts of them; which are the constitution, the rules, and the order and economy in the inside. You will, I hope, go deeper, and make your way into the substance of things. For example, should you see a regiment reviewed at Berlin or Potsdam, instead of contenting yourself with the general glitter of the collective corps, and saying, 'par maniere d'acquit', that is very fine, I hope you will ask what number of troops or companies it consists of; what number of officers of the Etat Major, and what number of subalternes; how many 'bas officiers', or non-commissioned officers, as sergeants, corporals, 'anspessades, frey corporals', etc., their pay, their clothing, and by whom; whether by the colonels, or captains, or commissaries appointed for that purpose; to whom they are accountable; the method of recruiting, completing, etc.

The same in civil matters: inform yourself of the jurisdiction of a court of justice; of the rules and numbers and endowments of a college, or an academy, and not only of the dimensions of the respective edifices; and let your letters to me contain these informations, in proportion as you acquire them.

I often reflect, with the most flattering hopes, how proud I shall be of you, if you should profit, as you may, of the opportunities which you have had, still have, and will have, of arriving at perfection; and, on the other hand, with dread of the grief and shame you will give me if you do not. May the first be the case! God bless you!

LETTER LXIV

LONDON, February 7, O. S. 1749.

DEAR BOY: You are now come to an age capable of reflection, and I hope you will do, what, however, few people at your age do, exert it for your own sake in the search of truth and sound knowledge. I will confess (for I am not unwilling to discover my secrets to you) that it is not many years since I have presumed to reflect for myself. Till sixteen or seventeen I had no reflection; and for many years after that, I made no use of what I had. I adopted the notions of the books I read, or the company I kept, without examining whether they were just or not; and I rather chose to run the risk of easy error, than to take the time and trouble of investigating truth. Thus, partly from laziness, partly from dissipation, and partly from the 'mauvaise honte' of rejecting fashionable notions, I was (as I have since found) hurried away by prejudices, instead of being guided by reason; and quietly cherished error, instead of seeking for truth. But since I have taken the trouble of reasoning for myself, and have had the courage to own that I do so, you cannot imagine how much my notions of things are altered, and in how different a light I now see them, from that in which I formerly viewed them, through the deceitful medium of prejudice or authority. Nay, I may possibly still retain many errors, which, from long habit, have perhaps grown into real opinions; for it is very difficult to distinguish habits, early acquired and long entertained, from the result of our reason and reflection.

My first prejudice (for I do not mention the prejudices of boys, and women, such as hobgoblins, ghosts, dreams, spilling salt, etc.) was my classical enthusiasm, which I received from the books I read, and the masters who explained them to me. I was convinced there had been no common sense nor common honesty in the world for these last fifteen hundred years; but that they were totally extinguished with the ancient Greek and Roman governments. Homer and Virgil could have no faults, because they were ancient; Milton and Tasso could have no merit, because they were modern. And I could almost have said, with regard to the ancients, what Cicero, very absurdly and unbecomingly for a philosopher, says with regard to Plato, 'Cum quo errare malim quam cum aliis recte sentire'. Whereas now, without any extraordinary effort of genius, I have discovered that nature was the same three thousand years ago as it is at present; that men were but men then as well as now; that modes and customs vary often, but that human nature is always the same. And I can no more suppose that men were better, braver, or wiser, fifteen hundred or three thousand years ago, than I can suppose that the animals or vegetables were better then than they are now. I dare assert too, in defiance of the favorers of the ancients, that Homer's hero, Achilles, was both a brute and a scoundrel, and consequently an improper character for the hero of an epic poem; he had so little regard for his country, that he would not act in defense of it, because he had quarreled with Agamemnon about a w——e; and then afterward, animated by private resentment only, he went about killing people basely, I will call it, because he knew himself invulnerable; and yet, invulnerable as he was, he wore the strongest armor in the world; which I humbly apprehend to be a blunder; for a horse-shoe clapped to his vulnerable heel would have been sufficient. On the other hand, with submission to the favorers of the moderns, I assert with Mr. Dryden, that the devil is in truth the hero of Milton's poem; his plan, which he lays, pursues, and at last executes, being the subject of the poem. From all which considerations I impartially conclude that the ancients had their excellencies and their defects, their virtues and their vices, just like the moderns; pedantry and affectation of learning decide clearly in favor of the former; vanity and ignorance, as peremptorily in favor of the latter. Religious prejudices kept pace with my classical ones; and there was a time when I thought it impossible for the honestest man in the world to be saved out of the pale of the Church of England, not considering that matters of opinion do not depend upon the will; and that it is as natural, and as allowable, that another man should differ in opinion from me, as that I should differ from him; and that if we are both sincere, we are both blameless; and should consequently have mutual indulgence for each other.

The next prejudices that I adopted were those of the 'beau monde', in which as I was determined to shine, I took what are commonly called the genteel vices to be necessary. I had heard them reckoned so, and without further inquiry I believed it, or at least should have been ashamed to have denied it, for fear of exposing myself to the ridicule of those whom I considered as the models of fine gentlemen. But I am now neither ashamed nor afraid to assert that those genteel vices, as they are falsely called, are only so many blemishes in the character of even a man of the world and what is called a fine gentleman, and degrade him in the opinions of those very people, to whom he, hopes to recommend himself by them. Nay, this prejudice often extends so far, that I have known people pretend to vices they had not, instead of carefully concealing those they had.

Use and assert your own reason; reflect, examine, and analyze everything, in order to form a sound and mature judgment; let no (authority) impose upon your understanding, mislead your actions, or dictate your conversation. Be early what, if you are not, you will when too late wish you had been. Consult your reason betimes: I do not say that it will always prove an unerring guide; for human reason is not infallible; but it will prove the least erring guide that you can follow. Books and conversation may assist it; but adopt neither blindly and implicitly; try both by that best rule, which God has given to direct us, reason. Of all the troubles, do not decline, as many people do, that of thinking. The herd of mankind can hardly be said to think; their notions are almost all adoptive; and, in general, I believe it is better that it should be so, as such common prejudices contribute more to order and quiet than their own separate reasonings would do, uncultivated and unimproved as they are. We have many of those useful prejudices in this country, which I should be very sorry to see removed. The good Protestant conviction, that the Pope is both Antichrist and the Whore of Babylon, is a more effectual preservative in this country against popery, than all the solid and unanswerable arguments of Chillingworth.

The idle story of the pretender's having been introduced in a warming pan into the queen's bed, though as destitute of all probability as of all foundation, has been much more prejudicial to the cause of Jacobitism than all that Mr. Locke and others have written, to show the unreasonableness and absurdity of the doctrines of indefeasible hereditary right, and unlimited passive obedience. And that silly, sanguine notion, which is firmly entertained here, that one Englishman can beat three Frenchmen, encourages, and has sometimes enabled, one Englishman in reality to beat two.

A Frenchman ventures, his life with alacrity 'pour l'honneur du Roi'; were you to change the object, which he has been taught to have in view, and tell him that it was 'pour le bien de la Patrie', he would very probably run away. Such gross local prejudices prevail with the herd of mankind, and do not impose upon cultivated, informed, and reflecting minds. But then they are notions equally false, though not so glaringly absurd, which are entertained by people of superior and improved understandings, merely for want of the necessary pains to investigate, the proper attention to examine, and the penetration requisite to determine the truth. Those are the prejudices which I would have you guard against by a manly exertion and attention of your reasoning faculty.

To mention one instance of a thousand that I could give you: It is a general prejudice, and has been propagated for these sixteen hundred years, that arts and sciences cannot flourish under an absolute government; and that genius must necessarily be cramped where freedom is restrained. This sounds plausible, but is false in fact. Mechanic arts, as agriculture, etc., will indeed be discouraged where the profits and property are, from the nature of the government, insecure. But why the despotism of a government should cramp the genius of a mathematician, an astronomer, a poet, or an orator, I confess I never could discover. It may indeed deprive the poet or the orator of the liberty of treating of certain subjects in the manner they would wish, but it leaves them subjects enough to exert genius upon, if they have it. Can an author with reason complain that he is cramped and shackled, if he is not at liberty to publish blasphemy, bawdry, or sedition? all which are equally prohibited in the freest governments, if they are wise and well regulated ones. This is the present general complaint of the French authors; but indeed chiefly of the bad ones. No wonder, say they, that England produces so many great geniuses; people there may think as they please, and publish what they think. Very true, but what hinders them from thinking as they please? If indeed they think in manner destructive of all religion, morality, or good manners, or to the disturbance of the state, an absolute government will certainly more effectually prohibit them from, or punish them for publishing such thoughts, than a free one could do. But how does that cramp the genius of an epic, dramatic, or lyric poet? or how does it corrupt the eloquence of an orator in the pulpit or at the bar? The number of good French authors, such as Corneille, Racine, Moliere, Boileau, and La Fontaine, who seemed to dispute it with the Augustan age, flourished under the despotism of Lewis XIV.; and the celebrated authors of the Augustan age did not shine till after the fetters were riveted upon the Roman people by that cruel and worthless Emperor. The revival of letters was not owing, neither, to any free government, but to the encouragement and protection of Leo X. and Francis I; the one as absolute a pope, and the other as despotic a prince, as ever reigned. Do not mistake, and imagine that while I am only exposing a prejudice, I am speaking in favor of arbitrary power; which from my soul I abhor, and look upon as a gross and criminal violation of the natural rights of mankind. Adieu.

EARL OF PHILIP DORMER STANHOPE CHESTERFIELD

LETTER LXV

LONDON, February 28, O. S. 1749.

DEAR BOY: I was very much pleased with the account that you gave me of your reception at Berlin; but I was still better pleased with the account which Mr. Harte sent me of your manner of receiving that reception; for he says that you behaved yourself to those crowned heads with all the respect and modesty due to them; but at the same time, without being any more embarrassed than if you had been conversing with your equals. This easy respect is the perfection of good-breeding, which nothing but superior good sense, or a long usage of the world, can produce, and as in your case it could not be the latter, it is a pleasing indication to me of the former.

You will now, in the course of a few months, have been rubbed at three of the considerable courts of Europe,- Berlin, Dresden, and Vienna; so that I hope you will arrive at Turin tolerably smooth and fit for the last polish. There you may get the best, there being no court I know of that forms more well-bred, and agreeable people. Remember now, that good-breeding, genteel carriage, address, and even dress (to a certain degree), are become serious objects, and deserve a part of your attention.

The day, if well employed, is long enough for them all. One half of it bestowed upon your studies and your exercises, will finish your mind and your body; the remaining part of it, spent in good company, will form your manners, and complete your character. What would I not give to have you read Demosthenes critically in the morning, and understand him better than anybody; at noon, behave yourself better than any person at court; and in the evenings, trifle more agreeably than anybody in mixed companies? All this you may compass if you please; you have the means, you have the opportunities. Employ them, for God's sake, while you may, and make yourself that all-accomplished man that I wish to have you. It entirely depends upon these two years; they are the decisive ones.

I send you here inclosed a letter of recommendation to Monsieur Capello, at Venice, which you will deliver him immediately upon your arrival, accompanying it with compliments from me to him and Madame, both of whom you have seen here. He will, I am sure, be both very civil and very useful to you there, as he will also be afterward at Rome, where he is appointed to go ambassador. By the way, wherever you are, I would advise you to frequent, as much as you can, the Venetian Ministers; who are always better informed of the courts they reside at than any other minister; the strict and regular accounts, which they are obliged to give to their own government, making them very diligent and inquisitive.

You will stay at Venice as long as the Carnival lasts; for though I am impatient to have you at Turin, yet I would wish you to see thoroughly all that is to be seen at so singular a place as Venice, and at so showish a time as the Carnival. You will take also particular care to view all those meetings of the government, which strangers are allowed to see; as the Assembly of the Senate, etc., and also to inform yourself of that peculiar and intricate form of government. There are books which give an account of it, among which the best is Amelot de la Houssaye, which I would advise you to read previously; it will not only give you a general notion of that constitution, but also furnish you with materials for proper questions and oral informations upon the place, which are always the best. There are likewise many very valuable remains, in sculpture and paintings, of the best masters, which deserve your attention.

I suppose you will be at Vienna as soon as this letter will get thither; and I suppose, too, that I must not direct above one more to you there. After which, my next shall be directed to you at Venice, the only place where a letter will be likely to find you, till you are at Turin; but you may, and I desire that you will write to me, from the several places in your way, from whence the post goes.

I will send you some other letters for Venice, to Vienna, or to your banker at Venice, to whom you will, upon your arrival there, send for them: For I will take care to have you so recommended from place to place, that you shall not run through them, as most of your countrymen do, without the advantage of seeing and knowing what best deserves to be seen and known; I mean the men and the manners.

God bless you, and make you answer my wishes: I will now say, my hopes! Adieu.

LETTER LXVI

DEAR BOY: I direct this letter to your banker at Venice, the surest place for you to meet with it, though I suppose that it will be there some time before you; for, as your intermediate stay anywhere else will be short, and as the post from hence, in this season of easterly winds is uncertain, I direct no more letters to Vienna; where I hope both you and Mr. Harte will have received the two letters which I sent you respectively; with a letter of recommendation to Monsieur Capello, at Venice, which was inclosed in mine to you. I will suppose too, that the inland post on your side of the water has not done you justice; for I received but one single letter from you, and one from Mr. Harte, during your whole stay at Berlin; from whence I hoped for, and expected very particular accounts.

I persuade myself, that the time you stay at Venice will be properly employed, in seeing all that is to be seen in that extraordinary place: and in conversing with people who can inform you, not of the raree-shows of the town, but of the constitution of the government; for which purpose I send you the inclosed letters of recommendation from Sir James Grey, the King's Resident at Venice, but who is now in England. These, with mine to Monsieur Capello, will carry you, if you will go, into all the best company at Venice.

But the important point; and the important place, is Turin; for there I propose your staying a considerable time, to pursue your studies, learn your exercises, and form your manners. I own, I am not without my anxiety for the consequence of your stay there, which must be either very good or very bad. To you it will be entirely a new scene. Wherever you have hitherto been, you have conversed, chiefly, with people wiser and discreeter than yourself; and have been equally out of the way of bad advice or bad example; but in the Academy at Turin you will probably meet with both, considering the variety of young fellows about your own age; among whom it is to be expected that some will be dissipated and idle, others vicious and profligate. I will believe, till the contrary appears, that you have sagacity enough to distinguish the good from the bad characters; and both sense and virtue enough to shun the latter, and connect yourself with the former: but however, for greater security, and for your sake alone, I must acquaint you that I have sent positive orders to Mr. Harte to carry you off, instantly, to a place which I have named to him, upon the very first symptom which he shall discover in you, of drinking, gaming, idleness, or disobedience to his orders; so that, whether Mr. Harte informs me or not of the particulars, I shall be able to judge of your conduct in general by the time of your stay at Turin. If it is short, I shall know why; and I promise you, that you shall soon find that I do; but if Mr. Harte lets you continue there, as long as I propose that you should, I shall then be convinced that you make the proper use of your time; which is the only thing I have to ask of you. One year is the most that I propose you should stay at Turin; and that year, if you employ it well, perfects you. One year more of your late application, with Mr. Harte, will complete your classical studies. You will be likewise master of your exercises in that time; and will have formed yourself so well at that court, as to be fit to appear advantageously at any other. These will be the happy effects of your year's stay at Turin, if you behave, and apply yourself there as you have done at Leipsig; but if either ill advice, or ill example, affect and seduce you, you are ruined forever. I look upon that year as your decisive year of probation; go through it well, and you will be all accomplished, and fixed in my tenderest affection forever; but should the contagion of vice of idleness lay hold of you there, your character, your fortune, my hopes, and consequently my favor are all blasted, and you are undone. The more I love you now, from the good opinion I have of you, the greater will be my indignation if I should have reason to change it. Hitherto you have had every possible proof of my affection, because you have deserved it; but when you cease to deserve it, you may expect every possible mark of my resentment. To leave nothing doubtful upon this important point I will tell you fairly, beforehand, by what rule I shall judge of your conduct—by Mr. Harte's accounts. He will not I am sure, nay, I will say more, he cannot be in the wrong with regard to you. He can have no other view but your good; and you will, I am sure, allow that he must be a better judge of it than you can possibly be at your age. While he is satisfied, I shall be so too; but whenever he is dissatisfied with you, I shall be much more so. If he complains, you must be guilty; and I shall not have the least regard for anything that you may allege in your own defense.

I will now tell you what I expect and insist upon from you at Turin: First, that you pursue your classical and other studies every morning with Mr. Harte, as long and in whatever manner Mr. Harte shall be pleased to require; secondly, that you learn, uninterruptedly, your exercises of riding, dancing, and fencing; thirdly, that you make yourself master of the Italian language; and lastly, that you pass your evenings in the best company. I also require a strict conformity to the hours and rules of the Academy. If you will but finish your year in this manner at Turin, I have nothing further to ask of you; and I will give you everything that you can ask of me. You shall after that be entirely your own master; I shall think you safe; shall lay aside all authority over you, and friendship shall be our mutual and only tie. Weigh this, I beg of you, deliberately in your own mind; and consider whether the application and the degree of restraint which I require but for one year more, will not be amply repaid by all the advantages, and the perfect liberty, which you will receive at the end of it. Your own good sense will, I am sure, not allow you to hesitate one moment in your choice. God bless you!
Adieu.

P. S. Sir James Grey's letters not being yet sent to me, as I thought they would, I shall inclose them in my next, which I believe will get to Venice as soon as you.

LETTER LXVII

LONDON, April 12, O. S. 1749.

DEAR BOY: I received, by the last mail, a letter from Mr. Harte, dated Prague, April the 1st, N. S., for which I desire you will return him my thanks, and assure him that I extremely approve of what he has done, and proposes eventually to do, in your way to Turin. Who would have thought you were old enough to have been so well acquainted with the heroes of the 'Bellum Tricennale', as to be looking out for their great-grandsons in Bohemia, with that affection with which, I am informed, you seek for the Wallsteins, the Kinskis, etc. As I cannot ascribe it to your age, I must to your consummate knowledge of history, that makes every country, and every century, as it were, your own. Seriously, I am told, that you are both very strong and very correct in history; of which I am extremely glad. This is useful knowledge.

Comte du Perron and Comte Lascaris are arrived here: the former gave me a letter from Sir Charles Williams, the latter brought me your orders. They are very pretty men, and have both knowledge and manners; which, though they always ought, seldom go together. I examined them, particularly Comte Lascaris, concerning you; their report is a very favorable one, especially on the side of knowledge; the quickness of conception which they allow you I can easily credit; but the attention which they add to it pleases me the more, as I own I expected it less. Go on in the pursuit and the increase of knowledge; nay, I am sure you will, for you now know too much to stop; and, if Mr. Harte would let you be idle, I am convinced you would not. But now that you have left Leipsig, and are entered into the great world, remember there is another object that must keep pace with, and accompany knowledge; I mean manners, politeness, and the Graces; in which Sir Charles Williams, though very much your friend, owns that you are very deficient. The manners of Leipsig must be shook off; and in that respect you must put on the new man. No scrambling at your meals, as at a German ordinary; no awkward overturns of glasses, plates, and salt-cellars; no horse play. On the contrary, a gentleness of manners, a graceful carriage, and an insinuating address, must take their place. I repeat, and shall never cease repeating to you, THE GRACES, THE GRACES.

I desire that as soon as ever you get to Turin you will apply yourself diligently to the Italian language; that before you leave that place, you may know it well enough to be able to speak tolerably when you get to Rome; where you will soon make yourself perfectly master of Italian, from the daily necessity you will be under of speaking it. In the mean time, I insist upon your not neglecting, much less forgetting, the German you already know; which you may not only continue but improve, by speaking it constantly to your Saxon boy, and as often as you can to the several Germans you will meet in your travels. You remember, no doubt, that you must never write to me from Turin, but in the German language and character.

I send you the inclosed letter of recommendation to Mr. Smith the King's Consul at Venice; who can, and I daresay will, be more useful to you there than anybody. Pray make your court, and behave your best, to Monsieur and Madame Capello, who will be of great use to you at Rome. Adieu! Yours tenderly.

LETTER LXVIII

LONDON, April 19, O. S. 1749.

DEAR BOY: This letter will, I believe, still find you at Venice in all the dissipation of masquerades, ridottos, operas, etc. With all my heart; they are decent evening's amusements, and very properly succeed that serious application to which I am sure you devote your mornings. There are liberal and illiberal pleasures as well as liberal and illiberal arts: There are some pleasures that degrade a gentleman as much as some trades could do. Sottish drinking, indiscriminate gluttony, driving coaches, rustic sports, such as fox-chases, horse-races, etc., are in my opinion infinitely below the honest and industrious profession of a tailor and a shoemaker, which are said to 'deroger'.

As you are now in a musical country, where singing, fiddling, and piping, are not only the common topics of conversation, but almost the principal objects of attention, I cannot help cautioning you against giving in to those (I will call them illiberal) pleasures (though music is commonly reckoned one of the liberal arts) to the degree that most of your countrymen do, when they travel in Italy. If you love music, hear it; go to operas, concerts, and pay fiddlers to play to you; but I insist upon your neither piping nor fiddling yourself. It puts a gentleman in a very frivolous, contemptible light; brings him into a great deal of bad company; and takes up a great deal of time, which might be much better employed. Few things would mortify me more, than to see you bearing a part in a concert, with a fiddle under your chin, or a pipe in your mouth.

I have had a great deal of conversation with Comte du Perron and Comte Lascaris upon your subject: and I will tell you, very truly, what Comte du Perron (who is, in my opinion, a very pretty man) said of you: 'Il a de l'esprit, un savoir peu commun a son age, une grande vivacite, et quand il aura pris des manieres il sera parfait; car il faut avouer qu'il sent encore le college; mars cela viendra'. I was very glad to hear, from one whom I think so good a judge, that you wanted nothing but 'des manieres', which I am convinced you will now soon acquire, in the company which henceforward you are likely to keep. But I must add, too, that if you should not acquire them, all the rest will be of little use to you. By 'manieres', I do not mean bare common civility; everybody must have that who would not be kicked out of company; but I mean engaging, insinuating, shining manners; distinguished politeness, an almost irresistible address; a superior gracefulness in all you say and do. It is this alone that can give all your other talents their full lustre and value; and, consequently, it is this which should now be thy principal object of your attention. Observe minutely, wherever you go, the allowed and established models of good-breeding, and form yourself upon them. Whatever pleases you most in others, will infallibly please others in you. I have often repeated this to you; now is your time of putting it in practice.

Pray make my compliments to Mr. Harte, and tell him I have received his letter from Vienna of the 16th N. S., but that I shall not trouble him with an answer to it till I have received the other letter which he promises me, upon the subject of one of my last. I long to hear from him after your settlement at Turin: the months that you are to pass there will be very decisive ones for you. The exercises of the Academy, and the manners of courts must be attended to and acquired; and, at the same time, your other studies continued. I am sure you will not pass, nor desire, one single idle hour there: for I do not foresee that you can, in any part of your life, put out six months to greater interest, than those next six at Turin.

We will talk hereafter about your stay at Rome and in other parts of Italy. This only I will now recommend to you; which is, to extract the spirit of every place you go to. In those places which are only distinguished by classical fame, and valuable remains of antiquity, have your classics in your hand and in your head; compare the ancient geography and descriptions with the modern, and never fail to take notes. Rome will furnish you with business enough of that sort; but then it furnishes you with many other objects well deserving your attention, such as deep ecclesiastical craft and policy. Adieu.

LETTER LXIX

LONDON, April 27, O. S. 1749.

DEAR BOY: I have received your letter from Vienna, of the 19th N. S., which gives me great uneasiness upon Mr. Harte's account. You and I have reason to interest ourselves very particularly in everything that relates to him. I am glad, however, that no bone is broken or dislocated; which being the case, I hope he will have been able to pursue his journey to Venice. In that supposition I direct this letter to you at Turin; where it will either find, or at least not wait very long for you, as I calculate that you will be there by the end of next month, N. S. I hope you reflect how much you have to do there, and that you are determined to employ every moment of your time accordingly. You have your classical and severer studies to continue with Mr. Harte; you have your exercises to learn; the turn and manners of a court to acquire; reserving always some time for the decent amusements and pleasures of a gentleman. You see I am never against pleasures; I loved them myself when I was of your age, and it is as reasonable that you should love them now. But I insist upon it that pleasures are very combinable with both business and studies, and have a much better relish from the mixture. The man who cannot join business and pleasure is either a formal coxcomb in the one, or a sensual beast in the other. Your evenings I therefore allot for company, assemblies, balls, and such sort of amusements, as I look upon those to be the best schools for the manners of a gentleman; which nothing can give but use, observation, and experience. You have, besides, Italian to learn, to which I desire you will diligently apply; for though French is, I believe, the language of the court at Turin, yet Italian will be very necessary for you at Rome, and in other parts of Italy; and if you are well grounded in it while you are at Turin (as you easily may, for it is a very easy language), your subsequent stay at Rome will make you perfect in it. I would also have you acquire a general notion of fortification; I mean so far as not to be ignorant of the terms, which you will often hear mentioned in company, such as ravelin, bastion; glacis, contrescarpe, etc. In order to this, I do not propose that you should make a study of fortification, as if you were to be an engineer, but a very easy way of knowing as much as you need know of them, will be to visit often the fortifications of Turin, in company with some old officer or engineer, who will show and explain to you the several works themselves; by which means you will get a clearer notion of them than if you were to see them only upon paper for seven years together. Go to originals whenever you can, and trust to copies and descriptions as little as possible. At your idle hours, while you are at Turin, pray read the history of the House of Savoy, which has produced a great many very great men. The late king, Victor Amedee, was undoubtedly one, and the present king is, in my opinion, another. In general, I believe that little princes are more likely to be great men than those whose more extensive dominions and superior strength flatter them with a security, which commonly produces negligence and indolence. A little prince, in the neighborhood of great ones, must be alert and look out sharp, if he would secure his own dominions: much more still if he would enlarge them. He must watch for conjunctures or endeavor to make them. No princes have ever possessed this art better than those of the House of Savoy; who have enlarged their dominions prodigiously within a century by profiting of conjunctures.

I send you here inclosed a letter from Comte Lascaris, who is a warm friend of yours: I desire that you will answer it very soon and cordially, and remember to make your compliments in it to Comte du Perron. A young man should never be wanting in those attentions; they cost little and bring in a great deal, by getting you people's good word and affection. They gain the heart, to which I have always advised you to apply yourself particularly; it guides ten thousand for one that, reason influences.

I cannot end this letter or (I believe) any other, without repeating my recommendation of THE GRACES. They are to be met with at Turin: for God's sake, sacrifice to them, and they will be propitious. People mistake grossly, to imagine that the least awkwardness, either in matter or manner, mind or body, is an indifferent thing and not worthy of attention. It may possibly be a weakness in me, but in short we are all so made: I confess to you fairly, that when you shall come home and that I first see you, if I find you ungraceful in your address, and awkward in your person and dress, it will be impossible for me to love you half so well as I should otherwise do, let your intrinsic merit and knowledge be ever so great. If that would be your case with me, as it really would, judge how much worse it might be with others, who have not the same affection and partiality for you, and to whose hearts you must make your own way.

Remember to write to me constantly while you are in Italy, in the German language and character, till you can write to me in Italian; which will not be till you have been some time at Rome.

Adieu, my dear boy: may you turn out what Mr. Harte and I wish you. I must add that if you do not, it will be both your own fault and your own misfortune.

LETTER LXX

LONDON, May 15, O. S. 1749.

DEAR BOY: This letter will, I hope, find you settled to your serious studies, and your necessary exercises at Turin, after the hurry and the dissipation of the Carnival at Venice. I mean that your stay at Turin should, and I flatter myself that it will, be an useful and ornamental period of your education; but at the same time I must tell you, that all my affection for you has never yet given me so much anxiety, as that which I now feel. While you are in danger, I shall be in fear; and you are in danger at Turin. Mr. Harte will by his care arm you as well as he can against it; but your own good sense and resolution can alone make you invulnerable. I am informed, there are now many English at the Academy at Turin; and I fear those are just so many dangers for you to encounter. Who they are, I do not know; but I well know the general ill conduct, the indecent behavior, and the illiberal views, of my young countrymen. abroad; especially wherever they are in numbers together. Ill example is of itself dangerous enough; but those who give it seldom stop there; they add their infamous exhortations and invitations; and, if they fail, they have recourse to ridicule, which is harder for one of your age and inexperience to withstand than either of the former. Be upon your guard, therefore, against these batteries, which will all be played upon you. You are not sent abroad to converse with your own countrymen: among them, in general, you will get, little knowledge, no languages, and, I am sure, no manners. I desire that you will form no connections, nor (what they impudently call) friendships with these people; which are, in truth, only combinations and conspiracies against good morals and good manners. There is commonly, in young people, a facility that makes them unwilling to refuse anything that is asked of them; a 'mauvaise honte' that makes them ashamed to refuse; and, at the same time, an ambition of pleasing and shining in the company they keep: these several causes produce the best effect in good company, but the very worst in bad. If people had no vices but their own, few would have so many as they have. For my own part, I would sooner wear other people's clothes than their vices; and they would sit upon me just as well. I hope you will have none; but if ever you have, I beg, at least, they may be all your own. Vices of adoption are, of all others, the most disgraceful and unpardonable. There are degrees in vices, as well as in virtues; and I must do my countrymen the justice to say, that they generally take their vices in the lower degree. Their gallantry is the infamous mean debauchery of stews, justly attended and rewarded by the loss of their health, as well as their character. Their pleasures of the table end in beastly drunkenness, low riot, broken windows, and very often (as they well deserve), broken bones. They game for the sake of the vice, not of the amusement; and therefore carry it to excess; undo, or are undone by their companions. By such conduct, and in such company abroad, they come home, the unimproved, illiberal, and ungentlemanlike creatures that one daily sees them, that is, in the park and in the streets, for one never meets them in good company; where they have neither manners to present themselves, nor merit to be received. But, with the manners of footmen and grooms, they assume their dress too; for you must have observed them in the streets here, in dirty blue frocks, with oaken sticks in their ends, and their hair greasy and unpowdered, tucked up under their hats of an enormous size. Thus finished and adorned by their travels, they become the disturbers of play-houses; they break the windows, and commonly the landlords, of the taverns where they drink; and are at once the support, the terror, and the victims, of the bawdy-houses they frequent. These poor mistaken people think they shine, and so they do indeed; but it is as putrefaction shines in the dark.

I am not now preaching to you, like an old fellow, upon their religious or moral texts; I am persuaded that you do not want the best instructions of that kind: but I am advising you as a friend, as a man of the world, as one who would not have you old while you are young, but would have you to take all the pleasures that reason points out, and that decency warrants. I will therefore suppose, for argument's sake (for upon no other account can it be supposed), that all the vices above mentioned were perfectly innocent in themselves: they would still degrade, vilify, and sink those who practiced them; would obstruct their rising in the world by debasing their characters; and give them low turn of mind, and manners absolutely inconsistent with their making any figure in upper life and great business.

What I have now said, together with your own good sense, is, I hope, sufficient to arm you against the seduction, the invitations, or the profligate exhortations (for I cannot call them temptations) of those unfortunate young people. On the other hand, when they would engage you in these schemes, content yourself with a decent but steady refusal; avoid controversy upon such plain points. You are too young to convert them; and, I trust, too wise to be converted by them. Shun them not only in reality, but even in appearance, if you would be well received in good company; for people will always be shy of receiving a man who comes from a place where the plague rages, let him look ever so healthy. There are some expressions, both in French and English, and some characters, both in those two and in other countries, which have, I dare say, misled many young men to their ruin. 'Une honnete debauche, une jolie debauche; "An agreeable rake, a man of pleasure." Do not think that this means debauchery and profligacy; nothing like it. It means, at most, the accidental and unfrequent irregularities of youth and vivacity, in opposition to dullness, formality, and want of spirit. A 'commerce galant', insensibly formed with a woman of fashion; a glass of wine or two too much, unwarily taken in the warmth and joy of good company; or some innocent frolic, by which nobody is injured, are the utmost bounds of that life of pleasure, which a man of sense and decency, who has a regard for his character, will allow himself, or be allowed by others. Those who transgress them in the hopes of shining, miss their aim, and become infamous, or at least, contemptible.

The length or shortness of your stay at Turin will sufficiently inform me (even though Mr. Harte should not) of your conduct there; for, as I have told you before, Mr. Harte has the strictest orders to carry you away immediately from thence, upon the first and least symptom of infection that he discovers about you; and I know him to be too conscientiously scrupulous, and too much your friend and mine not to execute them exactly. Moreover, I will inform you, that I shall have constant accounts of your behavior from Comte Salmour, the Governor of the Academy, whose son is now here, and my particular friend. I have, also, other good channels of intelligence, of which I do not apprise you. But, supposing that all turns out well at Turin, yet, as I propose your being at Rome for the jubilee, at Christmas, I desire that you will apply yourself diligently to your exercises of dancing, fencing, and riding at the Academy; as well for the sake of your health and growth, as to fashion and supple you. You must not neglect your dress neither, but take care to be 'bien mis'. Pray send for the best operator for the teeth at Turin, where I suppose there is some famous one; and let him put yours in perfect order; and then take care to keep them so, afterward, yourself. You had very good teeth, and I hope they are so still; but even those who have bad ones, should keep them clean; for a dirty mouth is, in my mind, ill manners. In short, neglect nothing that can possibly please. A thousand nameless little things, which nobody can describe, but which everybody feels, conspire to form that WHOLE of pleasing; as the several pieces of a Mosaic work though, separately, of little beauty or value, when properly joined, form those beautiful figures which please everybody. A look, a gesture, an attitude, a tone of voice, all bear their parts in the great work of pleasing. The art of pleasing is more particularly necessary in your intended profession than perhaps any other; it is, in truth, the first half of your business; for if you do not please the court you are sent to, you will be of very little use to the court you are sent from. Please the eyes and the ears, they will introduce you to the heart; and nine times in ten, the heart governs the understanding.

Make your court particularly, and show distinguished attentions to such men and women as are best at court, highest in the fashion, and in the opinion of the public; speak advantageously of them behind their backs, in companies whom you have reason to believe will tell them again. Express your admiration of the many great men that the House of Savoy has produced; observe that nature, instead of being exhausted by those efforts, seems to have redoubled them, in the person of the present King, and the Duke of Savoy; wonder, at this rate, where it will end, and conclude that it must end in the government of all Europe. Say this, likewise, where it will probably be repeated; but say it unaffectedly, and, the last especially, with a kind of 'enjouement'. These little arts are very allowable, and must be made use of in the course of the world; they are pleasing to one party, useful to the other, and injurious to nobody.

What I have said with regard to my countrymen in general, does not extend to them all without exception; there are some who have both merit and manners. Your friend, Mr. Stevens, is among the latter; and I approve of your connection with him. You may happen to meet with some others, whose friendship may be of great use to you hereafter, either from their superior talents, or their rank and fortune; cultivate them; but then I desire that Mr. Harte may be the judge of those persons.

Adieu my dear child! Consider seriously the importance of the two next years to your character, your figure, and your fortune.

LETTER LXXI

LONDON, May 22, O. S. 1749.

DEAR BOY: I recommended to you, in my last, an innocent piece of art; that of flattering people behind their backs, in presence of those who, to make their own court, much more than for your sake, will not fail to repeat and even amplify the praise to the party concerned. This is, of all flattery, the most pleasing, and consequently the most effectual. There are other, and many other, inoffensive arts of this kind, which are necessary in the course of the world, and which he who practices the earliest, will please the most, and rise the soonest. The spirits and vivacity of youth are apt to neglect them as useless, or reject them as troublesome. But subsequent knowledge and experience of the world reminds us of their importance, commonly when it is too late. The principal of these things is the mastery of one's temper, and that coolness of mind, and serenity of countenance, which hinders us from discovering by words, actions, or even looks, those passions or sentiments by which we are inwardly moved or agitated; and the discovery of which gives cooler and abler people such infinite advantages over us, not only in great business, but in all the most common occurrences of life. A man who does not possess himself enough to hear disagreeable things without visible marks of anger and change of countenance, or agreeable ones, without sudden bursts of joy and expansion of countenance, is at the mercy of every artful knave or pert coxcomb; the former will provoke or please you by design, to catch unguarded words or looks by which he will easily decipher the secrets of your heart, of which you should keep the key yourself, and trust it with no man living. The latter will, by his absurdity, and without intending it, produce the same discoveries of which other people will avail themselves. You will say, possibly, that this coolness must be constitutional, and consequently does not depend upon the will: and I will allow that constitution has some power over us; but I will maintain, too, that people very often, to excuse themselves, very unjustly accuse their constitutions. Care and reflection, if properly used, will get the better: and a man may as surely get a habit of letting his reason prevail over his constitution, as of letting, as most people do, the latter prevail over the former. If you find yourself subject to sudden starts of passion or madness (for I see no difference between them but in their duration), resolve within yourself, at least, never to speak one word while you feel that emotion within you. Determine, too, to keep your countenance as unmoved and unembarrassed as possible; which steadiness you may get a habit of, by constant attention. I should desire nothing better, in any negotiation, than to have to do with one of those men of warm, quick passions; which I would take care to set in motion. By artful provocations I would extort rash unguarded expressions; and, by hinting at all the several things that I could suspect, infallibly discover the true one, by the alteration it occasioned in the countenance of the person. 'Volto sciolto con pensieri stretti', is a most useful maxim in business. It is so necessary at some games, such as 'Berkan Quinze', etc., that a man who had not the command of his temper and countenance, would infallibly be outdone by those who had, even though they played fair. Whereas, in business, you always play with sharpers; to whom, at least, you should give no fair advantages. It may be objected, that I am now recommending dissimulation to you; I both own and justify it. It has been long said, 'Qui nescit dissimulare nescit regnare': I go still further, and say, that without some dissimulation no business can be carried on at all. It is SIMULATION that is false, mean, and criminal: that is the cunning which Lord Bacon calls crooked or left-handed wisdom, and which is never made use of but by those who have not true wisdom. And the same great man says, that dissimulation is only to hide our own cards, whereas simulation is put on, in order to look into other people's. Lord Bolingbroke, in his "Idea of a Patriot King," which he has lately published, and which I will send you by the first opportunity, says very justly that simulation is a STILETTO,—not only an unjust but an unlawful weapon, and the use of it very rarely to be excused, never justified. Whereas dissimulation is a shield, as secrecy is armor; and it is no more possible to preserve secrecy in business, without same degree of dissimulation, than it is to succeed in business without secrecy. He goes on, and says, that those two arts of dissimulation and secrecy are like the alloy mingled with pure ore: a little is necessary, and will not debase the coin below its proper standard; but if more than that little be employed (that is, simulation and cunning), the coin loses its currency, and the coiner his credit.

Make yourself absolute master, therefore, of your temper and your countenance, so far, at least, as that no visible change do appear in either, whatever you may feel inwardly. This may be difficult, but it is by no means impossible; and, as a man of sense never attempts impossibilities on one hand, on the other, he is never discouraged by difficulties: on the contrary, he redoubles his industry and his diligence; he perseveres, and infallibly prevails at last. In any point which prudence bids you pursue, and which a manifest utility attends, let difficulties only animate your industry, not deter you from the pursuit. If one way has failed, try another; be active, persevere, and you will conquer. Some people are to be reasoned, some flattered, some intimidated, and some teased into a thing; but, in general, all are to be brought into it at last, if skillfully applied to, properly managed, and indefatigably attacked in their several weak places. The time should likewise be judiciously chosen; every man has his 'mollia tempora', but that is far from being all day long; and you would choose your time very ill, if you applied to a man about one business, when his head was full of another, or when his heart was full of grief, anger, or any other disagreeable sentiment.

In order to judge of the inside of others, study your own; for men in general are very much alike; and though one has one prevailing passion, and another has another, yet their operations are much the same; and whatever engages or disgusts, pleases or offends you, in others will, 'mutatis mutandis', engage, disgust, please, or offend others, in you. Observe with the utmost attention all the operations of your own mind, the nature of your passions, and the various motives that determine your will; and you may, in a great degree, know all mankind. For instance, do you find yourself hurt and mortified when another makes you feel his superiority, and your own inferiority, in knowledge, parts, rank, or fortune? You will certainly take great care not to make a person whose good will, good word, interest, esteem, or friendship, you would gain, feel that superiority in you, in case you have it. If disagreeable insinuations, sly sneers, or repeated contradictions, tease and irritate you, would you use them where you wish to engage and please? Surely not, and I hope you wish to engage and please, almost universally. The temptation of saying a smart and witty thing, or 'bon mot'; and the malicious applause with which it is commonly received, has made people who can say them, and, still oftener, people who think they can, but cannot, and yet try, more enemies, and implacable ones too, than any one other thing that I know of: When such things, then, shall happen to be said at your expense (as sometimes they certainly will), reflect seriously upon the sentiments of uneasiness, anger, and resentment which they excite in you; and consider whether it can be prudent, by the same means, to excite the same sentiments in others against you. It is a decided folly to lose a friend for a jest; but, in my mind, it is not a much less degree of folly to make an enemy of an indifferent and neutral person, for the sake of a 'bon mot'. When things of this kind happen to be said of you, the most prudent way is to seem not to suppose that they are meant at you, but to dissemble and conceal whatever degree of anger you may feel inwardly; but, should they be so plain that you cannot be supposed ignorant of their meaning, to join in the laugh of the company against yourself; acknowledge the hit to be a fair one, and the jest a good one, and play off the whole thing in seeming good humor; but by no means reply in the same way; which only shows that you are hurt, and publishes the victory which you might have concealed. Should the thing said, indeed injure your honor or moral character, there is but one proper reply; which I hope you never will have occasion to make.

As the female part of the world has some influence, and often too much, over the male, your conduct with regard to women (I mean women of fashion, for I cannot suppose you capable of conversing with any others) deserves some share in your reflections. They are a numerous and loquacious body: their hatred would be more prejudicial than their friendship can be advantageous to you. A general complaisance and attention to that sex is therefore established by custom, and certainly necessary. But where you would particularly please anyone, whose situation, interest, or connections, can be of use to you, you must show particular preference.

The least attentions please, the greatest charm them. The innocent but pleasing flattery of their persons, however gross, is greedily swallowed and kindly digested: but a seeming regard for their understandings, a seeming desire of, and deference for, their advice, together with a seeming confidence in their moral virtues, turns their heads entirely in your favor. Nothing shocks them so much as the least appearance of that contempt which they are apt to suspect men of entertaining of their capacities; and you may be very sure of gaining their friendship if you seem to think it worth gaining. Here dissimulation is very often necessary, and even simulation sometimes allowable; which, as it pleases them, may, be useful to you, and is injurious to nobody.

This torn sheet, which I did not observe when I began upon it, as it alters the figure, shortens, too, the length of my letter. It may very well afford it: my anxiety for you carries me insensibly to these lengths. I am apt to flatter myself, that my experience, at the latter end of my life, may be of use to you at the beginning of yours; and I do not grudge the greatest trouble, if it can procure you the least advantage. I even repeat frequently the same things, the better to imprint them on your young, and, I suppose, yet giddy mind; and I shall think that part of my time the best employed, that contributes to make you employ yours well. God bless you, child!

LETTER LXXII

LONDON, June 16, O. S. 1749.

DEAR BOY: I do not guess where this letter will find you, but I hope it will find you well: I direct it eventually to Laubach; from whence I suppose you have taken care to have your letters sent after you. I received no account from Mr. Harte by last post, and the mail due this day is not yet come in; so that my informations come down no lower than the 2d June, N. S., the date of Mr. Harte's last letter. As I am now easy about your health, I am only curious about your motions, which I hope have been either to Inspruck or Verona; for I disapprove extremely of your proposed long and troublesome journey to Switzerland. Wherever you may be, I recommend to you to get as much Italian as you can, before you go either to Rome or Naples: a little will be of great use to you upon the road; and the knowledge of the grammatical part, which you can easily acquire in two or three months, will not only facilitate your progress, but accelerate your perfection in that language, when you go to those places where it is generally spoken; as Naples, Rome, Florence, etc.

Should the state of your health not yet admit of your usual application to books, you may, in a great degree, and I hope you will, repair that loss by useful and instructive conversations with Mr. Harte: you may, for example, desire him to give you in conversation the outlines, at least, of Mr. Locke's logic; a general notion of ethics, and a verbal epitome of rhetoric; of all which Mr. Harte will give you clearer ideas in half an hour, by word of mouth, than the books of most of the dull fellows who have written upon those subjects would do in a week.

I have waited so long for the post, which I hoped would come, that the post, which is just going out, obliges me to cut this letter short. God bless you, my dear child! and restore you soon to perfect health!

My compliments to Mr. Harte; to whose care your life is the least thing that you owe.

LETTER LXXIII

LONDON, June 22, O. S. 1749.

DEAR BOY: The outside of your letter of the 7th N. S., directed by your own hand, gave me more pleasure than the inside of any other letter ever did. I received it yesterday at the same time with one from Mr. Harts of the 6th. They arrived at a very proper time, for they found a consultation of physicians in my room, upon account of a fever which I had for four or five days, but which has now entirely left me. As Mr. Harte Says THAT YOUR LUNGS NOW AND THEN GIVE YOU A LITTLE PAIN, and that YOUR SWELLINGS COME AND GO VARIABLY, but as he mentions nothing of your coughing, spitting, or sweating, the doctors take it for granted that you are entirely free from those three bad symptoms: and from thence conclude, that, the pain which you sometimes feel upon your lungs is only symptomatical of your rheumatic disorder, from the pressure of the muscles which hinders the free play of the lungs. But, however, as the lungs are a point of the utmost importance and delicacy, they insist upon your drinking, in all events, asses' milk twice a day, and goats' whey as often as you please, the oftener the better: in your common diet, they recommend an attention to pectorals, such as sago, barley, turnips, etc. These rules are equally good in rheumatic as in consumptive cases; you will therefore, I hope, strictly observe them; for I take it for granted that you are above the silly likings or dislikings, in which silly people indulge their tastes, at the expense of their health.

I approve of your going to Venice, as much as I disapproved of your going to Switzerland. I suppose that you are by this time arrived; and, in that supposition, I direct this letter there. But if you should find the heat too great, or the water offensive, at this time of the year, I would have you go immediately to Verona, and stay there till the great heats are over, before you return to Venice.

The time which you will probably pass at Venice will allow you to make yourself master of that intricate and singular form of government, of which few of our travelers know anything. Read, ask, and see everything that is relative to it. There are likewise many valuable remains of the remotest antiquity, and many fine pieces of the Antico-moderno, all which deserve a different sort of attention from that which your countrymen commonly give them. They go to see them, as they go to see the lions, and kings on horseback, at the Tower here, only to say that they have seen them. You will, I am sure, view them in another light; you will consider them as you would a poem, to which indeed they are akin. You will observe whether the sculptor has animated his stone, or the painter his canvas, into the just expression of those sentiments and passions which should characterize and mark their several figures. You will examine, likewise, whether in their groups there be a unity of action, or proper relation; a truth of dress and manners. Sculpture and painting are very justly called liberal arts; a lively and strong imagination, together with a just observation, being absolutely necessary to excel in either; which, in my opinion, is by no means the case of music, though called a liberal art, and now in Italy placed even above the other two; a proof of the decline of that country. The Venetian school produced many great painters, such as Paul Veronese, Titian, Palma, etc., of whom you will see, as well in private houses as in churches, very fine pieces. The Last Supper, of Paul Veronese, in the church of St. George, is reckoned his capital performance, and deserves your attention; as does also the famous picture of the Cornaro Family, by Titian. A taste for sculpture and painting is, in my mind, as becoming as a taste for fiddling and piping is unbecoming, a man of fashion. The former is connected with history and poetry; the latter, with nothing that I know of but bad company.

Learn Italian as fast as ever you can, that you may be able to understand it tolerably, and speak it a little before you go to Rome and Naples: There are many good historians in that language, and excellent translations of the ancient Greek and Latin authors; which are called the Collana; but the only two Italian poets that deserve your acquaintance are Ariosto and Tasso; and they undoubtedly have great merit.

Make my compliments to Mr. Harte, and tell him that I have consulted about his leg, and that if it was only a sprain, he ought to keep a tight bandage about the part, for a considerable time, and do nothing else to it. Adieu! 'Jubeo te bene valere'.

LETTER LXXIV

LONDON, July 6, O. S. 1749.

DEAR BOY: As I am now no longer in pain about your health, which I trust is perfectly restored; and as, by the various accounts I have had of you, I need not be in pain about your learning, our correspondence may, for the future, turn upon less important points, comparatively; though still very important ones: I mean, the knowledge of the world, decorum, manners, address, and all those (commonly called little) accomplishments, which are absolutely necessary to give greater accomplishments their full, value and lustre.

Had I the admirable ring of Gyges, which rendered the wearer invisible; and had I, at the same time, those magic powers, which were very common formerly, but are now very scarce, of transporting myself, by a wish, to any given place, my first expedition would be to Venice, there to RECONNOITRE you, unseen myself. I would first take you in the morning, at breakfast with Mr. Harte, and attend to your natural and unguarded conversation with him; from whence, I think, I could pretty well judge of your natural turn of mind. How I should rejoice if I overheard you asking him pertinent questions upon useful subjects! or making judicious reflections upon the studies of that morning, or the occurrences of the former day! Then I would follow you into the different companies of the day, and carefully observe in what manner you presented yourself to, and behaved yourself with, men of sense and dignity; whether your address was respectful, and yet easy; your air modest, and yet unembarrassed; and I would, at the same time, penetrate into their thoughts, in order to know whether your first 'abord' made that advantageous impression upon their fancies, which a certain address, air, and manners, never fail doing. I would afterward follow you to the mixed companies of the evening; such as assemblies, suppers, etc., and there watch if you trifled gracefully and genteelly: if your good-breeding and politeness made way for your parts and knowledge. With what pleasure should I hear people cry out, 'Che garbato cavaliere, com' e pulito, disinvolto, spiritoso'! If all these things turned out to my mind, I would immediately assume my own shape, become visible, and embrace you: but if the contrary happened, I would preserve my invisibility, make the best of my way home again, and sink my disappointment upon you and the world. As, unfortunately, these supernatural powers of genii, fairies, sylphs, and gnomes, have had the fate of the oracles they succeeded, and have ceased for some time, I must content myself (till we meet naturally, and in the common way) with Mr. Harte's written accounts of you, and the verbal ones which I now and then receive from people who have seen you. However, I believe it would do you no harm, if you would always imagine that I were present, and saw and heard everything you did and said.

There is a certain concurrence of various little circumstances which compose what the French call 'l'aimable'; and which, now that you are entering into the world, you ought to make it your particular study to acquire. Without them, your learning will be pedantry, your conversation often improper, always unpleasant, and your figure, however good in itself, awkward and unengaging. A diamond, while rough, has indeed its intrinsic value; but, till polished, is of no use, and would neither be sought for nor worn. Its great lustre, it is true, proceeds from its solidity and strong cohesion of parts; but without the last polish, it would remain forever a dirty, rough mineral, in the cabinets of some few curious collectors. You have; I hope, that solidity and cohesion of parts; take now as much pains to get the lustre. Good company, if you make the right use of it, will cut you into shape, and give you the true brilliant polish. A propos of diamonds: I have sent you by Sir James Gray, the King's Minister, who will be at Venice about the middle of September, my own diamond buckles; which are fitter for your young feet than for my old ones: they will properly adorn you; they would only expose me. If Sir James finds anybody whom he can trust, and who will be at Venice before him, he will send them by that person; but if he should not, and that you should be gone from Venice before he gets there, he will in that case give them to your banker, Monsieur Cornet, to forward to you, wherever you may then be. You are now of an age, at which the adorning your person is not only not ridiculous, but proper and becoming. Negligence would imply either an indifference about pleasing, or else an insolent security of pleasing, without using those means to which others are obliged to have recourse. A thorough cleanliness in your person is as necessary for your own health, as it is not to be offensive to other people. Washing yourself, and rubbing your body and limbs frequently with a fleshbrush, will conduce as much to health as to cleanliness. A particular attention to the cleanliness of your mouth, teeth, hands, and nails, is but common decency, in order not to offend people's eyes and noses.

I send you here inclosed a letter of recommendation to the Duke of Nivernois, the French Ambassador at Rome; who is, in my opinion, one of the prettiest men I ever knew in my life. I do not know a better model for you to form yourself upon; pray observe and frequent him as much as you can. He will show you what manners and graces are. I shall, by successive posts, send you more letters, both for Rome and Naples, where it will be your own fault entirely if you do not keep the very best company.

As you will meet swarms of Germans wherever you go, I desire that you will constantly converse with them in their own language, which will improve you in that language, and be, at the same time, an agreeable piece of civility to them.

Your stay in Italy will, I do not doubt, make you critically master of Italian; I know it may, if you please, for it is a very regular, and consequently a very easy language. Adieu! God bless you!

LETTER LXXV

LONDON, July 20, O. S. 1749.

DEAR BOY: I wrote to Mr. Harte last Monday, the 17th, O. S., in answer to his letter of the 20th June, N. S., which I had received but the day before, after an interval of eight posts; during which I did not know whether you or he existed, and indeed I began to think that you did not. By that letter you ought at this time to be at Venice; where I hope you are arrived in perfect health, after the baths of Tiefler, in case you have made use of them. I hope they are not hot baths, if your lungs are still tender.

Your friend, the Comte d'Einsiedlen, is arrived here: he has been at my door, and I have been at his; but we have not yet met. He will dine with me some day this week. Comte Lascaris inquires after you very frequently, and with great affection; pray answer the letter which I forwarded to you a great while ago from him. You may inclose your answer to me, and I will take care to give it him. Those attentions ought never to be omitted; they cost little, and please a great deal; but the neglect of them offends more than you can yet imagine. Great merit, or great failings, will make you be respected or despised; but trifles, little attentions, mere nothings, either done, or neglected, will make you either liked or disliked, in the general run of the world. Examine yourself why you like such and such people, and dislike such and such others; and you will find, that those different sentiments proceed from very slight causes. Moral virtues are the foundation of society in general, and of friendship in particular; but attentions, manners, and graces, both adorn and strengthen them. My heart is so set upon your pleasing, and consequently succeeding in the world, that possibly I have already (and probably shall again) repeat the same things over and over to you. However, to err, if I do err, on the surer side, I shall continue to communicate to you those observations upon the world which long experience has enabled me to make, and which I have generally found to hold true. Your youth and talents, armed with my experience, may go a great way; and that armor is very much at your service, if you please to wear it. I premise that it is not my imagination, but my memory, that gives you these rules: I am not writing pretty; but useful reflections. A man of sense soon discovers, because he carefully observes, where, and how long, he is welcome; and takes care to leave the company, at least as soon as he is wished out of it. Fools never perceive where they are either ill-timed or illplaced.

I am this moment agreeably stopped, in the course of my reflections, by the arrival of Mr. Harte's letter of the 13th July, N. S., to Mr. Grevenkop, with one inclosed for your Mamma. I find by it that many of his and your letters to me must have miscarried; for he says that I have had regular accounts of you: whereas all those accounts have been only his letter of the 6th and yours of the 7th June, N. S.; his of the 20th June, N. S., to me; and now his of the 13th July, N. S., to Mr. Grevenkop. However, since you are so well, as Mr. Harte says you are, all is well. I am extremely glad that you have no complaint upon your lungs; but I desire that you will think you have, for three or four months to come. Keep in a course of asses' or goats' milk, for one is as good as the other, and possibly the latter is the best; and let your common food be as pectoral as you can conveniently make it. Pray tell Mr. Harte that, according to his desire, I have wrote a letter of thanks to Mr. Firmian. I hope you write to him too, from time to time. The letters of recommendation of a man of his merit and learning will, to be sure, be of great use to you among the learned world in Italy; that is, provided you take care to keep up to the character he gives you in them; otherwise they will only add to your disgrace.

Consider that you have lost a good deal of time by your illness; fetch it up now that you are well. At present you should be a good economist of your moments, of which company and sights will claim a considerable share; so that those which remain for study must be not only attentively, but greedily employed. But indeed I do not suspect you of one single moment's idleness in the whole day. Idleness is only the refuge of weak minds, and the holiday of fools. I do not call good company and liberal pleasures, idleness; far from it: I recommend to you a good share of both.

I send you here inclosed a letter for Cardinal Alexander Albani, which you will give him, as soon as you get to Rome, and before you deliver any others; the Purple expects that preference; go next to the Duc de Nivernois, to whom you are recommended by several people at Paris, as well as by myself. Then you may carry your other letters occasionally.

Remember to pry narrowly into every part of the government of Venice: inform yourself of the history of that republic, especially of its most remarkable eras; such as the Ligue de eambray, in 1509, by which it had like to have been destroyed; and the conspiracy formed by the Marquis de Bedmar, the Spanish Ambassador, to subject it to the Crown of Spain. The famous disputes between that republic and the Pope are worth your knowledge; and the writings of the celebrated and learned Fra Paolo di Sarpi, upon that occasion, worth your reading. It was once the greatest commercial power in Europe, and in the 14th and 15th centuries made a considerable figure; but at present its commerce is decayed, and its riches consequently decreased; and, far from meddling now with the affairs of the Continent, it owes its security to its neutrality and inefficiency; and that security will last no longer than till one of the great Powers in Europe engrosses the rest of Italy; an event which this century possibly may, but which the next probably will see.

Your friend Comte d'Ensiedlen and his governor, have been with me this moment, and delivered me your letter from Berlin, of February the 28th, N. S. I like them both so well that I am glad you did; and still gladder to hear what they say of you. Go on, and continue to deserve the praises of those who deserve praises themselves. Adieu.

I break open this letter to acknowledge yours of the 30th June, N. S., which I have but this instant received, though thirteen days antecedent in date to Mr. Harte's last. I never in my life heard of bathing four hours a day; and I am impatient to hear of your safe arrival at Venice, after so extraordinary an operation.

LETTER LXXVI

LONDON, July 30, O. S. 1749.

DEAR BOY: Mr. Harte's letters and yours drop in upon me most irregularly; for I received, by the last post, one from Mr. Harte, of the 9th, N. S., and that which Mr. Grevenkop had received from him, the post before, was of the 13th; at last, I suppose, I shall receive them all.

I am very glad that my letter, with Dr. Shaw's opinion, has lessened your bathing; for since I was born, I never heard of bathing four hours a-day; which would surely be too much, even in Medea's kettle, if you wanted (as you do not yet) new boiling.

Though, in that letter of mine, I proposed your going to Inspruck, it was only in opposition to Lausanne, which I thought much too long and painful a journey for you; but you will have found, by my subsequent letters, that I entirely approved of Venice; where I hope you have now been some time, and which is a much better place for you to reside at, till you go to Naples, than either Tieffer or Laubach. I love capitals extremely; it is in capitals that the best company is always to be found; and consequently, the best manners to be learned. The very best provincial places have some awkwardness, that distinguish their manners from those of the metropolis. 'A propos' of capitals, I send you here two letters of recommendation to Naples, from Monsieur Finochetti, the Neapolitan Minister at The Hague; and in my next I shall send you two more, from the same person, to the same place.

I have examined Comte d'Einsiedlen so narrowly concerning you, that I have extorted from him a confession that you do not care to speak German, unless to such as understand no other language. At this rate, you will never speak it well, which I am very desirous that you should do, and of which you would, in time, find the advantage. Whoever has not the command of a language, and does not speak it with facility, will always appear below himself when he converses in that language; the want of words and phrases will cramp and lame his thoughts. As you now know German enough to express yourself tolerably, speaking it very often will soon make you speak it very well: and then you will appear in it whatever you are. What with your own Saxon servant and the swarms of Germans you will meet with wherever you go, you may have opportunities of conversing in that language half the day; and I do very seriously desire that you will, or else all the pains that you have already taken about it are lost. You will remember likewise, that, till you can write in Italian, you are always to write to me in German.

Mr. Harte's conjecture concerning your distemper seems to be a very reasonable one; it agrees entirely with mine, which is the universal rule by which every man judges of another man's opinion. But, whatever may have been the cause of your rheumatic disorder, the effects are still to be attended to; and as there must be a remaining acrimony in your blood, you ought to have regard to that, in your common diet as well as in your medicines; both which should be of a sweetening alkaline nature, and promotive of perspiration. Rheumatic complaints are very apt to return, and those returns would be very vexatious and detrimental to you; at your age, and in your course of travels. Your time is, now particularly, inestimable; and every hour of it, at present, worth more than a year will be to you twenty years hence. You are now laying the foundation of your future character and fortune; and one single stone wanting in that foundation is of more consequence than fifty in the superstructure; which can always be mended and embellished if the foundation is solid. To carry on the metaphor of building: I would wish you to be a Corinthian edifice upon a Tuscan foundation; the latter having the utmost strength and solidity to support, and the former all possible ornaments to decorate. The Tuscan column is coarse, clumsy, and unpleasant; nobody looks at it twice; the Corinthian fluted column is beautiful and attractive; but without a solid foundation, can hardly be seen twice, because it must soon tumble down. Yours affectionately.

LETTER LXXVII

LONDON, August 7, O. S. 1749.

DEAR BOY: By Mr. Harte's letter to me of the 18th July N. S., which I received by the last post, I am at length informed of the particulars both of your past distemper, and of your future motions. As to the former, I am now convinced, and so is Dr. Shaw, that your lungs were only symptomatically affected; and that the rheumatic tendency is what you are chiefly now to guard against, but (for greater security) with due attention still to your lungs, as if they had been, and still were, a little affected. In either case, a cooling, pectoral regimen is equally good. By cooling, I mean cooling in its consequences, not cold to the palate; for nothing is more dangerous than very cold liquors, at the very time that one longs for them the most; which is, when one is very hot. Fruit, when full ripe, is very wholesome; but then it must be within certain bounds as to quantity; for I have known many of my countrymen die of bloody-fluxes, by indulging in too great a quantity of fruit, in those countries where, from the goodness and ripeness of it, they thought it could do them no harm. 'Ne quid nimis', is a most excellent rule in everything; but commonly the least observed, by people of your age, in anything.

As to your future motions, I am very well pleased with them, and greatly prefer your intended stay at Verona to Venice, whose almost stagnating waters must, at this time of the year, corrupt the air. Verona has a pure and clear air, and, as I am informed, a great deal of good company. Marquis Maffei, alone, would be worth going there for. You may, I think, very well leave Verona about the middle of September, when the great heats will be quite over, and then make the best of your way to Naples; where, I own, I want to have you by way of precaution (I hope it is rather over caution) in case of the last remains of a pulmonic disorder. The amphitheatre at Verona is worth your attention; as are also many buildings there and at Vicenza, of the famous Andrea Palladio, whose taste and style of buildings were truly antique. It would not be amiss, if you employed three or four days in learning the five orders of architecture, with their general proportions; and you may know all that you need know of them in that time. Palladio's own book of architecture is the best you can make use of for that purpose, skipping over the mechanical part of it, such as the materials, the cement, etc.

Mr. Harte tells me, that your acquaintance with the classics is renewed; the suspension of which has been so short, that I dare say it has produced no coldness. I hope and believe, you are now so much master of them, that two hours every day, uninterruptedly, for a year or two more, will make you perfectly so; and I think you cannot now allot them a greater share than that of your time, considering the many other things you have to learn and to do. You must know how to speak and write Italian perfectly; you must learn some logic, some geometry, and some astronomy; not to mention your exercises, where they are to be learned; and, above all, you must learn the world, which is not soon learned; and only to be learned by frequenting good and various companies.

Consider, therefore, how precious every moment of time is to you now. The more you apply to your business, the more you will taste your pleasures. The exercise of the mind in the morning whets the appetite for the pleasures of the evening, as much as the exercise of the body whets the appetite for dinner. Business and pleasure, rightly understood, mutually assist each other, instead of being enemies, as silly or dull people often think them. No man tastes pleasures truly, who does not earn them by previous business, and few people do business well, who do nothing else. Remember that when I speak of pleasures, I always mean the elegant pleasures of a rational being, and, not the brutal ones of a swine. I mean 'la bonne Chere', short of gluttony; wine, infinitely short of drunkenness; play, without the least gaming; and gallantry without debauchery. There is a line in all these things which men of sense, for greater security, take care to keep a good deal on the right side of; for sickness, pain, contempt and infamy, lie immediately on the other side of it. Men of sense and merit, in all other respects, may have had some of these failings; but then those few examples, instead of inviting us to imitation, should only put us the more upon our guard against such weaknesses: and whoever thinks them fashionable, will not be so himself; I have often known a fashionable man have some one vice; but I never in my life knew a vicious man a fashionable man. Vice is as degrading as it is criminal. God bless you, my dear child!

LETTER LXXVIII

LONDON, August 20, O. S. 1749.

DEAR BOY: Let us resume our reflections upon men, their characters, their manners, in a word, our reflections upon the world. They may help you to form yourself, and to know others; a knowledge very useful at all ages, very rare at yours. It seems as if it were nobody's business to communicate it to young men. Their masters teach them, singly, the languages or the sciences of their several departments; and are indeed generally incapable of teaching them the world: their parents are often so too, or at least neglect doing it, either from avocations, indifference, or from an opinion that throwing them into the world (as they call it) is the best way of teaching it them. This last notion is in a great degree true; that is, the world can doubtless never be well known by theory: practice is absolutely necessary; but surely it is of great use to a young man, before he sets out for that country full of mazes, windings, and turnings, to have at least a general map of it, made by some experienced traveler.

There is a certain dignity of manners absolutely necessary, to make even the most valuable character either respected or respectable.—[Meaning worthy of respect.]

Horse-play, romping, frequent and loud fits of laughter, jokes, waggery, and indiscriminate familiarity, will sink both merit and knowledge into a degree of contempt. They compose at most a merry fellow; and a merry fellow was never yet a respectable man. Indiscriminate familiarity either offends your superiors, or else dubbs you their dependent and led captain. It gives your inferiors just, but troublesome and improper claims of equality. A joker is near akin to a buffoon; and neither of them is the least related to wit. Whoever is admitted or sought for, in company, upon any other account than that of his merit and manners, is never respected there, but only made use of. We will have such-a-one, for he sings prettily; we will invite such-a-one to a ball, for he dances well; we will have such-a-one at supper, for he is always joking and laughing; we will ask another, because he plays deep at all games, or because he can drink a great deal. These are all vilifying distinctions, mortifying preferences, and exclude all ideas of esteem and regard. Whoever is HAD (as it is called) in company for the sake of any one thing singly, is singly that thing and will never be considered in any other light; consequently never respected, let his merits be what they will.

This dignity of manners, which I recommend so much to you, is not only as different from pride, as true courage is from blustering, or true wit from joking; but is absolutely inconsistent with it; for nothing vilifies and degrades more than pride. The pretensions of the proud man are oftener treated with sneer and contempt, than with indignation; as we offer ridiculously too little to a tradesman, who asks ridiculously too much for his goods; but we do not haggle with one who only asks a just and reasonable price.

Abject flattery and indiscriminate assentation degrade as much as indiscriminate contradiction and noisy debate disgust. But a modest assertion of one's own opinion, and a complaisant acquiescence to other people's, preserve dignity.

Vulgar, low expressions, awkward motions and address, vilify, as they imply either a very low turn of mind, or low education and low company.

Frivolous curiosity about trifles, and a laborious attention to little objects which neither require nor deserve a moment's thought, lower a man; who from thence is thought (and not unjustly) incapable of greater matters. Cardinal de Retz, very sagaciously, marked out Cardinal Chigi for a little mind, from the moment that he told him he had wrote three years with the same pen, and that it was an excellent good one still.

A certain degree of exterior seriousness in looks and motions gives dignity, without excluding wit and decent cheerfulness, which are always serious themselves. A constant smirk upon the face, and a whifing activity of the body, are strong indications of futility. Whoever is in a hurry, shows that the thing he is about is too big for him. Haste and hurry are very different things.

I have only mentioned some of those things which may, and do, in the opinion of the world, lower and sink characters, in other respects valuable enough,—but I have taken no notice of those that affect and sink the moral characters. They are sufficiently obvious. A man who has patiently been kicked may as well pretend to courage, as a man blasted by vices and crimes may to dignity of any kind. But an exterior decency and dignity of manners will even keep such a man longer from sinking, than otherwise he would be: of such consequence is the [****], even though affected and put on! Pray read frequently, and with the utmost attention, nay, get by heart, if you can, that incomparable chapter in Cicero's "Offices," upon the [****], or the Decorum. It contains whatever is necessary for the dignity of manners.

In my next I will send you a general map of courts; a region yet unexplored by you, but which you are one day to inhabit. The ways are generally crooked and full of turnings, sometimes strewed with flowers, sometimes choked up with briars; rotten ground and deep pits frequently lie concealed under a smooth and pleasing surface; all the paths are slippery, and every slip is dangerous. Sense and discretion must accompany you at your first setting out; but, notwithstanding those, till experience is your guide, you will every now and then step out of your way, or stumble.

Lady Chesterfield has just now received your German letter, for which she thanks you; she says the language is very correct; and I can plainly see that the character is well formed, not to say better than your English character. Continue to write German frequently, that it may become quite familiar to you. Adieu.

LETTER LXXIX

LONDON, August 21, O. S. 1749.

DEAR BOY: By the last letter that I received from Mr. Harte, of the 31st July, N. S., I suppose you are now either at Venice or Verona, and perfectly re covered of your late illness: which I am daily more and more convinced had no consumptive tendency; however, for some time still, 'faites comme s'il y en avoit', be regular, and live pectorally.

You will soon be at courts, where, though you will not be concerned, yet reflection and observation upon what you see and hear there may be of use to you, when hereafter you may come to be concerned in courts yourself. Nothing in courts is exactly as it appears to be; often very different; sometimes directly contrary. Interest, which is the real spring of everything there, equally creates and dissolves friendship, produces and reconciles enmities: or, rather, allows of neither real friendships nor enmities; for, as Dryden very justly observes, POLITICIANS NEITHER LOVE NOR HATE. This is so true, that you may think you connect yourself with two friends to-day, and be obliged tomorrow to make your option between them as enemies; observe, therefore, such a degree of reserve with your friends as not to put yourself in their power, if they should become your enemies; and such a degree of moderation with your enemies, as not to make it impossible for them to become your friends.

Courts are, unquestionably, the seats of politeness and good-breeding; were they not so, they would be the seats of slaughter and desolation. Those who now smile upon and embrace, would affront and stab each other, if manners did not interpose; but ambition and avarice, the two prevailing passions at courts, found dissimulation more effectual than violence; and dissimulation introduced that habit of politeness, which distinguishes the courtier from the country gentleman. In the former case the strongest body would prevail; in the latter, the strongest mind.

A man of parts and efficiency need not flatter everybody at court; but he must take great care to offend nobody personally; it being in the power of every man to hurt him, who cannot serve him. Homer supposes a chain let down from Jupiter to the earth, to connect him with mortals. There is, at all courts, a chain which connects the prince or the minister with the page of the back stairs, or the chamber-maid. The king's wife, or mistress, has an influence over him; a lover has an influence over her; the chambermaid, or the valet de chambre, has an influence over both, and so ad infinitum. You must, therefore, not break a link of that chain, by which you hope to climb up to the prince.

You must renounce courts if you will not connive at knaves, and tolerate fools. Their number makes them considerable. You should as little quarrel as connect yourself with either.

Whatever you say or do at court, you may depend upon it, will be known; the business of most of those, who crowd levees and antichambers, being to repeat all that they see or hear, and a great deal that they neither see nor hear, according as they are inclined to the persons concerned, or according to the wishes of those to whom they hope to make their court. Great caution is therefore necessary; and if, to great caution, you can join seeming frankness and openness, you will unite what Machiavel reckons very difficult but very necessary to be united; 'volto sciolto e pensieri stretti'.

Women are very apt to be mingled in court intrigues; but they deserve attention better than confidence; to hold by them is a very precarious tenure.

I am agreeably interrupted in these reflections by a letter which I have this moment received from Baron Firmian. It contains your panegyric, and with the strongest protestations imaginable that he does you only justice. I received this favorable account of you with pleasure, and I communicate it to you with as much. While you deserve praise, it is reasonable you should know that you meet with it; and I make no doubt, but that it will encourage you in persevering to deserve it. This is one paragraph of the Baron's letter: Ses moeurs dans un age si tendre, reglees selon toutes les loix d'une morale exacte et sensee; son application (that is what I like) a tout ce qui s'appelle etude serieuse, et Belles Lettres,—"Notwithstanding his great youth, his manners are regulated by the most unexceptionable rules of sense and of morality. His application THAT IS WHAT I LIKE to every kind of serious study, as well as to polite literature, without even the least appearance of ostentatious pedantry, render him worthy of your most tender affection; and I have the honor of assuring you, that everyone cannot but be pleased with the acquisition of his acquaintance or of his friendship. I have profited of it, both here and at Vienna; and shall esteem myself very happy to make use of the permission he has given me of continuing it by letter." Reputation, like health, is preserved and increased by the same means by which it is acquired. Continue to desire and deserve praise, and you will certainly find it. Knowledge, adorned by manners, will infallibly procure it. Consider, that you have but a little way further to get to your journey's end; therefore, for God's sake, do not slacken your pace; one year and a half more of sound application, Mr. Harte assures me, will finish this work; and when this work is finished well, your own will be very easily done afterward. 'Les Manieres et les Graces' are no immaterial parts of that work; and I beg that you will give as much of your attention to them as to your books. Everything depends upon them; 'senza di noi ogni fatica e vana'. The various companies you now go into will procure them you, if you will carefully observe, and form yourself upon those who have them.

Adieu! God bless you! and may you ever deserve that affection with which I am now, Yours.

LETTER LXXX

LONDON, September 5, O. S. 1749.

DEAR BOY: I have received yours from Laubach, of the 17th of August, N. S., with the inclosed for Comte Lascaris; which I have given him, and with which he is extremely pleased, as I am with your account of Carniola. I am very glad that you attend to, and inform yourself of, the political objects of the country you go through. Trade and manufactures are very considerable, not to say the most important ones; for, though armies and navies are the shining marks of the strength of countries, they would be very ill paid, and consequently fight very ill, if manufactures and commerce did not support them. You have certainly observed in Germany the inefficiency of great powers, with great tracts of country and swarms of men; which are absolutely useless, if not paid by other powers who have the resources of manufactures and commerce. This we have lately experienced to be the case of the two empresses of Germany and Russia: England, France, and Spain, must pay their respective allies, or they may as well be without them.

I have not the least objection to your taking, into the bargain, the observation of natural curiosities; they are very welcome, provided they do not take up the room of better things. But the forms of government, the maxims of policy, the strength or weakness, the trade and commerce, of the several countries you see or hear of are the important objects, which I recommend to your most minute inquiries, and most serious attention. I thought that the republic of Venice had by this time laid aside that silly and frivolous piece of policy, of endeavoring to conceal their form of government; which anybody may know, pretty nearly, by taking the pains to read four or five books, which explain all the great parts of it; and as for some of the little wheels of that machine, the knowledge of them would be as little useful to others as dangerous to themselves. Their best policy (I can tell them) is to keep quiet, and to offend no one great power, by joining with another. Their escape, after the Ligue of Cambray, should prove a useful lesson to them.

I am glad you frequent the assemblies at Venice. Have you seen Monsieur and Madame Capello, and how did they receive you? Let me know who are the ladies whose houses you frequent the most. Have you seen the Comptesse d'Orselska, Princess of Holstein? Is Comte Algarotti, who was the TENANT there, at Venice?

You will, in many parts of Italy, meet with numbers of the Pretender's people (English, Scotch, and Irish fugitives), especially at Rome; probably the Pretender himself. It is none of your business to declare war to these people, as little as it is your interest, or, I hope, your inclination, to connect yourself with them; and therefore I recommend to you a perfect neutrality. Avoid them as much as you can with decency and good manners; but when you cannot, avoid any political conversation or debates with them; tell them that you do not concern yourself with political matters: that you are neither maker nor a deposer of kings; that when you left England, you left a king in it, and have not since heard either of his death, or of any revolution that has happened; and that you take kings and kingdoms as you find them; but enter no further into matters with them, which can be of no use, and might bring on heats and quarrels. When you speak of the old Pretender, you will call him only the Chevalier de St. George;—but mention him as seldom as possible. Should he chance to speak to you at any assembly (as, I am told, he sometimes does to the English), be sure that you seem not to know him; and answer him civilly, but always either in French or in Italian; and give him, in the former, the appellation of Monsieur, and in the latter, of Signore. Should you meet with the Cardinal of York, you will be under no difficulty; for he has, as Cardinal, an undoubted right to 'Eminenza'. Upon the whole, see any of those people as little as possible; when you do see them, be civil to them, upon the footing of strangers; but never be drawn into any altercations with them about the imaginary right of their king, as they call him.

It is to no sort of purpose to talk to those people of the natural rights of mankind, and the particular constitution of this country. Blinded by prejudices, soured by misfortunes, and tempted by their necessities, they are as incapable of reasoning rightly, as they have hitherto been of acting wisely. The late Lord Pembroke never would know anything that he had not a mind to know; and, in this case, I advise you to follow his example. Never know either the father or the two sons, any otherwise than as foreigners; and so, not knowing their pretensions, you have no occasion to dispute them.

I can never help recommending to you the utmost attention and care, to acquire 'les Manieres, la Tournure, et les Graces, d'un galant homme, et d'un homme de cour'. They should appear in every look, in every action; in your address, and even in your dress, if you would either please or rise in the world. That you may do both (and both are in your power) is most ardently wished you, by Yours.

P. S. I made Comte Lascaris show me your letter, which I liked very well; the style was easy and natural, and the French pretty correct. There were so few faults in the orthography, that a little more observation of the best French authors would make you a correct master of that necessary language.

I will not conceal from you, that I have lately had extraordinary good accounts of you, from an unexpected and judicious person, who promises me that, with a little more of the world, your manners and address will equal your knowledge. This is the more pleasing to me, as those were the two articles of which I was the most doubtful. These commendations will not, I am persuaded, make you vain and coxcomical, but only encourage you to go on in the right way.

LETTER LXXXI

LONDON, September 12, O. S. 1749.

DEAR BOY: It seems extraordinary, but it is very true, that my anxiety for you increases in proportion to the good accounts which I receive of you from all hands. I promise myself so much from you, that I dread the least disappointment. You are now so near the port, which I have so long wished and labored to bring you safe into, that my concern would be doubled, should you be shipwrecked within sight of it. The object, therefore, of this letter is (laying aside all the authority of a parent) to conjure you as a friend, by the affection you have for me (and surely you have reason to have some), and by the regard you have for yourself, to go on, with assiduity and attention, to complete that work which, of late, you have carried on so well, and which is now so near being finished. My wishes and my plan were to make you shine and distinguish yourself equally in the learned and the polite world. Few have been able to do it. Deep learning is generally tainted with pedantry, or at least unadorned by manners: as, on the other hand, polite manners and the turn of the world are too often unsupported by knowledge, and consequently end contemptibly, in the frivolous dissipation of drawing-rooms and ruelles. You are now got over the dry and difficult parts of learning; what remains requires much more time than trouble. You have lost time by your illness; you must regain it now or never. I therefore most earnestly desire, for your own sake, that for these next six months, at least six hours every morning, uninterruptedly, may be inviolably sacred to your studies with Mr. Harte. I do not know whether he will require so much; but I know that I do, and hope you will, and consequently prevail with him to give you that time; I own it is a good deal: but when both you and he consider that the work will be so much better, and so much sooner done, by such an assiduous and continued application, you will, neither of you, think it too much, and each will find his account in it. So much for the mornings, which from your own good sense, and Mr. Harte's tenderness and care of you, will, I am sure, be thus well employed. It is not only reasonable, but useful too, that your evenings should be devoted to amusements and pleasures: and therefore I not only allow, but recommend, that they should be employed at assemblies, balls, SPECTACLES, and in the best companies; with this restriction only, that the consequences of the evening's diversions may not break in upon the morning's studies, by breakfastings, visits, and idle parties into the country. At your age, you need not be ashamed, when any of these morning parties are proposed, to say that you must beg to be excused, for you are obliged to devote your mornings to Mr. Harte; that I will have it so; and that you dare not do otherwise. Lay it all upon me; though I am persuaded it will be as much your own inclination as it is mine. But those frivolous, idle people, whose time hangs upon their own hands, and who desire to make others lose theirs too, are not to be reasoned with: and indeed it would be doing them too much honor. The shortest civil answers are the best; I CANNOT, I DARE NOT, instead of I WILL NOT; for if you were to enter with them into the necessity of study end the usefulness of knowledge, it would only furnish them with matter for silly jests; which, though I would not have you mind, I would not have you invite. I will suppose you at Rome studying six hours uninterruptedly with Mr. Harte, every morning, and passing your evenings with the best company of Rome, observing their manners and forming your own; and I will suppose a number of idle, sauntering, illiterate English, as there commonly is there, living entirely with one another, supping, drinking, and sitting up late at each other's lodgings; commonly in riots and scrapes when drunk, and never in good company when sober. I will take one of these pretty fellows, and give you the dialogue between him and yourself; such as, I dare say, it will be on his side; and such as, I hope, it will be on yours:—

Englishman. Will you come and breakfast with me tomorrow? there will be four or five of our countrymen; we have provided chaises, and we will drive somewhere out of town after breakfast.

Stanhope. I am very sorry I cannot; but I am obliged to be at home all morning.

Englishman. Why, then, we will come and breakfast with you.

Stanhope. I can't do that neither; I am engaged.

Englishman. Well, then, let it be the next day.

Stanhope. To tell you the truth, it can be no day in the morning; for I neither go out, nor see anybody at home before twelve.

Englishman. And what the devil do you do with yourself till twelve o'clock?

Stanhope. I am not by myself; I am with Mr. Harte.

LETTERS TO HIS SON, COMPLETE

Englishman. Then what the devil do you do with him?

Stanhope. We study different things; we read, we converse.

Englishman. Very pretty amusement indeed! Are you to take orders then?

Stanhope. Yes, my father's orders, I believe I must take.

Englishman. Why hast thou no more spirit, than to mind an old fellow a thousand miles off?

Stanhope. If I don't mind his orders he won't mind my draughts.

Englishman. What, does the old prig threaten then? threatened folks live long; never mind threats.

Stanhope. No, I can't say that he has ever threatened me in his life; but I believe I had best not provoke him.

Englishman. Pooh! you would have one angry letter from the old fellow, and there would be an end of it.

Stanhope. You mistake him mightily; he always does more than he says. He has never been angry with me yet, that I remember, in his life; but if I were to provoke him, I am sure he would never forgive me; he would be coolly immovable, and I might beg and pray, and write my heart out to no purpose.

Englishman. Why, then, he is an old dog, that's all I can say; and pray are you to obey your dry-nurse too, this same, and what's his name—Mr. Harte?

Stanhope. Yes.

Englishman. So he stuffs you all morning with Greek, and Latin, and Logic, and all that. Egad I have a dry-nurse too, but I never looked into a book with him in my life; I have not so much as seen the face of him this week, and don't care a louse if I never see it again.

Stanhope. My dry-nurse never desires anything of me that is not reasonable, and for my own good; and therefore I like to be with him.

Englishman. Very sententious and edifying, upon my word! at this rate you will be reckoned a very good young man.

Stanhope. Why, that will do me no harm.

Englishman. Will you be with us to-morrow in the evening, then? We shall be ten with you; and I have got some excellent good wine; and we'll be very merry.

Stanhope. I am very much obliged to you, but I am engaged for all the evening, to-morrow; first at Cardinal Albani's; and then to sup at the Venetian Ambassadress's.

Englishman. How the devil can you like being always with these foreigners? I never go among them with all their formalities and ceremonies. I am never easy in company with them, and I don't know why, but I am ashamed.

Stanhope. I am neither ashamed nor afraid; I am very, easy with them; they are very easy with me; I get the language, and I see their characters, by conversing with them; and that is what we are sent abroad for, is it not?

Englishman. I hate your modest women's company; your women of fashion as they call 'em; I don't know what to say to them, for my part.

Stanhope. Have you ever conversed with them?

Englishman. No; I never conversed with them; but have been sometimes in their company, though much against my will.

Stanhope. But at least they have done you no hurt; which is, probably, more than you can say of the women you do converse with.

Englishman. That's true, I own; but for all that, I would rather keep company with my surgeon half the year, than with your women of fashion the year round.

Stanhope. Tastes are different, you know, and every man follows his own.

Englishman. That's true; but thine's a devilish odd one, Stanhope. All morning with thy dry-nurse; all the evening in formal fine company; and all day long afraid of Old Daddy in England. Thou art a queer fellow, and I am afraid there is nothing to be made of thee.

Stanhope. I am afraid so too.

Englishman. Well, then, good night to you; you have no objection, I hope, to my being drunk to-night, which I certainly will be.

Stanhope. Not in the least; nor to your being sick tomorrow, which you as certainly will be; and so good night, too.

You will observe, that I have not put into your mouth those good arguments which upon such an occasion would, I am sure, occur to you; as piety and affection toward me; regard and friendship for Mr. Harte; respect for your own moral character, and for all the relative duties of man, son, pupil, and citizen. Such solid arguments would be thrown away upon such shallow puppies. Leave them to their ignorance and to their dirty, disgraceful vices. They will severely feel the effects of them, when it will be too late. Without the comfortable refuge of learning, and with all the sickness and pains of a ruined stomach, and a rotten carcass, if they happen to arrive at old age, it is an uneasy and ignominious one. The ridicule which such fellows endeavor to throw upon those who are not like them, is, in the opinion of all men of sense, the most authentic panegyric. Go on, then, my dear child, in the way you are in, only for a year and a half more: that is all I ask of you. After that, I promise that you shall be your own master, and that I will pretend to no other title than that of your best and truest friend. You shall receive advice, but no orders, from me; and in truth you will want no other advice but such as youth and inexperience must necessarily require. You shall certainly want nothing that is requisite, not only for your conveniency, but also for your pleasures; which I always desire shall be gratified. You will suppose that I mean the pleasures 'd'un honnete homme'.

While you are learning Italian, which I hope you do with diligence, pray take care to continue your German, which you may have frequent opportunities of speaking. I would also have you keep up your knowledge of the 'Jus Publicum Imperii', by looking over, now and then, those INESTIMABLE MANUSCRIPTS which Sir Charles Williams, who arrived here last week, assures me you have made upon that subject. It will be of very great use to you, when you come to be concerned in foreign affairs; as you shall be (if you qualify yourself for them) younger than ever any other was: I mean before you are twenty. Sir Charles tells me, that he will answer for your learning; and that, he believes, you will acquire that address, and those graces, which are so necessary to give it its full lustre and value. But he confesses, that he doubts more of the latter than of the former. The justice which he does Mr. Harte, in his panegyrics of him, makes me hope that there is likewise a great deal of truth in his encomiums of you. Are you pleased with, and proud of the reputation which you have already acquired? Surely you are, for I am sure I am. Will you do anything to lessen or forfeit it? Surely you will not. And will you not do all you can to extend and increase it? Surely you will. It is only going on for a year and a half longer, as you have gone on for the two years last past, and devoting half the day only to application; and you will be sure to make the earliest figure and fortune in the world, that ever man made. Adieu.

LETTER LXXXII

LONDON, September 22, O. S. 1749.

DEAR BOY: If I had faith in philters and love potions, I should suspect that you had given Sir Charles Williams some, by the manner in which he speaks of you, not only to me, but to everybody else. I will not repeat to you what he says of the extent and correctness of your knowledge, as it might either make you vain, or persuade you that you had already enough of what nobody can have too much. You will easily imagine how many questions I asked, and how narrowly I sifted him upon your subject; he answered me, and I dare say with truth, just as I could have wished; till satisfied entirely with his accounts of your character and learning, I inquired into other matters, intrinsically indeed of less consequence, but still of great consequence to every man, and of more to you than to almost any man: I mean, your address, manners, and air. To these questions, the same truth which he had observed before, obliged him to give me much less satisfactory answers. And as he thought himself, in friendship both to you and me, obliged to tell me the disagreeable as well as the agreeable truths, upon the same principle I think myself obliged to repeat them to you.

He told me then, that in company you were frequently most PROVOKINGLY inattentive, absent; and distrait; that you came into a room, and presented yourself, very awkwardly; that at table you constantly threw down knives, forks, napkins, bread, etc., and that you neglected your person and dress, to a degree unpardonable at any age, and much more so at yours.

These things, howsoever immaterial they may seem to people who do not know the world, and the nature of mankind, give me, who know them to be exceedingly material, very great concern. I have long distrusted you, and therefore frequently admonished you, upon these articles; and I tell you plainly, that I shall not be easy till I hear a very different account of them. I know no one thing more offensive to a company than that inattention and DISTRACTION. It is showing them the utmost contempt; and people never forgive contempt. No man is distrait with the man he fears, or the woman he loves; which is a proof that every man can get the better of that DISTRACTION, when he thinks it worth his while to do so; and, take my word for it, it is always worth his while. For my own part, I would rather be in company with a dead man, than with an absent one; for if the dead man gives me no pleasure; at least he shows me no contempt; whereas, the absent man, silently indeed, but very plainly, tells me that he does not think me worth his attention. Besides, can an absent man make any observations upon the characters customs, and manners of the company? No. He may be in the best companies all his lifetime (if they will admit him, which, if I were they, I would not) and never be one jot the wiser. I never will converse with an absent man; one may as well talk to a deaf one. It is, in truth, a practical blunder, to address ourselves to a man who we see plainly neither hears, minds, or understands us. Moreover, I aver that no man is, in any degree, fit for either business or conversation, who cannot and does not direct and command his attention to the present object, be that what it will. You know, by experience, that I grudge no expense in your education, but I will positively not keep you a Flapper. You may read, in Dr. Swift, the description of these flappers, and the use they were of to your friends the Laputans; whose minds (Gulliver says) are so taken up with intense speculations, that they neither can speak nor attend to the discourses of others, without being roused by some external traction upon the organs of speech and hearing; for which reason, those people who are able to afford it, always keep a flapper in their family, as one of their domestics; nor ever walk about, or make visits without him. This flapper is likewise employed diligently to attend his master in his walks; and, upon occasion, to give a soft flap upon his eyes, because he is always so wrapped up in cogitation, that he is in manifest danger of falling down every precipice, and bouncing his head against every post, and, in the streets, of jostling others, or being jostled into the kennel himself. If CHRISTIAN will undertake this province into the bargain, with all my heart; but I will not allow him any increase of wages upon that score. In short, I give you fair warning, that, when we meet, if you are absent in mind, I will soon be absent in body; for it will be impossible for me to stay in the room; and if at table you throw down your knife, plate, bread, etc., and hack the wing of a chicken for half an hour, without being able to cut it off, and your sleeve all the time in another dish, I must rise from the table to escape the fever you would certainly give me. Good God! how I should be shocked, if you came into my room, for the first time, with two left legs, presenting yourself with all the graces and dignity of a tailor, and your clothes hanging upon you, like those in Monmouth street, upon tenter-hooks! whereas, I expect, nay, require, to see you present yourself with the easy and genteel air of a man of fashion, who has kept good company. I expect you not only well dressed but very well dressed; I expect a gracefulness in all your motions, and something particularly engaging in your address, All this I expect, and all this it is in your power, by care and attention, to make me find; but to tell you the plain truth, if I do not find it, we shall not converse very much together; for I cannot stand inattention and awkwardness; it would endanger my health. You have often seen, and I have as often made you observe L——'s distinguished inattention and awkwardness. Wrapped up, like a Laputan, in intense thought, and possibly sometimes in no thought at all (which, I believe, is very often the case with absent people), he does not know his most intimate acquaintance by sight, or answers them as if he were at cross purposes. He leaves his hat in one room, his sword in another, and would leave his shoes in a third, if his buckles, though awry, did not save them: his legs and arms, by his awkward management of them, seem to have undergone the question extraordinaire; and his head, always hanging upon one or other of his shoulders, seems to have received the first stroke upon a block. I sincerely value and esteem him for his parts, learning, and virtue; but, for the soul of me, I cannot love him in company. This will be universally the case, in common life, of every inattentive, awkward man, let his real merit and knowledge be ever so great. When I was of your age, I desired to shine, as far as I was able, in every part of life; and was as attentive to my manners, my dress, and my air, in company of evenings, as to my books and my tutor in the mornings. A young fellow should be ambitious to shine in everything—and, of the two, always rather overdo than underdo. These things are by no means trifles: they are of infinite consequence to those who are to be thrown into the great world, and who would make a figure or a fortune in it. It is not sufficient to deserve well; one must please well too. Awkward, disagreeable merit will never carry anybody far. Wherever you find a good dancing-master, pray let him put you upon your haunches; not so much for the sake of dancing, as for coming into a room, and presenting yourself genteelly and gracefully. Women, whom you ought to endeavor to please, cannot forgive vulgar and awkward air and gestures; 'il leur faut du brillant'. The generality of men are pretty like them, and are equally taken by the same exterior graces.

I am very glad that you have received the diamond buckles safe; all I desire in return for them is, that they may be buckled even upon your feet, and that your stockings may not hide them. I should be sorry that you were an egregious fop; but, I protest, that of the two, I would rather have you a fop than a sloven. I think negligence in my own dress, even at my age, when certainly I expect no advantages from my dress, would be indecent with regard to others. I have done with fine clothes; but I will have my plain clothes fit me, and made like other people's: In the evenings, I recommend to you the company of women of fashion, who have a right to attention and will be paid it. Their company will smooth your manners, and give you a habit of attention and respect, of which you will find the advantage among men.

My plan for you, from the beginning, has been to make you shine equally in the learned and in the polite world; the former part is almost completed to my wishes, and will, I am persuaded, in a little time more, be quite so. The latter part is still in your power to complete; and I flatter myself that you will do it, or else the former part will avail you very little; especially in your department, where the exterior address and graces do half the business; they must be the harbingers of your merit, or your merit will be very coldly received; all can, and do judge of the former, few of the latter.

Mr. Harte tells me that you have grown very much since your illness; if you get up to five feet ten, or even nine inches, your figure will probably be a good one; and if well dressed and genteel, will probably please; which is a much greater advantage to a man than people commonly think. Lord Bacon calls it a letter of recommendation.

I would wish you to be the omnis homo, 'l'homme universel'. You are nearer it, if you please, than ever anybody was at your age; and if you will but, for the course of this next year only, exert your whole attention to your studies in the morning, and to your address, manners, air and tournure in the evenings, you will be the man I wish you, and the man that is rarely seen.

Our letters go, at best, so irregularly, and so often miscarry totally, that for greater security I repeat the same things. So, though I acknowledged by last post Mr. Harte's letter of the 8th September, N. S., I acknowledge it again by this to you. If this should find you still at Verona, let it inform you that I wish you would set out soon for Naples; unless Mr. Harte should think it better for you to stay at Verona, or any other place on this side Rome, till you go there for the Jubilee. Nay, if he likes it better, I am very willing that you should go directly from Verona to Rome; for you cannot have too much of Rome, whether upon account of the language, the curiosities, or the company. My only reason for mentioning Naples, is for the sake of the climate, upon account of your health; but if Mr. Harte thinks that your health is now so well restored as to be above climate, he may steer your course wherever he thinks proper: and, for aught I know, your going directly to Rome, and consequently staying there so much the longer, may be as well as anything else. I think you and I cannot put our affairs in better hands than in Mr. Harte's; and I will stake his infallibility against the Pope's, with some odds on his side. Apropos of the Pope: remember to be presented to him before you leave Rome, and go through the necessary ceremonies for it, whether of kissing his slipper or his b——h; for I would never deprive myself of anything that I wanted to do or see, by refusing to comply with an established custom. When I was in Catholic countries, I never declined kneeling in their churches at the elevation, nor elsewhere, when the Host went by. It is a complaisance due to the custom of the place, and by no means, as some silly people have imagined, an implied approbation of their doctrine. Bodily attitudes and situations are things so very indifferent in themselves, that I would quarrel with nobody about them. It may, indeed, be improper for Mr. Harte to pay that tribute of complaisance, upon account of his character.

This letter is a very long, and possibly a very tedious one; but my anxiety for your perfection is so great, and particularly at this critical and decisive period of your life, that I am only afraid of omitting, but never of repeating, or dwelling too long upon anything that I think may be of the least use to you. Have the same anxiety for yourself, that I have for you, and all will do well. Adieu! my dear child.

LETTER LXXXIII

LONDON, September 27, O. S. 1749.

DEAR BOY: A vulgar, ordinary way of thinking, acting, or speaking, implies a low education, and a habit of low company. Young people contract it at school, or among servants, with whom they are too often used to converse; but after they frequent good company, they must want attention and observation very much, if they do not lay it quite aside; and, indeed, if they do not, good company will be very apt to lay them aside. The various kinds of vulgarisms are infinite; I cannot pretend to point them out to you; but I will give some samples, by which you may guess at the rest.

A vulgar man is captious and jealous; eager and impetuous about trifles. He suspects himself to be slighted, thinks everything that is said meant at him: if the company happens to laugh, he is persuaded they laugh at him; he grows angry and testy, says something very impertinent, and draws himself into a scrape, by showing what he calls a proper spirit, and asserting himself. A man of fashion does not suppose himself to be either the sole or principal object of the thoughts, looks, or words of the company; and never suspects that he is either slighted or laughed at, unless he is conscious that he deserves it. And if (which very seldom happens) the company is absurd or ill-bred enough to do either, he does not care twopence, unless the insult be so gross and plain as to require satisfaction of another kind. As he is above trifles, he is never vehement and eager about them; and, wherever they are concerned, rather acquiesces than wrangles. A vulgar man's conversation always savors strongly of the lowness of his education and company. It turns chiefly upon his domestic affairs, his servants, the excellent order he keeps in his own family, and the little anecdotes of the neighborhood; all which he relates with emphasis, as interesting matters. He is a man gossip.

Vulgarism in language is the next and distinguishing characteristic of bad company and a bad education. A man of fashion avoids nothing with more care than that. Proverbial expressions and trite sayings are the flowers of the rhetoric of a vulgar man. Would he say that men differ in their tastes; he both supports and adorns that opinion by the good old saying, as he respectfully calls it, that WHAT IS ONE MAN'S MEAT, IS ANOTHER MAN'S POISON. If anybody attempts being SMART, as he calls it, upon him, he gives them TIT FOR TAT, aye, that he does. He has always some favorite word for the time being; which, for the sake of using often, he commonly abuses. Such as VASTLY angry, VASTLY kind, VASTLY handsome, and VASTLY ugly. Even his pronunciation of proper words carries the mark of the beast along with it. He calls the earth YEARTH; he is OBLEIGED, not OBLIGED to you. He goes TO WARDS, and not TOWARDS, such a place. He sometimes affects hard words, by way of ornament, which he always mangles like a learned woman. A man of fashion never has recourse to proverbs and vulgar aphorisms; uses neither favorite words nor hard words; but takes great care to speak very correctly and grammatically, and to pronounce properly; that is, according to the usage of the best companies.

An awkward address, ungraceful attitudes and actions, and a certain left-handedness (if I may use that word), loudly proclaim low education and low company; for it is impossible to suppose that a man can have frequented good company, without having catched something, at least, of their air and motions. A new raised man is distinguished in a regiment by his awkwardness; but he must be impenetrably dull, if, in a month or two's time, he cannot perform at least the common manual exercise, and look like a soldier. The very accoutrements of a man of fashion are grievous encumbrances to a vulgar man. He is at a loss what to do with his hat, when it is not upon his head; his cane (if unfortunately he wears one) is at perpetual war with every cup of tea or coffee he drinks; destroys them first, and then accompanies them in their fall. His sword is formidable only to his own legs, which would possibly carry him fast enough out of the way of any sword but his own. His clothes fit him so ill, and constrain him so much, that he seems rather, their prisoner than their proprietor. He presents himself in company like a criminal in a court of justice; his very air condemns him; and people of fashion will no more connect themselves with the one, than people of character will with the other. This repulse drives and sinks him into low company; a gulf from whence no man, after a certain age, ever emerged.

'Les manieres nobles et aisees, la tournure d'un homme de condition, le ton de la bonne compagnie, les graces, le jeune sais quoi, qui plait', are as necessary to adorn and introduce your intrinsic merit and knowledge, as the polish is to the diamond; which, without that polish, would never be worn, whatever it might weigh. Do not imagine that these accomplishments are only useful with women; they are much more so with men. In a public assembly, what an advantage has a graceful speaker, with genteel motions, a handsome figure, and a liberal air, over one who shall speak full as much good sense, but destitute of these ornaments? In business, how prevalent are the graces, how detrimental is the want of them? By the help of these I have known some men refuse favors less offensively than others granted them. The utility of them in courts and negotiations is inconceivable. You gain the hearts, and consequently the secrets, of nine in ten, that you have to do with, in spite even of their prudence; which will, nine times in ten, be the dupe of their hearts and of their senses. Consider the importance of these things as they deserve, and you will not lose one minute in the pursuit of them.

You are traveling now in a country once so famous both for arts and arms, that (however degenerate at present) it still deserves your attention and reflection. View it therefore with care, compare its former with its present state, and examine into the causes of its rise and its decay. Consider it classically and politically, and do not run through it, as too many of your young countrymen do, musically, and (to use a ridiculous word) KNICK-KNACKICALLY. No piping nor fiddling, I beseech you; no days lost in poring upon almost imperceptible 'intaglios and cameos': and do not become a virtuoso of small wares. Form a taste of painting, sculpture, and architecture, if you please, by a careful examination of the works of the best ancient and modern artists; those are liberal arts, and a real taste and knowledge of them become a man of fashion very well. But, beyond certain bounds, the man of taste ends, and the frivolous virtuoso begins.

Your friend Mendes, the good Samaritan, dined with me yesterday. He has more good-nature and generosity than parts. However, I will show him all the civilities that his kindness to you so justly deserves. He tells me that you are taller than I am, which I am very glad of: I desire that you may excel me in everything else too; and, far from repining, I shall rejoice at your superiority. He commends your friend Mr. Stevens extremely; of whom too I have heard so good a character from other people, that I am very glad of your connection with him. It may prove of use to you hereafter. When you meet with such sort of Englishmen abroad, who, either from their parts or their rank, are likely to make a figure at home, I would advise you to cultivate them, and get their favorable testimony of you here, especially those who are to return to England before you. Sir Charles Williams has puffed you (as the mob call it) here extremely. If three or four more people of parts do the same, before you come back, your first appearance in London will be to great advantage. Many people do, and indeed ought, to take things upon trust; many more do, who need not; and few dare dissent from an established opinion. Adieu!

LETTER LXXXIV

LONDON, October 2, O. S. 1749.

DEAR BOY: I received by the last post your letter of the 22d September, N. S., but I have not received that from Mr. Harte to which you refer, and which you say contained your reasons for leaving Verona, and returning to Venice; so that I am entirely ignorant of them. Indeed the irregularity and negligence of the post provoke me, as they break the thread of the accounts I want to receive from you, and of the instructions and orders which I send you, almost every post. Of these last twenty posts.

I am sure that I have wrote eighteen, either to you or to Mr. Harte, and it does not appear by your letter, that all or even any of my letters have been received. I desire for the future, that both you and Mr. Harte will constantly, in your letters, mention the dates of mine. Had it not been for their miscarriage, you would not have, been in the uncertainty you seem to be in at present, with regard to your future motions. Had you received my letters, you would have been by this time at Naples: but we must now take things where they are.

Upon the receipt, then, of this letter, you will as soon as conveniently you can, set out for Rome; where you will not arrive too long before the jubilee, considering the difficulties of getting lodgings, and other accommodations there at this time. I leave the choice of the route to you; but I do by no means intend that you should leave Rome after the jubilee, as you seem to hint in your letter: on the contrary, I will have Rome your headquarters for six months at least; till you shall have, in a manner, acquired the 'Jus Civitatis' there. More things are to be seen and learned there, than in any other town in Europe; there are the best masters to instruct, and the best companies to polish you. In the spring you may make (if you please) frequent excursions to Naples; but Rome must still be your headquarters, till the heats of June drive you from thence to some other place in Italy, which we shall think of by that time. As to the expense which you mention, I do not regard it in the least; from your infancy to this day, I never grudged any expense in your education, and still less do it now, that it is become more important and decisive: I attend to the objects of your expenses, but not to the sums. I will certainly not pay one shilling for your losing your nose, your money, or your reason; that is, I will not contribute to women, gaming, and drinking. But I will most cheerfully supply, not only every necessary, but every decent expense you can make. I do not care what the best masters cost. I would have you as well dressed, lodged, and attended, as any reasonable man of fashion is in his travels. I would have you have that pocket-money that should enable you to make the proper expense 'd'un honnete homme'. In short, I bar no expense, that has neither vice nor folly for its object; and under those two reasonable restrictions, draw, and welcome.

As for Turin, you may go there hereafter, as a traveler, for a month or two; but you cannot conveniently reside there as an academician, for reasons which I have formerly communicated to Mr. Harte, and which Mr. Villettes, since his return here, has shown me in a still stronger light than he had done by his letters from Turin, of which I sent copies to Mr. Harte, though probably he never received them.

After you have left Rome, Florence is one of the places with which you should be thoroughly acquainted. I know that there is a great deal of gaming there; but, at the same time, there are in every place some people whose fortunes are either too small, or whose understandings are too good to allow them to play for anything above trifles; and with those people you will associate yourself, if you have not (as I am assured you have not, in the least) the spirit of gaming in you. Moreover, at suspected places, such as Florence, Turin, and Paris, I shall be more attentive to your draughts, and such as exceed a proper and handsome expense will not be answered; for I can easily know whether you game or not without being told.

Mr. Harte will determine your route to Rome as he shall think best; whether along the coast of the Adriatic, or that of the Mediterranean, it is equal to me; but you will observe to come back a different way from that you went.

Since your health is so well restored, I am not sorry that you have returned to Venice, for I love capitals. Everything is best at capitals; the best masters, the best companions, and the best manners. Many other places are worth seeing, but capitals only are worth residing at. I am very glad that Madame Capello received you so well. Monsieur I was sure would: pray assure them both of my respects, and of my sensibility of their kindness to you. Their house will be a very good one for you at Rome; and I would advise you to be domestic in it if you can. But Madame, I can tell you, requires great attentions. Madame Micheli has written a very favorable account of you to my friend the Abbe Grossa Testa, in a letter which he showed me, and in which there are so many civil things to myself, that I would wish to tell her how much I think myself obliged to her. I approve very much of the allotment of your time at Venice; pray go on so for a twelvemonth at least, wherever you are. You will find your own account in it.

I like your last letter, which gives me an account of yourself, and your own transactions; for though I do not recommend the EGOTISM to you, with regard to anybody else, I desire that you will use it with me, and with me only. I interest myself in all that you do; and as yet (excepting Mr. Harte) nobody else does. He must of course know all, and I desire to know a great deal.

I am glad you have received, and that you like the diamond buckles. I am very willing that you should make, but very unwilling that you should CUT a figure with them at the jubilee; the CUTTING A FIGURE being the very lowest vulgarism in the English language; and equal in elegancy to Yes, my Lady, and No, my Lady. The word VAST and VASTLY, you will have found by my former letter that I had proscribed out of the diction of a gentleman, unless in their proper signification of sizes and BULK. Not only in language, but in everything else, take great care that the first impressions you give of yourself may be not only favorable, but pleasing, engaging, nay, seducing. They are often decisive; I confess they are a good deal so with me: and I cannot wish for further acquaintance with a man whose first 'abord' and address displease me.

So many of my letters have miscarried, and I know so little which, that I am forced to repeat the same thing over and over again eventually. This is one. I have wrote twice to Mr. Harte, to have your picture drawn in miniature, while you were at Venice; and send it me in a letter: it is all one to me whether in enamel or in watercolors, provided it is but very like you. I would have you drawn exactly as you are, and in no whimsical dress: and I lay more stress upon the likeness of the picture, than upon the taste and skill of the painter. If this be not already done, I desire that you will have it done forthwith before you leave Venice; and inclose it in a letter to me, which letter, for greater security, I would have you desire Sir James Gray to inclose in his packet to the office; as I, for the same, reason, send this under his cover. If the picture be done upon vellum, it will be the most portable. Send me, at the same time, a thread of silk of your own length exactly. I am solicitous about your figure; convinced, by a thousand instances, that a good one is a real advantage. 'Mens sana in corpore sano', is the first and greatest blessing. I would add 'et pulchro', to complete it. May you have that and every other! Adieu.

Have you received my letters of recommendation to Cardinal Albani and the Duke de Nivernois, at Rome?

LETTER LXXXV

LONDON, October 9, O. S. 1749.

DEAR BOY: If this letter finds you at all, of which I am very doubtful, it will find you at Venice, preparing for your journey to Rome; which, by my last letter to Mr. Harte, I advised you to make along the coast of the Adriatic, through Rimini, Loretto, Ancona, etc., places that are all worth seeing; but not worth staying at. And such I reckon all places where the eyes only are employed. Remains of antiquity, public buildings, paintings, sculptures, etc., ought to be seen, and that with a proper degree of attention; but this is soon done, for they are only outsides. It is not so with more important objects; the insides of which must be seen; and they require and deserve much more attention. The characters, the heads, and the hearts of men, are the useful science of which I would have you perfect master. That science is best taught and best learned in capitals, where every human passion has its object, and exerts all its force or all its art in the pursuit. I believe there is no place in the world, where every passion is busier, appears in more shapes, and is conducted with more art, than at Rome. Therefore, when you are there, do not imagine that the Capitol, the Vatican, and the Pantheon, are the principal objects of your curiosity. But for one minute that you bestow upon those, employ ten days in informing yourself of the nature of that government, the rise and decay of the papal power, the politics of that court, the 'Brigues' of the cardinals, the tricks of the Conclaves; and, in general, everything that relates to the interior of that extraordinary government, founded originally upon the ignorance and superstition of mankind, extended by the weakness of some princes, and the ambition of others; declining of late in proportion as knowledge has increased; and owing its present precarious security, not to the religion, the affection, or the fear of the temporal powers, but to the jealousy of each other. The Pope's excommunications are no longer dreaded; his indulgences little solicited, and sell very cheap; and his territories formidable to no power, are coveted by many, and will, most undoubtedly, within a century, be scantled out among the great powers, who have now a footing in Italy, whenever they can agree upon the division of the bear's skin. Pray inform yourself thoroughly of the history of the popes and the popedom; which, for many centuries, is interwoven with the history of all Europe. Read the best authors who treat of these matters, and especially Fra Paolo, 'De Beneficiis', a short, but very material book. You will find at Rome some of all the religious orders in the Christian world. Inform yourself carefully of their origin, their founders, their rules, their reforms, and even their dresses: get acquainted with some of all of them, but particularly with the Jesuits; whose society I look upon to be the most able and best governed society in the world. Get acquainted, if you can, with their General, who always resides at Rome; and who, though he has no seeming power out of his own society, has (it may be) more real influence over the whole world, than any temporal prince in it. They have almost engrossed the education of youth; they are, in general, confessors to most of the princes of Europe; and they are the principal missionaries out of it; which three articles give them a most extensive influence and solid advantages; witness their settlement in Paraguay. The Catholics in general declaim against that society; and yet are all governed by individuals of it. They have, by turns, been banished, and with infamy, almost every country in Europe; and have always found means to be restored, even with triumph. In short, I know no government in the world that is carried on upon such deep principles of policy, I will not add morality. Converse with them, frequent them, court them; but know them.

Inform yourself, too, of that infernal court, the Inquisition; which, though not so considerable at Rome as in Spain and Portugal, will, however, be a good sample to you of what the villainy of some men can contrive, the folly of others receive, and both together establish, in spite of the first natural principles of reason, justice, and equity.

These are the proper and useful objects of the attention of a man of sense, when he travels; and these are the objects for which I have sent you abroad; and I hope you will return thoroughly informed of them.

I receive this very moment Mr. Harte's letter of the 1st October, N. S., but I never received his former, to which he refers in this, and you refer in your last; in which he gave me the reasons for your leaving Verona so soon; nor have I ever received that letter in which your case was stated by your physicians. Letters to and from me have worse luck than other people's; for you have written to me, and I to you, for these last three months, by way of Germany, with as little success as before.

I am edified with your morning applications, and your evening gallantries at Venice, of which Mr. Harte gives me an account. Pray go on with both there, and afterward at Rome; where, provided you arrive in the beginning of December, you may stay at Venice as much longer as you please.

Make my compliments to Sir James Gray and Mr. Smith, with my acknowledgments for the great civilities they show you.

I wrote to Mr. Harte by the last post, October the 6th, O. S., and will write to him in a post or two upon the contents of his last. Adieu! 'Point de distractions'; and remember the GRACES.

LETTER LXXXVI

LONDON, October 17, O. S. 1749.

DEAR BOY: I have at last received Mr. Harte's letter of the 19th September, N. S., from Verona. Your reasons for leaving that place were very good ones; and as you stayed there long enough to see what was to be seen, Venice (as a capital) is, in my opinion, a much better place for your residence. Capitals are always the seats of arts and sciences, and the best companies. I have stuck to them all my lifetime, and I advise you to do so too.

You will have received in my three or four last letters my directions for your further motions to another capital, where I propose that your stay shall be pretty considerable. The expense, I am well aware, will be so too; but that, as I told you before, will have no weight when your improvement and advantage are in the other scale. I do not care a groat what it is, if neither vice nor folly are the objects of it, and if Mr. Harte gives his sanction.

I am very well pleased with your account of Carniola; those are the kind of objects worthy of your inquiries and knowledge. The produce, the taxes, the trade, the manufactures, the strength, the weakness, the government of the several countries which a man of sense travels through, are the material points to which he attends; and leaves the steeples, the market-places, and the signs, to the laborious and curious researches of Dutch and German travelers.

Mr. Harte tells me, that he intends to give you, by means of Signor Vicentini, a general notion of civil and military architecture; with which I am very well pleased. They are frequent subjects of conversation; and it is very right that you should have some idea of the latter, and a good taste of the former; and you may very soon learn as much as you need know of either. If you read about one-third of Palladio's book of architecture with some skillful person, and then, with that person, examine the best buildings by those rules, you will know the different proportions of the different orders; the several diameters of their columns; their intercolumniations, their several uses, etc. The Corinthian Order is chiefly used in magnificent buildings, where ornament and decoration are the principal objects; the Doric is calculated for strength, and the Ionic partakes of the Doric strength, and of the Corinthian ornaments. The Composite and the Tuscan orders are more modern, and were unknown to the Greeks; the one is too light, the other too clumsy. You may soon be acquainted with the considerable parts of civil architecture; and for the minute and mechanical parts of it, leave them to masons, bricklayers, and Lord Burlington, who has, to a certain extent, lessened himself by knowing them too well. Observe the same method as to military architecture; understand the terms, know the general rules, and then see them in execution with some skillful person. Go with some engineer or old officer, and view with care the real fortifications of some strong place; and you will get a clearer idea of bastions, half-moons, horn-works, ravelins, glacis, etc., than all the masters in the world could give you upon paper. And thus much I would, by all means, have you know of both civil and military architecture.

I would also have you acquire a liberal taste of the two liberal arts of painting and sculpture; but without descending into those minutia, which our modern virtuosi most affectedly dwell upon. Observe the great parts attentively; see if nature be truly represented; if the passions are strongly expressed; if the characters are preserved; and leave the trifling parts, with their little jargon, to affected puppies. I would advise you also, to read the history of the painters and sculptors, and I know none better than Felibien's. There are many in Italian; you will inform yourself which are the best. It is a part of history very entertaining, curious enough, and not quite useless. All these sort of things I would have you know, to a certain degree; but remember, that they must only be the amusements, and not the business of a man of parts.

Since writing to me in German would take up so much of your time, of which I would not now have one moment wasted, I will accept of your composition, and content myself with a moderate German letter once a fortnight, to Lady Chesterfield or Mr. Gravenkop. My meaning was only that you should not forget what you had already learned of the German language and character; but, on the contrary, that by frequent use it should grow more easy and familiar. Provided you take care of that, I do not care by what means: but I do desire that you will every day of your life speak German to somebody or other (for you will meet with Germans enough), and write a line or two of it every day to keep your hand in. Why should you not (for instance) write your little memorandums and accounts in that language and character? by which, too, you would have this advantage into the bargain, that, if mislaid, few but yourself could read them.

I am extremely glad to hear that you like the assemblies at Venice well enough to sacrifice some suppers to them; for I hear that you do not dislike your suppers neither. It is therefore plain, that there is somebody or something at those assemblies, which you like better than your meat. And as I know that there is none but good company at those assemblies, I am very glad to find that you like good company so well. I already imagine that you are a little, smoothed by it; and that you have either reasoned yourself, or that they have laughed you out of your absences and DISTRACTIONS; for I cannot suppose that you go there to insult them. I likewise imagine, that you wish to be welcome where you wish to go; and consequently, that you both present and behave yourself there 'en galant homme, et pas in bourgeois'.

If you have vowed to anybody there one of those eternal passions which I have sometimes known, by great accident, last three months, I can tell you that without great attention, infinite politeness, and engaging air and manners, the omens will be sinister, and the goddess unpropitious. Pray tell me what are the amusements of those assemblies? Are they little commercial play, are they music, are they 'la belle conversation', or are they all three? 'Y file-t-on le parfait amour? Y debite-t-on les beaux sentiments? Ou est-ce yu'on y parle Epigramme? And pray which is your department? 'Tutis depone in auribus'. Whichever it is, endeavor to shine and excel in it. Aim at least at the perfection of everything that is worth doing at all; and you will come nearer it than you would imagine; but those always crawl infinitely short of it whose aim is only mediocrity.
Adieu.

P. S. By an uncommon diligence of the post, I have this moment received yours of the 9th, N. S.

LETTER LXXXVII

LONDON, October 24, O. S. 1749.

DEAR BOY: By my last I only acknowledged, by this I answer, your letter of the 9th October, N. S.

I am very glad that you approved of my letter of September the 12th, O. S., because it is upon that footing that I always propose living with you. I will advise you seriously, as a friend of some experience, and I will converse with you cheerfully as a companion; the authority of a parent shall forever be laid aside; for, wherever it is exerted, it is useless; since, if you have neither sense nor sentiments enough to follow my advice as a friend, your unwilling obedience to my orders as a father will be a very awkward and unavailing one both to yourself and me. Tacitus, speaking of an army that awkwardly and unwillingly obeyed its generals only from the fear of punishment, says, they obeyed indeed, 'Sed ut qua mallent jussa Imperatorum interpretari, quam exequi'. For my own part, I disclaim such obedience.

You think, I find, that you do not understand Italian; but I can tell you, that, like the 'Bourgeois Gentilhomme', who spoke prose without knowing it, you understand a great deal, though you do not know that you do; for whoever understands French and Latin so well as you do, understands at least half the Italian language, and has very little occasion for a dictionary. And for the idioms, the phrases, and the delicacies of it, conversation and a little attention will teach them you, and that soon; therefore, pray speak it in company, right or wrong, 'a tort ou a travers', as soon as ever you have got words enough to ask a common question, or give a common answer. If you can only say 'buon giorno', say it, instead of saying 'bon jour', I mean to every Italian; the answer to it will teach you more words, and insensibly you will be very soon master of that easy language. You are quite right in not neglecting your German for it, and in thinking that it will be of more use to you; it certainly will, in the course of your business; but Italian has its use too, and is an ornament into the bargain; there being many very polite and good authors in that language. The reason you assign for having hitherto met with none of my swarms of Germans in Italy, is a very solid one; and I can easily conceive, that the expense necessary for a traveler must amount to a number of thalers, groschen, and kreutzers, tremendous to a German fortune. However, you will find several at Rome, either ecclesiastics, or in the suite of the Imperial Minister; and more, when you come into the Milanese, among the Queen of Hungary's officers. Besides, you have a Saxon servant, to whom I hope you speak nothing but German.

I have had the most obliging letter in the world from Monsieur Capello, in which he speaks very advantageously of you, and promises you his protection at Rome. I have wrote him an answer by which I hope I have domesticated you at his hotel there; which I advise you to frequent as much as you can. 'Il est vrai qui'il ne paie pas beaucaup de sa figure'; but he has sense and knowledge at bottom, with a great experience of business, having been already Ambassador at Madrid, Vienna, and London. And I am very sure that he will be willing to give you any informations, in that way, that he can.

Madame was a capricious, whimsical, fine lady, till the smallpox, which she got here, by lessening her beauty, lessened her humors too; but, as I presume it did not change her sex, I trust to that for her having such a share of them left, as may contribute to smooth and polish you. She, doubtless, still thinks that she has beauty enough remaining to entitle her to the attentions always paid to beauty; and she has certainly rank enough to require respect. Those are the sort of women who polish a young man the most, and who give him that habit of complaisance, and that flexibility and versatility of manners which prove of great use to him with men, and in the course of business.

You must always expect to hear, more or less, from me, upon that important subject of manners, graces, address, and that undefinable 'je ne sais quoi' that ever pleases. I have reason to believe that you want nothing else; but I have reason to fear too, that you want those: and that want will keep you poor in the midst of all the plenty of knowledge which you may have treasured up. Adieu.

LETTER LXXXVIII

LONDON, November 3, O. S. 1749.

DEAR BOY: From the time that you have had life, it has been the principle and favorite object of mine, to make you as perfect as the imperfections of human nature will allow: in this view, I have grudged no pains nor expense in your education; convinced that education, more than nature, is the cause of that great difference which you see in the characters of men. While you were a child, I endeavored to form your heart habitually to virtue and honor, before your understanding was capable of showing you their beauty and utility. Those principles, which you then got, like your grammar rules, only by rote, are now, I am persuaded, fixed and confirmed by reason. And indeed they are so plain and clear, that they require but a very moderate degree of understanding, either to comprehend or practice them. Lord Shaftesbury says, very prettily, that he would be virtuous for his own sake, though nobody were to know it; as he would be clean for his own sake, though nobody were to see him. I have therefore, since you have had the use of your reason, never written to you upon those subjects: they speak best for themselves; and I should now just as soon think of warning you gravely not to fall into the dirt or the fire, as into dishonor or vice. This view of mine, I consider as fully attained. My next object was sound and useful learning. My own care first, Mr. Harte's afterward, and OF LATE (I will own it to your praise) your own application, have more than answered my expectations in that particular; and, I have reason to believe, will answer even my wishes. All that remains for me then to wish, to recommend, to inculcate, to order, and to insist upon, is good-breeding; without which, all your other qualifications will be lame, unadorned, and to a certain degree unavailing. And here I fear, and have too much reason to believe, that you are greatly deficient. The remainder of this letter, therefore, shall be (and it will not be the last by a great many) upon that subject.

A friend of yours and mine has very justly defined good-breeding to be, THE RESULT OF MUCH GOOD SENSE, SOME GOOD NATURE, AND A LITTLE SELF-DENIAL FOR THE SAKE OF OTHERS, AND WITH A VIEW TO OBTAIN THE SAME INDULGENCE FROM THEM. Taking this for granted (as I think it cannot be disputed), it is astonishing to me that anybody who has good sense and good nature (and I believe you have both), can essentially fail in good-breeding. As to the modes of it, indeed, they vary according to persons, and places, and circumstances; and are only to be acquired by observation and experience: but the substance of it is everywhere and eternally the same. Good manners are, to particular societies, what good morals are to society in general; their cement and their security. And, as laws are enacted to enforce good morals, or at least to prevent the ill effects of bad ones; so there are certain rules of civility, universally implied and received, to enforce good manners and punish bad ones. And, indeed, there seems to me to be less difference, both between the crimes and between the punishments than at first one would imagine. The immoral man, who invades another man's property, is justly hanged for it; and the ill-bred man, who, by his ill-manners, invades and disturbs the quiet and comforts of private life, is by common consent as justly banished society. Mutual complaisances, attentions, and sacrifices of little conveniences, are as natural an implied compact between civilized people, as protection and obedience are between kings and subjects; whoever, in either case, violates that compact, justly forfeits all advantages arising from it. For my own part, I really think, that next to the consciousness of doing a good action, that of doing a civil one is the most pleasing; and the epithet which I should covet the most, next to that of Aristides, would be that of well-bred. Thus much for good-breeding in general; I will now consider some of the various modes and degrees of it.

Very few, scarcely any, are wanting in the respect which they should show to those whom they acknowledge to be infinitely their superiors; such as crowned heads, princes, and public persons of distinguished and eminent posts. It is the manner of showing that respect which is different. The man of fashion and of the world, expresses it in its fullest extent; but naturally, easily, and without concern: whereas a man, who is not used to keep good company, expresses it awkwardly; one sees that he is not used to it, and that it costs him a great deal: but I never saw the worst-bred man living guilty of lolling, whistling, scratching his head, and such-like indecencies, in company that he respected. In such companies, therefore, the only point to be attended to is to show that respect, which everybody means to show, in an easy, unembarrassed, and graceful manner. This is what observation and experience must teach you.

In mixed companies, whoever is admitted to make part of them, is, for the time at least, supposed to be upon a footing of equality with the rest: and consequently, as there is no one principal object of awe and respect, people are apt to take a greater latitude in their behavior, and to be less upon their guard; and so they may, provided it be within certain bounds, which are upon no occasion to be transgressed. But, upon these occasions, though no one is entitled to distinguished marks of respect, everyone claims, and very justly, every mark of civility and good-breeding. Ease is allowed, but carelessness and negligence are strictly forbidden. If a man accosts you, and talks to you ever so dully or frivolously, it is worse than rudeness, it is brutality, to show him, by a manifest inattention to what he says, that you think him a fool or a blockhead, and not worth hearing. It is much more so with regard to women; who, of whatever rank they are, are entitled, in consideration of their sex, not only to an attentive, but an officious good-breeding from men. Their little wants, likings, dislikes, preferences, antipathies, fancies, whims, and even impertinencies, must be officiously attended to, flattered, and, if possible, guessed at and anticipated by a well-bred man. You must never usurp to yourself those conveniences and 'agremens' which are of common right; such as the best places, the best dishes, etc., but on the contrary, always decline them yourself, and offer them to others; who, in their turns, will offer them to you; so that, upon the whole, you will in your turn enjoy your share of the common right. It would be endless for me to enumerate all the particular instances in which a well-bred man shows his good-breeding in good company; and it would be injurious to you to suppose that your own good sense will not point them out to you; and then your own good-nature will recommend, and your self-interest enforce the practice.

There is a third sort of good-breeding, in which people are the most apt to fail, from a very mistaken notion that they cannot fail at all. I mean with regard to one's most familiar friends and acquaintances, or those who really are our inferiors; and there, undoubtedly, a greater degree of ease is not only allowed, but proper, and contributes much to the comforts of a private, social life. But that ease and freedom have their bounds too, which must by no means be violated. A certain degree of negligence and carelessness becomes injurious and insulting, from the real or supposed inferiority of the persons: and that delightful liberty of conversation among a few friends is soon destroyed, as liberty often has been, by being carried to licentiousness. But example explains things best, and I will put a pretty strong case. Suppose you and me alone together; I believe you will allow that I have as good a right to unlimited freedom in your company, as either you or I can possibly have in any other; and I am apt to believe too, that you would indulge me in that freedom as far as anybody would. But, notwithstanding this, do you imagine that I should think there were no bounds to that freedom? I assure you, I should not think so; and I take myself to be as much tied down by a certain degree of good manners to you, as by other degrees of them to other people. Were I to show you, by a manifest inattention to what you said to me, that I was thinking of something else the whole time; were I to yawn extremely, snore, or break wind in your company, I should think that I behaved myself to you like a beast, and should not expect that you would care to frequent me. No. The most familiar and intimate habitudes, connections, and friendships, require a degree of good-breeding, both to preserve and cement them. If ever a man and his wife, or a man and his mistress, who pass nights as well as days together, absolutely lay aside all good-breeding, their intimacy will soon degenerate into a coarse familiarity, infallibly productive of contempt or disgust. The best of us have our bad sides, and it is as imprudent, as it is ill-bred, to exhibit them. I shall certainly not use ceremony with you; it would be misplaced between us: but I shall certainly observe that degree of good-breeding with you, which is, in the first place, decent, and which I am sure is absolutely necessary to make us like one another's company long.

I will say no more, now, upon this important subject of good-breeding, upon which I have already dwelt too long, it may be, for one letter; and upon which I shall frequently refresh your memory hereafter; but I will conclude with these axioms:

That the deepest learning, without good-breeding, is unwelcome and tiresome pedantry, and of use nowhere but in a man's own closet; and consequently of little or no use at all.

That a man, Who is not perfectly well-bred, is unfit for good company and unwelcome in it; will consequently dislike it soon, afterward renounce it; and be reduced to solitude, or, what is worse, low and bad company.

That a man who is not well-bred, is full as unfit for business as for company.

Make then, my dear child, I conjure you, good-breeding the great object of your thoughts and actions, at least half the day. Observe carefully the behavior and manners of those who are distinguished by their good-breeding; imitate, nay, endeavor to excel, that you may at least reach them; and be convinced that good-breeding is, to all worldly qualifications, what charity is to all Christian virtues. Observe how it adorns merit, and how often it covers the want of it. May you wear it to adorn, and not to cover you! Adieu.

LETTER LXXXIX

EARL OF PHILIP DORMER STANHOPE CHESTERFIELD

LONDON, November 14, O. S. 1749.

DEAR BOY: There is a natural good-breeding which occurs to every man of common sense, and is practiced by every man, of common good-nature. This good-breeding is general, independent of modes, and consists in endeavors to please and oblige our fellow-creatures by all good offices, short of moral duties. This will be practiced by a good-natured American savage, as essentially as by the best-bred European. But then, I do not take it to extend to the sacrifice of our own conveniences, for the sake of other people's. Utility introduced this sort of good-breeding as it introduced commerce; and established a truck of the little 'agremens' and pleasures of life. I sacrifice such a conveniency to you, you sacrifice another to me; this commerce circulates, and every individual finds his account in it upon the whole. The third sort of good-breeding is local, and is variously modified, in not only different countries, but in different towns of the same country. But it must be founded upon the two former sorts; they are the matter to which, in this case, fashion and custom only give the different shapes and impressions. Whoever has the two first sorts will easily acquire this third sort of good-breeding, which depends singly upon attention and observation. It is, properly, the polish, the lustre, the last finishing stroke of good-breeding. It is to be found only in capitals, and even there it varies; the good-breeding of Rome differing, in some things, from that of Paris; that of Paris, in others, from that of Madrid; and that of Madrid, in many things, from that of London. A man of sense, therefore, carefully attends to the local manners of the respective places where he is, and takes for his models those persons whom he observes to be at the head of fashion and good-breeding. He watches how they address themselves to their superiors, how they accost their equals, and how they treat their inferiors; and lets none of those little niceties escape him which are to good-breeding what the last delicate and masterly touches are to a good picture; and of which the vulgar have no notion, but by which good judges distinguish the master. He attends even to their air, dress, and motions, and imitates them, liberally, and not servilely; he copies, but does not mimic. These personal graces are of very great consequence. They anticipate the sentiments, before merit can engage the understanding; they captivate the heart, and give rise, I believe, to the extravagant notions of charms and philters. Their effects were so surprising, that they were reckoned supernatural. The most graceful and best-bred men, and the handsomest and genteelest women, give the most philters; and, as I verily believe, without the least assistance of the devil. Pray be not only well dressed, but shining in your dress; let it have 'du brillant'. I do not mean by a clumsy load of gold and silver, but by the taste and fashion of it. The women like and require it; they think it an attention due to them; but, on the other hand, if your motions and carriage are not graceful, genteel, and natural, your fine clothes will only display your awkwardness the more. But I am unwilling to suppose you still awkward; for surely, by this time, you must have catched a good air in good company. When you went from hence you were naturally awkward; but your awkwardness was adventitious and Westmonasterial. Leipsig, I apprehend, is not the seat of the Graces; and I presume you acquired none there. But now, if you will be pleased to observe what people of the first fashion do with their legs and arms, heads and bodies, you will reduce yours to certain decent laws of motion. You danced pretty well here, and ought to dance very well before you come home; for what one is obliged to do sometimes, one ought to be able to do well. Besides, 'la belle danse donne du brillant a un jeune homme'. And you should endeavor to shine. A calm serenity, negative merit and graces, do not become your age. You should be 'alerte, adroit, vif'; be wanted, talked of, impatiently expected, and unwillingly parted with in company. I should be glad to hear half a dozen women of fashion say, 'Ou est donc le petit Stanhope? due ne vient-il? Il faut avouer qu'il est aimable'. All this I do not mean singly with regard to women as the principal object; but, with regard to men, and with a view of your making yourself considerable. For with very small variations, the same things that please women please men; and a man whose manners are softened and polished by women of fashion, and who is formed by them to an habitual attention and complaisance, will please, engage, and connect men, much easier and more than he would otherwise. You must be sensible that you cannot rise in the world, without forming connections, and engaging different characters to conspire in your point. You must make them your dependents without their knowing it, and dictate to them while you seem to be directed by them.

Those necessary connections can never be formed, or preserved, but by an uninterrupted series of complaisance, attentions, politeness, and some constraint. You must engage their hearts, if you would have their support; you must watch the 'mollia tempora', and captivate them by the 'agremens' and charms of conversation. People will not be called out to your service, only when you want them; and, if you expect to receive strength from them, they must receive either pleasure or advantage from you.

I received in this instant a letter from Mr. Harte, of the 2d N. S., which I will answer soon; in the meantime, I return him my thanks for it, through you. The constant good accounts which he gives me of you, will make me suspect him of partiality, and think him 'le medecin tant mieux'. Consider, therefore, what weight any future deposition of his against you must necessarily have with me. As, in that case, he will be a very unwilling, he must consequently be a very important witness. Adieu!

LETTER XC

DEAR Boy: My last was upon the subject of good-breeding; but I think it rather set before you the unfitness and disadvantages of ill-breeding, than the utility and necessity of good; it was rather negative than positive. This, therefore, should go further, and explain to you the necessity, which you, of all people living, lie under, not only of being positively and actively well-bred, but of shining and distinguishing yourself by your good-breeding. Consider your own situation in every particular, and judge whether it is not essentially your interest, by your own good-breeding to others, to secure theirs to you and that, let me assure you, is the only way of doing it; for people will repay, and with interest too, inattention with inattention, neglect with neglect, and ill manners with worse: which may engage you in very disagreeable affairs. In the next place, your profession requires, more than any other, the nicest and most distinguished good-breeding. You will negotiate with very little success, if you do not previously, by your manners, conciliate and engage the affections of those with whom you are to negotiate. Can you ever get into the confidence and the secrets of the courts where you may happen to reside, if you have not those pleasing, insinuating manners, which alone can procure them? Upon my word, I do not say too much, when I say that superior good-breeding, insinuating manners, and genteel address, are half your business. Your knowledge will have but very little influence upon the mind, if your manners prejudice the heart against you; but, on the other hand, how easily will you DUPE the understanding, where you have first engaged the heart? and hearts are by no means to be gained by that mere common civility which everybody practices. Bowing again to those who bow to you, answering dryly those who speak to you, and saying nothing offensive to anybody, is such negative good-breeding that it is only not being a brute; as it would be but a very poor commendation of any man's cleanliness to say that he did not stink. It is an active, cheerful, officious, seducing, good-breeding that must gain you the good-will and first sentiments of men, and the affections of the women. You must carefully watch and attend to their passions, their tastes, their little humors and weaknesses, and 'aller au devant'. You must do it at the same time with alacrity and 'empressement', and not as if you graciously condescended to humor their weaknesses.

For instance, suppose you invited anybody to dine or sup with you, you ought to recollect if you had observed that they had any favorite dish, and take care to provide it for them; and when it came you should say, You SEEMED TO ME, AT SUCH AND SUCH A PLACE, TO GIVE THIS DISH A PREFERENCE, AND THEREFORE I ORDERED IT; THIS IS THE WINE THAT I OBSERVED YOU LIKED, AND THEREFORE I PROCURED SOME. The more trifling these things are, the more they prove your attention for the person, and are consequently the more engaging. Consult your own breast, and recollect how these little attentions, when shown you by others, flatter that degree of self-love and vanity from which no man living is free. Reflect how they incline and attract you to that person, and how you are propitiated afterward to all which that person says or does. The same causes will have the same effects in your favor. Women, in a great degree, establish or destroy every man's reputation of good-breeding; you must, therefore, in a manner, overwhelm them with these attentions: they are used to them, they expect them, and, to do them justice, they commonly requite them. You must be sedulous, and rather over officious than under, in procuring them their coaches, their chairs, their conveniences in public places: not see what you should not see; and rather assist, where you cannot help seeing. Opportunities of showing these attentions present themselves perpetually; but if they do not, make them. As Ovid advises his lover, when he sits in the Circus near his mistress, to wipe the dust off her neck, even if there be none: 'Si nullus, tamen excute nullum'. Your conversation with women should always be respectful; but, at the same time, enjoue, and always addressed to their vanity. Everything you say or do should convince them of the regard you have (whether you have it or not) for their beauty, their wit, or their merit. Men have possibly as much vanity as women, though of another kind; and both art and good-breeding require, that, instead of mortifying, you should please and flatter it, by words and looks of approbation. Suppose (which is by no means improbable) that, at your return to England, I should place you near the person of some one of the royal family; in that situation, good-breeding, engaging address, adorned with all the graces that dwell at courts, would very probably make you a favorite, and, from a favorite, a minister; but all the knowledge and learning in the world, without them, never would. The penetration of princes seldom goes deeper than the surface.

It is the exterior that always engages their hearts; and I would never advise you to give yourself much trouble about their understanding. Princes in general (I mean those 'Porphyrogenets' who are born and bred in purple) are about the pitch of women; bred up like them, and are to be addressed and gained in the same manner. They always see, they seldom weigh. Your lustre, not your solidity, must take them; your inside will afterward support and secure what your outside has acquired. With weak people (and they undoubtedly are three parts in four of mankind) good-breeding, address, and manners are everything; they can go no deeper; but let me assure you that they are a great deal even with people of the best understandings. Where the eyes are not pleased, and the heart is not flattered, the mind will be apt to stand out. Be this right or wrong, I confess I am so made myself. Awkwardness and ill-breeding shock me to that degree, that where I meet with them, I cannot find in my heart to inquire into the intrinsic merit of that person—I hastily decide in myself that he can have none; and am not sure that I should not even be sorry to know that he had any. I often paint you in my imagination, in your present 'lontananza', and, while I view you in the light of ancient and modern learning, useful and ornamental knowledge, I am charmed with the prospect; but when I view you in another light, and represent you awkward, ungraceful, ill-bred, with vulgar air and manners, shambling toward me with inattention and DISTRACTIONS, I shall not pretend to describe to you what I feel; but will do as a skillful painter did formerly—draw a veil before the countenance of the father.

I dare say you know already enough of architecture, to know that the Tuscan is the strongest and most solid of all the orders; but at the same time, it is the coarsest and clumsiest of them. Its solidity does extremely well for the foundation and base floor of a great edifice; but if the whole building be Tuscan, it will attract no eyes, it will stop no passengers, it will invite no interior examination; people will take it for granted that the finishing and furnishing cannot be worth seeing, where the front is so unadorned and clumsy. But if, upon the solid Tuscan foundation, the Doric, the Ionic, and the Corinthian orders rise gradually with all their beauty, proportions, and ornaments, the fabric seizes the most incurious eye, and stops the most careless passenger; who solicits admission as a favor, nay, often purchases it. Just so will it fare with your little fabric, which, at present, I fear, has more of the Tuscan than of the Corinthian order. You must absolutely change the whole front, or nobody will knock at the door. The several parts, which must compose this new front, are elegant, easy, natural, superior good-breeding; an engaging address; genteel motions; an insinuating softness in your looks, words, and actions; a spruce, lively air, fashionable dress; and all the glitter that a young fellow should have.

I am sure you would do a great deal for my sake; and therefore consider at your return here, what a disappointment and concern it would be to me, if I could not safely depute you to do the honors of my house and table; and if I should be ashamed to present you to those who frequent both. Should you be awkward, inattentive, and distrait, and happen to meet Mr. L——-at my table, the consequences of that meeting must be fatal; you would run your heads against each other, cut each other's fingers, instead of your meat, or die by the precipitate infusion of scalding soup.

This is really so copious a subject, that there is no end of being either serious or ludicrous upon it. It is impossible, too, to enumerate or state to you the various cases in good-breeding; they are infinite; there is no situation or relation in the world so remote or so intimate, that does not require a degree of it. Your own good sense must point it out to you; your own good-nature must incline, and your interest prompt you to practice it; and observation and experience must give you the manner, the air and the graces which complete the whole.

This letter will hardly overtake you, till you are at or near Rome. I expect a great deal in every way from your six months' stay there. My morning hopes are justly placed in Mr. Harte, and the masters he will give you; my evening ones, in the Roman ladies: pray be attentive to both. But I must hint to you, that the Roman ladies are not 'les femmes savantes, et ne vous embrasseront point pour l'amour du Grec. They must have 'ilgarbato, il leggiadro, it disinvolto, il lusinghiero, quel non so che, che piace, che alletta, che incanta'.

I have often asserted, that the profoundest learning and the politest manners were by no means incompatible, though so seldom found united in the same person; and I have engaged myself to exhibit you, as a proof of the truth of this assertion. Should you, instead of that, happen to disprove me, the concern indeed would be mine, but the loss will be yours. Lord Bolingbroke is a strong instance on my side of the question; he joins to the deepest erudition, the most elegant politeness and good-breeding that ever any courtier and man of the world was adorned with. And Pope very justly called him "All-accomplished St. John," with regard to his knowledge and his manners. He had, it is true, his faults; which proceeded from unbounded ambition, and impetuous passions; but they have now subsided by age and experience; and I can wish you nothing better than to be, what he is now, without being what he has been formerly. His address pre-engages, his eloquence persuades, and his knowledge informs all who approach him. Upon the whole, I do desire, and insist, that from after dinner till you go to bed, you make good-breeding, address, and manners, your serious object and your only care. Without them, you will be nobody; with them, you may be anything.

Adieu, my dear child! My compliments to Mr. Harte.

LETTER XCI

LONDON, November 24, O. S. 1749.

DEAR Boy: Every rational being (I take it for granted) proposes to himself some object more important than mere respiration and obscure animal existence. He desires to distinguish himself among his fellow-creatures; and, 'alicui negotio intentus, prreclari facinoris, aut artis bonae, faman quaerit'. Caesar, when embarking in a storm, said, that it was not necessary he should live; but that it was absolutely necessary he should get to the place to which he was going. And Pliny leaves mankind this only alternative; either of doing what deserves to be written, or of writing what deserves to be read. As for those who do neither, 'eorum vitam mortemque juxta aestumo; quoniam de utraque siletur'. You have, I am convinced, one or both of these objects in view; but you must know and use the necessary means, or your pursuit will be vain and frivolous. In either case, 'Sapere est princihium et fons'; but it is by no means all. That knowledge must be adorned, it must have lustre as well as weight, or it will be oftener taken, for lead than for gold. Knowledge you have, and will have: I am easy upon that article. But my business, as your friend, is not to compliment you upon what you have, but to tell you with freedom what you want; and I must tell you plainly, that I fear you want everything but knowledge.

EARL OF PHILIP DORMER STANHOPE CHESTERFIELD

I have written to you so often, of late, upon good-breeding, address, 'les manieres liantes', the Graces, etc., that I shall confine this letter to another subject, pretty near akin to them, and which, I am sure, you are full as deficient in; I mean Style.

Style is the dress of thoughts; and let them be ever so just, if your style is homely, coarse, and vulgar, they will appear to as much disadvantage, and be as ill received as your person, though ever so well proportioned, would, if dressed in rags, dirt, and tatters. It is not every understanding that can judge of matter; but every ear can and does judge, more or less, of style: and were I either to speak or write to the public, I should prefer moderate matter, adorned with all the beauties and elegancies of style, to the strongest matter in the world, ill-worded and ill-delivered. Your business is negotiation abroad, and oratory in the House of Commons at home. What figure can you make, in either case, if your style be inelegant, I do not say bad? Imagine yourself writing an office-letter to a secretary of state, which letter is to be read by the whole Cabinet Council, and very possibly afterward laid before parliament; any one barbarism, solecism, or vulgarism in it, would, in a very few days, circulate through the whole kingdom, to your disgrace and ridicule. For instance, I will suppose you had written the following letter from The Hague to the Secretary of State at London; and leave you to suppose the consequences of it:

MY LORD: I HAD, last night, the honor of your Lordship's letter of the 24th; and will SET ABOUT DOING the orders contained THEREIN; and IF so BE that I can get that affair done by the next post, I will not fail FOR TO give your Lordship an account of it by NEXT POST. I have told the French Minister, AS HOW THAT IF that affair be not soon concluded, your Lordship would think it ALL LONG OF HIM; and that he must have neglected FOR TO have wrote to his court about it. I must beg leave to put your Lordship in mind AS HOW, that I am now full three quarter in arrear; and if SO BE that I do not very soon receive at least one half year, I shall CUT A VERY BAD FIGURE; FOR THIS HERE place is very dear. I shall be VASTLY BEHOLDEN to your Lordship for THAT THERE mark of your favor; and so I REST or REMAIN, Your, etc.

You will tell me, possibly, that this is a caricatura of an illiberal and inelegant style: I will admit it; but assure you, at the same time, that a dispatch with less than half these faults would blow you up forever. It is by no means sufficient to be free from faults, in speaking and writing; but you must do both correctly and elegantly. In faults of this kind, it is not 'ille optimus qui minimis arguetur'; but he is unpardonable who has any at all, because it is his own fault: he need only attend to, observe, and imitate the best authors.

It is a very true saying, that a man must be born a poet, but that he may make himself an orator; and the very first principle of an orator is to speak his own language, particularly, with the utmost purity and elegance. A man will be forgiven even great errors in a foreign language; but in his own, even the least slips are justly laid hold of and ridiculed.

A person of the House of Commons, speaking two years ago upon naval affairs; asserted, that we had then the finest navy UPON THE FACE OF THE YEARTH. This happy mixture of blunder and vulgarism, you may easily imagine, was matter of immediate ridicule; but I can assure you that it continues so still, and will be remembered as long as he lives and speaks. Another, speaking in defense of a gentleman, upon whom a censure was moved, happily said that he thought that gentleman was more LIABLE to be thanked and rewarded, than censured. You know, I presume, that LIABLE can never be used in a good sense.

LETTERS TO HIS SON, COMPLETE

You have with you three or four of the best English authors, Dryden, Atterbury, and Swift; read them with the utmost care, and with a particular view to their language, and they may possibly correct that CURIOUS INFELICITY OF DICTION, which you acquired at Westminster. Mr. Harte excepted, I will admit that you have met with very few English abroad, who could improve your style; and with many, I dare say, who speak as ill as yourself, and, it may be, worse; you must, therefore, take the more pains, and consult your authors and Mr. Harte the more. I need not tell you how attentive the Romans and Greeks, particularly the Athenians, were to this object. It is also a study among the Italians and the French; witness their respective academies and dictionaries for improving and fixing their languages. To our shame be it spoken, it is less attended to here than in any polite country; but that is no reason why you should not attend to it; on the contrary, it will distinguish you the more. Cicero says, very truly, that it is glorious to excel other men in that very article, in which men excel brutes; SPEECH.

Constant experience has shown me, that great purity and elegance of style, with a graceful elocution, cover a multitude of faults, in either a speaker or a writer. For my own part, I confess (and I believe most people are of my mind) that if a speaker should ungracefully mutter or stammer out to me the sense of an angel, deformed by barbarism and solecisms, or larded with vulgarisms, he should never speak to me a second time, if I could help it. Gain the heart, or you gain nothing; the eyes and the ears are the only roads to the heart. Merit and knowledge will not gain hearts, though they will secure them when gained. Pray, have that truth ever in your mind. Engage the eyes by your address, air, and motions; soothe the ears by the elegance and harmony of your diction; the heart will certainly follow; and the whole man, or woman, will as certainly follow the heart. I must repeat it to you, over and over again, that with all the knowledge which you may have at present, or hereafter acquire, and with all merit that ever man had, if you have not a graceful address, liberal and engaging manners, a prepossessing air, and a good degree of eloquence in speaking and writing; you will be nobody; but will have the daily mortification of seeing people, with not one-tenth part of your merit or knowledge, get the start of you, and disgrace you, both in company and in business.

You have read "Quintilian," the best book in the world to form an orator; pray read 'Cicero de Oratore', the best book in the world to finish one. Translate and retranslate from and to Latin, Greek, and English; make yourself a pure and elegant English style: it requires nothing but application. I do not find that God has made you a poet; and I am very glad that he has not: therefore, for God's sake, make yourself an orator, which you may do. Though I still call you boy, I consider you no longer as such; and when I reflect upon the prodigious quantity of manure that has been laid upon you, I expect that you should produce more at eighteen, than uncultivated soils do at eight-and-twenty.

Pray tell Mr. Harte that I have received his letter of the 13th, N. S. Mr. Smith was much in the right not to let you go, at this time of the year, by sea; in the summer you may navigate as much as you please; as, for example, from Leghorn to Genoa, etc. Adieu.

LETTER XCII

LONDON, November 27, O. S. 1749.

EARL OF PHILIP DORMER STANHOPE CHESTERFIELD

DEAR BOY: While the Roman Republic flourished, while glory was pursued, and virtue practiced, and while even little irregularities and indecencies, not cognizable by law, were, however, not thought below the public care, censors were established, discretionally to supply, in particular cases, the inevitable defects of the law, which must and can only be general. This employment I assume to myself with regard to your little republic, leaving the legislative power entirely to Mr. Harte; I hope, and believe, that he will seldom, or rather never, have occasion to exert his supreme authority; and I do by no means suspect you of any faults that may require that interposition. But, to tell you the plain truth, I am of opinion that my censorial power will not be useless to you, nor a sinecure to me. The sooner you make it both, the better for us both. I can now exercise this employment only upon hearsay, or, at most, written evidence; and therefore shall exercise it with great lenity and some diffidence; but when we meet, and that I can form my judgment upon ocular and auricular evidence, I shall no more let the least impropriety, indecorum, or irregularity pass uncensured, than my predecessor Cato did. I shall read you with the attention of a critic, not with the partiality of an author: different in this respect, indeed, from most critics, that I shall seek for faults only to correct and not to expose them. I have often thought, and still think, that there are few things which people in general know less, than how to love and how to hate. They hurt those they love by a mistaken indulgence, by a blindness, nay, often by a partiality to their faults. Where they hate they hurt themselves, by ill-timed passion and rage. Fortunately for you, I never loved you in that mistaken manner. From your infancy, I made you the object of my most serious attention, and not my plaything. I consulted your real good, not your humors or fancies; and I shall continue to do so while you want it, which will probably be the case during our joint lives; for, considering the difference of our ages, in the course of nature, you will hardly have acquired experience enough of your own, while I shall be in condition of lending you any of mine. People in general will much better bear being told of their vices or crimes, than of their little failings and weaknesses. They, in some degree, justify or excuse (as they think) the former, by strong passions, seductions, and artifices of others, but to be told of, or to confess, their little failings and weaknesses, implies an inferiority of parts, too mortifying to that self-love and vanity, which are inseparable from our natures. I have been intimate enough with several people to tell them that they had said or done a very criminal thing; but I never was intimate enough with any man, to tell him, very seriously, that he had said or done a very foolish one. Nothing less than the relation between you and me can possibly authorize that freedom; but fortunately for you, my parental rights, joined to my censorial powers, give it me in its fullest extent, and my concern for you will make me exert it. Rejoice, therefore, that there is one person in the world who can and will tell you what will be very useful to you to know, and yet what no other man living could or would tell you. Whatever I shall tell you of this kind, you are very sure, can have no other motive than your interest; I can neither be jealous nor envious of your reputation or fortune, which I must be both desirous and proud to establish and promote; I cannot be your rival either in love or in business; on the contrary, I want the rays of your rising to reflect new lustre upon my setting light. In order to this, I shall analyze you minutely, and censure you freely, that you may not (if possible) have one single spot, when in your meridian.

There is nothing that a young fellow, at his first appearance in the world, has more reason to dread, and consequently should take more pains to avoid, than having any ridicule fixed upon him. It degrades him with the most reasonable part of mankind; but it ruins him with the rest; and I have known many a man undone by acquiring a ridiculous nickname: I would not, for all the riches in the world, that you should acquire one when you return to England. Vices and crimes excite hatred and reproach; failings, weaknesses, and awkwardnesses, excite ridicule; they are laid hold of by mimics, who, though very contemptible wretches themselves, often, by their buffoonery, fix ridicule upon their betters. The little defects in manners, elocution, address, and air (and even of figure, though very unjustly), are the objects of ridicule, and the causes of nicknames. You cannot imagine the grief it would give me, and the prejudice it would do you, if, by way of distinguishing you from others of your name, you should happen to be called Muttering Stanhope, Absent Stanhope, Ill-bred Stanhope, or Awkward, Left-legged Stanhope: therefore, take great care to put it out of the power of Ridicule itself to give you any of these ridiculous epithets; for, if you get one, it will stick to you, like the envenomed shirt. The very first day that I see you, I shall be able to tell you, and certainly shall tell you, what degree of danger you are in; and I hope that my admonitions, as censor, may prevent the censures of the public. Admonitions are always useful; is this one or not? You are the best judge; it is your own picture which I send you, drawn, at my request, by a lady at Venice: pray let me know how far, in your conscience, you think it like; for there are some parts of it which I wish may, and others, which I should be sorry were. I send you, literally, the copy of that part of her letter, to her friend here, which relates to you.—[In compliance to your orders, I have examined young Stanhope carefully, and think I have penetrated into his character. This is his portrait, which I take to be a faithful one. His face is pleasing, his countenance sensible, and his look clever. His figure is at present rather too square; but if he shoots up, which he has matter and years for, he will then be of a good size. He has, undoubtedly, a great fund of acquired knowledge; I am assured that he is master of the learned languages. As for French, I know he speaks it perfectly, and, I am told, German as well. The questions he asks are judicious; and denote a thirst after knowledge. I cannot say that he appears equally desirous of pleasing, for he seems to neglect attentions and the graces. He does not come into a room well, nor has he that easy, noble carriage, which would be proper for him. It is true, he is as yet young and inexperienced; one may therefore reasonably hope that his exercises, which he has not yet gone through, and good company, in which he is still a novice, will polish, and give all that is wanting to complete him. What seems necessary for that purpose, would, be an attachment to some woman of fashion, and who knows the world. Some Madame de l'Ursay would be the proper person. In short, I can assure you, that he has everything which Lord Chesterfield can wish him, excepting that carriage, those graces, and the style used in the best company; which he will certainly acquire in time, and by frequenting the polite world. If he should not, it would be great pity, since he so well deserves to possess them. You know their importance. My Lord, his father, knows it too, he being master of them all. To conclude, if little Stanhope acquires the graces, I promise you he will make his way; if not, he will be stopped in a course, the goal of which he might attain with honor.]

Tell Mr. Harte that I have this moment received his letter of the 22d, N. S., and that I approve extremely of the long stay you have made at Venice. I love long residences at capitals; running post through different places is a most unprofitable way of traveling, and admits of no application. Adieu.

You see, by this extract, of what consequence other people think these things. Therefore, I hope you will no longer look upon them as trifles. It is the character of an able man to despise little things in great business: but then he knows what things are little, and what not. He does not suppose things are little, because they are commonly called so: but by the consequences that may or may not attend them. If gaining people's affections, and interesting their hearts in your favor, be of consequence, as it undoubtedly is, he knows very well that a happy concurrence of all those, commonly called little things, manners, air, address, graces, etc., is of the utmost consequence, and will never be at rest till he has acquired them. The world is taken by the outside of things, and we must take the world as it is; you nor I cannot set it right. I know, at this time, a man of great quality and station, who has not the parts of a porter; but raised himself to the station he is in, singly by having a graceful figure, polite manners, and an engaging address; which, by the way, he only acquired by habit; for he had not sense enough to get them by reflection. Parts and habit should conspire to complete you. You will have the habit of good company, and you have reflection in your power.

LETTER XCIII

LONDON, December 5, O. S. 1749.

DEAR BOY: Those who suppose that men in general act rationally, because they are called rational creatures, know very little of the world, and if they act themselves upon that supposition, will nine times in ten find themselves grossly mistaken. That man is, 'animal bipes, implume, risibile', I entirely agree; but for the 'rationale', I can only allow it him 'in actu primo' (to talk logic) and seldom in 'actu secundo'. Thus, the speculative, cloistered pedant, in his solitary cell, forms systems of things as they should be, not as they are;

and writes as decisively and absurdly upon war, politics, manners, and characters, as that pedant talked, who was so kind as to instruct Hannibal in the art of war. Such closet politicians never fail to assign the deepest motives for the most trifling actions; instead of often ascribing the greatest actions to the most trifling causes, in which they would be much seldomer mistaken. They read and write of kings, heroes, and statesmen, as never doing anything but upon the deepest principles of sound policy. But those who see and observe kings, heroes, and statesmen, discover that they have headaches, indigestions, humors, and passions, just like other people; everyone of which, in their turns, determine their wills, in defiance of their reason. Had we only read in the "Life of Alexander," that he burned Persepolis, it would doubtless have been accounted for from deep policy: we should have been told, that his new conquest could not have been secured without the destruction of that capital, which would have been the constant seat of cabals, conspiracies, and revolts. But, luckily, we are informed at the same time, that this hero, this demi-god, this son and heir of Jupiter Ammon, happened to get extremely drunk with his w——e; and, by way of frolic, destroyed one of the finest cities in the world.

Read men, therefore, yourself, not in books but in nature. Adopt no systems, but study them yourself. Observe their weaknesses, their passions, their humors, of all which their understandings are, nine times in ten, the dupes. You will then know that they are to be gained, influenced, or led, much oftener by little things than by great ones; and, consequently, you will no longer think those things little, which tend to such great purposes.

Let us apply this now to the particular object of this letter; I mean, speaking in, and influencing public assemblies. The nature of our constitution makes eloquence more useful, and more necessary, in this country than in any other in Europe. A certain degree of good sense and knowledge is requisite for that, as well as for everything else; but beyond that, the purity of diction, the elegance of style, the harmony of periods, a pleasing elocution, and a graceful action, are the things which a public speaker should attend to the most; because his audience certainly does, and understands them the best; or rather indeed understands little else.

The late Lord Chancellor Cowper's strength as an orator lay by no means in his reasonings, for he often hazarded very weak ones. But such was the purity and elegance of his style, such the propriety and charms of his elocution, and such the gracefulness of his action, that he never spoke without universal applause; the ears and the eyes gave him up the hearts and the understandings of the audience. On the contrary, the late Lord Townshend always spoke materially, with argument and knowledge, but never pleased. Why? His diction was not only inelegant, but frequently ungrammatical, always vulgar; his cadences false, his voice unharmonious, and his action ungraceful. Nobody heard him with patience; and the young fellows used to joke upon him, and repeat his inaccuracies. The late Duke of Argyle, though the weakest reasoner, was the most pleasing speaker I ever knew in my life. He charmed, he warmed, he forcibly ravished the audience; not by his matter certainly, but by his manner of delivering it. A most genteel figure, a graceful, noble air, an harmonious voice, an elegance of style, and a strength of emphasis, conspired to make him the most affecting, persuasive, and applauded speaker I ever saw. I was captivated like others; but when I came home, and coolly considered what he had said, stripped of all those ornaments in which he had dressed it, I often found the matter flimsy, the arguments weak, and I was convinced of the power of those adventitious concurring circumstances, which ignorance of mankind only calls trifling ones. Cicero, in his book 'De Oratore', in order to raise the dignity of that profession which he well knew himself to be at the head of, asserts that a complete orator must be a complete everything, lawyer, philosopher, divine, etc. That would be extremely well, if it were possible: but man's life is not long enough; and I hold him to be the completest orator, who speaks the best upon that subject which occurs; whose happy choice of words, whose lively imagination, whose elocution and action adorn and grace his matter, at the same time that they excite the attention and engage the passions of his audience.

You will be of the House of Commons as soon as you are of age; and you must first make a figure there, if you would make a figure, or a fortune, in your country. This you can never do without that correctness and elegance in your own language, which you now seem to neglect, and which you have entirely to learn. Fortunately for you, it is to be learned. Care and observation will do it; but do not flatter yourself, that all the knowledge, sense, and reasoning in the world will ever make you a popular and applauded speaker, without the ornaments and the graces of style, elocution, and action. Sense and argument, though coarsely delivered, will have their weight in a private conversation, with two or three people of sense; but in a public assembly they will have none, if naked and destitute of the advantages I have mentioned. Cardinal de Retz observes, very justly, that every numerous assembly is a mob, influenced by their passions, humors, and affections, which nothing but eloquence ever did or ever can engage. This is so important a consideration for everybody in this country, and more particularly for you, that I earnestly recommend it to your most serious care and attention. Mind your diction, in whatever language you either write or speak; contract a habit of correctness and elegance. Consider your style, even in the freest conversation and most familiar letters. After, at least, if not before, you have said a thing, reflect if you could not have said it better. Where you doubt of the propriety or elegance of a word or a phrase, consult some good dead or living authority in that language. Use yourself to translate, from various languages into English; correct those translations till they satisfy your ear, as well as your understanding. And be convinced of this truth, that the best sense and reason in the world will be as unwelcome in a public assembly, without these ornaments, as they will in public companies, without the assistance of manners and politeness. If you will please people, you must please them in their own way; and, as you cannot make them what they should be, you must take them as they are. I repeat it again, they are only to be taken by 'agremens', and by what flatters their senses and their hearts. Rabelais first wrote a most excellent book, which nobody liked; then, determined to conform to the public taste, he wrote Gargantua and Pantagruel, which everybody liked, extravagant as it was. Adieu.

LETTER XCIV

LONDON, December 9, O. S. 1749.

DEAR BOY: It is now above forty years since I have never spoken nor written one single word, without giving myself at least one moment's time to consider whether it was a good or a bad one, and whether I could not find out a better in its place. An unharmonious and rugged period, at this time, shocks my ears; and I, like all the rest of the world, will willingly exchange and give up some degree of rough sense, for a good degree of pleasing sound. I will freely and truly own to you, without either vanity or false modesty, that whatever reputation I have acquired as a speaker, is more owing to my constant attention to my diction than to my matter, which was necessarily just the same as other people's. When you come into parliament, your reputation as a speaker will depend much more upon your words, and your periods, than upon the subject. The same matter occurs equally to everybody of common sense, upon the same question; the dressing it well, is what excites the attention and admiration of the audience.

It is in parliament that I have set my heart upon your making a figure; it is there that I want to have you justly proud of yourself, and to make me justly proud of you. This means that you must be a good speaker there; I use the word MUST, because I know you may if you will. The vulgar, who are always mistaken, look upon a speaker and a comet with the same astonishment and admiration, taking them both for preternatural phenomena. This error discourages many young men from attempting that character; and good speakers are willing to have their talent considered as something very extraordinary, if not, a peculiar gift of God to his elect. But let you and me analyze and simplify this good speaker; let us strip him of those adventitious plumes with which his own pride, and the ignorance of others, have decked him, and we shall find the true definition of him to be no more than this: A man of good common sense who reasons justly and expresses himself elegantly on that subject upon which he speaks. There is, surely, no witchcraft in this. A man of sense, without a superior and astonishing degree of parts, will not talk nonsense upon any subject; nor will he, if he has the least taste or application, talk inelegantly. What then does all this mighty art and mystery of speaking in parliament amount to? Why, no more than this: that the man who speaks in the House of Commons, speaks in that House, and to four hundred people, that opinion upon a given subject which he would make no difficulty of speaking in any house in England, round the fire, or at table, to any fourteen people whatsoever; better judges, perhaps, and severer critics of what he says, than any fourteen gentlemen of the House of Commons.

I have spoken frequently in parliament, and not always without some applause; and therefore I can assure you, from my experience, that there is very little in it. The elegance of the style, and the turn of the periods, make the chief impression upon the hearers. Give them but one or two round and harmonious periods in a speech, which they will retain and repeat; and they will go home as well satisfied as people do from an opera, humming all the way one or two favorite tunes that have struck their ears, and were easily caught. Most people have ears, but few have judgment; tickle those ears, and depend upon it, you will catch their judgments, such as they are.

Cicero, conscious that he was at the top of his profession (for in his time eloquence was a profession), in order to set himself off, defines in his treatise 'De Oratore', an orator to be such a man as never was, nor never will be; and, by his fallacious argument, says that he must know every art and science whatsoever, or how shall he speak upon them? But, with submission to so great an authority, my definition of an orator is extremely different from, and I believe much truer than his. I call that man an orator, who reasons justly, and expresses himself elegantly, upon whatever subject he treats. Problems in geometry, equations in algebra, processes in chemistry, and experiments in anatomy, are never, that I have heard of, the object of eloquence; and therefore I humbly conceive, that a man may be a very fine speaker, and yet know nothing of geometry, algebra, chemistry, or anatomy. The subjects of all parliamentary debates are subjects of common sense singly.

Thus I write whatever occurs to me, that I think may contribute either to form or inform you. May my labor not be in vain! and it will not, if you will but have half the concern for yourself that I have for you. Adieu.

LETTER XCV

LONDON; December 12, O. S. 1749.

DEAR BOY: Lord Clarendon in his history says of Mr. John Hampden THAT HE HAD A HEAD TO CONTRIVE, A TONGUE TO PERSUADE, AND A HAND TO EXECUTE ANY MISCHIEF. I shall not now enter into the justness of this character of Mr. Hampden, to whose brave stand against the illegal demand of ship-money we owe our present liberties; but I mention it to you as the character, which with the alteration of one single word, GOOD, instead of MISCHIEF, I would have you aspire to, and use your utmost endeavors to deserve. The head to contrive, God must to a certain degree have given you; but it is in your own power greatly to improve it, by study, observation, and reflection. As for the TONGUE TO PERSUADE, it wholly depends upon yourself; and without it the best head will contrive to very little purpose. The hand to execute depends likewise, in my opinion, in a great measure upon yourself. Serious reflection will always give courage in a good cause; and the courage arising from reflection is of a much superior nature to the animal and constitutional courage of a foot soldier. The former is steady and unshaken, where the 'nodus' is 'dignus vindice'; the latter is oftener improperly than properly exerted, but always brutally.

The second member of my text (to speak ecclesiastically) shall be the subject of my following discourse; THE TONGUE TO PERSUADE—as judicious, preachers recommend those virtues, which they think their several audiences want the most; such as truth and continence, at court; disinterestedness, in the city; and sobriety, in the country.

You must certainly, in the course of your little experience, have felt the different effects of elegant and inelegant speaking. Do you not suffer, when people accost you in a stammering or hesitating manner, in an untuneful voice, with false accents and cadences; puzzling and blundering through solecisms, barbarisms, and vulgarisms; misplacing even their bad words, and inverting all method? Does not this prejudice you against their matter, be it what it will; nay, even against their persons? I am sure it does me. On the other hand, do you not feel yourself inclined, prepossessed, nay, even engaged in favor of those who address you in the direct contrary manner? The effects of a correct and adorned style of method and perspicuity, are incredible toward persuasion; they often supply the want of reason and argument, but, when used in the support of reason and argument, they are irresistible. The French attend very much to the purity and elegance of their style, even in common conversation; insomuch that it is a character to say of a man 'qu'il narre bien'. Their conversations frequently turn upon the delicacies of their language, and an academy is employed in fixing it. The 'Crusca', in Italy, has the same object; and I have met with very few Italians, who did not speak their own language correctly and elegantly. How much more necessary is it for an Englishman to do so, who is to speak it in a public assembly, where the laws and liberties of his country are the subjects of his deliberation? The tongue that would persuade there, must not content itself with mere articulation. You know what pains Demosthenes took to correct his naturally bad elocution; you know that he declaimed by the seaside in storms, to prepare himself for the noise of the tumultuous assemblies he was to speak to; and you can now judge of the correctness and elegance of his style. He thought all these things of consequence, and he thought right; pray do you think so too? It is of the utmost consequence to you to be of that opinion. If you have the least defect in your elocution, take the utmost care and pains to correct it. Do not neglect your style, whatever language you speak in, or whoever you speak to, were it your footman. Seek always for the best words and the happiest expressions you can find. Do not content yourself with being barely understood; but adorn your thoughts, and dress them as you would your person; which, however well proportioned it might be, it would be very improper and indecent to exhibit naked, or even worse dressed than people of your sort are.

I have sent you in a packet which your Leipsig acquaintance, Duval, sends to his correspondent at Rome, Lord Bolingbroke's book,—["Letters on the Spirit of Patriotism," on the Idea of a Patriot King which he published about a year ago.]—I desire that you will read it over and over again, with particular attention to the style, and to all those beauties of oratory with which it is adorned. Till I read that book, I confess I did not know all the extent and powers of the English language. Lord Bolingbroke has both a tongue and a pen to persuade; his manner of speaking in private conversation is full as elegant as his writings; whatever subject he either speaks or writes upon, he adorns with the most splendid eloquence; not a studied or labored eloquence, but such a flowing happiness of diction, which (from care perhaps at first) is become so habitual to him, that even his most familiar conversations, if taken down in writing, would bear the press, without the least correction either as to method or style. If his conduct, in the former part of his life, had been equal to all his natural and acquired talents, he would most justly have merited the epithet of all-accomplished. He is himself sensible of his past errors: those violent passions which seduced him in his youth, have now subsided by age; and take him as he is now, the character of all-accomplished is more his due than any man's I ever knew in my life.

But he has been a most mortifying instance of the violence of human passions and of the weakness of the most exalted human reason. His virtues and his vices, his reason and his passions, did not blend themselves by a gradation of tints, but formed a shining and sudden contrast. Here the darkest, there the most splendid colors; and both rendered more shining from their proximity. Impetuosity, excess, and almost extravagance, characterized not only his passions, but even his senses. His youth was distinguished by all the tumult and storm of pleasures, in which he most licentiously triumphed, disdaining all decorum. His fine imagination has often been heated and exhausted, with his body, in celebrating and deifying the prostitute of the night; and his convivial joys were pushed to all the extravagance of frantic Bacchanals. Those passions were interrupted but by a stronger ambition. The former impaired both his constitution and his character, but the latter destroyed both his fortune and his reputation.

He has noble and generous sentiments, rather than fixed reflected principles of good nature and friendship; but they are more violent than lasting, and suddenly and often varied to their opposite extremes, with regard to the same persons. He receives the common attentions of civility as obligations, which he returns with interest; and resents with passion the little inadvertencies of human nature, which he repays with interest too. Even a difference of opinion upon a philosophical subject would provoke, and prove him no practical philosopher at least.

Notwithstanding the dissipation of his youth, and the tumultuous agitation of his middle age, he has an infinite fund of various and almost universal knowledge, which, from the clearest and quickest conception, and happiest memory, that ever man was blessed with, he always carries about him. It is his pocket-money, and he never has occasion to draw upon a book for any sum. He excels more particularly in history, as his historical works plainly prove. The relative political and commercial interests of every country in Europe, particularly of his own, are better known to him, than perhaps to any man in it; but how steadily he has pursued the latter, in his public conduct, his enemies, of all parties and denominations, tell with joy.

He engaged young, and distinguished himself in business; and his penetration was almost intuition. I am old enough to have heard him speak in parliament. And I remember that, though prejudiced against him by party, I felt all the force and charms of his eloquence. Like Belial in Milton, "he made the worse appear the better cause." All the internal and external advantages and talents of an orator are undoubtedly his. Figure, voice, elocution, knowledge, and, above all, the purest and most florid diction, with the justest metaphors and happiest images, had raised him to the post of Secretary at War, at four-and-twenty years old, an age at which others are hardly thought fit for the smallest employments.

During his long exile in France, he applied himself to study with his characteristical ardor; and there he formed and chiefly executed the plan of a great philosophical work. The common bounds of human knowledge are too narrow for his warm and aspiring imagination. He must go 'extra flammantia maenia Mundi', and explore the unknown and unknowable regions of metaphysics; which open an unbounded field for the excursion of an ardent imagination; where endless conjectures supply the defect of unattainable knowledge, and too often usurp both its name and its influence.

He has had a very handsome person, with a most engaging address in his air and manners; he has all the dignity and good-breeding which a man of quality should or can have, and which so few, in this country at least, really have.

He professes himself a deist; believing in a general Providence, but doubting of, though by no means rejecting (as is commonly supposed) the immortality of the soul and a future state.

Upon the whole, of this extraordinary man, what can we say, but, alas, poor human nature!

In your destination, you will have frequent occasions to speak in public; to princes and states abroad; to the House of Commons at home; judge, then, whether eloquence is necessary for you or not; not only common eloquence, which is rather free from faults than adorned by beauties; but the highest, the most shining degree of eloquence. For God's sake, have this object always in your view and in your thoughts. Tune your tongue early to persuasion; and let no jarring, dissonant accents ever fall from it, Contract a habit of speaking well upon every occasion, and neglect yourself in no one. Eloquence and good-breeding, alone, with an exceeding small degree of parts and knowledge, will carry a man a great way; with your parts and knowledge, then, how far will they not carry you? Adieu.

LETTER XCVI

LONDON, December 16, O. S. 1749.

DEAR Boy: This letter will, I hope, find you safely arrived and well settled at Rome, after the usual distresses and accidents of a winter journey; which are very proper to teach you patience. Your stay there I look upon as a very important period of your life; and I do believe that you will fill it up well. I hope you will employ the mornings diligently with Mr. Harte, in acquiring weight; and the evenings in the best companies at Rome, in acquiring lustre. A formal, dull father, would recommend to you to plod out the evenings, too, at home, over a book by a dim taper; but I recommend to you the evenings for your pleasures, which are as much a part of your education, and almost as necessary a one, as your morning studies. Go to whatever assemblies or SPECTACLES people of fashion go to, and when you are there do as they do. Endeavor to outshine those who shine there the most, get the 'Garbo', the 'Gentilezza', the 'Leggeadria' of the Italians; make love to the most impertinent beauty of condition that you meet with, and be gallant with all the rest. Speak Italian, right or wrong, to everybody; and if you do but laugh at yourself first for your bad Italian, nobody else will laugh at you for it. That is the only way to speak it perfectly; which I expect you will do, because I am sure you may, before you leave Rome. View the most curious remains of antiquity with a classical spirit; and they will clear up to you many passages of the classical authors; particularly the Trajan and Antonine Columns; where you find the warlike instruments, the dresses, and the triumphal ornaments of the Romans. Buy also the prints and explanations of all those respectable remains of Roman grandeur, and compare them with the originals. Most young travelers are contented with a general view of those things, say they are very fine, and then go about their business. I hope you will examine them in a very different way. 'Approfondissez' everything you see or hear; and learn, if you can, the WHY and the WHEREFORE. Inquire into the meaning and the objects of the innumerable processions, which you will see at Rome at this time. Assist at all the ceremonies, and know the reason, or at least the pretenses of them, and however absurd they may be, see and speak of them with great decency. Of all things, I beg of you not to herd with your own countrymen, but to be always either with the Romans, or with the foreign ministers residing at Rome. You are sent abroad to see the manners and characters, and learn the languages of foreign countries; and not to converse with English, in English; which would defeat all those ends. Among your graver company, I recommend (as I have done before) the Jesuits to you; whose learning and address will both please and improve you; inform yourself, as much as you can, of the history, policy, and practice of that society, from the time of its founder, Ignatius of Loyola, who was himself a madman. If you would know their morality, you will find it fully and admirably stated in 'Les Lettres d'un Provincial', by the famous Monsieur Pascal; and it is a book very well worth your reading. Few people see what they see, or hear what they hear; that is, they see and hear so inattentively and superficially, that they are very little the better for what they do see and hear. This, I dare say, neither is, nor will be your case. You will understand, reflect upon, and consequently retain, what you see and hear. You have still two years good, but no more, to form your character in the world decisively; for, within two months after your arrival in England, it will be finally and irrevocably determined, one way or another, in the opinion of the public. Devote, therefore, these two years to the pursuit of perfection; which ought to be everybody's object, though in some particulars unattainable; those who strive and labor the most, will come the nearest to it. But, above all things, aim at it in the two important arts of speaking and pleasing; without them all your other talents are maimed and crippled. They are the wings upon which you must soar above other people; without them you will only crawl with the dull mass of mankind. Prepossess by your air, address, and manners; persuade by your tongue; and you will easily execute what your head has contrived. I desire that you will send me very minute accounts from Rome, not of what you see, but, of who you see; of your pleasures and entertainments. Tell me what companies you frequent most, and how you are received.

LETTER XCVII

LONDON, December 19, O. S. 1749.

DEAR BOY: The knowledge of mankind is a very use ful knowledge for everybody; a most necessary one for you, who are destined to an active, public life. You will have to do with all sorts of characters; you should, therefore, know them thoroughly, in order to manage them ably. This knowledge is not to be gotten systematically; you must acquire it yourself by your own observation and sagacity; I will give you such hints as I think may be useful land-marks in your intended progress.

I have often told you (and it is most true) that, with regard to mankind, we must not draw general conclusions from certain particular principles, though, in the main, true ones. We must not suppose that, because a man is a rational animal, he will therefore always act rationally; or, because he has such or such a predominant passion, that he will act invariably and consequentially in the pursuit of it. No. We are complicated machines: and though we have one main-spring, that gives motion to the whole, we have an infinity of little wheels, which, in their turns, retard, precipitate, and sometimes stop that motion. Let us exemplify. I will suppose ambition to be (as it commonly is) the predominant passion of a minister of state; and I will suppose that minister to be an able one. Will he, therefore, invariably pursue the object of that predominant passion? May I be sure that he will do so and so, because he ought? Nothing less. Sickness or low spirits, may damp this predominant passion; humor and peevishness may triumph over it; inferior passions may, at times, surprise it and prevail. Is this ambitious statesman amorous? Indiscreet and unguarded confidences, made in tender moments, to his wife or his mistress, may defeat all his schemes. Is he avaricious? Some great lucrative object, suddenly presenting itself, may unravel all the work of his ambition. Is he passionate? Contradiction and provocation (sometimes, it may be, too, artfully intended) may extort rash and inconsiderate expressions, or actions destructive of his main object. Is he vain, and open to flattery? An artful, flattering favorite may mislead him; and even laziness may, at certain moments, make him neglect or omit the necessary steps to that height at which he wants to arrive. Seek first, then, for the predominant passion of the character which you mean to engage and influence, and address yourself to it; but without defying or despising the inferior passions; get them in your interest too, for now and then they will have their turns. In many cases, you may not have it in your power to contribute to the gratification of the prevailing passion; then take the next best to your aid. There are many avenues to every man; and when you cannot get at him through the great one, try the serpentine ones, and you will arrive at last.

There are two inconsistent passions, which, however, frequently accompany each other, like man and wife; and which, like man and wife too, are commonly clogs upon each other. I mean ambition and avarice: the latter is often the true cause of the former, and then is the predominant passion. It seems to have been so in Cardinal Mazarin, who did anything, submitted to anything, and forgave anything, for the sake of plunder. He loved and courted power, like a usurer, because it carried profit along with it. Whoever should have formed his opinion, or taken his measures, singly, from the ambitious part of Cardinal Mazarin's character, would have found himself often mistaken. Some who had found this out, made their fortunes by letting him cheat them at play. On the contrary, Cardinal Richelieu's prevailing passion seems to have been ambition, and his immense riches only the natural consequences of that ambition gratified; and yet, I make no doubt, but that ambition had now and then its turn with the former, and avarice with the latter. Richelieu (by the way) is so strong a proof of the inconsistency of human nature, that I cannot help observing to you, that while he absolutely governed both his king and his country, and was, in a great degree, the arbiter of the fate of all Europe, he was more jealous of the great reputation of Corneille than of the power of Spain; and more flattered with being thought (what he was not) the best poet, than with being thought (what he certainly was) the greatest statesman in Europe; and affairs stood still while he was concerting the criticism upon the Cid. Could one think this possible, if one did not know it to be true? Though men are all of one composition, the several ingredients are so differently proportioned in each individual, that no two are exactly alike; and no one at all times like himself. The ablest man will sometimes do weak things; the proudest man, mean things; the honestest man, ill things; and the wickedest man, good ones. Study individuals then, and if you take (as you ought to do,) their outlines from their prevailing passion, suspend your last finishing strokes till you have attended to, and discovered the operations of their inferior passions, appetites, and humors. A man's general character may be that of the honestest man of the world: do not dispute it; you might be thought envious or ill-natured; but, at the same time, do not take this probity upon trust to such a degree as to put your life, fortune, or reputation in his power. This honest man may happen to be your rival in power, in interest, or in love; three passions that often put honesty to most severe trials, in which it is too often cast; but first analyze this honest man yourself; and then only you will be able to judge how far you may, or may not, with safety trust him.

Women are much more like each other than men: they have, in truth, but two passions, vanity and love; these are their universal characteristics. An Agrippina may sacrifice them to ambition, or a Messalina to lust; but those instances are rare; and, in general, all they say, and all they do, tends to the gratification of their vanity or their love. He who flatters them most, pleases them best; and they are the most in love with him, who they think is the most in love with them. No adulation is too strong for them; no assiduity too great; no simulation of passion too gross; as, on the other hand, the least word or action that can possibly be construed into a slight or contempt, is unpardonable, and never forgotten. Men are in this respect tender too, and will sooner forgive an injury than an insult. Some men are more captious than others; some are always wrongheaded; but every man living has such a share of vanity, as to be hurt by marks of slight and contempt. Every man does not pretend to be a poet, a mathematician, or a statesman, and considered as such; but every man pretends to common sense, and to fill his place in the world with common decency; and, consequently, does not easily forgive those negligences, inattentions and slights which seem to call in question, or utterly deny him both these pretensions.

Suspect, in general, those who remarkably affect any one virtue; who raise it above all others, and who, in a manner, intimate that they possess it exclusively. I say suspect them, for they are commonly impostors; but do not be sure that they are always so; for I have sometimes known saints really religious, blusterers really brave, reformers of manners really honest, and prudes really chaste. Pry into the recesses of their hearts yourself, as far as you are able, and never implicitly adopt a character upon common fame; which, though generally right as to the great outlines of characters, is always wrong in some particulars.

Be upon your guard against those who upon very slight acquaintance, obtrude their unasked and unmerited friendship and confidence upon you; for they probably cram you with them only for their own eating; but, at the same time, do not roughly reject them upon that general supposition. Examine further, and see whether those unexpected offers flow from a warm heart and a silly head, or from a designing head and a cold heart; for knavery and folly have often the same symptoms. In the first case, there is no danger in accepting them, 'valeant quantum valere possunt'. In the latter case, it may be useful to seem to accept them, and artfully to turn the battery upon him who raised it.

There is an incontinency of friendship among young fellows, who are associated by their mutual pleasures only, which has, very frequently, bad consequences. A parcel of warm hearts and inexperienced heads, heated by convivial mirth, and possibly a little too much wine, vow, and really mean at the time, eternal friendships to each other, and indiscreetly pour out their whole souls in common, and without the least reserve. These confidences are as indiscreetly repealed as they were made; for new pleasures and new places soon dissolve this ill-cemented connection; and then very ill uses are made of these rash confidences. Bear your part, however, in young companies; nay, excel, if you can, in all the social and convivial joy and festivity that become youth. Trust them with your love tales, if you please; but keep your serious views secret. Trust those only to some tried friend, more experienced than yourself, and who, being in a different walk of life from you, is not likely to become your rival; for I would not advise you to depend so much upon the heroic virtue of mankind, as to hope or believe that your competitor will ever be your friend, as to the object of that competition.

These are reserves and cautions very necessary to have, but very imprudent to show; the 'volto sciolto' should accompany them. Adieu.

LETTER XCVIII

DEAR BOY: Great talents and great virtues (if you should have them) will procure you the respect and the admiration of mankind; but it is the lesser talents, the 'leniores virtutes', which must procure you their love and affection. The former, unassisted and unadorned by the latter, will extort praise; but will, at the same time, excite both fear and envy; two sentiments absolutely incompatible with love and affection.

Caesar had all the great vices, and Cato all the great virtues, that men could have. But Caesar had the 'leniores virtutes' which Cato wanted, and which made him beloved, even by his enemies, and gained him the hearts of mankind, in spite of their reason: while Cato was not even beloved by his friends, notwithstanding the esteem and respect which they could not refuse to his virtues; and I am apt to think, that if Caesar had wanted, and Cato possessed, those 'leniores virtutes', the former would not have attempted (at least with success), and the latter could have protected, the liberties of Rome. Mr. Addison, in his "Cato," says of Caesar (and I believe with truth),

"Curse on his virtues, they've undone his country."

By which he means those lesser, but engaging virtues of gentleness, affability, complaisance, and good humor. The knowledge of a scholar, the courage of a hero, and the virtue of a Stoic, will be admired; but if the knowledge be accompanied with arrogance, the courage with ferocity, and the virtue with inflexible severity, the man will never be loved. The heroism of Charles XII. of Sweden (if his brutal courage deserves that name) was universally admired, but the man nowhere beloved. Whereas Henry IV. of France, who had full as much courage, and was much longer engaged in wars, was generally beloved upon account of his lesser and social virtues. We are all so formed, that our understandings are generally the DUPES of our hearts, that is, of our passions; and the surest way to the former is through the latter, which must be engaged by the 'leniores virtutes' alone, and the manner of exerting them. The insolent civility of a proud man is (for example) if possible, more shocking than his rudeness could be; because he shows you by his manner that he thinks it mere condescension in him; and that his goodness alone bestows upon you what you have no pretense to claim. He intimates his protection, instead of his friendship, by a gracious nod, instead of a usual bow; and rather signifies his consent that you may, than his invitation that you should sit, walk, eat, or drink with him.

The costive liberality of a purse-proud man insults the distresses it sometimes relieves; he takes care to make you feel your own misfortunes, and the difference between your situation and his; both which he insinuates to be justly merited: yours, by your folly; his, by his wisdom. The arrogant pedant does not communicate, but promulgates his knowledge. He does not give it you, but he inflicts it upon you; and is (if possible) more desirous to show you your own ignorance than his own learning. Such manners as these, not only in the particular instances which I have mentioned, but likewise in all others, shock and revolt that little pride and vanity which every man has in his heart; and obliterate in us the obligation for the favor conferred, by reminding us of the motive which produced, and the manner which accompanied it.

These faults point out their opposite perfections, and your own good sense will naturally suggest them to you.

But besides these lesser virtues, there are what may be called the lesser talents, or accomplishments, which are of great use to adorn and recommend all the greater; and the more so, as all people are judges of the one, and but few are of the other. Everybody feels the impression, which an engaging address, an agreeable manner of speaking, and an easy politeness, makes upon them; and they prepare the way for the favorable reception of their betters. Adieu.

LETTER XCIX

LONDON, December 26, O. S. 1749.

MY DEAR FRIEND: The new year is the season in which custom seems more particularly to authorize civil and harmless lies, under the name of compliments. People reciprocally profess wishes which they seldom form; and concern, which they seldom feel. This is not the case between you and me, where truth leaves no room for compliments.

'Dii tibi dent annos, de to nam caetera sumes', was said formerly to one by a man who certainly did not think it. With the variation of one word only, I will with great truth say it to you. I will make the first part conditional by changing, in the second, the 'nam' into 'si'. May you live as long as you are fit to live, but no longer! or may you rather die before you cease to be fit to live, than after! My true tenderness for you makes me think more of the manner than of the length of your life, and forbids me to wish it prolonged, by a single day, that should bring guilt, reproach, and shame upon you. I have not malice enough in my nature, to wish that to my greatest enemy. You are the principal object of all my cares, the only object of all my hopes; I have now reason to believe, that you will reward the former, and answer the latter; in that case, may you live long, for you must live happy; 'de te nam caetera sumes'. Conscious virtue is the only solid foundation of all happiness; for riches, power, rank, or whatever, in the common acceptation of the word, is supposed to constitute happiness, will never quiet, much less cure, the inward pangs of guilt. To that main wish, I will add those of the good old nurse of Horace, in his epistle to Tibullus: 'Sapere', you have it in a good degree already. 'Et fari ut possit quae sentiat'. Have you that? More, much more is meant by it, than common speech or mere articulation. I fear that still remains to be wished for, and I earnestly wish it to you. 'Gratia and Fama' will inevitably accompany the above-mentioned qualifications. The 'Valetudo' is the only one that is not in your own power; Heaven alone can grant it you, and may it do so abundantly! As for the 'mundus victus, non deficiente crumena', do you deserve, and I will provide them.

It is with the greatest pleasure that I consider the fair prospect which you have before you. You have seen, read, and learned more, at your age, than most young fellows have done at two or three-and-twenty. Your destination is a shining one, and leads to rank, fortune, and distinction. Your education has been calculated for it; and, to do you justice, that education has not been thrown away upon you. You want but two things, which do not want conjuration, but only care, to acquire: eloquence and manners; that is, the graces of speech, and the graces of behavior. You may have them; they are as much in your power as powdering your hair is; and will you let the want of them obscure (as it certainly will do) that shining prospect which presents itself to you. I am sure you will not. They are the sharp end, the point of the nail that you are driving, which must make way first for the larger and more solid parts to enter. Supposing your moral character as pure, and your knowledge as sound, as I really believe them both to be; you want nothing for that perfection, which I have so constantly wished you, and taken so much pains to give you, but eloquence and politeness. A man who is not born with a poetical genius, can never be a poet, or at best an extremely bad one; but every man, who can speak at all, can speak elegantly and correctly if he pleases, by attending to the best authors and orators; and, indeed, I would advise those who do not speak elegantly, not to speak at all; for I am sure they will get more by their silence than by their speech. As for politeness: whoever keeps good company, and is not polite, must have formed a resolution, and take some pains not to be so; otherwise he would naturally and insensibly take the air, the address, and the turn of those he converses with. You will, probably, in the course of this year, see as great a variety of good company in the several capitals you will be at, as in any one year of your life; and consequently must (I should hope) catch some of their manners, almost whether you will or not; but, as I dare say you will endeavor to do it, I am convinced you will succeed, and that I shall have pleasure of finding you, at your return here, one of the best-bred men in Europe.

I imagine, that when you receive my letters, and come to those parts of them which relate to eloquence and politeness, you say, or at least think, What, will he never have done upon those two subjects? Has he not said all he can say upon them? Why the same thing over and over again? If you do think or say so, it must proceed from your not yet knowing the infinite importance of these two accomplishments, which I cannot recommend to you too often, nor inculcate too strongly. But if, on the contrary, you are convinced of the utility, or rather the necessity of those two accomplishments, and are determined to acquire them, my repeated admonitions are only unnecessary; and I grudge no trouble which can possibly be of the least use to you.

I flatter myself, that your stay at Rome will go a great way toward answering all my views: I am sure it will, if you employ your time, and your whole time, as you should. Your first morning hours, I would have you devote to your graver studies with Mr. Harte; the middle part of the day I would have employed in seeing things; and the evenings in seeing people. You are not, I hope, of a lazy, inactive turn, in either body or mind; and, in that case, the day is full long enough for everything; especially at Rome, where it is not the fashion, as it is here and at Paris, to embezzle at least half of it at table. But if, by accident, two or three hours are sometimes wanting for some useful purpose, borrow them from your sleep. Six, or at most seven hours sleep is, for a constancy, as much as you or anybody can want; more is only laziness and dozing; and is, I am persuaded, both unwholesome and stupefying. If, by chance, your business, or your pleasures, should keep you up till four or five o'clock in the morning, I would advise you, however, to rise exactly at your usual time, that you may not lose the precious morning hours; and that the want of sleep may force you to go to bed earlier the next night. This is what I was advised to do when very young, by a very wise man; and what, I assure you, I always did in the most dissipated part of my life. I have very often gone to bed at six in the morning and rose, notwithstanding, at eight; by which means I got many hours in the morning that my companions lost; and the want of sleep obliged me to keep good hours the next, or at least the third night. To this method I owe the greatest part of my reading: for, from twenty to forty, I should certainly have read very little, if I had not been up while my acquaintances were in bed. Know the true value of time; snatch, seize, and enjoy every moment of it. No idleness, no laziness, no procrastination; never put off till to-morrow what you can do today. That was the rule of the famous and unfortunate Pensionary De Witt; who, by strictly following it, found time, not only to do the whole business of the republic, but to pass his evenings at assemblies and suppers, as if he had had nothing else to do or think of.

Adieu, my dear friend, for such I shall call you, and as such I shall, for the future, live with you; for I disclaim all titles which imply an authority, that I am persuaded you will never give me occasion to exercise.

'Multos et felices', most sincerely, to Mr. Harte.

1750

LETTER C

LONDON, January 8, O. S. 1750

DEAR BOY: I have seldom or never written to you upon the subject of religion and morality; your own reason, I am persuaded, has given you true notions of both; they speak best for themselves; but if they wanted assistance, you have Mr. Harte at hand, both for precept and example; to your own reason, therefore, and to Mr. Harte, shall I refer you for the reality of both, and confine myself in this letter to the decency, the utility, and the necessity of scrupulously preserving the appearances of both. When I say the appearances of religion, I do not mean that you should talk or act like a missionary or an enthusiast, nor that you should take up a controversial cudgel against whoever attacks the sect you are of; this would be both useless and unbecoming your age; but I mean that you should by no means seem to approve, encourage, or applaud, those libertine notions, which strike at religions equally, and which are the poor threadbare topics of halfwits and minute philosophers. Even those who are silly enough to laugh at their jokes, are still wise enough to distrust and detest their characters; for putting moral virtues at the highest, and religion at the lowest, religion must still be allowed to be a collateral security, at least, to virtue, and every prudent man will sooner trust to two securities than to one. Whenever, therefore, you happen to be in company with those pretended 'Esprits forts', or with thoughtless libertines, who laugh at all religion to show their wit, or disclaim it, to complete their riot, let no word or look of yours intimate the least approbation; on the contrary, let a silent gravity express your dislike: but enter not into the subject and decline such unprofitable and indecent controversies. Depend upon this truth, that every man is the worse looked upon, and the less trusted for being thought to have no religion; in spite of all the pompous and specious epithets he may assume, of 'Esprit fort', freethinker, or moral philosopher; and a wise atheist (if such a thing there is) would, for his own interest and character in this world, pretend to some religion.

Your moral character must be not only pure, but, like Caesar's wife, unsuspected. The least speck or blemish upon it is fatal. Nothing degrades and vilifies more, for it excites and unites detestation and contempt. There are, however, wretches in the world profligate enough to explode all notions of moral good and evil; to maintain that they are merely local, and depend entirely upon the customs and fashions of different countries; nay, there are still, if possible, more unaccountable wretches; I mean those who affect to preach and propagate such absurd and infamous notions without believing them themselves. These are the devil's hypocrites. Avoid, as much as possible, the company of such people; who reflect a degree of discredit and infamy upon all who converse with them. But as you may, sometimes, by accident, fall into such company, take great care that no complaisance, no good-humor, no warmth of festal mirth, ever make you seem even to acquiesce, much less to approve or applaud, such infamous doctrines. On the other hand, do not debate nor enter into serious argument upon a subject so much below it: but content yourself with telling these APOSTLES that you know they are not, serious; that you have a much better opinion of them than they would have you have; and that, you are very sure, they would not practice the doctrine they preach. But put your private mark upon them, and shun them forever afterward.

There is nothing so delicate as your moral character, and nothing which it is your interest so much to preserve pure. Should you be suspected of injustice, malignity, perfidy, lying, etc., all the parts and knowledge in the world will never procure you esteem, friendship, or respect. A strange concurrence of circumstances has sometimes raised very bad men to high stations, but they have been raised like criminals to a pillory, where their persons and their crimes, by being more conspicuous, are only the more known, the more detested, and the more pelted and insulted. If, in any case whatsoever, affectation and ostentation are pardonable, it is in the case of morality; though even there, I would not advise you to a pharisaical pomp of virtue. But I will recommend to you a most scrupulous tenderness for your moral character, and the utmost care not to say or do the least thing that may ever so slightly taint it. Show yourself, upon all occasions, the advocate, the friend, but not the bully of virtue. Colonel Chartres, whom you have certainly heard of (who was, I believe, the most notorious blasted rascal in the world, and who had, by all sorts of crimes, amassed immense wealth), was so sensible of the disadvantage of a bad character, that I heard him once say, in his impudent, profligate manner, that though he would not give one farthing for virtue, he would give ten thousand pounds for a character; because he should get a hundred thousand pounds by it; whereas, he was so blasted, that he had no longer an opportunity of cheating people. Is it possible, then, that an honest man can neglect what a wise rogue would purchase so dear?

There is one of the vices above mentioned, into which people of good education, and, in the main, of good principles, sometimes fall, from mistaken notions of skill, dexterity, and self-defense, I mean lying; though it is inseparably attended with more infamy and loss than any other. The prudence and necessity of often concealing the truth, insensibly seduces people to violate it. It is the only art of mean capacities, and the only refuge of mean spirits. Whereas, concealing the truth, upon proper occasions, is as prudent and as innocent, as telling a lie, upon any occasion, is infamous and foolish. I will state you a case in your own department. Suppose you are employed at a foreign court, and that the minister of that court is absurd or impertinent enough to ask you what your instructions are? will you tell him a lie, which as soon as found out (and found out it certainly will be) must destroy your credit, blast your character, and render you useless there? No. Will you tell him the truth then, and betray your trust? As certainly, No. But you will answer with firmness, That you are surprised at such a question, that you are persuaded he does not expect an answer to it; but that, at all events, he certainly will not have one. Such an answer will give him confidence in you; he will conceive an opinion of your veracity, of which opinion you may afterward make very honest and fair advantages. But if, in negotiations, you are looked upon as a liar and a trickster, no confidence will be placed in you, nothing will be communicated to you, and you will be in the situation of a man who has been burned in the cheek; and who, from that mark, cannot afterward get an honest livelihood if he would, but must continue a thief.

Lord Bacon, very justly, makes a distinction between simulation and dissimulation; and allows the latter rather than the former; but still observes, that they are the weaker sort of politicians who have recourse to either. A man who has strength of mind and strength of parts, wants neither of them. Certainly (says he) the ablest men that ever were, have all had an openness and frankness of dealing, and a name of certainty and veracity; but then, they were like horses well managed; for they could tell, passing well, when to stop or turn; and at such times, when they thought the case indeed required some dissimulation, if then they used it, it came to pass that the former opinion spread abroad of their good faith and clearness of dealing, made them almost invisible.

There are people who indulge themselves in a sort of lying, which they reckon innocent, and which in one sense is so; for it hurts nobody but themselves. This sort of lying is the spurious offspring of vanity, begotten upon folly: these people deal in the marvelous; they have seen some things that never existed; they have seen other things which they never really saw, though they did exist, only because they were thought worth seeing. Has anything remarkable been said or done in any place, or in any company? they immediately present and declare themselves eye or ear witnesses of it. They have done feats themselves, unattempted, or at least unperformed by others. They are always the heroes of their own fables; and think that they gain consideration, or at least present attention, by it. Whereas, in truth, all that they get is ridicule and contempt, not without a good degree of distrust; for one must naturally conclude, that he who will tell any lie from idle vanity, will not scruple telling a greater for interest. Had I really seen anything so very extraordinary as to be almost incredible I would keep it to myself, rather than by telling it give anybody room to doubt, for one minute, of my veracity. It is most certain, that the reputation of chastity is not so necessary for a women, as that of veracity is for a man; and with reason; for it is possible for a woman to be virtuous, though not strictly chaste, but it is not possible for a man to be virtuous without strict veracity. The slips of the poor women are sometimes mere bodily frailties; but a lie in a man is a vice of the mind and of the heart. For God's sake be scrupulously jealous of the purity of your moral character; keep it immaculate, unblemished, unsullied; and it will be unsuspected. Defamation and calumny never attack, where there is no weak place; they magnify, but they do not create.

There is a very great difference between the purity of character, which I so earnestly recommend to you, and the stoical gravity and austerity of character, which I do by no means recommend to you. At your age, I would no more wish you to be a Cato than a Clodius. Be, and be reckoned, a man of pleasure as well as a man of business. Enjoy this happy and giddy time of your life; shine in the pleasures, and in the company of people of your own age. This is all to be done, and indeed only can be done, without the least taint to the purity of your moral character; for those mistaken young fellows, who think to shine by an impious or immoral licentiousness, shine only from their stinking, like corrupted flesh, in the dark. Without this purity, you can have no dignity of character; and without dignity of character it is impossible to rise in the world. You must be respectable, if you will be respected. I have known people slattern away their character, without really polluting it; the consequence of which has been, that they have become innocently contemptible; their merit has been dimmed, their pretensions unregarded, and all their views defeated. Character must be kept bright, as well as clean. Content yourself with mediocrity in nothing. In purity of character and in politeness of manners labor to excel all, if you wish to equal many. Adieu.

LETTER CI

LONDON, January 11, O. S. 1750

MY DEAR FRIEND: Yesterday I received a letter from Mr. Harte, of the 31st December, N. S., which I will answer soon; and for which I desire you to return him my thanks now. He tells me two things that give me great satisfaction: one is that there are very few English at Rome; the other is, that you frequent the best foreign companies. This last is a very good symptom; for a man of sense is never desirous to frequent those companies, where he is not desirous to please, or where he finds that he displeases; it will not be expected in those companies, that, at your age, you should have the 'Garbo', the 'Disinvoltura', and the 'Leggiadria' of a man of five-and-twenty, who has been long used to keep the best companies; and therefore do not be discouraged, and think yourself either slighted or laughed at, because you see others, older and more used to the world, easier, more familiar, and consequently rather better received in those companies than yourself. In time your turn will come; and if you do but show an inclination, a desire to please, though you should be embarrassed or even err in the means, which must necessarily happen to you at first, yet the will (to use a vulgar expression) will be taken for the deed; and people, instead of laughing at you, will be glad to instruct you. Good sense can only give you the great outlines of good-breeding; but observation and usage can alone give you the delicate touches, and the fine coloring. You will naturally endeavor to show the utmost respect to people of certain ranks and characters, and consequently you will show it; but the proper, the delicate manner of showing that respect, nothing but observation and time can give.

I remember that when, with all the awkwardness and rust of Cambridge about me, I was first introduced into good company, I was frightened out of my wits. I was determined to be, what I thought, civil; I made fine low bows, and placed myself below everybody; but when I was spoken to, or attempted to speak myself, 'obstupui, steteruntque comae, et vox faucibus haesit'. If I saw people whisper, I was sure it was at me; and I thought myself the sole object of either the ridicule or the censure of the whole company, who, God knows, did not trouble their heads about me. In this way I suffered, for some time, like a criminal at the bar; and should certainly have renounced all polite company forever, if I had not been so convinced of the absolute necessity of forming my manners upon those of the best companies, that I determined to persevere and suffer anything, or everything, rather than not compass that point. Insensibly it grew easier to me; and I began not to bow so ridiculously low, and to answer questions without great hesitation or stammering: if, now and then, some charitable people, seeing my embarrassment, and being 'desoevre' themselves, came and spoke to me, I considered them as angels sent to comfort me, and that gave me a little courage. I got more soon afterward, and was intrepid enough to go up to a fine woman, and tell her that I thought it a warm day; she answered me, very civilly, that she thought so too; upon which the conversation ceased, on my part, for some time, till she, good-naturedly resuming it, spoke to me thus: "I see your embarrassment, and I am sure that the few words you said to me cost you a great deal; but do not be discouraged for that reason, and avoid good company. We see that you desire to please, and that is the main point; you want only the manner, and you think that you want it still more than you do. You must go through your noviciate before you can profess good-breeding: and, if you will be my novice, I will present you my acquaintance as such."

You will easily imagine how much this speech pleased me, and how awkwardly I answered it; I hemmed once or twice (for it gave me a bur in my throat) before I could tell her that I was very much obliged to her; that it was true, that I had a great deal of reason to distrust my own behavior, not being used to fine company; and that I should be proud of being her novice, and receiving her instructions.

As soon as I had fumbled out this answer, she called up three or four people to her, and said: Savez-vous (for she was a foreigner, and I was abroad) que j'ai entrepris ce jeune homme, et qu'il le faut rassurer? Pour moi, je crois en avoir fait——[Do you know that I have undertaken this young man, and he must be encouraged? As for me, I think I have made a conquest of him; for he just now ventured to tell me, although tremblingly, that it is warm. You will assist me in polishing him. He must necessarily have a passion for somebody; if he does not think me worthy of being the object, he will seek out some other. However, my novice, do not disgrace yourself by frequenting opera girls and actresses; who will not require of you sentiments and politeness, but will be your ruin in every respect. I repeat it to you, my friend, if you should get into low, mean company, you will be undone. Those creatures will destroy your fortune and your health, corrupt your morals, and you will never acquire the style of good company.]

The company laughed at this lecture, and I was stunned with it. I did not know whether she was serious or in jest. By turns I was pleased, ashamed, encouraged, and dejected. But when I found afterward, that both she, and those to whom she had presented me, countenanced and protected me in company, I gradually got more assurance, and began not to be ashamed of endeavoring to be civil. I copied the best masters, at first servilely, afterward more freely, and at last I joined habit and invention.

All this will happen to you, if you persevere in the desire of pleasing and shining as a man of the world; that part of your character is the only one about which I have at present the least doubt. I cannot entertain the least suspicion of your moral character; your learned character is out of question. Your polite character is now the only remaining object that gives me the least anxiety; and you are now in the right way of finishing it. Your constant collision with good company will, of course, smooth and polish you. I could wish that you would say, to the five or six men or women with whom you are the most acquainted, that you are sensible that, from youth and inexperience, you must make many mistakes in good-breeding; that you beg of them to correct you, without reserve, wherever they see you fail; and that you shall take such admonition as the strongest proofs of their friendship. Such a confession and application will be very engaging to those to whom you make them. They will tell others of them, who will be pleased with that disposition, and, in a friendly manner, tell you of any little slip or error. The Duke de Nivernois—[At that time Ambassador from the Court of France to Rome.]—would, I am sure, be charmed, if you dropped such a thing to him; adding, that you loved to address yourself always to the best masters. Observe also the different modes of good-breeding of several nations, and conform yourself to them respectively. Use an easy civility with the French, more ceremony with the Italians, and still more with the Germans; but let it be without embarrassment and with ease. Bring it by use to be habitual to you; for, if it seems unwilling and forced; it will never please. 'Omnis Aristippum decuit color, et res'. Acquire an easiness and versatility of manners, as well as of mind; and, like the chameleon, take the hue of the company you are with.

There is a sort of veteran women of condition, who having lived always in the 'grande monde', and having possibly had some gallantries, together with the experience of five-and-twenty, or thirty years, form a young fellow better than all the rules that can be given him. These women, being past their bloom, are extremely flattered by the least attention from a young fellow; and they will point out to him those manners and ATTENTIONS that pleased and engaged them, when they were in the pride of their youth and beauty. Wherever you go, make some of those women your friends; which a very little matter will do. Ask their advice, tell them your doubts or difficulties as to your behavior; but take great care not to drop one word of their experience; for experience implies age; and the suspicion of age, no woman, let her be ever so old, ever forgives. I long for your picture, which Mr. Harte tells me is now drawing. I want to see your countenance, your air, and even your dress; the better they all three are, the better I am not wise enough to despise any one of them. Your dress, at least, is in your own power, and I hope that you mind it to a proper degree. Yours,
Adieu.

LETTER CII

LONDON, January 18, O. S. 1750

MY DEAR FRIEND: I consider the solid part of your little edifice as so near being finished and completed, that my only remaining care is about the embellishments; and that must now be your principal care too. Adorn yourself with all those graces and accomplishments, which, without solidity, are frivolous; but without which solidity is, to a great degree, useless. Take one man, with a very moderate degree of knowledge, but with a pleasing figure, a prepossessing address, graceful in all that he says and does, polite, 'liant', and, in short, adorned with all the lesser talents: and take another man, with sound sense and profound knowledge, but without the above-mentioned advantages; the former will not only get the better of the latter, in every pursuit of every KIND, but in truth there will be no sort of competition between them. But can every man acquire these advantages? I say, Yes, if he please, suppose he is in a situation and in circumstances to frequent good company. Attention, observation, and imitation, will most infallibly do it.

When you see a man whose first 'abord' strikes you, prepossesses you in his favor, and makes you entertain a good opinion of him, you do not know why, analyze that 'abord', and examine, within yourself, the several parts that composed it; and you will generally find it to be the result, the happy assemblage of modesty unembarrassed, respect without timidity, a genteel, but unaffected attitude of body and limbs, an open, cheerful, but unsmirking countenance, and a dress, by no means negligent, and yet not foppish. Copy him, then, not servilely, but as some of the greatest masters of painting have copied others; insomuch that their copies have been equal to the originals, both as to beauty and freedom. When you see a man who is universally allowed to shine as an agreeable, well-bred man, and a fine gentleman (as, for example, the Duke de Nivernois), attend to him, watch him carefully; observe in what manner he addresses himself to his superiors, how he lives with his equals, and how he treats his inferiors. Mind his turn of conversation in the several situations of morning visits, the table, and the evening amusements. Imitate, without mimicking him; and be his duplicate, but not his ape. You will find that he takes care never to say or do any thing that can be construed into a slight, or a negligence; or that can, in any degree, mortify people's vanity and self-love; on the contrary, you will perceive that he makes people pleased with him, by making them first pleased with themselves: he shows respect, regard, esteem and attention, where they are severally proper: he sows them with care, and he reaps them in plenty.

These amiable accomplishments are all to be acquired by use and imitation; for we are, in truth, more than half what we are by imitation. The great point is, to choose good models and to study them with care. People insensibly contract, not only the air, the manners, and the vices, of those with whom they commonly converse, but their virtues too, and even their way of thinking. This is so true, that I have known very plain understandings catch a certain degree of wit, by constantly conversing with those who had a great deal. Persist, therefore, in keeping the best company, and you will insensibly become like them; but if you add attention and observation, you will very soon become one of them. The inevitable contagion of company shows you the necessity of keeping the best, and avoiding all other; for in everyone, something will stick. You have hitherto, I confess, had very few opportunities of keeping polite company. Westminster school is, undoubtedly, the seat of illiberal manners and brutal behavior. Leipsig, I suppose, is not the seat of refined and elegant manners. Venice, I believe, has done something; Rome, I hope, will do a great deal more; and Paris will, I dare say, do all that you want; always supposing that you frequent the best companies, and in the intention of improving and forming yourself; for without that intention nothing will do.

LETTERS TO HIS SON, COMPLETE

I here subjoin a list of all those necessary, ornamental accomplishments (without which, no man living can either please, or rise in the world) which hitherto I fear you want, and which only require your care and attention to possess.

To speak elegantly, whatever language you speak in; without which nobody will hear you with pleasure, and consequently you will speak to very little purpose.

An agreeable and distinct elocution; without which nobody will hear you with patience: this everybody may acquire, who is not born with some imperfection in the organs of speech. You are not; and therefore it is wholly in your power. You need take much less pains for it than Demosthenes did.

A distinguished politeness of manners and address; which common sense, observation, good company, and imitation, will infallibly give you if you will accept it.

A genteel carriage and graceful motions, with the air of a man of fashion: a good dancing-master, with some care on your part, and some imitation of those who excel, will soon bring this about.

To be extremely clean in your person, and perfectly well dressed, according to the fashion, be that what it will: Your negligence of your dress while you were a schoolboy was pardonable, but would not be so now.

Upon the whole, take it for granted, that without these accomplishments, all you know, and all you can do, will avail you very little. Adieu.

LETTER CIII

LONDON, January 25, O. S. 1750

MY DEAR FRIEND: It is so long since I have heard from you, that I suppose Rome engrosses every moment of your time; and if it engrosses it in the manner I could wish, I willingly give up my share of it. I would rather 'prodesse quam conspici'. Put out your time, but to good interest; and I do not desire to borrow much of it. Your studies, the respectable remains of antiquity, and your evening amusements cannot, and indeed ought not, to leave you much time to write. You will, probably, never see Rome again; and therefore you ought to see it well now; by seeing it well, I do not mean only the buildings, statues, and paintings, though they undoubtedly deserve your attention: but I mean seeing into the constitution and government of it. But these things certainly occur to your own common sense.

How go, your pleasures at Rome? Are you in fashion there? that is, do you live with the people who are?—the only way of being so yourself, in time. Are you domestic enough in any considerable house to be called 'le petit Stanhope'? Has any woman of fashion and good-breeding taken the trouble of abusing and laughing at you amicably to your face? Have you found a good 'decrotteuse'. For those are the steps by which you must rise to politeness. I do not presume to ask if you have any attachment, because I believe you will not make me your confident; but this I will say, eventually, that if you have one, 'il faut bien payer d'attentions et de petits soin', if you would have your sacrifice propitiously received. Women are not so much taken by beauty as men are, but prefer those men who show them the most attention.

Would you engage the lovely fair?

With gentlest manners treat her;

With tender looks and graceful air,

In softest accents greet her.

Verse were but vain, the Muses fail,

Without the Graces' aid;

The God of Verse could not prevail

To stop the flying maid.

Attention by attentions gain,

And merit care by cares;

So shall the nymph reward your pain;

And Venus crown your prayers.

Probatum est.

A man's address and manner weigh much more with them than his beauty; and, without them, the Abbati and Monsignori will get the better of you. This address and manner should be exceedingly respectful, but at the same time easy and unembarrassed. Your chit-chat or 'entregent' with them neither can, nor ought to be very solid; but you should take care to turn and dress up your trifles prettily, and make them every now and then convey indirectly some little piece of flattery. A fan, a riband, or a head-dress, are great materials for gallant dissertations, to one who has got 'le ton leger et aimable de la bonne compagnie'. At all events, a man had better talk too much to women, than too little; they take silence for dullness, unless where they think that the passion they have inspired occasions it; and in that case they adopt the notion, that

Silence in love betrays more woe

> Than words, though ne'er so witty;
>
> The beggar that is dumb, we know,
>
> Deserves a double pity.

'A propos' of this subject: what progress do you make in that language, in which Charles the Fifth said that he would choose to speak to his mistress? Have you got all the tender diminutives, in 'etta, ina', and 'ettina', which, I presume, he alluded to? You already possess, and, I hope, take care not to forget, that language which he reserved for his horse. You are absolutely master, too, of that language in which he said he would converse with men; French. But, in every language, pray attend carefully to the choice of your words, and to the turn of your expression. Indeed, it is a point of very great consequence. To be heard with success, you must be heard with pleasure: words are the dress of thoughts; which should no more be presented in rags, tatters, and dirt, than your person should. By the way, do you mind your person and your dress sufficiently? Do you take great care of your teeth? Pray have them put in order by the best operator at Rome. Are you be-laced, bepowdered, and be-feathered, as other young fellows are, and should be? At your age, 'il faut du brillant, et meme un peu de fracas, mais point de mediocre; il faut un air vif, aise et noble. Avec les hommes, un maintien respectueux et en meme tems respectable; avec les femmes, un caquet leger, enjoue, et badin, mais toujours fort poli'.

To give you an opportunity of exerting your talents, I send you, here inclosed, a letter of recommendation from Monsieur Villettes to Madame de Simonetti at Milan; a woman of the first fashion and consideration there; and I shall in my next send you another from the same person to Madame Clerici, at the same place. As these two ladies' houses are the resort of all the people of fashion at Milan, those two recommendations will introduce you to them all. Let me know, in due time, if you have received these two letters, that I may have them renewed, in case of accidents.

Adieu, my dear friend! Study hard; divert yourself heartily; distinguish carefully between the pleasures of a man of fashion, and the vices of a scoundrel; pursue the former, and abhor the latter, like a man of sense.

LETTER CIV

LONDON, February 5, O. S. 1750

MY DEAR FRIEND: Very few people are good economists of their fortune, and still fewer of their time; and yet of the two, the latter is the most precious. I heartily wish you to be a good economist of both: and you are now of an age to begin to think seriously of those two important articles. Young people are apt to think that they have so much time before them, that they may squander what they please of it, and yet have enough left; as very great fortunes have frequently seduced people to a ruinous profusion. Fatal mistakes, always repented of, but always too late! Old Mr. Lowndes, the famous Secretary of the Treasury in the reigns of King William, Queen Anne, and King George the First, used to say,—TAKE CARE OF THE PENCE, AND THE POUNDS WILL TAKE CARE OF THEMSELVES. To this maxim, which he not only preached but practiced, his two grandsons at this time owe the very considerable fortunes that he left them.

This holds equally true as to time; and I most earnestly recommend to you the care of those minutes and quarters of hours, in the course of the day, which people think too short to deserve their attention; and yet, if summed up at the end of the year, would amount to a very considerable portion of time. For example: you are to be at such a place at twelve, by appointment; you go out at eleven, to make two or three visits first; those persons are not at home, instead of sauntering away that intermediate time at a coffeehouse, and possibly alone, return home, write a letter, beforehand, for the ensuing post, or take up a good book, I do not mean Descartes, Malebranche, Locke, or Newton, by way of dipping; but some book of rational amusement and detached pieces, as Horace, Boileau, Waller, La Bruyere, etc. This will be so much time saved, and by no means ill employed. Many people lose a great deal of time by reading: for they read frivolous and idle books, such as the absurd romances of the two last centuries; where characters, that never existed, are insipidly displayed, and sentiments that were never felt, pompously described: the Oriental ravings and extravagances of the "Arabian Nights," and Mogul tales; or, the new flimsy brochures that now swarm in France, of fairy tales, 'Reflections sur le coeur et l'esprit, metaphysique de l'amour, analyse des beaux sentimens', and such sort of idle frivolous stuff, that nourishes and improves the mind just as much as whipped cream would the body. Stick to the best established books in every language; the celebrated poets, historians, orators, or philosophers. By these means (to use a city metaphor) you will make fifty PER CENT. Of that time, of which others do not make above three or four, or probably nothing at all.

Many people lose a great deal of their time by laziness; they loll and yawn in a great chair, tell themselves that they have not time to begin anything then, and that it will do as well another time. This is a most unfortunate disposition, and the greatest obstruction to both knowledge and business. At your age, you have no right nor claim to laziness; I have, if I please, being emeritus. You are but just listed in the world, and must be active, diligent, indefatigable. If ever you propose commanding with dignity, you must serve up to it with diligence. Never put off till tomorrow what you can do to-day.

Dispatch is the soul of business; and nothing contributes more to dispatch than method. Lay down a method for everything, and stick to it inviolably, as far as unexpected incidents may allow. Fix one certain hour and day in the week for your accounts, and keep them together in their proper order; by which means they will require very little time, and you can never be much cheated. Whatever letters and papers you keep, docket and tie them up in their respective classes, so that you may instantly have recourse to any one. Lay down a method also for your reading, for which you allot a certain share of your mornings; let it be in a consistent and consecutive course, and not in that desultory and unmethodical manner, in which many people read scraps of different authors, upon different subjects. Keep a useful and short commonplace book of what you read, to help your memory only, and not for pedantic quotations. Never read history without having maps and a chronological book, or tables, lying by you, and constantly recurred to; without which history is only a confused heap of facts. One method more I recommend to you, by which I have found great benefit, even in the most dissipated part of my life; that is, to rise early, and at the same hour every morning, how late soever you may have sat up the night before. This secures you an hour or two, at least, of reading or reflection before the common interruptions of the morning begin; and it will save your constitution, by forcing you to go to bed early, at least one night in three.

You will say, it may be, as many young people would, that all this order and method is very troublesome, only fit for dull people, and a disagreeable restraint upon the noble spirit and fire of youth. I deny it; and assert, on the contrary, that it will procure you both more time and more taste for your pleasures; and, so far from being troublesome to you, that after you have pursued it a month, it would be troublesome to you to lay it aside. Business whets the appetite, and gives a taste to pleasure, as exercise does to food; and business can never be done without method; it raises the spirits for pleasures; and a SPECTACLE, a ball, an assembly, will much more sensibly affect a man who has employed, than a man who has lost, the preceding part of the day; nay, I will venture to say, that a fine lady will seem to have more charms to a man of study or business, than to a saunterer. The same listlessness runs through his whole conduct, and he is as insipid in his pleasures, as inefficient in everything else.

I hope you earn your pleasures, and consequently taste them; for, by the way, I know a great many men, who call themselves men of pleasure, but who, in truth, have none. They adopt other people's indiscriminately, but without any taste of their own. I have known them often inflict excesses upon themselves because they thought them genteel; though they sat as awkwardly upon them as other people's clothes would have done. Have no pleasures but your own, and then you will shine in them. What are yours? Give me a short history of them. 'Tenez-vous votre coin a table, et dans les bonnes compagnies? y brillez-vous du cote de la politesse, de d'enjouement, du badinage? Etes-vous galant? Filex-vous le parfait amour? Est-il question de flechir par vos soins et par vos attentions les rigueurs de quelque fiere Princesse'? You may safely trust me; for though I am a severe censor of vice and folly, I am a friend and advocate for pleasures, and will contribute all in my power to yours.

There is a certain dignity to be kept up in pleasures, as well as in business. In love, a man may lose his heart with dignity; but if he loses his nose, he loses his character into the bargain. At table, a man may with decency have a distinguishing palate; but indiscriminate voraciousness degrades him to a glutton. A man may play with decency; but if he games, he is disgraced. Vivacity and wit make a man shine in company; but trite jokes and loud laughter reduce him to a buffoon. [see Mark Twain's identical advice in his 'Speeches' D.W.] Every virtue, they say, has its kindred vice; every pleasure, I am sure, has its neighboring disgrace. Mark carefully, therefore, the line that separates them, and rather stop a yard short, than step an inch beyond it.

I wish to God that you had as much pleasure in following my advice, as I have in giving it you! and you may the more easily have it, as I give you none that is inconsistent with your pleasure. In all that I say to you, it is your interest alone that I consider: trust to my experience; you know you may to my affection. Adieu.

I have received no letter yet from you or Mr. Harte.

LETTER CV

LONDON, February 8, O. S. 1750

MY DEAR FRIEND: You have, by this time, I hope and believe, made such a progress in the Italian language, that you can read it with ease; I mean, the easy books in it; and indeed, in that, as well as in every other language, the easiest books are generally the best; for, whatever author is obscure and difficult in his own language, certainly does not think clearly. This is, in my opinion, the case of a celebrated Italian author; to whom the Italians, from the admiration they have of him, have given the epithet of il divino; I mean Dante. Though I formerly knew Italian extremely well, I could never understand him; for which reason I had done with him, fully convinced that he was not worth the pains necessary to understand him.

The good Italian authors are, in my mind, but few; I mean, authors of invention; for there are, undoubtedly, very good historians and excellent translators. The two poets worth your reading, and, I was going to say, the only two, are Tasso and Ariosto. Tasso's 'Gierusalemme Liberata' is altogether unquestionably a fine poem, though—it has some low, and many false thoughts in it: and Boileau very justly makes it the mark of a bad taste, to compare 'le Clinquant Tasse a l' Or de Virgile'. The image, with which he adorns the introduction of his epic poem, is low and disgusting; it is that of a froward, sick, puking child, who is deceived into a dose of necessary physic by 'du bon-bon'. These verses are these:

"Cosi all'egro fanciul porgiamo aspersi

Di soavi licor gli orli del vaso:

Succhi amari ingannato intanto ei beve,

E dall' inganno suo vita riceve."

However, the poem, with all its faults about it, may justly be called a fine one.

If fancy, imagination, invention, description, etc., constitute a poet, Ariosto is, unquestionably, a great one. His "Orlando," it is true, is a medley of lies and truths—sacred and profane—wars, loves, enchantments, giants, madheroes, and adventurous damsels, but then, he gives it you very fairly for what it is, and does not pretend to put it upon you for the true 'epopee', or epic poem. He says:

"Le Donne, i Cavalier, l'arme, gli amori

Le cortesie, l'audaci imprese, io canto."

The connections of his stories are admirable, his reflections just, his sneers and ironies incomparable, and his painting excellent. When Angelica, after having wandered over half the world alone with Orlando, pretends, notwithstanding,

"——-ch'el fior virginal cosi avea salvo,

Come selo porto dal matern' alvo."

The author adds, very gravely,—

"Forse era ver, ma non pero credibile

A chi del senso suo fosse Signore."

Astolpho's being carried to the moon by St. John, in order to look for Orlando's lost wits, at the end of the 34th book, and the many lost things that he finds there, is a most happy extravagancy, and contains, at the same time, a great deal of sense. I would advise you to read this poem with attention. It is, also, the source of half the tales, novels, and plays, that have been written since.

The 'Pastor Fido' of Guarini is so celebrated, that you should read it; but in reading it, you will judge of the great propriety of the characters. A parcel of shepherds and shepherdesses, with the TRUE PASTORAL' SIMPLICITY, talk metaphysics, epigrams, 'concetti', and quibbles, by the hour to each other.

The Aminto del Tasso, is much more what it is intended to be, a pastoral: the shepherds, indeed, have their 'concetti' and their antitheses; but are not quite so sublime and abstracted as those in Pastor Fido. I think that you will like it much the best of the two.

Petrarca is, in my mind, a sing-song, love-sick poet; much admired, however, by the Italians: but an Italian who should think no better of him than I do, would certainly say that he deserved his 'Laura' better than his 'Lauro'; and that wretched quibble would be reckoned an excellent piece of Italian wit.

The Italian prose-writers (of invention I mean) which I would recommend to your acquaintance, are Machiavello and Boccacio; the former, for the established reputation which he has acquired, of a consummate politician (whatever my own private sentiments may be of either his politics or his morality): the latter, for his great invention, and for his natural and agreeable manner of telling his stories.

Guicciardini, Bentivoglio, Davila, etc., are excellent historians, and deserved being read with attention. The nature of history checks, a little, the flights of Italian imaginations; which, in works of invention, are very high indeed. Translations curb them still more: and their translations of the classics are incomparable; particularly the first ten, translated in the time of Leo the Tenth, and inscribed to him, under the title of Collana. That original Collana has been lengthened since; and if I mistake not, consist now of one hundred and ten volumes.

From what I have said, you will easily guess that I meant to put you upon your guard; and not let your fancy be dazzled and your taste corrupted by the concetti, the quaintnesses, and false thoughts, which are too much the characteristics of the Italian and Spanish authors. I think you are in no great danger, as your taste has been formed upon the best ancient models, the Greek and Latin authors of the best ages, who indulge themselves in none of the puerilities I have hinted at. I think I may say, with truth; that true wit, sound taste, and good sense, are now, as it were, engrossed by France and England. Your old acquaintances, the Germans, I fear, are a little below them; and your new acquaintances, the Italians, are a great deal too much above them. The former, I doubt, crawl a little; the latter, I am sure, very often fly out of sight.

I recommended to you a good many years ago, and I believe you then read, La maniere de bien penser dans les ouvrages d'esprit par le Pere Bouhours; and I think it is very well worth your reading again, now that you can judge of it better. I do not know any book that contributes more to form a true taste; and you find there, into the bargain, the most celebrated passages, both of the ancients and the moderns, which refresh your memory with what you have formerly read in them separately. It is followed by a book much of the same size, by the same author, entitled, 'Suite des Pensees ingenieuses'.

To do justice to the best English and French authors, they have not given into that false taste; they allow no thoughts to be good, that are not just and founded upon truth. The age of Lewis XIV. was very like the Augustan; Boileau, Moliere, La Fontaine, Racine, etc., established the true, and exposed the false taste. The reign of King Charles II. (meritorious in no other respect) banished false taste out of England, and proscribed puns, quibbles, acrostics, etc. Since that, false wit has renewed its attacks, and endeavored to recover its lost empire, both in England and France; but without success; though, I must say, with more success in France than in England. Addison, Pope, and Swift, have vigorously defended the rights of good sense, which is more than can be said of their contemporary French authors, who have of late had a great tendency to 'le faux brillant', 'le raffinement, et l'entortillement'. And Lord Roscommon would be more in the right now, than he was then, in saying that,

"The English bullion of one sterling line,

Drawn to French wire, would through whole pages shine."

Lose no time, my dear child, I conjure you, in forming your taste, your manners, your mind, your everything; you have but two years' time to do it in; for whatever you are, to a certain degree, at twenty, you will be, more or less, all the rest of your life. May it be a long and happy one. Adieu.

LETTER CVI

LONDON, February 22, O. S. 1750

MY DEAR FRIEND: If the Italian of your letter to Lady Chesterfield was all your own, I am very well satisfied with the progress which you have made in that language in so short a time; according to that gradation, you will, in a very little time more, be master of it. Except at the French Ambassador's, I believe you hear only Italian spoke; for the Italians speak very little French, and that little generally very ill. The French are even with them, and generally speak Italian as ill; for I never knew a Frenchman in my life who could pronounce the Italian ce, ci, or ge, gi. Your desire of pleasing the Roman ladies will of course give you not only the desire, but the means of speaking to them elegantly in their own language. The Princess Borghese, I am told, speaks French both ill and unwillingly; and therefore you should make a merit to her of your application to her language. She is, by a kind of prescription (longer than she would probably wish), at the head of the 'beau monde' at Rome; and can, consequently, establish or destroy a young fellow's fashionable character. If she declares him 'amabile e leggiadro', others will think him so, or at least those who do not will not dare to say so. There are in every great town some such women, whose rank, beauty, and fortune have conspired to place them at the head of the fashion. They have generally been gallant, but within certain decent bounds. Their gallantries have taught, both them and their admirers, good-breeding; without which they could keep up no dignity, but would be vilified by those very gallantries which put them in vogue. It is with these women, as with ministers and favorites at court; they decide upon fashion and characters, as these do of fortunes and preferments. Pay particular court, therefore, wherever you are, to these female sovereigns of the 'beau monde'; their recommendation is a passport through all the realms of politeness. But then, remember that they require minute officious attentions. You should, if possible, guess at and anticipate all their little fancies and inclinations; make yourself familiarly and domestically useful to them, by offering yourself for all their little commissions, and assisting in doing the honors of their houses, and entering with seeming unction into all their little grievances, bustles, and views; for they are always busy. If you are once 'ben ficcato' at the Palazzo Borghese, you twill soon be in fashion at Rome; and being in fashion will soon fashion you; for that is what you must now think of very seriously.

I am sorry that there is no good dancing-master at Rome, to form your exterior air and carriage; which, I doubt, are not yet the genteelest in the world. But you may, and I hope you will, in the meantime, observe the air and carriage of those who are reckoned to have the best, and form your own upon them. Ease, gracefulness, and dignity, compose the air and address of a man of fashion; which is as unlike the affected attitudes and motions of a 'petit maitre', as it is to the awkward, negligent, clumsy, and slouching manner of a booby.

I am extremely pleased with the account Mr. Harte has given me of the allotment of your time at Rome. Those five hours every morning, which you employ in serious studies with Mr. Harte, are laid out with great interest, and will make you rich all the rest of your life. I do not look upon the subsequent morning hours, which you pass with your Ciceroni, to be ill-disposed of; there is a kind of connection between them; and your evening diversions in good company are, in their way, as useful and necessary. This is the way for you to have both weight and lustre in the world; and this is the object which I always had in view in your education.

Adieu, my friend! go on and prosper.

Mr. Grevenkop has just received Mr. Harte's letter of the 19th N. S.

LETTER CVII

LONDON, March 8, O. S. 1750

Young as you are, I hope you are in haste to live; by living, I mean living with lustre and honor to yourself, with utility to society; doing what may deserve to be written, or writing what may deserve to be read; I should wish both. Those who consider life in that light, will not idly lavish one moment. The present moments are the only ones we are sure of, and as such the most valuable; but yours are doubly so at your age; for the credit, the dignity, the comfort, and the pleasure of all your future moments, depend upon the use you make of your present ones.

EARL OF PHILIP DORMER STANHOPE CHESTERFIELD

I am extremely satisfied with your present manner of employing your time; but will you always employ it as well? I am far from meaning always in the same way; but I mean as well in proportion, in the variation of age and circumstances. You now, study five hours every morning; I neither suppose that you will, nor desire that you should do so for the rest of your life. Both business and pleasure will justly and equally break in upon those hours. But then, will you always employ the leisure they leave you in useful studies? If you have but an hour, will you improve that hour, instead of idling it away? While you have such a friend and monitor with you as Mr. Harte, I am sure you will. But suppose that business and situations should, in six or seen months, call Mr. Harte away from you; tell me truly, what may I expect and depend upon from you, when left to yourself? May I be sure that you will employ some part of every day, in adding something to that stock of knowledge which he will have left you? May I hope that you will allot one hour in the week to the care of your own affairs, to keep them in that order and method which every prudent man does? But, above all, may I be convinced that your pleasures, whatever they may be, will be confined within the circle of good company, and people of fashion? Those pleasures I recommend to you; I will promote them I will pay for them; but I will neither pay for, nor suffer, the unbecoming, disgraceful, and degrading pleasures (they should not be called pleasures), of low and profligate company. I confess the pleasures of high life are not always strictly philosophical; and I believe a Stoic would blame, my indulgence; but I am yet no Stoic, though turned of five-and-fifty; and I am apt to think that you are rather less so, at eighteen. The pleasures of the table, among people of the first fashion, may indeed sometimes, by accident, run into excesses: but they will never sink into a continued course of gluttony and drunkenness. The gallantry of high life, though not strictly justifiable, carries, at least, no external marks of infamy about it. Neither the heart nor the constitution is corrupted by it; neither nose nor character lost by it; manners, possibly, improved. Play, in good company, is only play, and not gaming; not deep, and consequently not dangerous nor dishonorable. It is only the interacts of other amusements.

This, I am sure, is not talking to you like an old man, though it is talking to you like an old friend; these are not hard conditions to ask of you. I am certain you have sense enough to know how reasonable they are on my part, how advantageous they are on yours: but have you resolution enough to perform them? Can you withstand the examples, and the invitations, of the profligate, and their infamous missionaries? For I have known many a young fellow seduced by a 'mauvaise honte', that made him ashamed to refuse. These are resolutions which you must form, and steadily execute for yourself, whenever you lose the friendly care and assistance of your Mentor. In the meantime, make a greedy use of him; exhaust him, if you can, of all his knowledge; and get the prophet's mantle from him, before he is taken away himself.

You seem to like Rome. How do you go on there? Are you got into the inside of that extraordinary government? Has your Abbate Foggini discovered many of those mysteries to you? Have you made an acquaintance with some eminent Jesuits? I know no people in the world more instructive. You would do very well to take one or two such sort of people home with you to dinner every day. It would be only a little 'minestra' and 'macaroni' the more; and a three or four hours' conversation 'de suite' produces a thousand useful informations, which short meetings and snatches at third places do not admit of; and many of those gentlemen are by no means unwilling to dine 'gratis'. Whenever you meet with a man eminent in any way, feed him, and feed upon him at the same time; it will not only improve you, but give you a reputation of knowledge, and of loving it in others.

I have been lately informed of an Italian book, which I believe may be of use to you, and which, I dare say, you may get at Rome, written by one Alberti, about fourscore or a hundred years ago, a thick quarto. It is a classical description of Italy; from whence, I am assured, that Mr. Addison, to save himself trouble, has taken most of his remarks and classical references. I am told that it is an excellent book for a traveler in Italy.

What Italian books have you read, or are you reading? Ariosto. I hope, is one of them. Pray apply yourself diligently to Italian; it is so easy a language, that speaking it constantly, and reading it often, must, in six months more, make you perfect master of it: in which case you will never forget it; for we only forget those things of which we know but little.

But, above all things, to all that you learn, to all that you say, and to all that you do, remember to join the Graces. All is imperfect without them; with them everything is at least tolerable. Nothing could hurt me more than to find you unattended by them. How cruelly should I be shocked, if, at our first meeting, you should present yourself to me without them! Invoke them, and sacrifice to them every moment; they are always kind, where they are assiduously courted. For God's sake, aim at perfection in everything: 'Nil actum reputans si quid superesset agendum. Adieu. Yours most tenderly.

LETTER CVIII

LONDON, March 19, O. S. 1750.

MY DEAR FRIEND: I acknowledge your last letter of the 24th February, N. S. In return for your earthquake, I can tell you that we have had here more than our share of earthquakes; for we had two very strong ones in eight-and-twenty days. They really do too much honor to our cold climate; in your warm one, they are compensated by favors from the sun, which we do not enjoy.

I did not think that the present Pope was a sort of man to build seven modern little chapels at the expense of so respectable a piece of antiquity as the Coliseum. However, let his Holiness's taste of 'virtu' be ever so bad, pray get somebody to present you to him before you leave Rome; and without hesitation kiss his slipper, or whatever else the etiquette of that Court requires. I would have you see all those ceremonies; and I presume that you are, by this time, ready enough at Italian to understand and answer 'il Santo Padre' in that language. I hope, too, that you have acquired address and usage enough of the world to be presented to anybody, without embarrassment or disapprobation. If that is not yet quite perfect, as I cannot suppose it is entirely, custom will improve it daily, and habit at last complete it. I have for some time told you, that the great difficulties are pretty well conquered. You have acquired knowledge, which is the 'principium et fons'; but you have now a variety of lesser things to attend to, which collectively make one great and important object. You easily guess that I mean the graces, the air, address, politeness, and, in short, the whole 'tournure' and 'agremens' of a man of fashion; so many little things conspire to form that 'tournure', that though separately they seem too insignificant to mention, yet aggregately they are too material for me (who think for you down to the very lowest things) to omit. For instance, do you use yourself to carve, eat and drink genteelly, and with ease? Do you take care to walk, sit, stand, and present yourself gracefully? Are you sufficiently upon your guard against awkward attitudes, and illiberal, ill-bred, and disgusting habits, such as scratching yourself, putting your fingers in your mouth, nose, and ears? Tricks always acquired at schools, often too much neglected afterward; but, however, extremely ill-bred and nauseous. For I do not conceive that any man has a right to exhibit, in company, any one excrement more than another. Do you dress well, and think a little of the brillant in your person? That, too, is necessary, because it is 'prevenant'. Do you aim at easy, engaging, but, at the same time, civil or respectful manners, according to the company you are in? These, and a thousand other things, which you will observe in people of fashion better than I can describe them, are absolutely necessary for every man; but still more for you, than for almost any man living. The showish, the shining, the engaging parts of the character of a fine gentleman, should (considering your destination) be the principal objects, of your present attention.

When you return here, I am apt to think that you will find something better to do than to run to Mr. Osborne's at Gray's Inn, to pick up scarce books. Buy good books and read them; the best books are the commonest, and the last editions are always the best, if the editors are not blockheads, for they may profit of the former. But take care not to understand editions and title-pages too well. It always smells of pedantry, and not always of learning. What curious books I have—they are indeed but few—shall be at your service. I have some of the old Collana, and the Machiavel of 1550. Beware of the 'Bibliomanie'.

In the midst of either your studies or your pleasures, pray never lose view of the object of your destination: I mean the political affairs of Europe. Follow them politically, chronologically, and geographically, through the newspapers, and trace up the facts which you meet with there to their sources: as, for example, consult the treaties Neustadt and Abo, with regard to the disputes, which you read of every day in the public papers, between Russia and Sweden. For the affairs of Italy, which are reported to be the objects of present negotiations, recur to the quadruple alliance of the year 1718, and follow them down through their several variations to the treaty of Aix-la-Chapelle, 1748; in which (by the bye) you will find the very different tenures by which the Infant Don Philip, your namesake, holds Parma and Placentia. Consult, also, the Emperor Charles the Sixth's Act of Cession of the kingdoms of Naples and Sicily, being a point which, upon the death of the present King of Spain, is likely to occasion some disputes; do not lose the thread of these matters; which is carried on with great ease, but if once broken, is resumed with difficulty.

Pray tell Mr. Harte, that I have sent his packet to Baron Firmian by Count Einsiedlen, who is gone from hence this day for Germany, and passes through Vienna in his way to Italy; where he is in hopes of crossing upon you somewhere or other. Adieu, my friend.

LETTER CIX

LONDON, March 29, O. S. 1750

MY DEAR FRIEND: You are now, I suppose, at Naples, in a new scene of 'Virtu', examining all the curiosities of Herculaneum, watching the eruptions of Mount Vesuvius, and surveying the magnificent churches and public buildings, by which Naples is distinguished.

You have a court there into the bargain, which, I hope, you frequent and attend to. Polite manners, a versatility of mind, a complaisance even to enemies, and the 'volto sciolto', with the 'pensieri stretti', are only to be learned at courts, and must be well learned by whoever would either shine or thrive in them. Though they do not change the nature, they smooth and soften the manners of mankind. Vigilance, dexterity, and flexibility supply the place of natural force; and it is the ablest mind, not the strongest body that prevails there. Monsieur and Madame Fogliani will, I am sure, show you all the politeness of courts; for I know no better bred people than they are. Domesticate yourself there while you stay at Naples, and lay aside the English coldness and formality. You have also a letter to Comte Mahony, whose house I hope you frequent, as it is the resort of the best company. His sister, Madame Bulkeley, is now here; and had I known of your going so soon to Naples, I would have got you, 'ex abundanti', a letter from her to her brother. The conversation of the moderns in the evening is full as necessary for you, as that of the ancients in the morning.

You would do well, while you are at Naples, to read some very short history of that kingdom. It has had great variety of masters, and has occasioned many wars; the general history of which will enable you to ask many proper questions, and to receive useful informations in return. Inquire into the manner and form of that government; for constitution it has none, being an absolute one; but the most absolute governments have certain customs and forms, which are more or less observed by their respective tyrants. In China it is the fashion for the emperors, absolute as they are, to govern with justice and equity; as in the other Oriental monarchies, it is the custom to govern by violence and cruelty. The King of France, as absolute, in fact, as any of them, is by custom only more gentle; for I know of no constitutional bar to his will. England is now, the only monarchy in the world, that can properly be said to have a constitution; for the people's rights and liberties are secured by laws; and I cannot reckon Sweden and Poland to be monarchies, those two kings having little more to say than the Doge of Venice. I do not presume to say anything of the constitution of the empire to you, who are 'jurisperitorum Germanicorum facile princeps'.

When you write to me, which, by the way, you do pretty seldom, tell me rather whom you see, than what you see. Inform me of your evening transactions and acquaintances; where, and how you pass your evenings; what people of learning you have made acquaintance with; and, if you will trust me with so important an affair, what belle passion inflames you. I interest myself most in what personally concerns you most; and this is a very critical year in your life. To talk like a virtuoso, your canvas is, I think, a good one, and RAPHAEL HARTE has drawn the outlines admirably; nothing is now wanting but the coloring of Titian, and the Graces, the 'morbidezza' of Guido; but that is a great deal. You must get them soon, or you will never get them at all. 'Per la lingua Italiana, sono sicuro ch'ella n'e adesso professore, a segno tale ch'io non ardisca dirle altra cosa in quela lingua se non. Addio'.

LETTER CX

LONDON, April 26, O. S. 1756.

MY DEAR FRIEND: As your journey to Paris approaches, and as that period will, one way or another, be of infinite consequence to you, my letters will henceforward be principally calculated for that meridian. You will be left there to your own discretion, instead of Mr. Harte's, and you will allow me, I am sure, to distrust a little the discretion of eighteen. You will find in the Academy a number of young fellows much less discreet than yourself. These will all be your acquaintances; but look about you first, and inquire into their respective characters, before you form any connections among them; and, 'caeteris paribus', single out those of the most considerable rank and family. Show them a distinguishing attention; by which means you will get into their respective houses, and keep the best company. All those French young fellows are excessively 'etourdis'; be upon your guard against scrapes and quarrels; have no corporal pleasantries with them, no 'jeux de mains', no 'coups de chambriere', which frequently bring on quarrels. Be as lively as they, if you please, but at the same time be a little wiser than they. As to letters, you will find most of them ignorant; do not reproach them with that ignorance, nor make them feel your superiority. It is not their faults, they are all bred up for the army; but, on the other, hand, do not allow their ignorance and idleness to break in upon those morning hours which you may be able to allot to your serious, studies. No breakfastings with them, which consume a great deal of time; but tell them (not magisterially and sententiously) that you will read two or three hours in the morning, and that for the rest of the day you are very much at their service. Though, by the way, I hope you will keep wiser company in the evenings.

I must insist upon your never going to what is called the English coffee-house at Paris, which is the resort of all the scrub English, and also of the fugitive and attainted Scotch and Irish; party quarrels and drunken squabbles are very frequent there; and I do not know a more degrading place in all Paris. Coffee-houses and taverns are by no means creditable at Paris. Be cautiously upon your guard against the infinite number of fine-dressed and fine-spoken 'chevaliers d'industrie' and 'avanturiers' which swarm at Paris: and keep everybody civilly at arm's length, of whose real character or rank you are not previously informed. Monsieur le Comte or Monsieur le Chevalier, in a handsome laced coat, 'et tres bien mis', accosts you at the play, or some other public place; he conceives at first sight an infinite regard for you: he sees that you are a stranger of the first distinction; he offers you his services, and wishes nothing more ardently than to contribute, as far as may be in his little power, to procure you 'les agremens de Paris'. He is acquainted with some ladies of condition, 'qui prefrent une petite societe agreable, et des petits soupers aimables d'honnetes gens, au tumulte et a la dissipation de Paris'; and he will with the greatest pleasure imaginable have the honor of introducing you to those ladies of quality. Well, if you were to accept of this kind offer, and go with him, you would find 'au troisieme; a handsome, painted and p——d strumpet, in a tarnished silver or gold second-hand robe, playing a sham party at cards for livres, with three or four sharpers well dressed enough, and dignified by the titles of Marquis, Comte, and Chevalier. The lady receives you in the most polite and gracious manner, and with all those 'complimens de routine' which every French woman has equally. Though she loves retirement, and shuns 'le grande monde', yet she confesses herself obliged to the Marquis for having procured her so inestimable, so accomplished an acquaintance as yourself; but her concern is how to amuse you: for she never suffers play at her house for above a livre; if you can amuse yourself with that low play till supper, 'a la bonne heure'. Accordingly you sit down to that little play, at which the good company takes care that you shall win fifteen or sixteen livres, which gives them an opportunity of celebrating both your good luck and your good play. Supper comes up, and a good one it is, upon the strength of your being able to pay for it. 'La Marquise en fait les honneurs au mieux, talks sentiments, 'moeurs et morale', interlarded with 'enjouement', and accompanied with some oblique ogles, which bid you not despair in time. After supper, pharaoh, lansquenet, or quinze, happen accidentally to be mentioned: the Marquise exclaims against it, and vows she will not suffer it, but is at last prevailed upon by being assured 'que ce ne sera que pour des riens'. Then the wished-for moment is come, the operation begins: you are cheated, at best, of all the money in your pocket, and if you stay late, very probably robbed of your watch and snuff-box, possibly murdered for greater security. This I can assure you, is not an exaggerated, but a literal description of what happens every day to some raw and inexperienced stranger at Paris. Remember to receive all these civil gentlemen, who take such a fancy to you at first sight, very coldly, and take care always to be previously engaged, whatever party they propose to you. You may happen sometimes, in very great and good companies, to meet with some dexterous gentlemen, who may be very desirous, and also very sure, to win your money, if they can but engage you to play with them. Therefore lay it down as an invariable rule never to play with men, but only with women of fashion, at low play, or with women and men mixed. But, at the same time, whenever you are asked to play deeper than you would, do not refuse it gravely and sententiously, alleging the folly of staking what would be very inconvenient to one to lose, against what one does not want to win; but parry those invitations ludicrously, 'et en badinant'. Say that, if you were sure to lose, you might possibly play, but that as you may as well win, you dread 'l'embarras des richesses', ever since you have seen what an encumbrance they were to poor Harlequin, and that, therefore, you are determined never to venture the winning above two louis a-day; this sort of light trifling way of declining invitations to vice and folly, is more becoming your age, and at the same time more effectual, than grave philosophical refusals. A young fellow who seems to have no will of his own, and who does everything that is asked of him, is called a very good-natured, but at the same time, is thought a very silly young fellow. Act wisely, upon solid principles, and from true motives, but keep them to yourself, and never talk sententiously. When you are invited to drink, say that you wish you could, but that so little makes you both drunk and sick, 'que le jeu me vaut pas la chandelle'.

Pray show great attention, and make your court to Monsieur de la Gueriniere; he is well with Prince Charles and many people of the first distinction at Paris; his commendations will raise your character there, not to mention that his favor will be of use to you in the Academy itself. For the reasons which I mentioned to you in my last, I would have you be interne in the Academy for the first six months; but after that, I promise you that you shall have lodgings of your own 'dans un hotel garni', if in the meantime I hear well of you, and that you frequent, and are esteemed in the best French companies. You want nothing now, thank God, but exterior advantages, that last polish, that 'tournure du monde', and those graces, which are so necessary to adorn, and give efficacy to, the most solid merit. They are only to be acquired in the best companies, and better in the best French companies than in any other. You will not want opportunities, for I shall send you letters that will establish you in the most distinguished companies, not only of the beau monde, but of the beaux esprits, too. Dedicate, therefore, I beg of you, that whole year to your own advantage and final improvement, and do not be diverted from those objects by idle dissipations, low seduction, or bad example. After that year, do whatever you please; I will interfere no longer in your conduct; for I am sure both you and I shall be safe then. Adieu!

LETTER CXI

LONDON, April 30, O. S. 1750

MY DEAR FRIEND: Mr. Harte, who in all his letters gives you some dash of panegyric, told me in his last a thing that pleases me extremely; which was that at Rome you had constantly preferred the established Italian assemblies to the English conventicles setup against them by dissenting English ladies. That shows sense, and that you know what you are sent abroad for. It is of much more consequence to know the 'mores multorem hominum' than the 'urbes'. Pray continue this judicious conduct wherever you go, especially at Paris, where, instead of thirty, you will find above three hundred English, herding together and conversing with no one French body.

The life of 'les Milords Anglois' is regularly, or, if you will, irregularly, this. As soon as they rise, which is very late, they breakfast together, to the utter loss of two good morning hours. Then they go by coachfuls to the Palais, the Invalides, and Notre-Dame; from thence to the English coffee-house, where they make up their tavern party for dinner. From dinner, where they drink quick, they adjourn in clusters to the play, where they crowd up the stage, dressed up in very fine clothes, very ill-made by a Scotch or Irish tailor. From the play to the tavern again, where they get very drunk, and where they either quarrel among themselves, or sally forth, commit some riot in the streets, and are taken up by the watch. Those who do not speak French before they go, are sure to learn none there. Their tender vows are addressed to their Irish laundress, unless by chance some itinerant Englishwoman, eloped from her husband, or her creditors, defrauds her of them. Thus they return home, more petulant, but not more informed, than when they left it; and show, as they think, their improvement by affectedly both speaking and dressing in broken French:—

"Hunc to Romane caveito."

Connect yourself, while you are in France, entirely with the French; improve yourself with the old, divert yourself with the young; conform cheerfully to their customs, even to their little follies, but not to their vices. Do not, however, remonstrate or preach against them, for remonstrances do not suit with your age. In French companies in general you will not find much learning, therefore take care not to brandish yours in their faces. People hate those who make them feel their own inferiority. Conceal all your learning carefully, and reserve it for the company of les Gens d'Eglise, or les Gens de Robe; and even then let them rather extort it from you, than find you over-willing to draw it. Your are then thought, from that seeming unwillingness, to have still more knowledge than it may be you really have, and with the additional merit of modesty into the bargain. A man who talks of, or even hints at, his 'bonnes fortunes', is seldom believed, or, if believed, much blamed; whereas a man who conceals with care is often supposed to have more than he has, and his reputation of discretion gets him others. It is just so with a man of learning; if he affects to show it, it is questioned, and he is reckoned only superficial; but if afterward it appears that he really has it, he is pronounced a pedant. Real merit of any kind, 'ubi est non potest diu celari'; it will be discovered, and nothing can depreciate it but a man's exhibiting it himself. It may not always be rewarded as it ought, but it will always be known. You will in general find the women of the beau monde at Paris more instructed than the men, who are bred up singly for the army, and thrown into it at twelve or thirteen years old; but then that sort of education, which makes them ignorant of books, gives them a great knowledge of the world, an easy address, and polite manners.

Fashion is more tyrannical at Paris than in any other place in the world; it governs even more absolutely than their king, which is saying a great deal. The least revolt against it is punished by proscription. You must observe, and conform to all the 'minutiae' of it, if you will be in fashion there yourself; and if you are not in fashion, you are nobody. Get, therefore, at all events, into the company of those men and women 'qui donnent le ton'; and though at first you should be admitted upon that shining theatre only as a 'persona muta', persist, persevere, and you will soon have a part given you. Take great care never to tell in one company what you see or hear in another, much less to divert the present company at the expense of the last; but let discretion and secrecy be known parts of your character. They will carry you much further, and much safer than more shining talents. Be upon your guard against quarrels at Paris; honor is extremely nice there, though the asserting of it is exceedingly penal. Therefore, 'point de mauvaises plaisanteries, point de jeux de main, et point de raillerie piquante'.

Paris is the place in the world where, if you please, you may the best unite the 'utile' and the 'dulce'. Even your pleasures will be your improvements, if you take them with the people of the place, and in high life. From what you have hitherto done everywhere else, I have just reason to believe, that you will do everything that you ought at Paris. Remember that it is your decisive moment; whatever you do there will be known to thousands here, and your character there, whatever it is, will get before you here. You will meet with it at London. May you and I both have reason to rejoice at that meeting! Adieu.

LETTER CXII

LONDON, May 8, O. S. 1750

MY DEAR FRIEND: At your age the love of pleasures is extremely natural, and the enjoyment of them not unbecoming: but the danger, at your age, is mistaking the object, and setting out wrong in the pursuit. The character of a man of pleasure dazzles young eyes; they do not see their way to it distinctly, and fall into vice and profligacy. I remember a strong instance of this a great many years ago. A young fellow, determined to shine as a man of pleasure, was at the play called the "Libertine Destroyed," a translation of 'Le Festin de Pierre' of Molieire's. He was so struck with what he thought the fine character of the libertine, that he swore he would be the LIBERTINE DESTROYED. Some friends asked him, whether he had not better content himself with being only the libertine, but without being DESTROYED? to which he answered with great warmth, "No, for that being destroyed was the perfection of the whole." This, extravagant as it seems in this light, is really the case of many an unfortunate young fellow, who, captivated by the name of pleasures, rushes indiscriminately, and without taste, into them all, and is finally DESTROYED. I am not stoically advising, nor parsonically preaching to you to be a Stoic at your age; far from it: I am pointing out to you the paths to pleasures, and am endeavoring only to quicken and heighten them for you. Enjoy pleasures, but let them be your own, and then you will taste them; but adopt none; trust to nature for genuine ones. The pleasures that you would feel you must earn; the man who gives himself up to all, feels none sensibly. Sardanapalus, I am convinced, never felt any in his life. Those only who join serious occupations with pleasures, feel either as they should do. Alcibiades, though addicted to the most shameful excesses, gave some time to philosophy, and some to business. Julius Caesar joined business with pleasure so properly, that they mutually assisted each other; and though he was the husband of all the wives at Rome, he found time to be one of the best scholars, almost the best orator, and absolutely the best general there. An uninterrupted life of pleasures is as insipid as contemptible. Some hours given every day to serious business must whet both the mind and the senses, to enjoy those of pleasure. A surfeited glutton, an emaciated sot, and an enervated rotten whoremaster, never enjoy the pleasures to which they devote themselves; but they are only so many human sacrifices to false gods. The pleasures of low life are all of this mistaken, merely sensual, and disgraceful nature; whereas, those of high life, and in good company (though possibly in themselves not more moral) are more delicate, more refined, less dangerous, and less disgraceful; and, in the common course of things, not reckoned disgraceful at all. In short, pleasure must not, nay, cannot, be the business of a man of sense and character; but it may be, and is, his relief, his reward. It is particularly so with regard to the women; who have the utmost contempt for those men, that, having no character nor consideration with their own sex, frivolously pass their whole time in 'ruelles' and at 'toilettes'. They look upon them as their lumber, and remove them whenever they can get better furniture. Women choose their favorites more by the ear than by any other of their senses or even their understandings. The man whom they hear the most commended by the men, will always be the best received by them. Such a conquest flatters their vanity, and vanity is their universal, if not their strongest passion. A distinguished shining character is irresistible with them; they crowd to, nay, they even quarrel for the danger in hopes of the triumph. Though, by the way (to use a vulgar expression), she who conquers only catches a Tartar, and becomes the slave of her captive. 'Mais c'est la leur affaire'. Divide your time between useful occupations and elegant pleasures. The morning seems to belong to study, business, or serious conversations with men of learning and figure; not that I exclude an occasional hour at a toilette. From sitting down to dinner, the proper business of the day is pleasure, unless real business, which must never be postponed for pleasure, happens accidentally to interfere. In good company, the pleasures of the table are always carried to a certain point of delicacy and gratification, but never to excess and riot. Plays, operas, balls, suppers, gay conversations in polite and cheerful companies, properly conclude the evenings; not to mention the tender looks that you may direct and the sighs that you may offer, upon these several occasions, to some propitious or unpropitious female deity, whose character and manners will neither disgrace nor corrupt yours. This is the life of a man of real sense and pleasure; and by this distribution of your time, and choice of your pleasures, you will be equally qualified for the busy, or the 'beau monde'. You see I am not rigid, and do not require that you and I should be of the same age. What I say to you, therefore, should have the more weight, as coming from a friend, not a father. But low company, and their low vices, their indecent riots and profligacy, I never will bear nor forgive.

I have lately received two volumes of treaties, in German and Latin, from Hawkins, with your orders, under your own hand, to take care of them for you, which orders I shall most dutifully and punctually obey, and they wait for you in my library, together with your great collection of rare books, which your Mamma sent me upon removing from her old house.

I hope you not only keep up, but improve in your German, for it will be of great use to you when you cone into business; and the more so, as you will be almost the only Englishman who either can speak or understand it. Pray speak it constantly to all Germans, wherever you meet them, and you will meet multitudes of them at

Paris. Is Italian now become easy and familiar to you? Can you speak it with the same fluency that you can speak German? You cannot conceive what an advantage it will give you in negotiations to possess Italian, German, and French perfectly, so as to understand all the force and finesse of those three languages. If two men of equal talents negotiate together, he who best understands the language in which the negotiation is carried on, will infallibly get the better of the other. The signification and force of one single word is often of great consequence in a treaty, and even in a letter.

Remember the GRACES, for without them 'ogni fatica e vana'. Adieu.

LETTER CXIII

LONDON, May 17, O. S. 1750

MY DEAR FRIEND: Your apprenticeship is near out, and you are soon to set up for yourself; that approaching moment is a critical one for you, and an anxious one for me. A tradesman who would succeed in his way, must begin by establishing a character of integrity and good manners; without the former, nobody will go to his shop at all; without the latter, nobody will go there twice. This rule does not exclude the fair arts of trade. He may sell his goods at the best price he can, within certain bounds. He may avail himself of the humor, the whims, and the fantastical tastes of his customers; but what he warrants to be good must be really so, what he seriously asserts must be true, or his first fraudulent profits will soon end in a bankruptcy. It is the same in higher life, and in the great business of the world. A man who does not solidly establish, and really deserve, a character of truth, probity, good manners, and good morals, at his first setting out in the world, may impose, and shine like a meteor for a very short time, but will very soon vanish, and be extinguished with contempt. People easily pardon, in young men, the common irregularities of the senses: but they do not forgive the least vice of the heart. The heart never grows better by age; I fear rather worse; always harder. A young liar will be an old one; and a young knave will only be a greater knave as he grows older. But should a bad young heart, accompanied with a good head (which, by the way, very seldom is the case), really reform in a more advanced age, from a consciousness of its folly, as well as of its guilt; such a conversion would only be thought prudential and political, but never sincere. I hope in God, and I verily. believe, that you want no moral virtue. But the possession of all the moral virtues, in 'actu primo', as the logicians call it, is not sufficient; you must have them in 'actu secundo' too; nay, that is not sufficient neither—you must have the reputation of them also. Your character in the world must be built upon that solid foundation, or it will soon fall, and upon your own head. You cannot, therefore, be too careful, too nice, too scrupulous, in establishing this character at first, upon which your whole depends. Let no conversation, no example, no fashion, no 'bon mot', no silly desire of seeming to be above, what most knaves, and many fools, call prejudices, ever tempt you to avow, excuse, extenuate, or laugh at the least breach of morality; but show upon all occasions, and take all occasions to show, a detestation and abhorrence of it. There, though young, you ought to be strict; and there only, while young, it becomes you to be strict and severe. But there, too, spare the persons while you lash the crimes. All this relates, as you easily judge, to the vices of the heart, such as lying, fraud, envy, malice, detraction, etc., and I do not extend it to the little frailties of youth, flowing from high spirits and warm blood. It would ill become you, at your age, to declaim against them, and sententiously censure a gallantry, an accidental excess of the table, a frolic, an inadvertency; no, keep as free from them yourself as you can: but say nothing against them in others. They certainly mend by time, often by reason; and a man's worldly character is not affected by them, provided it be pure in all other respects.

To come now to a point of much less, but yet of very great consequence at your first setting out. Be extremely upon your guard against vanity, the common failing of inexperienced youth; but particularly against that kind of vanity that dubs a man a coxcomb; a character which, once acquired, is more indelible than that of the priesthood. It is not to be imagined by how many different ways vanity defeats its own purposes. One man decides peremptorily upon every subject, betrays his ignorance upon many, and shows a disgusting presumption upon the rest. Another desires to appear successful among the women; he hints at the encouragement he has received, from those of the most distinguished rank and beauty, and intimates a particular connection with some one; if it is true, it is ungenerous; if false, it is infamous: but in either case he destroys the reputation he wants to get. Some flatter their vanity by little extraneous objects, which have not the least relation to themselves; such as being descended from, related to, or acquainted with, people of distinguished merit and eminent characters. They talk perpetually of their grandfather such-a-one, their uncle such-a-one, and their intimate friend Mr. Such-a-one, with whom, possibly, they are hardly acquainted. But admitting it all to be as they would have it, what then? Have they the more merit for those accidents? Certainly not. On the contrary, their taking up adventitious, proves their want of intrinsic merit; a rich man never borrows. Take this rule for granted, as a never-failing one: That you must never seem to affect the character in which you have a mind to shine. Modesty is the only sure bait when you angle for praise. The affectation of courage will make even a brave man pass only for a bully; as the affectation of wit will make a man of parts pass for a coxcomb. By this modesty I do not mean timidity and awkward bashfulness. On the contrary, be inwardly firm and steady, know your own value whatever it may be, and act upon that principle; but take great care to let nobody discover that you do know your own value. Whatever real merit you have, other people will discover, and people always magnify their own discoveries, as they lessen those of others.

For God's sake, revolve all these things seriously in your thoughts, before you launch out alone into the ocean of Paris. Recollect the observations that you have yourself made upon mankind, compare and connect them with my instructions, and then act systematically and consequentially from them; not 'au jour la journee'. Lay your little plan now, which you will hereafter extend and improve by your own observations, and by the advice of those who can never mean to mislead you; I mean Mr. Harte and myself.

LETTER CXIV

LONDON, May 24., O. S. 1750

MY DEAR FRIEND: I received yesterday your letter of the 7th, N. S., from Naples, to which place I find you have traveled, classically, critically, and 'da virtuoso'. You did right, for whatever is worth seeing at, all, is worth seeing well, and better than most people see it. It is a poor and frivolous excuse, when anything curious is talked of that one has seen, to say, I SAW IT, BUT REALLY I DID NOT MUCH MIND IT. Why did they go to see it, if they would not mind it? or why not mind it when they saw it? Now that you are at Naples, you pass part of your time there 'en honnete homme, da garbato cavaliere', in the court and the best companies. I am told that strangers are received with the utmost hospitality at Prince————'s, 'que lui il fait bonne chere, et que Madame la Princesse donne chere entire; mais que sa chair est plus que hazardee ou mortifiee meme'; which in plain English means, that she is not only tender, but rotten. If this be true, as I am pretty sure it is, one may say to her in a little sense, 'juvenumque prodis, publics cura'.

Mr. Harte informs me that you are clothed in sumptuous apparel; a young fellow should be so; especially abroad, where fine clothes are so generally the fashion. Next to their being fine, they should be well made, and worn easily for a man is only the less genteel for a fine coat, if, in wearing it, he shows a regard for it, and is not as easy in it as if it were a plain one.

I thank you for your drawing, which I am impatient to see, and which I shall hang up in a new gallery that I am building at Blackheath, and very fond of; but I am still more impatient for another copy, which I wonder I have not yet received, I mean the copy of your countenance. I believe, were that a whole length, it would still fall a good deal short of the dimensions of the drawing after Dominichino, which you say is about eight feet high; and I take you, as well as myself, to be of the family of the Piccolomini. Mr. Bathurst tells me that he thinks you rather taller than I am; if so, you may very possibly get up to five feet eight inches, which I would compound for, though I would wish you five feet ten. In truth, what do I not wish you, that has a tendency to perfection? I say a tendency only, for absolute perfection is not in human nature, so that it would be idle to wish it. But I am very willing to compound for your coming nearer to perfection than the generality of your contemporaries: without a compliment to you, I think you bid fair for that. Mr. Harte affirms (and if it were consistent with his character would, I believe, swear) that you have no vices of the heart; you have undoubtedly a stock of both ancient and modern learning, which I will venture to say nobody of your age has, and which must now daily increase, do what you will. What, then, do you want toward that practicable degree of perfection which I wish you? Nothing but the knowledge, the turn, and the manners of the world; I mean the 'beau monde'. These it is impossible that you can yet have quite right; they are not given, they must be learned. But then, on the other hand, it is impossible not to acquire them, if one has a mind to them; for they are acquired insensibly, by keeping good company, if one has but the least attention to their characters and manners.

Every man becomes, to a certain degree, what the people he generally converses with are. He catches their air, their manners, and even their way of thinking. If he observes with attention, he will catch them soon, but if he does not, he will at long run contract them insensibly. I know nothing in the world but poetry that is not to be acquired by application and care. The sum total of this is a very comfortable one for you, as it plainly amounts to this in your favor, that you now want nothing but what even your pleasures, if they are liberal ones, will teach you. I congratulate both you and myself upon your being in such a situation, that, excepting your exercises, nothing is now wanting but pleasures to complete you. Take them, but (as I am sure you will) with people of the first fashion, wherever you are, and the business is done; your exercises at Paris, which I am sure you will attend to, will supple and fashion your body; and the company you will keep there will, with some degree of observation on your part, soon give you their air, address, manners, in short, 'le ton de la bonne compagnie'. Let not these considerations, however, make you vain: they are only between you and me but as they are very comfortable ones, they may justly give you a manly assurance, a firmness, a steadiness, without which a man can neither be well-bred, or in any light appear to advantage, or really what he is. They may justly remove all, timidity, awkward bashfulness, low diffidence of one's self, and mean abject complaisance to every or anybody's opinion. La Bruyere says, very truly, 'on ne vaut dans ce monde, que ce que l'on veut valoir'. It is a right principle to proceed upon in the world, taking care only to guard against the appearances and outward symptoms of vanity. Your whole then, you see, turns upon the company you keep for the future. I have laid you in variety of the best at Paris, where, at your arrival you will find a cargo of letters to very different sorts of people, as 'beaux esprits, savants, et belles dames'. These, if you will frequent them, will form you, not only by their examples, advice, and admonitions in private, as I have desired them to do; and consequently add to what you have the only one thing now needful.

Pray tell me what Italian books you have read, and whether that language is now become familiar to you.

Read Ariosto and Tasso through, and then you will have read all the Italian poets who in my opinion are worth reading. In all events, when you get to Paris, take a good Italian master to read Italian with you three times a week; not only to keep what you have already, which you would otherwise forget, but also to perfect you in the rest. It is a great pleasure, as well as a great advantage, to be able to speak to people of all nations, and well, in their own language. Aim at perfection in everything, though in most things it is unattainable; however, they who aim at it, and persevere, will come much nearer it, than those whose laziness and despondency make them give it up as unattainable. 'Magnis tamen excidit ausis' is a degree of praise which will always attend a noble and shining temerity, and a much better sign in a young fellow, than 'serpere humi, tutus nimium timidusque procellae'. For men as well as women:

"————-born to be controlled,

Stoop to the forward and the bold."

A man who sets out in the world with real timidity and diffidence has not an equal chance for it; he will be discouraged, put by, or trampled upon. But to succeed, a man, especially a young one, should have inward firmness, steadiness, and intrepidity, with exterior modesty and SEEMING diffidence. He must modestly, but resolutely, assert his own rights and privileges. 'Suaviter in modo', but 'fortiter in re'. He should have an apparent frankness and openness, but with inward caution and closeness. All these things will come to you by frequenting and observing good company. And by good company, I mean that sort of company which is called good company by everybody of that place. When all this is over, we shall meet; and then we will talk over, tete-a-tete, the various little finishing strokes which conversation and, acquaintance occasionally suggest, and which cannot be methodically written.

Tell Mr. Harte that I have received his two letters of the 2d and 8th N. S., which, as soon as I have received a third, I will answer. Adieu, my dear! I find you will do.

LETTER CXV

LONDON, June 5, O. S. 1750

MY DEAR FRIEND: I have received your picture, which I have long waited for with impatience: I wanted to see your countenance from whence I am very apt, as I believe most people are, to form some general opinion of the mind. If the painter has taken you as well as he has done Mr. Harte (for his picture is by far the most like I ever saw in my life), I draw good conclusions from your countenance, which has both spirit and finesse in it. In bulk you are pretty well increased since I saw you; if your height has not increased in proportion, I desire that you will make haste to, complete it. Seriously, I believe that your exercises at Paris will make you shoot up to a good size; your legs, by all accounts, seem to promise it. Dancing excepted, the wholesome part is the best part of those academical exercises. 'Ils degraissent leur homme'.

'A propos' of exercises, I have prepared everything for your reception at Monsieur de la Gueriniere's, and your room, etc., will be ready at your arrival. I am sure you must be sensible how much better it will be for you to be interne in the Academy for the first six or seven months at least, than to be 'en hotel garni', at some distance from it, and obliged to go to it every morning, let the weather be what it will, not to mention the loss of time too; besides, by living and boarding in the Academy, you will make an acquaintance with half the young fellows of fashion at Paris; and in a very little while be looked upon as one of them in all French companies: an advantage that has never yet happened to any one Englishman that I have known. I am sure you do not suppose that the difference of the expense, which is but a trifle, has any weight with me in this resolution. You have the French language so perfectly, and you will acquire the French 'tournure' so soon, that I do not know anybody likely to pass their time so well at Paris as yourself. Our young countrymen have generally too little French, and too bad address, either to present themselves, or be well received in the best French companies; and, as a proof of it, there is no one instance of an Englishman's having ever been suspected of a gallantry with a French woman of condition, though every French woman of condition is more than suspected of having a gallantry. But they take up with the disgraceful and dangerous commerce of prostitutes, actresses, dancing-women, and that sort of trash; though, if they had common address, better achievements would be extremely easy. 'Un arrangement', which is in plain English a gallantry, is, at Paris, as necessary a part of a woman of fashion's establishment, as her house, stable, coach, etc. A young fellow must therefore be a very awkward one, to be reduced to, or of a very singular taste, to prefer drabs and danger to a commerce (in the course of the world not disgraceful) with a woman of health, education, and rank. Nothing sinks a young man into low company, both of women and men, so surely as timidity and diffidence of himself. If he thinks that he shall not, he may depend upon it he will not please. But with proper endeavors to please, and a degree of persuasion that he shall, it is almost certain that he will. How many people does one meet with everywhere, who, with very moderate parts, and very little knowledge, push themselves pretty far, simply by being sanguine, enterprising, and persevering? They will take no denial from man or woman; difficulties do not discourage them; repulsed twice or thrice, they rally, they charge again, and nine times in ten prevail at last. The same means will much sooner, and, more certainly, attain the same ends, with your parts and knowledge. You have a fund to be sanguine upon, and good forces to rally. In business (talents supposed) nothing is more effectual or successful, than a good, though concealed opinion of one's self, a firm resolution, and an unwearied perseverance. None but madmen attempt impossibilities; and whatever is possible, is one way or another to be brought about. If one method fails, try another, and suit your methods to the characters you have to do with. At the treaty of the Pyrenees, which Cardinal Mazarin and Don Louis de Haro concluded, 'dans l'Isle des Faisans', the latter carried some very important points by his constant and cool perseverance.

The Cardinal had all the Italian vivacity and impatience; Don Louis all the Spanish phlegm and tenaciousness. The point which the Cardinal had most at heart was, to hinder the re-establishment of the Prince of Conde, his implacable enemy; but he was in haste to conclude, and impatient to return to Court, where absence is always dangerous. Don Louis observed this, and never failed at every conference to bring the affair of the Prince of Conde upon the tapis. The Cardinal for some time refused even to treat upon it. Don Louis, with the same 'sang froid', as constantly persisted, till he at last prevailed: contrary to the intentions and the interest both of the Cardinal and of his Court. Sense must distinguish between what is impossible, and what is only difficult; and spirit and perseverance will get the better of the latter. Every man is to be had one way or another, and every woman almost any way. I must not omit one thing, which is previously necessary to this, and, indeed, to everything else; which is attention, a flexibility of attention; never to be wholly engrossed by any past or future object, but instantly directed to the present one, be it what it will. An absent man can make but few observations; and those will be disjointed and imperfect ones, as half the circumstance must necessarily escape him. He can pursue nothing steadily, because his absences make him lose his way. They are very disagreeable, and hardly to be tolerated in old age; but in youth they cannot be forgiven. If you find that you have the least tendency to them, pray watch yourself very carefully, and you may prevent them now; but if you let them grow into habit, you will find it very difficult to cure them hereafter, and a worse distemper I do not know.

I heard with great satisfaction the other day, from one who has been lately at Rome, that nobody was better received in the best companies than yourself. The same thing, I dare say, will happen to you at Paris; where they are particularly kind to all strangers, who will be civil to them, and show a desire of pleasing. But they must be flattered a little, not only by words, but by a seeming preference given to their country, their manners, and their customs; which is but a very small price to pay for a very good reception. Were I in Africa, I would pay it to a negro for his goodwill. Adieu.

LETTER CXVI

LONDON, June 11, O. S. 1750

MY DEAR FRIEND: The President Montesquieu (whom you will be acquainted with at Paris), after having laid down in his book, 'De l'Esprit des Lois', the nature and principles of the three different kinds of government, viz, the democratical, the monarchical, and the despotic, treats of the education necessary for each respective form. His chapter upon the education proper for the monarchical I thought worth transcribing and sending to you. You will observe that the monarchy which he has in his eye is France:—

"In monarchies, the principal branch of education is not taught in colleges or academies. It commences, in some measure, at our setting out in the world; for this is the school of what we call honor, that universal preceptor, which ought everywhere to be our guide.

"Here it is that we constantly hear three rules or maxims, viz: That we should have a certain nobleness in our virtues, a kind of frankness in our morals, and a particular politeness in our behavior.

"The virtues we are here taught, are less what we owe to others, than to ourselves; they are not so much what draws us toward society, as what distinguishes us from our fellow-citizens.

"Here the actions of men are judged, not as virtuous, but as shining; not as just, but as great; not as reasonable, but as extraordinary.

"When honor here meets with anything noble in our actions, it is either a judge that approves them, or a sophister by whom they are excused.

"It allows of gallantry, when united with the idea of sensible affection, or with that of conquest; this is the reason why we never meet with so strict a purity of morals in monarchies as in republican governments.

EARL OF PHILIP DORMER STANHOPE CHESTERFIELD

"It allows of cunning and craft, when joined with the notion of greatness of soul or importance of affairs; as, for instance, in politics, with whose finenesses it is far from being offended.

"It does not forbid adulation, but when separate from the idea of a large fortune, and connected only with the sense of our mean condition.

"With regard to morals, I have observed, that the education of monarchies ought to admit of a certain frankness and open carriage. Truth, therefore, in conversation, is here a necessary point. But is it for the sake of truth. By no means. Truth is requisite only, because a person habituated to veracity has an air of boldness and freedom. And, indeed, a man of this stamp seems to lay a stress only on the things themselves, not on the manner in which they are received.

"Hence it is, that in proportion as this kind of frankness is commended, that of the common people is despised, which has nothing but truth and simplicity for its object.

"In fine, the education of monarchies requires a certain politeness of behavior. Man, a sociable animal, is formed to please in society; and a person that would break through the rules of decency, so as to shock those he conversed with, would lose the public esteem, and become incapable of doing any good.

"But politeness, generally speaking, does not derive its original from so pure a source. It arises from a desire of distinguishing ourselves. It is pride that renders us polite; we are flattered with being taken notice of for a behavior that shows we are not of a mean condition, and that we have not been bred up with those who in all ages are considered as the scum of the people.

"Politeness, in monarchies, is naturalized at court. One man excessively great renders everybody else little. Hence that regard which is paid to our fellow-subjects; hence that politeness, equally pleasing to those by whom, as to those toward whom, it is practiced; because it gives people to understand that a person actually belongs, or at least deserves to belong, to the court.

"A court air consists in quitting a real for a borrowed greatness. The latter pleases the courtier more than the former. It inspires him with a certain disdainful modesty, which shows itself externally, but whose pride insensibly diminishes in proportion to his distance from the source of this greatness.

"At court we find a delicacy of taste in everything; a delicacy arising from the constant use of the superfluities of life; from the variety, and especially the satiety of pleasures; from the multiplicity and even confusion of fancies, which, if they are not agreeable, are sure of being well received.

"These are the things which properly fall within the province of education, in order to form what we call a man of honor, a man possessed of all the qualities and virtues requisite in this kind of government.

"Here it is that honor interferes with everything, mixing even with people's manner of thinking, and directing their very principles.

"To this whimsical honor it is owing that the virtues are only just what it pleases; it adds rules of its own invention to everything prescribed to us; it extends or limits our duties according to its own fancy, whether they proceed from religion, politics, or morality.

"There is nothing so strongly inculcated in monarchies, by the laws, by religion, and honor, as submission to the Prince's will, but this very honor tells us, that the Prince never ought to command a dishonorable action, because this would render us incapable of serving him.

"Crillon refused to assassinate the Duke of Guise, but offered to fight him. After the massacre of St. Bartholomew, Charles IX., having sent orders to the governors in the several provinces for the Huguenots to be murdered, Viscount Dorte, who commanded at Bayonne, wrote thus to the King: 'Sire, Among the inhabitants of this town, and your Majesty's troops, I could not find so much as one executioner; they are honest citizens and brave soldiers. We jointly, therefore, beseech your Majesty to command our arms and lives in things that are practicable.' This great and generous soul looked upon a base action as a thing impossible.

"There is nothing that honor more strongly recommends to the nobility, than to serve their Prince in a military capacity. And indeed this is their favorite profession, because its dangers, its success, and even its miscarriages, are the road to grandeur. Yet this very law, of its own making, honor chooses to explain; and in case of any affront, it requires or permits us to retire.

"It insists also, that we should be at liberty either to seek or to reject employments; a liberty which it prefers even to an ample fortune.

"Honor, therefore, has its supreme laws, to which education is obliged to conform. The chief of these are, that we are permitted to set a value upon our fortune, but are absolutely forbidden to set any upon our lives.

"The second is, that when we are raised to a post or preferment, we should never do or permit anything which may seem to imply that we look upon ourselves as inferior to the rank we hold.

"The third is, that those things which honor forbids are more rigorously forbidden, when the laws do not concur in the prohibition; and those it commands are more strongly insisted upon, when they happen not to be commanded by law."

Though our government differs considerably from the French, inasmuch as we have fixed laws and constitutional barriers for the security of our liberties and properties, yet the President's observations hold pretty near as true in England as in France. Though monarchies may differ a good deal, kings differ very little. Those who are absolute desire to continue so, and those who are not, endeavor to become so; hence the same maxims and manners almost in all courts: voluptuousness and profusion encouraged, the one to sink the people into indolence, the other into poverty—consequently into dependence. The court is called the world here as well as at Paris; and nothing more is meant by saying that a man knows the world, than that he knows courts. In all courts you must expect to meet with connections without friendship, enmities without hatred, honor without virtue, appearances saved, and realities sacrificed; good manners with bad morals; and all vice and virtues so disguised, that whoever has only reasoned upon both would know neither when he first met them at court. It is well that you should know the map of that country, that when you come to travel in it, you may do it with greater safety.

From all this you will of yourself draw this obvious conclusion: That you are in truth but now going to the great and important school, the world; to which Westminster and Leipsig were only the little preparatory schools, as Marylebone, Windsor, etc., are to them. What you have already acquired will only place you in the second form of this new school, instead of the first. But if you intend, as I suppose you do, to get into the shell, you have very different things to learn from Latin and Greek: and which require much more sagacity and attention than those two dead languages; the language of pure and simple nature; the language of nature variously modified and corrupted by passions, prejudices, and habits; the language of simulation and dissimulation: very hard, but very necessary to decipher. Homer has not half so many, nor so difficult dialects, as the great book of the school you are now going to. Observe, therefore, progressively, and with the greatest attention, what the best scholars in the form immediately above you do, and so on, until you get into the shell yourself. Adieu.

Pray tell Mr. Harte that I have received his letter of the 27th May, N. S., and that I advise him never to take the English newswriters literally, who never yet inserted any one thing quite right. I have both his patent and his mandamus, in both which he is Walter, let the newspapers call him what they please.

LETTER CXVII

LONDON, July 9, O. S. 1750.

MY DEAR FRIEND: I should not deserve that appellation in return from you, if I did not freely and explicitly inform you of every corrigible defect which I may either hear of, suspect, or at any time discover in you. Those who, in the common course of the world, will call themselves your friends; or whom, according to the common notions of friendship, you may possibly think such, will never tell you of your faults, still less of your weaknesses. But, on the contrary, more desirous to make you their friend, than to prove themselves yours, they will flatter both, and, in truth, not be sorry for either. Interiorly, most people enjoy the inferiority of their best friends. The useful and essential part of friendship, to you, is reserved singly for Mr. Harte and myself: our relations to you stand pure and unsuspected of all private views. In whatever we say to you, we can have no interest but yours. We are therefore authorized to represent, advise, and remonstrate; and your reason must tell you that you ought to attend to and believe us.

I am credibly informed, that there is still a considerable hitch or hobble in your enunciation; and that when you speak fast you sometimes speak unintelligibly. I have formerly and frequently laid my thoughts before you so fully upon this subject, that I can say nothing new upon it now. I must therefore only repeat, that your whole depends upon it. Your trade is to speak well, both in public and in private. The manner of your speaking is full as important as the matter, as more people have ears to be tickled, than understandings to judge. Be your productions ever so good, they will be of no use, if you stifle and strangle them in their birth. The best compositions of Corelli, if ill executed and played out of tune, instead of touching, as they do when well performed, would only excite the indignation of the hearer's, when murdered by an unskillful performer. But to murder your own productions, and that 'coram Populo', is a MEDEAN CRUELTY, which Horace absolutely forbids. Remember of what importance Demosthenes, and one of the Gracchi, thought ENUNCIATION; and read what stress Cicero and Quintilian lay upon it; even the herb-women at Athens were correct judges of it. Oratory, with all its graces, that of enunciation in particular, is full as necessary in our government as it ever was in Greece or Rome. No man can make a fortune or a figure in this country, without speaking, and speaking well in public. If you will persuade, you must first please; and if you will please, you must tune your voice to harmony, you must articulate every syllable distinctly, your emphasis and cadences must be strongly and properly marked; and the whole together must be graceful and engaging: If you do not speak in that manner, you had much better not speak at all. All the learning you have, or ever can have, is not worth one groat without it. It may be a comfort and an amusement to you in your closet, but can be of no use to you in the world. Let me conjure you, therefore, to make this your only object, till you have absolutely conquered it, for that is in your power; think of nothing else, read and speak for nothing else. Read aloud, though alone, and read articulately and distinctly, as if you were reading in public, and on the most important occasion. Recite pieces of eloquence, declaim scenes of tragedies to Mr. Harte, as if he were a numerous audience. If there is any particular consonant which you have a difficulty in articulating, as I think you had with the R, utter it millions and millions of times, till you have uttered it right. Never speak quick, till you have first learned to speak well. In short, lay aside every book, and every thought, that does not directly tend to this great object, absolutely decisive of your future fortune and figure.

The next thing necessary in your destination, is writing correctly, elegantly, and in a good hand too; in which three particulars, I am sorry to tell you, that you hitherto fail. Your handwriting is a very bad one, and would make a scurvy figure in an office-book of letters, or even in a lady's pocket-book. But that fault is easily cured by care, since every man, who has the use of his eyes and of his right hand, can write whatever hand he pleases. As to the correctness and elegance of your writing, attention to grammar does the one, and to the best authors the other. In your letter to me of the 27th June, N. S., you omitted the date of the place, so that I only conjectured from the contents that you were at Rome.

Thus I have, with the truth and freedom of the tenderest affection, told you all your defects, at least all that I know or have heard of. Thank God, they are all very curable; they must be cured, and I am sure, you will cure them. That once done, nothing remains for you to acquire, or for me to wish you, but the turn, the manners, the address, and the GRACES, of the polite world; which experience, observation, and good company; will insensibly give you. Few people at your age have read, seen, and known, so much as you have; and consequently few are so near as yourself to what I call perfection, by which I only, mean being very near as well as the best. Far, therefore, from being discouraged by what you still want, what you already have should encourage you to attempt, and convince you that by attempting you will inevitably obtain it. The difficulties which you have surmounted were much greater than any you have now to encounter. Till very lately, your way has been only through thorns and briars; the few that now remain are mixed with roses. Pleasure is now the principal remaining part of your education. It will soften and polish your manners; it will make you pursue and at last overtake the GRACES. Pleasure is necessarily reciprocal; no one feels, who does not at the same time give it. To be pleased one must please. What pleases you in others, will in general please them in you. Paris is indisputably the seat of the GRACES; they will even court you, if you are not too coy. Frequent and observe the best companies there, and you will soon be naturalized among them; you will soon find how particularly attentive they are to the correctness and elegance of their language, and to the graces of their enunciation: they would even call the understanding of a man in question, who should neglect or not know the infinite advantages arising from them. 'Narrer, reciter, declamer bien', are serious studies among them, and well deserve to be so everywhere. The conversations, even among the women, frequently turn upon the elegancies and minutest delicacies of the French language. An 'enjouement', a gallant turn, prevails in all their companies, to women, with whom they neither are, nor pretend to be, in love; but should you (as may very possibly happen) fall really in love there with some woman of fashion and sense (for I do not suppose you capable of falling in love with a strumpet), and that your rival, without half your parts or knowledge, should get the better of you, merely by dint of manners, 'enjouement, badinage', etc., how would you regret not having sufficiently attended to those accomplishments which you despised as superficial and trifling, but which you would then find of real consequence in the course of the world! And men, as well as women, are taken by those external graces. Shut up your books, then, now as a business, and open them only as a pleasure; but let the great book of the world be your serious study; read it over and over, get it by heart, adopt its style, and make it your own.

When I cast up your account as it now stands, I rejoice to see the balance so much in your favor; and that the items per contra are so few, and of such a nature, that they may be very easily cancelled. By way of debtor and creditor, it stands thus:

Creditor. By French	Debtor. To English
German	Enunciation
Italian	Manners
	Latin
	Greek
	Logic
	Ethics
	History
	|Naturae
Jus	|Gentium
	|Publicum

This, my dear friend, is a very true account; and a very encouraging one for you. A man who owes so little can clear it off in a very little time, and, if he is a prudent man, will; whereas a man who, by long negligence, owes a great deal, despairs of ever being able to pay; and therefore never looks into his account at all.

When you go to Genoa, pray observe carefully all the environs of it, and view them with somebody who can tell you all the situations and operations of the Austrian army, during that famous siege, if it deserves to be called one; for in reality the town never was besieged, nor had the Austrians any one thing necessary for a siege. If Marquis Centurioni, who was last winter in England, should happen to be there, go to him with my compliments, and he will show you all imaginable civilities.

I could have sent you some letters to Florence, but that I knew Mr. Mann would be of more use to you than all of them. Pray make him my compliments. Cultivate your Italian, while you are at Florence, where it is spoken in its utmost purity, but ill pronounced.

Pray save me the seed of some of the best melons you eat, and put it up dry in paper. You need not send it me; but Mr. Harte will bring it in his pocket when he comes over. I should likewise be glad of some cuttings of the best figs, especially la Pica gentile and the Maltese; but as this is not the season for them, Mr. Mann will, I dare say, undertake that commission, and send them to me at the proper time by Leghorn. Adieu. Endeavor to please others, and divert yourself as much as ever you can, in 'honnete et galant homme'.

P. S. I send you the inclosed to deliver to Lord Rochford, upon your arrival at Turin.

LETTER CXVIII.

LONDON, August 6, O. S. 1750

MY DEAR FRIEND: Since your letter from Sienna, which gave me a very imperfect account both of your illness and your recovery, I have not received one word either from you or Mr. Harte. I impute this to the carelessness of the post simply: and the great distance between us at present exposes our letters to those accidents. But when you come to Paris, from whence the letters arrive here very regularly, I shall insist upon you writing to me constantly once a week; and that upon the same day, for instance, every Thursday, that I may know by what mail to expect your letter. I shall also require you to be more minute in your account of yourself than you have hitherto been, or than I have required, because of the informations which I receive from time to time from Mr. Harte. At Paris you will be out of your time, and must set up for yourself; it is then that I shall be very solicitous to know how you carry on your business. While Mr. Harte was your partner, the care was his share, and the profit yours. But at Paris, if you will have the latter, you must take the former along with it. It will be quite a new world to you; very different from the little world that you have hitherto seen; and you will have much more to do in it. You must keep your little accounts constantly every morning, if you would not have them run into confusion, and swell to a bulk that would frighten you from ever looking into them at all. You must allow some time for learning what you do not know, and some for keeping what you do know; and you must leave a great deal of time for your pleasures; which (I repeat it, again) are now become the most necessary part of your education. It is by conversations, dinners, suppers, entertainments, etc., in the best companies, that you must be formed for the world. 'Les manieres les agremens, les graces' cannot be learned by theory; they are only to be got by use among those who have them; and they are now the main object of your life, as they are the necessary steps to your fortune. A man of the best parts, and the greatest learning, if he does not know the world by his own experience and observation, will be very absurd; and consequently very unwelcome in company. He may say very good things; but they will probably be so ill-timed, misplaced, or improperly addressed, that he had much better hold his tongue. Full of his own matter, and uninformed of; or inattentive to, the particular circumstances and situations of the company, he vents it indiscriminately; he puts some people out of countenance; he shocks others; and frightens all, who dread what may come out next. The most general rule that I can give you for the world, and which your experience will convince you of the truth of, is, Never to give the tone to the company, but to take it from them; and to labor more to put them in conceit with themselves, than to make them admire you. Those whom you can make like themselves better, will, I promise you, like you very well.

A system-monger, who, without knowing anything of the world by experience, has formed a system, of it in his dusty cell, lays it down, for example, that (from the general nature of mankind) flattery is pleasing. He will therefore flatter. But how? Why, indiscriminately. And instead of repairing and heightening the piece judiciously, with soft colors and a delicate pencil,—with a coarse brush and a great deal of whitewash, he daubs and besmears the piece he means to adorn. His flattery offends even his patron; and is almost too gross for his mistress. A man of the world knows the force of flattery as well as he does; but then he knows how, when, and where to give it; he proportions his dose to the constitution of the patient. He flatters by application, by inference, by comparison, by hint, and seldom directly. In the course of the world, there is the same difference in everything between system and practice.

I long to have you at Paris, which is to be your great school; you will be then in a manner within reach of me.

Tell me, are you perfectly recovered, or do you still find any remaining complaint upon your lungs? Your diet should be cooling, and at the same time nourishing. Milks of all kinds are proper for you; wines of all kinds bad. A great deal of gentle, and no violent exercise, is good for you. Adieu. 'Gratia, fama, et valetudo, contingat, abunde!'

LETTER CXIX

LONDON, October 22, O. S. 1750

MY DEAR FRIEND: This letter will, I am persuaded, find you, and I hope safely, arrived at Montpelier; from whence I trust that Mr. Harte's indisposition will, by being totally removed, allow you to get to Paris before Christmas. You will there find two people who, though both English, I recommend in the strongest manner possible to your attention; and advise you to form the most intimate connections with them both, in their different ways. The one is a man whom you already know something of, but not near enough: it is the Earl of Huntingdon; who, next to you, is the truest object of my affection and esteem; and who (I am proud to say it) calls me, and considers me as his adopted father. His parts are as quick as his knowledge is extensive; and if quality were worth putting into an account, where every other item is so much more valuable, he is the first almost in this country: the figure he will make in it, soon after he returns to it, will, if I am not more mistaken than ever I was in my life, equal his birth and my hopes. Such a connection will be of infinite advantage to you; and, I can assure you, that he is extremely disposed to form it upon my account; and will, I hope and believe, desire to improve and cement it upon your own.

In our parliamentary government, connections are absolutely necessary; and, if prudently formed and ably maintained, the success of them is infallible. There are two sorts of connections, which I would always advise you to have in view. The first I will call equal ones; by which I mean those, where the two connecting parties reciprocally find their account, from pretty near an equal degree of parts and abilities. In those, there must be a freer communication; each must see that the other is able, and be convinced that he is willing to be of use to him. Honor must be the principle of such connections; and there must be a mutual dependence, that present and separate interest shall not be able to break them. There must be a joint system of action; and, in case of different opinions, each must recede a little, in order at last to form an unanimous one. Such, I hope, will be your connection with Lord Huntingdon. You will both come into parliament at the same time; and if you have an equal share of abilities and application, you and he, with other young people, with whom you will naturally associate, may form a band which will be respected by any administration, and make a figure in the public. The other sort of connections I call unequal ones; that is, where the parts are all on one side, and the rank and fortune on the other. Here, the advantage is all on one side; but that advantage must be ably and artfully concealed. Complaisance, an engaging manner, and a patient toleration of certain airs of superiority, must cement them. The weaker party must be taken by the heart, his head giving no hold; and he must be governed by being made to believe that he governs. These people, skillfully led, give great weight to their leader. I have formerly pointed out to you a couple that I take to be proper objects for your skill; and you will meet with twenty more, for they are very rife.

The other person whom I recommended to you is a woman; not as a woman, for that is not immediately my business; besides, I fear that she is turned of fifty. It is Lady Hervey, whom I directed you to call upon at Dijon, but who, to my great joy, because to your great advantage, passes all this winter at Paris. She has been bred all her life at courts; of which she has acquired all the easy good-breeding and politeness, without the frivolousness. She has all the reading that a woman should have; and more than any woman need have; for she understands Latin perfectly well, though she wisely conceals it. As she will look upon you as her son, I desire that you will look upon her as my delegate: trust, consult, and apply to her without reserve. No woman ever had more than she has, 'le ton de la parfaitement bonne compagnie, les manieres engageantes, et le je ne sais quoi qui plait'. Desire her to reprove and correct any, and every, the least error and inaccuracy in your manners, air, address, etc. No woman in Europe can do it so well; none will do it more willingly, or in a more proper and obliging manner. In such a case she will not put you out of countenance, by telling you of it in company; but either intimate it by some sign, or wait for an opportunity when you are alone together. She is also in the best French company, where she will not only introduce but PUFF you, if I may use so low a word. And I can assure you that it is no little help, in the 'beau monde', to be puffed there by a fashionable woman. I send you the inclosed billet to carry her, only as a certificate of the identity of your person, which I take it for granted she could not know again.

You would be so much surprised to receive a whole letter from me without any mention of the exterior ornaments necessary for a gentleman, as manners, elocution, air, address, graces, etc., that, to comply with your expectations, I will touch upon them; and tell you, that when you come to England, I will show you some people, whom I do not now care to name, raised to the highest stations singly by those exterior and adventitious ornaments, whose parts would never have entitled them to the smallest office in the excise. Are they then necessary, and worth acquiring, or not? You will see many instances of this kind at Paris, particularly a glaring one, of a person—[M. le Marechal de Richelieu]—raised to the highest posts and dignities in France, as well as to be absolute sovereign of the 'beau monde', simply by the graces of his person and address; by woman's chit-chat, accompanied with important gestures; by an imposing air and pleasing abord. Nay, by these helps, he even passes for a wit, though he hath certainly no uncommon share of it. I will not name him, because it would be very imprudent in you to do it. A young fellow, at his first entrance into the 'beau monde', must not offend the king 'de facto' there. It is very often more necessary to conceal contempt than resentment, the former forgiven, but the latter sometimes forgot.

There is a small quarto book entitled, 'Histoire Chronologique de la France', lately published by Le President Henault, a man of parts and learning, with whom you will probably get acquainted at Paris. I desire that it may always lie upon your table, for your recourse as often as you read history. The chronology, though chiefly relative to the history of France, is not singly confined to it; but the most interesting events of all the rest of Europe are also inserted, and many of them adorned by short, pretty, and just reflections. The new edition of 'Les Memoires de Sully', in three quarto volumes, is also extremely well worth your reading, as it will give you a clearer, and truer notion of one of the most interesting periods of the French history, than you can yet have formed from all the other books you may have read upon the subject. That prince, I mean Henry the Fourth, had all the accomplishments and virtues of a hero, and of a king, and almost of a man. The last are the most rarely seen. May you possess them all! Adieu.

Pray make my compliments to Mr. Harte, and let him know that I have this moment received his letter of the 12th, N. S., from Antibes. It requires no immediate answer; I shall therefore delay mine till I have another from him. Give him the inclosed, which I have received from Mr. Eliot.

LETTER CXX

LONDON, November 1, O. S. 1750

MY DEAR FRIEND: I hope that this letter will not find you still at Montpelier, but rather be sent after you from thence to Paris, where, I am persuaded, that Mr. Harte could find as good advice for his leg as at Montpelier, if not better; but if he is of a different opinion, I am sure you ought to stay there, as long as he desires.

While you are in France, I could wish that the hours you allot for historical amusement should be entirely devoted to the history of France. One always reads history to most advantage in that country to which it is relative; not only books, but persons being ever at hand to solve doubts and clear up difficulties. I do by no means advise you to throw away your time in ransacking, like a dull antiquarian, the minute and unimportant parts of remote and fabulous times. Let blockheads read what blockheads wrote. And a general notion of the history of France, from the conquest of that country by the Franks, to the reign of Louis the Eleventh, is sufficient for use, consequently sufficient for you. There are, however, in those remote times, some remarkable eras that deserve more particular attention; I mean those in which some notable alterations happened in the constitution and form of government. As, for example, in the settlement of Clovis in Gaul, and the form of government which he then established; for, by the way; that form of government differed in this particular from all the other Gothic governments, that the people, neither collectively nor by representatives, had any share in it. It was a mixture of monarchy and aristocracy: and what were called the States General of France consisted only of the nobility and clergy till the time of Philip le Bel, in the very beginning of the fourteenth century, who first called the people to those assemblies, by no means for the good of the people, who were only amused by this pretended honor, but, in truth, to check the nobility and clergy, and induce them to grant the money he wanted for his profusion; this was a scheme of Enguerrand de Marigny, his minister, who governed both him and his kingdom to such a degree as to, be called the coadjutor and governor of the kingdom. Charles Martel laid aside these assemblies, and governed by open force. Pepin restored them, and attached them to him, and with them the nation; by which means he deposed Childeric and mounted the throne. This is a second period worth your attention. The third race of kings, which begins with Hugues Capet, is a third period. A judicious reader of history will save himself a great deal of time and trouble by attending with care only to those interesting periods of history which furnish remarkable events, and make eras, and going slightly over the common run of events. Some people read history as others read the "Pilgrim's Progress"; giving equal attention to, and indiscriminately loading their memories with every part alike. But I would have you read it in a different manner; take the shortest general history you can find of every country; and mark down in that history the most important periods, such as conquests, changes of kings, and alterations of the form of government; and then have recourse to more extensive histories or particular treatises, relative to those great points. Consider them well, trace up their causes, and follow their consequences. For instance, there is a most excellent, though very short history of France, by Le Gendre. Read that with attention, and you will know enough of the general history; but when you find there such remarkable periods as are above mentioned, consult Mezeray, and other of the best and minutest historians, as well as political treatises upon those subjects. In later times, memoirs, from those of Philip de Commines, down to the innumerble ones in the reign of Louis the Fourteenth, have been of great use, and thrown great light upon particular parts of history.

Conversation in France, if you have the address and dexterity to turn it upon useful subjects, will exceedingly improve your historical knowledge; for people there, however classically ignorant they may be, think it a shame to be ignorant of the history of their own country: they read that, if they read nothing else, and having often read nothing else, are proud of having read that, and talk of it willingly; even the women are well instructed in that sort of reading. I am far from meaning by this that you should always be talking wisely in company, of books, history, and matters of knowledge. There are many companies which you will, and ought to keep, where such conversations would be misplaced and ill-timed; your own good sense must distinguish the company and the time. You must trifle only with triflers; and be serious only with the serious, but dance to those who pipe. 'Cur in theatrum Cato severs venisti?' was justly said to an old man: how much more so would it be to one of your age? From the moment that you are dressed and go out, pocket all your knowledge with your watch, and never pull it out in company unless desired: the producing of the one unasked, implies that you are weary of the company; and the producing of the other unrequired, will make the company weary of you. Company is a republic too jealous of its liberties, to suffer a dictator even for a quarter of an hour; and yet in that, as in republics, there are some few who really govern; but then it is by seeming to disclaim, instead of attempting to usurp the power; that is the occasion in which manners, dexterity, address, and the undefinable 'je ne sais quoi' triumph; if properly exerted, their conquest is sure, and the more lasting for not being perceived. Remember, that this is not only your first and greatest, but ought to be almost your only object, while you are in France.

I know that many of your countrymen are apt to call the freedom and vivacity of the French petulancy and illbreeding; but, should you think so, I desire upon many accounts that you will not say so; I admit that it may be so in some instances of 'petits maitres Etourdis', and in some young people unbroken to the world; but I can assure you, that you will find it much otherwise with people of a certain rank and age, upon whose model you will do very well to form yourself. We call their steady assurance, impudence why? Only because what we call modesty is awkward bashfulness and 'mauvaise honte'. For my part, I see no impudence, but, on the contrary, infinite utility and advantage in presenting one's self with the same coolness and unconcern in any and every company. Till one can do that, I am very sure that one can never present one's self well. Whatever is done under concern and embarrassment, must be ill done, and, till a man is absolutely easy and unconcerned in every company, he will never be thought to have kept good company, nor be very welcome in it. A steady assurance, with seeming modesty, is possibly the most useful qualification that a man can have in every part of life. A man would certainly make a very considerable fortune and figure in the world, whose modesty and timidity should often, as bashfulness always does (put him in the deplorable and lamentable situation of the pious AEneas, when 'obstupuit, steteruntque comae; et vox faucibus haesit!). Fortune (as well as women)—

"————-born to be controlled,

Stoops to the forward and the bold."

Assurance and intrepidity, under the white banner of seeming modesty, clear the way for merit, that would otherwise be discouraged by difficulties in its journey; whereas barefaced impudence is the noisy and blustering harbinger of a worthless and senseless usurper.

You will think that I shall never have done recommending to you these exterior worldly accomplishments, and you will think right, for I never shall; they are of too great consequence to you for me to be indifferent or negligent about them: the shining part of your future figure and fortune depends now wholly upon them.

These are the acquisitions which must give efficacy and success to those you have already made. To have it said and believed that you are the most learned man in England, would be no more than was said and believed of Dr. Bentley; but to have it said, at the same time, that you are also the best-bred, most polite, and agreeable man in the kingdom, would be such a happy composition of a character as I never yet knew any one man deserve; and which I will endeavor, as well as ardently wish, that you may. Absolute perfection is, I well know, unattainable; but I know too, that a man of parts may be unweariedly aiming at it, and arrive pretty near it. Try, labor, persevere. Adieu.

LETTER CXXI

LONDON, November 8, O. S. 1750

MY DEAR FRIEND: Before you get to Paris, where you will soon be left to your own discretion, if you have any, it is necessary that we should understand one another thoroughly; which is the most probable way of preventing disputes. Money, the cause of much mischief in the world, is the cause of most quarrels between fathers and sons; the former commonly thinking that they cannot give too little, and the latter, that they cannot have enough; both equally in the wrong. You must do me the justice to acknowledge, that I have hitherto neither stinted nor grudged any expense that could be of use or real pleasure to you; and I can assure you, by the way, that you have traveled at a much more considerable expense than I did myself; but I never so much as thought of that, while Mr. Harte was at the head of your finances; being very sure that the sums granted were scrupulously applied to the uses for which they were intended. But the case will soon be altered, and you will be your own receiver and treasurer. However, I promise you, that we will not quarrel singly upon the quantum, which shall be cheerfully and freely granted: the application and appropriation of it will be the material point, which I am now going to clear up and finally settle with you. I will fix, or even name, no settled allowance; though I well know in my own mind what would be the proper one; but I will first try your draughts, by which I can in a good degree judge of your conduct. This only I tell you in general, that if the channels through which my money is to go are the proper ones, the source shall not be scanty; but should it deviate into dirty, muddy, and obscure ones (which by the bye, it cannot do for a week without my knowing it); I give you fair and timely notice, that the source will instantly be dry. Mr. Harte, in establishing you at Paris, will point out to you those proper channels; he will leave you there upon the foot of a man of fashion, and I will continue you upon the same; you will have your coach, your valet de chambre, your own footman, and a valet de place; which, by the way, is one servant more than I had. I would have you very well dressed, by which I mean dressed as the generality of people of fashion are; that is, not to be taken notice of, for being either more or less fine than other people: it is by being well dressed, not finely dressed, that a gentleman should be distinguished. You must frequent 'les spectacles', which expense I shall willingly supply. You must play 'a des petits jeux de commerce' in mixed companies; that article is trifling; I shall pay it cheerfully. All the other articles of pocket-money are very inconsiderable at Paris, in comparison of what they are here, the silly custom of giving money wherever one dines or sups, and the expensive importunity of subscriptions, not being yet introduced there. Having thus reckoned up all the decent expenses of a gentleman, which I will most readily defray, I come now to those which I will neither bear nor supply. The first of these is gaming, of which, though I have not the least reason to suspect you, I think it necessary eventually to assure you, that no consideration in the world shall ever make me pay your play debts; should you ever urge to me that your honor is pawned, I should most immovably answer you, that it was your honor, not mine, that was pawned; and that your creditor might e'en take the pawn for the debt.

Low company, and low pleasures, are always much more costly than liberal and elegant ones. The disgraceful riots of a tavern are much more expensive, as well as dishonorable, than the sometimes pardonable excesses in good company. I must absolutely hear of no tavern scrapes and squabbles.

I come now to another and very material point; I mean women; and I will not address myself to you upon this subject, either in a religious, a moral, or a parental style. I will even lay aside my age, remember yours, and speak to you as one man of pleasure, if he had parts too, would speak to another. I will by no means pay for whores, and their never-failing consequences, surgeons; nor will I, upon any account, keep singers, dancers, actresses, and 'id genus omne'; and, independently of the expense, I must tell you, that such connections would give me, and all sensible people, the utmost contempt for your parts and address; a young fellow must have as little sense as address, to venture, or more properly to sacrifice, his health and ruin his fortune, with such sort of creatures; in such a place as Paris especially, where gallantry is both the profession and the practice of every woman of fashion. To speak plainly, I will not forgive your understanding c————s and p————s; nor will your constitution forgive them you. These distempers, as well as their cures, fall nine times in ten upon the lungs. This argument, I am sure, ought to have weight with you: for I protest to you, that if you meet with any such accident, I would not give one year's purchase for your life. Lastly, there is another sort of expense that I will not allow, only because it is a silly one; I mean the fooling away your money in baubles at toy shops. Have one handsome snuff-box (if you take snuff), and one handsome sword; but then no more pretty and very useless things.

By what goes before, you will easily perceive that I mean to allow you whatever is necessary, not only for the figure, but for the pleasures of a gentleman, and not to supply the profusion of a rake. This, you must confess, does not savor of either the severity or parsimony of old age. I consider this agreement between us, as a subsidiary treaty on my part, for services to be performed on yours. I promise you, that I will be as punctual in the payment of the subsidies, as England has been during the last war; but then I give you notice at the same time, that I require a much more scrupulous execution of the treaty on your part, than we met with on that of our allies; or else that payment will be stopped. I hope all that I have now said was absolutely unnecessary, and that sentiments more worthy and more noble than pecuniary ones, would of themselves have pointed out to you the conduct I recommend; but, at all events, I resolved to be once for all explicit with you, that, in the worst that can happen, you may not plead ignorance, and complain that I had not sufficiently explained to you my intentions.

Having mentioned the word rake, I must say a word or two more on that subject, because young people too frequently, and always fatally, are apt to mistake that character for that of a man of pleasure; whereas, there are not in the world two characters more different. A rake is a composition of all the lowest, most ignoble, degrading, and shameful vices; they all conspire to disgrace his character, and to ruin his fortune; while wine and the p————s contend which shall soonest and most effectually destroy his constitution. A dissolute, flagitious footman, or porter, makes full as good a rake as a man of the first quality. By the bye, let me tell you, that in the wildest part of my youth, I never was a rake, but, on the contrary, always detested and despised that character.

A man of pleasure, though not always so scrupulous as he should be, and as one day he will wish he had been, refines at least his pleasures by taste, accompanies them with decency, and enjoys them with dignity. Few men can be men of pleasure, every man may be a rake. Remember that I shall know everything you say or do at Paris, as exactly as if, by the force of magic, I could follow you everywhere, like a sylph or a gnome, invisible myself. Seneca says, very prettily, that one should ask nothing of God, but what one should be willing that men should know; nor of men, but what one should be willing that God should know. I advise you to say and do nothing at Paris, but what you would be willing that I should know. I hope, nay, I believe, that will be the case. Sense, I dare say, you do not want; instruction, I am sure, you have never wanted: experience you are daily gaining: all which together must inevitably (I should think) make you both 'respectable et aimable', the perfection of a human character. In that case nothing shall be wanting on my part, and you shall solidly experience all the extent and tenderness of my affection for you; but dread the reverse of both! Adieu!

P. S. When you get to Paris, after you have been to wait on Lord Albemarle, go to see Mr. Yorke, whom I have particular reasons for desiring that you should be well with, as I shall hereafter explain to you. Let him know that my orders, and your own inclinations, conspired to make you desire his friendship and protection.

LETTER CXXII

MY DEAR FRIEND: I have sent you so many preparatory letters for Paris, that this, which will meet you there, shall only be a summary of them all.

You have hitherto had more liberty than anybody of your age ever had; and I must do you the justice to own, that you have made a better use of it than most people of your age would have done; but then, though you had not a jailer, you had a friend with you. At Paris, you will not only be unconfined, but unassisted. Your own good sense must be your only guide: I have great confidence in it, and am convinced that I shall receive just such accounts of your conduct at Paris as I could wish; for I tell you beforehand, that I shall be most minutely informed of all that you do, and almost of all that you say there. Enjoy the pleasures of youth, you cannot do better: but refine and dignify them like a man, of parts; let them raise, and not sink; let them adorn and not vilify your character; let them, in short, be the pleasures of a gentleman, and taken with your equals at least, but rather with your superiors, and those chiefly French.

Inquire into the characters of the several Academicians, before you form a connection with any of them; and be most upon your guard against those who make the most court to you.

You cannot study much in the Academy; but you may study usefully there, if you are an economist of your time, and bestow only upon good books those quarters and halves of hours, which occur to everybody in the course of almost every day; and which, at the year's end, amount to a very considerable sum of time. Let Greek, without fail, share some part of every day; I do not mean the Greek poets, the catches of Anacreon, or the tender complaints of Theocritus, or even the porter-like language of Homer's heroes; of whom all smatterers in Greek know a little, quote often, and talk of always; but I mean Plato, Aristoteles, Demosthenes, and Thucydides, whom none but adepts know. It is Greek that must distinguish you in the learned world, Latin alone will not: and Greek must be sought to be retained, for it never occurs like Latin. When you read history or other books of amusement, let every language you are master of have its turn, so that you may not only retain, but improve in everyone. I also desire that you will converse in German and Italian, with all the Germans and the Italians with whom you converse at all. This will be a very agreeable and flattering thing to them, and a very useful one to you.

LETTERS TO HIS SON, COMPLETE

Pray apply yourself diligently to your exercises; for though the doing them well is not supremely meritorious, the doing them ill is illiberal, vulgar, and ridiculous.

I recommend theatrical representations to you; which are excellent at Paris. The tragedies of Corneille and Racine, and the comedies of Moliere, well attended to, are admirable lessons, both for the heart and the head. There is not, nor ever was, any theatre comparable to the French. If the music of the French operas does not please your Italian ear, the words of them, at least, are sense and poetry, which is much more than I can, say of any Italian opera that I ever read or heard in my life.

I send you the inclosed letter of recommendation to Marquis Matignon, which I would have you deliver to him as soon as you can; you will, I am sure, feel the good effects of his warm friendship for me and Lord Bolingbroke, who has also wrote to him upon your subject. By that, and by the other letters which I have sent you, you will be at once so thoroughly introduced into the best French company, that you must take some pains if you will keep bad; but that is what I do not suspect you of. You have, I am sure, too much right ambition to prefer low and disgraceful company to that of your superiors, both in rank and age. Your character, and consequently your fortune, absolutely depends upon the company you keep, and the turn you take at Paris. I do not in the least mean a grave turn; on the contrary, a gay, a sprightly, but, at the same time, an elegant and liberal one.

Keep carefully out of all scrapes and quarrels. They lower a character extremely; and are particularly dangerous in France; where a man is dishonored by not resenting an affront, and utterly ruined by resenting it. The young Frenchmen are hasty, giddy, and petulant; extremely national, and 'avantageux'. Forbear from any national jokes or reflections, which are always improper, and commonly unjust. The colder northern nations generally look upon France as a whistling, singing, dancing, frivolous nation; this notion is very far from being a true one, though many 'Petits maitres' by their behavior seem to justify it; but those very 'petits maltres', when mellowed by age and experience, very often turn out very able men. The number of great generals and statesmen, as well as excellent authors, that France has produced, is an undeniable proof, that it is not that frivolous, unthinking, empty nation that northern prejudices suppose it. Seem to like and approve of everything at first, and I promise you that you will like and approve of many things afterward.

I expect that you will write to me constantly, once every week, which I desire may be every Thursday; and that your letters may inform me of your personal transactions: not of what you see, but of whom you see, and what you do.

Be your own monitor, now that you will have no other. As to enunciation, I must repeat it to you again and again, that there is no one thing so necessary: all other talents, without that, are absolutely useless, except in your own closet.

It sounds ridiculously to bid you study with your dancing-master; and yet I do. The bodily-carriage and graces are of infinite consequence to everybody, and more particularly to you.

Adieu for this time, my dear child. Yours tenderly.

LETTER CXXIII

LONDON, November 12, O. S. 1750

MY DEAR FRIEND: You will possibly think, that this letter turns upon strange, little, trifling objects; and you will think right, if you consider them separately; but if you take them aggregately, you will be convinced that as parts, which conspire to form that whole, called the exterior of a man of fashion, they are of importance. I shall not dwell now upon these personal graces, that liberal air, and that engaging address, which I have so often recommended to you; but descend still lower, to your dress, cleanliness, and care of your person.

When you come to Paris, you may take care to be extremely well dressed; that is, as the fashionable people are; this does by no means consist in the finery, but in the taste, fitness, and manner of wearing your clothes; a fine suit ill-made, and slatternly or stiffly worn, far from adorning, only exposes the awkwardness of the wearer. Get the best French tailor to make your clothes, whatever they are, in the fashion, and to fit you: and then wear them, button them, or unbutton them, as the genteelest people you see do. Let your man learn of the best friseur to do your hair well, for that is a very material part of your dress. Take care to have your stockings well gartered up, and your shoes well buckled; for nothing gives a more slovenly air to a man than ill-dressed legs. In your person you must be accurately clean; and your teeth, hands, and nails, should be superlatively so; a dirty mouth has real ill consequences to the owner, for it infallibly causes the decay, as well as the intolerable pain of the teeth, and it is very offensive to his acquaintance, for it will most inevitably stink. I insist, therefore, that you wash your teeth the first thing you do every morning, with a soft sponge and swarm water, for four or five minutes; and then wash your mouth five or six times. Mouton, whom I desire you will send for upon your arrival at Paris, will give you an opiate, and a liquor to be used sometimes. Nothing looks more ordinary, vulgar, and illiberal, than dirty hands, and ugly, uneven, and ragged nails: I do not suspect you of that shocking, awkward trick, of biting yours; but that is not enough: you must keep the ends of them smooth and clean, not tipped with black, as the ordinary people's always are. The ends of your nails should be small segments of circles, which, by a very little care in the cutting, they are very easily brought to; every time that you wipe your hands, rub the skin round your nails backward, that it may not grow up, and shorten your nails too much. The cleanliness of the rest of your person, which, by the way, will conduce greatly to your health, I refer from time to time to the bagnio. My mentioning these particulars arises (I freely own) from some suspicion that the hints are not unnecessary; for, when you were a schoolboy, you were slovenly and dirty above your fellows. I must add another caution, which is that upon no account whatever, you put your fingers, as too many people are apt to do, in your nose or ears. It is the most shocking, nasty, vulgar rudeness, that can be offered to company; it disgusts one, it turns one's stomach; and, for my own part, I would much rather know that a man's fingers were actually in his breech, than see them in his nose. Wash your ears well every morning, and blow your nose in your handkerchief whenever you have occasion; but, by the way, without looking at it afterward. There should be in the least, as well as in the greatest parts of a gentleman, 'les manieres nobles'. Sense will teach you some, observation others; attend carefully to the manners, the diction, the motions, of people of the first fashion, and form your own upon them. On the other hand, observe a little those of the vulgar, in order to avoid them: for though the things which they say or do may be the same, the manner is always totally different: and in that, and nothing else, consists the characteristic of a man of fashion. The lowest peasant speaks, moves, dresses, eats, and drinks, as much as a man of the first fashion, but does them all quite differently; so that by doing and saying most things in a manner opposite to that of the vulgar, you have a great chance of doing and saying them right. There are gradations in awkwardness and vulgarism, as there are in everything else. 'Les manieres de robe', though not quite right, are still better than 'les manieres bourgeoises'; and these, though bad, are still better than 'les manieres de campagne'. But the language, the air, the dress, and the manners of the court, are the only true standard 'des manieres nobles, et d'un honnete homme. Ex pede Herculem' is an old and true saying, and very applicable to our present subject; for a man of parts, who has been bred at courts, and used to keep the best company, will distinguish himself, and is to be known from the vulgar by every word, attitude, gesture, and even look. I cannot leave these seeming 'minutiae', without repeating to you the necessity of your carving well; which is an article, little as it is, that is useful twice every day of one's life; and the doing it ill is very troublesome to one's self, and very disagreeable, often ridiculous, to others.

Having said all this, I cannot help reflecting, what a formal dull fellow, or a cloistered pedant, would say, if they were to see this letter: they would look upon it with the utmost contempt, and say that surely a father might find much better topics for advice to a son. I would admit it, if I had given you, or that you were capable of receiving, no better; but if sufficient pains have been taken to form your heart and improve your mind, and, as I hope, not without success, I will tell those solid gentlemen, that all these trifling things, as they think them, collectively, form that pleasing 'je ne sais quoi', that ensemble, which they are utter strangers to both in themselves and others. The word aimable is not known in their language, or the thing in their manners. Great usage of the world, great attention, and a great desire of pleasing, can alone give it; and it is no trifle. It is from old people's looking upon these things as trifles, or not thinking of them at all, that so many young people are so awkward and so ill-bred. Their parents, often careless and unmindful of them, give them only the common run of education, as school, university, and then traveling; without examining, and very often without being able to judge, if they did examine, what progress they make in any one of these stages. Then, they carelessly comfort themselves, and say, that their sons will do like other people's sons; and so they do, that is, commonly very ill. They correct none of the childish nasty tricks, which they get at school; nor the illiberal manners which they contract at the university; nor the frivolous and superficial pertness, which is commonly all that they acquire by their travels. As they do not tell them of these things, nobody else can; so they go on in the practice of them, without ever hearing, or knowing, that they are unbecoming, indecent, and shocking. For, as I have often formerly observed to you, nobody but a father can take the liberty to reprove a young fellow, grown up, for those kinds of inaccuracies and improprieties of behavior. The most intimate friendship, unassisted by the paternal superiority, will not authorize it. I may truly say, therefore, that you are happy in having me for a sincere, friendly, and quick-sighted monitor. Nothing will escape me: I shall pry for your defects, in order to correct them, as curiously as I shall seek for your perfections, in order to applaud and reward them, with this difference only, that I shall publicly mention the latter, and never hint at the former, but in a letter to, or a tete-d-tete with you. I will never put you out of countenance before company; and I hope you will never give me reason to be out of countenance for you, as any one of the above-mentioned defects would make me. 'Praetor non, curat de minimis', was a maxim in the Roman law; for causes only of a certain value were tried by him but there were inferior jurisdictions, that took cognizance of the smallest. Now I shall try you, not only as 'praetor' in the greatest, but as 'censor' in lesser, and as the lowest magistrate in the least cases.

I have this moment received Mr. Harte's letter of the 1st November, N. S., by which I am very glad to find that he thinks of moving toward Paris, the end of this month, which looks as if his leg were better; besides, in my opinion, you both of you only lose time at Montpelier; he would find better advice, and you better company, at Paris. In the meantime, I hope you go into the best company there is at Montpelier; and there always is some at the Intendant's, or the Commandant's. You will have had full time to learn 'les petites chansons Languedociennes', which are exceedingly pretty ones, both words and tunes. I remember, when I was in those parts, I was surprised at the difference which I found between the people on one side, and those on the other side of the Rhone. The Provencaux were, in general, surly, ill-bred, ugly, and swarthy; the Languedocians the very reverse: a cheerful, well-bred, handsome people. Adieu! Yours most affectionately.

P. S. Upon reflection, I direct this letter to Paris; I think you must have left Montpelier before it could arrive there.

LETTER CXXIV

LONDON, November 19, O. S. 1750

MY DEAR FRIEND: I was very glad to find by your letter of the 12th, N. S., that you had informed yourself so well of the state of the French marine at Toulon, and of the commerce at Marseilles; they are objects that deserve the inquiry and attention of every man who intends to be concerned in public affairs. The French are now wisely attentive to both; their commerce is incredibly increased within these last thirty years; they have beaten us out of great part of our Levant trade; their East India trade has greatly affected ours; and, in the West Indies, their Martinico establishment supplies, not only France itself, but the greatest part of Europe, with sugars whereas our islands, as Jamaica, Barbadoes, and the Leeward, have now no other market for theirs but England. New France, or Canada, has also greatly lessened our fur and skin trade. It is true (as you say) that we have no treaty of commerce subsisting (I do not say WITH MARSEILLES) but with France. There was a treaty of commerce made between England and France, immediately after the treaty of Utrecht; but the whole treaty was conditional, and to depend upon the parliament's enacting certain things which were stipulated in two of the articles; the parliament, after a very famous debate, would not do it; so the treaty fell to the ground: however, the outlines of that treaty are, by mutual and tacit consent, the general rules of our present commerce with France. It is true, too, that our commodities which go to France, must go in our bottoms; the French having imitated in many respects our famous Act of Navigation, as it is commonly called. This act was made in the year 1652, in the parliament held by Oliver Cromwell. It forbids all foreign ships to bring into England any merchandise or commodities whatsoever, that were not of the growth and produce of that country to which those ships belonged, under penalty of the forfeiture of such ships. This act was particularly leveled at the Dutch, who were at that time the carriers of almost all Europe, and got immensely by freight. Upon this principle, of the advantages arising from freight, there is a provision in the same act, that even the growth and produce of our own colonies in America shall not be carried from thence to any other country in Europe, without first touching in England; but this clause has lately been repealed, in the instances of some perishable commodities, such as rice, etc., which are allowed to be carried directly from our American colonies to other countries. The act also provides, that two-thirds, I think, of those who navigate the said ships shall be British subjects. There is an excellent, and little book, written by the famous Monsieur Huet Eveque d'Avranches, 'Sur le Commerce des Anciens', which is very well worth your reading, and very soon read. It will give you a clear notion of the rise and progress of commerce. There are many other books, which take up the history of commerce where Monsieur d'Avranches leaves it, and bring it down to these times. I advise you to read some of them with care; commerce being a very essential part of political knowledge in every country; but more particularly in that which owes all its riches and power to it.

I come now to another part of your letter, which is the orthography, if I may call bad spelling ORTHOGRAPHY. You spell induce, ENDUCE; and grandeur, you spell grandURE; two faults of which few of my housemaids would have been guilty. I must tell you that orthography, in the true sense of the word, is so absolutely necessary for a man of letters; or a gentleman, that one false spelling may fix ridicule upon him for the rest of his life; and I know a man of quality, who never recovered the ridicule of having spelled WHOLESOME without the w.

Reading with care will secure everybody from false spelling; for books are always well spelled, according to the orthography of the times. Some words are indeed doubtful, being spelled differently by different authors of equal authority; but those are few; and in those cases every man has his option, because he may plead his authority either way; but where there is but one right way, as in the two words above mentioned, it is unpardonable and ridiculous for a gentleman to miss it; even a woman of a tolerable education would despise and laugh, at a lover, who should send her an ill-spelled billet-doux. I fear and suspect, that you have taken it into your head, in most cases, that the matter is all, and the manner little or nothing. If you have, undeceive yourself, and be convinced that, in everything, the manner is full as important as the matter. If you speak the sense of an angel, in bad words and with a disagreeable utterance, nobody will hear you twice, who can help it. If you write epistles as well as Cicero, but in a very bad hand, and very ill-spelled, whoever receives will laugh at them; and if you had the figure of Adonis, with an awkward air and motions, it will disgust instead of pleasing. Study manner, therefore, in everything, if you would be anything. My principal inquiries of my friends at Paris, concerning you, will be relative to your manner of doing whatever you do. I shall not inquire whether you understand Demosthenes, Tacitus, or the 'Jus Publicum Imperii'; but I shall inquire, whether your utterance is pleasing, your style not only pure, but elegant, your manners noble and easy, your air and address engaging in short, whether you are a gentleman, a man of fashion, and fit to keep good company, or not; for, till I am satisfied in these particulars, you and I must by no means meet; I could not possibly stand it.

It is in your power to become all this at Paris, if you please. Consult with Lady Hervey and Madame Monconseil upon all these matters; and they will speak to you, and advise you freely. Tell them, that 'bisogna compatire ancora', that you are utterly new in the world; that you are desirous to form yourself; that you beg they will reprove, advise, and correct you; that you know that none can do it so well; and that you will implicitly follow their directions. This, together with your careful observation of the manners of the best company, will really form you.

Abbe Guasco, a friend of mine, will come to you as soon as he knows of your arrival at Paris; he is well received in the best companies there, and will introduce you to them. He will be desirous to do you any service he can; he is active and curious, and can give you information upon most things. He is a sort of 'complaisant' of the President Montesquieu, to whom you have a letter.

I imagine that this letter will not wait for you very long at Paris, where I reckon you will be in about a fortnight. Adieu.

LETTER CXXV

LONDON, December 24, 1750

DEAR FRIEND: At length you are become a Parisian, and consequently must be addressed in French; you will also answer me in the same language, that I may be able to judge of the degree in which you possess the elegance, the delicacy, and the orthography of that language which is, in a manner, become the universal one of Europe. I am assured that you speak it well, but in that well there are gradations. He, who in the provinces might be reckoned to speak correctly, would at Paris be looked upon as an ancient Gaul. In that country of mode, even language is subservient to fashion, which varies almost as often as their clothes.

The AFFECTED, the REFINED, the NEOLOGICAL, OR NEW FASHIONABLE STYLE are at present too much in vogue at Paris. Know, observe, and occasionally converse (if you please) according to those different styles; but do not let your taste be infected by them. Wit, too, is there subservient to fashion; and actually, at Paris, one must have wit, even in despite of Minerva. Everybody runs after it; although if it does not come naturally and of itself; it never can be overtaken. But, unfortunately for those who pursue, they seize upon what they take for wit, and endeavor to pass it for such upon others. This is, at best, the lot of Ixion, who embraced a cloud instead of the goddess he pursued. Fine sentiments, which never existed, false and unnatural thoughts, obscure and far-sought expressions, not only unintelligible, but which it is even impossible to decipher, or to guess at, are all the consequences of this error; and two-thirds of the new French books which now appear are made up of those ingredients. It is the new cookery of Parnassus, in which the still is employed instead of the pot and the spit, and where quintessences and extracts ate chiefly used. N. B. The Attic salt is proscribed.

You will now and then be obliged to eat of this new cookery, but do not suffer your taste to be corrupted by it. And when you, in your turn, are desirous of treating others, take the good old cookery of Lewis XIV.'s reign for your rule. There were at that time admirable head cooks, such as Corneille, Boileau, Racine, and La Fontaine. Whatever they prepared was simple, wholesome, and solid. But laying aside all metaphors, do not suffer yourself to be dazzled by false brilliancy, by unnatural expressions, nor by those antitheses so much in fashion: as a protection against such innovations, have a recourse to your own good sense, and to the ancient authors. On the other hand, do not laugh at those who give into such errors; you are as yet too young to act the critic, or to stand forth a severe avenger of the violated rights of good sense. Content yourself with not being perverted, but do not think of converting others; let them quietly enjoy their errors in taste, as well as in religion. Within the course of the last century and a half, taste in France has (as well as that kingdom itself) undergone many vicissitudes. Under the reign of I do not say Lewis XIII. but of Cardinal de Richelieu, good taste first began to make its way. It was refined under that of Lewis XIV., a great king, at least, if not a great man. Corneille was the restorer of true taste, and the founder of the French theatre; although rather inclined to the Italian 'Concetti' and the Spanish 'Agudeze'. Witness those epigrams which he makes Chimene utter in the greatest excess of grief.

Before his time, those kind of itinerant authors, called troubadours or romanciers, were a species of madmen who attracted the admiration of fools. Toward the end of Cardinal de Richelieu's reign, and the beginning of Lewis XIV.'s, the Temple of Taste was established at the Hotel of Rambouillet; but that taste was not judiciously refined this Temple of Taste might more properly have been named a Laboratory of Wit, where good sense was put to the torture, in order to extract from it the most subtile essence. There it was that Voiture labored hard and incessantly to create wit. At length, Boileau and Moliere fixed the standard of true taste. In spite of the Scuderys, the Calprenedes, etc., they defeated and put to flight ARTAMENES, JUBA, OROONDATES, and all those heroes of romance, who were, notwithstanding (each of them), as good as a whole Army. Those madmen then endeavored to obtain an asylum in libraries; this they could not accomplish, but were under a necessity of taking shelter in the chambers of some few ladies. I would have you read one volume of "Cleopatra," and one of "Clelia"; it will otherwise be impossible for you to form any idea of the extravagances they contain; but God keep you from ever persevering to the twelfth.

During almost the whole reign of Lewis XIV., true taste remained in its purity, until it received some hurt, although undesignedly, from a very fine genius, I mean Monsieur de Fontenelle; who, with the greatest sense and the most solid learning, sacrificed rather too much to the Graces, whose most favorite child and pupil he was. Admired with reason, others tried to imitate him; but, unfortunately for us, the author of the "Pastorals," of the "History of Oracles," and of the "French Theatre," found fewer imitators than the Chevalier d'Her did mimics. He has since been taken off by a thousand authors: but never really imitated by anyone that I know of.

At this time, the seat of true taste in France seems to me not well established. It exists, but torn by factions. There is one party of petits maitres, one of half-learned women, another of insipid authors whose works are 'verba et voces, et praeterea nihil'; and, in short, a numerous and very fashionable party of writers, who, in a metaphysical jumble, introduce their false and subtle reasonings upon the movements and the sentiments of THE SOUL, THE HEART, and THE MIND.

Do not let yourself be overpowered by fashion, nor by particular sets of people with whom you may be connected; but try all the different coins before you receive any in payment. Let your own good sense and reason judge of the value of each; and be persuaded, that NOTHING CAN BE BEAUTIFUL UNLESS TRUE: whatever brilliancy is not the result of the solidity and justness of a thought, it is but a false glare. The Italian saying upon a diamond is equally just with regard to thoughts, 'Quanto Piu sodezza, tanto piu splendore'.

All this ought not to hinder you from conforming externally to the modes and tones of the different companies in which you may chance to be. With the 'petits maitres' speak epigrams; false sentiments, with frivolous women; and a mixture of all these together, with professed beaux esprits. I would have you do so; for at your age you ought not to aim at changing the tone of the company, but conform to it. Examine well, however; weigh all maturely within yourself; and do not mistake the tinsel of Tasso for the gold of Virgil.

You will find at Paris good authors, and circles distinguished by the solidity of their reasoning. You will never hear TRIFLING, AFFECTED, and far-sought conversations, at Madame de Monconseil's, nor at the hotels of Matignon and Coigni, where she will introduce you. The President Montesquieu will not speak to you in the epigrammatic style. His book, the "Spirit of the Laws," written in the vulgar tongue, will equally please and instruct you.

Frequent the theatre whenever Corneille, Racine, and Moliere's pieces are played. They are according to nature and to truth. I do not mean by this to give an exclusion to several admirable modern plays, particularly "Cenie,"—[Imitated in English by Mr. Francis, in a play called "Eugenia."]—replete with sentiments that are true, natural, and applicable to one's self. If you choose to know the characters of people now in fashion, read Crebillon the younger, and Marivaux's works. The former is a most excellent painter; the latter has studied, and knows the human heart, perhaps too well. Crebillon's 'Egaremens du Coeur et de l'Esprit is an excellent work in its kind; it will be of infinite amusement to you, and not totally useless. The Japanese history of "Tanzar and Neadarne," by the same author, is an amiable extravagancy, interspersed with the most just reflections. In short, provided you do not mistake the objects of your attention, you will find matter at Paris to form a good and true taste.

As I shall let you remain at Paris without any person to direct your conduct, I flatter myself that you will not make a bad use of the confidence I repose in you. I do not require that you should lead the life of a Capuchin friar; quite the contrary: I recommend pleasures to you; but I expect that they shall be the pleasures of a gentleman. Those add brilliancy to a young man's character; but debauchery vilifies and degrades it. I shall have very true and exact accounts of your conduct; and, according to the informations I receive, shall be more, or less, or not at all, yours. Adieu.

P. S. Do not omit writing to me once a-week; and let your answer to this letter be in French. Connect yourself as much as possible with the foreign ministers; which is properly traveling into different countries, without going from one place. Speak Italian to all the Italians, and German to all the Germans you meet, in order not to forget those two languages.

I wish you, my dear friend, as many happy new years as you deserve, and not one more. May you deserve a great number!

1751

LETTER CXXVI

LONDON, January 8, O.S. 1751

MY DEAR FRIEND: By your letter of the 5th, N. S., I find that your 'debut' at Paris has been a good one; you are entered into good company, and I dare say you will, not sink into bad. Frequent the houses where you have been once invited, and have none of that shyness which makes most of your countrymen strangers, where they might be intimate and domestic if they pleased. Wherever you have a general invitation to sup when you please, profit of it, with decency, and go every now and then. Lord Albemarle will, I am sure, be extremely kind to you, but his house is only a dinner house; and, as I am informed, frequented by no French people. Should he happen to employ you in his bureau, which I much doubt, you must write a better hand than your common one, or you will get no credit by your manuscripts; for your hand is at present an illiberal one; it is neither a hand of business nor of a gentleman, but the hand of a school-boy writing his exercise, which he hopes will never be read.

Madame de Monconseil gives me a favorable account of you; and so do Marquis de Matignon and Madame du Boccage; they all say that you desire to please, and consequently promise me that you will; and they judge right; for whoever really desires to please, and has (as you now have) the means of learning how, certainly will please and that is the great point of life; it makes all other things easy. Whenever you are with Madame de Monconseil, Madame du Boccage, or other women of fashion, with whom you are tolerably free, say frankly and naturally: "I know little of the world; I am quite a novice in it; and although very desirous of pleasing, I am at a loss for the means. Be so good, Madame, as to let me into your secret of pleasing everybody. I shall owe my success to it, and you will always have more than falls to your share." When, in consequence of this request, they shall tell you of any little error, awkwardness, or impropriety, you should not only feel, but express the warmest acknowledgment. Though nature should suffer, and she will at first hearing them, tell them, that you will look upon the most severe criticisms as the greatest proof of their friendship. Madame du Boccage tells me, particularly, to inform you: "I shall always, receive the honor of his visits with pleasure; it is true, that at his age the pleasures of conversation are cold; but I will endeavor to make him acquainted with young people," etc.

Make use of this invitation, and as you live, in a manner, next door to her, step in and out there frequently. Monsieur du Boccage will go with you, he tells me, with great pleasure, to the plays, and point out to you whatever deserves your knowing there. This is worth your acceptance too; he has a very good taste. I have not yet heard from Lady Hervey upon your subject; but as you inform me that you have already supped with her once, I look upon you as adopted by her; consult her in all your little matters; tell her any difficulties that may occur to you; ask her what you should do or say in such or such cases; she has 'l'usage du monde en perfection', and will help you to acquire it. Madame de Berkenrode 'est paitrie de graces', and your quotation is very applicable to her. You may be there, I dare say, as often as you please, and I would advise you to sup there once a week.

You say, very justly, that as Mr. Harte is leaving you, you shall want advice more than ever; you shall never want mine; and as you have already had so much of it, I must rather repeat than add to what I have already given you; but that I will do, and add to it occasionally, as circumstances may require. At present I shall only remind you of your two great objects, which you should always attend to; they are parliament and foreign affairs. With regard to the former, you can do nothing while abroad but attend carefully to the purity, correctness, and elegance of your diction; the clearness and gracefulness of your utterance, in whatever language you speak. As for the parliamentary knowledge, I will take care of that when you come home. With regard to foreign affairs, everything you do abroad may and ought to tend that way. Your reading should be chiefly historical; I do not mean of remote, dark, and fabulous history, still less of jimcrack natural history of fossils, minerals, plants, etc., but I mean the useful, political, and constitutional history of Europe, for these last three centuries and a half. The other thing necessary for your foreign object, and not less necessary than either ancient or modern knowledge, is a great knowledge of the world, manners, politeness, address, and 'le ton de la bonne compagnie'. In that view, keeping a great deal of good company, is the principal point to which you are now to attend. It seems ridiculous to tell you, but it is most certainly true, that your dancing-master is at this time the man in all Europe of the greatest importance to you. You must dance well, in order to sit, stand, and walk well; and you must do all these well in order to please. What with your exercises, some reading, and a great deal of company, your day is, I confess, extremely taken up; but the day, if well employed, is long enough for everything; and I am sure you will not slattern away one moment of it in inaction. At your age, people have strong and active spirits, alacrity and vivacity in all they do; are 'impigri', indefatigable, and quick. The difference is, that a young fellow of parts exerts all those happy dispositions in the pursuit of proper objects; endeavors to excel in the solid, and in the showish parts of life; whereas a silly puppy, or a dull rogue, throws away all his youth and spirit upon trifles, where he is serious or upon disgraceful vices, while he aims at pleasures. This I am sure will not be your case; your good sense and your good conduct hitherto are your guarantees with me for the future. Continue only at Paris as you have begun, and your stay there will make you, what I have always wished you to be, as near perfection as our nature permits.

Adieu, my dear; remember to write to me once a-week, not as to a father, but, without reserve, as to a friend.

LETTER CXXVII

LONDON, January 14, O. S. 1751

MY DEAR FRIEND: Among the many good things Mr. Harte has told me of you, two in particular gave me great pleasure. The first, that you are exceedingly careful and jealous of the dignity of your character; that is the sure and solid foundation upon which you must both stand and rise. A man's moral character is a more delicate thing than a woman's reputation of chastity. A slip or two may possibly be forgiven her, and her character may be clarified by subsequent and continued good conduct: but a man's moral character once tainted is irreparably destroyed. The second was, that you had acquired a most correct and extensive knowledge of foreign affairs, such as the history, the treaties, and the forms of government of the several countries of Europe. This sort of knowledge, little attended to here, will make you not only useful, but necessary, in your future destination, and carry you very far. He added that you wanted from hence some books relative to our laws and constitution, our colonies, and our commerce; of which you know less than of those of any other part of Europe. I will send you what short books I can find of that sort, to give you a general notion of those things: but you cannot have time to go into their depths at present—you cannot now engage with new folios; you and I will refer the constitutional part of this country to our meeting here, when we will enter seriously into it, and read the necessary books together. In the meantime, go on in the course you are in, of foreign matters; converse with ministers and others of every country, watch the transactions of every court, and endeavor to trace them up to their source. This, with your physics, your geometry, and your exercises, will be all that you can possibly have time for at Paris; for you must allow a great deal for company and pleasures: it is they that must give you those manners, that address, that 'tournure' of the 'beau monde', which will qualify you for your future destination. You must first please, in order to get the confidence, and consequently the secrets, of the courts and ministers for whom and with whom you negotiate.

I will send you by the first opportunity a short book written by Lord Bolingbroke, under the name of Sir John Oldcastle, containing remarks upon the history of England; which will give you a clear general notion of our constitution, and which will serve you, at the same time, like all Lord Bolingbroke's works, for a model of eloquence and style. I will also send you Sir Josiah Childe's little book upon trade, which may properly be called the "Commercial Grammar." He lays down the true principles of commerce, and his conclusions from them are generally very just.

Since you turn your thoughts a little toward trade and commerce, which I am very glad you do, I will recommend a French book to you, which you will easily get at Paris, and which I take to be the best book in the world of that kind: I mean the 'Dictionnaire de Commerce de Savory', in three volumes in folio; where you will find every one thing that relates to trade, commerce, specie, exchange, etc., most clearly stated; and not only relative to France, but to the whole world. You will easily suppose, that I do not advise you to read such a book 'tout de suite'; but I only mean that you should have it at hand, to have recourse to occasionally.

With this great stock of both useful and ornamental knowledge, which you have already acquired, and which, by your application and industry, you are daily increasing, you will lay such a solid foundation of future figure and fortune, that if you complete it by all the accomplishments of manners, graces, etc., I know nothing which you may not aim at, and in time hope for. Your great point at present at Paris, to which all other considerations must give way, is to become entirely a man of fashion: to be well-bred without ceremony, easy without negligence, steady and intrepid with modesty, genteel without affectation, insinuating without meanness, cheerful without being noisy, frank without indiscretion, and secret without mysteriousness; to know the proper time and place for whatever you say or do, and to do it with an air of condition all this is not so soon nor so easily learned as people imagine, but requires observation and time. The world is an immense folio, which demands a great deal of time and attention to be read and understood as it ought to be; you have not yet read above four or five pages of it; and you will have but barely time to dip now and then in other less important books.

Lord Albemarle has, I know, wrote {It is a pleasure for an ordinary mortal to find Lord Chesterfield in gramatical error—and he did it again in the last sentence of this paragraph—but this was 1751? D.W.} to a friend of his here, that you do not frequent him so much as he expected and desired; that he fears somebody or other has given you wrong impressions of him; and that I may possibly think, from your being seldom at his house, that he has been wanting in his attentions to you. I told the person who told me this, that, on the contrary, you seemed, by your letters to me, to be extremely pleased with Lord Albemarle's behavior to you: but that you were obliged to give up dining abroad during your course of experimental philosophy. I guessed the true reason, which I believe was, that, as no French people frequent his house, you rather chose to dine at other places, where you were likely to meet with better company than your countrymen and you were in the right of it. However, I would have you show no shyness to Lord Albemarle, but go to him, and dine with him oftener than it may be you would wish, for the sake of having him speak well of you here when he returns. He is a good deal in fashion here, and his PUFFING you (to use an awkward expression) before you return here, will be of great use to you afterward. People in general take characters, as they do most things, upon trust, rather than be at the trouble of examining them themselves; and the decisions of four or five fashionable people, in every place, are final, more particularly with regard to characters, which all can hear, and but few judge of. Do not mention the least of this to any mortal; and take care that Lord Albemarle do not suspect that you know anything of the matter.

Lord Huntingdon and Lord Stormount are, I hear, arrived at Paris; you have, doubtless, seen them. Lord Stormount is well spoken of here; however, in your connections, if you form any with them, show rather a preference to Lord Huntingdon, for reasons which you will easily guess.

Mr. Harte goes this week to Cornwall, to take possession of his living; he has been installed at Windsor; he will return here in about a month, when your literary correspondence with him will be regularly carried on. Your mutual concern at parting was a good sign for both.

I have this moment received good accounts of you from Paris. Go on 'vous etes en bon train'. Adieu.

LETTER CXXVIII

LONDON, January 21, O. S.. 1751

MY DEAR FRIEND: In all my letters from Paris, I have the pleasure of finding, among many other good things, your docility mentioned with emphasis; this is the sure way of improving in those things, which you only want. It is true they are little, but it is as true too that they are necessary things. As they are mere matters of usage and mode, it is no disgrace for anybody of your age to be ignorant of them; and the most compendious way of learning them is, fairly to avow your ignorance, and to consult those who, from long usage and experience, know them best. Good sense and good-nature suggest civility in general; but, in good-breeding there are a thousand little delicacies, which are established only by custom; and it is these little elegances of manners which distinguish a courtier and a man of fashion from the vulgar. I am assured by different people, that your air is already much improved; and one of my correspondents makes you the true French compliment of saying, 'F'ose vous promettre qu'il sera bientot comme un de nos autres'. However unbecoming this speech may be in the mouth of a Frenchman, I am very glad that they think it applicable to you; for I would have you not only adopt, but rival, the best manners and usages of the place you are at, be they what they will; that is the versatility of manners which is so useful in the course of the world. Choose your models well at Paris, and then rival them in their own way. There are fashionable words, phrases, and even gestures, at Paris, which are called 'du bon ton'; not to mention 'certaines Petites politesses et attentions, qui ne sont rien en elle-memes', which fashion has rendered necessary. Make yourself master of all these things; and to such a degree, as to make the French say, 'qu'on diroit que c'est un Francois'; and when hereafter you shall be at other courts, do the same thing there; and conform to the fashionable manners and usage of the place; that is what the French themselves are not apt to do; wherever they go, they retain their own manners, as thinking them the best; but, granting them to be so, they are still in the wrong not to conform to those of the place. One would desire to please, wherever one is; and nothing is more innocently flattering than an approbation, and an imitation of the people one converses with.

I hope your colleges with Marcel go on prosperously. In these ridiculous, though, at the same time, really important lectures, pray attend, and desire your professor also to attend, more particularly to the chapter of the arms. It is they that decide of a man's being genteel or otherwise, more than any other part of the body. A twist or stiffness in the wrist, will make any man in Europe look awkward. The next thing to be attended to is, your coming into a room, and presenting yourself to a company. This gives the first impression; and the first impression is often a lasting one. Therefore, pray desire Professor Marcel to make you come in and go out of his room frequently, and in the supposition of different companies being there; such as ministers, women, mixed companies, etc. Those who present themselves well, have a certain dignity in their air, which, without the least seeming mixture of pride, at once engages, and is respected.

I should not so often repeat, nor so long dwell upon such trifles, with anybody that had less solid and valuable knowledge than you have. Frivolous people attend to those things, 'par preference'; they know nothing else; my fear with you is, that, from knowing better things, you should despise these too much, and think them of much less consequence than they really are; for they are of a great deal, and more especially to you.

Pleasing and governing women may, in time, be of great service to you. They often please and govern others. 'A propos', are you in love with Madame de Berkenrode still, or has some other taken her place in your affections? I take it for granted, that 'qua to cumque domat Venus, non erubescendis adurit ignibus. Un arrangement honnete sied bien a un galant homme'. In that case I recommend to you the utmost discretion, and the profoundest silence. Bragging of, hinting at, intimating, or even affectedly disclaiming and denying such an arrangement will equally discredit you among men and women. An unaffected silence upon that subject is the only true medium.

In your commerce with women, and indeed with men too, 'une certaine douceur' is particularly engaging; it is that which constitutes that character which the French talk of so much, and so justly value, I mean 'l'aimable'. This 'douceur' is not so easily described as felt. It is the compound result of different things; a complaisance, a flexibility, but not a servility of manners; an air of softness in the countenance, gesture, and expression, equally whether you concur or differ with the person you converse with. Observe those carefully who have that 'douceur' that charms you and others; and your own good sense will soon enable you to discover the different ingredients of which it is composed. You must be more particularly attentive to this 'douceur', whenever you are obliged to refuse what is asked of you, or to say what in itself cannot be very agreeable to those to whom you say it. It is then the necessary gilding of a disagreeable pill. 'L'aimable' consists in a thousand of these little things aggregately. It is the 'suaviter in modo', which I have so often recommended to you. The respectable, Mr. Harte assures me, you do not want, and I believe him. Study, then, carefully; and acquire perfectly, the 'Aimable', and you will have everything.

Abbe Guasco, who is another of your panegyrists, writes me word that he has taken you to dinner at Marquis de St. Germain's; where you will be welcome as often as you please, and the oftener the better. Profit of that, upon the principle of traveling in different countries, without changing places. He says, too, that he will take you to the parliament, when any remarkable cause is to be tried. That is very well; go through the several chambers of the parliament, and see and hear what they are doing; join practice and observation to your theoretical knowledge of their rights and privileges. No Englishman has the least notion of them.

I need not recommend you to go to the bottom of the constitutional and political knowledge of countries; for Mr. Harte tells me that you have a peculiar turn that way, and have informed yourself most correctly of them.

I must now put some queries to you, as to a 'juris publici peritus', which I am sure you can answer me, and which I own I cannot answer myself; they are upon a subject now much talked of.

1st. Are there any particular forms requisite for the election of a King of the Romans, different from those which are necessary for the election of an Emperor?

2d. Is not a King of the Romans as legally elected by the votes of a majority of the electors, as by two-thirds, or by the unanimity of the electors?

3d. Is there any particular law or constitution of the empire, that distinguishes, either in matter or in, form, the election of a King of the Romans from that of an Emperor? And is not the golden bull of Charles the Fourth equally the rule for both?

4th. Were there not, at a meeting of a certain number of the electors (I have forgotten when), some rules and limitations agreed upon concerning the election of a King of the Romans? And were those restrictions legal, and did they obtain the force of law?

How happy am I, my dear child, that I can apply to you for knowledge, and with a certainty of being rightly informed! It is knowledge, more than quick, flashy parts, that makes a man of business. A man who is master of his matter, twill, with inferior parts, be too hard in parliament, and indeed anywhere else, for a man of-better parts, who knows his subject but superficially: and if to his knowledge he joins eloquence and elocution, he must necessarily soon be at the head of that assembly; but without those two, no knowledge is sufficient.

Lord Huntingdon writes me word that he has seen you, and that you have renewed your old school-acquaintance.

Tell me fairly your opinion of him, and of his friend Lord Stormount: and also of the other English people of fashion you meet with. I promise you inviolable secrecy on my part. You and I must now write to each other—as friends, and without the least reserve; there will for the future be a thousand-things in my letters, which I would not have any mortal living but yourself see or know. Those you will easily distinguish, and neither show nor repeat; and I will do the same by you.

To come to another subject (for I have a pleasure in talking over every subject with you): How deep are you in Italian? Do you understand Ariosto, Tasso, Boccaccio and Machiavelli? If you do, you know enough of it and may know all the rest, by reading, when you have time. Little or no business is written in Italian, except in Italy; and if you know enough of it to understand the few Italian letters that may in time come in your way, and to speak Italian tolerably to those very few Italians who speak no French, give yourself no further trouble about that language till you happen to have full leisure to perfect yourself in it. It is not the same with regard to German; your speaking and writing it well, will particularly distinguish you from every other man in England; and is, moreover, of great use to anyone who is, as probably you will be, employed in the Empire. Therefore, pray cultivate them sedulously, by writing four or five lines of German every day, and by speaking it to every German you meet with.

You have now got a footing in a great many good houses at Paris, in which I advise you to make yourself domestic. This is to be done by a certain easiness of carriage, and a decent familiarity. Not by way of putting yourself upon the frivolous footing of being 'sans consequence', but by doing in some degree, the honors of the house and table, calling yourself 'en badinant le galopin d'ici', saying to the masters or mistress, 'ceci est de mon departement; je m'en charge; avouez, que je m'en acquitte a merveille.' This sort of 'badinage' has something engaging and 'liant' in it, and begets that decent familiarity, which it is both agreeable and useful to establish in good houses and with people of fashion. Mere formal visits, dinners, and suppers, upon formal invitations, are not the thing; they add to no connection nor information; but it is the easy, careless ingress and egress at all hours, that forms the pleasing and profitable commerce of life.

The post is so negligent, that I lose some letters from Paris entirely, and receive others much later than I should. To this I ascribe my having received no letter from you for above a fortnight, which to my impatience seems a long time. I expect to hear from you once a-week. Mr. Harte is gone to Cornwall, and will be back in about three weeks. I have a packet of books to send you by the first opportunity, which I believe will be Mr. Yorke's return to Paris. The Greek books come from Mr. Harte, and the English ones from your humble servant. Read Lord Bolingbroke's with great attention, as well to the style as to the matter. I wish you could form yourself such a style in every language. Style is the dress of thoughts; and a well-dressed thought, like a well-dressed man, appears to great advantage. Yours. Adieu.

LETTER CXXIX

LONDON, August 28, O. S. 1751

MY DEAR FRIEND: A bill for ninety pounds sterling was brought me the other day, said to be drawn upon me by you: I scrupled paying it at first, not upon account of the sum, but because you had sent me no letter of advice, which is always done in those transactions; and still more, because I did not perceive that you had signed it. The person who presented it, desired me to look again, and that I should discover your name at the bottom: accordingly I looked again, and, with the help of my magnifying glass, did perceive that what I had first taken only for somebody's mark, was, in truth, your name, written in the worst and smallest hand I ever saw in my life.

However, I paid it at a venture; though I would almost rather lose the money, than that such a signature should be yours. All gentlemen, and all men of business, write their names always in the same way, that their signature may be so well known as not to be easily counterfeited; and they generally sign in rather larger character than their common hand; whereas your name was in a less, and a worse, than your common writing. This suggested to me the various accidents which may very probably happen to you, while you write so ill. For instance, if you were to write in such a character to the Secretary's office, your letter would immediately be sent to the decipherer, as containing matters of the utmost secrecy, not fit to be trusted to the common character. If you were to write so to an antiquarian, he (knowing you to be a man of learning) would certainly try it by the Runic, Celtic, or Sclavonian alphabet, never suspecting it to be a modern character. And, if you were to send a 'poulet' to a fine woman, in such a hand, she would think that it really came from the 'poulailler'; which, by the bye, is the etymology of the word 'poulet'; for Henry the Fourth of France used to send billets-doux to his mistresses by his 'poulailler', under pretense of sending them chickens; which gave the name of poulets to those short, but expressive manuscripts. I have often told you that every man who has the use of his eyes and of his hand, can write whatever hand he pleases; and it is plain that you can, since you write both the Greek and German characters, which you never learned of a writing-master, extremely well, though your common hand, which you learned of a master, is an exceedingly bad and illiberal one; equally unfit for business or common use. I do not desire that you should write the labored, stiff character of a writing-master: a man of business must write quick and well, and that depends simply upon use. I would therefore advise you to get some very good writing-master at Paris, and apply to it for a month only, which will be sufficient; for, upon my word, the writing of a genteel plain hand of business is of much more importance than you think. You will say, it may be, that when you write so very ill, it is because you are in a hurry, to which I answer, Why are you ever in a hurry? A man of sense may be in haste, but can never be in a hurry, because he knows that whatever he does in a hurry, he must necessarily do very ill. He may be in haste to dispatch an affair, but he will care not to let that haste hinder his doing it well. Little minds are in a hurry, when the object proves (as it commonly does) too big for them; they run, they hare, they puzzle, confound, and perplex themselves: they want to do everything at once, and never do it at all. But a man of sense takes the time necessary for doing the thing he is about, well; and his haste to dispatch a business only appears by the continuity of his application to it: he pursues it with a cool steadiness, and finishes it before he begins any other. I own your time is much taken up, and you have a great many different things to do; but remember that you had much better do half of them well and leave the other half undone, than do them all indifferently.

Moreover, the few seconds that are saved in the course of the day, by writing ill instead of well, do not amount to an object of time by any means equivalent to the disgrace or ridicule of writing the scrawl of a common whore. Consider, that if your very bad writing could furnish me with matter of ridicule, what will it not do to others who do not view you in that partial light that I do? There was a pope, I think it was Cardinal Chigi, who was justly ridiculed for his attention to little things, and his inability in great ones: and therefore called maximus in minimis, and minimus in maximis. Why? Because he attended to little things when he had great ones to do. At this particular period of your life, and at the place you are now in, you have only little things to do; and you should make it habitual to you to do them well, that they may require no attention from you when you have, as I hope you will have, greater things to mind. Make a good handwriting familiar to you now, that you may hereafter have nothing but your matter to think of, when you have occasion to write to kings and ministers. Dance, dress, present yourself, habitually well now, that you may have none of those little things to think of hereafter, and which will be all necessary to be done well occasionally, when you will have greater things to do.

As I am eternally thinking of everything that can be relative to you, one thing has occurred to me, which I think necessary to mention to you, in order to prevent the difficulties which it might otherwise lay you under; it is this as you get more acquaintances at Paris, it will be impossible for you to frequent your first acquaintances so much as you did, while you had no others. As, for example, at your first 'debut', I suppose you were chiefly at Madame Monconseil's, Lady Hervey's, and Madame du Boccage's. Now, that you have got so many other houses, you cannot be at theirs so often as you used; but pray take care not to give them the least reason to think that you neglect, or despise them, for the sake of new and more dignified and shining acquaintances; which would be ungrateful and imprudent on your part, and never forgiven on theirs. Call upon them often, though you do not stay with them so long as formerly; tell them that you are sorry you are obliged to go away, but that you have such and such engagements, with which good-breeding obliges you to comply; and insinuate that you would rather stay with them. In short, take care to make as many personal friends, and as few personal enemies, as possible. I do not mean, by personal friends, intimate and confidential friends, of which no man can hope to have half a dozen in the whole course of his life; but I mean friends, in the common acceptation of the word; that is, people who speak well of you, and who would rather do you good than harm, consistently with their own interest, and no further. Upon the whole, I recommend to you, again and again, 'les Graces'. Adorned by them, you may, in a manner, do what you please; it will be approved of; without them, your best qualities will lose half their efficacy. Endeavor to be fashionable among the French, which will soon make you fashionable here. Monsieur de Matignon already calls you 'le petit Francois'. If you can get that name generally at Paris, it will put you 'a la mode'. Adieu, my dear child.

LETTER CXXX

LONDON, February 4, O. S. 1751

MY DEAR FRIEND: The accounts which I receive of you from Paris grow every day more and more satisfactory. Lord Albemarle has wrote a sort of panegyric of you, which has been seen by many people here, and which will be a very useful forerunner for you. Being in fashion is an important point for anybody anywhere; but it would be a very great one for you to be established in the fashion here before you return. Your business will be half done by it, as I am sure you would not give people reason to change their favorable presentiments of you. The good that is said of you will not, I am convinced, make you a coxcomb; and, on the other hand, the being thought still to want some little accomplishments, will, I am persuaded, not mortify you, but only animate you to acquire them: I will, therefore, give you both fairly, in the following extract of a letter which I lately received from an impartial and discerning friend:—

"Permit me to assure you, Sir, that Mr. Stanhope will succeed. He has a great fund of knowledge, and an uncommonly good memory, although he does not make any parade of either the one or the other. He is desirous of pleasing, and he will please. He has an expressive countenance; his figure is elegant, although little. He has not the least awkwardness, though he has not as yet acquired all-the graces requisite; which Marcel and the ladies will soon give him. In short, he wants nothing but those things, which, at his age, must unavoidably be wanting; I mean, a certain turn and delicacy of manners, which are to be acquired only by time, and in good company. Ready as he is, he will soon learn them; particularly as he frequents such companies as are the most proper to give them."

By this extract, which I can assure you is a faithful one, you and I have both of us the satisfaction of knowing how much you have, and how little you want. Let what you have give you (if possible) rather more SEEMING modesty, but at the same time more interior firmness and assurance; and let what you want, which you see is very attainable, redouble your attention and endeavors to acquire it. You have, in truth, but that one thing to apply to and a very pleasing application it is, since it is through pleasures you must arrive at it. Company, suppers, balls, spectacles, which show you the models upon which you should form yourself, and all the little usages, customs, and delicacies, which you must adopt and make habitual to you, are now your only schools and universities; in which young fellows and fine women will give you the best lectures.

Monsieur du Boccage is another of your panegyrists; and he tells me that Madame Boccage 'a pris avec vous le ton de mie et de bonne'; and that you like it very well. You are in the right of it; it is the way of improving;

endeavor to be upon that footing with every woman you converse with; excepting where there may be a tender point of connection; a point which I have nothing to do with; but if such a one there is, I hope she has not 'de mauvais ni de vilains bras', which I agree with you in thinking a very disagreeable thing.

I have sent you, by the opportunity of Pollok the courier, who was once my servant, two little parcels of Greek and English books; and shall send you two more by Mr. Yorke: but I accompany them with this caution, that as you have not much time to read, you should employ it in reading what is the most necessary, and that is, indisputably modern historical, geographical, chronological, and political knowledge; the present constitution, maxims, force, riches, trade, commerce, characters, parties, and cabals of the several courts of Europe. Many who are reckoned good scholars, though they know pretty accurately the governments of Athens and Rome, are totally ignorant of the constitution of any one country now in Europe, even of their own. Read just Latin and Greek enough to keep up your classical learning, which will be an ornament to you while young, and a comfort to you when old. But the true useful knowledge, and especially for you, is the modern knowledge above mentioned. It is that must qualify you both for domestic and foreign business, and it is to that, therefore, that you should principally direct your attention; and I know, with great pleasure, that you do so. I would not thus commend you to yourself, if I thought commendations would have upon you those ill effects, which they frequently have upon weak minds. I think you are much above being a vain coxcomb, overrating your own merit, and insulting others with the superabundance of it. On the contrary, I am convinced that the consciousness of merit makes a man of sense more modest, though more firm. A man who displays his own merit is a coxcomb, and a man who does not know it is a fool. A man of sense knows it, exerts it, avails himself of it, but never boasts of it; and always SEEMS rather to under than over value it, though in truth, he sets the right value upon it. It is a very true maxim of La Bruyere's (an author well worth your studying), 'qu'on ne vaut dans ce monde, que ce que l'on veut valoir'. A man who is really diffident, timid, and bashful, be his merit what it will, never can push himself in the world; his despondency throws him into inaction; and the forward, the bustling, and the petulant, will always get the better of him. The manner makes the whole difference. What would be impudence in one manner, is only a proper and decent assurance in another. A man of sense, and of knowledge in the world, will assert his own rights, and pursue his own objects, as steadily and intrepidly as the most impudent man living, and commonly more so; but then he has art enough to give an outward air of modesty to all he does. This engages and prevails, while the very same things shock and fail, from the overbearing or impudent manner only of doing them. I repeat my maxim, 'Suaviter in modo, sed fortiter in re'. Would you know the characters, modes and manners of the latter end of the last age, which are very like those of the present, read La Bruyere. But would you know man, independently of modes, read La Rochefoucault, who, I am afraid, paints him very exactly.

Give the inclosed to Abbe Guasco, of whom you make good use, to go about with you, and see things. Between you and me, he has more knowledge than parts. 'Mais un habile homme sait tirer parti de tout', and everybody is good for something. President Montesquieu is, in every sense, a most useful acquaintance. He has parts, joined to great reading and knowledge of the world. 'Puisez dans cette source tant que vous pourrez'.

Adieu. May the Graces attend you! for without them 'ogni fatica e vana'. If they do not come to you willingly, ravish them, and force them to accompany you in all you think, all you say, and all you do.

EARL OF PHILIP DORMER STANHOPE CHESTERFIELD

LETTER CXXXI

LONDON, February 11, O. S. 1751

MY DEAR FRIEND: When you go to the play, which I hope you do often, for it is a very instructive amusement, you must certainly have observed the very different effects which the several parts have upon you, according as they are well or ill acted. The very best tragedy of, Corneille's, if well spoken and acted, interests, engages, agitates, and affects your passions. Love, terror, and pity alternately possess you. But, if ill spoken and acted, it would only excite your indignation or your laughter. Why? It is still Corneille's; it is the same sense, the same matter, whether well or ill acted. It is, then, merely the manner of speaking and acting that makes this great difference in the effects. Apply this to yourself, and conclude from it, that if you would either please in a private company, or persuade in a public assembly, air, looks, gestures, graces, enunciation, proper accents, just emphasis, and tuneful cadences, are full as necessary as the matter itself. Let awkward, ungraceful, inelegant, and dull fellows say what they will in behalf of their solid matter and strong reasonings; and let them despise all those graces and ornaments which engage the senses and captivate the heart; they will find (though they will possibly wonder why) that their rough, unpolished matter, and their unadorned, coarse, but strong arguments, will neither please nor persuade; but, on the contrary, will tire out attention, and excite disgust. We are so made, we love to be pleased better than to be informed; information is, in a certain degree, mortifying, as it implies our previous ignorance; it must be sweetened to be palatable.

To bring this directly to you: know that no man can make a figure in this country, but by parliament. Your fate depends upon your success there as a speaker; and, take my word for it, that success turns much more upon manner than matter. Mr. Pitt and Mr. Murray the solicitor-general, uncle to Lord Stormount, are, beyond comparison, the best speakers; why? only because they are the best orators. They alone can inflame or quiet the House; they alone are so attended to, in that numerous and noisy assembly, that you might hear a pin fall while either of them is speaking. Is it that their matter is better, or their arguments stronger, than other people's? Does the House expect extraordinary informations from them? Not, in the least: but the House expects pleasure from them, and therefore attends; finds it, and therefore approves. Mr. Pitt, particularly, has very little parliamentary knowledge; his matter is generally flimsy, and his arguments often weak; but his eloquence is superior, his action graceful, his enunciation just and harmonious; his periods are well turned, and every word he makes use of is the very best, and the most expressive, that can be used in that place. This, and not his matter, made him Paymaster, in spite of both king and ministers. From this draw the obvious conclusion. The same thing holds full as true in conversation; where even trifles, elegantly expressed, well looked, and accompanied with graceful action, will ever please, beyond all the homespun, unadorned sense in the world. Reflect, on one side, how you feel within yourself, while you are forced to suffer the tedious, muddy, and ill-turned narration of some awkward fellow, even though the fact may be interesting; and, on the other hand, with what pleasure you attend to the relation of a much less interesting matter, when elegantly expressed, genteelly turned, and gracefully delivered. By attending carefully to all these agremens in your daily conversation, they will become habitual to you, before you come into parliament; and you will have nothing then, to do, but to raise them a little when you come there. I would wish you to be so attentive to this object, that I, would not have you speak to your footman, but in the very best words that the subject admits of, be the language what it will. Think of your words, and of their arrangement, before you speak; choose the most elegant, and place them in the best order. Consult your own ear, to avoid cacophony, and, what is very near as bad, monotony. Think also of your gesture and looks, when you are speaking even upon the most trifling subjects. The same things, differently expressed, looked, and delivered, cease to be the same things.

The most passionate lover in the world cannot make a stronger declaration of love than the 'Bourgeois gentilhomme' does in this happy form of words, 'Mourir d'amour me font belle Marquise vos beaux yeux'. I defy anybody to say more; and yet I would advise nobody to say that, and I would recommend to you rather to smother and conceal your passion entirely than to reveal it in these words. Seriously, this holds in everything, as well as in that ludicrous instance. The French, to do them justice, attend very minutely to the purity, the correctness, and the elegance of their style in conversation and in their letters. 'Bien narrer' is an object of their study; and though they sometimes carry it to affectation, they never sink into inelegance, which is much the worst extreme of the two. Observe them, and form your French style upon theirs: for elegance in one language will reproduce itself in all. I knew a young man, who, being just elected a member of parliament, was laughed at for being discovered, through the keyhole of his chamber-door, speaking to himself in the glass, and forming his looks and gestures. I could not join in that laugh; but, on the contrary, thought him much wiser than those who laughed at him; for he knew the importance of those little graces in a public assembly, and they did not. Your little person (which I am told, by the way, is not ill turned), whether in a laced coat or a blanket, is specifically the same; but yet, I believe, you choose to wear the former, and you are in the right, for the sake of pleasing more. The worst-bred man in Europe, if a lady let fall her fan, would certainly take it up and give it her; the best-bred man in Europe could do no more. The difference, however, would be considerable; the latter would please by doing it gracefully; the former would be laughed at for doing it awkwardly. I repeat it, and repeat it again, and shall never cease repeating it to you: air, manners, graces, style, elegance, and all those ornaments, must now be the only objects of your attention; it is now, or never, that you must acquire them. Postpone, therefore, all other considerations; make them now your serious study; you have not one moment to lose. The solid and the ornamental united, are undoubtedly best; but were I reduced to make an option, I should without hesitation choose the latter.

I hope you assiduously frequent Marcell—[At that time the most celebrated dancing-master at Paris.]—and carry graces from him; nobody had more to spare than he had formerly. Have you learned to carve? for it is ridiculous not to carve well. A man who tells you gravely that he cannot carve, may as well tell you that he cannot blow his nose: it is both as necessary, and as easy.

Make my compliments to Lord Huntingdon, whom I love and honor extremely, as I dare say you do; I will write to him soon, though I believe he has hardly time to read a letter; and my letters to those I love are, as you know by experience, not very short ones: this is one proof of it, and this would have been longer, if the paper had been so. Good night then, my dear child.

LETTER CXXXII

LONDON, February 28, O. S. 1751.

MY DEAR FRIEND: This epigram in Martial—

"Non amo te, Sabidi, nec possum dicere quare;

Hoc tantum possum dicere, non amo te"—

[OR: "I do not love thee Dr. Fell

The reason why I cannot tell.

But this I know and know full well:

EARL OF PHILIP DORMER STANHOPE CHESTERFIELD

I do not love thee Dr. Fell." D.W.]

has puzzled a great many people, who cannot conceive how it is possible not to love anybody, and yet not to know the reason why. I think I conceive Martial's meaning very clearly, though the nature of epigram, which is to be short, would not allow him to explain it more fully; and I take it to be this: O Sabidis, you are a very worthy deserving man; you have a thousand good qualities, you have a great deal of learning; I esteem, I respect, but for the soul of me I cannot love you, though I cannot particularly say why. You are not aimable: you have not those engaging manners, those pleasing attentions, those graces, and that address, which are absolutely necessary to please, though impossible to define. I cannot say it is this or that particular thing that hinders me from loving you; it is the whole together; and upon the whole you are not agreeable.

How often have I, in the course of my life, found myself in this situation, with regard to many of my acquaintance, whom I have honored and respected, without being able to love. I did not know why, because, when one is young, one does not take the trouble, nor allow one's self the time, to analyze one's sentiments and to trace them up to their source. But subsequent observation and reflection have taught me why. There is a man, whose moral character, deep learning, and superior parts, I acknowledge, admire, and respect; but whom it is so impossible for me to love, that I am almost in a fever whenever I am in his company. His figure (without being deformed) seems made to disgrace or ridicule the common structure of the human body. His legs and arms are never in the position which, according to the situation of his body, they ought to be in, but constantly employed in committing acts of hostility upon the Graces. He throws anywhere, but down his throat, whatever he means to drink, and only mangles what he means to carve. Inattentive to all the regards of social life, he mistimes or misplaces everything. He disputes with heat, and indiscriminately, mindless of the rank, character, and situation of those with whom he disputes; absolutely ignorant of the several gradations of familiarity or respect, he is exactly the same to his superiors, his equals, and his inferiors; and therefore, by a necessary consequence, absurd to two of the three. Is it possible to love such a man? No. The utmost I can do for him, is to consider him as a respectable Hottentot.—[This 'mot' was aimed at Dr. Johnson in retaliation for his famous letter.]

I remember, that when I came from Cambridge, I had acquired, among the pedants of that illiberal seminary, a sauciness of literature, a turn to satire and contempt, and a strong tendency to argumentation and contradiction. But I had been but a very little while in the world, before I found that this would by no means do; and I immediately adopted the opposite character; I concealed what learning I had; I applauded often, without approving; and I yielded commonly without conviction. 'Suaviter in modo' was my law and my prophets; and if I pleased (between you and me) it was much more owing to that, than to any superior knowledge or merit of my own. Apropos, the word PLEASING puts one always in mind of Lady Hervey; pray tell her, that I declare her responsible to me for your pleasing; that I consider her as a pleasing Falstaff, who not only pleases, herself, but is the cause of pleasing in others; that I know she can make anything of anybody; and that, as your governess, if she does not make you please, it must be only because she will not, and not because she cannot. I hope you are 'dubois don't on en fait'; and if so, she is so good a sculptor, that I am sure she can give you whatever form she pleases. A versatility of manners is as necessary in social, as a versatility of parts is in political life. One must often yield, in order to prevail; one must humble one's self, to be exalted; one must, like St. Paul, become all things to all men, to gain some; and, by the way, men are taken by the same means, 'mutatis mutandis', that women are gained—by gentleness, insinuation, and submission: and these lines of Mr. Dryden will hold to a minister as well as to a mistress:

"The prostrate lover, when he lowest lies,

But stoops to conquer, and but kneels to rise."

In the course of the world, the qualifications of the chameleon are often necessary; nay, they must be carried a little further, and exerted a little sooner; for you should, to a certain degree, take the hue of either the man or the woman that you want, and wish to be upon terms with. 'A propos', have you yet found out at Paris, any friendly and hospitable Madame de Lursay, 'qui veut bien se charger du soin de vous eduquer'? And have you had any occasion of representing to her, 'qu'elle faisoit donc des noeuds'? But I ask your pardon, Sir, for the abruptness of the question, and acknowledge that I am meddling with matters that are out of my department. However, in matters of less importance, I desire to be 'de vos secrets le fidele depositaire'. Trust me with the general turn and color of your amusements at Paris. Is it 'le fracas du grand monde, comedies, bals, operas, cour,' etc.? Or is it 'des petites societes, moins bruyantes, mais pas pour cela moins agreables'? Where are you the most 'etabli'? Where are you 'le petit Stanhope'? Voyez vous encore jour, a quelque arrangement honnete? Have you made many acquaintances among the young Frenchmen who ride at your Academy; and who are they? Send to me this sort of chit-chat in your letters, which, by the bye, I wish you would honor me with somewhat oftener. If you frequent any of the myriads of polite Englishmen who infest Paris, who are they? Have you finished with Abbe Nolet, and are you 'au fait' of all the properties and effects of air? Were I inclined to quibble, I would say, that the effects of air, at least, are best to be learned of Marcel. If you have quite done with l'Abbes Nolet, ask my friend l'Abbe Sallier to recommend to you some meagre philomath, to teach you a little geometry and astronomy; not enough to absorb your attention and puzzle your intellects, but only enough not to be grossly ignorant of either. I have of late been a sort of 'astronome malgre moi', by bringing in last Monday into the House of Lords a bill for reforming our present Calendar and taking the New Style. Upon which occasion I was obliged to talk some astronomical jargon, of which I did not understand one word, but got it by heart, and spoke it by rote from a master. I wished that I had known a little more of it myself; and so much I would have you know. But the great and necessary knowledge of all is, to know, yourself and others: this knowledge requires great attention and long experience; exert the former, and may you have the latter! Adieu!

P. S. I have this moment received your letters of the 27th February, and the 2d March, N. S. The seal shall be done as soon as possible. I am, glad that you are employed in Lord Albemarle's bureau; it will teach you, at least, the mechanical part of that business, such as folding, entering, and docketing letters; for you must not imagine that you are let into the 'fin fin' of the correspondence, nor indeed is it fit that you should, at, your age. However, use yourself to secrecy as to the letters you either read or write, that in time you may be trusted with SECRET, VERY SECRET, SEPARATE, APART, etc. I am sorry that this business interferes with your riding; I hope it is seldom; but I insist upon its not interfering with your dancing-master, who is at this time the most useful and necessary of all the masters you have or can have.

LETTER CXXXIII

MY DEAR FRIEND: I mentioned to you, some time ago a sentence which I would most earnestly wish you always to retain in your thoughts, and observe in your conduct. It is 'suaviter in modo, fortiter in re' [gentleness of manners, with firmness of mind D.W.]. I do not know any one rule so unexceptionably useful and necessary in every part of life. I shall therefore take it for my text to-day, and as old men love preaching, and I have some right to preach to you, I here present you with my sermon upon these words. To proceed, then, regularly and PULPITICALLY, I will first show you, my beloved, the necessary connection of the two members of my text 'suaviter in modo: fortiter in re'. In the next place, I shall set forth the advantages and utility resulting from a strict observance of the precept contained in my text; and conclude with an application of the whole. The 'suaviter in modo' alone would degenerate and sink into a mean, timid complaisance and passiveness, if not supported and dignified by the 'fortiter in re', which would also run into impetuosity and brutality, if not tempered and softened by the 'suaviter in modo': however, they are seldom united.

The warm, choleric man, with strong animal spirits, despises the 'suaviter in modo', and thinks to, carry all before him by the 'fortiter in re'. He may, possibly, by great accident, now and then succeed, when he has only weak and timid people to deal with; but his general fate will be, to shock offend, be hated, and fail. On the other hand, the cunning, crafty man thinks to gain all his ends by the 'suaviter in modo' only; HE BECOMES ALL THINGS TO ALL MEN; he seems to have no opinion of his own, and servilely adopts the present opinion of the present person; he insinuates himself only into the esteem of fools, but is soon detected, and surely despised by everybody else. The wise man (who differs as much from the cunning, as from the choleric man) alone joins the 'suaviter in modo' with the 'fortiter in re'. Now to the advantages arising from the strict observance of this precept:

If you are in authority, and have a right to command, your commands delivered 'suaviter in modo' will be willingly, cheerfully, and consequently well obeyed; whereas, if given only 'fortiter', that is brutally, they will rather, as Tacitus says, be interrupted than executed. For my own part, if I bid my footman bring me a glass of wine, in a rough insulting manner, I should expect that, in obeying me, he would contrive to spill some of it upon me: and I am sure I should deserve it. A cool, steady resolution should show that where you have a right to command you will be obeyed; but at the same time, a gentleness in the manner of enforcing that obedience should make it a cheerful one, and soften as much as possible the mortifying consciousness of inferiority. If you are to ask a favor, or even to solicit your due, you must do it 'suaviter in modo', or you will give those who have a mind to refuse you, either a pretense to do it, by resenting the manner; but, on the other hand, you must, by a steady perseverance and decent tenaciousness, show the 'fortiter in re'. The right motives are seldom the true ones of men's actions, especially of kings, ministers, and people in high stations; who often give to importunity and fear, what they would refuse to justice or to merit. By the 'suaviter in modo' engage their hearts, if you can; at least prevent the pretense of offense but take care to show enough of the 'fortiter in re' to extort from their love of ease, or their fear, what you might in vain hope for from their justice or good-nature. People in high life are hardened to the wants and distresses of mankind, as surgeons are to their bodily pains; they see and hear of them all day long, and even of so many simulated ones, that they do not know which are real, and which not. Other sentiments are therefore to be applied to, than those of mere justice and humanity; their favor must be captivated by the 'suaviter in modo'; their love of ease disturbed by unwearied importunity, or their fears wrought upon by a decent intimation of implacable, cool resentment; this is the true 'fortiter in re'. This precept is the only way I know in the world of being loved without being despised, and feared without being hated. It constitutes the dignity of character which every wise man must endeavor to establish.

Now to apply what has been said, and so conclude.

If you find that you have a hastiness in your temper, which unguardedly breaks out into indiscreet sallies, or rough expressions, to either your superiors, your equals, or your inferiors, watch it narrowly, check it carefully, and call the 'suaviter in modo' to your assistance: at the first impulse of passion, be silent till you can be soft. Labor even to get the command of your countenance so well, that those emotions may not be read in it; a most unspeakable advantage in business! On the other hand, let no complaisance, no gentleness of temper, no weak desire of pleasing on your part,—no wheedling, coaxing, nor flattery, on other people's,— make you recede one jot from any point that reason and prudence have bid you pursue; but return to the charge, persist, persevere, and you will find most things attainable that are possible. A yielding, timid meekness is always abused and insulted by the unjust and the unfeeling; but when sustained by the 'fortiter in re', is always respected, commonly successful. In your friendships and connections, as well as in your enemies, this rule is particularly useful; let your firmness and vigor preserve and invite attachments to you; but, at the same time, let your manner hinder the enemies of your friends and dependents from becoming yours; let your enemies be disarmed by the gentleness of your manner, but let them feel, at the same time, the steadiness of your just resentment; for there is a great difference between bearing malice, which is always ungenerous, and a resolute self-defense, which is always prudent and justifiable. In negotiations with foreign ministers, remember the 'fortiter in re'; give up no point, accept of no expedient, till the utmost necessity reduces you to it, and even then, dispute the ground inch by inch; but then, while you are contending with the minister 'fortiter in re', remember to gain the man by the 'suaviter in modo'. If you engage his heart, you have a fair chance for imposing upon his understanding, and determining his will. Tell him, in a frank, gallant manner, that your ministerial wrangles do not lessen your personal regard for his merit; but that, on the contrary, his zeal and ability in the service of his master, increase it; and that, of all things, you desire to make a good friend of so good a servant. By these means you may, and will very often be a gainer: you never can be a loser. Some people cannot gain upon themselves to be easy and civil to those who are either their rivals, competitors, or opposers, though, independently of those accidental circumstances, they would like and esteem them. They betray a shyness and an awkwardness in company with them, and catch at any little thing to expose them; and so, from temporary and only occasional opponents, make them their personal enemies. This is exceedingly weak and detrimental, as indeed is all humor in business; which can only be carried on successfully by, unadulterated good policy and right reasoning. In such situations I would be more particularly and 'noblement', civil, easy, and frank with the man whose designs I traversed: this is commonly called generosity and magnanimity, but is, in truth, good sense and policy. The manner is often as important as the matter, sometimes more so; a favor may make an enemy, and an injury may make a friend, according to the different manner in which they are severally done. The countenance, the address, the words, the enunciation, the Graces, add great efficacy to the 'suaviter in modo', and great dignity to the 'fortiter in re', and consequently they deserve the utmost attention.

From what has been said, I conclude with this observation, that gentleness of manners, with firmness of mind, is a short, but full description of human perfection on this side of religious and moral duties. That you may be seriously convinced of this truth, and show it in your life and conversation, is the most sincere and ardent wish of, Yours.

LETTER CXXXIV

LONDON, March 11, O. S. 1751.

MY DEAR FRIEND: I received by the last post a letter from Abbe Guasco, in which he joins his representations to those of Lord Albemarle, against your remaining any longer in your very bad lodgings at the Academy; and, as I do not find that any advantage can arise to you from being 'interne' in an academy which is full as far from the riding-house and from all your other masters, as your lodgings will probably be, I agree to your removing to an 'hotel garni'; the Abbe will help you to find one, as I desire him by the inclosed, which you will give him. I must, however, annex one condition to your going into private lodgings, which is an absolute exclusion of English breakfasts and suppers at them; the former consume the whole morning, and the latter employ the evenings very ill, in senseless toasting a l'Angloise in their infernal claret. You will be sure to go to the riding-house as often as possible, that is, whenever your new business at Lord Albemarle's does not hinder you. But, at all events, I insist upon your never missing Marcel, who is at present of more consequence to you than all the bureaux in Europe; for this is the time for you to acquire 'tous ces petits riens', which, though in an arithmetical account, added to one another 'ad infinitum', they would amount to nothing, in the account of the world amount to a great and important sum. 'Les agremens et les graces', without which you will never be anything, are absolutely made up of all those 'riens', which are more easily felt than described. By the way, you may take your lodgings for one whole year certain, by which means you may get them much cheaper; for though I intend to see you here in less than a year, it will be but for a little time, and you will return to Paris again, where I intend you shall stay till the end of April twelvemonth, 1752, at which time, provided you have got all 'la politesse, les manieres, les attentions, et les graces du beau monde', I shall place you in some business suitable to your destination.

I have received, at last, your present of the cartoon, from Dominichino, by Planchet. It is very finely done, it is pity that he did not take in all the figures of the original. I will hang it up, where it shall be your own again some time or other.

Mr. Harte is returned in perfect health from Cornwall, and has taken possession of his prebendal house at Windsor, which is a very pretty one. As I dare say you will always feel, I hope you will always express, the strongest sentiments of gratitude and friendship for him. Write to him frequently, and attend to the letters you receive from him. He shall be with us at Blackheath, alias BABIOLE, all the time that I propose you shall be there, which I believe will be the month of August next.

Having thus mentioned to you the probable time of our meeting, I will prepare you a little for it. Hatred; jealousy, or envy, make, most people attentive to discover the least defects of those they do not love; they rejoice at every new discovery they make of that kind, and take care to publish it. I thank God, I do not know what those three ungenerous passions are, having never felt them in my own breast; but love has just the same effect upon me, except that I conceal, instead of publishing, the defeats which my attention makes me discover in those I love. I curiously pry into them; I analyze them; and, wishing either to find them perfect, or to make them so, nothing escapes me, and I soon discover every the least gradation toward or from that perfection. You must therefore expect the most critical 'examen' that ever anybody underwent. I shall discover your least, as well as your greatest defects, and I shall very freely tell you of them, 'Non quod odio habeam sed quod amem'. But I shall tell them you 'tete-a-tete', and as MICIO not as DEMEA; and I will tell them to nobody else. I think it but fair to inform you beforehand, where I suspect that my criticisms are likely to fall; and that is more upon the outward, than upon the inward man; I neither suspect your heart nor your head; but to be plain with you, I have a strange distrust of your air, your address, your manners, your 'tournure', and particularly of your ENUNCIATION and elegance of style. These will be all put to the trial; for while you are with me, you must do the honors of my house and table; the least inaccuracy or inelegance will not escape me; as you will find by a LOOK at the time, and by a remonstrance afterward when we are alone. You will see a great deal of company of all sorts at BABIOLE, and particularly foreigners. Make, therefore, in the meantime, all these exterior and ornamental qualifications your peculiar care, and disappoint all my imaginary schemes of criticism. Some authors have criticised their own works first, in hopes of hindering others from doing it afterward: but then they do it themselves with so much tenderness and partiality for their own production, that not only the production itself, but the preventive criticism is criticised. I am not one of those authors; but, on the contrary, my severity increases with my fondness for my work; and if you will but effectually correct all the faults I shall find, I will insure you from all subsequent criticisms from other quarters.

Are you got a little into the interior, into the constitution of things at Paris? Have you seen what you have seen thoroughly? For, by the way, few people see what they see, or hear what they hear. For example, if you go to les Invalides, do you content yourself with seeing the building, the hall where three or four hundred cripples dine, and the galleries where they lie? or do you inform yourself of the numbers, the conditions of their admission, their allowance, the value and nature of the fund by which the whole is supported? This latter I call seeing, the former is only starting. Many people take the opportunity of 'les vacances', to go and see the empty rooms where the several chambers of the parliament did sit; which rooms are exceedingly like all other large rooms; when you go there, let it be when they are full; see and hear what is doing in them; learn their respective constitutions, jurisdictions, objects, and methods of proceeding; hear some causes tried in every one of the different chambers; 'Approfondissez les choses'.

I am glad to hear that you are so well at Marquis de St. Germain's, —[At that time Ambassador from the King of Sardinia at the Court of France.]—of whom I hear a very good character. How are you with the other foreign ministers at Paris? Do you frequent the Dutch Ambassador or Ambassadress? Have you any footing at the Nuncio's, or at the Imperial and Spanish ambassadors? It is useful. Be more particular in your letters to me, as to your manner of passing your time, and the company you keep. Where do you dine and sup oftenest? whose house is most your home? Adieu. 'Les Graces, les Graces'.

LETTER CXXXV

LONDON, March 18, O. S. 1751.

MY DEAR FRIEND: I acquainted you in a former letter, that I had brought a bill into the House of Lords for correcting and reforming our present calendar, which is the Julian, and for adopting the Gregorian. I will now give you a more particular account of that affair; from which reflections will naturally occur to you that I hope may be useful, and which I fear you have not made. It was notorious, that the Julian calendar was erroneous, and had overcharged the solar year with eleven days. Pope Gregory the Thirteenth corrected this error; his reformed calendar was immediately received by all the Catholic powers of Europe, and afterward adopted by all the Protestant ones, except Russia, Sweden, and England. It was not, in my opinion, very honorable for England to remain, in a gross and avowed error, especially in such company; the inconveniency of it was likewise felt by all those who had foreign correspondences, whether political or mercantile. I determined, therefore, to attempt the reformation; I consulted the best lawyers and the most skillful astronomers, and we cooked up a bill for that purpose. But then my difficulty began: I was to bring in this bill, which was necessarily composed of law jargon and astronomical calculations, to both which I am an utter stranger. However, it was absolutely necessary to make the House of Lords think that I knew something of the matter; and also to make them believe that they knew something of it themselves, which they do not. For my own part, I could just as soon have talked Celtic or Sclavonian to them as astronomy, and they would have understood me full as well: so I resolved to do better than speak to the purpose, and to please instead of informing them. I gave them, therefore, only an historical account of calendars, from the Egyptian down to the Gregorian, amusing them now and then with little episodes; but I was particularly attentive to the choice of my words, to the harmony and roundness of my periods, to my elocution, to my action. This succeeded, and ever will succeed; they thought I informed, because I pleased them; and many of them said that I had made the whole very clear to them; when, God knows, I had not even attempted it. Lord Macclesfield, who had the greatest share in forming the bill, and who is one of the greatest mathematicians and astronomers in Europe, spoke afterward with infinite knowledge, and all the clearness that so intricate a matter would admit of: but as his words, his periods, and his utterance, were not near so good as mine, the preference was most unanimously, though most unjustly, given to me. This will ever be the case; every numerous assembly is MOB, let the individuals who compose it be what they will. Mere reason and good sense is never to be talked to a mob; their passions, their sentiments, their senses, and their seeming interests, are alone to be applied to. Understanding they have collectively none, but they have ears and eyes, which must be flattered and seduced; and this can only be done by eloquence, tuneful periods, graceful action, and all the various parts of oratory.

When you come into the House of Commons, if you imagine that speaking plain and unadorned sense and reason will do your business, you will find yourself most grossly mistaken. As a speaker, you will be ranked only according to your eloquence, and by no means according to your matter; everybody knows the matter almost alike, but few can adorn it. I was early convinced of the importance and powers of eloquence; and from that moment I applied myself to it. I resolved not to utter one word, even in common conversation, that should not be the most expressive and the most elegant that the language could supply me with for that purpose; by which means I have acquired such a certain degree of habitual eloquence, that I must now really take some pains, if, I would express myself very inelegantly. I want to inculcate this known truth into you, which, you seem by no means to be convinced of yet, that ornaments are at present your only objects. Your sole business now is to shine, not to weigh. Weight without lustre is lead. You had better talk trifles elegantly to the most trifling woman, than coarse in elegant sense to the most solid man; you had better, return a dropped fan genteelly, than give a thousand pounds awkwardly; and you had better refuse a favor gracefully, than to grant it clumsily. Manner is all, in everything: it is by manner only that you can please, and consequently rise. All your Greek will never advance you from secretary to envoy, or from envoy to ambassador; but your address, your manner, your air, if good, very probably may. Marcel can be of much more use to you than Aristotle. I would, upon my word, much rather that you had Lord Bolingbroke's style and eloquence in speaking and writing, than all the learning of the Academy of Sciences, the Royal Society, and the two Universities united.

Having mentioned Lord Bolingbroke's style, which is, undoubtedly, infinitely superior to anybody's, I would have you read his works, which you have, over-and-over again, with particular attention to his style. Transcribe, imitate, emulate it, if possible: that would be of real use to you in the House of Commons, in negotiations, in conversation; with that, you may justly hope to please, to persuade, to seduce, to impose; and you will fail in those articles, in proportion as you fall short of it. Upon the whole, lay aside, during your year's residence at Paris, all thoughts of all that dull fellows call solid, and exert your utmost care to acquire what people of fashion call shining. 'Prenez l'eclat et le brillant d'un galant homme'.

Among the commonly called little things, to which you, do not attend, your handwriting is one, which is indeed shamefully bad and illiberal; it is neither the hand of a man of business, nor of a gentleman, but of a truant school-boy; as soon, therefore, as you have done with Abbe Nolet, pray get an excellent writing-master (since you think that you cannot teach yourself to write what hand you please), and let him teach you to write a genteel, legible, liberal hand, and quick; not the hand of a procureur or a writing-master, but that sort of hand in which the first 'Commis' in foreign bureaus commonly write; for I tell you truly, that were I Lord Albemarle, nothing should remain in my bureau written in your present hand. From hand to arms the transition is natural; is the carriage and motion of your arms so too? The motion of the arms is the most material part of a man's air, especially in dancing; the feet are not near so material. If a man dances well from the waist upward, wears his hat well, and moves his head properly, he dances well. Do the women say that you dress well? for that is necessary too for a young fellow. Have you 'un gout vif', or a passion for anybody? I do not ask for whom: an Iphigenia would both give you the desire, and teach you the means to please.

In a fortnight or three weeks you will see Sir Charles Hotham at Paris, in his way to Toulouse, where he is to stay a year or two. Pray be very civil to him, but do not carry him into company, except presenting him to Lord Albemarle; for, as he is not to stay at Paris above a week, we do not desire that he should taste of that dissipation: you may show him a play and an opera. Adieu, my dear child.

LETTERS TO HIS SON, COMPLETE

LETTER CXXXVI

LONDON, March 25, O. S. 1751.

MY DEAR FRIEND: What a happy period of your life is this? Pleasure is now, and ought to be, your business. While you were younger, dry rules, and unconnected words, were the unpleasant objects of your labors. When you grow older, the anxiety, the vexations, the disappointments inseparable from public business, will require the greatest share of your time and attention; your pleasures may, indeed, conduce to your business, and your business will quicken your pleasures; but still your time must, at least, be divided: whereas now it is wholly your own, and cannot be so well employed as in the pleasures of a gentleman. The world is now the only book you want, and almost the only one you ought to read: that necessary book can only be read in company, in public places, at meals, and in 'ruelles'. You must be in the pleasures, in order to learn the manners of good company. In premeditated, or in formal business, people conceal, or at least endeavor to conceal, their characters: whereas pleasures discover them, and the heart breaks out through the guard of the understanding. Those are often propitious moments for skillful negotiators to improve. In your destination particularly, the able conduct of pleasures is of infinite use; to keep a good table, and to do the honors of it gracefully, and 'sur le ton de la bonne compagnie', is absolutely necessary for a foreign minister. There is a certain light table chit-chat, useful to keep off improper and too serious subjects, which is only to be learned in the pleasures of good company. In truth it may be trifling; but, trifling as it is, a man of parts and experience of the world will give an agreeable turn to it. 'L'art de badiner agreablement' is by no means to be despised.

An engaging address, and turn to gallantry, is often of very great service to foreign ministers. Women have, directly or indirectly; a good deal to say in most courts. The late Lord Strafford governed, for a considerable time, the Court of Berlin and made his own fortune, by being well with Madame de Wartenberg, the first King of Prussia's mistress. I could name many other instances of that kind. That sort of agreeable 'caquet de femmes', the necessary fore-runners of closer conferences, is only to be got by frequenting women of the first fashion, 'et, qui donnent le ton'. Let every other book then give way to this great and necessary book, the world, of which there are so many various readings, that it requires a great deal of time and attention to understand it well: contrary to all other books, you must not stay home, but go abroad to read it; and when you seek it abroad, you will not find it in booksellers' shops and stalls, but in courts, in hotels, at entertainments, balls, assemblies, spectacles, etc. Put yourself upon the footing of an easy, domestic, but polite familiarity and intimacy in the several French houses to which you have been introduced: Cultivate them, frequent them, and show a desire of becoming 'enfant de la maison'. Get acquainted as much as you can with 'les gens de cour'; and observe, carefully, how politely they can differ, and how civilly they can hate; how easy and idle they can seem in the multiplicity of their business; and how they can lay hold of the proper moments to carry it on, in the midst of their pleasures. Courts, alone, teach versatility and politeness; for there is no living there without them. Lord Albermarle has, I hear, and am very glad of it, put you into the hands of Messieurs de Bissy. Profit of that, and beg of them to let you attend them in all the companies of Versailles and Paris. One of them, at least, will naturally carry you to Madame de la Valiores, unless he is discarded by this time, and Gelliot—[A famous opera-singer at Paris.]—retaken. Tell them frankly, 'que vous cherchez a vous former, que vous etes en mains de maitres, s'ils veulent bien s'en donner la peine'. Your profession has this agreeable peculiarity in it, which is, that it is connected with, and promoted by pleasures; and it is the only one in which a thorough knowledge of the world, polite manners, and an engaging address, are absolutely necessary. If a lawyer knows his law, a parson his divinity, and a financier his calculations, each may make a figure and a fortune in his profession, without great knowledge of the world, and without the manners of gentlemen. But your profession throws you into all the intrigues and cabals, as well as pleasures, of courts: in those windings and labyrinths, a knowledge of the world, a discernment of characters, a suppleness and versatility of mind, and an elegance of manners, must be your clue; you must know how to soothe and lull the monsters that guard, and how to address and gain the fair that keep, the golden fleece. These are the arts and the accomplishments absolutely necessary for a foreign minister; in which it must be owned, to our shame, that most other nations outdo the English; and, 'caeteris paribus', a French minister will get the better of an English one at any third court in Europe. The French have something more 'liant', more insinuating and engaging in their manner, than we have. An English minister shall have resided seven years at a court, without having made any one personal connection there, or without being intimate and domestic in any one house. He is always the English minister, and never naturalized. He receives his orders, demands an audience, writes an account of it to his Court, and his business is done. A French minister, on the contrary, has not been six weeks at a court without having, by a thousand little attentions, insinuated himself into some degree of favor with the Prince, his wife, his mistress, his favorite, and his minister. He has established himself upon a familiar and domestic footing in a dozen of the best houses of the place, where he has accustomed the people to be not only easy, but unguarded, before him; he makes himself at home there, and they think him so. By these means he knows the interior of those courts, and can almost write prophecies to his own, from the knowledge he has of the characters, the humors, the abilities, or the weaknesses of the actors. The Cardinal d'Ossat was looked upon at Rome as an Italian, and not as a French cardinal; and Monsieur d'Avaux, wherever he went, was never considered as a foreign minister, but as a native, and a personal friend. Mere plain truth, sense, and knowledge, will by no means do alone in courts; art and ornaments must come to their assistance. Humors must be flattered; the 'mollia tempora' must be studied and known: confidence acquired by seeming frankness, and profited of by silent skill. And, above all; you must gain and engage the heart, to betray the understanding to you. 'Ha tibi erunt artes'.

The death of the Prince of Wales, who was more beloved for his affability and good-nature than esteemed for his steadiness and conduct, has given concern to many, and apprehensions to all. The great difference of the ages of the King and Prince George presents the prospect of a minority; a disagreeable prospect for any nation! But it is to be hoped, and is most probable, that the King, who is now perfectly recovered of his late indisposition, may live to see his grandson of age. He is, seriously, a most hopeful boy: gentle and good-natured, with good sound sense. This event has made all sorts of people here historians, as well as politicians. Our histories are rummaged for all the particular circumstances of the six minorities we have had since the Conquest, viz, those of Henry III., Edward III., Richard II., Henry VI., Edward V., and Edward VI.; and the reasonings, the speculations, the conjectures, and the predictions, you will easily imagine, must be innumerable and endless, in this nation, where every porter is a consummate politician. Dr. Swift says, very humorously, that "Every man knows that he understands religion and politics, though he never learned them; but that many people are conscious that they do not understand many other sciences, from having never learned them." Adieu.

LETTER CXXXVII

LONDON, April 7, O. S. 1751

MY DEAR FRIEND: Here you have, altogether, the pocketbooks, the compasses, and the patterns. When your three Graces have made their option, you need only send me, in a letter small pieces of the three mohairs they fix upon. If I can find no way of sending them safely and directly to Paris, I will contrive to have them left with Madame Morel, at Calais, who, being Madame Monconseil's agent there, may find means of furthering them to your three ladies, who all belong to your friend Madame Monconseil. Two of the three, I am told, are handsome; Madame Polignac, I can swear, is not so; but, however, as the world goes, two out of three is a very good composition.

You will also find in the packet a compass ring set round with little diamonds, which I advise you to make a present of to Abbe Guasco, who has been useful to you, and will continue to be so; as it is a mere bauble, you must add to the value of it by your manner of giving it him. Show it him first, and, when he commends it, as probably he will, tell him that it is at his service, 'et que comme il est toujours par vole et par chemins, il est absolument necessaire qu'il ale une boussole'. All those little gallantries depend entirely upon the manner of doing them; as, in truth, what does not? The greatest favors may be done so awkwardly and bunglingly as to offend; and disagreeable things may be done so agreeably as almost to oblige. Endeavor to acquire this great secret; it exists, it is to be found, and is worth a great deal more than the grand secret of the alchemists would be if it were, as it is not, to be found. This is only to be learned in courts, where clashing views, jarring opinions, and cordial hatreds, are softened and kept within decent bounds by politeness and manners. Frequent, observe, and learn courts. Are you free of that of St. Cloud? Are you often at Versailles? Insinuate and wriggle yourself into favor at those places. L'Abbe de la Ville, my old friend, will help you at the latter; your three ladies may establish you in the former. The good-breeding 'de la ville et de la cour' [of the city and of the court] are different; but without deciding which is intrinsically the best, that of the court is, without doubt, the most necessary for you, who are to live, to grow, and to rise in courts. In two years' time, which will be as soon as you are fit for it, I hope to be able to plant you in the soil of a YOUNG COURT here: where, if you have all the address, the suppleness and versatility of a good courtier, you will have a great chance of thriving and flourishing. Young favor is easily acquired if the proper means are employed; and, when acquired, it is warm, if not durable; and the warm moments must be snatched and improved. 'Quitte pour ce qui en pent arriver apres'. Do not mention this view of mine for you to any one mortal; but learn to keep your own secrets, which, by the way, very few people can do.

If your course of experimental philosophy with Abbe Nolot is over, I would have you apply to Abbe Sallier, for a master to give you a general notion of astronomy and geometry; of both of which you may know as much, as I desire you should, in six months' time. I only desire that you should have a clear notion of the present planetary system, and the history of all the former systems. Fontenelle's 'Pluralites des Mondes' will almost teach you all you need know upon that subject. As for geometry, the seven first books of Euclid will be a sufficient portion of it for you. It is right to have a general notion of those abstruse sciences, so as not to appear quite ignorant of them, when they happen, as sometimes they do, to be the topics of conversation; but a deep knowledge of them requires too much time, and engrosses the mind too much. I repeat it again and again to you, Let the great book of the world be your principal study. 'Nocturna versate manu, versate diurna'; which may be rendered thus in English: Turn Over MEN BY DAY, AND WOMEN BY NIGHT. I mean only the best editions.

Whatever may be said at Paris of my speech upon the bill for the reformation of the present calendar, or whatever applause it may have met with here, the whole, I can assure you, is owing to the words and to the delivery, but by no means to the matter; which, as I told you in a former letter, I was not master of. I mention this again, to show you the importance of well-chosen words, harmonious periods, and good delivery; for, between you and me, Lord Macclefield's speech was, in truth, worth a thousand of mine. It will soon be printed, and I will send it you. It is very instructive. You say, that you wish to speak but half as well as I did; you may easily speak full as well as ever I did, if you will but give the same attention to the same objects that I did at your age, and for many years afterward; I mean correctness, purity, and elegance of style, harmony of periods, and gracefulness of delivery. Read over and over again the third book of 'Cicero de Oratore', in which he particularly treats of the ornamental parts of oratory; they are indeed properly oratory, for all the rest depends only upon common sense, and some knowledge of the subject you speak upon. But if you would please, persuade, and prevail in speaking, it must be by the ornamental parts of oratory. Make them therefore habitual to you; and resolve never to say the most common things, even to your footman, but in the best words you can find, and with the best utterance. This, with 'les manieres, la tournure, et les usages du beau monde', are the only two things you want; fortunately, they are both in your power; may you have them both! Adieu.

EARL OF PHILIP DORMER STANHOPE CHESTERFIELD

LETTER CXXXVIII

LONDON, April 15, O. S. 1751

MY DEAR FRIEND: What success with the graces, and in the accomplishments, elegancies, and all those little nothings so indispensably necessary to constitute an amiable man? Do you take them, do you make a progress in them? The great secret is the art of pleasing; and that art is to be attained by every man who has a good fund of common sense. If you are pleased with any person, examine why; do as he does; and you will charm others by the same things which please you in him. To be liked by women, you must be esteemed by men; and to please men, you must be agreeable to women. Vanity is unquestionably the ruling passion in women; and it is much flattered by the attentions of a man who is generally esteemed by men; when his merit has received the stamp of their approbation, women make it current, that is to say, put him in fashion. On the other hand, if a man has not received the last polish from women, he may be estimable among men, but will never be amiable. The concurrence of the two sexes is as necessary to the perfection of our being, as to the formation of it. Go among women with the good qualities of your sex, and you will acquire from them the softness and the graces of theirs. Men will then add affection to the esteem which they before had for you. Women are the only refiners of the merit of men; it is true, they cannot add weight, but they polish and give lustre to it. 'A propos', I am assured, that Madame de Blot, although she has no great regularity of features, is, notwithstanding, excessively pretty; and that, for all that, she has as yet been scrupulously constant to her husband, though she has now been married above a year. Surely she does not reflect, that woman wants polishing. I would have you polish one another reciprocally. Force, assiduities, attentions, tender looks, and passionate declarations, on your side will produce some irresolute wishes, at least, on hers; and when even the slightest wishes arise, the rest will soon follow.

As I take you to be the greatest 'juris peritus' and politician of the whole Germanic body, I suppose you will have read the King of Prussia's letter to the Elector of Mayence, upon the election of a King of the Romans; and on the other side, a memorial entitled, IMPARTIAL REPRESENTATION OF WHAT IS JUST WITH REGARD TO THE ELECTION OF A KING OF THE ROMANS, etc. The first is extremely well written, but not grounded upon the laws and customs of the empire. The second is very ill written (at least in French), but well grounded. I fancy the author is some German, who has taken into his head that he understands French. I am, however, persuaded that the elegance and delicacy of the King of Prussia's letter will prevail with two-thirds of the public, in spite of the solidity and truth contained in the other piece. Such is the force of an elegant and delicate style!

I wish you would be so good as to give me a more particular and circumstantial account of the method of passing your time at Paris. For instance, where it is that you dine every Friday, in company with that amiable and respectable old man, Fontenelle? Which is the house where you think yourself at home? For one always has such a one, where one is better established, and more at ease than anywhere else. Who are the young Frenchmen with whom you are most intimately connected? Do you frequent the Dutch Ambassador's. Have you penetrated yet into Count Caunitz's house? Has Monsieur de Pignatelli the honor of being one of your humble servants? And has the Pope's nuncio included you in the jubilee? Tell me also freely how you are with Lord Huntingdon: Do you see him often? Do you connect yourself with him? Answer all these questions circumstantially in your first letter.

I am told that Du Clos's book is not in vogue at Paris, and that it is violently criticised: I suppose that is because one understands it; and being intelligible is now no longer the fashion. I have a very great respect for fashion, but a much greater for this book; which is, all at once, true, solid, and bright. It contains even epigrams; what can one wish for more?

Mr.———will, I suppose, have left Paris by this time for his residence at Toulouse. I hope he will acquire manners there; I am sure he wants them. He is awkward, he is silent, and has nothing agreeable in his address,—most necessary qualifications to distinguish one's self in business, as well as in the POLITE WORLD! In truth, these two things are so connected, that a man cannot make a figure in business, who is not qualified to shine in the great world; and to succeed perfectly in either the one or the other, one must be in 'utrumque paratus'. May you be that, my dear friend! and so we wish you a good night.

P. S. Lord and Lady Blessington, with their son Lord Mountjoy, will be at Paris next week, in their way to the south of France; I send you a little packet of books by them. Pray go wait upon them, as soon as you hear of their arrival, and show them all the attentions you can.

LETTER CXXXIX

LONDON, April 22, O. S. 1751

MY DEAR FRIEND: I apply to you now, as to the greatest virtuoso of this, or perhaps any other age; one whose superior judgment and distinguishing eye hindered the King of Poland from buying a bad picture at Venice, and whose decisions in the realms of 'virtu' are final, and without appeal. Now to the point. I have had a catalogue sent me, 'd'une Trente a l'aimable de Tableaux des plus Grands Maitres, appartenans au Sieur Araignon Aperen, valet de chambre de la Reine, sur le quai de la Megisserie, au coin de Arche Marion'. There I observe two large pictures of Titian, as described in the inclosed page of the catalogue, No. 18, which I should be glad to purchase upon two conditions: the first is, that they be undoubted originals of Titian, in good preservation; and the other that they come cheap. To ascertain the first (but without disparaging your skill), I wish you would get some undoubted connoisseurs to examine them carefully: and if, upon such critical examination, they should be unanimously allowed to be undisputed originals of Titian, and well preserved, then comes the second point, the price: I will not go above two hundred pounds sterling for the two together; but as much less as you can get them for. I acknowledge that two hundred pounds seems to be a very small sum for two undoubted Titians of that size; but, on the other hand, as large Italian pictures are now out of fashion at Paris, where fashion decides of everything, and as these pictures are too large for common rooms, they may possibly come within the price above limited. I leave the whole of this transaction (the price excepted, which I will not exceed) to your consummate skill and prudence, with proper advice joined to them. Should you happen to buy them for that price, carry them to your own lodgings, and get a frame made to the second, which I observe has none, exactly the same with the other frame, and have the old one new gilt; and then get them carefully packed up, and sent me by Rouen.

I hear much of your conversing with 'les beaux esprits' at Paris: I am very glad of it; it gives a degree of reputation, especially at Paris; and their conversation is generally instructive, though sometimes affected. It must be owned, that the polite conversation of the men and women of fashion at Paris, though not always very deep, is much less futile and frivolous than ours here. It turns at least upon some subject, something of taste, some point of history, criticism, and even philosophy; which, though probably not quite so solid as Mr. Locke's, is, however, better, and more becoming rational beings, than our frivolous dissertations upon the weather, or upon whist. Monsieur du Clos observes, and I think very justly, 'qu'il y a a present en France une fermentation universelle de la raison qui tend a se developper'. Whereas, I am sorry to say, that here that fermentation seems to have been over some years ago, the spirit evaporated, and only the dregs left. Moreover, 'les beaux esprits' at Paris are commonly well-bred, which ours very frequently are not; with the former your manners will be formed; with the latter, wit must generally be compounded for at the expense of manners. Are you acquainted with Marivaux, who has certainly studied, and is well acquainted with the heart; but who refines so much upon its 'plis et replis', and describes them so affectedly, that he often is unintelligible to his readers, and sometimes so, I dare say, to himself? Do you know 'Crebillon le fils'? He is a fine painter and a pleasing writer; his characters are admirable and his reflections just. Frequent these people, and be glad, but not proud of frequenting them: never boast of it, as a proof of your own merit, nor insult, in a manner, other companies by telling them affectedly what you, Montesquieu and Fontenelle were talking of the other day; as I have known many people do here, with regard to Pope and Swift, who had never been twice in company with either; nor carry into other companies the 'ton' of those meetings of 'beaux esprits'. Talk literature, taste, philosophy, etc., with them, 'a la bonne heure'; but then, with the same ease, and more 'enjouement', talk 'pom-pons, moires', etc., with Madame de Blot, if she requires it. Almost every subject in the world has its proper time and place; in which no one is above or below discussion. The point is, to talk well upon the subject you talk upon; and the most trifling, frivolous subjects will still give a man of parts an opportunity of showing them. 'L'usage du grand monde' can alone teach that. That was the distinguishing characteristic of Alcibiades, and a happy one it was, that he could occasionally, and with so much ease, adopt the most different, and even the most opposite habits and manners, that each seemed natural to him. Prepare yourself for the great world, as the 'athletae' used to do for their exercises: oil (if I may use that expression) your mind and your manners, to give them the necessary suppleness and flexibility; strength alone will not do, as young people are too apt to think.

How do your exercises go on? Can you manage a pretty vigorous 'sauteur' between the pillars? Are you got into stirrups yet? 'Faites-vous assaut aux armes? But, above all, what does Marcel say of you? Is he satisfied? Pray be more particular in your accounts of yourself, for though I have frequent accounts of you from others, I desire to have your own too. Adieu. Yours, truly and friendly.

LETTER CXL

LONDON, May 2, O. S. 1751

DEAR FRIEND: Two accounts, which I have very lately received of you, from two good judges, have put me into great spirits, as they have given me reasonable hopes that you will soon acquire all that I believe you want: I mean the air, the address; the graces, and the manners of a man of fashion. As these two pictures of you are very unlike that which I received, and sent you some months ago, I will name the two painters: the first is an old friend and acquaintance of mine, Monsieur d'Aillon. His picture is, I hope, like you; for it is a very good one: Monsieur Tollot's is still a better, and so advantageous a one, that I will not send you a copy of it, for fear of making you too vain. So far only I will tell you, that there was but one BUT in either of their accounts; and it was this: I gave d'Aillon the question ordinary and extraordinary, upon the important article of manners; and extorted this from him: But, since you will know it, he still wants that last beautiful varnish, which raises the colors, and gives brilliancy to the piece. Be persuaded that he will acquire it: he has too much sense not to know its value; and if I am not greatly mistaken, more persons than one are now endeavoring to give it him. Monsieur Tollot says: "In order to be exactly all that you wish him, he only wants those little nothings, those graces in detail, and that amiable ease, which can only be acquired by usage of the great world. I am assured that he is, in that respect, in good hands. I do not know whether that does not rather imply in fine arms." Without entering into a nice discussion of the last question, I congratulate you and myself upon your being so near that point at which I so anxiously wish you to arrive. I am sure that all your attention and endeavors will be exerted; and, if exerted, they will succeed. Mr. Tollot says, that you are inclined to be fat, but I hope you will decline it as much as you can; not by taking anything corrosive to make you lean, but by taking as little as you can of those things that would make you fat. Drink no chocolate; take your coffee without cream: you cannot possibly avoid suppers at Paris, unless you avoid company too, which I would by no means have you do; but eat as little at supper as you can, and make even an allowance for that little at your dinners. Take occasionally a double dose of riding and fencing; and now that summer is come, walk a good deal in the Tuileries. It is a real inconvenience to anybody to be fat, and besides it is ungraceful for a young fellow. 'A propos', I had like to have forgot to tell you, that I charged Tollot to attend particularly to your utterence and diction; two points of the utmost importance. To the first he says: "His enunciation is not bad, but it is to be wished that it were still better; and he expresses himself with more fire than elegance. Usage of good company will instruct him likewise in that." These, I allow, are all little things, separately; but aggregately, they make a most important and great article in the account of a gentleman. In the House of Commons you can never make a figure without elegance of style, and gracefulness of utterance; and you can never succeed as a courtier at your own Court, or as a minister at any other, without those innumerable 'petite riens dans les manieres, et dans les attentions'. Mr. Yorke is by this time at Paris; make your court to him, but not so as to disgust, in the least, Lord Albemarle, who may possibly dislike your considering Mr. Yorke as the man of business, and him as only 'pour orner la scene'. Whatever your opinion may be upon THAT POINT, take care not to let it appear; but be well with them both by showing no public preference to either.

Though I must necessarily fall into repetitions by treating the same subject so often, I cannot help recommending to you again the utmost attention to your air and address. Apply yourself now to Marcel's lectures, as diligently as you did formerly to Professor Mascow's; desire him to teach you every genteel attitude that the human body can be put into; let him make you go in and out of his room frequently, and present yourself to him, as if he were by turns different persons; such as a minister, a lady, a superior, an equal, and inferior, etc. Learn to seat genteelly in different companies; to loll genteelly, and with good manners, in those companies where you are authorized to be free, and to sit up respectfully where the same freedom is not allowable. Learn even to compose your countenance occasionally to the respectful, the cheerful, and the insinuating. Take particular care that the motions of your hands and arms be easy and graceful; for the genteelness of a man consists more in them than in anything else, especially in his dancing. Desire some women to tell you of any little awkwardness that they observe in your carriage; they are the best judges of those things; and if they are satisfied, the men will be so too. Think now only of the decorations. Are you acquainted with Madame Geoffrain, who has a great deal of wit; and who, I am informed, receives only the very best company in her house? Do you know Madame du Pin, who, I remember, had beauty, and I hear has wit and reading? I could wish you to converse only with those who, either from their rank, their merit, or their beauty, require constant attention; for a young man can never improve in company where he thinks he may neglect himself. A new bow must be constantly kept bent; when it grows older, and has taken the right turn, it may now and then be relaxed.

I have this moment paid your draft of L89 75s.; it was signed in a very good hand; which proves that a good hand may be written without the assistance of magic. Nothing provokes me much more, than to hear people indolently say that they cannot do, what is in everybody's power to do, if it be but in their will. Adieu.

LETTER CXLI

LONDON, May 6, O. S. 1751.

MY DEAR FRIEND: The best authors are always the severest critics of their own works; they revise, correct, file, and polish them, till they think they have brought them to perfection. Considering you as my work, I do not look upon myself as a bad author, and am therefore a severe critic. I examine narrowly into the least inaccuracy or inelegance, in order to correct, not to expose them, and that the work may be perfect at last. You are, I know, exceedingly improved in your air, address, and manners, since you have been at Paris; but still there is, I believe, room for further improvement before you come to that perfection which I have set my heart upon seeing you arrive at; and till that moment I must continue filing and polishing. In a letter that I received by last post, from a friend of yours at Paris, there was this paragraph: "I have the honor to assure you, without flattery, that Mr. Stanhope succeeds beyond what might be expected from a person of his age. He goes into very good company; and that kind of manner, which was at first thought to be too decisive and peremptory, is now judged otherwise; because it is acknowledged to be the effect of an ingenuous frankness, accompanied by politeness, and by a proper deference. He studies to please, and succeeds. Madame du Puisieux was the other day speaking of him with complacency and friendship. You will be satisfied with him in all respects." This is extremely well, and I rejoice at it: one little circumstance only may, and I hope will, be altered for the better. Take pains to undeceive those who thought that 'petit ton un peu delcide et un peu brusceur'; as it is not meant so, let it not appear so. Compose your countenance to an air of gentleness and 'douceur', use some expressions of diffidence of your own opinion, and deference to other people's; such as, "If I might be permitted to say—I should think—Is it not rather so? At least I have the greatest reason to be diffident of myself." Such mitigating, engaging words do by no means weaken your argument; but, on the contrary, make it more powerful by making it more pleasing. If it is a quick and hasty manner of speaking that people mistake 'pour decide et brusque', prevent their mistakes for the future by speaking more deliberately, and taking a softer tone of voice; as in this case you are free from the guilt, be free from the suspicion, too. Mankind, as I have often told you, are more governed by appearances than by realities; and with regard to opinion, one had better be really rough and hard, with the appearance of gentleness and softness, than just the reverse. Few people have penetration enough to discover, attention enough to observe, or even concern enough to examine beyond the exterior; they take their notions from the surface, and go no deeper: they commend, as the gentlest and best-natured man in the world, that man who has the most engaging exterior manner, though possibly they have been but once in his company. An air, a tone of voice, a composure of countenance to mildness and softness, which are all easily acquired, do the business: and without further examination, and possibly with the contrary qualities, that man is reckoned the gentlest, the modestest, and the best-natured man alive. Happy the man, who, with a certain fund of parts and knowledge, gets acquainted with the world early enough to make it his bubble, at an age when most people are the bubbles of the world! for that is the common case of youth. They grow wiser when it is too late; and, ashamed and vexed at having been bubbles so long, too often turn knaves at last. Do not therefore trust to appearances and outside yourself, but pay other people with them; because you may be sure that nine in ten of mankind do, and ever will trust to them. This is by no means a criminal or blamable simulation, if not used with an ill intention. I am by no means blamable in desiring to have other people's good word, good-will, and affection, if I do not mean to abuse them. Your heart, I know, is good, your sense is sound, and your knowledge extensive. What then remains for you to do? Nothing, but to adorn those fundamental qualifications, with such engaging and captivating manners, softness, and gentleness, as will endear you to those who are able to judge of your real merit, and which always stand in the stead of merit with those who are not. I do not mean by this to recommend to you 'le fade doucereux', the insipid softness of a gentle fool; no, assert your own opinion, oppose other people's when wrong; but let your manner, your air, your terms, and your tone of voice, be soft and gentle, and that easily and naturally, not affectedly. Use palliatives when you contradict; such as I MAY BE MISTAKEN, I AM NOT SURE, BUT I BELIEVE, I SHOULD RATHER THINK, etc. Finish any argument or dispute with some little good-humored pleasantry, to show that you are neither hurt yourself, nor meant to hurt your antagonist; for an argument, kept up a good while, often occasions a temporary alienation on each side. Pray observe particularly, in those French people who are distinguished by that character, 'cette douceur de moeurs et de manieres', which they talk of so much, and value so justly; see in what it consists; in mere trifles, and most easy to be acquired, where the heart is really good. Imitate, copy it, till it becomes habitual and easy to you. Without a compliment to you, I take it to be the only thing you now want: nothing will sooner give it you than a real passion, or, at least, 'un gout vif', for some woman of fashion; and, as I suppose that you have either the one or the other by this time, you are consequently in the best school. Besides this, if you were to say to Lady Hervey, Madame Monconseil, or such others as you look upon to be your friends, It is said that I have a kind of manner which is rather too decisive and too peremptory; it is not, however, my intention that it should be so; I entreat you to correct, and even publicly to punish me whenever I am guilty. Do not treat me with the least indulgence, but criticise to the utmost. So clear-sighted a judge as you has a right to be severe; and I promise you that the criminal will endeavor to correct himself. Yesterday I had two of your acquaintances to dine with me, Baron B. and his companion Monsieur S. I cannot say of the former, 'qu'il est paitri de graces'; and I would rather advise him to go and settle quietly at home, than to think of improving himself by further travels. 'Ce n'est pas le bois don't on en fait'. His companion is much better, though he has a strong 'tocco di tedesco'. They both spoke well of you, and so far I liked them both. How go you on with the amiable little Blot? Does she listen to your Battering tale? Are you numbered among the list of her admirers? Is Madame———your Madame de Lursay? Does she sometimes knot, and are you her Meilcour? They say she has softness, sense, and engaging manners; in such an apprenticeship much may be learned.—[This whole passage, and several others, allude to Crebillon's 'Egaremens du Coeur et de l'Esprit', a sentimental novel written about that time, and then much in vogue at Paris.]

A woman like her, who has always pleased, and often been pleased, can best teach the art of pleasing; that art, without which, 'ogni fatica vana'. Marcel's lectures are no small part of that art: they are the engaging forerunner of all other accomplishments. Dress is also an article not to be neglected, and I hope you do not neglect it; it helps in the 'premier abord', which is often decisive. By dress, I mean your clothes being well made, fitting you, in the fashion and not above it; your hair well done, and a general cleanliness and spruceness in your person. I hope you take infinite care of your teeth; the consequences of neglecting the mouth are serious, not only to one's self, but to others. In short, my dear child, neglect nothing; a little more will complete the whole. Adieu. I have not heard from you these three weeks, which I think a great while.

LETTER CXLII

LONDON, May 10, O. S. 1751.

MY DEAR FRIEND: I received yesterday, at the same time, your letters of the 4th and 11th, N. S., and being much more careful of my commissions than you are of yours, I do not delay one moment sending you my final instructions concerning the pictures. The man you allow to be a Titian, and in good preservation; the woman is an indifferent and a damaged picture; but as I want them for furniture for a particular room, companions are necessary; and therefore I am willing to take the woman for better for worse, upon account of the man; and if she is not too much damaged, I can have her tolerably repaired, as many a fine woman is, by a skillful hand here; but then I expect that the lady should be, in a manner, thrown into the bargain with the man; and, in this state of affairs, the woman being worth little or nothing, I will not go above fourscore Louis for the two together. As for the Rembrandt you mention, though it is very cheap, if good, I do not care for it. I love 'la belle nature'; Rembrandt paints caricatures. Now for your own commissions, which you seem to have forgotten. You mention nothing of the patterns which you received by Monsieur Tollot, though I told you in a former letter, which you must have had before the date of your last, that I should stay till I received the patterns pitched upon by your ladies; for as to the instructions which you sent me in Madame Monconseil's hand, I could find no mohairs in London that exactly answered that description; I shall, therefore, wait till you send me (which you may easily do in a letter) the patterns chosen by your three graces.

I would, by all means, have you go now and then, for two or three days, to Marechal Coigny's, at Orli; it is but a proper civility to that family, which has been particularly civil to you; and, moreover, I would have you familiarize yourself with, and learn the interior and domestic manners of, people of that rank and fashion. I also desire that you will frequent Versailles and St. Cloud, at both of which courts you have been received with distinction. Profit of that distinction, and familiarize yourself at both. Great courts are the seats of true good-breeding; you are to live at courts, lose no time in learning them. Go and stay sometimes at Versailles for three or four days, where you will be domestic in the best families, by means of your friend Madame de Puisieux; and mine, l'Abbe de la Ville. Go to the King's and the Dauphin's levees, and distinguish yourself from the rest of your countrymen, who, I dare say, never go there when they can help it. Though the young Frenchmen of fashion may not be worth forming intimate connections with, they are well worth making acquaintance of; and I do not see how you can avoid it, frequenting so many good French houses as you do, where, to be sure, many of them come. Be cautious how you contract friendships, but be desirous, and even industrious, to obtain a universal acquaintance. Be easy, and even forward, in making new acquaintances; that is the only way of knowing manners and characters in general, which is, at present, your great object. You are 'enfant de famille' in three ministers' houses; but I wish you had a footing, at least, in thirteen and that, I should think, you might easily bring about, by that common chain, which, to a certain degree, connects those you do not with those you do know.

For instance, I suppose that neither Lord Albemarle, nor Marquis de St. Germain, would make the least difficulty to present you to Comte Caunitz, the Nuncio, etc. 'Il faut etre rompu du monde', which can only be done by an extensive, various, and almost universal acquaintance.

When you have got your emaciated Philomath, I desire that his triangles, rhomboids, etc., may not keep you one moment out of the good company you would otherwise be in. Swallow all your learning in the morning, but digest it in company in the evenings. The reading of ten new characters is more your business now, than the reading of twenty old books; showish and shining people always get the better of all others, though ever so solid. If you would be a great man in the world when you are old, shine and be showish in it while you are young, know everybody, and endeavor to please everybody, I mean exteriorly; for fundamentally it is impossible. Try to engage the heart of every woman, and the affections of almost every man you meet with. Madame Monconseil assures me that you are most surprisingly improved in your air, manners, and address: go on, my dear child, and never think that you are come to a sufficient degree of perfection; 'Nil actum reputans, si quid superesset agendum'; and in those shining parts of the character of a gentleman, there is always something remaining to be acquired. Modes and manners vary in different places, and at different times; you must keep pace with them, know them, and adopt them, wherever you find them. The great usage of the world, the knowledge of characters, the brillant dun 'galant homme,' is all that you now want. Study Marcel and the 'beau monde' with great application, but read Homer and Horace only when you have nothing else to do. Pray who is 'la belle Madame de Case', whom I know you frequent? I like the epithet given her very well: if she deserves it, she deserves your attention too. A man of fashion should be gallant to a fine woman, though he does not make love to her, or may be otherwise engaged. On 'lui doit des politesses, on fait l'eloge de ses charmes, et il n'en est ni plus ni moins pour cela': it pleases, it flatters; you get their good word, and you lose nothing by it. These 'gentillesses' should be accompanied, as indeed everything else should, with an air: 'un air, un ton de douceur et de politesse'. Les graces must be of the party, or it will never do; and they are so easily had, that it is astonishing to me that everybody has them not; they are sooner gained than any woman of common reputation and decency. Pursue them but with care and attention, and you are sure to enjoy them at last: without them, I am sure, you will never enjoy anybody else. You observe, truly, that Mr.———is gauche; it is to be hoped that will mend with keeping company; and is yet pardonable in him, as just come from school. But reflect what you would think of a man, who had been any time in the world, and yet should be so awkward. For God's sake, therefore, now think of nothing but shining, and even distinguishing yourself in the most polite courts, by your air, your address, your manners, your politeness, your 'douceur', your graces. With those advantages (and not without them) take my word for it, you will get the better of all rivals, in business as well as in 'ruelles'. Adieu. Send me your patterns, by the next post, and also your instructions to Grevenkop about the seal, which you seem to have forgotten.

LETTER CXLIII

LONDON, May 16, O. S. 1751.

MY DEAR FRIEND: In about three months from this day, we shall probably meet. I look upon that moment as a young woman does upon her bridal night; I expect the greatest pleasure, and yet cannot help fearing some little mixture of pain. My reason bids me doubt a little, of what my imagination makes me expect. In some articles I am very sure that my most sanguine wishes will not be disappointed; and those are the most material ones. In others, I fear something or other, which I can better feel than describe. However, I will attempt it. I fear the want of that amiable and engaging 'je ne sais quoi', which as some philosophers have, unintelligibly enough, said of the soul, is all in all, and all in every part; it should shed its influence over every word and action. I fear the want of that air, and first 'abord', which suddenly lays hold of the heart, one does not know distinctly how or why. I fear an inaccuracy, or, at least, inelegance of diction, which will wrong, and lower, the best and justest matter. And, lastly, I fear an ungraceful, if not an unpleasant utterance, which would disgrace and vilify the whole. Should these fears be at present founded, yet the objects of them are (thank God) of such a nature, that you may, if you please, between this and our meeting, remove everyone of them. All these engaging and endearing accomplishments are mechanical, and to be acquired by care and observation, as easily as turning, or any mechanical trade. A common country fellow, taken from the plow, and enlisted in an old corps, soon lays aside his shambling gait, his slouching air, his clumsy and awkward motions: and acquires the martial air, the regular motions, and whole exercise of the corps, and particularly of his right and left hand man. How so? Not from his parts; which were just the same before as after he was enlisted; but either from a commendable ambition of being like, and equal to those he is to live with; or else from the fear of being punished for not being so. If then both or either of these motives change such a fellow, in about six months' time, to such a degree, as that he is not to be known again, how much stronger should both these motives be with you, to acquire, in the utmost perfection, the whole exercise of the people of fashion, with whom you are to live all your life? Ambition should make you resolve to be at least their equal in that exercise, as well as the fear of punishment; which most inevitably will attend the want of it. By that exercise, I mean the air, the manners, the graces, and the style of people of fashion. A friend of yours, in a letter I received from him by the last post, after some other commendations of you, says, "It is surprising that, thinking with so much solidity as he does, and having so true and refined a taste, he should express himself with so little elegance and delicacy. He even totally neglects the choice of words and turn of phrases."

This I should not be so much surprised or concerned at, if it related only to the English language; which hitherto you have had no opportunity of studying, and but few of speaking, at least to those who could correct your inaccuracies. But if you do not express yourself elegantly and delicately in French and German, (both which languages I know you possess perfectly and speak eternally) it can be only from an unpardonable inattention to what you most erroneously think a little object, though, in truth, it is one of the most important of your life. Solidity and delicacy of thought must be given us: it cannot be acquired, though it may be improved; but elegance and delicacy of expression may be acquired by whoever will take the necessary care and pains. I am sure you love me so well; that you would be very sorry when we meet, that I should be either disappointed or mortified; and I love you so well, that I assure you I should be both, if I should find you want any of those exterior accomplishments which are the indispensably necessary steps to that figure and fortune, which I so earnestly wish you may one day make in the world.

I hope you do not neglect your exercises of riding, fencing, and dancing, but particularly the latter: for they all concur to 'degourdir', and to give a certain air. To ride well, is not only a proper and graceful accomplishment for a gentleman, but may also save you many a fall hereafter; to fence well, may possibly save your life; and to dance well, is absolutely necessary in order to sit, stand, and walk well. To tell you the truth, my friend, I have some little suspicion that you now and then neglect or omit your exercises, for more serious studies. But now 'non est his locus', everything has its time; and this is yours for your exercises; for when you return to Paris I only propose your continuing your dancing; which you shall two years longer, if you happen to be where there is a good dancing-master. Here I will see you take some lessons with your old master Desnoyers, who is our Marcel.

What says Madame du Pin to you? I am told she is very handsome still; I know she was some few years ago. She has good parts, reading, manners, and delicacy: such an arrangement would be both creditable and advantageous to you. She will expect to meet with all the good-breeding and delicacy that she brings; and as she is past the glare and 'eclat' of youth, may be the more willing to listen to your story, if you tell it well. For an attachment, I should prefer her to 'la petite Blot'; and, for a mere gallantry, I should prefer 'la petite Blot' to her; so that they are consistent, et 'l'un n'emplche pas l'autre'. Adieu. Remember 'la douceur et les graces'.

LETTER CXLIV

LONDON, May 23, O. S. 1751.

MY DEAR FRIEND: I have this moment received your letter of the 25th N. S., and being rather something more attentive to my commissions than you are to yours, return you this immediate answer to the question you ask me about the two pictures: I will not give one livre more than what I told you in my last; having no sort of occasion for them, and not knowing very well where to put them if I had them.

I wait with impatience for your final orders about the mohairs; the mercer persecuting me every day for three pieces which I thought pretty, and which I have kept by me eventually, to secure them in case your ladies should pitch upon them.

If I durst! what should hinder you from daring? One always dares if there are hopes of success; and even if there are none, one is no loser by daring. A man of fashion knows how, and when, to dare. He begins his approaches by distant attacks, by assiduities, and by attentions. If he is not immediately and totally repulsed, he continues to advance. After certain steps success is infallible; and none but very silly fellows can then either doubt, or not attempt it. Is it the respectable character of Madame de la Valiere which prevents your daring, or are you intimidated at the fierce virtue of Madame du Pin? Does the invincible modesty of the handsome Madame Case discourage, more than her beauty invites you? Fie, for shame! Be convinced that the most virtuous woman, far from being offended at a declaration of love, is flattered by it, if it is made in a polite and agreeable manner. It is possible that she may not be propitious to your vows; that is to say, if she has a liking or a passion for another person. But, at all events, she will not be displeased with you for it; so that, as there is no danger, this cannot even be called daring. But if she attends, if she listens, and allows you to repeat your declaration, be persuaded that if you do not dare all the rest, she will laugh at you. I advise you to begin rather by Madame du Pin, who has still more than beauty enough for such a youngster as you. She has, besides, knowledge of the world, sense, and delicacy. As she is not so extremely young, the choice of her lovers cannot be entirely at her option. I promise you, she will not refuse the tender of your most humble services. Distinguish her, then, by attentions and by tender looks. Take favorable opportunities of whispering that you wish esteem and friendship were the only motives of your regard for her; but that it derives from sentiments of a much more tender nature: that you made not this declaration without pain; but that the concealing your passion was a still greater torment.

I am sensible, that in saying this for the first time, you will look silly, abashed, and even express yourself very ill. So much the better; for, instead of attributing your confusion to the little usage you have of the world, particularly in these sort of subjects, she will think that excess of love is the occasion of it. In such a case, the lover's best friend is self-love. Do not then be afraid; behave gallantly. Speak well, and you will be heard. If you are not listened to the first time, try a second, a third, and a fourth. If the place is not already taken, depend upon it, it may be conquered.

I am very glad you are going to Orli, and from thence to St. Cloud; go to both, and to Versailles also, often. It is that interior domestic familiarity with people of fashion, that alone can give you 'l'usage du monde, et les manieres aisees'. It is only with women one loves, or men one respects, that the desire of pleasing exerts itself; and without the desire of pleasing no man living can please. Let that desire be the spring of all your words and actions. That happy talent, the art of pleasing, which so few do, though almost all might possess, is worth all your learning and knowledge put together. The latter can never raise you high without the former; but the former may carry you, as it has carried thousands, a great way without the latter.

I am glad that you dance so well, as to be reckoned by Marcel among his best scholars; go on, and dance better still. Dancing well is pleasing 'pro tanto', and makes a part of that necessary whole, which is composed of a thousand parts, many of them of 'les infiniment petits quoi qu'infiniment necessaires'.

I shall never have done upon this subject which is indispensably necessary toward your making any figure or fortune in the world; both which I have set my heart upon, and for both which you now absolutely want no one thing but the art of pleasing; and I must not conceal from you that you have still a good way to go before you arrive at it. You still want a thousand of those little attentions that imply a desire of pleasing: you want a 'douceur' of air and expression that engages: you want an elegance and delicacy of expression, necessary to adorn the best sense and most solid matter: in short, you still want a great deal of the 'brillant' and the 'poli'. Get them at any rate: sacrifice hecatombs of books to them: seek for them in company, and renounce your closet till you have got them. I never received the letter you refer to, if ever you wrote it. Adieu, et bon soir, Monseigneur.

EARL OF PHILIP DORMER STANHOPE CHESTERFIELD

LETTER CXLV

GREENWICH, June 6, O. S. 1751.

MY DEAR FRIEND: Solicitous and anxious as I have ever been to form your heart, your mind, and your manners, and to bring you as near perfection as the imperfection of our natures will allow, I have exhausted, in the course of our correspondence, all that my own mind could suggest, and have borrowed from others whatever I thought could be useful to you; but this has necessarily been interruptedly and by snatches. It is now time, and you are of an age to review and to weigh in your own mind all that you have heard, and all that you have read, upon these subjects; and to form your own character, your conduct, and your manners, for the rest of your life; allowing for such improvements as a further knowledge of the world will naturally give you. In this view I would recommend to you to read, with the greatest attention, such books as treat particularly of those subjects; reflecting seriously upon them, and then comparing the speculation with the practice.

For example, if you read in the morning some of La Rochefoucault's maxims; consider them, examine them well, and compare them with the real characters you meet with in the evening. Read La Bruyere in the morning, and see in the evening whether his pictures are like. Study the heart and the mind of man, and begin with your own. Meditation and reflection must lay the foundation of that knowledge: but experience and practice must, and alone can, complete it. Books, it is true, point out the operations of the mind, the sentiments of the heart, the influence of the passions; and so far they are of previous use: but without subsequent practice, experience, and observation, they are as ineffectual, and would even lead you into as many errors in fact, as a map would do, if you were to take your notions of the towns and provinces from their delineations in it. A man would reap very little benefit by his travels, if he made them only in his closet upon a map of the whole world. Next to the two books that I have already mentioned, I do not know a better for you to read, and seriously reflect upon, than 'Avis d'une Mere d'un Fils, par la Marquise de Lambert'.

She was a woman of a superior understanding and knowledge of the world, had always kept the best company, was solicitous that her son should make a figure and a fortune in the world, and knew better than anybody how to point out the means. It is very short, and will take you much less time to read, than you ought to employ in reflecting upon it, after you have read it. Her son was in the army, she wished he might rise there; but she well knew, that, in order to rise, he must first please: she says to him, therefore, With regard to those upon whom you depend, the chief merit is to please. And, in another place, in subaltern employments, the art of pleasing must be your support. Masters are like mistresses: whatever services they may be indebted to you for, they cease to love when you cease to be agreeable. This, I can assure you, is at least as true in courts as in camps, and possibly more so. If to your merit and knowledge you add the art of pleasing, you may very probably come in time to be Secretary of State; but, take my word for it, twice your merit and knowledge, without the art of pleasing, would, at most, raise you to the IMPORTANT POST of Resident at Hamburgh or Ratisbon. I need not tell you now, for I often have, and your own discernment must have told you, of what numberless little ingredients that art of pleasing is compounded, and how the want of the least of them lowers the whole; but the principal ingredient is, undoubtedly, 'la douceur dans le manieres': nothing will give you this more than keeping company with your superiors. Madame Lambert tells her son, Let your connections be with people above you; by that means you will acquire a habit of respect and politeness. With one's equals, one is apt to become negligent, and the mind grows torpid. She advises him, too, to frequent those people, and to see their inside; In order to judge of men, one must be intimately connected; thus you see them without, a veil, and with their mere every-day merit. A happy expression! It was for this reason that I have so often advised you to establish and domesticate yourself, wherever you can, in good houses of people above you, that you may see their EVERY-DAY character, manners, habits, etc. One must see people undressed to judge truly of their shape; when they are dressed to go abroad, their clothes are contrived to conceal, or at least palliate the defects of it: as full-bottomed wigs were contrived for the Duke of Burgundy, to conceal his hump back. Happy those who have no faults to disguise, nor weaknesses to conceal! there are few, if any such; but unhappy those who know little enough of the world to judge by outward appearances. Courts are the best keys to characters; there every passion is busy, every art exerted, every character analyzed; jealousy, ever watchful, not only discovers, but exposes, the mysteries of the trade, so that even bystanders 'y apprennent a deviner'. There too the great art of pleasing is practiced, taught, and learned with all its graces and delicacies. It is the first thing needful there: It is the absolutely necessary harbinger of merit and talents, let them be ever so great. There is no advancing a step without it. Let misanthropes and would-be philosophers declaim as much as they please against the vices, the simulation, and dissimulation of courts; those invectives are always the result of ignorance, ill-humor, or envy. Let them show me a cottage, where there are not the same vices of which they accuse courts; with this difference only, that in a cottage they appear in their native deformity, and that in courts, manners and good-breeding make them less shocking, and blunt their edge. No, be convinced that the good-breeding, the 'tournure, la douceur dans les manieres', which alone are to be acquired at courts, are not the showish trifles only which some people call or think them; they are a solid good; they prevent a great deal of real mischief; they create, adorn, and strengthen friendships; they keep hatred within bounds; they promote good-humor and good-will in families, where the want of good-breeding and gentleness of manners is commonly the original cause of discord. Get then, before it is too late, a habit of these 'mitiores virtutes': practice them upon every the least occasion, that they may be easy and familiar to you upon the greatest; for they lose a great degree of their merit if they seem labored, and only called in upon extraordinary occasions. I tell you truly, this is now the only doubtful part of your character with me; and it is for that reason that I dwell upon it so much, and inculcate it so often. I shall soon see whether this doubt of mine is founded; or rather I hope I shall soon see that it is not.

This moment I receive your letter of the 9th N. S. I am sorry to find that you have had, though ever so slight a return of your Carniolan disorder; and I hope your conclusion will prove a true one, and that this will be the last. I will send the mohairs by the first opportunity. As for the pictures, I am already so full, that I am resolved not to buy one more, unless by great accident I should meet with something surprisingly good, and as surprisingly cheap.

I should have thought that Lord————, at his age, and with his parts and address, need not have been reduced to keep an opera w——e, in such a place as Paris, where so many women of fashion generously serve as volunteers. I am still more sorry that he is in love with her; for that will take him out of good company, and sink him into bad; such as fiddlers, pipers, and 'id genus omne'; most unedifying and unbecoming company for a man of fashion!

Lady Chesterfield makes you a thousand compliments. Adieu, my dear child.

LETTER CXLVI

GREENWICH, June 10, O. S. 1751

MY DEAR FRIEND: Your ladies were so slow in giving their specific orders, that the mohairs, of which you at last sent me the patterns, were all sold. However, to prevent further delays (for ladies are apt to be very impatient, when at last they know their own minds), I have taken the quantities desired of three mohairs which come nearest to the description you sent me some time ago, in Madame Monconseil's own hand; and I will send them to Calais by the first opportunity. In giving 'la petite Blot' her piece, you have a fine occasion of saying fine things, if so inclined.

Lady Hervey, who is your puff and panegyrist, writes me word that she saw you lately dance at a ball, and that you dance very genteelly. I am extremely glad to hear it; for (by the maxim, that 'omne majus continet in se minus'), if you dance genteelly, I presume you walk, sit, and stand genteelly too; things which are much more easy, though much more necessary, than dancing well. I have known many very genteel people, who could not dance well; but I never knew anybody dance very well, who was not genteel in other things. You will probably often have occasion to stand in circles, at the levees of princes and ministers, when it is very necessary 'de payer de sa personne, et d'etre bien plante', with your feet not too near nor too distant from each other. More people stand and walk, than sit genteelly. Awkward, ill-bred people, being ashamed, commonly sit bolt upright and stiff; others, too negligent and easy, 'se vautrent dans leur fauteuil', which is ungraceful and ill-bred, unless where the familiarity is extreme; but a man of fashion makes himself easy, and appears so by leaning gracefully instead of lolling supinely; and by varying those easy attitudes instead of that stiff immobility of a bashful booby. You cannot conceive, nor can I express, how advantageous a good air, genteel motions, and engaging address are, not only among women, but among men, and even in the course of business; they fascinate the affections, they steal a preference, they play about the heart till they engage it. I know a man, and so do you, who, without a grain of merit, knowledge, or talents, has raised himself millions of degrees above his level, simply by a good air and engaging manners; insomuch that the very Prince who raised him so high, calls him, 'mon aimable vaut-rien';—[The Marichal de Richelieu.]—but of this do not open your lips, 'pour cause'. I give you this secret as the strongest proof imaginable of the efficacy of air, address, 'tournure, et tout ces Petits riens'.

Your other puff and panegyrist, Mr. Harte, is gone to Windsor in his way to Cornwall, in order to be back soon enough to meet you here: I really believe he is as impatient for that moment as I am, 'et c'est tout dire': but, however, notwithstanding my impatience, if by chance you should then be in a situation, that leaving Paris would cost your heart too many pangs, I allow you to put off your journey, and to tell me, as Festus did Paul, AT A MORE CONVENIENT SEASON I WILL SPEAK TO THEE. You see by this that I eventually sacrifice my sentiments to yours, and this in a very uncommon object of paternal complaisance. Provided always, and be it understood (as they say in acts of Parliament), that 'quae te cumque domat Venus, non erubescendis adurit ignibus'. If your heart will let you come, bring with you only your valet de chambre, Christian, and your own footman; not your valet de place, whom you may dismiss for the time, as also your coach; but you had best keep on your lodgings, the intermediate expense of which will be but inconsiderable, and you will want them to leave your books and baggage in. Bring only the clothes you travel in, one suit of black, for the mourning for the Prince will not be quite out by that time, and one suit of your fine clothes, two or three of your laced shirts, and the rest plain ones; of other things, as bags, feathers, etc., as you think proper. Bring no books, unless two or three for your' amusement upon the road; for we must apply simply to English, in which you are certainly no 'puriste'; and I will supply you sufficiently with the proper English authors. I shall probably keep you here till about the middle of October, and certainly not longer; it being absolutely necessary for you to pass the next winter at Paris; so that; should any fine eyes shed tears for your departure, you may dry them by the promise of your return in two months.

Have you got a master for geometry? If the weather is very hot, you may leave your riding at the 'manege' till you return to Paris, unless you think the exercise does you more good than the heat can do you harm; but I desire you will not leave off Marcel for one moment; your fencing likewise, if you have a mind, may subside for the summer; but you will do well to resume it in the winter and to be adroit at it, but by no means for offense, only for defense in case of necessity. Good night. Yours.

P. S. I forgot to give you one commission, when you come here; which is, not to fail bringing the GRACES along with you.

LETTERS TO HIS SON, COMPLETE

LETTER CXLVII

GREENWICH, June 13, O. S. 1751.

MY DEAR FRIEND: 'Les bienseances'—[This single word implies decorum, good-breeding, and propriety]—are a most necessary part of the knowledge of the world. They consist in the relations of persons, things, time, and place; good sense points them out, good company perfects them (supposing always an attention and a desire to please), and good policy recommends them.

Were you to converse with a king, you ought to be as easy and unembarrassed as with your own valet de chambre; but yet, every look, word and action, should imply the utmost respect. What would be proper and well-bred with others, much your superiors, would be absurd and ill-bred with one so very much so. You must wait till you are spoken to; you must receive, not give, the subject of conversation; and you must even take care that the given subject of such conversation do not lead you into any impropriety. The art would be to carry it, if possible, to some indirect flattery; such as commending those virtues in some other person, in which that prince either thinks he does, or at least would be thought by others to excel. Almost the same precautions are necessary to be used with ministers, generals, etc., who expect to be treated with very near the same respect as their masters, and commonly deserve it better. There is, however, this difference, that one may begin the conversation with them, if on their side it should happen to drop, provided one does not carry it to any subject upon which it is improper either for them to speak, or be spoken to. In these two cases, certain attitudes and actions would be extremely absurd, because too easy, and consequently disrespectful. As, for instance, if you were to put your arms across in your bosom, twirl your snuff-box, trample with your feet, scratch your head, etc., it would be shockingly ill-bred in that company; and, indeed, not extremely well-bred in any other. The great difficulty in those cases, though a very surmountable one by attention and custom, is to join perfect inward ease with perfect outward respect.

In mixed companies with your equals (for in mixed companies all people are to a certain degree equal), greater ease and liberty are allowed; but they too have their bounds within 'bienseance'. There is a social respect necessary: you may start your own subject of conversation with modesty, taking great care, however, 'de ne jamais parler de cordes dans la maison d'un pendu.—[Never to mention a rope in the family of a man who has been hanged]—Your words, gestures, and attitudes, have a greater degree of latitude, though by no means an unbounded one. You may have your hands in your pockets, take snuff, sit, stand, or occasionally walk, as you like; but I believe you would not think it very 'bienseant' to whistle, put on your hat, loosen your garters or your buckles, lie down upon a couch, or go to bed, and welter in an easychair. These are negligences and freedoms which one can only take when quite alone; they are injurious to superiors, shocking and offensive to equals, brutal and insulting to inferiors. That easiness of carriage and behavior, which is exceedingly engaging, widely differs from negligence and inattention, and by no means implies that one may do whatever one pleases; it only means that one is not to be stiff, formal, embarrassed, disconcerted, and ashamed, like country bumpkins, and, people who have never been in good company; but it requires great attention to, and a scrupulous observation of 'les bienseances': whatever one ought to do, is to be done with ease and unconcern; whatever is improper must not be done at all. In mixed companies also, different ages and sexes are to be differently addressed. You would not talk of your pleasures to men of a certain age, gravity, and dignity; they justly expect from young people a degree of deference and regard. You should be full as easy with them as with people of your own years: but your manner must be different; more respect must be implied; and it is not amiss to insinuate that from them you expect to learn. It flatters and comforts age for not being able to take a part in the joy and titter of youth. To women you should always address yourself with great outward respect and attention, whatever you feel inwardly; their sex is by long prescription entitled to it; and it is among the duties of 'bienseance'; at the same time that respect is very properly and very agreeably mixed with a degree of 'enjouement', if you have it; but then, that badinage must either directly or indirectly tend to their praise, and even not be liable to a malicious construction to their disadvantage. But here, too, great attention must be had to the difference of age, rank, and situation. A 'marechale' of fifty must not be played with like a young coquette of fifteen; respect and serious 'enjouement', if I may couple those two words, must be used with the former, and mere 'badinage, zeste meme d'un peu de polissonerie', is pardonable with the latter.

Another important point of 'les bienseances', seldom enough attended to, is, not to run your own present humor and disposition indiscriminately against everybody, but to observe, conform to, and adopt them. For example, if you happened to be in high good humor and a flow of spirits, would you go and sing a 'pont neuf',—[a ballad]—or cut a caper, to la Marechale de Coigny, the Pope's nuncio, or Abbe Sallier, or to any person of natural gravity and melancholy, or who at that time should be in grief? I believe not; as, on the other hand, I suppose, that if you were in low spirits or real grief, you would not choose to bewail your situation with 'la petite Blot'. If you cannot command your present humor and disposition, single out those to converse with, who happen to be in the humor the nearest to your own.

Loud laughter is extremely inconsistent with 'les bienseances', as it is only the illiberal and noisy testimony of the joy of the mob at some very silly thing. A gentleman is often seen, but very seldom heard to laugh. Nothing is more contrary to 'les bienseances' than horse-play, or 'jeux de main' of any kind whatever, and has often very serious, sometimes very fatal consequences. Romping, struggling, throwing things at one another's head, are the becoming pleasantries of the mob, but degrade a gentleman: 'giuoco di mano, giuoco di villano', is a very true saying, among the few true sayings of the Italians.

Peremptoriness and decision in young people is 'contraire aux bienseances', and they should seldom seem to assert, and always use some softening mitigating expression; such as, 's'il m'est permis de le dire, je croirais plutot, si j'ose m'expliquer', which soften the manner, without giving up or even weakening the thing. People of more age and experience expect, and are entitled to, that degree of deference.

There is a 'bienseance' also with regard to people of the lowest degree: a gentleman observes it with his footman—even with the beggar in the street. He considers them as objects of compassion, not of insult; he speaks to neither 'd'un ton brusque', but corrects the one coolly, and refuses the other with humanity. There is one occasion in the world in which 'le ton brusque' is becoming a gentleman. In short, 'les bienseances' are another word for MANNERS, and extend to every part of life. They are propriety; the Graces should attend, in order to complete them; the Graces enable us to do, genteelly and pleasingly, what 'les bienseances' require to be done at all. The latter are an obligation upon every man; the former are an infinite advantage and ornament to any man. May you unite both!

Though you dance well, do not think that you dance well enough, and consequently not endeavor to dance still better. And though you should be told that you are genteel, still aim at being genteeler. If Marcel should, do not you be satisfied. Go on, court the Graces all your lifetime; you will find no better friends at court: they will speak in your favor, to the hearts of princes, ministers, and mistresses.

Now that all tumultuous passions and quick sensations have subsided with me, and that I have no tormenting cares nor boisterous pleasures to agitate me, my greatest joy is to consider the fair prospect you have before you, and to hope and believe you will enjoy it. You are already in the world, at an age when others have hardly heard of it. Your character is hitherto not only unblemished in its mortal part, but even unsullied by any low, dirty, and ungentleman-like vice; and will, I hope, continue so. Your knowledge is sound, extensive and avowed, especially in everything relative to your destination. With such materials to begin with, what then is wanting! Not fortune, as you have found by experience. You have had, and shall have, fortune sufficient to assist your merit and your industry; and if I can help it, you never shall have enough to make you negligent of either. You have, too, 'mens sana in corpore sano', the greatest blessing of all. All, therefore, that you want is as much in your power to acquire, as to eat your breakfast when set before you; it is only that knowledge of the world, that elegance of manners, that universal politeness, and those graces which keeping good company, and seeing variety of places and characters, must inevitably, with the least attention on your part, give you. Your foreign destination leads to the greatest things, and your parliamentary situation will facilitate your progress. Consider, then, this pleasing prospect as attentively for yourself as I consider it for you. Labor on your part to realize it, as I will on mine to assist, and enable you to do it. 'Nullum numen abest, si sit prudentia'.

Adieu, my dear child! I count the days till I have the pleasure of seeing you; I shall soon count the hours, and at last the minutes, with increasing impatience.

P. S. The mohairs are this day gone from hence for Calais, recommended to the care of Madame Morel, and directed, as desired, to the Comptroller-general. The three pieces come to six hundred and eighty French livres.

LETTER CXLVIII

GREENWICH, June 20, O. S. 1751

MY DEAR FRIEND: So very few people, especially young travelers, see what they see, or hear what they hear, that though I really believe it may be unnecessary with you, yet there can be no harm in reminding you, from time to time, to see what you see, and to hear what you hear; that is, to see and hear as you should do. Frivolous, futile people, who make at least three parts in four of mankind, only desire to see and hear what their frivolous and futile precursors have seen and heard: as St. Peter's, the Pope, and High Mass, at Rome; Notre Dame, Versailles, the French King, and the French Comedy, in France. A man of parts sees and hears very differently from these gentlemen, and a great deal more. He examines and informs himself thoroughly of everything he sees or hears; and, more particularly, as it is relative to his own profession or destination. Your destination is political; the object, therefore, of your inquiries and observations should be the political interior of things; the forms of government, laws, regulations, customs, trade, manufactures, etc., of the several nations of Europe. This knowledge is much better acquired by conversation with sensible and well-informed people, than by books, the best of which upon these subjects are always imperfect. For example, there are "Present States" of France, as there are of England; but they are always defective, being published by people uninformed, who only copy one another; they are, however, worth looking into because they point out objects for inquiry, which otherwise might possibly never have occurred to one's mind; but an hour's conversation with a sensible president or 'conseiller' will let you more into the true state of the parliament of Paris, than all the books in France. In the same manner, the 'Almanack Militaire' is worth your having; but two or three conversations with officers will inform you much better of their military regulations. People have, commonly, a partiality for their own professions, love to talk of them, and are even flattered by being consulted upon the subject; when, therefore, you are with any of those military gentlemen (and you can hardly be in any company without some), ask them military questions, inquire into their methods of discipline, quartering, and clothing their men; inform yourself of their pay, their perquisites, 'lours montres, lours etapes', etc. Do the same as to the marine, and make yourself particularly master of that detail; which has, and always will have, a great relation to the affairs of England; and, in proportion as you get good informations, take minutes of them in writing.

The regulations of trade and commerce in France are excellent, as appears but too plainly for us, by the great increase of both, within these thirty years; for not to mention their extensive commerce in both the East and West Indies, they have got the whole trade of the Levant from us; and now supply all the foreign markets with their sugars, to the ruin almost of our sugar colonies, as Jamaica, Barbadoes, and the Leeward Islands. Get, therefore, what informations you can of these matters also.

Inquire too into their church matters; for which the present disputes between the court and the clergy give you fair and frequent opportunities. Know the particular rights of the Gallican church, in opposition to the pretensions of the See of Rome. I need not recommend ecclesiastical history to you, since I hear that you study 'Du Pin' very assiduously.

You cannot imagine how much this solid and useful knowledge of other countries will distinguish you in your own (where, to say the truth, it is very little known or cultivated), besides the great use it is of in all foreign negotiations; not to mention that it enables a man to shine in all companies. When kings and princes have any knowledge, it is of this sort, and more particularly; and therefore it is the usual topic of their levee conversations, in which it will qualify you to bear a considerable part; it brings you more acquainted with them; and they are pleased to have people talk to them on a subject in which they think to shine.

There is a sort of chit-chat, or SMALL TALK, which is the general run of conversation at courts, and in most mixed companies. It is a sort of middling conversation, neither silly nor edifying; but, however, very necessary for you to become master of. It turns upon the public events of Europe, and then is at its best; very often upon the number, the goodness or badness, the discipline, or the clothing of the troops of different princes; sometimes upon the families, the marriages, the relations of princes, and considerable people; and sometimes 'sur le bon chere', the magnificence of public entertainments, balls, masquerades, etc. I would wish you to be able to talk upon all these things better, and with more knowledge than other people; insomuch that upon those occasions, you should be applied to, and that people should say, I DARE SAY MR. STANHOPE CAN TELL US.

Second-rate knowledge and middling talents carry a man further at courts, and in the busy part of the world, than superior knowledge and shining parts. Tacitus very justly accounts for a man's having always kept in favor and enjoyed the best employments under the tyrannical reigns of three or four of the very worst emperors, by saying that it was not 'propter aliquam eximiam artem, sed quia par negotiis neque supra erat'. Discretion is the great article; all these things are to be learned, and only learned by keeping a great deal of the best company. Frequent those good houses where you have already a footing, and wriggle yourself somehow or other into every other. Haunt the courts particularly in order to get that ROUTINE.

This moment I receive yours of the 18th N. S. You will have had some time ago my final answers concerning the pictures; and, by my last, an account that the mohairs were gone to Madame Morel, at Calais, with the proper directions.

I am sorry that your two sons-in-law [?? D.W.], the Princes B——, are such boobies; however, as they have the honor of being so nearly related to you, I will show them what civilities I can.

I confess you have not time for long absences from Paris, at present, because of your various masters, all which I would have you apply to closely while you are now in that capital; but when you return thither, after the visit you intend me the honor of, I do not propose your having any master at all, except Marcel, once or twice a week. And then the courts will, I hope, be no longer strange countries to you; for I would have you run down frequently to Versailles and St. Cloud, for three or four days at a time. You know the Abbe de la Ville, who will present you to others, so that you will soon be 'faufile' with the rest of the court. Court is the soil in which you are to grow and flourish; you ought to be well acquainted with the nature of it; like all other soil, it is in some places deeper, in others lighter, but always capable of great improvement by cultivation and experience.

You say that you want some hints for a letter to Lady Chesterfield; more use and knowledge of the world will teach you occasionally to write and talk genteelly, 'sup des riens', which I can tell you is a very useful part upon worldly knowledge; for in some companies, it would be imprudent to talk of anything else; and with very many people it is impossible to talk of anything else; they would not understand you. Adieu.

LETTER CXLIX

LONDON, June 24, O. S. 1751

MY DEAR FRIEND: Air, address, manners, and graces are of such infinite advantage to whoever has them, and so peculiarly and essentially necessary for you, that now, as the time of our meeting draws near, I tremble for fear I should not find you possessed of them; and, to tell you the truth, I doubt you are not yet sufficiently convinced for their importance. There is, for instance, your intimate friend, Mr. H——, who with great merit, deep knowledge, and a thousand good qualities, will never make a figure in the world while he lives. Why? Merely for want of those external and showish accomplishments, which he began the world too late to acquire; and which, with his studious and philosophical turn, I believe he thinks are not worth his attention. He may, very probably, make a figure in the republic of letters, but he had ten thousand times better make a figure as a man of the world and of business in the republic of the United Provinces, which, take my word for it, he never will.

As I open myself, without the least reserve, whenever I think that my doing so can be of any use to you, I will give you a short account of myself. When I first came into the world, which was at the age you are of now, so that, by the way, you have got the start of me in that important article by two or three years at least,—at nineteen I left the University of Cambridge, where I was an absolute pedant; when I talked my best, I quoted Horace; when I aimed at being facetious, I quoted Martial; and when I had a mind to be a fine gentleman, I talked Ovid. I was convinced that none but the ancients had common sense; that the classics contained everything that was either necessary, useful, or ornamental to men; and I was not without thoughts of wearing the 'toga virilis' of the Romans, instead of the vulgar and illiberal dress of the moderns. With these excellent notions I went first to The Hague, where, by the help of several letters of recommendation, I was soon introduced into all the best company; and where I very soon discovered that I was totally mistaken in almost every one notion I had entertained. Fortunately, I had a strong desire to please (the mixed result of good-nature and a vanity by no means blamable), and was sensible that I had nothing but the desire. I therefore resolved, if possible, to acquire the means, too. I studied attentively and minutely the dress, the air, the manner, the address, and the turn of conversation of all those whom I found to be the people in fashion, and most generally allowed to please. I imitated them as well as I could; if I heard that one man was reckoned remarkably genteel, I carefully watched his dress, motions and attitudes, and formed my own upon them. When I heard of another, whose conversation was agreeable and engaging, I listened and attended to the turn of it. I addressed myself, though 'de tres mauvaise grace', to all the most fashionable fine ladies; confessed, and laughed with them at my own awkwardness and rawness, recommending myself as an object for them to try their skill in forming. By these means, and with a passionate desire of pleasing everybody, I came by degrees to please some; and, I can assure you, that what little figure I have made in the world, has been much more owing to that passionate desire of pleasing universally than to any intrinsic merit or sound knowledge I might ever have been master of. My passion for pleasing was so strong (and I am very glad it was so), that I own to you fairly, I wished to make every woman I saw in love with me, and every man I met with admire me. Without this passion for the object, I should never have been so attentive to the means; and I own I cannot conceive how it is possible for any man of good-nature and good sense to be without this passion. Does not good-nature incline us to please all those we converse with, of whatever rank or station they may be? And does not good sense and common observation, show of what infinite use it is to please? Oh! but one may please by the good qualities of the heart, and the knowledge of the head, without that fashionable air, address and manner, which is mere tinsel. I deny it. A man may be esteemed and respected, but I defy him to please without them. Moreover, at your age, I would not have contented myself with barely pleasing; I wanted to shine and to distinguish myself in the world as a man of fashion and gallantry, as well as business. And that ambition or vanity, call it what you please, was a right one; it hurt nobody, and made me exert whatever talents I had. It is the spring of a thousand right and good things.

I was talking you over the other day with one very much your friend, and who had often been with you, both at Paris and in Italy. Among the innumerable questions which you may be sure I asked him concerning you, I happened to mention your dress (for, to say the truth, it was the only thing of which I thought him a competent judge) upon which he said that you dressed tolerably well at Paris; but that in Italy you dressed so ill, that he used to joke with you upon it, and even to tear your clothes. Now, I must tell you, that at your age it is as ridiculous not to be very well dressed, as at my age it would be if I were to wear a white feather and red-heeled shoes. Dress is one of various ingredients that contribute to the art of pleasing; it pleases the eyes at least, and more especially of women. Address yourself to the senses, if you would please; dazzle the eyes, soothe and flatter the ears of mankind; engage their hearts, and let their reason do its worst against you. 'Suaviter in modo' is the great secret. Whenever you find yourself engaged insensibly, in favor of anybody of no superior merit nor distinguished talents, examine, and see what it is that has made those impressions upon you: and you will find it to be that 'douceur', that gentleness of manners, that air and address, which I have so often recommended to you; and from thence draw this obvious conclusion, that what pleases you in them, will please others in you; for we are all made of the same clay, though some of the lumps are a little finer, and some a little coarser; but in general, the surest way to judge of others, is to examine and analyze one's self thoroughly. When we meet I will assist you in that analysis, in which every man wants some assistance against his own self-love. Adieu.

LETTERS TO HIS SON, COMPLETE

LETTER CL

GREENWICH, June 30, O. S. 1751.

MY DEAR FRIEND: Pray give the inclosed to our friend the Abbe; it is to congratulate him upon his 'Canonicat', which I am really very glad of, and I hope it will fatten him up to Boileau's 'Chanoine'; at present he is as meagre as an apostle or a prophet. By the way, has he ever introduced you to la Duchesse d'Aiguillon? If he has not, make him present you; and if he has, frequent her, and make her many compliments from me. She has uncommon, sense and knowledge for a woman, and her house is the resort of one set of 'les beaux esprits. It is a satisfaction and a sort of credit to be acquainted with those gentlemen; and it puts a young fellow in fashion. 'A propos des beaux esprits', you have 'les entries' at Lady Sandwich's; who, old as she was, when I saw her last, had the strongest parts of any woman I ever knew in my life? If you are not acquainted with her, either the Duchesse d'Aiguillon or Lady Hervey can, and I dare say will; introduce you. I can assure you, it is very well worth your while, both upon her own account, and for the sake of the people of wit and learning who frequent her. In such companies there is always something to be learned as well as manners; the conversation turns upon something above trifles; some point of literature, criticism, history, etc., is discussed with ingenuity and good manners; for I must do the French people of learning justice; they are not bears, as most of ours are: they are gentlemen.

Our Abbe writes me word that you were gone to Compiegne: I am very glad of it; other courts must form you for your own. He tells me too, that you have left off riding at the 'manege'; I have no objection to that, it takes up a great deal of the morning; and if you have got a genteel and firm seat on horseback, it is enough for you, now that tilts and tournaments are laid aside. I suppose you have hunted at Compiegne. The King's hunting there, I am told, is a fine sight. The French manner of hunting is gentlemanlike; ours is only for bumpkins and boobies. The poor beasts are here pursued and run down by much greater beasts than themselves, and the true British fox-hunter is most undoubtedly a species appropriated and peculiar to this country, which no other part of the globe produces.

I hope you apply the time you have saved from the riding-house to useful more than to learned purposes; for I can assure you they are very different things. I would have you allow but one hour a-day for Greek; and that more to keep what you have than to increase it: by Greek, I mean useful Greek books, such as Demosthenes, Thucydides, etc., and not the poets, with whom you are already enough acquainted. Your Latin will take care of itself. Whatever more time you may have for reading, pray bestow it upon those books which are immediately relative to your destination; such as modern history, in the modern languages, memoirs, anecdotes, letters, negotiations, etc. Collect also, if you can, authentically, the present state of all the courts and countries in Europe, the characters of the kings and princes, their wives, their ministers, and their w——s; their several views, connections, and interests; the state of their FINANCES, their military force, their trade, manufactures, and commerce. That is the useful, the necessary knowledge for you, and indeed for every gentleman. But with all this, remember, that living books are much better than dead ones; and throw away no time (for it is thrown away) with the latter, which you can employ well with the former; for books must now be your only amusement, but, by no means your business. I had much rather that you were passionately in love with some determined coquette of condition (who would lead you a dance, fashion, supple, and polish you), than that you knew all Plato and Aristotle by heart: an hour at Versailles, Compiegne, or St. Cloud, is now worth more to you than three hours in your closet, with the best books that ever were written.

I hear the dispute between the court and the clergy is made up amicably, both parties have yielded something; the king being afraid of losing more of his soul, and the clergy more of their revenue. Those gentlemen are very skillful in making the most of the vices and the weaknesses of the laity. I hope you have read and informed yourself fully of everything relative to that affair; it is a very important question, in which the priesthood of every country in Europe is highly concerned. If you would be thoroughly convinced that their tithes are of divine institution, and their property the property of God himself, not to be touched by any power on earth, read Fra Paolo De Beneficiis, an excellent and short book; for which, and some other treaties against the court of Rome, he was stilettoed; which made him say afterward, upon seeing an anonymous book written against him by order of the Pope, 'Conosco bene to stile Romano'.

The parliament of Paris, and the states of Languedoc, will, I believe, hardly scramble off; having only reason and justice, but no terrors on their side. Those are political and constitutional questions that well deserve your attention and inquiries. I hope you are thoroughly master of them. It is also worth your while to collect and keep all the pieces written upon those subjects.

I hope you have been thanked by your ladies, at least, if not paid in money, for the mohairs, which I sent by a courier to Paris, some time ago, instead of sending them to Madame Morel, at Calais, as I told you I should. Do they like them; and do they like you the better for getting them? 'Le petite Blot devroit au moins payer de sa personne'. As for Madame de Polignac, I believe you will very willingly hold her excused from personal payment.

Before you return to England, pray go again to Orli, for two or three days, and also to St. Cloud, in order to secure a good reception there at your return. Ask the Marquis de Matignon too, if he has any orders for you in England, or any letters or packets for Lord Bolingbroke. Adieu! Go on and prosper.

LETTER CLI

GREENWICH, July 8, O. S. 1751.

MY DEAR FRIEND: The last mail brought me your letter of the 3d July, N. S. I am glad that you are so well with Colonel Yorke, as to be let into secret correspondences. Lord Albemarle's reserve to you is, I believe, more owing to his secretary than to himself; for you seem to be much in favor with him; and possibly too HE HAS NO VERY SECRET LETTERS to communicate. However, take care not to discover the least dissatisfaction upon this score: make the proper acknowledgments to Colonel Yorke, for what he does show you; but let neither Lord Albemarle nor his people perceive the least coldness on your part, upon account of what they do not show you. It is very often necessary, not to manifest all one feels. Make your court to, and connect yourself as much as possible with Colonel Yorke; he may be of great use to you hereafter; and when you take leave, not only offer to bring over any letters or packets, by way of security; but even ask, as a favor, to be the carrier of a letter from him to his father, the Chancellor. 'A propos' of your coming here; I confess that I am weakly impatient for it, and think a few days worth getting; I would, therefore, instead of the 25th of next month, N. S., which was the day that I some time ago appointed for your leaving Paris, have you set out on Friday the 20th of August, N. S.; in consequence of which you will be at Calais some time on the Sunday following, and probably at Dover within four-and-twenty hours afterward. If you land in the morning, you may, in a postchaise, get to Sittingborne that day; if you come on shore in the evening, you can only get to Canterbury, where you will be better lodged than at Dover. I will not have you travel in the night, nor fatigue and overheat yourself by running on fourscore miles the moment you land. You will come straight to Blackheath, where I shall be ready to meet you, and which is directly upon the Dover road to London; and we will go to town together, after you have rested yourself a day or two here. All the other directions, which I gave you in my former letter, hold still the same. But, notwithstanding this regulation, should you have any particular reasons for leaving Paris two or three days sooner or later, than the above mentioned, 'vous etes maitre'. Make all your arrangements at Paris for about a six weeks stay in England at farthest.

I had a letter the other day from Lord Huntingdon, of which one-half at least was your panegyric; it was extremely welcome to me from so good a hand. Cultivate that friendship; it will do you honor and give you strength. Connections, in our mixed parliamentary government, are of great use.

I send you here inclosed the particular price of each of the mohairs; but I do not suppose that you will receive a shilling for anyone of them. However, if any of your ladies should take an odd fancy to pay, the shortest way, in the course of business, is for you to keep the money, and to take so much less from Sir John Lambert in your next draught upon him.

I am very sorry to hear that Lady Hervey is ill. Paris does not seem to agree with her; she used to have great health here. 'A propos' of her; remember, when you are with me, not to mention her but when you and I are quite alone, for reasons which I will tell you when we meet: but this is only between you and me; and I desire that you will not so much as hint it to her, or to anybody else.

If old Kurzay goes to the valley of Jehoshaphat, I cannot help it; it will be an ease to our friend Madame Montconseil, who I believe maintains her, and a little will not satisfy her in any way.

Remember to bring your mother some little presents; they need not be of value, but only marks of your affection and duty for one who has always been tenderly fond of you. You may bring Lady Chesterfield a little Martin snuffbox of about five Louis; and you need bring over no other presents; you and I not wanting 'les petits presens pour entretenir l'amitee'.

Since I wrote what goes before, I have talked you over minutely with Lord Albemarle, who told me, that he could very sincerely commend you upon every article but one; but upon that one you were often joked, both by him and others. I desired to know what that was; he laughed and told me it was the article of dress, in which you were exceedingly negligent. Though he laughed, I can assure you that it is no laughing matter for you; and you will possibly be surprised when I assert (but, upon my word, it is literally true), that to be very well dressed is of much more importance to you, than all the Greek you know will, be of these thirty years. Remember that the world is now your only business; and that you must adopt its customs and manners, be they silly or be they not. To neglect your dress, is an affront to all the women you keep company with; as it implies that you do not think them worth that attention which everybody else doth; they mind dress, and you will never please them if you neglect yours; and if you do not please the women, you will not please half the men you otherwise might. It is the women who put a young fellow in fashion even with the men. A young fellow ought to have a certain fund of coquetry; which should make him try all the means of pleasing, as much as any coquette in Europe can do. Old as I am, and little thinking of women, God knows, I am very far from being negligent of my dress; and why? From conformity to custom, and out of decency to men, who expect that degree of complaisance. I do not, indeed, wear feathers and red heels, which would ill suit my age; but I take care to have my clothes well made, my wig well combed and powdered, my linen and person extremely clean. I even allow my footman forty shillings a year extraordinary, that they may be spruce and neat. Your figure especially, which from its stature cannot be very majestic and interesting, should be the more attended to in point of dress as it cannot be 'imposante', it should be 'gentile, aimable, bien mise'. It will not admit of negligence and carelessness.

I believe Mr. Hayes thinks that you have slighted him a little of late, since you have got into so much other company. I do not by any means blame you for not frequenting his house so much as you did at first, before you had got into so many other houses more entertaining and more instructing than his; on the contrary, you do very well; but, however, as he was extremely civil to you, take care to be so to him, and make up in manner what you omit in matter. See him, dine with him before you come away, and ask his commands for England.

Your triangular seal is done, and I have given it to an English gentleman, who sets out in a week for Paris, and who will deliver it to Sir John Lambert for you.

I cannot conclude this letter without returning again to the showish, the ornamental, the shining parts of your character; which, if you neglect, upon my word you will render the solid ones absolutely useless; nay, such is the present turn of the world, that some valuable qualities are even ridiculous, if not accompanied by the genteeler accomplishments. Plainness, simplicity, and quakerism, either in dress or manners, will by no means do; they must both be laced and embroidered; speaking, or writing sense, without elegance and turn, will be very little persuasive; and the best figure in the world, without air and address, will be very ineffectual. Some pedants may have told you that sound sense and learning stand in, need of no ornaments; and, to support that assertion, elegantly quote the vulgar proverb, that GOOD WINE NEEDS NO BUSH; but surely the little experience you have already had of the world must have convinced you that the contrary of that assertion is true. All those accomplishments are now in your power; think of them, and of them only. I hope you frequent La Foire St. Laurent, which I see is now open; you will improve more by going there with your mistress, than by staying at home and reading Euclid with your geometry master. Adieu. 'Divertissez-vous, il n'y a rien de tel'.

LETTER CLII

GREENWICH, July 15, O. S. 1751

MY DEAR FRIEND: As this is the last, or last letter but one, that I think I shall write before I have the pleasure of seeing you here, it may not be amiss to prepare you a little for our interview, and for the time we shall pass together. Before kings and princes meet, ministers on each side adjust the important points of precedence, arm chairs, right hand and left, etc., so that they know previously what they are to expect, what they have to trust to; and it is right they should; for they commonly envy or hate, but most certainly distrust each other. We shall meet upon very different terms; we want no such preliminaries: you know my tenderness, I know your affection. My only object, therefore, is to make your short stay with me as useful as I can to you; and yours, I hope, is to co-operate with me. Whether, by making it wholesome, I shall make it pleasant to you, I am not sure. Emetics and cathartics I shall not administer, because I am sure you do not want them; but for alteratives you must expect a great many; and I can tell you that I have a number of NOSTRUMS, which I shall communicate to nobody but yourself. To speak without a metaphor, I shall endeavor to assist your youth with all the experience that I have purchased, at the price of seven and fifty years. In order to this, frequent reproofs, corrections, and admonitions will be necessary; but then, I promise you, that they shall be in a gentle, friendly, and secret manner; they shall not put you out of countenance in company, nor out of humor when we are alone. I do not expect that, at nineteen, you should have that knowledge of the world, those manners, that dexterity, which few people have at nine-and-twenty. But I will endeavor to give them you; and I am sure you will endeavor to learn them, as far as your youth, my experience, and the time we shall pass together, will allow. You may have many inaccuracies (and to be sure you have, for who has not at your age?) which few people will tell you of, and some nobody can tell you of but myself. You may possibly have others, too, which eyes less interested, and less vigilant than mine, do not discover; all those you shall hear of from one whose tenderness for you will excite his curiosity and sharpen his penetration. The smallest inattention or error in manners, the minutest inelegance of diction, the least awkwardness in your dress and carriage, will not escape my observation, nor pass without amicable correction. Two, the most intimate friends in the world, can freely tell each other their faults, and even their crimes, but cannot possibly tell each other of certain little weaknesses; awkwardnesses, and blindnesses of self-love; to authorize that unreserved freedom, the relation between us is absolutely necessary. For example, I had a very worthy friend, with whom I was intimate enough to tell him his faults; he had but few; I told him of them; he took it kindly of me, and corrected them. But then, he had some weaknesses that I could never tell him of directly, and which he was so little sensible of himself, that hints of them were lost upon him. He had a scrag neck, of about a yard long; notwithstanding which, bags being in fashion, truly he would wear one to his wig, and did so; but never behind him, for, upon every motion of his head, his bag came forward over one shoulder or the other. He took it into his head too, that he must occasionally dance minuets, because other people did; and he did so, not only extremely ill, but so awkward, so disjointed, slim, so meagre, was his figure, that had he danced as well as ever Marcel did, it would have been ridiculous in him to have danced at all. I hinted these things to him as plainly as friendship would allow, and to no purpose; but to have told him the whole, so as to cure him, I must have been his father, which, thank God, I am not. As fathers commonly go, it is seldom a misfortune to be fatherless; and, considering the general run of sons, as seldom a misfortune to be childless. You and I form, I believe, an exception to that rule; for, I am persuaded that we would neither of us change our relation, were it in our power. You will, I both hope and believe, be not only the comfort, but the pride of my age; and, I am sure, I will be the support, the friend, the guide of your youth. Trust me without reserve; I will advise you without private interest, or secret envy. Mr. Harte will do so too; but still there may be some little things proper for you to know, and necessary for you to correct, which even his friendship would not let him tell you of so freely as I should; and some, of which he may not possibly be so good a judge of as I am, not having lived so much in the great world.

One principal topic of our conversation will be, not only the purity but the elegance of the English language; in both which you are very deficient. Another will be the constitution of this country, of which, I believe, you know less than of most other countries in Europe. Manners, attentions, and address, will also be the frequent subjects of our lectures; and whatever I know of that important and necessary art, the art of pleasing. I will unreservedly communicate to you. Dress too (which, as things are, I can logically prove, requires some attention) will not always escape our notice. Thus, my lectures will be more various, and in some respects more useful than Professor Mascow's, and therefore, I can tell you, that I expect to be paid for them; but, as possibly you would not care to part with your ready money, and as I do not think that it would be quite handsome in me to accept it, I will compound for the payment, and take it in attention and practice.

Pray remember to part with all your friends, acquaintances, and mistresses, if you have any at Paris, in such a manner as may make them not only willing but impatient to see you there again. Assure them of your desire of returning to them; and do it in a manner that they may think you in earnest, that is 'avec onction et une espece d'attendrissement'. All people say, pretty near the same things upon those occasions; it is the manner only that makes the difference; and that difference is great. Avoid, however, as much as you can, charging yourself with commissions, in your return from hence to Paris; I know, by experience, that they are exceedingly troublesome, commonly expensive, and very seldom satisfactory at last, to the persons who gave them; some you cannot refuse, to people to whom you are obliged, and would oblige in your turn; but as to common fiddle-faddle commissions, you may excuse yourself from them with truth, by saying that you are to return to Paris through Flanders, and see all those great towns; which I intend you shall do, and stay a week or ten days at Brussels. Adieu! A good journey to you, if this is my last; if not, I can repeat again what I shall wish constantly.

EARL OF PHILIP DORMER STANHOPE CHESTERFIELD

LETTER CLIII

LONDON, December 19, O. S. 1751—[Note the date, which indicates that the sojourn with the author has ended.]

MY DEAR FRIEND: You are now entered upon a scene of business, where I hope you will one day make a figure. Use does a great deal, but care and attention must be joined to it. The first thing necessary in writing letters of business, is extreme clearness and perspicuity; every paragraph should be so clear and unambiguous, that the dullest fellow in the world may not be able to mistake it, nor obliged to read it twice in order to understand it. This necessary clearness implies a correctness, without excluding an elegance of style. Tropes, figures, antitheses, epigrams, etc., would be as misplaced and as impertinent in letters of business, as they are sometimes (if judiciously used) proper and pleasing in familiar letters, upon common and trite subjects. In business, an elegant simplicity, the result of care, not of labor, is required. Business must be well, not affectedly dressed; but by no means negligently. Let your first attention be to clearness, and read every paragraph after you have written it, in the critical view of discovering whether it is possible that any one man can mistake the true sense of it: and correct it accordingly.

Our pronouns and relatives often create obscurity or ambiguity; be therefore exceedingly attentive to them, and take care to mark out with precision their particular relations. For example, Mr. Johnson acquainted me that he had seen Mr. Smith, who had promised him to speak to Mr. Clarke, to return him (Mr. Johnson) those papers, which he (Mr. Smith) had left some time ago with him (Mr. Clarke): it is better to repeat a name, though unnecessarily, ten times, than to have the person mistaken once. WHO, you know, is singly relative to persons, and cannot be applied to things; WHICH and THAT are chiefly relative to things, but not absolutely exclusive of persons; for one may say, the man THAT robbed or killed such-a-one; but it is better to say, the man WHO robbed or killed. One never says, the man or the woman WHICH. WHICH and THAT, though chiefly relative to things, cannot be always used indifferently as to things, and the 'euoovca' must sometimes determine their place. For instance, the letter WHICH I received from you, WHICH you referred to in your last, WHICH came by Lord Albemarle's messenger WHICH I showed to such-a-one; I would change it thus—The letter THAT I received from you; WHICH you referred to in your last, THAT came by Lord Albemarle's messenger, and WHICH I showed to such-a-one.

Business does not exclude (as possibly you wish it did) the usual terms of politeness and good-breeding; but, on the contrary, strictly requires them: such as, I HAVE THE HONOR TO ACQUAINT YOUR LORDSHIP; PERMIT ME TO ASSURE YOU; IF I MAY BE ALLOWED TO GIVE MY OPINION, etc. For the minister abroad, who writes to the minister at home, writes to his superior; possibly to his patron, or at least to one who he desires should be so.

Letters of business will not only admit of, but be the better for CERTAIN GRACES—but then, they must be scattered with a sparing and skillful hand; they must fit their place exactly. They must decently adorn without encumbering, and modestly shine without glaring. But as this is the utmost degree of perfection in letters of business, I would not advise you to attempt those embellishments, till you have first laid your foundation well.

Cardinal d'Ossat's letters are the true letters of business; those of Monsieur d'Avaux are excellent; Sir William Temple's are very pleasing, but, I fear, too affected. Carefully avoid all Greek or Latin quotations; and bring no precedents from the VIRTUOUS SPARTANS, THE POLITE ATHENIANS, AND THE BRAVE ROMANS. Leave all that to futile pedants. No flourishes, no declamation. But (I repeat it again) there is an elegant simplicity and dignity of style absolutely necessary for good letters of business; attend to that carefully. Let your periods be harmonious, without seeming to be labored; and let them not be too long, for that always occasions a degree of obscurity. I should not mention correct orthography, but that you very often fail in that particular, which will bring ridicule upon you; for no man is allowed to spell ill. I wish too that your handwriting were much better; and I cannot conceive why it is not, since every man may certainly write whatever hand he pleases. Neatness in folding up, sealing, and directing your packets, is by no means to be neglected; though, I dare say, you think it is. But there is something in the exterior, even of a packet, that may please or displease; and consequently worth some attention.

You say that your time is very well employed; and so it is, though as yet only in the outlines, and first ROUTINE of business. They are previously necessary to be known; they smooth the way for parts and dexterity. Business requires no conjuration nor supernatural talents, as people unacquainted with it are apt to think. Method, diligence, and discretion, will carry a man, of good strong common sense, much higher than the finest parts, without them, can do. 'Par negotiis, neque supra', is the true character of a man of business; but then it implies ready attention and no ABSENCES, and a flexibility and versatility of attention from one object to another, without being engrossed by anyone.

Be upon your guard against the pedantry and affectation of business which young people are apt to fall into, from the pride of being concerned in it young. They look thoughtful, complain of the weight of business, throw out mysterious hints, and seem big with secrets which they do not know. Do you, on the contrary, never talk of business but to those with whom you are to transact it; and learn to seem vacuus and idle, when you have the most business. Of all things, the 'volte sciollo', and the 'pensieri stretti', are necessary. Adieu.

LETTER CLIV

LONDON, December 30, O. S. 1751

MY DEAR FRIEND: The parliaments are the courts of justice of France, and are what our courts of justice in Westminster-Hall are here. They used anciently to follow the court, and administer justice in presence of the King. Philip le Bel first fixed it at Paris, by an edict of 1302. It consisted then of but one chambre, which was called 'la Chambre des Prelats', most of the members being ecclesiastics; but the multiplicity of business made it by degrees necessary to create several other chambres. It consists now of seven chambres:

'La Grande Chambre', which is the highest court of justice, and to which appeals lie from the others.

'Les cinq Chambres des Enquetes', which are like our Common Pleas, and Court of Exchequer.

'La Tournelle', which is the court for criminal justice, and answers to our Old Bailey and King's Bench.

There are in all twelve parliaments in France: 1. Paris 2. Toulouse 3. Grenoble 4. Bourdeaux 5. Dijon 6. Rouen 7. Aix en Provence 8. Rennes en Bretagne 9. Pau en Navarre 10. Metz 11. Dole en Franche Comte 12. Douay

There are three 'Conseils Souverains', which may almost be called parliaments; they are those of:

Perpignan Arras Alsace

For further particulars of the French parliaments, read 'Bernard de la Rochefavin des Parlemens de France', and other authors, who have treated that subject constitutionally. But what will be still better, converse upon it with people of sense and knowledge, who will inform you of the particular objects of the several chambres, and the businesses of the respective members, as, 'les Presidens, les Presidens a Mortier' (these last so called from their black velvet caps laced with gold), 'les Maitres tres des Requetes, les Greffiers, le Procureur General, les Avocats Generaux, les Conseillers', etc. The great point in dispute is concerning the powers of the parliament of Paris in matters of state, and relatively to the Crown. They pretend to the powers of the States-General of France when they used to be assembled (which, I think, they have not been since the reign of Lewis the Thirteenth, in the year 1615). The Crown denies those pretensions, and considers them only as courts of justice. Mezeray seems to be on the side of the parliament in this question, which is very well worth your inquiry. But, be that as it will, the parliament of Paris is certainly a very respectable body, and much regarded by the whole kingdom. The edicts of the Crown, especially those for levying money on the subjects, ought to be registered in parliament; I do not say to have their effect, for the Crown would take good care of that; but to have a decent appearance, and to procure a willing acquiescence in the nation. And the Crown itself, absolute as it is, does not love that strong opposition, and those admirable remonstrances, which it sometimes meets with from the parliaments. Many of those detached pieces are very well worth your collecting; and I remember, a year or two ago, a remonstrance of the parliament of Douay, upon the subject, as I think, of the 'Vingtieme', which was in my mind one of the finest and most moving compositions I ever read. They owned themselves, indeed, to be slaves, and showed their chains: but humbly begged of his Majesty to make them a little lighter, and less galling.

THE STATES OF FRANCE were general assemblies of the three states or orders of the kingdom; the Clergy, the Nobility, and the 'Tiers Etat', that is, the people. They used to be called together by the King, upon the most important affairs of state, like our Lords and Commons in parliament, and our Clergy in convocation. Our parliament is our states, and the French parliaments are only their courts of justice. The Nobility consisted of all those of noble extraction, whether belonging to the SWORD or to the ROBE, excepting such as were chosen (which sometimes happened) by the Tiers Etat as their deputies to the States-General. The Tiers Etat was exactly our House of Commons, that is, the people, represented by deputies of their own choosing. Those who had the most considerable places, 'dans la robe', assisted at those assemblies, as commissioners on the part of the Crown. The States met, for the first time that I can find (I mean by the name of 'les etats'), in the reign of Pharamond, 424, when they confirmed the Salic law. From that time they have been very frequently assembled, sometimes upon important occasions, as making war and peace, reforming abuses, etc.; at other times, upon seemingly trifling ones, as coronations, marriages, etc. Francis the First assembled them, in 1526, to declare null and void his famous treaty of Madrid, signed and sworn to by him during his captivity there. They grew troublesome to the kings and to their ministers, and were but seldom called after the power of the Crown grew strong; and they have never been heard of since the year 1615. Richelieu came and shackled the nation, and Mazarin and Lewis the Fourteenth riveted the shackles.

There still subsist in some provinces in France, which are called 'pais d etats', an humble local imitation, or rather mimicry, of the great 'etats', as in Languedoc, Bretagne, etc. They meet, they speak, they grumble, and finally submit to whatever the King orders.

Independently of the intrinsic utility of this kind of knowledge to every man of business, it is a shame for any man to be ignorant of it, especially relatively to any country he has been long in. Adieu.

1752

LETTER CLV

LONDON, January 2, O. S. 1752.

MY DEAR FRIEND: Laziness of mind, or inattention, are as great enemies to knowledge as incapacity; for, in truth, what difference is there between a man who will not, and a man who cannot be informed? This difference only, that the former is justly to be blamed, the latter to be pitied. And yet how many there are, very capable of receiving knowledge, who from laziness, inattention, and incuriousness, will not so much as ask for it, much less take the least pains to acquire it!

Our young English travelers generally distinguish themselves by a voluntary privation of all that useful knowledge for which they are sent abroad; and yet, at that age, the most useful knowledge is the most easy to be acquired; conversation being the book, and the best book in which it is contained. The drudgery of dry grammatical learning is over, and the fruits of it are mixed with, and adorned by, the flowers of conversation. How many of our young men have been a year at Rome, and as long at Paris, without knowing the meaning and institution of the Conclave in the former, and of the parliament in the latter? and this merely for want of asking the first people they met with in those several places, who could at least have given them some general notions of those matters.

You will, I hope, be wiser, and omit no opportunity (for opportunities present themselves every hour of the day) of acquainting yourself with all those political and constitutional particulars of the kingdom and government of France. For instance, when you hear people mention le Chancelier, or 'le Garde de Sceaux', is it any great trouble for you to ask, or for others to tell you, what is the nature, the powers, the objects, and the profits of those two employments, either when joined together, as they often are, or when separate, as they are at present? When you hear of a gouverneur, a lieutenant du Roi, a commandant, and an intendant of the same province, is, it not natural, is it not becoming, is it not necessary, for a stranger to inquire into their respective rights and privileges? And yet, I dare say, there are very few Englishmen who know the difference between the civil department of the Intendant, and the military powers of the others. When you hear (as I am persuaded you must) every day of the 'Vingtieme', which is one in twenty, and consequently five per cent., inquire upon what that tax is laid, whether upon lands, money, merchandise, or upon all three; how levied, and what it is supposed to produce. When you find in books: (as you will sometimes) allusion to particular laws and customs, do not rest till you have traced them up to their source. To give you two examples: you will meet in some French comedies, 'Cri', or 'Clameur de Haro'; ask what it means, and you will be told that it is a term of the law in Normandy, and means citing, arresting, or obliging any person to appear in the courts of justice, either upon a civil or a criminal account; and that it is derived from 'a Raoul', which Raoul was anciently Duke of Normandy, and a prince eminent for his justice; insomuch, that when any injustice was committed, the cry immediately was, 'Venez, a Raoul, a Raoul', which words are now corrupted and jumbled into 'haro'. Another, 'Le vol du Chapon, that is, a certain district of ground immediately contiguous to the mansion-seat of a family, and answers to what we call in English DEMESNES. It is in France computed at about 1,600 feet round the house, that being supposed to be the extent of the capon's flight from 'la basse cour'. This little district must go along with the mansion-seat, however the rest of the estate may be divided.

I do not mean that you should be a French lawyer; but I would not have you unacquainted with the general principles of their law, in matters that occur every day: Such is the nature of their descents, that is, the inheritance of lands: Do they all go to the eldest son, or are they equally divided among the children of the deceased? In England, all lands unsettled descend to the eldest son, as heir-at-law, unless otherwise disposed of by the father's will, except in the county of Kent, where a particular custom prevails, called Gavelkind; by which, if the father dies intestate, all his children divide his lands equally among them. In Germany, as you know, all lands that, are not fiefs are equally divided among all the children, which ruins those families; but all male fiefs of the empire descend unalienably to the next male heir, which preserves those families. In France, I believe, descents vary in different provinces.

The nature of marriage contracts deserves inquiry. In England, the general practice is, the husband takes all the wife's fortune; and in consideration of it settles upon her a proper pin-money, as it is called; that is, an annuity during his life, and a jointure after his death. In France it is not so, particularly at Paris; where 'la communaute des biens' is established. Any married woman at Paris (IF YOU ARE ACQUAINTED WITH ONE) can inform you of all these particulars.

These and other things of the same nature, are the useful and rational objects of the curiosity of a man of sense and business. Could they only be attained by laborious researches in folio-books, and wormeaten manuscripts, I should not wonder at a young fellow's being ignorant of them; but as they are the frequent topics of conversation, and to be known by a very little degree of curiosity, inquiry and attention, it is unpardonable not to know them.

Thus I have given you some hints only for your inquiries; 'l'Etat de la France, l'Almanach Royal', and twenty other such superficial books, will furnish you with a thousand more. 'Approfondissez.'

LETTERS TO HIS SON, COMPLETE

How often, and how justly, have I since regretted negligences of this kind in my youth! And how often have I since been at great trouble to learn many things which I could then have learned without any! Save yourself now, then, I beg of you, that regret and trouble hereafter. Ask questions, and many questions; and leave nothing till you are thoroughly informed of it. Such pertinent questions are far from being illbred or troublesome to those of whom you ask them; on the contrary, they are a tacit compliment to their knowledge; and people have a better opinion of a young man, when they see him desirous to be informed.

I have by last post received your two letters of the 1st and 5th of January, N. S. I am very glad that you have been at all the shows at Versailles: frequent the courts. I can conceive the murmurs of the French at the poorness of the fireworks, by which they thought their king of their country degraded; and, in truth, were things always as they should be, when kings give shows they ought to be magnificent.

I thank you for the 'These de la Sorbonne', which you intend to send me, and which I am impatient to receive. But pray read it carefully yourself first; and inform yourself what the Sorbonne is by whom founded, and for what puraoses.

Since you have time, you have done very well to take an Italian and a German master; but pray take care to leave yourelf time enough for company; for it is in company only that you can learn what will be much more useful to you than either Italian or German; I mean 'la politesse, les manieres et les graces, without which, as I told you long ago, and I told you true, 'ogni fatica a vana'. Adieu.

Pray make my compliments to Lady Brown.

LETTER CLVI

LONDON, January 6, O. S. 1752. MY DEAR FRIEND

I recommended to you, in my last, some inquiries into the constitution of that famous society the Sorbonne; but as I cannot wholly trust to the diligence of those inquiries, I will give you here the outlines of that establishment; which may possibly excite you to inform yourself of particulars, which you are more 'a portee' to know than I am.

It was founded by Robert de Sorbon, in the year 1256 for sixteen poor scholars in divinity; four of each nation, of the university of which it made a part; since that it hath been much extended and enriched, especially by the liberality and pride of Cardinal Richelieu; who made it a magnificent building for six-and-thirty doctors of that society to live in; besides which, there are six professors and schools for divinity. This society has long been famous for theological knowledge and exercitations. There unintelligible points are debated with passion, though they can never be determined by reason. Logical subtilties set common sense at defiance; and mystical refinements disfigure and disguise the native beauty and simplicity of true natural religion; wild imaginations form systems, which weak minds adopt implicitly, and which sense and reason oppose in vain; their voice is not strong enough to be heard in schools of divinity. Political views are by no means neglected in those sacred places; and questions are agitated and decided, according to the degree of regard, or rather submission, which the Sovereign is pleased to show the Church. Is the King a slave to the Church, though a tyrant to the laity? The least resistance to his will shall be declared damnable. But if he will not acknowledge the superiority of their spiritual over his temporal, nor even admit their 'imperium in imperio', which is the least they will compound for, it becomes meritorious not only to resist, but to depose him. And I suppose that the bold propositions in the thesis you mention, are a return for the valuation of 'les biens du Clergé'.

I would advise you, by all means, to attend to two or three of their public disputations, in order to be informed both of the manner and the substance of those scholastic exercises. Pray remember to go to all those kind of things. Do not put it off, as one is too apt to do those things which one knows can be done every day, or any day; for one afterward repents extremely, when too late, the not having done them.

But there is another (so-called) religious society, of which the minutest circumstance deserves attention, and furnishes great matter for useful reflections. You easily guess that I mean the society of 'les R. R. P. P. Jesuites', established but in the year 1540, by a Bull of Pope Paul III. Its progress, and I may say its victories, were more rapid than those of the Romans; for within the same century it governed all Europe; and, in the next, it extended its influence over the whole world. Its founder was an abandoned profligate Spanish officer, Ignatius Loyola; who, in the year 1521, being wounded in the leg at the 'siege of Pampeluna, went mad from the smart of his wound, the reproaches of his conscience, and his confinement, during which he read the lives of the Saints. Consciousness of guilt, a fiery temper, and a wild imagination, the common ingredients of enthusiasm, made this madman devote himself to the particular service of the Virgin Mary; whose knight-errant he declared himself, in the very same form in which the old knight-errants in romances used to declare themselves the knights and champions of certain beautiful and incomparable princesses, whom sometimes they had, but oftener had not, seen. For Dulcinea del Toboso was by no means the first princess whom her faithful and valorous knight had never seen in his life. The enthusiast went to the Holy Land, from whence he returned to Spain, where he began to learn Latin and philosophy at three-and-thirty years old, so that no doubt but he made great progress in both. The better to carry on his mad and wicked designs, he chose four disciples, or rather apostles, all Spaniards, viz, Laynes, Salmeron, Bobadilla, and Rodriguez. He then composed the rules and constitutions of his order; which, in the year 1547, was called the order of Jesuits, from the church of Jesus in Rome, which was given them. Ignatius died in 1556, aged sixty-five, thirty-five years after his conversion, and sixteen years after the establishment of his society. He was canonized in the year 1609, and is doubtless now a saint in heaven.

If the religious and moral principles of this society are to be detested, as they justly are, the wisdom of their political principles is as justly to be admired. Suspected, collectively as an order, of the greatest crimes, and convicted of many, they have either escaped punishment, or triumphed after it; as in France, in the reign of Henry IV. They have, directly or indirectly, governed the consciences and the councils of all the Catholic princes in Europe; they almost governed China in the reign of Cangghi; and they are now actually in possession of the Paraguay in America, pretending, but paying no obedience to the Crown of Spain. As a collective body they are detested, even by all the Catholics, not excepting the clergy, both secular and regular, and yet, as individuals, they are loved, respected, and they govern wherever they are.

Two things, I believe, contribute to their success. The first, that passive, implicit, unlimited obedience to their General (who always resides at Rome), and to the superiors of their several houses, appointed by him. This obedience is observed by them all to a most astonishing degree; and, I believe, there is no one society in the world, of which so many individuals sacrifice their private interest to the general one of the society itself. The second is the education of youth, which they have in a manner engrossed; there they give the first, and the first are the lasting impressions; those impressions are always calculated to be favorable to the society. I have known many Catholics, educated by the Jesuits, who, though they detested the society, from reason and knowledge, have always remained attached to it, from habit and prejudice. The Jesuits know, better than any set of people in the world, the importance of the art of pleasing, and study it more; they become all things to all men in order to gain, not a few, but many. In Asia, Africa, and America they become more than half pagans, in order to convert the pagans to be less than half Christians. In private families they begin by insinuating themselves as friends, they grow to be favorites, and they end DIRECTORS. Their manners are not like those of any other regulars in the world, but gentle, polite, and engaging. They are all carefully bred up to that particular destination, to which they seem to have a natural turn; for which reason one sees most Jesuits excel in some particular thing. They even breed up some for martyrdom in case of need; as the superior of a Jesuit seminary at Rome told Lord Bolingbroke. 'E abbiamo anche martiri per il martirio, se bisogna'.

Inform yourself minutely of everything concerning this extraordinary establishment; go into their houses, get acquainted with individuals, hear some of them preach. The finest preacher I ever heard in my life is le Pere Neufville, who, I believe, preaches still at Paris, and is so much in the best company, that you may easily get personally acquainted with him.

If you would know their 'morale' read Pascal's 'Lettres Provinciales', in which it is very truly displayed from their own writings.

Upon the whole, this is certain, that a society of which so little good is said, and so much ill believed, and that still not only subsists, but flourishes, must be a very able one. It is always mentioned as a proof of the superior abilities of the Cardinal Richelieu, that, though hated by all the nation, and still more by his master, he kept his power in spite of both.

I would earnestly wish you to do everything now, which I wish, that I had done at your age, and did not do. Every country has its peculiarities, which one can be much better informed of during one's residence there, than by reading all the books in the world afterward. While you are in Catholic countries, inform yourself of all the forms and ceremonies of that tawdry church; see their converts both of men and women, know their several rules and orders, attend their most remarkable ceremonies; have their terms of art explained to you, their 'tierce, sexte, nones, matines; vepres, complies'; their 'breviares, rosaires, heures, chapelets, agnus', etc., things that many people talk of from habit, though few people know the true meaning of anyone of them. Converse with, and study the characters of some of those incarcerated enthusiasts. Frequent some 'parloirs', and see the air and manners of those Recluse, who are a distinct nation themselves, and like no other.

I dined yesterday with Mrs. F——d, her mother and husband. He is an athletic Hibernian, handsome in his person, but excessively awkward and vulgar in his air and manner. She inquired much after you, and, I thought, with interest. I answered her as a 'Mezzano' should do: 'Et je pronai votre tendresse, vos soins, et vos soupirs'.

When you meet with any British returning to their own country, pray send me by them any little 'brochures, factums, theses', etc., 'qui font du bruit ou du plaisir a Paris'. Adieu, child.

LETTER CLVII

LONDON, January 23, O. S. 1752.

MY DEAR FRIEND: Have you seen the new tragedy of Varon,—[Written by the Vicomte de Grave; and at that time the general topic of conversation at Paris.]—and what do you think of it? Let me know, for I am determined to form my taste upon yours. I hear that the situations and incidents are well brought on, and the catastrophe unexpected and surprising, but the verses bad. I suppose it is the subject of all conversations at Paris, where both women and men are judges and critics of all such performances; such conversations, that both form and improve the taste, and whet the judgment; are surely preferable to the conversations of our mixed companies here; which, if they happen to rise above bragg and whist, infallibly stop short of everything either pleasing or instructive.

I take the reason of this to be, that (as women generally give the 'ton' to the conversation) our English women are not near so well informed and cultivated as the French; besides that they are naturally more serious and silent.

I could wish there were a treaty made between the French and English theatres, in which both parties should make considerable concessions. The English ought to give up their notorious violations of all the unities; and all their massacres, racks, dead bodies, and mangled carcasses, which they so frequently exhibit upon their stage. The French should engage to have more action and less declamation; and not to cram and crowd things together, to almost a degree of impossibility, from a too scrupulous adherence to the unities. The English should restrain the licentiousness of their poets, and the French enlarge the liberty of theirs; their poets are the greatest slaves in their country, and that is a bold word; ours are the most tumultuous subjects in England, and that is saying a good deal. Under such regulations one might hope to see a play in which one should not be lulled to sleep by the length of a monotonical declamation, nor frightened and shocked by the barbarity of the action. The unity of time extended occasionally to three or four days, and the unity of place broke into, as far as the same street, or sometimes the same town; both which, I will affirm, are as probable as four-and-twenty hours, and the same room.

More indulgence too, in my mind, should be shown, than the French are willing to allow, to bright thoughts, and to shining images; for though, I confess, it is not very natural for a hero or a princess to say fine things in all the violence of grief, love, rage, etc., yet, I can as well suppose that, as I can that they should talk to themselves for half an hour; which they must necessarily do, or no tragedy could be carried on, unless they had recourse to a much greater absurdity, the choruses of the ancients. Tragedy is of a nature, that one must see it with a degree of self-deception; we must lend ourselves a little to the delusion; and I am very willing to carry that complaisance a little farther than the French do.

Tragedy must be something bigger than life, or it would not affect us. In nature the most violent passions are silent; in tragedy they must speak, and speak with dignity too. Hence the necessity of their being written in verse, and unfortunately for the French, from the weakness of their language, in rhymes. And for the same reason, Cato the Stoic, expiring at Utica, rhymes masculine and feminine at Paris; and fetches his last breath at London, in most harmmonious and correct blank verse.

It is quite otherwise with Comedy, which should be mere common life, and not one jot bigger. Every character should speak upon the stage, not only what it would utter in the situation there represented, but in the same manner in which it would express it. For which reason I cannot allow rhymes in comedy, unless they were put into the mouth, and came out of the mouth of a mad poet. But it is impossible to deceive one's self enough (nor is it the least necessary in comedy) to suppose a dull rogue of an usurer cheating, or 'gross Jean' blundering in the finest rhymes in the world.

As for Operas, they are essentially too absurd and extravagant to mention; I look upon them as a magic scene, contrived to please the eyes and the ears, at the expense of the understanding; and I consider singing, rhyming, and chiming heroes, and princesses, and philosophers, as I do the hills, the trees, the birds, and the beasts, who amicably joined in one common country dance, to the irresistible turn of Orpheus's lyre. Whenever I go to an opera, I leave my sense and reason at the door with my half guinea, and deliver myself up to my eyes and my ears.

Thus I have made you my poetical confession; in which I have acknowledged as many sins against the established taste in both countries, as a frank heretic could have owned against the established church in either, but I am now privileged by my age to taste and think for myself, and not to care what other people think of me in those respects; an advantage which youth, among its many advantages, hath not. It must occasionally and outwardly conform, to a certain degree, to establish tastes, fashions, and decisions. A young man may, with a becoming modesty, dissent, in private companies, from public opinions and prejudices: but he must not attack them with warmth, nor magisterially set up his own sentiments against them. Endeavor to hear, and know all opinions; receive them with complaisance; form your own with coolness, and give it with modesty.

I have received a letter from Sir John Lambert, in which he requests me to use my interest to procure him the remittance of Mr. Spencer's money, when he goes abroad and also desires to know to whose account he is to place the postage of my letters. I do not trouble him with a letter in answer, since you can execute the commission. Pray make my compliments to him, and assure him that I will do all I can to procure him Mr. Spencer's business; but that his most effectual way will be by Messrs. Hoare, who are Mr. Spencer's cashiers, and who will undoubtedly have their choice upon whom they will give him his credit. As for the postage of the letters, your purse and mine being pretty near the same, do you pay it, over and above your next draught.

Your relations, the Princes B———, will soon be with you at Paris; for they leave London this week: whenever you converse with them, I desire it may be in Italian; that language not being yet familiar enough to you.

By our printed papers, there seems to be a sort of compromise between the King and the parliament, with regard to the affairs of the hospitals, by taking them out of the hands of the Archbishop of Paris, and placing them in Monsieur d'Argenson's: if this be true, that compromise, as it is called, is clearly a victory on the side of the court, and a defeat on the part of the parliament; for if the parliament had a right, they had it as much to the exclusion of Monsieur d'Argenson as of the Archbishop. Adieu.

LETTER CLVIII

LONDON, February 6, O. S. 1752.

MY DEAR FRIEND: Your criticism of Varon is strictly just; but, in truth, severe. You French critics seek for a fault as eagerly as I do for a beauty: you consider things in the worst light, to show your skill, at the expense of your pleasure; I view them in the best, that I may have more pleasure, though at the expense of my judgment. A 'trompeur trompeur et demi' is prettily said; and, if you please, you may call 'Varon, un Normand', and 'Sostrate, un Manceau, qui vaut un Normand et demi'; and, considering the 'denouement' in the light of trick upon trick, it would undoubtedly be below the dignity of the buskin, and fitter for the sock.

But let us see if we cannot bring off the author. The great question upon which all turns, is to discover and ascertain who Cleonice really is. There are doubts concerning her 'etat'; how shall they be cleared? Had the truth been extorted from Varon (who alone knew) by the rack, it would have been a true tragical 'denouement'. But that would probably not have done with Varon, who is represented as a bold, determined, wicked, and at that time desperate fellow; for he was in the hands of an enemy who he knew could not forgive him, with common prudence or safety. The rack would, therefore, have extorted no truth from him; but he would have died enjoying the doubts of his enemies, and the confusion that must necessarily attend those doubts. A stratagem is therefore thought of to discover what force and terror could not, and the stratagem such as no king or minister would disdain, to get at an important discovery. If you call that stratagem a TRICK, you vilify it, and make it comical; but call that trick a STRATAGEM, or a MEASURE, and you dignify it up to tragedy: so frequently do ridicule or dignity turn upon one single word. It is commonly said, and more particularly by Lord Shaftesbury, that ridicule is the best test of truth; for that it will not stick where it is not just. I deny it. A truth learned in a certain light, and attacked in certain words, by men of wit and humor, may, and often doth, become ridiculous, at least so far that the truth is only remembered and repeated for the sake of the ridicule. The overturn of Mary of Medicis into a river, where she was half-drowned, would never have been remembered if Madame de Vernuel, who saw it, had not said 'la Reine boit'. Pleasure or malignity often gives ridicule a weight which it does not deserve. The versification, I must confess, is too much neglected and too often bad: but, upon the whole, I read the play with pleasure.

If there is but a great deal of wit and character in your new comedy, I will readily compound for its having little or no plot. I chiefly mind dialogue and character in comedies. Let dull critics feed upon the carcasses of plays; give me the taste and the dressing.

I am very glad you went to Versailles to see the ceremony of creating the Prince de Conde 'Chevalier de l' Ordre'; and I do not doubt but that upon this occasion you informed yourself thoroughly of the institution and rules of that order. If you did, you were certainly told it was instituted by Henry III. immediately after his return, or rather his flight from Poland; he took the hint of it at Venice, where he had seen the original manuscript of an order of the 'St. Esprit, ou droit desir', which had been instituted in 1352, by Louis d'Anjou, King of Jerusalem and Sicily, and husband to Jane, Queen of Naples, Countess of Provence. This Order was under the protection of St. Nicholas de Bari, whose image hung to the collar. Henry III. found the Order of St. Michael prostituted and degraded, during the civil wars; he therefore joined it to his new Order of the St. Esprit, and gave them both together; for which reason every knight of the St. Esprit is now called Chevalier des Ordres du Roi. The number of the knights hath been different, but is now fixed to ONE HUNDRED, exclusive of the sovereign. There, are many officers who wear the riband of this Order, like the other knights; and what is very singular is, that these officers frequently sell their employments, but obtain leave to wear the blue riband still, though the purchasers of those offices wear it also.

As you will have been a great while in France, people will expect that you should be 'au fait' of all these sort of things relative to that country. But the history of all the Orders of all countries is well worth your knowledge; the subject occurs often, and one should not be ignorant of it, for fear of some such accident as happened to a solid Dane at Paris, who, upon seeing 'L'Ordre du St. Esprit', said, 'Notre St. Esprit chez nous c'est un Elephant'. Almost all the princes in Germany have their Orders too; not dated, indeed, from any important events, or directed to any great object, but because they will have orders, to show that they may; as some of them, who have the 'jus cudendae monetae', borrow ten shillings worth of gold to coin a ducat. However, wherever you meet with them, inform yourself, and minute down a short account of them; they take in all the colors of Sir Isaac Newton's prisms. N. B: When you inquire about them, do not seem to laugh.

I thank you for le Mandement de Monseigneur l'Archeveyue; it is very well drawn, and becoming an archbishop. But pray do not lose sight of a much more important object, I mean the political disputes between the King and the parliament, and the King and the clergy; they seem both to be patching up; but, however, get the whole clue to them, as far as they have gone.

I received a letter yesterday from Madame Monconseil, who assures me you have gained ground 'du cote des maniires', and that she looks upon you to be 'plus qu'a moitie chemin'. I am very glad to hear this, because, if you are got above half way of your journey, surely you will finish it, and not faint in the course. Why do you think I have this affair so extremely at heart, and why do I repeat it so often? Is it for your sake, or for mine? You can immediately answer yourself that question; you certainly have—I cannot possibly have any interest in it. If then you will allow me, as I believe you may, to be a judge of what is useful and necessary to you, you must, in consequence, be convinced of the infinite importance of a point which I take so much pains to inculcate.

I hear that the new Duke of Orleans 'a remercie Monsieur de Melfort, and I believe, 'pas sans raison', having had obligations to him; 'mais il ne l'a pas remercie en mari poli', but rather roughly. Il faut que ce soit un bourru'. I am told, too, that people get bits of his father's rags, by way of relies; I wish them joy, they will do them a great deal of good. See from hence what weaknesses human nature is capable of, and make allowances for such in all your plans and reasonings. Study the characters of the people you have to do with, and know what they are, instead of thinking them what they should be; address yourself generally to the senses, to the heart, and to the weaknesses of mankind, but very rarely to their reason.

Good-night or good-morrow to you, according to the time you shall receive this letter from, Yours.

LETTER CLIX

LONDON, February 14, O. S. 1752.

MY DEAR FRIEND: In a month's time, I believe I shall have the pleasure of sending you, and you will have the pleasure of reading, a work of Lord Bolingbroke's, in two volumes octavo, "Upon the Use of History," in several letters to Lord Hyde, then Lord Cornbury. It is now put into the press. It is hard to determine whether this work will instruct or please most: the most material historical facts, from the great era of the treaty of Munster, are touched upon, accompanied by the most solid reflections, and adorned by all that elegance of style which was peculiar to himself, and in which, if Cicero equals, he certainly does not exceed him; but every other writer falls short of him. I would advise you almost to get this book by heart. I think you have a turn to history, you love it, and have a memory to retain it: this book will teach you the proper use of it. Some people load their memories indiscriminately with historical facts, as others do their stomachs with food; and bring out the one, and bring up the other, entirely crude and undigested. You will find in Lord Bolingbroke's book an infallible specific against that epidemical complaint.—[It is important to remember that at this time Lord Bolingbroke's philosophical works had not appeared; which accounts for Lord Chesterfield's recommending to his son, in this, as well as in some foregoing passages, the study of Lord Bolingbroke's writings.]

I remember a gentleman who had read history in this thoughtless and undistinguishing manner, and who, having traveled, had gone through the Valtelline. He told me that it was a miserable poor country, and therefore it was, surely, a great error in Cardinal Richelieu to make such a rout, and put France to so much expense about it. Had my friend read history as he ought to have done, he would have known that the great object of that great minister was to reduce the power of the House of Austria; and in order to that, to cut off as much as he could the communication between the several parts of their then extensive dominions; which reflections would have justified the Cardinal to him, in the affair of the Valtelline. But it was easier to him to remember facts, than to combine and reflect.

One observation I hope you will make in reading history; for it is an obvious and a true one. It is, that more people have made great figures and great fortunes in courts by their exterior accomplishments, than by their interior qualifications. Their engaging address, the politeness of their manners, their air, their turn, hath almost always paved the way for their superior abilities, if they have such, to exert themselves. They have been favorites before they have been ministers. In courts, an universal gentleness and 'douceur dans les manieres' is most absolutely necessary: an offended fool, or a slighted valet de chambre, may very possibly do you more hurt at court, than ten men of merit can do you good. Fools, and low people, are always jealous of their dignity, and never forget nor forgive what they reckon a slight: on the other hand, they take civility and a little attention as a favor; remember, and acknowledge it: this, in my mind, is buying them cheap; and therefore they are worth buying. The prince himself, who is rarely the shining genius of his court, esteems you only by hearsay but likes you by his senses; that is, from your air, your politeness, and your manner of addressing him, of which alone he is a judge. There is a court garment, as well as a wedding garment, without which you will not be received. That garment is the 'volto sciolto'; an imposing air, an elegant politeness, easy and engaging manners, universal attention, an insinuating gentleness, and all those 'je ne sais quoi' that compose the GRACES.

I am this moment disagreeably interrupted by a letter; not from you, as I expected, but from a friend of yours at Paris, who informs me that you have a fever which confines you at home. Since you have a fever, I am glad you have prudence enough in it to stay at home, and take care of yourself; a little more prudence might probably have prevented it. Your blood is young, and consequently hot; and you naturally make a great deal by your good stomach and good digestion; you should, therefore, necessarily attenuate and cool it, from time to time, by gentle purges, or by a very low diet, for two or three days together, if you would avoid fevers. Lord Bacon, who was a very great physician in both senses of the word, hath this aphorism in his "Essay upon Health," 'Nihil magis ad Sanitatem tribuit quam crebrae et domesticae purgationes'. By 'domesticae', he means those simple uncompounded purgatives which everybody can administer to themselves; such as senna-tea, stewed prunes and senria, chewing a little rhubarb, or dissolving an ounce and a half of manna in fair water, with the juice of a lemon to make it palatable. Such gentle and unconfining evacuations would certainly prevent those feverish attacks to which everybody at your age is subject.

By the way, I do desire, and insist, that whenever, from any indisposition, you are not able to write to me upon the fixed days, that Christian shall; and give me a TRUE account how you are. I do not expect from him the Ciceronian epistolary style; but I will content myself with the Swiss simplicity and truth.

I hope you extend your acquaintance at Paris, and frequent variety of companies; the only way of knowing the world; every set of company differs in some particulars from another; and a man of business must, in the course of his life, have to do with all sorts. It is a very great advantage to know the languages of the several countries one travels in; and different companies may, in some degree, be considered as different countries; each hath its distinctive language, customs, and manners: know them all, and you will wonder at none.

Adieu, child. Take care of your health; there are no pleasures without it.

LETTER CLX

LONDON, February 20, O. S. 1752.

MY DEAR FRIEND: In all systems whatsoever, whether of religion, government, morals, etc., perfection is the object always proposed, though possibly unattainable; hitherto, at least, certainly unattained. However, those who aim carefully at the mark itself, will unquestionably come nearer it, than those who from despair, negligence, or indolence, leave to chance the work of skill. This maxim holds equally true in common life; those who aim at perfection will come infinitely nearer it than those desponding or indolent spirits, who foolishly say to themselves: Nobody is perfect; perfection is unattainable; to attempt it is chimerical; I shall do as well as others; why then should I give myself trouble to be what I never can, and what, according to the common course of things, I need not be, PERFECT?

I am very sure that I need not point out to you the weakness and the folly of this reasoning, if it deserves the name of reasoning. It would discourage and put a stop to the exertion of any one of our faculties. On the contrary, a man of sense and spirit says to himself: Though the point of perfection may (considering the imperfection of our nature) be unattainable, my care, my endeavors, my attention, shall not be wanting to get as near it as I can. I will approach it every day, possibly, I may arrive at it at last; at least, what I am sure is in my own power, I will not be distanced. Many fools (speaking of you) say to me: What! would you have him perfect? I answer: Why not? What hurt would it do him or me? O, but that is impossible, say they; I reply, I am not sure of that: perfection in the abstract, I admit to be unattainable, but what is commonly called perfection in a character I maintain to be attainable, and not only that, but in every man's power. He hath, continue they, a good head, a good heart, a good fund of knowledge, which would increase daily: What would you have more? Why, I would have everything more that can adorn and complete a character. Will it do his head, his heart, or his knowledge any harm, to have the utmost delicacy of manners, the most shining advantages of air and address, the most endearing attentions, and the most engaging graces? But as he is, say they, he is loved wherever he is known. I am very glad of it, say I; but I would have him be liked before he is known, and loved afterward. I would have him, by his first abord and address, make people wish to know him, and inclined to love him: he will save a great deal of time by it. Indeed, reply they, you are too nice, too exact, and lay too much stress upon things that are of very little consequence. Indeed, rejoin I, you know very little of the nature of mankind, if you take those things to be of little consequence: one cannot be too attentive to them; it is they that always engage the heart, of which the understanding is commonly the bubble. And I would much rather that he erred in a point of grammar, of history, of philosophy, etc., than in point of manners and address. But consider, he is very young; all this will come in time. I hope so; but that time must be when he is young, or it will never be at all; the right 'pli' must be taken young, or it will never be easy or seem natural. Come, come, say they (substituting, as is frequently done, assertion instead of argument), depend upon it he will do very well: and you have a great deal of reason to be satisfied with him. I hope and believe he will do well, but I would have him do better than well. I am very well pleased with him, but I would be more, I would be proud of him. I would have him have lustre as well as weight. Did you ever know anybody that reunited all these talents? Yes, I did; Lord Bolingbroke joined all the politeness, the manners, and the graces of a courtier, to the solidity of a statesman, and to the learning of a pedant. He was 'omnis homo'; and pray what should hinder my boy from being so too, if he 'hath, as I think he hath, all the other qualifications that you allow him? Nothing can hinder him, but neglect of or inattention to, those objects which his own good sense must tell him are, of infinite consequence to him, and which therefore I will not suppose him capable of either neglecting or despising.

This (to tell you the whole truth) is the result of a controversy that passed yesterday, between Lady Hervey and myself, upon your subject, and almost in the very words. I submit the decision of it to yourself; let your own good sense determine it, and make you act in consequence of that determination. The receipt to make this composition is short and infallible; here I give it to you:

Take variety of the best company, wherever you are; be minutely attentive to every word and action; imitate respectively those whom you observe to be distinguished and considered for any one accomplishment; then mix all those several accomplishments together, and serve them up yourself to others.

I hope your fair, or rather your brown AMERICAN is well. I hear that she makes very handsome presents, if she is not so herself. I am told there are people at Paris who expect, from this secret connection, to see in time a volume of letters, superior to Madame de Graffiny's Peruvian ones; I lay in my claim to one of the first copies.

Francis's Genie—[Francis's "Eugenia."]—hath been acted twice, with most universal applause; to-night is his third night, and I am going to it. I did not think it would have succeeded so well, considering how long our British audiences have been accustomed to murder, racks, and poison, in every tragedy; but it affected the heart so much, that it triumphed over habit and prejudice. All the women cried, and all the men were moved. The prologue, which is a very good one, was made entirely by Garrick. The epilogue is old Cibber's; but corrected, though not enough, by Francis. He will get a great deal of, money by it; and, consequently, be better able to lend you sixpence, upon any emergency.

The parliament of Paris, I find by the newspapers, has not carried its point concerning the hospitals, and, though the King hath given up the Archbishop, yet as he has put them under the management and direction 'du Grand Conseil', the parliament is equally out of the question. This will naturally put you upon inquiring into the constitution of the 'Grand Conseil'. You will, doubtless, inform yourself who it is composed of, what things are 'de son ressort', whether or not there lies an appeal from thence to any other place; and of all other particulars, that may give you a clear notion of this assembly. There are also three or four other Conseils in France, of which you ought to know the constitution and the objects; I dare say you do know them already; but if you do not, lose no time in informing yourself. These things, as I have often told you, are best learned in various French companies: but in no English ones, for none of our countrymen trouble their heads about them. To use a very trite image, collect, like the bee, your store from every quarter. In some companies ('parmi les fermiers generaux nommement') you may, by proper inquiries, get a general knowledge, at least, of 'les affaires des finances'. When you are with 'des gens de robe', suck them with regard to the constitution, and civil government, and 'sic de caeteris'. This shows you the advantage of keeping a great deal of different French company; an advantage much superior to any that you can possibly receive from loitering and sauntering away evenings in any English company at Paris, not even excepting Lord A———. Love of ease, and fear of restraint (to both which I doubt you are, for a young fellow, too much addicted) may invite you among your countrymen: but pray withstand those mean temptations, 'et prenez sur vous', for the sake of being in those assemblies, which alone can inform your mind and improve your manners. You have not now many months to continue at Paris; make the most of them; get into every house there, if you can; extend acquaintance, know everything and everybody there; that when you leave it for other places, you may be 'au fait', and even able to explain whatever you may hear mentioned concerning it. Adieu.

LETTER CLXI

LONDON, March 2, O. S. 1752.

MY DEAR FRIEND: Whereabouts are you in Ariosto? Or have you gone through that most ingenious contexture of truth and lies, of serious and extravagant, of knights-errant, magicians, and all that various matter which he announces in the beginning of his poem:

Le Donne, I Cavalier, l'arme, gli amori,

Le cortesie, l'audaci impreso io canto.

I am by no means sure that Homer had superior invention, or excelled more in description than Ariosto. What can be more seducing and voluptuous, than the description of Alcina's person and palace? What more ingeniously extravagant, than the search made in the moon for Orlando's lost wits, and the account of other people's that were found there? The whole is worth your attention, not only as an ingenious poem, but as the source of all modern tales, novels, fables, and romances; as Ovid's "Metamorphoses;" was of the ancient ones; besides, that when you have read this work, nothing will be difficult to you in the Italian language. You will read Tasso's 'Gierusalemme', and the 'Decamerone di Boccacio', with great facility afterward; and when you have read those three authors, you will, in my opinion, have read all the works of invention that are worth reading in that language; though the Italians would be very angry at me for saying so.

A gentleman should know those which I call classical works, in every language; such as Boileau, Corneille, Racine, Moliere, etc., in French; Milton, Dryden, Pope, Swift, etc., in English; and the three authors above mentioned in Italian; whether you have any such in German I am not quite sure, nor, indeed, am I inquisitive. These sort of books adorn the mind, improve the fancy, are frequently alluded to by, and are often the subjects of conversations of the best companies. As you have languages to read, and memory to retain them, the knowledge of them is very well worth the little pains it will cost you, and will enable you to shine in company. It is not pedantic to quote and allude to them, which it would be with regard to the ancients.

Among the many advantages which you have had in your education, I do not consider your knowledge of several languages as the least. You need not trust to translations; you can go to the source; you can both converse and negotiate with people of all nations, upon equal terms; which is by no means the case of a man, who converses or negotiates in a language which those with whom he hath to do know much better than himself. In business, a great deal may depend upon the force and extent of one word; and, in conversation, a moderate thought may gain, or a good one lose, by the propriety or impropriety, the elegance or inelegance of one single word. As therefore you now know four modern languages well, I would have you study (and, by the way, it will be very little trouble to you) to know them correctly, accurately, and delicately. Read some little books that treat of them, and ask questions concerning their delicacies, of those who are able to answer you. As, for instance, should I say in French, 'la lettre que je vous ai ECRIT', or, 'la lettre que je vous ai ECRITE'? in which, I think, the French differ among themselves. There is a short French grammar by the Port Royal, and another by Pere Buffier, both which are worth your reading; as is also a little book called 'Les Synonymes Francois. There are books of that kind upon the Italian language, into some of which I would advise you to dip; possibly the German language may have something of the same sort, and since you already speak it, the more properly you speak it the better; one would, I think, as far as possible, do all one does correctly and elegantly. It is extremely engaging to people of every nation, to meet with a foreigner who hath taken pains enough to speak their language correctly; it flatters that local and national pride and prejudice of which everybody hath some share.

Francis's "Eugenia," which I will send you, pleased most people of good taste here; the boxes were crowded till the sixth night, when the pit and gallery were totally deserted, and it was dropped. Distress, without death, was not sufficient to affect a true British audience, so long accustomed to daggers, racks, and bowls of poison: contrary to Horace's rule, they desire to see Medea murder her children upon the stage. The sentiments were too delicate to move them; and their hearts are to be taken by storm, not by parley.

Have you got the things, which were taken from you at Calais, restored? and, among them, the little packet which my sister gave you for Sir Charles Hotham? In this case, have you forwarded it to him? If you have not had an opportunity, you will have one soon; which I desire you will not omit; it is by Monsieur d'Aillion, whom you will see in a few days at Paris, in his way to Geneva, where Sir Charles now is, and will remain some time. Adieu:

LETTER CLXII

LETTERS TO HIS SON, COMPLETE

LONDON, March 5, O. S. 1752

MY DEAR FRIEND: As I have received no letter from you by the usual post, I am uneasy upon account of your health; for, had you been well, I am sure you would have written, according to your engagement and my requisition. You have not the least notion of any care of your health; but though I would not have you be a valetudinarian, I must tell you that the best and most robust health requires some degree of attention to preserve. Young fellows, thinking they have so much health and time before them, are very apt to neglect or lavish both, and beggar themselves before they are aware: whereas a prudent economy in both would make them rich indeed; and so far from breaking in upon their pleasures, would improve, and almost perpetuate them. Be you wiser, and, before it is too late, manage both with care and frugality; and lay out neither, but upon good interest and security.

I will now confine myself to the employment of your time, which, though I have often touched upon formerly, is a subject that, from its importance, will bear repetition. You have it is true, a great deal of time before you; but, in this period of your life, one hour usefully employed may be worth more than four-and-twenty hereafter; a minute is precious to you now, whole days may possibly not be so forty years hence.

Whatever time you allow, or can snatch for serious reading (I say snatch, because company and the knowledge of the world is now your chief object), employ it in the reading of some one book, and that a good one, till you have finished it: and do not distract your mind with various matters at the same time. In this light I would recommend to you to read 'tout de suite' Grotius 'de Jure Belli et Pacis', translated by Barbeyrac, and Puffendorff's 'Jus Gentium', translated by the same hand. For accidental quarters of hours, read works of invention, wit and humor, of the best, and not of trivial authors, either ancient or modern.

Whatever business you have, do it the first moment you can; never by halves, but finish it without interruption, if possible. Business must not be sauntered and trifled with; and you must not say to it, as Felix did to Paul, "At a more convenient season I will speak to thee." The most convenient season for business is the first; but study and business in some measure point out their own times to a man of sense; time is much oftener squandered away in the wrong choice and improper methods of amusement and pleasures.

Many people think that they are in pleasures, provided they are neither in study nor in business. Nothing like it; they are doing nothing, and might just as well be asleep. They contract habitudes from laziness, and they only frequent those places where they are free from all restraints and attentions. Be upon your guard against this idle profusion of time; and let every place you go to be either the scene of quick and lively pleasures, or the school of your own improvements; let every company you go into either gratify your senses, extend your knowledge, or refine your manners. Have some decent object of gallantry in view at some places; frequent others, where people of wit and taste assemble; get into others, where people of superior rank and dignity command respect and attention from the rest of the company; but pray frequent no neutral places, from mere idleness and indolence. Nothing forms a young man so much as being used to keep respectable and superior company, where a constant regard and attention is necessary. It is true, this is at first a disagreeable state of restraint; but it soon grows habitual, and consequently easy; and you are amply paid for it, by the improvement you make, and the credit it gives you. What you said some time ago was very true, concerning 'le Palais Royal'; to one of your age the situation is disagreeable enough: you cannot expect to be much taken notice of; but all that time you can take notice of others; observe their manners, decipher their characters, and insensibly you will become one of the company.

All this I went through myself, when I was of your age. I have sat hours in company without being taken the least notice of; but then I took notice of them, and learned in their company how to behave myself better in the next, till by degrees I became part of the best companies myself. But I took great care not to lavish away my time in those companies where there were neither quick pleasures nor useful improvements to be expected.

Sloth, indolence, and 'mollesse' are pernicious and unbecoming a young fellow; let them be your 'ressource' forty years hence at soonest. Determine, at all events, and however disagreeable it may to you in some respects, and for some time, to keep the most distinguished and fashionable company of the place you are at, either for their rank, or for their learning, or 'le bel esprit et le gout'. This gives you credentials to the best companies, wherever you go afterward. Pray, therefore, no indolence, no laziness; but employ every minute in your life in active pleasures, or useful employments. Address yourself to some woman of fashion and beauty, wherever you are, and try how far that will go. If the place be not secured beforehand, and garrisoned, nine times in ten you will take it. By attentions and respect you may always get into the highest company: and by some admiration and applause, whether merited or not, you may be sure of being welcome among 'les savans et les beaux esprits'. There are but these three sorts of company for a young fellow; there being neither pleasure nor profit in any other.

My uneasiness with regard to your health is this moment removed by your letter of the 8th N. S., which, by what accident I do not know, I did not receive before.

I long to read Voltaire's 'Rome Sauvee', which, by the very faults that your SEVERE critics find with it, I am sure I shall like; for I will at an any time give up a good deal of regularity for a great deal of brillant; and for the brillant surely nobody is equal to Voltaire. Catiline's conspiracy is an unhappy subject for a tragedy; it is too single, and gives no opportunity to the poet to excite any of the tender passions; the whole is one intended act of horror, Crebillon was sensible of this defect, and to create another interest, most absurdly made Catiline in love with Cicero's daughter, and her with him.

I am very glad that you went to Versailles, and dined with Monsieur de St. Contest. That is company to learn 'les bonnes manieres' in; and it seems you had 'les bonnes morceaux' into the bargain. Though you were no part of the King of France's conversation with the foreign ministers, and probably not much entertained with it, do you think that it is not very useful to you to hear it, and to observe the turn and manners of people of that sort? It is extremely useful to know it well. The same in the next rank of people, such as ministers of state, etc., in whose company, though you cannot yet, at your age, bear a part, and consequently be diverted, you will observe and learn, what hereafter it may be necessary for you to act.

Tell Sir John Lambert that I have this day fixed Mr. Spencer's having his credit upon him; Mr. Hoare had also recommended him. I believe Mr. Spencer will set out next month for some place in France, but not Paris. I am sure he wants a great deal of France, for at present he is most entirely English: and you know very well what I think of that. And so we bid you heartily good-night.

LETTER CLXIII

LETTERS TO HIS SON, COMPLETE

LONDON, March 16, O. S. 1752

MY DEAR FRIEND: How do you go on with the most useful and most necessary of all studies, the study of the world? Do you find that you gain knowledge? And does your daily experience at once extend and demonstrate your improvement? You will possibly ask me how you can judge of that yourself. I will tell you a sure way of knowing. Examine yourself, and see whether your notions of the world are changed, by experience, from what they were two years ago in theory; for that alone is one favorable symptom of improvement. At that age (I remember it in myself) every notion that one forms is erroneous; one hath seen few models, and those none of the best, to form one's self upon. One thinks that everything is to be carried by spirit and vigor; that art is meanness, and that versatility and complaisance are the refuge of pusilanimity and weakness. This most mistaken opinion gives an indelicacy, a 'brusquerie', and a roughness to the manners. Fools, who can never be undeceived, retain them as long as they live: reflection, with a little experience, makes men of sense shake them off soon. When they come to be a little better acquainted with themselves, and with their own species, they discover that plain right reason is, nine times in ten, the fettered and shackled attendant of the triumph of the heart and the passions; and, consequently, they address themselves nine times in ten to the conqueror, not to the conquered: and conquerors, you know, must be applied to in the gentlest, the most engaging, and the most insinuating manner. Have you found out that every woman is infallibly to be gained by every sort of flattery, and every man by one sort or other? Have you discovered what variety of little things affect the heart, and how surely they collectively gain it? If you have, you have made some progress. I would try a man's knowledge of the world, as I would a schoolboy's knowledge of Horace: not by making him construe 'Maecenas atavis edite regibus', which he could do in the first form; but by examining him as to the delicacy and 'curiosa felicitas' of that poet. A man requires very little knowledge and experience of the world, to understand glaring, high-colored, and decided characters; they are but few, and they strike at first: but to distinguish the almost imperceptible shades, and the nice gradations of virtue and vice, sense and folly, strength and weakness (of which characters are commonly composed), demands some experience, great observation, and minute attention. In the same cases, most people do the same things, but with this material difference, upon which the success commonly turns: A man who hath studied the world knows when to time, and where to place them; he hath analyzed the characters he applies to, and adapted his address and his arguments to them: but a man, of what is called plain good sense, who hath only reasoned by himself, and not acted with mankind, mistimes, misplaces, runs precipitately and bluntly at the mark, and falls upon his nose in the way. In the common manners of social life, every man of common sense hath the rudiments, the A B C of civility; he means not to offend, and even wishes to please: and, if he hath any real merit, will be received and tolerated in good company. But that is far from being enough; for, though he may be received, he will never be desired; though he does not offend, he will never be loved; but, like some little, insignificant, neutral power, surrounded by great ones, he will neither be feared nor courted by any; but, by turns, invaded by all, whenever it is their interest. A most contemptible situation! Whereas, a man who hath carefully attended to, and experienced, the various workings of the heart, and the artifices of the head; and who, by one shade, can trace the progression of the whole color; who can, at the proper times, employ all the several means of persuading the understanding, and engaging the heart, may and will have enemies; but will and must have friends: he may be opposed, but he will be supported too; his talents may excite the jealousy of some, but his engaging arts will make him beloved by many more; he will be considerable; he will be considered. Many different qualifications must conspire to form such a man, and to make him at once respectable and amiable; the least must be joined to the greatest; the latter would be unavailing without the former; and the former would be futile and frivolous, without the latter. Learning is acquired by reading books; but the much more necessary learning, the knowledge of the world, is only to be acquired by reading men, and studying all the various editions of them. Many words in every language are generally thought to be synonymous; but those who study the language attentively will find, that there is no such thing; they will discover some little difference, some distinction between all those words that are vulgarly called synonymous; one hath always more energy, extent, or delicacy, than another. It is the same with men; all are in general, and yet no two in particular, exactly alike. Those who have not accurately studied, perpetually mistake them; they do not discern the shades and gradations that distinguish characters seemingly alike. Company, various company, is the only school for this knowledge. You ought to be, by this time, at least in the third form of that school, from whence the rise to the uppermost is easy and quick; but then you must have application and vivacity; and you must not only bear with, but even seek restraint in most companies, instead of stagnating in one or two only, where indolence and love of ease may be indulged.

In the plan which I gave you in my last,—[That letter is missing.]—for your future motions, I forgot to tell you; that, if a king of the Romans should be chosen this year, you shall certainly be at that election; and as, upon those occasions, all strangers are excluded from the place of the election, except such as belong to some ambassador, I have already eventually secured you a place in the suite of the King's Electoral Ambassador, who will be sent upon that account to Frankfort, or wherever else the election may be. This will not only secure you a sight of the show, but a knowledge of the whole thing; which is likely to be a contested one, from the opposition of some of the electors, and the protests of some of the princes of the empire. That election, if there is one, will, in my opinion, be a memorable era in the history of the empire; pens at least, if not swords, will be drawn; and ink, if not blood, will be plentifully shed by the contending parties in that dispute. During the fray, you may securely plunder, and add to your present stock of knowledge of the 'jus publicum imperii'. The court of France hath, I am told, appointed le President Ogier, a man of great abilities, to go immediately to Ratisbon, 'pour y souffler la discorde'. It must be owned that France hath always profited skillfully of its having guaranteed the treaty of Munster; which hath given it a constant pretense to thrust itself into the affairs of the empire. When France got Alsace yielded by treaty, it was very willing to have held it as a fief of the empire; but the empire was then wiser. Every power should be very careful not to give the least pretense to a neighboring power to meddle with the affairs of its interior. Sweden hath already felt the effects of the Czarina's calling herself Guarantee of its present form of government, in consequence of the treaty of Neustadt, confirmed afterward by that of Abo; though, in truth, that guarantee was rather a provision against Russia's attempting to alter the then new established form of government in Sweden, than any right given to Russia to hinder the Swedes from establishing what form of government they pleased. Read them both, if you can get them. Adieu.

LETTER CLXIV

LONDON, April 73, O. S. 1752

MY DEAR FRIEND: I receive this moment your letter of the 19th, N. S., with the inclosed pieces relative to the present dispute between the King and the parliament. I shall return them by Lord Huntingdon, whom you will soon see at Paris, and who will likewise carry you the piece, which I forgot in making up the packet I sent you by the Spanish Ambassador. The representation of the parliament is very well drawn, 'suaviter in modo, fortiter in re'. They tell the King very respectfully, that, in a certain case, WHICH THEY SHOULD THINK IT CRIMINAL To SUPPOSE, they would not obey him. This hath a tendency to what we call here revolution principles. I do not know what the Lord's anointed, his vicegerent upon earth, divinely appointed by him, and accountable to none but him for his actions, will either think or do, upon these symptoms of reason and good sense, which seem to be breaking out all over France: but this I foresee, that, before the end of this century, the trade of both king and priest will not be half so good a one as it has been. Du Clos, in his "Reflections," hath observed, and very truly, 'qu'il y a un germe de raison qui commence a se developper en France';—a developpement that must prove fatal to Regal and Papal pretensions. Prudence may, in many cases, recommend an occasional submission to either; but when that ignorance, upon which an implicit faith in both could only be founded, is once removed, God's Vicegerent, and Christ's Vicar, will only be obeyed and believed, as far as what the one orders, and the other says, is conformable to reason and to truth.

I am very glad (to use a vulgar expression) that You MAKE AS IF YOU WERE NOT WELL, though you really are; I am sure it is the likeliest way to keep so. Pray leave off entirely your greasy, heavy pastry, fat creams, and indigestible dumplings; and then you need not confine yourself to white meats, which I do not take to be one jot wholesomer than beef, mutton, and partridge.

Voltaire sent me, from Berlin, his 'History du Siecle de Louis XIV. It came at a very proper time; Lord Bolingbroke had just taught me how history should be read; Voltaire shows me how it should be written. I am sensible that it will meet with almost as many critics as readers. Voltaire must be criticised; besides, every man's favorite is attacked: for every prejudice is exposed, and our prejudices are our mistresses; reason is at best our wife, very often heard indeed, but seldom minded. It is the history of the human understanding, written by a man of parts, for the use of men of parts. Weak minds will not like it, even though they do not understand it; which is commonly the measure of their admiration. Dull ones will want those minute and uninteresting details with which most other histories are encumbered. He tells me all I want to know, and nothing more. His reflections are short, just, and produce others in his readers. Free from religious, philosophical, political and national prejudices, beyond any historian I ever met with, he relates all those matters as truly and as impartially, as certain regards, which must always be to some degree observed, will allow him; for one sees plainly that he often says much less than he would say, if he might. He hath made me much better acquainted with the times of Lewis XIV., than the innumerable volumes which I had read could do; and hath suggested this reflection to me, which I have never made before—His vanity, not his knowledge, made him encourage all, and introduce many arts and sciences in his country. He opened in a manner the human understanding in France, and brought it to its utmost perfection; his age equalled in all, and greatly exceeded in many things (pardon me, Pedants!) the Augustan. This was great and rapid; but still it might be done, by the encouragement, the applause, and the rewards of a vain, liberal, and magnificent prince. What is much more surprising is, that he stopped the operations of the human mind just where he pleased; and seemed to say, "Thus far shalt thou go, and no farther." For, a bigot to his religion, and jealous of his power, free and rational thoughts upon either, never entered into a French head during his reign; and the greatest geniuses that ever any age produced, never entertained a doubt of the divine right of Kings, or the infallibility of the Church. Poets, Orators, and Philosophers, ignorant of their natural rights, cherished their chains; and blind, active faith triumphed, in those great minds, over silent and passive reason. The reverse of this seems now to be the case in France: reason opens itself; fancy and invention fade and decline.

I will send you a copy of this history by Lord Huntingdon, as I think it very probable that it is not allowed to be published and sold at Paris. Pray read it more than once, and with attention, particularly the second volume, which contains short, but very clear accounts of many very interesting things, which are talked of by everybody, though fairly. understood by very few. There are two very puerile affectations which I wish this book had been free from; the one is, the total subversion of all the old established French orthography; the other is, the not making use of any one capital letter throughout the whole book, except at the beginning of a paragraph. It offends my eyes to see rome, paris, france, Caesar, I henry the fourth, etc., begin with small letters; and I do not conceive that there can be any reason for doing it, half so strong as the reason of long usage is to the contrary. This is an affectation below Voltaire; who, I am not ashamed to say, that I admire and delight in, as an author, equally in prose and in verse.

I had a letter a few days ago from Monsieur du Boccage, in which he says, 'Monsieur Stanhope s'est jete dans la politique, et je crois qu'il y reussira': You do very well, it is your destination; but remember that, to succeed in great things, one must first learn to please in little ones. Engaging manners and address must prepare the way for superior knowledge and abilities to act with effect. The late Duke of Marlborough's manners and address prevailed with the first king of Prussia, to let his troops remain in the army of the Allies, when neither their representations, nor his own share in the common cause could do it. The Duke of Marlborough had no new matter to urge to him; but had a manner, which he could not, nor did not, resist. Voltaire, among a thousand little delicate strokes of that kind, says of the Duke de la Feuillade, 'qu'il etoit l'homme le plus brillant et le plus aimable du royaume; et quoique gendre du General et Ministre, il avoit pour lui la faveur publique'. Various little circumstances of that sort will often make a man of great real merit be hated, if he hath not address and manners to make him be loved. Consider all your own circumstances seriously; and you will find that, of all arts, the art of pleasing is the most necessary for you to study and possess. A silly tyrant said, 'oderint modo timeant'; a wise man would have said, 'modo ament nihil timendum est mihi'. Judge from your own daily experience, of the efficacy of that pleasing 'je ne sais quoi', when you feel, as you and everybody certainly does, that in men it is more engaging than knowledge, in women than beauty.

I long to see Lord and Lady———-(who are not yet arrived), because they have lately seen you; and I always fancy, that I can fish out something new concerning you, from those who have seen you last: not that I shall much rely upon their accounts, because I distrust the judgment of Lord and Lady———-, in those matters about which I am most inquisitive. They have ruined their own son by what they called and thought loving him. They have made him believe that the world was made for him, not he for the world; and unless he stays abroad a great while, and falls into very good company, he will expect, what he will never find, the attentions and complaisance from others, which he has hitherto been used to from Papa and Mamma. This, I fear, is too much the case of Mr. ----; who, I doubt, will be run through the body, and be near dying, before he knows how to live. However you may turn out, you can never make me any of these reproaches. I indulged no silly, womanish fondness for you; instead of inflicting my tenderness upon you, I have taken all possible methods to make you deserve it; and thank God you do; at least, I know but one article, in which you are different from what I could wish you; and you very well know what that is I want: That I and all the world should like you, as well as I love you. Adieu.

LETTER CLXV

LONDON, April 30, O. S. 1752.

MY DEAR FRIEND: 'Avoir du monde' is, in my opinion, a very just and happy expression for having address, manners, and for knowing how to behave properly in all companies; and it implies very truly that a man who hath not those accomplishments is not of the world. Without them, the best parts are inefficient, civility is absurd, and freedom offensive. A learned parson, rusting in his cell, at Oxford or Cambridge, will season admirably well upon the nature of man; will profoundly analyze the head, the heart, the reason, the will, the passions, the senses, the sentiments, and all those subdivisions of we know not what; and yet, unfortunately, he knows nothing of man, for he hath not lived with him; and is ignorant of all the various modes, habits, prejudices, and tastes, that always influence and often determine him. He views man as he does colors in Sir Isaac Newton's prism, where only the capital ones are seen; but an experienced dyer knows all their various shades and gradations, together with the result of their several mixtures. Few men are of one plain, decided color; most are mixed, shaded, and blended; and vary as much, from different situations, as changeable silks do form different lights. The man 'qui a du monde' knows all this from his own experience and observation: the conceited, cloistered philosopher knows nothing of it from his own theory; his practice is absurd and improper, and he acts as awkwardly as a man would dance, who had never seen others dance, nor learned of a dancing-master; but who had only studied the notes by which dances are now pricked down as well as tunes. Observe and imitate, then, the address, the arts, and the manners of those 'qui ont du monde': see by what methods they first make, and afterward improve impressions in their favor. Those impressions are much oftener owing to little causes than to intrinsic merit; which is less volatile, and hath not so sudden an effect. Strong minds have undoubtedly an ascendant over weak ones, as Galigai Marachale d'Ancre very justly observed, when, to the disgrace and reproach of those times, she was executed for having governed Mary of Medicis by the arts of witchcraft and magic. But then ascendant is to be gained by degrees, and by those arts only which experience and the knowledge of the world teaches; for few are mean enough to be bullied, though most are weak enough to be bubbled. I have often seen people of superior, governed by people of much inferior parts, without knowing or even suspecting that they were so governed. This can only happen when those people of inferior parts have more worldly dexterity and experience, than those they govern. They see the weak and unguarded part, and apply to it they take it, and all the rest follows. Would you gain either men or women, and every man of sense desires to gain both, 'il faut du monde'. You have had more opportunities than ever any man had, at your age, of acquiring 'ce monde'. You have been in the best companies of most countries, at an age when others have hardly been in any company at all. You are master of all those languages, which John Trott seldom speaks at all, and never well; consequently you need be a stranger nowhere. This is the way, and the only way, of having 'du monde', but if you have it not, and have still any coarse rusticity about you, may not one apply to you the 'rusticus expectat' of Horace?

This knowledge of the world teaches us more particularly two things, both which are of infinite consequence, and to neither of which nature inclines us; I mean, the command of our temper, and of our countenance. A man who has no 'monde' is inflamed with anger, or annihilated with shame, at every disagreeable incident: the one makes him act and talk like a madman, the other makes him look like a fool. But a man who has 'du monde', seems not to understand what he cannot or ought not to resent. If he makes a slip himself, he recovers it by his coolness, instead of plunging deeper by his confusion like a stumbling horse. He is firm, but gentle; and practices that most excellent maxim, 'suaviter in modo, fortiter in re'. The other is the 'volto sciolto a pensieri stretti'. People unused to the world have babbling countenances; and are unskilful enough to show what they have sense enough not to tell. In the course of the world, a man must very often put on an easy, frank countenance, upon very disagreeable occasions; he must seem pleased when he is very much otherwise; he must be able to accost and receive with smiles, those whom he would much rather meet with swords. In courts he must not turn himself inside out. All this may, nay must be done, without falsehood and treachery; for it must go no further than politeness and manners, and must stop short of assurances and professions of simulated friendship. Good manners, to those one does not love, are no more a breach of truth, than "your humble servant" at the bottom of a challenge is; they are universally agreed upon and understood, to be things of course. They are necessary guards of the decency and peace of society; they must only act defensively; and then not with arms poisoned by perfidy. Truth, but not the whole truth, must be the invariable principle of every man, who hath either religion, honor, or prudence. Those who violate it may be cunning, but they are not able. Lies and perfidy are the refuge of fools and cowards. Adieu!

P. S. I must recommend to you again, to take your leave of all your French acquaintance, in such a manner as may make them regret your departure, and wish to see and welcome you at Paris again, where you may possibly return before it is very long. This must not be done in a cold, civil manner, but with at least seeming warmth, sentiment, and concern. Acknowledge the obligations you have to them for the kindness they have shown you during your stay at Paris: assure them that wherever you are, you will remember them with gratitude; wish for opportunities of giving them proofs of your 'plus tendre et respectueux souvenir; beg of them in case your good fortune should carry them to any part of the world where you could be of any the least use to them, that they would employ you without reserve. Say all this, and a great deal more, emphatically and pathetically; for you know 'si vis me flere'. This can do you no harm, if you never return to Paris; but if you do, as probably you may, it will be of infinite use to you. Remember too, not to omit going to every house where you have ever been once, to take leave and recommend yourself to their remembrance. The reputation which you leave at one place, where you have been, will circulate, and you will meet with it at twenty places where you are to go. That is a labor never quite lost.

This letter will show you, that the accident which happened to me yesterday, and of which Mr. Grevenkop gives you account, hath had no bad consequences. My escape was a great one.

LETTER CLXVI

LONDON, May 11, O. S. 1752.

DEAR FRIEND: I break my word by writing this letter; but I break it on the allowable side, by doing more than I promised. I have pleasure in writing to you; and you may possibly have some profit in reading what I write; either of the motives were sufficient for me, both for you I cannot withstand. By your last I calculate that you will leave Paris upon this day se'nnight; upon that supposition, this letter may still find you there.

Colonel Perry arrived here two or three days ago, and sent me a book from you; Cassandra abridged. I am sure it cannot be too much abridged. The spirit of that most voluminous work, fairly extracted, may be contained in the smallest duodecimo; and it is most astonishing, that there ever could have been people idle enough to write or read such endless heaps of the same stuff. It was, however, the occupation of thousands in the last century, and is still the private, though disavowed, amusement of young girls, and sentimental ladies. A lovesick girl finds, in the captain with whom she is in love, all the courage and all the graces of the tender and accomplished Oroondates: and many a grown-up, sentimental lady, talks delicate Clelia to the hero, whom she would engage to eternal love, or laments with her that love is not eternal.

"Ah! qu'il est doux d'aimer, si l'on aimoit toujours!

Mais helas! il'n'est point d'eternelles amours."

It is, however, very well to have read one of those extravagant works (of all which La Calprenede's are the best), because it is well to be able to talk, with some degree of knowledge, upon all those subjects that other people talk sometimes upon: and I would by no means have anything, that is known to others, be totally unknown to you. It is a great advantage for any man, to be able to talk or to hear, neither ignorantly nor absurdly, upon any subject; for I have known people, who have not said one word, hear ignorantly and absurdly; it has appeared in their inattentive and unmeaning faces.

This, I think, is as little likely to happen to you as to anybody of your age: and if you will but add a versatility and easy conformity of manners, I know no company in which you are likely to be de trop.

This versatility is more particularly necessary for you at this time, now that you are going to so many different places: for, though the manners and customs of the several courts of Germany are in general the same, yet everyone has its particular characteristic; some peculiarity or other, which distinguishes it from the next. This you should carefully attend to, and immediately adopt. Nothing flatters people more, nor makes strangers so welcome, as such an occasional conformity. I do not mean by this, that you should mimic the air and stiffness of every awkward German court; no, by no means; but I mean that you should only cheerfully comply, and fall in with certain local habits, such as ceremonies, diet, turn of conversation, etc. People who are lately come from Paris, and who have been a good while there, are generally suspected, and especially in Germany, of having a degree of contempt for every other place. Take great care that nothing of this kind appear, at least outwardly, in your behavior; but commend whatever deserves any degree of commendation, without comparing it with what you may have left, much better of the same kind, at Paris. As for instance, the German kitchen is, without doubt, execrable, and the French delicious; however, never commend the French kitchen at a German table; but eat of what you can find tolerable there, and commend it, without comparing it to anything better. I have known many British Yahoos, who though while they were at Paris conformed to no one French custom, as soon as they got anywhere else, talked of nothing but what they did, saw, and eat at

LETTERS TO HIS SON, COMPLETE

Paris. The freedom of the French is not to be used indiscriminately at all the courts in Germany, though their easiness may, and ought; but that, too, at some places more than others. The courts of Manheim and Bonn, I take to be a little more unbarbarized than some others; that of Mayence, an ecclesiastical one, as well as that of Treves (neither of which is much frequented by foreigners), retains, I conceive, a great deal of the Goth and Vandal still. There, more reserve and ceremony are necessary; and not a word of the French. At Berlin, you cannot be too French. Hanover, Brunswick, Cassel, etc., are of the mixed kind, 'un peu decrottes, mais pas assez'.

Another thing, which I most earnestly recommend to you, not only in Germany, but in every part of the world where you may ever be, is not only real, but seeming attention, to whoever you speak to, or to whoever speaks to you. There is nothing so brutally shocking, nor so little forgiven, as a seeming inattention to the person who is speaking to you: and I have known many a man knocked down, for (in my opinion) a much lighter provocation, than that shocking inattention which I mean. I have seen many people, who, while you are speaking to them, instead of looking at, and attending to you, fix their eyes upon the ceiling or some other part of the room, look out of the window, play with a dog, twirl their snuff-box, or pick their nose. Nothing discovers a little, futile, frivolous mind more than this, and nothing is so offensively ill-bred; it is an explicit declaration on your part, that every the most trifling object, deserves your attention more than all that can be said by the person who is speaking to you. Judge of the sentiments of hatred and resentment, which such treatment must excite in every breast where any degree of self-love dwells; and I am sure I never yet met with that breast where there was not a great deal: I repeat it again and again (for it is highly necessary for you to remember it), that sort of vanity and self-love is inseparable from human nature, whatever may be its rank or condition; even your footmen will sooner forget and forgive a beating, than any manifest mark of slight and contempt. Be therefore, I beg of you, not only really, but seemingly and manifestly attentive to whoever speaks to you; nay, more, take their 'ton', and tune yourself to their unison. Be serious with the serious, gay with the gay, and trifle with the triflers. In assuming these various shapes, endeavor to make each of them seem to sit easy upon you, and even to appear to be your own natural one. This is the true and useful versatility, of which a thorough knowledge of the world at once teaches the utility and the means of acquiring.

I am very sure, at least I hope, that you will never make use of a silly expression, which is the favorite expression, and the absurd excuse of all fools and blockheads; I CANNOT DO SUCH A THING; a thing by no means either morally or physically impossible. I CANNOT attend long together to the same thing, says one fool; that is, he is such a fool that he will not. I remember a very awkward fellow, who did not know what to do with his sword, and who always took it off before dinner, saying that he could not possibly dine with his sword on; upon which I could not help telling him, that I really believed he could without any probable danger either to himself or others. It is a shame and an absurdity, for any man to say that he cannot do all those things, which are commonly done by all the rest of mankind.

Another thing that I must earnestly warn you against is laziness; by which more people have lost the fruit of their travels than, perhaps, by any other thing. Pray be always in motion. Early in the morning go and see things; and the rest of the day go and see people. If you stay but a week at a place, and that an insignificant one, see, however, all that is to be seen there; know as many people, and get into as many houses, as ever you can.

I recommend to you likewise, though probably you have thought of it yourself, to carry in your pocket a map of Germany, in which the postroads are marked; and also some short book of travels through Germany. The former will help to imprint in your memory situations and distances; and the latter will point out many things for you to see, that might otherwise possibly escape you, and which, though they may be in themselves of little consequence, you would regret not having seen, after having been at the places where they were.

Thus warned and provided for your journey, God speed you; 'Felix faustumque sit! Adieu.

LETTER CLXVII

LONDON, May 27, O. S. 1752

MY DEAR FRIEND: I send you the inclosed original from a friend of ours, with my own commentaries upon the text; a text which I have so often paraphrased, and commented upon already, that I believe I can hardly say anything new upon it; but, however, I cannot give it over till I am better convinced, than I yet am, that you feel all the utility, the importance, and the necessity of it; nay, not only feel, but practice it. Your panegyrist allows you, what most fathers would be more than satisified with, in a son, and chides me for not contenting myself with 'l'essentiellement bon'; but I, who have been in no one respect like other fathers, cannot neither, like them, content myself with 'l'essentiellement bon'; because I know that it will not do your business in the world, while you want 'quelques couches de vernis'. Few fathers care much for their sons, or, at least, most of them care more for their money: and, consequently, content themselves with giving them, at the cheapest rate, the common run of education: that is, a school till eighteen; the university till twenty; and a couple of years riding post through the several towns of Europe; impatient till their boobies come home to be married, and, as they call it, settled. Of those who really love their sons, few know how to do it. Some spoil them by fondling them while they are young, and then quarrel with them when they are grown up, for having been spoiled; some love them like mothers, and attend only to the bodily health and strength of the hopes of their family, solemnize his birthday, and rejoice, like the subjects of the Great Mogul, at the increase of his bulk; while others, minding, as they think, only essentials, take pains and pleasure to see in their heir, all their favorite weaknesses and imperfections. I hope and believe that I have kept clear of all of these errors in the education which I have given you. No weaknesses of my own have warped it, no parsimony has starved it, no rigor has deformed it. Sound and extensive learning was the foundation which I meant to lay—I have laid it; but that alone, I knew, would by no means be sufficient: the ornamental, the showish, the pleasing superstructure was to be begun. In that view, I threw you into the great world, entirely your own master, at an age when others either guzzle at the university, or are sent abroad in servitude to some awkward, pedantic Scotch governor. This was to put you in the way, and the only way of acquiring those manners, that address, and those graces, which exclusively distinguish people of fashion; and without which all moral virtues, and all acquired learning, are of no sort of use in the courts and 'le beau monde': on the contrary, I am not sure if they are not an hindrance. They are feared and disliked in those places, as too severe, if not smoothed and introduced by the graces; but of these graces, of this necessary 'beau vernis', it seems there are still 'quelque couches qui manquent'. Now, pray let me ask you, coolly and seriously, 'pourquoi ces couches manquent-elles'? For you may as easily take them, as you may wear more or less powder in your hair, more or less lace upon your coat. I can therefore account for your wanting them no other way in the world, than from your not being yet convinced of their full value. You have heard some English bucks say, "Damn these finical outlandish airs, give me a manly, resolute manner. They make a rout with their graces, and talk like a parcel of dancing-masters, and dress like a parcel of fops: one good Englishman will beat three of them." But let your own observation undeceive you of these prejudices. I will give you one instance only, instead of an hundred that I could give you, of a very shining fortune and figure, raised upon no other foundation whatsoever, than that of address, manners, and graces. Between you and me (for this example must go no further), what do you think made our friend, Lord A——e, Colonel of a regiment of guards, Governor of Virginia, Groom of the Stole, and Ambassador to Paris; amounting in all to sixteen or seventeen thousand pounds a year? Was it his birth? No, a Dutch gentleman only. Was it his estate? No, he had none. Was it his learning, his parts, his political abilities and application? You can answer these questions as easily, and as soon, as I can ask them. What was it then? Many people wondered, but I do not; for I know, and will tell you.

It was his air, his address, his manners, and his graces. He pleased, and by pleasing he became a favorite; and by becoming a favorite became all that he has been since. Show me any one instance, where intrinsic worth and merit, unassisted by exterior accomplishments, have raised any man so high. You know the Due de Richelieu, now 'Marechal, Cordon bleu, Gentilhomme de la Chambre', twice Ambassador, etc. By what means? Not by the purity of his character, the depth of his knowledge, or any uncommon penetration and sagacity. Women alone formed and raised him. The Duchess of Burgundy took a fancy to him, and had him before he was sixteen years old; this put him in fashion among the beau monde: and the late Regent's oldest daughter, now Madame de Modene, took him next, and was near marrying him. These early connections with women of the first distinction gave him those manners, graces, and address, which you see he has; and which, I can assure you, are all that he has; for, strip him of them, and he will be one of the poorest men in Europe. Man or woman cannot resist an engaging exterior; it will please, it will make its way. You want, it seems, but 'quelques couches'; for God's sake, lose no time in getting them; and now you have gone so far, complete the work. Think of nothing else till that work is finished; unwearied application will bring about anything: and surely your application can never be so well employed as upon that object, which is absolutely necessary to facilitate all others. With your knowledge and parts, if adorned by manners and graces, what may you not hope one day to be? But without them, you will be in the situation of a man who should be very fleet of one leg but very lame of the other. He could not run; the lame leg would check and clog the well one, which would be very near useless.

From my original plan for your education, I meant to make you 'un homme universel'; what depends on me is executed, the little that remains undone depends singly upon you. Do not then disappoint, when you can so easily gratify me. It is your own interest which I am pressing you to pursue, and it is the only return that I desire for all the care and affection of, Yours.

LETTER CLXVIII

LONDON, May 31, O. S. 1752

MY DEAR FRIEND: The world is the book, and the only one to which, at present, I would have you apply yourself; and the thorough knowledge of it will be of more use to you, than all the books that ever were read. Lay aside the best book whenever you can go into the best company; and depend upon it, you change for the better. However, as the most tumultuous life, whether of business or pleasure, leaves some vacant moments every day, in which a book is the refuge of a rational being, I mean now to point out to you the method of employing those moments (which will and ought to be but few) in the most advantageous manner. Throw away none of your time upon those trivial, futile books, published by idle or necessitous authors, for the amusement of idle and ignorant readers; such sort of books swarm and buzz about one every day; flap them away, they have no sting. 'Certum pete finem', have some one object for those leisure moments, and pursue that object invariably till you have attained it; and then take some other. For instance, considering your destination, I would advise you to single out the most remarkable and interesting eras of modern history, and confine all your reading to that ERA. If you pitch upon the Treaty of Munster (and that is the proper period to begin with, in the course which I am now recommending), do not interrupt it by dipping and deviating into other books, unrelative to it; but consult only the most authentic histories, letters, memoirs, and negotiations, relative to that great transaction; reading and comparing them, with all that caution and distrust which Lord Bolingbroke recommends to you, in a better manner, and in better words than I can. The next period worth your particular knowledge, is the Treaty of the Pyrenees: which was calculated to lay, and in effect did lay, the succession of the House of Bourbon to the crown of Spain. Pursue that in the same manner, singling, out of the millions of volumes written upon that occasion, the two or three most authentic ones, and particularly letters, which are the best authorities in matters of negotiation. Next come the Treaties of Nimeguen and Ryswick, postscripts in, a manner to those of Munster and the Pyrenees. Those two transactions have had great light thrown upon them by the publication of many authentic and original letters and pieces. The concessions made at the Treaty of Ryswick, by the then triumphant Lewis the Fourteenth, astonished all those who viewed things only superficially; but, I should think, must have been easily accounted for by those who knew the state of the kingdom of Spain, as well as of the health of its King, Charles the Second, at that time. The interval between the conclusion of the peace of Ryswick, and the breaking out of the great war in 1702, though a short, is a most interesting one. Every week of it almost produced some great event. Two partition treaties, the death of the King of Spain, his unexpected will, and the acceptance of it by Lewis the Fourteenth, in violation of the second treaty of partition, just signed and ratified by him. Philip the Fifth quietly and cheerfully received in Spain, and acknowledged as King of it, by most of those powers, who afterward joined in an alliance to dethrone him. I cannot help making this observation upon that occasion: That character has often more to do in great transactions, than prudence and sound policy; for Lewis the Fourteenth gratified his personal pride, by giving a Bourbon King to Spain, at the expense of the true interest of France; which would have acquired much more solid and permanent strength by the addition of Naples, Sicily, and Lorraine, upon the footing of the second partition treaty; and I think it was fortunate for Europe that he preferred the will. It is true, he might hope to influence his Bourbon posterity in Spain; he knew too well how weak the ties of blood are among men, and how much weaker still they are among princes. The Memoirs of Count Harrach, and of Las Torres, give a good deal of light into the transactions of the Court of Spain, previous to the death of that weak King; and the Letters of the Marachal d'Harcourt, then the French Ambassador in Spain, of which I have authentic copies in manuscript, from the year 1698 to 1701, have cleared up that whole affair to me. I keep that book for you. It appears by those letters, that the impudent conduct of the House of Austria, with regard to the King and Queen of Spain, and Madame Berlips, her favorite, together with the knowledge of the partition treaty, which incensed all Spain, were the true and only reasons of the will, in favor of the Duke of Anjou. Cardinal Portocarrero, nor any of the Grandees, were bribed by France, as was generally reported and believed at that time; which confirms Voltaire's anecdote upon that subject. Then opens a new scene and a new century; Lewis the Fourteenth's good fortune forsakes him, till the Duke of Marlborough and Prince Eugene make him amends for all the mischief they had done him, by making the allies refuse the terms of peace offered by him at Gertruydenberg. How the disadvantageous peace of Utrecht was afterward brought on, you have lately read; and you cannot inform yourself too minutely of all those circumstances, that treaty 'being the freshest source from whence the late transactions of Europe have flowed. The alterations that have since happened, whether by wars or treaties, are so recent, that all the written accounts are to be helped out, proved, or contradicted, by the oral ones of almost every informed person, of a certain age or rank in life. For the facts, dates, and original pieces of this century, you will find them in Lamberti, till the year 1715, and after that time in Rousset's 'Recueil'.

I do not mean that you should plod hours together in researches of this kind: no, you may employ your time more usefully: but I mean, that you should make the most of the moments you do employ, by method, and the pursuit of one single object at a time; nor should I call it a digression from that object, if when you meet with clashing and jarring pretensions of different princes to the same thing, you had immediately recourse to other books, in which those several pretensions were clearly stated; on the contrary, that is the only way of remembering those contested rights and claims: for, were a man to read 'tout de suite', Schwederus's 'Theatrum Pretensionum', he would only be confounded by the variety, and remember none of them; whereas, by examining them occasionally, as they happen to occur, either in the course of your historical reading, or as they are agitated in your own times, you will retain them, by connecting them with those historical facts which occasioned your inquiry. For example, had you read, in the course of two or three folios of Pretensions, those, among others, of the two Kings of England and Prussia to Oost Frise, it is impossible, that you should have remembered them; but now, that they are become the debated object at the Diet at Ratisbon, and the topic of all political conversations, if you consult both books and persons concerning them, and inform yourself thoroughly, you will never forget them as long as you live. You will hear a great deal of them ow one side, at Hanover, and as much on the other side, afterward, at Berlin: hear both sides, and form your own opinion; but dispute with neither.

Letters from foreign ministers to their courts, and from their courts to them, are, if genuine, the best and most authentic records you can read, as far as they go. Cardinal d'Ossat's, President Jeanin's, D'Estrade's, Sir William Temple's, will not only inform your mind, but form your style; which, in letters of business, should be very plain and simple, but, at the same time, exceedingly clear, correct, and pure.

All that I have said may be reduced to these two or three plain principles: 1st, That you should now read very little, but converse a great deal; 2d, To read no useless, unprofitable books; and 3d, That those which you do read, may all tend to a certain object, and be relative to, and consequential of each other. In this method, half an hour's reading every day will carry you a great way. People seldom know how to employ their time to the best advantage till they have too little left to employ; but if, at your age, in the beginning of life, people would but consider the value of it, and put every moment to interest, it is incredible what an additional fund of knowledge and pleasure such an economy would bring in. I look back with regret upon that large sum of time, which, in my youth, I lavished away idly, without either improvement or pleasure. Take warning betimes, and enjoy every moment; pleasures do not commonly last so long as life, and therefore should not be neglected; and the longest life is too short for knowledge, consequently every moment is precious.

I am surprised at having received no letter from you since you left Paris. I still direct this to Strasburgh, as I did my two last. I shall direct my next to the post house at Mayence, unless I receive, in the meantime, contrary instructions from you. Adieu. Remember les attentions: they must be your passports into good company.

LETTER CLXIX

LONDON, June, O. S. 1752.

MY DEAR FRIEND: Very few celebrated negotiators have been eminent for their learning. The most famous French negotiators (and I know no nation that can boast of abler) have been military men, as Monsieur d'Harcourt, Comte d'Estrades, Marechal d'Uxelles, and others. The late Duke of Marlborough, who was at least as able a negotiator as a general, was exceedingly ignorant of books, but extremely knowing in men, whereas the learned Grotius appeared, both in Sweden and in France, to be a very bungling minister. This is, in my opinion, very easily to be accounted for. A man of very deep learning must have employed the greatest part of his time in books; and a skillful negotiator must necessarily have employed much the greater part of his time with man. The sound scholar, when dragged out of his dusty closet into business, acts by book, and deals with men as he has read of them; not as he has known them by experience: he follows Spartan and Roman precedents, in what he falsely imagines to be similar cases; whereas two cases never were, since the beginning of the world, exactly alike; and he would be capable, where he thought spirit and vigor necessary, to draw a circle round the persons he treated with, and to insist upon a categorical answer before they went out of it, because he had read, in the Roman history, that once upon a time some Roman ambassador, did so.

No; a certain degree of learning may help, but no degree of learning will ever make a skillful minister whereas a great knowledge of the world, of the characters, passions, and habits of mankind, has, without one grain of learning, made a thousand. Military men have seldom much knowledge of books; their education does not allow it; but what makes great amends for that want is, that they generally know a great deal of the world; they are thrown into it young; they see variety of nations and characters; and they soon find, that to rise, which is the aim of them all, they must first please: these concurrent causes almost always give them manners and politeness. In consequence of which, you see them always distinguished at courts, and favored by the women. I could wish that you had been of an age to have made a campaign or two as a volunteer. It would have given you an attention, a versatility, and an alertness; all which I doubt you want; and a great want it is.

A foreign minister has not great business to transact every day; so that his knowledge and his skill in negotiating are not frequently put to the trial; but he has that to do every day, and every hour of the day, which is necessary to prepare and smooth the way for his business; that is, to insinuate himself by his manners, not only into the houses, but into the confidence of the most considerable people of that place; to contribute to their pleasures, and insensibly not to be looked upon as a stranger himself. A skillful minister may very possibly be doing his master's business full as well, in doing the honors gracefully and genteelly of a ball or a supper, as if he were laboriously writing a protocol in his closet. The Marechal d'Harcourt, by his magnificence, his manners, and his politeness, blunted the edge of the long aversion which the Spaniards had to the French. The court and the grandees were personally fond, of him, and frequented his house; and were at least insensibly brought to prefer a French to a German yoke; which I am convinced would never have happened, had Comte d'Harrach been Marechal d'Harcourt, or the Marechal d'Harcourt Comte d'Harrach. The Comte d'Estrades had, by 'ses manieres polies et liantes', formed such connections, and gained such an interest in the republic of the United Provinces, that Monsieur De Witt, the then Pensionary of Holland, often applied to him to use his interest with his friend, both in Holland and the other provinces, whenever he (De Witt) had a difficult point which he wanted to carry. This was certainly not brought about by his knowledge of books, but of men: dancing, fencing, and riding, with a little military architecture, were no doubt the top of his education; and if he knew that 'collegium' in Latin signified college in French, it must have been by accident. But he knew what was more useful: from thirteen years old he had been in the great world, and had read men and women so long, that he could then read them at sight.

Talking the other day, upon this and other subjects, all relative to you, with one who knows and loves you very well, and expressing my anxiety and wishes that your exterior accomplishments, as a man of fashion, might adorn, and at least equal your intrinsic merit as a man of sense and honor, the person interrupted me, and said: Set your heart at rest; that never will or can happen. It is not in character; that gentleness, that 'douceur', those attentions which you wish him to have, are not in his nature; and do what you will, nay, let him do what he will, he can never acquire them. Nature may be a little disguised and altered by care; but can by no means whatsoever be totally forced and changed. I denied this principle to a certain degree; but admitting, however, that in many respects our nature was not to be changed; and asserting, at the same time, that in others it might by care be very much altered and improved, so as in truth to be changed; that I took those exterior accomplishments, which we had been talking of, to be mere modes, and absolutely depending upon the will, and upon custom; and that, therefore, I was convinced that your good sense, which must show you the importance of them, would make you resolve at all events to acquire them, even in spite of nature, if nature be in the case. Our dispute, which lasted a great while, ended as Voltaire observes that disputes in England are apt to do, in a wager of fifty guineas; which I myself am to decide upon honor, and of which this is a faithful copy. If you think I shall win it, you may go my halves if you please; declare yourself in time. This I declare, that I would most cheerfully give a thousand guineas to win those fifty; you may secure them me if you please.

I grow very impatient for your future letters from the several courts of Manheim, Bonn, Hanover, etc. And I desire that your letters may be to me, what I do not desire they should be to anybody else, I mean full of yourself. Let the egotism, a figure which upon all other occasions I detest, be your only one to me. Trifles that concern you are not trifles to me; and my knowledge of them may possibly be useful to you. Adieu. 'Les graces, les graces, les graces'.

LETTERS TO HIS SON, COMPLETE

LETTER CLXX

LONDON, June 23, O. S. 1752

MY DEAR FRIEND: I direct this letter to Mayence, where I think it is likely to meet you, supposing, as I do, that you stayed three weeks at Manheim, after the date of your last from thence; but should you have stayed longer at Manheim, to which I have no objection, it will wait for you at Mayence. Mayence will not, I believe, have charms to detain you above a week; so that I reckon you will be at Bonn at the end of July, N. S. There you may stay just as little or as long as you please, and then proceed to Hanover.

I had a letter by the last post from a relation of mine at Hanover, Mr. Stanhope Aspinwall, who is in the Duke of Newcastle's office, and has lately been appointed the King's Minister to the Dey of Algiers; a post which, notwithstanding your views of foreign affairs, I believe you do not envy him. He tells me in that letter, there are very good lodgings to be had at one Mrs. Meyers's, the next door to the Duke of Newcastle's, which he offers to take for you; I have desired him to do it, in case Mrs. Meyers will wait for you till the latter end of August, or the beginning of September, N. S., which I suppose is about the time when you will be at Hanover. You will find this Mr. Aspinwall of great use to you there. He will exert himself to the utmost to serve you; he has been twice or thrice at Hanover, and knows all the allures there: he is very well with the Duke of Newcastle, and will puff you there. Moreover, if you have a mind to work there as a volunteer in that bureau, he will assist and inform you. In short, he is a very honest, sensible, and informed man; 'mais me paye pas beaucoup de sa figure; il abuse meme du privilege qu'ont les hommes d'etre laids; et il ne sera pas en reste avec les lions et les leopards qu'il trouvera a Alger'.

As you are entirely master of the time when you will leave Bonn and go to Hanover, so are you master to stay at Hanover as long as you please, and to go from thence where you please; provided that at Christmas you are at Berlin, for the beginning of the Carnival: this I would not have you say at Hanover, considering the mutual disposition of those two courts; but when anybody asks you where you are to go next, say that you propose rambling in Germany, at Brunswick, Cassel, etc., till the next spring; when you intend to be in Flanders, in your way to England. I take Berlin, at this time, to be the politest, the most shining, and the most useful court in Europe for a young fellow to be at: and therefore I would upon no account not have you there, for at least a couple of months of the Carnival. If you are as well received, and pass your time as well at Bonn as I believe you will, I would advise you to remain there till about the 20th of August, N. S., in four days you will be at Hanover. As for your stay there, it must be shorter or longer, according to certain circumstances WHICH YOU KNOW OF; supposing them, at the best, then, stay within a week or ten days of the King's return to England; but supposing them at the worst, your stay must not be too short, for reasons which you also know; no resentment must either appear or be suspected; therefore, at worst, I think you must remain there a month, and at best, as long as ever you please. But I am convinced that all will turn out very well for you there. Everybody is engaged or inclined to help you; the ministers, English and German, the principal ladies, and most of the foreign ministers; so that I may apply to you, 'nullum numen abest, si sit prudentia'. Du Perron will, I believe, be back there from Turin much about the time you get there: pray be very attentive to him, and connect yourself with him as much as ever you can; for, besides that he is a very pretty and well-informed man, he is very much in fashion at Hanover, is personally very well with the King and certain ladies; so that a visible intimacy and connection with him will do you credit and service. Pray cultivate Monsieur Hop, the Dutch minister, who has always been very much my friend, and will, I am sure, be yours; his manners, it is true, are not very engaging; he is rough, but he is sincere. It is very useful sometimes to see the things which one ought to avoid, as it is right to see very often those which one ought to imitate, and my friend Hop's manners will frequently point out to you, what yours ought to be by the rule of contraries.

Congreve points out a sort of critics, to whom he says that we are doubly obliged:—

"Rules for good writing they with pains indite,

Then show us what is bad, by what they write."

It is certain that Monsieur Hop, with the best heart in the world, and a thousand good qualities, has a thousand enemies, and hardly a friend; simply from the roughness of his manners.

N. B. I heartily wish you could have stayed long enough at Manheim to have been seriously and desperately in love with Madame de Taxis; who, I suppose, is a proud, insolent, fine lady, and who would consequently have expected attentions little short of adoration: nothing would do you more good than such a passion; and I live in hopes that somebody or other will be able to excite such an one in you; your hour may not yet be come, but it will come. Love has not been unaptly compared to the smallpox which most people have sooner or later. Iphigenia had a wonderful effect upon Cimon; I wish some Hanover Iphigenia may try her skill upon you.

I recommend to you again, though I have already done it twice or thrice, to speak German, even affectedly, while you are at Hanover; which will show that you prefer that language, and be of more use to you there with SOMEBODY, than you can imagine. When you carry my letters to Monsieur Munchausen and Monsieur Schwiegeldt, address yourself to them in German; the latter speaks French very well, but the former extremely ill. Show great attention to Madame, Munchausen's daughter, who is a great favorite; those little trifles please mothers, and sometimes fathers, extremely. Observe, and you will find, almost universally, that the least things either please or displease most; because they necessarily imply, either a very strong desire of obliging, or an unpardonable indifference about it. I will give you a ridiculous instance enough of this truth, from my own experience. When I was Ambassador the first time in Holland, Comte de Wassenaer and his wife, people of the first rank and consideration, had a little boy of about three years old, of whom they were exceedingly fond; in order to make my court to them, I was so too, and used to take the child often upon my lap, and play with him. One day his nose was very dirty, upon which I took out my handkerchief and wiped it for him; this raised a loud laugh, and they called me a very, handy nurse; but the father and mother were so pleased with it, that to this day it is an anecdote in the family, and I never receive a letter from Comte Wassenaer, but he makes me the compliments 'du morveux gue j'ai mouche autrefois'; who, by the way, I am assured, is now the prettiest young fellow in Holland. Where one would gain people, remember that nothing is little. Adieu.

LETTER CLXXI

LETTERS TO HIS SON, COMPLETE

LONDON, June 26, O. S. 1752.

MY DEAR FRIEND: As I have reason to fear, from your M last letter of the 18th, N. S., from Manheim, that all, or at least most of my letters to you, since you left Paris, have miscarried; I think it requisite, at all events, to repeat in this the necessary parts of those several letters, as far as they relate to your future motions.

I suppose that this will either find you, or be but a few days before you at Bonn, where it is directed; and I suppose too, that you have fixed your time for going from thence to Hanover. If things TURN OUT WELL AT HANOVER, as in my opinion they will, 'Chi sta bene non si muova', stay there till a week or ten days before the King sets out for England; but, should THEY TURN OUT ILL, which I cannot imagine, stay, however, a month, that your departure may not seem a step of discontent or peevishness; the very suspicion of which is by all means to be avoided. Whenever you leave Hanover, be it sooner or be it later, where would you go? 'Lei Padrone', and I give you your choice: would you pass the months of November and December at Brunswick, Cassel, etc.? Would you choose to go for a couple of months to Ratisbon, where you would be very well recommended to, and treated by the King's Electoral Minister, the Baron de Behr, and where you would improve your 'Jus publicum'? or would you rather go directly to Berlin, and stay there till the end of the Carnival? Two or three months at Berlin are, considering all circumstances, necessary for you; and the Carnival months are the best; 'pour le reste decidez en dernier ressort, et sans appel comme d'abus'. Let me know your decree, when you have formed it. Your good or ill success at Hanover will have a very great influence upon your subsequent character, figure, and fortune in the world; therefore I confess that I am more anxious about it, than ever bride was on her wedding night, when wishes, hopes, fears, and doubts, tumultuously agitate, please, and terrify her. It is your first crisis: the character which you will acquire there will, more or less, be that which will abide by you for the rest of your life. You will be tried and judged there, not as a boy, but as a man; and from that moment there is no appeal for character; it is fixed. To form that character advantageously, you have three objects particularly to attend to: your character as a man of morality, truth, and honor; your knowledge in the objects of your destination, as a man of business; and your engaging and insinuating address, air and manners, as a courtier; the sure and only steps to favor.

Merit at courts, without favor, will do little or nothing; favor, without merit, will do a good deal; but favor and merit together will do everything. Favor at courts depends upon so many, such trifling, such unexpected, and unforeseen events, that a good courtier must attend to every circumstance, however little, that either does, or can happen; he must have no absences, no DISTRACTIONS; he must not say, "I did not mind it; who would have thought it?" He ought both to have minded, and to have thought it. A chamber-maid has sometimes caused revolutions in courts which have produced others in kingdoms. Were I to make my way to favor in a court, I would neither willfully, nor by negligence, give a dog or a cat there reason to dislike me. Two 'pies grieches', well instructed, you know, made the fortune of De Luines with Lewis XIII. Every step a man makes at court requires as much attention and circumspection, as those which were made formerly between hot plowshares, in the Ordeal, or fiery trials; which, in those times of ignorance and superstition, were looked upon as demonstrations of innocence or guilt. Direct your principal battery, at Hanover, at the D of N 's: there are many very weak places in that citadel; where, with a very little skill, you cannot fail making a great impression. Ask for his orders in everything you do; talk Austrian and Anti-gallican to him; and, as soon as you are upon a foot of talking easily to him, tell him 'en badinant', that his skill and success in thirty or forty elections in England leave you no reason to doubt of his carrying his election for Frankfort; and that you look upon the Archduke as his Member for the Empire. In his hours of festivity and compotation, drop that he puts you in mind of what Sir William Temple says of the Pensionary De Witt,—who at that time governed half Europe,—that he appeared at balls, assemblies, and public places, as if he had nothing else to do or to think of. When he talks to you upon foreign affairs, which he will often do, say that you really cannot presume to give any opinion of your own upon those matters, looking upon yourself at present only as a postscript to the corps diplomatique; but that, if his Grace will be pleased to make you an additional volume to it, though but in duodecimo, you will do your best that he shall neither be ashamed nor repent of it. He loves to have a favorite, and to open himself to that favorite. He has now no such person with him; the place is vacant, and if you have dexterity you may fill it. In one thing alone do not humor him; I mean drinking; for, as I believe, you have never yet been drunk, you do not yourself know how you can bear your wine, and what a little too much of it may make you do or say; you might possibly kick down all you had done before.

You do not love gaming, and I thank God for it; but at Hanover I would have you show, and profess a particular dislike to play, so as to decline it upon all occasions, unless where one may be wanted to make a fourth at whist or quadrille; and then take care to declare it the result of your complaisance, not of your inclinations. Without such precaution you may very possibly be suspected, though unjustly, of loving play, upon account of my former passion for it; and such a suspicion would do you a great deal of hurt, especially with the King, who detests gaming. I must end this abruptly. God bless you!

LETTER CLXXII

MY DEAR FRIEND: Versatility as a courtier may be almost decisive to you hereafter; that is, it may conduce to, or retard your preferment in your own destination. The first reputation goes a great way; and if you fix a good one at Hanover, it will operate also to your advantage in England. The trade of a courtier is as much a trade as that of a shoemaker; and he who applies himself the most, will work the best: the only difficulty is to distinguish (what I am sure you have sense enough to distinguish) between the right and proper qualifications and their kindred faults; for there is but a line between every perfection and its neighboring imperfection. As, for example, you must be extremely well-bred and polite, but without the troublesome forms and stiffness of ceremony. You must be respectful and assenting, but without being servile and abject. You must be frank, but without indiscretion; and close, without being costive. You must keep up dignity of character, without the least pride of birth or rank. You must be gay within all the bounds of decency and respect; and grave without the affectation of wisdom, which does not become the age of twenty. You must be essentially secret, without being dark and mysterious. You must be firm, and even bold, but with great seeming modesty.

With these qualifications, which, by the way, are all in your own power, I will answer for your success, not only at Hanover, but at any court in Europe. And I am not sorry that you begin your apprenticeship at a little one; because you must be more circumspect, and more upon your guard there, than at a great one, where every little thing is not known nor reported.

When you write to me, or to anybody else, from thence, take care that your letters contain commendations of all that you see and hear there; for they will most of them be opened and read; but, as frequent couriers will come from Hanover to England, you may sometimes write to me without reserve; and put your letters into a very little box, which you may send safely by some of them.

I must not omit mentioning to you, that at the Duke of Newcastle's table, where you will frequently dine, there is a great deal of drinking; be upon your guard against it, both upon account of your health, which would not bear it, and of the consequences of your being flustered and heated with wine: it might engage you in scrapes and frolics, which the King (who is a very sober man himself) detests. On the other hand, you should not seem too grave and too wise to drink like the rest of the company; therefore use art: mix water with your wine; do not drink all that is in the glass; and if detected, and pressed to drink more do not cry out sobriety; but say that you have lately been out of order, that you are subject to inflammatory complaints, and that you must beg to be excused for the present. A young fellow ought to be wiser than he should seem to be; and an old fellow ought to seem wise whether he really' be so or not.

During your stay at Hanover I would have you make two or three excursions to parts of that Electorate: the Hartz, where the silver mines are; Gottingen, for the University; Stade, for what commerce there is. You should also go to Zell. In short, see everything that is to be seen there, and inform yourself well of all the details of that country. Go to Hamburg for three or four days, and know the constitution of that little Hanseatic Republic, and inform yourself well of the nature of the King of Denmark's pretensions to it.

If all things turn out right for you at Hanover, I would have you make it your head-quarters, till about a week or ten days before the King leaves it; and then go to Brunswick, which, though a little, is a very polite, pretty court. You may stay there a fortnight or three weeks, as you like it; and from thence go to Cassel, and stay there till you go to Berlin; where I would have you be by Christmas. At Hanover you will very easily get good letters of recommendation to Brunswick and to Cassel. You do not want any to Berlin; however, I will send you one for Voltaire. 'A propos' of Berlin, be very reserved and cautious while at Hanover, as to that King and that country; both which are detested, because feared by everybody there, from his Majesty down to the meanest peasant; but, however, they both extremely deserve your utmost attention and you will see the arts and wisdom of government better in that country, now, than in any other in Europe. You may stay three months at Berlin, if you like it, as I believe you will; and after that I hope we shall meet there again.

Of all the places in the world (I repeat it once more), establish a good reputation at Hanover, 'et faites vous valoir la, autant qu'il est possible, par le brillant, les manieres, et les graces'. Indeed it is of the greatest importance to you, and will make any future application to the King in your behalf very easy. He is more taken by those little things, than any man, or even woman, that I ever knew in my life: and I do not wonder at him. In short, exert to the utmost all your means and powers to please: and remember that he who pleases the most, will rise the soonest and the highest. Try but once the pleasure and advantage of pleasing, and I will answer that you will never more neglect the means.

I send you herewith two letters, the one to Monsieur Munchausen, the other to Monsieur Schweigeldt, an old friend of mine, and a very sensible knowing man. They will both I am sure, be extremely civil to you, and carry you into the best company; and then it is your business to please that company. I never was more anxious about any period of your life, than I am about this, your Hanover expedition, it being of so much more consequence to you than any other. If I hear from thence, that you are liked and loved there, for your air, your manners, and address, as well as esteemed for your knowledge, I shall be the happiest man in the world. Judge then what I must be, if it happens otherwise. Adieu.

LETTER CLXXIII

EARL OF PHILIP DORMER STANHOPE CHESTERFIELD

LONDON, July 21, O. S. 1752

MY DEAR FRIEND: By my calculation this letter may probably arrive at Hanover three or four days before you; and as I am sure of its arriving there safe, it shall contain the most material points that I have mentioned in my several letters to you since you left Paris, as if you had received but few of them, which may very probably be the case.

As for your stay at Hanover, it must not IN ALL EVENTS be less than a month; but if things turn out to Your SATISFACTION, it may be just as long as you please. From thence you may go wherever you like; for I have so good an opinion of your judgment, that I think you will combine and weigh all circumstances, and choose the properest places. Would you saunter at some of the small courts, as Brunswick, Cassel, etc., till the Carnival at Berlin? You are master. Would you pass a couple of months at Ratisbon, which might not be ill employed? 'A la bonne heure'. Would you go to Brussels, stay a month or two there with Dayrolles, and from thence to Mr. Yorke, at The Hague? With all my heart. Or, lastly, would you go to Copenhagen and Stockholm? 'Lei e anche Padrone': choose entirely for yourself, without any further instructions from me; only let me know your determination in time, that I may settle your credit, in case you go to places where at present you have none. Your object should be to see the 'mores multorum hominum et urbes'; begin and end it where you please.

By what you have already seen of the German courts, I am sure you must have observed that they are much more nice and scrupulous, in points of ceremony, respect and attention, than the greater courts of France and England. You will, therefore, I am persuaded, attend to the minutest circumstances of address and behavior, particularly during your stay at Hanover, which (I will repeat it, though I have said it often to you already) is the most important preliminary period of your whole life. Nobody in the world is more exact, in all points of good-breeding, than the King; and it is the part of every man's character, that he informs himself of first. The least negligence, or the slightest inattention, reported to him, may do you infinite prejudice: as their contraries would service.

If Lord Albemarle (as I believe he did) trusted you with the secret affairs of his department, let the Duke of Newcastle know that he did so; which will be an inducement to him to trust you too, and possibly to employ you in affairs of consequence. Tell him that, though you are young, you know the importance of secrecy in business, and can keep a secret; that I have always inculcated this doctrine into you, and have, moreover, strictly forbidden you ever to communicate, even to me, any matters of a secret nature, which you may happen to be trusted with in the course of business.

As for business, I think I can trust you to yourself; but I wish I could say as much for you with regard to those exterior accomplishments, which are absolutely necessary to smooth and shorten the way to it. Half the business is done, when one has gained the heart and the affections of those with whom one is to transact it. Air and address must begin, manners and attention must finish that work. I will let you into one secret concerning myself; which is, that I owe much more of the success which I have had in the world to my manners, than to any superior degree of merit or knowledge. I desired to please, and I neglected none of the means. This, I can assure you, without any false modesty, is the truth: You have more knowledge than I had at your age, but then I had much more attention and good-breeding than you. Call it vanity, if you please, and possibly it was so; but my great object was to make every man I met with like me, and every woman love me. I often succeeded; but why? By taking great pains, for otherwise I never should: my figure by no means entitled me to it; and I had certainly an up-hill game; whereas your countenance would help you, if you made the most of it, and proscribed for ever the guilty, gloomy, and funereal part of it. Dress, address, and air, would become your best countenance, and make your little figure pass very well.

LETTERS TO HIS SON, COMPLETE

If you have time to read at Hanover, pray let the books you read be all relative to the history and constitution of that country; which I would have you know as correctly as any Hanoverian in the whole Electorate. Inform yourself of the powers of the States, and of the nature and extent of the several judicatures; the particular articles of trade and commerce of Bremen, Harburg, and Stade; the details and value of the mines of the Hartz. Two or three short books will give you the outlines of all these things; and conversation turned upon those subjects will do the rest, and better than books can.

Remember of all things to speak nothing but German there; make it (to express myself pedantically) your vernacular language; seem to prefer it to any other; call it your favorite language, and study to speak it with purity and elegance, if it has any. This will not only make you perfect in it, but will please, and make your court there better than anything. A propos of languages: Did you improve your Italian while you were at Paris, or did you forget it? Had you a master there? and what Italian books did you read with him? If you are master of Italian, I would have you afterward, by the first convenient opportunity, learn Spanish, which you may very easily, and in a very little time do; you will then, in the course of your foreign business, never be obliged to employ, pay, or trust any translator for any European language.

As I love to provide eventually for everything that can possibly happen, I will suppose the worst that can befall you at Hanover. In that case I would have you go immediately to the Duke of Newcastle, and beg his Grace's advice, or rather orders, what you should do; adding, that his advice will always be orders to you. You will tell him that though you are exceedingly mortified, you are much less so than you should otherwise be, from the consideration that being utterly unknown to his M———, his objection could not be personal to you, and could only arise from circumstances which it was not in your power either to prevent or remedy; that if his Grace thought that your continuing any longer there would be disagreeable, you entreated him to tell you so; and that upon the whole, you referred yourself entirely to him, whose orders you should most scrupulously obey. But this precaution, I dare say, is 'ex abundanti', and will prove unnecessary; however, it is always right to be prepared for all events, the worst as well as the best; it prevents hurry and surprise, two dangerous, situations in business; for I know no one thing so useful, so necessary in all business, as great coolness, steadiness, and sangfroid: they give an incredible advantage over whoever one has to do with.

I have received your letter of the 15th, N. S., from Mayence, where I find that you have diverted yourself much better than I expected. I am very well acquainted with Comte Cobentzel's character, both of parts and business. He could have given you letters to Bonn, having formerly resided there himself. You will not be so agreeably ELECTRIFIED where this letter will find you, as you were both at Manheim and Mayence; but I hope you may meet with a second German Mrs. F———d, who may make you forget the two former ones, and practice your German. Such transient passions will do you no harm; but, on the contrary, a great deal of good; they will refine your manners and quicken your attention; they give a young fellow 'du brillant', and bring him into fashion; which last is a great article at setting out in the world.

I have wrote, about a month ago, to Lord Albemarle, to thank him for all his kindnesses to you; but pray have you done as much? Those are the necessary attentions which should never be omitted, especially in the beginning of life, when a character is to be established.

That ready wit; which you so partially allow me, and so justly Sir Charles Williams, may create many admirers; but, take my word for it, it makes few friends. It shines and dazzles like the noon-day sun, but, like that too, is very apt to scorch; and therefore is always feared. The milder morning and evening light and heat of that planet soothe and calm our minds. Good sense, complaisance, gentleness of manners, attentions and graces are the only things that truly engage, and durably keep the heart at long run. Never seek for wit; if it presents itself, well and good; but, even in that case, let your judgment interpose; and take care that it be not at the expense of anybody. Pope says very truly:

EARL OF PHILIP DORMER STANHOPE CHESTERFIELD

"There are whom heaven has blest with store of wit;

Yet want as much again to govern it."

And in another place, I doubt with too much truth:

"For wit and judgment ever are at strife

Though meant each other's aid, like man and wife."

The Germans are very seldom troubled with any extraordinary ebullitions or effervescenses of wit, and it is not prudent to try it upon them; whoever does, 'ofendet solido'.

Remember to write me very minute accounts of all your transactions at Hanover, for they excite both my impatience and anxiety. Adieu!

LETTER CLXXIV

LONDON, August 4, O. S. 1752

MY DEAR FRIEND: I am extremely concerned at the return of your old asthmatic complaint, of which your letter from Cassel of the 28th July, N. S., in forms me. I believe it is chiefly owing to your own negligence; for, notwithstanding the season of the year, and the heat and agitation of traveling, I dare swear you have not taken one single dose of gentle, cooling physic, since that which I made you take at Bath. I hope you are now better, and in better hands. I mean in Dr. Hugo's at Hanover: he is certainly a very skillful physician, and therefore I desire that you will inform him most minutely of your own case, from your first attack in Carniola, to this last at Marpurgh; and not only follow his prescriptions exactly at present, but take his directions, with regard to the regimen that he would have you observe to prevent the returns of this complaint; and, in case of any returns, the immediate applications, whether external or internal, that he would have you make use of. Consider, it is very worth your while to submit at present to any course of medicine or diet, to any restraint or confinement, for a time, in order to get rid, once for all, of so troublesome and painful a distemper; the returns of which would equally break in upon your business or your pleasures. Notwithstanding all this, which is plain sense and reason, I much fear that, as soon as ever you are got out of your present distress, you will take no preventive care, by a proper course of medicines and regimen; but, like most people of your age, think it impossible that you ever should be ill again. However, if you will not be wise for your own sake, I desire you will be so for mine, and most scrupulously observe Dr. Hugo's present and future directions.

Hanover, where I take it for granted you are, is at present the seat and centre of foreign negotiations; there are ministers from almost every court in Europe; and you have a fine opportunity of displaying with modesty, in conversation, your knowledge of the matters now in agitation. The chief I take to be the Election of the King of the Romans, which, though I despair of, heartily wish were brought about for two reasons. The first is, that I think it may prevent a war upon the death of the present Emperor, who, though young and healthy, may possibly die, as young and healthy people often do. The other is, the very reason that makes some powers oppose it, and others dislike it, who do not openly oppose it; I mean, that it may tend to make the imperial dignity hereditary in the House of Austria; which I heartily wish, together with a very great increase of power in the empire: till when, Germany will never be anything near a match for France. Cardinal Richelieu showed his superior abilities in nothing more, than in thinking no pains or expense too great to break the power of the House of Austria in the empire. Ferdinand had certainly made himself absolute, and the empire consequently formidable to France, if that Cardinal had not piously adopted the Protestant cause, and put the empire, by the treaty of Westphalia, in pretty much the same disjointed situation in which France itself was before Lewis the Eleventh; when princes of the blood, at the head of provinces, and Dukes of Brittany, etc., always opposed, and often gave laws to the crown. Nothing but making the empire hereditary in the House of Austria, can give it that strength and efficiency, which I wish it had, for the sake of the balance of power. For, while the princes of the empire are so independent of the emperor, so divided among themselves, and so open to the corruption of the best bidders, it is ridiculous to expect that Germany ever will, or can act as a compact and well-united body against France. But as this notion of mine would as little please SOME OF OUR FRIENDS, as many of our enemies, I would not advise you, though you should be of the same opinion, to declare yourself too freely so. Could the Elector Palatine be satisfied, which I confess will be difficult, considering the nature of his pretensions, the tenaciousness and haughtiness of the court of Vienna (and our inability to do, as we have too often done, their work for them); I say, if the Elector Palatine could be engaged to give his vote, I should think it would be right to proceed to the election with a clear majority of five votes; and leave the King of Prussia and the Elector of Cologne, to protest and remonstrate as much as ever they please. The former is too wise, and the latter too weak in every respect, to act in consequence of these protests. The distracted situation of France, with its ecclesiastical and parliamentary quarrels, not to mention the illness and possibly the death of the Dauphin, will make the King of Prussia, who is certainly no Frenchman in his heart, very cautious how he acts as one. The Elector of Saxony will be influenced by the King of Poland, who must be determined by Russia, considering his views upon Poland, which, by the by, I hope he will never obtain; I mean, as to making that crown hereditary in his family. As for his sons having it by the precarious tenure of election, by which his father now holds it, 'a la bonne heure'. But, should Poland have a good government under hereditary kings, there would be a new devil raised in Europe, that I do not know who could lay. I am sure I would not raise him, though on my own side for the present.

I do not know how I came to trouble my head so much about politics today, which has been so very free from them for some years: I suppose it was because I knew that I was writing to the most consummate politician of this, and his age. If I err, you will set me right; 'si quid novisti rectius istis, candidus imperti', etc.

I am excessively impatient for your next letter, which I expect by the first post from Hanover, to remove my anxiety, as I hope it will, not only with regard to your health, but likewise to OTHER THINGS; in the meantime in the language of a pedant, but with the tenderness of a parent, 'jubeo te bene valere'.

Lady Chesterfield makes you many compliments, and is much concerned at your indisposition.

LETTER CLXXV

TO MONSIEUR DE VOLTAIRE, NOW STAYING AT BERLIN.

LONDON, August 27, O. S. 1752.

SIR: As a most convincing proof how infinitely I am interested in everything which concerns Mr. Stanhope, who will have the honor of presenting you this letter, I take the liberty of introducing him to you. He has read a great deal, he has seen a great deal; whether or not he has made a proper use of that knowledge, is what I do not know: he is only twenty years of age. He was at Berlin some years ago, and therefore he returns thither; for at present people are attracted toward the north by the same motives which but lately drew them to the south.

Permit me, Sir, to return you thanks for the pleasure and instruction I have received from your 'History of Lewis XIV'. I have as yet read it but four times, because I wish to forget it a little before I read it a fifth; but I find that impossible: I shall therefore only wait till you give us the augmentation which you promised; let me entreat you not to defer it long. I thought myself pretty conversant in the history of the reign of Lewis XIV., by means of those innumerable histories, memoirs, anecdotes, etc., which I had read relative to that period of time. You have convinced me that I was mistaken, and had upon that subject very confused ideas in many respects, and very false ones in others. Above all, I cannot but acknowledge the obligation we have to you, Sir, for the light which you have thrown upon the follies and outrages of the different sects; the weapons you employ against those madmen, or those impostors, are the only suitable ones; to make use of any others would be imitating them: they must be attacked by ridicule, and, punished with contempt. 'A propos' of those fanatics; I send you here inclosed a piece upon that subject, written by the late Dean Swift: I believe you will not dislike it. You will easily guess why it never was printed: it is authentic, and I have the original in his own handwriting. His Jupiter, at the Day of judgment, treats them much as you do, and as they deserve to be treated.

Give me leave, Sir, to tell you freely, that I am embarrassed upon your account, as I cannot determine what it is that I wish from you. When I read your last history, I am desirous that you should always write history; but when I read your 'Rome Sauvee' (although ill-printed and disfigured), yet I then wish you never to deviate from poetry; however, I confess that there still remains one history worthy of your pen, and of which your pen alone is worthy. You have long ago given us the history of the greatest and most outrageous madman (I ask your pardon if I cannot say the greatest hero) of Europe; you have given us latterly the history of the greatest king; give us now the history of the greatest and most virtuous man in Europe; I should think it degrading to call him king. To you this cannot be difficult, he is always before your eyes: your poetical invention is not necessary to his glory, as that may safely rely upon your historical candor. The first duty of an historian is the only one he need require from his, 'Ne quid falsi dicere audeat, ne quid veri non audeat'. Adieu, Sir! I find that I must admire you every day more and more; but I also know that nothing ever can add to the esteem and attachment with which I am actually, your most humble and most obedient servant,
CHESTERFIELD.

LETTER CLXXVI

LONDON, September 19, 1752,

MY DEAR FRIEND: Since you have been at Hanover, your correspondence has been both unfrequent and laconic. You made indeed one great effort in folio on the 18th, with a postscript of the 22d August, N. S., and since that, 'vous avez rate in quarto'. On the 31st August, N. S., you give me no informations of what I want chiefly to know; which is, what Dr. Hugo (whom I charged you to consult) said of your asthmatic complaint, and what he prescribed you to prevent the returns of it; and also what is the company that, you keep there, who has been kind and civil to you, and who not.

You say that you go constantly to the parade; and you do very well; for though you are not of that trade, yet military matters make so great a part both of conversation and negotiation, that it is very proper not to be ignorant of them. I hope you mind more than the mere exercise of the troops you see; and that you inform yourself at the same time, of the more material details; such as their pay, and the difference of it when in and out of quarters; what is furnished them by the country when in quarters, and what is allowed them of ammunition, bread, etc., when in the field; the number of men and officers in the several troops and companies, together with the non-commissioned officers, as 'caporals, frey-caporals, anspessades', sergeants, quarter-masters, etc.; the clothing how frequent, how good, and how furnished; whether by the colonel, as here in England, from what we call the OFF-RECKONINGS, that is, deductions from the men's pay, or by commissaries appointed by the government for that purpose, as in France and Holland. By these inquiries you will be able to talk military with military men, who, in every country in Europe, except England, make at least half of all the best companies. Your attending the parades has also another good effect, which is, that it brings you, of course, acquainted with the officers, who, when of a certain rank and service, are generally very polite, well-bred people, 'et du bon ton'. They have commonly seen a great deal of the world, and of courts; and nothing else can form a gentleman, let people say what they will of sense and learning; with both which a man may contrive to be a very disagreeable companion. I dare say, there are very few captains of foot, who are not much better company than ever Descartes or Sir Isaac Newton were. I honor and respect such superior geniuses; but I desire to converse with people of this world, who bring into company their share, at least, of cheerfulness, good-breeding, and knowledge of mankind. In common life, one much oftener wants small money, and silver, than gold. Give me a man who has ready cash about him for present expenses; sixpences, shillings, half-crowns, and crowns, which circulate easily: but a man who has only an ingot of gold about him, is much above common purposes, and his riches are not handy nor convenient. Have as much gold as you please in one pocket, but take care always to keep change in the other; for you will much oftener have occasion for a shilling than for a guinea. In this the French must be allowed to excel all people in the world: they have 'un certain entregent, un enjouement, un aimable legerete dans la conversation, une politesse aisee et naturelle, qui paroit ne leur rien couter', which give society all its charms. I am sorry to add, but it is too true, that the English and the Dutch are the farthest from this, of all the people in the world; I do by no means except even the Swiss.

Though you do not think proper to inform me, I know from other hands that you were to go to the Gohr with a Comte Schullemburg, for eight or ten days only, to see the reviews. I know also that you had a blister upon your arm, which did you a great deal of good. I know too, you have contracted a great friendship with Lord Essex, and that you two were inseparable at Hanover. All these things I would rather have known from you than from others; and they are the sort of things that I am the most desirous of knowing, as they are more immediately relative to yourself.

EARL OF PHILIP DORMER STANHOPE CHESTERFIELD

I am very sorry for the Duchess of Newcastle's illness, full as much upon your as upon her account, as it has hindered you from being so much known to the Duke as I could have wished; use and habit going a great way with him, as indeed they do with most people. I have known many people patronized, pushed up, and preferred by those who could have given no other reason for it, than that they were used to them. We must never seek for motives by deep reasoning, but we must find them out by careful observation and attention, no matter what they should be, but the point is, what they are. Trace them up, step by step, from the character of the person. I have known 'de par le monde', as Brantome says, great effects from causes too little ever to have been suspected. Some things must be known, and can never be guessed.

God knows where this letter will find you, or follow you; not at Hanover, I suppose; but wherever it does, may it find you in health and pleasure! Adieu.

LETTER CLXXVII

LONDON, September 22, O. S. 1752

MY DEAR FRIEND: The day after the date of my last, I received your letter of the 8th. I approve extremely of your intended progress, and am very glad that you go to the Gohr with Comte Schullemburg. I would have you see everything with your own eyes, and hear everything with your own ears: for I know, by very long experience, that it is very unsafe to trust to other people's. Vanity and interest cause many misrepresentations, and folly causes many more. Few people have parts enough to relate exactly and judiciously: and those who have, for some reason or other, never fail to sink, or to add some circumstances.

The reception which you have met with at Hanover, I look upon as an omen of your being well received everywhere else; for to tell you the truth, it was the place that I distrusted the most in that particular. But there is a certain conduct, there are certaines 'manieres' that will, and must get the better of all difficulties of that kind; it is to acquire them that you still continue abroad, and go from court to court; they are personal, local, and temporal; they are modes which vary, and owe their existence to accidents, whim, and humor; all the sense and reason in the world would never point them out; nothing but experience, observation, and what is called knowledge of the world, can possibly teach them. For example, it is respectful to bow to the King of England, it is disrespectful to bow to the King of France; it is the rule to courtesy to the Emperor; and the prostration of the whole body is required by eastern monarchs. These are established ceremonies, and must be complied with: but why they were established, I defy sense and reason to tell us. It is the same among all ranks, where certain customs are received, and must necessarily be complied with, though by no means the result of sense and reason. As for instance, the very absurd, though almost universal custom of drinking people's healths. Can there be anything in the world less relative to any other man's health, than my drinking a glass of wine? Common sense certainly never pointed it out; but yet common sense tells me I must conform to it. Good sense bids one be civil and endeavor to please; though nothing but experience and observation can teach one the means, properly adapted to time, place, and persons. This knowledge is the true object of a gentleman's traveling, if he travels as he ought to do. By frequenting good company in every country, he himself becomes of every country; he is no longer an Englishman, a Frenchman, or an Italian; but he is an European; he adopts, respectively, the best manners of every country; and is a Frenchman at Paris, an Italian at Rome, an Englishman at London.

This advantage, I must confess, very seldom accrues to my countrymen from their traveling; as they have neither the desire nor the means of getting into good company abroad; for, in the first place, they are confoundedly bashful; and, in the next place, they either speak no foreign language at all, or if they do, it is barbarously. You possess all the advantages that they want; you know the languages in perfection, and have constantly kept the best company in the places where you have been; so that you ought to be an European.

Your canvas is solid and strong, your outlines are good; but remember that you still want the beautiful coloring of Titian, and the delicate, graceful touches of Guido. Now is your time to get them. There is, in all good company, a fashionable air, countenance, manner, and phraseology, which can only be acquired by being in good company, and very attentive to all that passes there. When you dine or sup at any well-bred man's house, observe carefully how he does the honors of his table to the different guests. Attend to the compliments of congratulation or condolence that you hear a well-bred man make to his superiors, to his equals, and to his inferiors; watch even his countenance and his tone of voice, for they all conspire in the main point of pleasing. There is a certain distinguishing diction of a man of fashion; he will not content himself with saying, like John Trott, to a new-married man, Sir, I wish you much joy; or to a man who lost his son, Sir, I am sorry for your loss; and both with a countenance equally unmoved; but he will say in effect the same thing in a more elegant and less trivial manner, and with a countenance adapted to the occasion. He will advance with warmth, vivacity, and a cheerful countenance, to the new-married man, and embracing him, perhaps say to him, "If you do justice to my attachment to you, you will judge of the joy that I feel upon this occasion, better than I can express it," etc.; to the other in affliction, he will advance slowly, with a grave composure of countenance, in a more deliberate manner, and with a lower voice, perhaps say, "I hope you do me the justice to be convinced that I feel whatever you feel, and shall ever be affected where you are concerned."

Your 'abord', I must tell you, was too cold and uniform; I hope it is now mended. It should be respectfully open and cheerful with your superiors, warm and animated with your equals, hearty and free with your inferiors. There is a fashionable kind of SMALL TALK which you should get; which, trifling as it is, is of use in mixed companies, and at table, especially in your foreign department; where it keeps off certain serious subjects, that might create disputes, or at least coldness for a time. Upon such occasions it is not amiss to know how to parley cuisine, and to be able to dissert upon the growth and flavor of wines. These, it is true, are very little things; but they are little things that occur very often, and therefore should be said 'avec gentillesse et grace'. I am sure they must fall often in your way; pray take care to catch them. There is a certain language of conversation, a fashionable diction, of which every gentleman ought to be perfectly master, in whatever language he speaks. The French attend to it carefully, and with great reason; and their language, which is a language of phrases, helps them out exceedingly. That delicacy of diction is characteristical of a man of fashion and good company.

I could write folios upon this subject, and not exhaust it; but I think, and hope, that to you I need not. You have heard and seen enough to be convinced of the truth and importance of what I have been so long inculcating into you upon these points. How happy am I, and how happy are you, my dear child, that these Titian tints, and Guido graces, are all that you want to complete my hopes and your own character! But then, on the other hand, what a drawback would it be to that happiness, if you should never acquire them? I remember, when I was of age, though I had not near so good an education as you have, or seen a quarter so much of the world, I observed those masterly touches and irresistible graces in others, and saw the necessity of acquiring them myself; but then an awkward 'mauvaise honte', of which I had brought a great deal with me from Cambridge, made me ashamed to attempt it, especially if any of my countrymen and particular acquaintances were by. This was extremely absurd in me: for, without attempting, I could never succeed. But at last, insensibly, by frequenting a great deal of good company, and imitating those whom I saw that everybody liked, I formed myself, 'tant bien que mal'. For God's sake, let this last fine varnish, so necessary to give lustre to the whole piece, be the sole and single object now of your utmost attention. Berlin may contribute a great deal to it if you please; there are all the ingredients that compose it.

EARL OF PHILIP DORMER STANHOPE CHESTERFIELD

'A Propos' of Berlin, while you are there, take care to seem ignorant of all political matters between the two courts; such as the affairs of Ost Frise, and Saxe Lawemburg, etc., and enter into no conversations upon those points; but, however, be as well at court as you possibly can; live at it, and make one of it. Should General Keith offer you civilities, do not decline them; but return them, however, without being 'enfant de la maison chez lui': say 'des chores flatteuses' of the Royal Family, and especially of his Prussian Majesty, to those who are the most like to repeat them. In short, make yourself well there, without making yourself ill SOMEWHERE ELSE. Make compliments from me to Algarotti, and converse with him in Italian.

I go next week to the Bath, for a deafness, which I have been plagued with these four or five months; and which I am assured that pumping my head will remove. This deafness, I own, has tried my patience; as it has cut me off from society, at an age when I had no pleasures but those left. In the meantime, I have, by reading and writing, made my eyes supply the defect of my ears. Madame H——, I suppose, entertained both yours alike; however, I am very glad that you were well with her; for she is a good 'proneuse', and puffs are very useful to a young fellow at his entrance into the world.

If you should meet with Lord Pembroke again, anywhere, make him many compliments from me; and tell him that I should have written to him, but that I knew how troublesome an old correspondent must be to a young one. He is much commended in the accounts from Hanover.

You will stay at Berlin just as long as you like it, and no longer; and from thence you are absolutely master of your own motions, either to The Hague, or to Brussels; but I think that you had better go to The Hague first, because that from thence Brussels will be in your way to Calais, which is a much better passage to England than from Helvoetsluys. The two courts of The Hague and Brussels are worth your seeing; and you will see them both to advantage, by means of Colonel Yorke and Dayrolles. Adieu. Here is enough for this time.

LETTER CLXXVIII

LONDON, September 26, 1752

MY DEAR FRIEND: As you chiefly employ, or rather wholly engross my thoughts, I see every day, with increasing pleasure, the fair prospect which you have before you. I had two views in your education; they draw nearer and nearer, and I have now very little reason to distrust your answering them fully. Those two were, parliamentary and foreign affairs. In consequence of those views, I took care, first, to give you a sufficient stock of sound learning, and next, an early knowledge of the world. Without making a figure in parliament, no man can make any in this country; and eloquence alone enables a man to make a figure in parliament, unless, it be a very mean and contemptible one, which those make there who silently vote, and who do 'pedibus ire in sententiam'. Foreign affairs, when skillfully managed, and supported by a parliamentary reputation, lead to whatever is most considerable in this country. You have the languages necessary for that purpose, with a sufficient fund of historical and treaty knowledge; that is to say, you have the matter ready, and only want the manner. Your objects being thus fixed, I recommend to you to have them constantly in your thoughts, and to direct your reading, your actions, and your words, to those views. Most people think only 'ex re nata', and few 'ex professo': I would have you do both, but begin with the latter. I explain myself: Lay down certain principles, and reason and act consequently from them. As, for example, say to yourself, I will make a figure in parliament, and in order to do that, I must not only speak, but speak very well. Speaking mere common sense will by no means do; and I must speak not only correctly but elegantly; and not only elegantly but eloquently. In order to do this, I will first take pains to get an habitual, but unaffected, purity, correctness and elegance of style in my common conversation; I will seek for the best words, and take care to reject improper, inexpressive, and vulgar ones. I will read the greatest masters of oratory, both ancient and modern, and I will read them singly in that view. I will study Demosthenes and Cicero, not to discover an old Athenian or Roman custom, nor to puzzle myself with the value of talents, mines, drachms, and sesterces, like the learned blockheads in us; but to observe their choice of words, their harmony of diction, their method, their distribution, their exordia, to engage the favor and attention of their audience; and their perorations, to enforce what they have said, and to leave a strong impression upon the passions. Nor will I be pedant enough to neglect the modern; for I will likewise study Atterbury, Dryden, Pope, and Bolingbroke; nay, I will read everything that I do read in that intention, and never cease improving and refining my style upon the best models, till at last I become a model of eloquence myself, which, by care, it is in every man's power to be. If you set out upon this principle, and keep it constantly in your mind, every company you go into, and every book you read, will contribute to your improvement, either by showing you what to imitate, or what to avoid. Are you to give an account of anything to a mixed company? or are you to endeavor to persuade either man or woman? This principle, fixed in your mind, will make you carefully attend to the choice of your words, and to the clearness and harmony of your diction.

So much for your parliamentary object; now to the foreign one.

Lay down first those principles which are absolutely necessary to form a skillful and successful negotiator, and form yourself accordingly. What are they? First, the clear historical knowledge of past transactions of that kind. That you have pretty well already, and will have daily more and more; for, in consequence of that principle, you will read history, memoirs, anecdotes, etc., in that view chiefly. The other necessary talents for negotiation are: the great art of pleasing and engaging the affection and confidence, not only of those with whom you are to cooperate, but even of those whom you are to oppose: to conceal your own thoughts and views, and to discover other people's: to engage other people's confidence by a seeming cheerful frankness and openness, without going a step too far: to get the personal favor of the king, prince, ministers, or mistresses of the court to which you are sent: to gain the absolute command over your temper and your countenance, that no heat may provoke you to say, nor no change of countenance to betray, what should be a secret: to familiarize and domesticate yourself in the houses of the most considerable people of the place, so as to be received there rather as a friend to the family than as a foreigner. Having these principles constantly in your thoughts, everything you do and everything you say will some way or other tend to your main view; and common conversation will gradually fit you for it. You will get a habit of checking any rising heat; you will be upon your guard against any indiscreet expression; you will by degrees get the command of your countenance, so as not to change it upon any the most sudden accident; and you will, above all things, labor to acquire the great art of pleasing, without which nothing is to be done. Company is, in truth, a constant state of negotiation; and, if you attend to it in that view, will qualify you for any. By the same means that you make a friend, guard against an enemy, or gain a mistress; you will make an advantageous treaty, baffle those who counteract you, and gain the court you are sent to. Make this use of all the company you keep, and your very pleasures will make you a successful negotiator. Please all who are worth pleasing; offend none. Keep your own secret, and get out other people's. Keep your own temper and artfully warm other people's. Counterwork your rivals, with diligence and dexterity, but at the same time with the utmost personal civility to them; and be firm without heat. Messieurs d'Avaux and Servien did no more than this. I must make one observation, in confirmation of this assertion; which is, that the most eminent negotiators have allways been the politest and bestbred men in company; even what the women call the PRETTIEST MEN. For God's sake, never lose view of these two your capital objects: bend everything to them, try everything by their rules, and calculate everything for their purposes. What is peculiar to these two objects, is, that they require nothing, but what one's own vanity, interest, and pleasure, would make one do independently of them. If a man were never to be in business, and always lead a private life, would he not desire to please and to persuade? So that, in your two destinations, your fortune and figure luckily conspire with your vanity and your pleasures. Nay more; a foreign minister, I will maintain it, can never be a good man of business if he is not an agreeable man of pleasure too. Half his business is done by the help of his pleasures; his views are carried on, and perhaps best and most unsuspectedly, at balls, suppers, assemblies, and parties of pleasure; by intrigues with women, and connections insensibly formed with men, at those unguarded hours of amusement.

These objects now draw very near you, and you have no time to lose in preparing yourself to meet them. You will be in parliament almost as soon as your age will allow, and I believe you will have a foreign department still sooner, and that will be earlier than ever any other body had one. If you set out well at one-and-twenty, what may you not reasonably hope to be at one-and-forty? All that I could wish you! Adieu.

LETTER CLXXIX

LONDON, September 29, 1752.

MY DEAR FRIEND: There is nothing so necessary, but at the same time there is nothing more difficult (I know it by experience) for you young fellows, than to know how to behave yourselves prudently toward those whom you do not like. Your passions are warm, and your heads are light; you hate all those who oppose your views, either of ambition or love; and a rival, in either, is almost a synonymous term for an enemy. Whenever you meet such a man, you are awkwardly cold to him, at best; but often rude, and always desirous to give him some indirect slap. This is unreasonable; for one man has as good a right to pursue an employment, or a mistress, as another; but it is, into the bargain, extremely imprudent; because you commonly defeat your own purpose by it, and while you are contending with each other, a third often prevails. I grant you that the situation is irksome; a man cannot help thinking as he thinks, nor feeling what he feels; and it is a very tender and sore point to be thwarted and counterworked in one's pursuits at court, or with a mistress; but prudence and abilities must check the effects, though they cannot remove the cause. Both the pretenders make themselves disagreeable to their mistress, when they spoil the company by their pouting, or their sparring; whereas, if one of them has command enough over himself (whatever he may feel inwardly) to be cheerful, gay, and easily and unaffectedly civil to the other, as if there were no manner of competition between them, the lady will certainly like him the best, and his rival will be ten times more humbled and discouraged; for he will look upon such a behavior as a proof of the triumph and security of his rival, he will grow outrageous with the lady, and the warmth of his reproaches will probably bring on a quarrel between them. It is the same in business; where he who can command his temper and his countenance the best, will always have an infinite advantage over the other. This is what the French call un 'procede honnete et galant', to PIQUE yourself upon showing particular civilities to a man, to whom lesser minds would, in the same case, show dislike, or perhaps rudeness. I will give you an instance of this in my own case; and pray remember it, whenever you come to be, as I hope you will, in a like situation.

When I went to The Hague, in 1744, it was to engage the Dutch to come roundly into the war, and to stipulate their quotas of troops, etc.; your acquaintance, the Abbe de la Ville, was there on the part of France, to endeavor to hinder them from coming into the war at all. I was informed, and very sorry to hear it, that he had abilities, temper, and industry. We could not visit, our two masters being at war; but the first time I met him at a third place, I got somebody to present me to him; and I told him, that though we were to be national enemies, I flattered myself we might be, however, personal friends, with a good deal more of the same kind; which he returned in full as polite a manner. Two days afterward, I went, early in the morning, to solicit the

Deputies of Amsterdam, where I found l'Abbe de la Ville, who had been beforehand with me; upon which I addressed myself to the Deputies, and said, smilingly, I am very sorry, Gentlemen, to find my enemy with you; my knowledge of his capacity is already sufficient to make me fear him; we are not upon equal terms; but I trust to your own interest against his talents. If I have not this day had the first word, I shall at least have the last. They smiled: the Abbe was pleased with the compliment, and the manner of it, stayed about a quarter of an hour, and then left me to my Deputies, with whom I continued upon the same tone, though in a very serious manner, and told them that I was only come to state their own true interests to them, plainly and simply, without any of those arts, which it was very necessary for my friend to make use of to deceive them. I carried my point, and continued my 'procede' with the Abbe; and by this easy and polite commerce with him, at third places, I often found means to fish out from him whereabouts he was.

Remember, there are but two 'procedes' in the world for a gentleman and a man of parts; either extreme politeness or knocking down. If a man notoriously and designedly insults and affronts you, knock him down; but if he only injures you, your best revenge is to be extremely civil to him in your outward behavior, though at the same time you counterwork him, and return him the compliment, perhaps with interest. This is not perfidy nor dissimulation; it would be so if you were, at the same time, to make professions of esteem and friendship to this man; which I by no means recommend, but on the contrary abhor. But all acts of civility are, by common consent, understood to be no more than a conformity to custom, for the quiet and conveniency of society, the 'agremens' of which are not to be disturbed by private dislikes and jealousies. Only women and little minds pout and spar for the entertainment of the company, that always laughs at, and never pities them. For my own part, though I would by no means give up any point to a competitor, yet I would pique myself upon showing him rather more civility than to another man. In the first place, this 'procede' infallibly makes all 'les rieurs' of your side, which is a considerable party; and in the next place, it certainly pleases the object of the competition, be it either man or woman; who never fail to say, upon such an occasion, that THEY MUST OWN YOU HAVE BEHAVED YOURSELF VERY, HANDSOMELY IN THE WHOLE AFFAIR. The world judges from the appearances of things, and not from the reality, which few are able, and still fewer are inclined to fathom: and a man, who will take care always to be in the right in those things, may afford to be sometimes a little in the wrong in more essential ones: there is a willingness, a desire to excuse him. With nine people in ten, good-breeding passes for good-nature, and they take attentions for good offices. At courts there will be always coldnesses, dislikes, jealousies, and hatred, the harvest being but small in proportion to the number of laborers; but then, as they arise often, they die soon, unless they are perpetuated by the manner in which they have been carried on, more than by the matter which occasioned them. The turns and vicissitudes of courts frequently make friends of enemies, and enemies of friends; you must labor, therefore, to acquire that great and uncommon talent of hating with good-breeding and loving with prudence; to make no quarrel irreconcilable by silly and unnecessary indications of anger; and no friendship dangerous, in case it breaks, by a wanton, indiscreet, and unreserved confidence.

Few, (especially young) people know how to love, or how to hate; their love is an unbounded weakness, fatal to the person they love; their hate is a hot, rash, and imprudent violence, always fatal to themselves.

Nineteen fathers in twenty, and every mother, who had loved you half as well as I do, would have ruined you; whereas I always made you feel the weight of my authority, that you might one day know the force of my love. Now, I both hope and believe, my advice will have the same weight with you from choice that my authority had from necessity. My advice is just eight-and-twenty years older than your own, and consequently, I believe you think, rather better. As for your tender and pleasurable passions, manage them yourself; but let me have the direction of all the others. Your ambition, your figure, and your fortune, will, for some time at least, be rather safer in my keeping than in your own. Adieu.

LETTER CLXXX

BATH, October 4, 1752

MY DEAR FRIEND: I consider you now as at the court of Augustus, where, if ever the desire of pleasing animated you, it must make you exert all the means of doing it. You will see there, full as well, I dare say, as Horace did at Rome, how states are defended by arms, adorned by manners, and improved by laws. Nay, you have an Horace there as well as an Augustus; I need not name Voltaire, 'qui nil molitur inept?' as Horace himself said of another poet. I have lately read over all his works that are published, though I had read them more than once before. I was induced to this by his 'Siecle de Louis XIV', which I have yet read but four times. In reading over all his works, with more attention I suppose than before, my former admiration of him is, I own, turned into astonishment. There is no one kind of writing in which he has not excelled. You are so severe a classic that I question whether you will allow me to call his 'Henriade' an epic poem, for want of the proper number of gods, devils, witches and other absurdities, requisite for the machinery; which machinery is, it seems, necessary to constitute the 'epopee'. But whether you do or not, I will declare (though possibly to my own shame) that I never read any epic poem with near so much pleasure. I am grown old, and have possibly lost a great deal of that fire which formerly made me love fire in others at any rate, and however attended with smoke; but now I must have all sense, and cannot, for the sake of five righteous lines, forgive a thousand absurd ones.

In this disposition of mind, judge whether I can read all Homer through 'tout de suite'. I admire its beauties; but, to tell you the truth, when he slumbers, I sleep. Virgil, I confess, is all sense, and therefore I like him better than his model; but he is often languid, especially in his five or six last books, during which I am obliged to take a good deal of snuff. Besides, I profess myself an ally of Turnus against the pious AEneas, who, like many 'soi-disant' pious people, does the most flagrant injustice and violence in order to execute what they impudently call the will of Heaven. But what will you say, when I tell you truly, that I cannot possibly read our countryman Milton through? I acknowledge him to have some most sublime passages, some prodigious flashes of light; but then you must acknowledge that light is often followed by darkness visible, to use his own expression. Besides, not having the honor to be acquainted with any of the parties in this poem, except the Man and the Woman, the characters and speeches of a dozen or two of angels and of as many devils, are as much above my reach as my entertainment. Keep this secret for me: for if it should be known, I should be abused by every tasteless pedant, and every solid divine in England.

'Whatever I have said to the disadvantage of these three poems, holds much stronger against Tasso's 'Gierusalemme': it is true he has very fine and glaring rays of poetry; but then they are only meteors, they dazzle, then disappear, and are succeeded by false thoughts, poor 'concetti', and absurd impossibilities; witness the Fish and the Parrot; extravagancies unworthy of an heroic poem, and would much better have become Ariosto, who professes 'le coglionerie'.

I have never read the "Lusiade of Camoens," except in prose translation, consequently I have never read it at all, so shall say nothing of it; but the Henriade is all sense from the beginning to the end, often adorned by the justest and liveliest reflections, the most beautiful descriptions, the noblest images, and the sublimest sentiments; not to mention the harmony of the verse, in which Voltaire undoubtedly exceeds all the French poets: should you insist upon an exception in favor of Racine, I must insist, on my part, that he at least equals him. What hero ever interested more than Henry the Fourth; who, according to the rules of epic poetry, carries on one great and long action, and succeeds in it at last? What descriptions ever excited more horror than those, first of the Massacre, and then of the Famine at Paris? Was love ever painted with more truth and 'morbidezza' than in the ninth book? Not better, in my mind, even in the fourth of Virgil. Upon the whole, with all your classical rigor, if you will but suppose St. Louis a god, a devil, or a witch, and that he appears in person, and not in a dream, the Henriade will be an epic poem, according to the strictest statute laws of the 'epopee'; but in my court of equity it is one as it is.

I could expatiate as much upon all his different works, but that I should exceed the bounds of a letter and run into a dissertation. How delightful is his history of that northern brute, the King of Sweden, for I cannot call him a man; and I should be sorry to have him pass for a hero, out of regard to those true heroes, such as Julius Caesar, Titus, Trajan, and the present King of Prussia, who cultivated and encouraged arts and sciences; whose animal courage was accompanied by the tender and social sentiments of humanity; and who had more pleasure in improving, than in destroying their fellow-creatures. What can be more touching, or more interesting—what more nobly thought, or more happily expressed, than all his dramatic pieces? What can be more clear and rational than all his philosophical letters? and whatever was so graceful, and gentle, as all his little poetical trifles? You are fortunately 'a porte' of verifying, by your knowledge of the man, all that I have said of his works.

Monsieur de Maupertius (whom I hope you will get acquainted with) is, what one rarely meets with, deep in philosophy and, mathematics, and yet 'honnete et aimable homme': Algarotti is young Fontenelle. Such men must necessarily give you the desire of pleasing them; and if you can frequent them, their acquaintance will furnish you the means of pleasing everybody else.

'A propos' of pleasing, your pleasing Mrs. F———-d is expected here in two or three days; I will do all that I can for you with her: I think you carried on the romance to the third or fourth volume; I will continue it to the eleventh; but as for the twelfth and last, you must come and conclude it yourself. 'Non sum qualis eram'.

Good-night to you, child; for I am going to bed, just at the hour at which I suppose you are going to live, at Berlin.

LETTER CLXXXI

BATH, November 11, O. S. 1752

MY DEAR FRIEND: It is a very old and very true maxim, that those kings reign the most secure and the most absolute, who reign in the hearts of their people. Their popularity is a better guard than their army, and the affections of their subjects a better pledge of their obedience than their fears. This rule is, in proportion, full as true, though upon a different scale, with regard to private people. A man who possesses that great art of pleasing universally, and of gaining the affections of those with whom he converses, possesses a strength which nothing else can give him: a strength which facilitates and helps his rise; and which, in case of accidents, breaks his fall. Few people of your age sufficiently consider this great point of popularity; and when they grow older and wiser, strive in vain to recover what they have lost by their negligence. There are three principal causes that hinder them from acquiring this useful strength: pride, inattention, and 'mauvaise honte'. The first I will not, I cannot suspect you of; it is too much below your understanding. You cannot, and I am sure you do not think yourself superior by nature to the Savoyard who cleans your room, or the footman who cleans your shoes; but you may rejoice, and with reason, at the difference that fortune has made in your favor. Enjoy all those advantages; but without insulting those who are unfortunate enough to want them, or even doing anything unnecessarily that may remind them of that want. For my own part, I am more upon my guard as to my behavior to my servants, and others who are called my inferiors, than I am toward my equals: for fear of being suspected of that mean and ungenerous sentiment of desiring to make others feel that difference which fortune has, and perhaps too, undeservedly, made between us. Young people do not enough attend to this; and falsely imagine that the imperative mood, and a rough tone of authority and decision, are indications of spirit and courage. Inattention is always looked upon, though sometimes unjustly, as the effect of pride and contempt; and where it is thought so, is never forgiven. In this article, young people are generally exceedingly to blame, and offend extremely. Their whole attention is engrossed by their particular set of acquaintance; and by some few glaring and exalted objects of rank, beauty, or parts; all the rest they think so little worth their care, that they neglect even common civility toward them. I will frankly confess to you, that this was one of my great faults when I was of your age. Very attentive to please that narrow court circle in which I stood enchanted, I considered everything else as bourgeois, and unworthy of common civility; I paid my court assiduously and skillfully enough to shining and distinguished figures, such as ministers, wits, and beauties; but then I most absurdly and imprudently neglected, and consequently offended all others. By this folly I made myself a thousand enemies of both sexes; who, though I thought them very insignificant, found means to hurt me essentially where I wanted to recommend myself the most. I was thought proud, though I was only imprudent. A general easy civility and attention to the common run of ugly women, and of middling men, both which I sillily thought, called, and treated, as odd people, would have made me as many friends, as by the contrary conduct I made myself enemies. All this too was 'a pure perte'; for I might equally, and even more successfully, have made my court, when I had particular views to gratify. I will allow that this task is often very unpleasant, and that one pays, with some unwillingness, that tribute of attention to dull and tedious men, and to old and ugly women; but it is the lowest price of popularity and general applause, which are very well worth purchasing were they much dearer. I conclude this head with this advice to you: Gain, by particular assiduity and address, the men and women you want; and, by an universal civility and attention, please everybody so far as to have their good word, if not their goodwill; or, at least, as to secure a partial neutrality.

'Mauvaise honte' not only hinders young people from making, a great many friends, but makes them a great many enemies. They are ashamed of doing the thing they know to be right, and would otherwise do, for fear of the momentary laugh of some fine gentleman or lady, or of some 'mauvais plaisant'. I have been in this case: and have often wished an obscure acquaintance at the devil, for meeting and taking notice of me when I was in what I thought and called fine company. I have returned their notice shyly, awkwardly, and consequently offensively; for fear of a momentary joke, not considering, as I ought to have done, that the very people who would have joked upon me at first, would have esteemed me the more for it afterward. An example explains a rule best: Suppose you were walking in the Tuileries with some fine folks, and that you should unexpectedly meet your old acquaintance, little crooked Grierson; what would you do? I will tell you what you should do, by telling you what I would now do in that case myself. I would run up to him, and embrace him; say some kind of things to him, and then return to my company. There I should be immediately asked: 'Mais qu'est ce que c'est donc que ce petit Sapajou que vous avez embrasse si tendrement? Pour cela, l'accolade a ete charmante'; with a great deal more festivity of that sort. To this I should answer, without being the least ashamed, but en badinant: O je ne vous dirai tas qui c'est; c'est un petit ami que je tiens incognito, qui a son merite, et qui, a force d'etre connu, fait oublier sa figure. Que me donnerez-vous, et je vous le presenterai'? And then, with a little more seriousness, I would add: 'Mais d'ailleurs c'est que je ne desavoue jamais mes connoissances, a cause de leur etat ou de leur figure. Il faut avoir bien peu de sentimens pour le faire'. This would at once put an end to that momentary pleasantry, and give them all a better opinion of me than they had before. Suppose another case, and that some of the finest ladies 'du bon ton' should come into a room, and find you sitting by, and talking politely to 'la vieille' Marquise de Bellefonds, the joke would, for a moment, turn upon that 'tete-a-tete': He bien! avez vous a la fin fixd la belle Marquise? La partie est-elle faite pour la petite maison? Le souper sera galant sans doute: Mais ne faistu donc point scrupule de seduire une jeune et aimable personne comme celle-la'? To this I should answer: 'La partie n'etoit pas encore tout-a fait liee, vous nous avez interrompu; mais avec le tems que fait-on? D'ailleurs moquezvous de mes amours tant qu'il vous plaira, je vous dirai que je respecte tant les jeunes dames, que je respecte meme les vieilles, pour l'avoir ete. Apre cela il y a souvent des liaisons entre les vieilles et les jeunes'. This would at once turn the pleasantry into an esteem for your good sense and your good-breeding. Pursue steadily, and without fear or shame, whatever your reason tells you is right, and what you see is practiced by people of more experience than yourself, and of established characters of good sense and good-breeding.

After all this, perhaps you will say, that it is impossible to please everybody. I grant it; but it does not follow that one should not therefore endeavor to please as many as one can. Nay, I will go further, and admit that it is impossible for any man not to have some enemies. But this truth from long experience I assert, that he who has the most friends and the fewest enemies, is the strongest; will rise the highest with the least envy; and fall, if he does fall, the gentlest, and the most pitied. This is surely an object worth pursuing. Pursue it according to the rules I have here given you. I will add one observation more, and two examples to enforce it; and then, as the parsons say, conclude.

There is no one creature so obscure, so low, or so poor, who may not, by the strange and unaccountable changes and vicissitudes of human affairs, somehow or other, and some time or other, become an useful friend or a trouble-some enemy, to the greatest and the richest. The late Duke of Ormond was almost the weakest but at the same time the best-bred, and most popular man in this kingdom. His education in courts and camps, joined to an easy, gentle nature, had given him that habitual affability, those engaging manners, and those mechanical attentions, that almost supplied the place of every talent he wanted; and he wanted almost every one. They procured him the love of all men, without the esteem of any. He was impeached after the death of Queen Anne, only because that, having been engaged in the same measures with those who were necessarily to be impeached, his impeachment, for form's sake, became necessary. But he was impeached without acrimony, and without the lest intention that he should suffer, notwithstanding the party violence of those times. The question for his impeachment, in the House of Commons, was carried by many fewer votes than any other question of impeachment; and Earl Stanhope, then Mr. Stanhope, and Secretary' of State, who impeached him, very soon after negotiated and concluded his accommodation with the late King; to whom he was to have been presented the next day. But the late Bishop of Rochester, Atterbury, who thought that the Jacobite cause might suffer by losing the Duke of Ormond, went in all haste, and prevailed with the poor weak man to run away; assuring him that he was only to be gulled into a disgraceful submission, and not to be pardoned in consequence of it. When his subsequent attainder passed, it excited mobs and disturbances in town. He had not a personal enemy in the world; and had a thousand friends. All this was simply owing to his natural desire of pleasing, and to the mechanical means that his education, not his parts, had given him of doing it. The other instance is the late Duke of Marlborough, who studied the art of pleasing, because he well knew the importance of it: he enjoyed and used it more than ever man did. He gained whoever he had a mind to gain; and he had a mind to gain everybody, because he knew that everybody was more or less worth gaining. Though his power, as Minister and General, made him many political and party enemies, they did not make him one personal one; and the very people who would gladly have displaced, disgraced, and perhaps attainted the Duke of Marlborough, at the same time personally loved Mr. Churchill, even though his private character was blemished by sordid avarice, the most unamiable of all vices. He had wound up and turned his whole machine to please and engage. He had an inimitable sweetness and gentleness in his countenance, a tenderness in his manner of speaking, a graceful dignity in every motion, and an universal and minute attention to the least things that could possibly please the least person. This was all art in him; art of which he well knew and enjoyed the advantages; for no man ever had more interior ambition, pride, and avarice, than he had.

Though you have more than most people of your age, you have yet very little experience and knowledge of the world; now, I wish to inoculate mine upon you, and thereby prevent both the dangers and the marks of youth and inexperience. If you receive the matter kindly, and observe my prescriptions scrupulously, you will secure the future advantages of time and join them to the present inestimable ones of one-and-twenty.

I most earnestly recommend one thing to you, during your present stay at Paris. I own it is not the most agreeable; but I affirm it to be the most useful thing in the world to one of your age; and therefore I do hope that you will force and constrain yourself to do it. I mean, to converse frequently, or rather to be in company frequently with both men and women much your superiors in age and rank. I am very sensible that, at your age, 'vous y entrez pour peu de chose, et meme souvent pour rien, et que vous y passerez meme quelques mauvais quart-d'heures'; but no matter; you will be a solid gainer by it: you will see, hear, and learn the turn and manners of those people; you will gain premature experience by it; and it will give you a habit of engaging and respectful attentions. Versailles, as much as possible, though probably unentertaining: the Palais Royal often, however dull: foreign ministers of the first rank, frequently, and women, though old, who are respectable and respected for their rank or parts; such as Madame de Pusieux, Madame de Nivernois, Madame d'Aiguillon, Madame Geoffrain, etc. This 'sujetion', if it be one to you, will cost you but very little in these three or four months that you are yet to pass in Paris, and will bring you in a great deal; nor will it, nor ought it, to hinder you from being in a more entertaining company a great part of the day. 'Vous pouvez, si vous le voulex, tirer un grand parti de ces quatre mois'. May God make you so, and bless you! Adieu.

LETTER CLXXXII

BATH, November 16, O. S. 1752.

MY DEAR FRIEND: Vanity, or to call it by a gentler name, the desire of admiration and applause, is, perhaps, the most universal principle of human actions; I do not say that it is the best; and I will own that it is sometimes the cause of both foolish and criminal effects. But it is so much oftener the principle of right things, that though they ought to have a better, yet, considering human nature, that principle is to be encouraged and cherished, in consideration of its effects. Where that desire is wanting, we are apt to be indifferent, listless, indolent, and inert; we do not exert our powers; and we appear to be as much below ourselves as the vainest man living can desire to appear above what he really is.

As I have made you my confessor, and do not scruple to confess even my weaknesses to you, I will fairly own that I had that vanity, that weakness, if it be one, to a prodigious degree; and, what is more, I confess it without repentance: nay, I am glad I had it; since, if I have had the good fortune to please in the world, it is to that powerful and active principle that I owe it. I began the world, not with a bare desire, but with an insatiable thirst, a rage of popularity, applause, and admiration. If this made me do some silly things on one hand, it made me, on the other hand, do almost all the right things that I did; it made me attentive and civil to the women I disliked, and to the men I despised, in hopes of the applause of both: though I neither desired, nor would I have accepted the favors of the one, nor the friendship of the other. I always dressed, looked, and talked my best; and, I own, was overjoyed whenever I perceived, that by all three, or by any one of them, the company was pleased with me. To men, I talked whatever I thought would give them the best opinion of my parts and learning; and to women, what I was sure would please them; flattery, gallantry, and love. And, moreover, I will own to you, under the secrecy of confession, that my vanity has very often made me take great pains to make a woman in love with me, if I could, for whose person I would not have given a pinch of snuff. In company with men, I always endeavored to outshine, or at least, if possible, to equal the most shining man in it. This desire elicited whatever powers I had to gratify it; and where I could not perhaps shine in the first, enabled me, at least, to shine in a second or third sphere. By these means I soon grew in fashion; and when a man is once in fashion, all he does is right. It was infinite pleasure to me to find my own fashion and popularity. I was sent for to all parties of pleasure, both of men or women; where, in some measure, I gave the 'ton'. This gave me the reputation of having had some women of condition; and that reputation, whether true or false, really got me others. With the men I was a Proteus, and assumed every shape, in order to please them all: among the gay, I was the gayest; among the grave, the gravest; and I never omitted the least attentions of good-breeding, or the least offices of friendship, that could either please, or attach them to me: and accordingly I was soon connected with all the men of any fashion or figure in town.

To this principle of vanity, which philosophers call a mean one, and which I do not, I owe great part of the figure which I have made in life. I wish you had as much, but I fear you have too little of it; and you seem to have a degree of laziness and listlessness about you that makes you indifferent as to general applause. This is not in character at your age, and would be barely pardonable in an elderly and philosophical man. It is a vulgar, ordinary saying, but it is a very true one, that one should always put the best foot foremost. One should please, shine, and dazzle, wherever it is possible. At Paris, I am sure you must observe 'que chacun se fait valoir autant qu'il est possible'; and La Bruyere observes, very justly, qu'on ne vaut dans ce monde que ce qu'on veut valoir': wherever applause is in question, you will never see a French man, nor woman, remiss or negligent. Observe the eternal attentions and politeness that all people have there for one another. 'Ce n'est pas pour leurs beaux yeux au moins'. No, but for their own sakes, for commendations and applause. Let me then recommend this principle of vanity to you; act upon it 'meo periculo'; I promise you it will turn to your account. Practice all the arts that ever coquette did, to please. Be alert and indefatigable in making every man admire, and every woman in love with you. I can tell you too, that nothing will carry you higher in the world.

I have had no letter from you since your arrival at Paris, though you must have been long enough there to have written me two or three. In about ten or twelve days I propose leaving this place, and going to London; I have found considerable benefit by my stay here, but not all that I want. Make my compliments to Lord Albemarle.

LETTER CLXXXIII

BATH, November 28, 1752

MY DEAR FRIEND: Since my last to you, I have read Madame Maintenon's "Letters"; I am sure they are genuine, and they both entertained and informed me. They have brought me acquainted with the character of that able and artful lady; whom I am convinced that I now know much better than her directeur the Abby de Fenelon (afterward Archbishop of Cambray) did, when he wrote her the 185th letter; and I know him the better too for that letter. The Abby, though brimful of the divine love, had a great mind to be first minister, and cardinal, in order, NO DOUBT, to have an opportunity of doing the more good. His being 'directeur' at that time to Madame Maintenon, seemed to be a good step toward those views. She put herself upon him for a saint, and he was weak enough to believe it; he, on the other hand, would have put himself upon her for a saint too, which, I dare say, she did not believe; but both of them knew that it was necessary for them to appear saints to Lewis the Fourteenth, who they were very sure was a bigot. It is to be presumed, nay, indeed, it is plain by that 185th letter that Madame Maintenon had hinted to her directeur some scruples of conscience, with relation to her commerce with the King; and which I humbly apprehend to have been only some scruples of prudence, at once to flatter the bigot character, and increase the desires of the King. The pious Abbe, frightened out of his wits, lest the King should impute to the 'directeur' any scruples or difficulties which he might meet with on the part of the lady, writes her the above-mentioned letter; in which he not only bids her not tease the King by advice and exhortations, but to have the utmost submission to his will; and, that she may not mistake the nature of that submission, he tells her it is the same that Sarah had for Abraham; to which submission Isaac perhaps was owing. No bawd could have written a more seducing letter to an innocent country girl, than the 'directeur' did to his 'penitente'; who I dare say had no occasion for his good advice. Those who would justify the good 'directeur', alias the pimp, in this affair, must not attempt to do it by saying that the King and Madame Maintenon were at that time privately married; that the directeur knew it; and that this was the meaning of his 'enigme'. That is absolutely impossible; for that private marriage must have removed all scruples between the parties; nay, could not have been contracted upon any other principle, since it was kept private, and consequently prevented no public scandal. It is therefore extremely evident that Madame Maintenon could not be married to the King at the time when she scrupled granting, and when the 'directeur' advised her to grant, those favors which Sarah with so much submission granted to Abraham: and what the 'directeur' is pleased to call 'le mystere de Dieu', was most evidently a state of concubinage. The letters are very well worth your reading; they throw light upon many things of those times.

I have just received a letter from Sir William Stanhope, from Lyons; in which he tells me that he saw you at Paris, that he thinks you a little grown, but that you do not make the most of it, for that you stoop still: 'd'ailleurs' his letter was a panegyric of you.

The young Comte de Schullemburg, the Chambellan whom you knew at Hanover, is come over with the King, 'et fait aussi vos eloges'.

Though, as I told you in my last, I have done buying pictures, by way of 'virtu', yet there are some portraits of remarkable people that would tempt me. For instance, if you could by chance pick up at Paris, at a reasonable price, and undoubted originals (whether heads, half lengths, or whole lengths, no matter) of Cardinals Richelieu, Mazarin, and Retz, Monsieur de Turenne, le grand Prince de Condo; Mesdames de Montespan, de Fontanges, de Montbazon, de Sevigne, de Maintenon, de Chevreuse, de Longueville, d'Olonne, etc., I should be tempted to purchase them. I am sensible that they can only be met with, by great accident, at family sales and auctions, so I only mention the affair to you eventually.

I do not understand, or else I do not remember, what affair you mean in your last letter; which you think will come to nothing, and for which, you say, I had once a mind that you should take the road again. Explain it to me.

I shall go to town in four or five days, and carry back with me a little more hearing than I brought; but yet, not half enough for common wants. One wants ready pocket-money much oftener than one wants great sums; and to use a very odd expression, I want to hear at sight. I love every-day senses, every-day wit and entertainment; a man who is only good on holydays is good for very little. Adieu.

LETTER CLXXXIV

Christmas Day, 1752

MY DEAR FRIEND: A tyrant with legions at his com mand may say, Oderint modo timeant; though he is a fool if he says it, and a greater fool if he thinks it. But a private man who can hurt but few, though he can please many, must endeavor to be loved, for he cannot be feared in general. Popularity is his only rational and sure foundation. The good-will, the affections, the love of the public, can alone raise him to any considerable height. Should you ask me how he is to acquire them, I will answer, By desiring them. No man ever deserved, who did not desire them; and no man both deserved and desired them who had them not, though many have enjoyed them merely by desiring, and without deserving them. You do not imagine, I believe, that I mean by this public love the sentimental love of either lovers or intimate friends; no, that is of another nature, and confined to a very narrow circle; but I mean that general good-will which a man may acquire in the world, by the arts of pleasing respectively exerted according to the rank, the situation, and the turn of mind of those whom he hath to do with. The pleasing impressions which he makes upon them will engage their affections and their good wishes, and even their good offices as far (that is) as they are not inconsistent with their own interests; for further than that you are not to expect from three people in the course of your life, even were it extended to the patriarchal term. Could I revert to the age of twenty, and carry back with me all the experience that forty years more have taught me, I can assure you, that I would employ much the greatest part of my time in engaging the good-will, and in insinuating myself into the predilection of people in general, instead of directing my endeavors to please (as I was too apt to do) to the man whom I immediately wanted, or the woman I wished for, exclusively of all others. For if one happens (and it will sometimes happen to the ablest man) to fail in his views with that man or that woman, one is at a loss to know whom to address one's self to next, having offended in general, by that exclusive and distinguished particular application. I would secure a general refuge in the good-will of the multitude, which is a great strength to any man; for both ministers and mistresses choose popular and fashionable favorites. A man who solicits a minister, backed by the general good-will and good wishes of mankind, solicits with great weight and great probability of success; and a woman is strangely biassed in favor of a man whom she sees in fashion, and hears everybody speak well of. This useful art of insinuation consists merely of various little things. A graceful motion, a significant look, a trifling attention, an obliging word dropped 'a propos', air, dress, and a thousand other undefinable things, all severally little ones, joined together, make that happy and inestimable composition, THE ART OF PLEASING. I have in my life seen many a very handsome woman who has not pleased me, and many very sensible men who have disgusted me. Why? only for want of those thousand little means to please, which those women, conscious of their beauty, and those men of their sense, have been grossly enough mistaken to neglect. I never was so much in love in my life, as I was with a woman who was very far from being handsome; but then she was made up of graces, and had all the arts of pleasing. The following verses, which I have read in some congratulatory poem prefixed to some work, I have forgot which, express what I mean in favor of what pleases preferably to what is generally called mare solid and instructive:

"I would an author like a mistress try,

Not by a nose, a lip, a cheek, or eye,

But by some nameless power to give me joy."

Lady Chesterfield bids me make you many compliments; she showed me your letter of recommendation of La Vestres; with which I was very well pleased: there is a pretty turn in it; I wish you would always speak as genteelly. I saw another letter from a lady at Paris, in which there was a high panegyrical paragraph concerning you. I wish it were every word of it literally true; but, as it comes from a very little, pretty, white hand, which is suspected, and I hope justly, of great partiality to you: 'il en faut rabattre quelque chose, et meme en le faisant it y aura toujours d'assez beaux restes'. Adieu.

EARL OF PHILIP DORMER STANHOPE CHESTERFIELD

1753-1754

LETTER CLXXXV

LONDON, New Years' Day, 1753

MY DEAR FRIEND: It is now above a fortnight since I have received a letter from you. I hope, however, that you are well, but engrossed by the business of Lord Albemarle's 'bureau' in the mornings, and by business of a genteeler nature in the evenings; for I willingly give up my own satisfaction to your improvement, either in business or manners.

Here have been lately imported from Paris two gentlemen, who, I find, were much acquainted with you there Comte Zinzendorf, and Monsieur Clairant the Academician. The former is a very pretty man, well-bred, and with a great deal of useful knowledge; for those two things are very consistent. I examined him about you, thinking him a competent judge. He told me, 'que vous parliez l'Allemand comme un Allemand; que vous saviez le droit public de l'empire parfaitement bien; que vous aviez le gout sur, et des connoissances fort etendues'. I told him that I knew all this very well; but that I wanted to know whether you had l'air, les manieres, les attentions, en fin le brillant d'un honnete homme': his answer was, 'Mais oui en verite, c'est fort bien'. This, you see, is but cold in comparison of what I do wish, and of what you ought to wish. Your friend Clairant interposed, and said, 'Mais je vous assure qu'il est fort poli'; to which I answered, 'Je le crois bien, vis-a-vis des Lapons vos amis; je vous recuse pour juge, jusqu'a ce que vous ayez ete delaponne, au moins dix ans, parmi les honnetes gens'. These testimonies in your favor are such as perhaps you are satisfied with, and think sufficient; but I am not; they are only the cold depositions of disinterested and unconcerned witnesses, upon a strict examination. When, upon a trial, a man calls witnesses to his character, and that those witnesses only say that they never heard, nor do not know any ill of him, it intimates at best a neutral and insignificant, though innocent character. Now I want, and you ought to endeavor, that 'les agremens, les graces, les attentions', etc., should be a distinguishing part of your character, and specified of you by people unasked. I wish to hear people say of you, 'Ah qu'il est aimable! Quelles manieres, quelles graces, quel art de Claire'! Nature, thank God, has given you all the powers necessary; and if she has not yet, I hope in God she will give you the will of exerting them.

I have lately read with great pleasure Voltaire's two little histories of 'Les Croisades', and 'l'Esprit Humain'; which I recommend to your perusal, if you have not already read them. They are bound up with a most poor performance called 'Micromegas', which is said to be Voltaire's too, but I cannot believe it, it is so very unworthy of him; it consists only of thoughts stolen from Swift, but miserably mangled and disfigured. But his history of the 'Croisades' shows, in a very short and strong light, the most immoral and wicked scheme that was ever contrived by knaves, and executed by madmen and fools, against humanity. There is a strange but never-failing relation between honest madmen and skillful knaves; and whenever one meets with collected numbers of the former, one may be very sure that they are secretly directed by the latter. The popes, who have generally been both the ablest and the greatest knaves in Europe, wanted all the power and money of the East; for they had all that was in Europe already. The times and the minds favored their design, for they were dark and uniformed; and Peter the Hermit, at once a knave and a madman, was a fine papal tool for so wild and wicked an undertaking. I wish we had good histories of every part of Europe, and indeed of the world, written upon the plan of Voltaire's 'de l'Esprit Humain'; for, I own, I am provoked at the contempt which most historians show for humanity in general: one would think by them that the whole human species consisted but of about a hundred and fifty people, called and dignified (commonly very undeservedly too) by the titles of emperors, kings, popes, generals, and ministers.

I have never seen in any of the newspapers any mention of the affairs of the Cevennes, or Grenoble, which you gave me an account of some time ago; and the Duke de Mirepoix pretends, at least, to know nothing of either. Were they false reports? or does the French court choose to stifle them? I hope that they are both true, because I am very willing that the cares of the French government should be employed and confined to themselves.

Your friend, the Electress Palatine, has sent me six wild boars' heads, and other 'pieces de sa chasse', in return for the fans, which she approved of extremely. This present was signified to me by one Mr. Harold, who wrote me a letter in very indifferent English; I suppose he is a Dane who has been in England.

Mr. Harte came to town yesterday, and dined with me to-day. We talked you over; and I can assure you, that though a parson, and no member 'du beau monde', he thinks all the most shining accomplishments of it full as necessary for you as I do. His expression was, THAT IS ALL THAT HE WANTS; BUT IF HE WANTS THAT, CONSIDERING HIS SITUATION AND DESTINATION, HE MIGHT AS WELL WANT EVERYTHING ELSE.

This is the day when people reciprocally offer and receive the kindest and the warmest wishes, though, in general, without meaning them on one side, or believing them on the other. They are formed by the head, in compliance with custom, though disavowed by the heart, in consequence of nature. His wishes upon this occasion are the best that are the best turned; you do not, I am sure, doubt the truth of mine, and therefore I will express them with a Quaker-like simplicity. May this new year be a very new one indeed to you; may you put off the old, and put on the new man! but I mean the outward, not the inward man. With this alteration, I might justly sum up all my wishes for you in these words:

Dii tibi dent annos, de to nam caetera sumes.

This minute, I receive your letter of the 26th past, which gives me a very disagreeable reason for your late silence. By the symptoms which you mention of your illness, I both hope and believe that it was wholly owing to your own want of care. You are rather inclined to be fat, you have naturally a good stomach, and you eat at the best tables; which must of course make you plethoric: and upon my word you will be very subject to these accidents, if you will not, from time to time, when you find yourself full, heated, or your head aching, take some little, easy, preventative purge, that would not confine you; such as chewing a little rhubarb when you go to bed at night; or some senna tea in the morning. You do very well to live extremely low, for some time; and I could wish, though I do not expect it, that you would take one gentle vomit; for those giddinesses and swimmings in the head always proceed from some foulness of the stomach. However, upon the whole, I am very glad that your old complaint has not mixed itself with this, which I am fully convinced arises simply from your own negligence. Adieu.

I am sorry for Monsieur Kurze, upon his sister's account.

LETTER CLXXXVI

LONDON, January 15, 1753

MY DEAR FRIEND: I never think my time so well employed, as when I think it employed to your advantage. You have long had the greatest share of it; you now engross it. The moment is now decisive; the piece is going to be exhibited to the public; the mere out lines and the general coloring are not sufficient to attract the eyes and to secure applause; but the last finishing, artful, and delicate strokes are necessary. Skillful judges will discern and acknowledge their merit; the ignorant will, without knowing why, feel their power. In that view, I have thrown together, for your perusal, some maxims; or, to speak more properly, observations on men and things; for I have no merit as to the invention: I am no system monger; and, instead of giving way to my imagination, I have only consulted my memory; and my conclusions are all drawn from facts, not from fancy. Most maxim mongers have preferred the prettiness to the justness of a thought, and the turn to the truth; but I have refused myself to everything that my own experience did not justify and confirm. I wish you would consider them seriously, and separately, and recur to them again 'pro re nata' in similar cases. Young men are as apt to think themselves wise enough, as drunken men are to think themselves sober enough. They look upon spirit to be a much better thing than experience; which they call coldness. They are but half mistaken; for though spirit, without experience, is dangerous, experience, without spirit, is languid and defective. Their union, which is very rare, is perfection; you may join them, if you please; for all my experience is at your service; and I do not desire one grain of your spirit in return. Use them both, and let them reciprocally animate and check each other. I mean here, by the spirit of youth, only the vivacity and presumption of youth, which hinder them from seeing the difficulties or dangers of an undertaking, but I do not mean what the silly vulgar call spirit, by which they are captious, jealous of their rank, suspicious of being undervalued, and tart (as they call it) in their repartees, upon the slightest occasions. This is an evil, and a very silly spirit, which should be driven out, and transferred to an herd of swine. This is not the spirit of a man of fashion, who has kept good company. People of an ordinary, low education, when they happen to fail into good company, imagine themselves the only object of its attention; if the company whispers, it is, to be sure, concerning them; if they laugh, it is at them; and if anything ambiguous, that by the most forced interpretation can be applied to them, happens to be said, they are convinced that it was meant at them; upon which they grow out of countenance first, and then angry. This mistake is very well ridiculed in the "Stratagem," where Scrub says, I AM SURE THEY TALKED OF ME FOR THEY LAUGHED CONSUMEDLY. A well-bred man seldom thinks, but never seems to think himself slighted, undervalued, or laughed at in company, unless where it is so plainly marked out, that his honor obliges him to resent it in a proper manner; 'mais les honnetes gens ne se boudent jamais'. I will admit that it is very difficult to command one's self enough, to behave with ease, frankness, and good-breeding toward those, who one knows dislike, slight, and injure one, as far as they can, without personal consequences; but I assert that it is absolutely necessary to do it: you must embrace the man you hate, if you cannot be justified in knocking him down; for otherwise you avow the injury which you cannot revenge. A prudent cuckold (and there are many such at Paris) pockets his horns when he cannot gore with them; and will not add to the triumph of his maker by only butting with them ineffectually. A seeming ignorance is very often a most necessary part of worldly knowledge. It is, for instance, commonly advisable to seem ignorant of what people offer to tell you; and when they say, Have you not heard of such a thing? to answer No, and to let them go on; though you know it already. Some have a pleasure in telling it, because they think that they tell it well; others have a pride in it, as being the sagacious discoverers; and many have a vanity in showing that they have been, though very undeservedly, trusted; all these would be disappointed, and consequently displeased, if you said Yes. Seem always ignorant (unless to one's most intimate friend) of all matters of private scandal and defamation, though you should hear them a thousand times; for the parties affected always look upon the receiver to be almost as bad as the thief: and, whenever they become the topic of conversation seem to be a skeptic, though you are really a serious believer; and always take the extenuating part. But all this seeming ignorance should be joined to thorough and extensive private informations: and, indeed, it is the best method of procuring them; for most people have such a vanity in showing a superiority over others, though but for a moment, and in the merest trifles, that they will tell you what they should not, rather than not show that they can tell what you did not know; besides that such seeming ignorance will make you pass for incurious and consequently undesigning. However, fish for facts, and take pains to be well informed of everything that passes; but fish judiciously, and not always, nor indeed often, in the shape of direct questions, which always put people upon their guard, and, often repeated, grow tiresome. But sometimes take the things that you would know for granted; upon which somebody will, kindly and officiously, set you right: sometimes say that you have heard so and so; and at other times seem to know more than you do, in order to know all that you want; but avoid direct questioning as much as you can. All these necessary arts of the world require constant attention, presence of mind, and coolness. Achilles, though invulnerable, never went to battle but completely armed. Courts are to be the theatres of your wars, where you should be always as completely armed, and even with the addition of a heel-piece. The least inattention, the least DISTRACTION, may prove fatal. I would fain see you what pedants call 'omnis homo', and what Pope much better calls ALL-ACCOMPLISHED: you have the means in your power; add the will; and you may bring it about. The vulgar have a coarse saying, of SPOILING A SHIP FOR A HALFPENNY WORTH OF TAR; prevent the application by providing the tar: it is very easily to be had in comparison with what you have already got.

The fine Mrs. Pitt, who it seems saw you often at Paris, speaking of you the other day, said, in French, for she speaks little English, . . . whether it is that you did not pay the homage due to her beauty, or that it did not strike you as it does others, I cannot determine; but I hope she had some other reason than truth for saying it. I will suppose that you did not care a pin for her; but, however, she surely deserved a degree of propitiatory adoration from you, which I am afraid you neglected. Had I been in your case, I should have endeavored, at least, to have supplanted Mr. Mackay in his office of nocturnal reader to her. I played at cards, two days ago, with your friend Mrs. Fitzgerald, and her most sublime mother, Mrs. Seagrave; they both inquired after you; and Mrs. Fitzgerald said, she hoped you went on with your dancing; I said, Yes, and that you assured me you had made such considerable improvements in it, that you had now learned to stand still, and even upright.

Your 'virtuosa', la Signora Vestri, sung here the other day, with great applause: I presume you are INTIMATELY acquainted with her merit. Good night to you, whoever you pass it with.

I have this moment received a packet, sealed with your seal, though not directed by your hand, for Lady Hervey. No letter from you! Are you not well?

LETTER CLXXXVII

LONDON, May 27, O. S. 1753.

MY DEAR FRIEND: I have this day been tired, jaded, nay, tormented, by the company of a most worthy, sensible, and learned man, a near relation of mine, who dined and passed the evening with me. This seems a paradox, but is a plain truth; he has no knowledge of the world, no manners, no address; far from talking without book, as is commonly said of people who talk sillily, he only talks by book; which in general conversation is ten times worse. He has formed in his own closet from books, certain systems of everything, argues tenaciously upon those principles, and is both surprised and angry at whatever deviates from them. His theories are good, but, unfortunately, are all impracticable. Why? because he has only read and not conversed. He is acquainted with books, and an absolute stranger to men. Laboring with his matter, he is delivered of it with pangs; he hesitates, stops in his utterance, and always expresses himself inelegantly. His actions are all ungraceful; so that, with all his merit and knowledge, I would rather converse six hours with the most frivolous tittle-tattle woman who knew something of the world, than with him. The preposterous notions of a systematical man who does not know the world, tire the patience of a man who does. It would be endless to correct his mistakes, nor would he take it kindly: for he has considered everything deliberately, and is very sure that he is in the right. Impropriety is a characteristic, and a never-failing one, of these people. Regardless, because ignorant, of customs and manners, they violate them every moment. They often shock, though they never mean to offend: never attending either to the general character, or the particular distinguishing circumstances of the people to whom, or before whom they talk; whereas the knowledge of the world teaches one, that the very same things which are exceedingly right and proper in one company, time and place, are exceedingly absurd in others. In short, a man who has great knowledge, from experience and observation, of the characters, customs, and manners of mankind, is a being as different from, and as superior to, a man of mere book and systematical knowledge, as a well-managed horse is to an ass. Study, therefore, cultivate, and frequent men and women; not only in their outward, and consequently, guarded, but in their interior, domestic, and consequently less disguised, characters and manners. Take your notions of things, as by observation and experience you find they really are, and not as you read that they are or should be; for they never are quite what they should be. For this purpose do not content yourself with general and common acquaintance; but wherever you can, establish yourself, with a kind of domestic familiarity, in good houses. For instance, go again to Orli, for two or three days, and so at two or three 'reprises'. Go and stay two or three days at a time at Versailles, and improve and extend the acquaintance you have there. Be at home at St. Cloud; and, whenever any private person of fashion invites you to, pass a few days at his country-house, accept of the invitation. This will necessarily give you a versatility of mind, and a facility to adopt various manners and customs; for everybody desires to please those in whose house they are; and people are only to be pleased in their own way. Nothing is more engaging than a cheerful and easy conformity to people's particular manners, habits, and even weaknesses; nothing (to use a vulgar expression) should come amiss to a young fellow. He should be, for good purposes, what Alcibiades was commonly for bad ones, a Proteus, assuming with ease, and wearing with cheerfulness, any shape. Heat, cold, luxury, abstinence, gravity, gayety, ceremony, easiness, learning, trifling, business, and pleasure, are modes which he should be able to take, lay aside, or change occasionally, with as much ease as he would take or lay aside his hat. All this is only to be acquired by use and knowledge of the world, by keeping a great deal of company, analyzing every character, and insinuating yourself into the familiarity of various acquaintance. A right, a generous ambition to make a figure in the world, necessarily gives the desire of pleasing; the desire of pleasing points out, to a great degree, the means of doing it; and the art of pleasing is, in truth, the art of rising, of distinguishing one's self, of making a figure and a fortune in the world. But without pleasing, without the graces, as I have told you a thousand times, 'ogni fatica e vana'. You are now but nineteen, an age at which most of your countrymen are illiberally getting drunk in port, at the university. You have greatly got the start of them in learning; and if you can equally get the start of them in the knowledge and manners of the world, you may be very sure of outrunning them in court and parliament, as you set out much earlier than they. They generally begin but to see the world at one-and-twenty; you will by that age have seen all Europe. They set out upon their travels unlicked cubs: and in their travels they only lick one another, for they seldom go into any other company. They know nothing but the English world, and the worst part of that too, and generally very little of any but the English language; and they come home, at three or four-and-twenty, refined and polished (as is said in one of Congreve's plays) like Dutch skippers from a whale-fishing. The care which has been taken of you, and (to do you justice) the care that you have taken of yourself, has left you, at the age of nineteen only, nothing to acquire but the knowledge of the world, manners, address, and those exterior accomplishments. But they are great and necessary acquisitions, to those who have sense enough to know their true value; and your getting them before you are one-and-twenty, and before you enter upon the active and shining scene of life, will give you such an advantage over all your contemporaries, that they cannot overtake you: they must be distanced. You may probably be placed about a young prince, who will probably be a young king. There all the various arts of pleasing, the engaging address, the versatility of manners, the brillant, the graces, will outweigh, and yet outrun all solid knowledge and unpolished merit. Oil yourself, therefore, and be both supple and shining, for that race, if you would be first, or early at the goal. Ladies will most probably too have something to say there; and those who are best with them will probably be best SOMEWHERE ELSE.

Labor this great point, my dear child, indefatigably; attend to the very smallest parts, the minutest graces, the most trifling circumstances, that can possibly concur in forming the shining character of a complete gentleman, 'un galant homme, un homme de cour', a man of business and pleasure; 'estime des hommes, recherche des femmes, aime de tout le monde'. In this view, observe the shining part of every man of fashion, who is liked and esteemed; attend to, and imitate that particular accomplishment for which you hear him chiefly celebrated and distinguished: then collect those various parts, and make yourself a mosiac of the whole. No one body possesses everything, and almost everybody possesses some one thing worthy of imitation: only choose your models well; and in order to do so, choose by your ear more than by your eye. The best model is always that which is most universally allowed to be the best, though in strictness it may possibly not be so. We must take most things as they are, we cannot make them what we would, nor often what they should be; and where moral duties are not concerned, it is more prudent to follow than to attempt to lead. Adieu.

LETTER CLXXXVIII

BATH, October 3, 1753

MY DEAR FRIEND: You have set out well at The Hague; you are in love with Madame Munter, which I am very glad of: you are in the fine company there, and I hope one of it: for it is not enough, at your age, to be merely in good company; but you should, by your address and attentions, make that good company think you one of them. There is a tribute due to beauty, even independently of further views; which tribute I hope you paid with alacrity to Madame Munter and Madame Degenfeldt: depend upon it, they expected it, and were offended in proportion as that tribute seemed either unwillingly or scantily paid. I believe my friend Kreuningen admits nobody now to his table, for fear of their communicating the plague to him, or at least the bite of a mad dog. Pray profit of the entrees libres that the French Ambassador has given you; frequent him, and SPEAK to him. I think you will not do amiss to call upon Mr. Burrish, at Aix-la-Chapelle, since it is so little out of your way; and you will do still better, if you would, which I know you will not, drink those waters for five or six days only, to scour your stomach and bowels a little; I am sure it would do you a great deal of good Mr. Burrish can, doubtless, give you the best letters to Munich; and he will naturally give you some to Comte Preysing, or Comte Sinsheim, and such sort of grave people; but I could wish that you would ask him for some to young fellows of pleasure, or fashionable coquettes, that, you may be 'dans l'honnete debauche de Munich'. A propos of your future motions; I leave you in a great measure the master of them, so shall only suggest my thoughts to you upon that subject.

You have three electoral courts in view, Bonn, Munich, and Manheim. I would advise you to see two of them rather cursorily, and fix your tabernacle at the third, whichever that may be, for a considerable time. For instance, should you choose (as I fancy you will), to make Manheim the place of your residence, stay only ten or twelve days at Bonn, and as long at Munich, and then go and fix at Manheim; and so, vice versa, if you should like Bonn or Munich better than you think you would Manheim, make that the place of your residence, and only visit the other two. It is certain that no man can be much pleased himself, or please others much, in any place where he is only a bird of passage for eight or ten days; neither party thinking it worth while to make an acquaintance, still less to form any connection, for so short a time; but when months are the case, a man may domesticate himself pretty well, and very soon not be looked upon as a stranger. This is the real utility of traveling, when, by contracting a familiarity at any place, you get into the inside of it, and see it in its undress. That is the only way of knowing the customs, the manners, and all the little characteristical peculiarities that distinguish one place from another; but then this familiarity is not to be brought about by cold, formal visits of half an hour: no; you must show a willingness, a desire, an impatience of forming connections, 'il faut s'y preter, et y mettre du liant, du desir de plaire. Whatever you do approve, you must be lavish in your praises of; and you must learn to commend what you do not approve of, if it is approved of there. You are not much given to praise, I know; but it is because you do not yet know how extremely people are engaged by a seeming sanction to their own opinions, prejudices, and weaknesses, even in the merest trifles. Our self-love is mortified when we think our opinions, and even our tastes, customs, and dresses, either arraigned or condemned; as on the contrary, it is tickled and flattered by approbation. I will give you a remarkable instance of this kind. The famous Earl of Shaftesbury, in the flagitious reign of Charles the Second, while he was Chancellor, had a mind to be a favorite, as well as a minister of the King; in order, therefore, to please his Majesty, whose prevailing passion was women, my Lord kept a w———e, whom he had no occasion for, and made no manner of use of. The King soon heard of it, and asked him if it was true; he owned it was; but that, though he kept that one woman, he had several others besides, for he loved variety. A few days afterward, the King, at his public levee, saw Lord Shaftesbury at some distance, and said in the circle, "One would not think that that little, weak man is the greatest whore-master in England; but I can assure you that he is." Upon Lord Shaftesbury's coming into the circle, there was a general smile; the King said, "This is concerning you, my Lord."—"Me, sir?" answered the Chancellor, with some surprise. "Yes, you," answered the King; "for I had just said that you were the greatest whore-master in England! Is it not true?"—"Of a SUBJECT, Sir," replied Lord Shaftesbury, "perhaps I am." It is the same in everything; we think a difference of opinion, of conduct, of manners, a tacit reproach, at least, upon our own; we must therefore use ourselves to a ready conformity to whatever is neither criminal nor dishonorable. Whoever differs from any general custom, is supposed both to think, and proclaim himself wiser than the rest of the world: which the rest of the world cannot bear, especially in a young man. A young fellow is always forgiven and often applauded, when he carries a fashion to an excess; but never if he stops short of it. The first is ascribed to youth and fire; but the latter is imputed to an affectation of singularity or superiority. At your age, one is allowed to 'outrer' fashion, dress, vivacity, gallantry, etc., but by no means to be behindhand in any one of them. And one may apply to youth in this case, 'Si non errasset, fecerat ille minus'. Adieu.

LETTER CLXXXIX

BATH, October 19, 1753

MY DEAR FRIEND: Of all the various ingredients that compose the useful and necessary art of pleasing, no one is so effectual and engaging as that gentleness, that 'douceur' of countenance and manner, to which you are no stranger, though (God knows why) a sworn enemy. Other people take great pains to conceal or disguise their natural imperfections; some by the make of their clothes and other arts, endeavor to conceal the defects of their shape; women, who unfortunately have natural bad complexions, lay on good ones; and both men and women upon whom unkind nature has inflicted a surliness and ferocity of countenance, do at least all they can, though often without success, to soften and mitigate it; they affect 'douceur', and aim at smiles, though often in the attempt, like the Devil in Milton, they GRIN HORRIBLY A GHASTLY SMILE. But you are the only person I ever knew in the whole course of my life, who not only disdain, but absolutely reject and disguise a great advantage that nature has kindly granted. You easily guess I mean COUNTENANCE; for she has given you a very pleasing one; but you beg to be excused, you will not accept it; but on the contrary, take singular pains to put on the most 'funeste', forbidding, and unpleasing one that can possibly be imagined. This one would think impossible; but you know it to be true. If you imagine that it gives you a manly, thoughtful, and decisive air, as some, though very few of your countrymen do, you are most exceedingly mistaken; for it is at best the air of a German corporal, part of whose exercise is to look fierce, and to 'blasemeer-op'. You will say, perhaps, What, am I always to be studying my countenance, in order to wear this 'douceur'? I answer, No; do it but for a fortnight, and you never will have occasion to think of it more. Take but half the pains to recover the countenance that nature gave you, that you must have taken to disguise and deform it as you have, and the business will be done. Accustom your eyes to a certain softness, of which they are very capable, and your face to smiles, which become it more than most faces I know. Give all your motions, too, an air of 'douceur', which is directly the reverse of their present celerity and rapidity. I wish you would adopt a little of 'l'air du Couvent' (you very well know what I mean) to a certain degree; it has something extremely engaging; there is a mixture of benevolence, affection, and unction in it; it is frequently really sincere, but is almost always thought so, and consequently pleasing. Will you call this trouble? It will not be half an hour's trouble to you in a week's time. But suppose it be, pray tell me, why did you give yourself the trouble of learning to dance so well as you do? It is neither a religious, moral, or civil duty. You must own, that you did it then singly to please, and you were, in the right on't. Why do you wear fine clothes, and curl your hair? Both are troublesome; lank locks, and plain flimsy rags are much easier. This then you also do in order to please, and you do very right. But then, for God's sake, reason and act consequentially; and endeavor to please in other things too, still more essential; and without which the trouble you have taken in those is wholly thrown away. You show your dancing, perhaps six times a year, at most; but you show your countenance and your common motions every day, and all day. Which then, I appeal to yourself, ought you to think of the most, and care to render easy, graceful, and engaging? Douceur of countenance and gesture can alone make them so. You are by no means ill-natured; and would you then most unjustly be reckoned so? Yet your common countenance intimates, and would make anybody who did not know you, believe it. 'A propos' of this, I must tell you what was said the other day to a fine lady whom you know, who is very good-natured in truth, but whose common countenance implies ill-nature, even to brutality. It was Miss H———n, Lady M—y's niece, whom you have seen both at Blackheath and at Lady Hervey's. Lady M—y was saying to me that you had a very engaging countenance when you had a mind to it, but that you had not always that mind; upon which Miss H———n said, that she liked your countenance best, when it was as glum as her own. Why then, replied Lady M—y, you two should marry; for while you both wear your worst countenances, nobody else will venture upon either of you; and they call her now Mrs. Stanhope. To complete this 'douceur' of countenance and motions, which I so earnestly recommend to you, you should carry it also to your expressions and manner of thinking, 'mettez y toujours de l'affectueux de l'onction'; take the gentle, the favorable, the indulgent side of most questions. I own that the manly and sublime John Trott, your countryman, seldom does; but, to show his spirit and decision, takes the rough and harsh side, which he generally adorns with an oath, to seem more formidable. This he only thinks fine; for to do John justice, he is commonly as good-natured as anybody. These are among the many little things which you have not, and I have, lived long enough in the world to know of what infinite consequence they are in the course of life. Reason then, I repeat it again, within yourself, CONSEQUENTIALLY; and let not the pains you have taken, and still take, to please in some things be a 'pure perte', by your negligence of, and inattention to others of much less trouble, and much more consequence.

I have been of late much engaged, or rather bewildered, in Oriental history, particularly that of the Jews, since the destruction of their temple, and their dispersion by Titus; but the confusion and uncertainty of the whole, and the monstrous extravagances and falsehoods of the greatest part of it, disgusted me extremely. Their Talmud, their Mischna, their Targums, and other traditions and writings of their Rabbins and Doctors, who were most of them Cabalists, are really more extravagant and absurd, if possible, than all that you have read in Comte de Gabalis; and indeed most of his stuff is taken from them. Take this sample of their nonsense, which is transmitted in the writings of one of their most considerable Rabbins: "One Abas Saul, a man of ten feet high, was digging a grave, and happened to find the eye of Goliah, in which he thought proper to bury himself, and so he did, all but his head, which the Giant's eye was unfortunately not quite deep enough to receive." This, I assure you, is the most modest lie of ten thousand. I have also read the Turkish history which, excepting the religious part, is not fabulous, though very possibly not true. For the Turks, having no notion of letters and being, even by their religion, forbid the use of them, except for reading and transcribing the Koran, they have no historians of their own, nor any authentic records nor memorials for other historians to work upon; so that what histories we have of that country are written by foreigners; as Platina, Sir Paul Rycaut, Prince Cantimer, etc., or else snatches only of particular and short periods, by some who happened to reside there at those times; such as Busbequius, whom I have just finished. I like him, as far as he goes, much the best of any of them: but then his account is, properly, only an account of his own Embassy, from the Emperor Charles the Fifth to Solyman the Magnificent. However, there he gives, episodically, the best account I know of the customs and manners of the Turks, and of the nature of that government, which is a most extraordinary one. For, despotic as it always seems, and sometimes is, it is in truth a military republic, and the real power resides in the Janissaries; who sometimes order their Sultan to strangle his Vizir, and sometimes the Vizir to depose or strangle his Sultan, according as they happen to be angry at the one or the other. I own I am glad that the capital strangler should, in his turn, be STRANGLE-ABLE, and now and then strangled; for I know of no brute so fierce, nor no criminal so guilty, as the creature called a Sovereign, whether King, Sultan, or Sophy, who thinks himself, either by divine or human right, vested with an absolute power of destroying his fellow-creatures; or who, without inquiring into his right, lawlessly exerts that power. The most excusable of all those human monsters are the Turks, whose religion teaches them inevitable fatalism. A propos of the Turks, my Loyola, I pretend, is superior to your Sultan. Perhaps you think this impossible, and wonder who this Loyola is. Know then, that I have had a Barbet brought me from France, so exactly like the Sultan that he has been mistaken for him several times; only his snout is shorter, and his ears longer than the Sultan's. He has also the acquired knowledge of the Sultan; and I am apt to think that he studied under the same master at Paris. His habit and his white band show him to be an ecclesiastic; and his begging, which he does very earnestly, proves him to be of a mendicant order; which, added to his flattery and insinuation, make him supposed to be a Jesuit, and have acquired him the name of Loyola. I must not omit too, that when he breaks wind he smells exactly like the Sultan.

I do not yet hear one jot the better for all my bathings and pumpings, though I have been here already full half my time; I consequently go very little into company, being very little fit for any. I hope you keep company enough for us both; you will get more by that, than I shall by all my reading. I read simply to amuse myself and fill up my time, of which I have too much; but you have two much better reasons for going into company, pleasure and profit. May you find a great deal of both in a great deal of company! Adieu.

LETTER CXC

LONDON, November 20, 1753

MY DEAR FRIEND: Two mails are now due from Holland, so that I have no letter from you to acknowledge; but that, you know, by long experience, does not hinder my writing to you. I always receive your letters with pleasure; but I mean, and endeavor, that you should receive mine with some profit; preferring always your advantage to my own pleasure.

If you find yourself well settled and naturalized at Manheim, stay there some time, and do not leave a certain for an uncertain good; but if you think you shall be as well, or better established at Munich, go there as soon as you please; and if disappointed, you can always return to Manheim I mentioned, in a former letter, your passing the Carnival at Berlin, which I think may be both useful and pleasing to you; however, do as you will; but let me know what you resolve: That King and that country have, and will have, so great a share in the affairs of Europe, that they are well worth being thoroughly known.

Whether, where you are now, or ever may be hereafter, you speak French, German, or English most, I earnestly recommend to you a particular attention to the propriety and elegance of your style; employ the best words you can find in the language, avoid cacophony, and make your periods as harmonious as you can. I need not, I am sure, tell you what you must often have felt, how much the elegance of diction adorns the best thoughts, and palliates the worst. In the House of Commons it is almost everything; and, indeed, in every assembly, whether public or private. Words, which are the dress of thoughts, deserve surely more care than clothes, which are only the dress of the person, and which, however, ought to have their share of attention. If you attend to your style in any one language, it will give you a habit of attending to it in every other; and if once you speak either French or German very elegantly, you will afterward speak much the better English for it. I repeat it to you again, for at least the thousandth time, exert your whole attention now in acquiring the ornamental parts of character. People know very little of the world, and talk nonsense, when they talk of plainness and solidity unadorned: they will do in nothing; mankind has been long out of a state of nature, and the golden age of native simplicity will never return. Whether for the better or the worse, no matter; but we are refined; and plain manners, plain dress, and plain diction, would as little do in life, as acorns, herbage, and the water of the neighboring spring, would do at table. Some people are just come, who interrupt me in the middle of my sermon; so good-night.

LETTER CXCI

LONDON, November 26, 1753

DEAR FRIEND: Fine doings at Manheim! If one may give credit to the weekly histories of Monsieur Roderigue, the finest writer among the moderns; not only 'des chasses brillantes et nombreuses des operas ou les acteurs se surpassent les jours des Saints de L. L. A. A. E. E. serenissimes celebres; en grand gala'; but to crown the whole, Monsieur Zuchmantel is happily arrived, and Monsieur Wartenslebeu hourly expected. I hope that you are 'pars magna' of all these delights; though, as Noll Bluff says, in the "Old Bachelor," THAT RASCALLY GAZETTEER TAKES NO MORE NOTICE OF YOU THAN IF YOU WERE NOT IN THE LAND OF THE LIVING. I should think that he might at least have taken notice that in these rejoicings you appeared with a rejoicing, and not a gloomy countenance; and you distinguished yourself in that numerous and shining company, by your air, dress, address, and attentions. If this was the case, as I will both hope and suppose it was, I will, if you require it, have him written to, to do you justice in his next 'supplement'. Seriously, I am very glad that you are whirled in that 'tourbillon' of pleasures; they smooth, polish, and rub off rough corners: perhaps too, you have some particular COLLISION, which is still more effectual.

Schannat's "History of the Palatinate" was, I find, written originally in German, in which language I suppose it is that you have read it; but, as I must humbly content myself with the French translation, Vaillant has sent for it for me from Holland, so that I have not yet read it. While you are in the Palatinate, you do very well to read everything relative to it; you will do still better if you make that reading the foundation of your inquiries into the more minute circumstances and anecdotes of that country, whenever you are in company with informed and knowing people.

The Ministers here, intimidated on the absurd and groundless clamors of the mob, have, very weakly in my mind, repealed, this session, the bill which they had passed in the last for rendering Jews capable of being naturalized by subsequent acts of parliament. The clamorers triumph, and will doubtless make further demands, which, if not granted, this piece of complaisance will soon be forgotten. Nothing is truer in politics, than this reflection of the Cardinal de Retz, 'Que le peuple craint toujours quand on ne le craint pas'; and consequently they grow unreasonable and insolent, when they find that they are feared. Wise and honest governors will never, if they can help it, give the people just cause to complain; but then, on the other hand, they will firmly withstand groundless clamor. Besides that this noise against the Jew bill proceeds from that narrow mobspirit of INTOLERATION in religious, and inhospitality in civil matters; both which all wise governments should oppose.

The confusion in France increases daily, as, no doubt, you are informed where you are. There is an answer of the clergy to the remonstrances of the parliament, lately published, which was sent me by the last post from France, and which I would have sent you, inclosed in this, were it not too bulky. Very probably you may see it at Manheim, from the French Minister: it is very well worth your reading, being most artfully and plausibly written, though founded upon false principles; the 'jus divinum' of the clergy, and consequently their supremacy in all matters of faith and doctrine are asserted; both which I absolutely deny. Were those two points allowed the clergy of any country whatsoever, they must necessarily govern that country absolutely; everything being, directly or indirectly, relative to faith or doctrine; and whoever is supposed to have the power of saving and damning souls to all eternity (which power the clergy pretend to), will be much more considered, and better obeyed, than any civil power that forms no pretensions beyond this world. Whereas, in truth, the clergy in every country are, like all other subjects, dependent upon the supreme legislative power, and are appointed by that power under whatever restrictions and limitations it pleases, to keep up decency and decorum in the church, just as constables are to keep peace in the parish. This Fra Paolo has clearly proved, even upon their own principles of the Old and New Testament, in his book 'de Beneficiis', which I recommend to you to read with attention; it is short. Adieu.

LETTER CXCII

LONDON, December 25, 1753

MY DEAR FRIEND: Yesterday again I received two letters at once from you, the one of the 7th, the other of the 15th, from Manheim.

You never had in your life so good a reason for not writing, either to me or to anybody else, as your sore finger lately furnished you. I believe it was painful, and I am glad it is cured; but a sore finger, however painful, is a much less evil than laziness, of either body or mind, and attended by fewer ill consequences.

I am very glad to hear that you were distinguished at the court of Manheim from the rest of your countrymen and fellow-travelers: it is a sign that you had better manners and address than they; for take it for granted, the best-bred people will always be the best received wherever they go. Good manners are the settled medium of social, as specie is of commercial life; returns are equally expected for both; and people will no more advance their civility to a bear, than their money to a bankrupt. I really both hope and believe, that the German courts will do you a great deal of good; their ceremony and restraint being the proper correctives and antidotes for your negligence and inattention. I believe they would not greatly relish your weltering in your own laziness, and an easy chair; nor take it very kindly, if, when they spoke to you or you to them, you looked another way, as much as to say, kiss my b——h. As they give, so they require attention; and, by the way, take this maxim for an undoubted truth, That no young man can possibly improve in any company, for which he has not respect enough to be under some degree of restraint.

I dare not trust to Meyssonier's report of his Rhenish, his Burgundy not having answered either his account or my expectations. I doubt, as a wine merchant, he is the 'perfidus caupo', whatever he may be as a banker. I shall therefore venture upon none of his wine; but delay making my provision of Old Hock, till I go abroad myself next spring: as I told you in the utmost secrecy, in my last, that I intend to do; and then probably I may taste some that I like, and go upon sure ground. There is commonly very good, both at Aix-la-Chapelle and Liege, where I formerly got some excellent, which I carried with me to Spa, where I drank no other wine.

As my letters to you frequently miscarry, I will repeat in this that part of my last which related to your future motions. Whenever you shall be tired of Berlin, go to Dresden; where Sir Charles Williams will be, who will receive you with open arms. He dined with me to-day, and sets out for Dresden in about six weeks. He spoke of you with great kindness and impatience to see you again. He will trust and employ you in business (and he is now in the whole secret of importance) till we fix our place to meet in: which probably will be Spa. Wherever you are, inform yourself minutely of, and attend particularly to the affairs of France; they grow serious, and in my opinion will grow more and more so every day. The King is despised and I do not wonder at it; but he has brought it about to be hated at the same time, which seldom happens to the same man. His ministers are known to be as disunited as incapable; he hesitates between the Church and the parliaments, like the ass in the fable, that starved between two hampers of hay: too much in love with his mistress to part with her, and too much afraid of his soul to enjoy her; jealous of the parliaments, who would support his authority; and a devoted bigot to the Church, that would destroy it. The people are poor, consequently discontented; those who have religion, are divided in their notions of it; which is saying that they hate one another. The clergy never do forgive; much less will they forgive the parliament; the parliament never will forgive them. The army must, without doubt, take, in their own minds at last, different parts in all these disputes, which upon occasion would break out. Armies, though always the supporters and tools of absolute power for the time being, are always the destroyers of it, too, by frequently changing the hands in which they think proper to lodge it. This was the case of the Praetorian bands, who deposed and murdered the monsters they had raised to oppress mankind. The Janissaries in turkey, and the regiments of guards in Russia, do the same now. The French nation reasons freely, which they never did before, upon matters of religion and government, and begin to be 'sprejiudicati'; the officers do so too; in short, all the symptoms, which I have ever met with in history previous to great changes and revolutions in government, now exist, and daily increase, in France. I am glad of it; the rest of Europe will be the quieter, and have time to recover. England, I am sure, wants rest, for it wants men and money; the Republic of the United Provinces wants both still more; the other Powers cannot well dance, when neither France, nor the maritime powers, can, as they used to do, pay the piper. The first squabble in Europe, that I foresee, will be about the Crown of Poland, should the present King die: and therefore I wish his Majesty a long life and a merry Christmas. So much for foreign politics; but 'a propos' of them, pray take care, while you are in those parts of Germany, to inform yourself correctly of all the details, discussions, and agreements, which the several wars, confiscations, bans, and treaties, occasioned between the Bavarian and Palatine Electorates; they are interesting and curious.

I shall not, upon the occasion of the approaching new year, repeat to you the wishes which I continue to form for you; you know them all already, and you know that it is absolutely in your power to satisfy most of them. Among many other wishes, this is my most earnest one: That you would open the new year with a most solemn and devout sacrifice to the Graces; who never reject those that supplicate them with fervor; without them, let me tell you, that your friend Dame Fortune will stand you in little stead; may they all be your friends! Adieu.

LETTER CXCIII

LONDON, January 15, 1754

MY DEAR FRIEND: I have this moment received your letter of the 26th past from Munich. Since you are got so well out of the distress and dangers of your journey from Manheim, I am glad that you were in them:

> "Condisce i diletti
>
> Memorie di pene,
>
> Ne sa che sia bene
>
> Chi mal non soffri."

They were but little samples of the much greater distress and dangers which you must expect to meet within your great, and I hope, long journey through life. In some parts of it, flowers are scattered, with profusion, the road is smooth, and the prospect pleasant: but in others (and I fear the greater number) the road is rugged, beset with thorns and briars, and cut by torrents. Gather the flowers in your way; but, at the same time, guard against the briars that are either mixed with them, or that most certainly succeed them.

I thank you for your wild boar; who, now he is dead, I assure him, 'se laissera bien manger malgre qu'il en ait'; though I am not so sure that I should have had that personal valor which so successfully distinguished you in single combat with him, which made him bite the dust like Homer's heroes, and, to conclude my period sublimely, put him into that PICKLE, from which I propose eating him. At the same time that I applaud your valor, I must do justice to your modesty; which candidly admits that you were not overmatched, and that your adversary was about your own age and size. A Maracassin, being under a year old, would have been below your indignation. 'Bete de compagne', being under two years old, was still, in my opinion, below your glory; but I guess that your enemy was 'un Ragot', that is, from two to three years old; an age and size which, between man and boar, answer pretty well to yours.

If accidents of bad roads or waters do not detain you at Munich, I do not fancy that pleasures will: and I rather believe you will seek for, and find them, at the Carnival at Berlin; in which supposition, I eventually direct this letter to your banker there. While you are at Berlin (I earnestly recommend it to you again and again) pray CARE to see, hear, know, and mind, everything there. THE ABLEST PRINCE IN EUROPE is surely an object that deserves attention; and the least thing that he does, like the smallest sketches of the greatest painters, has its value, and a considerable one too.

Read with care the Code Frederick, and inform yourself of the good effects of it in those parts of, his dominions where it has taken place, and where it has banished the former chicanes, quirks, and quibbles of the old law. Do not think any detail too minute or trifling for your inquiry and observation. I wish that you could find one hour's leisure every day, to read some good Italian author, and to converse in that language with our worthy friend Signor Angelo Cori; it would both refresh and improve your Italian, which, of the many languages you know, I take to be that in which you are the least perfect; but of which, too, you already know enough to make yourself master of, with very little trouble, whenever you please.

Live, dwell, and grow at the several courts there; use them so much to your face, that they may not look upon you as a stranger. Observe, and take their 'ton', even to their affectations and follies; for such there are, and perhaps should be, at all courts. Stay, in all events, at Berlin, till I inform you of Sir Charles Williams's arrival at Dresden; where I suppose you would not care to be before him, and where you may go as soon after him as ever you please. Your time there will neither be unprofitably nor disagreeably spent; he will introduce you into all the best company, though he can introduce you to none so good as his own. He has of late applied himself very seriously to foreign affairs, especially those of Saxony and Poland; he knows them perfectly well, and will tell you what he knows. He always expresses, and I have good reason to believe very sincerely, great kindness and affection for you.

The works of the late Lord Bolingbroke are just published, and have plunged me into philosophical studies; which hitherto I have not been much used to, or delighted with; convinced of the futility of those researches; but I have read his "Philosophical Essay" upon the extent of human knowledge, which, by the way, makes two large quartos and a half. He there shows very clearly, and with most splendid eloquence, what the human mind can and cannot do; that our understandings are wisely calculated for our place in this planet, and for the link which we form in the universal chain of things; but that they are by no means capable of that degree of knowledge, which our curiosity makes us search after, and which our vanity makes us often believe we arrive at. I shall not recommend to you the reading of that work; but, when you return hither, I shall recommend to your frequent and diligent perusal all his tracts that are relative to our history and constitution; upon which he throws lights, and scatters graces, which no other writer has ever done.

Reading, which was always a pleasure to me, in the time even of my greatest dissipation, is now become my only refuge; and, I fear, I indulge it too much at the expense of my eyes. But what can I do? I must do something; I cannot bear absolute idleness; my ears grow every day more useless to me, my eyes consequently more necessary; I will not hoard them like a miser, but will rather risk the loss, than not enjoy the use of them.

Pray let me know all the particulars, not only of your reception at Munich, but also at Berlin; at the latter, I believe, it will be a good one; for his Prussian Majesty knows, that I have long been AN ADMIRER AND RESPECTER OF HIS GREAT AND VARIOUS TALENTS. Adieu.

LETTER CXCIV

LONDON, February 1, 1754

EARL OF PHILIP DORMER STANHOPE CHESTERFIELD

MY DEAR FRIEND: I received, yesterday, yours of the 12th, from Munich; in consequence of which, I direct this to you there, though I directed my three last to Berlin, where I suppose you will find them at your arrival. Since you are not only domesticated, but 'niche' at Munich, you are much in the right to stay there. It is not by seeing places that one knows them, but by familiar and daily conversations with the people of fashion. I would not care to be in the place of that prodigy of beauty, whom you are to drive 'dans la course de Traineaux'; and I am apt to think you are much more likely to break her bones, than she is, though ever so cruel, to break your heart. Nay, I am not sure but that, according to all the rules of gallantry, you are obliged to overturn her on purpose; in the first place, for the chance of seeing her backside; in the next, for the sake of the contrition and concern which it would give you an opportunity of showing; and, lastly, upon account of all the 'gentillesses et epigrammes', which it would naturally suggest. Voiture has made several stanzas upon an accident of that kind, which happened to a lady of his acquaintance. There is a great deal of wit in them, rather too much; for, according to the taste of those times, they are full of what the Italians call 'concetti spiritosissimi'; the Spaniards 'agudeze'; and we, affectation and quaintness. I hope you have endeavored to suit your 'Traineau' to the character of the fair-one whom it is to contain. If she is of an irascible, impetuous disposition (as fine women can sometimes be), you will doubtless place her in the body of a lion, a tiger, a dragon, or some tremendous beast of prey and fury; if she is a sublime and stately beauty, which I think more probable (for unquestionably she is 'hogh gebohrne'), you will, I suppose, provide a magnificent swan or proud peacock for her reception; but if she is all tenderness and softness, you have, to be sure, taken care amorous doves and wanton sparrows should seem to flutter round her. Proper mottos, I take it for granted, that you have eventually prepared; but if not, you may find a great many ready-made ones in 'Les Entretiens d'Ariste et d'Eugene, sur les Devises', written by Pere Bouhours, and worth your reading at any time. I will not say to you, upon this occasion, like the father in Ovid,

"Parce, puer, stimulis, et fortius utere loris."

On the contrary, drive on briskly; it is not the chariot of the sun that you drive, but you carry the sun in your chariot; consequently, the faster it goes, the less it will be likely to scorch or consume. This is Spanish enough, I am sure.

If this finds you still at Munich, pray make many compliments from me to Mr. Burrish, to whom I am very much obliged for all his kindness to you; it is true, that while I had power I endeavored to serve him; but it is as true too, that I served many others more, who have neither returned nor remembered those services.

I have been very ill this last fortnight, of your old Carniolian complaint, the 'arthritis vaga'; luckily, it did not fall upon my breast, but seized on my right arm; there it fixed its seat of empire; but, as in all tyrannical governments, the remotest parts felt their share of its severity. Last post I was not able to hold a pen long enough to write to you, and therefore desired Mr. Grevenkop to do it for me; but that letter was directed to Berlin. My pain is now much abated, though I have still some fine remains of it in my shoulder, where I fear it will tease me a great while. I must be careful to take Horace's advice, and consider well, 'Quid valeant humeri, quid ferre recusent'.

Lady Chesterfield bids me make you her compliments, and assure you that the music will be much more welcome to her with you, than without you.

In some of my last letters, which were directed to, and will, I suppose, wait for you at Berlin, I complimented you, and with justice, upon your great improvement of late in the epistolary way, both with regard to the style and the turn of your letters; your four or five last to me have been very good ones, and one that you wrote to

Mr. Harte, upon the new year, was so pretty a one, and he was so much and so justly pleased with it, that he sent it me from Windsor the instant he had read it. This talent (and a most necessary one it is in the course of life) is to be acquired by resolving, and taking pains to acquire it; and, indeed, so is every talent except poetry, which is undoubtedly a gift. Think, therefore, night and day, of the turn, the purity, the correctness, the perspicuity, and the elegance of whatever you speak or write; take my word for it, your labor will not be in vain, but greatly rewarded by the harvest of praise and success which it will bring you. Delicacy of turn, and elegance of style, are ornaments as necessary to common sense, as attentions, address, and fashionable manners, are to common civility; both may subsist without them, but then, without being of the least use to the owner. The figure of a man is exactly the same in dirty rags, or in the finest and best chosen clothes; but in which of the two he is the most likely to please, and to be received in good company, I leave to you to determine.

Both my arm and my paper hint to me, to bid you good-night.

LETTER CXCV

LONDON, February 12, 1754.

MY DEAR FRIEND: I take my aim, and let off this letter at you at Berlin; I should be sorry it missed you, because I believe you will read it with as much pleasure as I write it. It is to inform you, that, after some difficulties and dangers, your seat in the new parliament is at last absolutely secured, and that without opposition, or the least necessity of your personal trouble or appearance. This success, I must further inform you, is in a great degree owing to Mr. Eliot's friendship to us both; for he brings you in with himself at his surest borough. As it was impossible to act with more zeal and friendship than Mr. Eliot has acted in this whole affair, I desire that you will, by the very next post, write him a letter of thanks, warm and young thanks, not old and cold ones. You may inclose it in yours to me, and, I will send it to him, for he is now in Cornwall.

Thus, sure of being a senator, I dare say you do not propose to be one of the 'pedarii senatores, et pedibus ire in sententiam; for, as the House of Commons is the theatre where you must make your fortune and figure in the world, you must resolve to be an actor, and not a 'persona muta', which is just equivalent to a candle snuffer upon other theatres. Whoever does not shine there, is obscure, insignificant and contemptible; and you cannot conceive how easy it is for a man of half your sense and knowledge to shine there if he pleases.

The receipt to make a speaker, and an applauded one too, is short and easy.—Take of common sense 'quantum sufcit', add a little application to the rules and orders of the House, throw obvious thoughts in a new light, and make up the whole with a large quantity of purity, correctness, and elegance of style. Take it for granted, that by far the greatest part of mankind do neither analyze nor search to the bottom; they are incapable of penetrating deeper than the surface. All have senses to be gratified, very few have reason to be applied to. Graceful utterance and action please their eyes, elegant diction tickles their ears; but strong reason would be thrown away upon them. I am not only persuaded by theory, but convinced by my experience, that (supposing a certain degree of common sense) what is called a good speaker is as much a mechanic as a good shoemaker; and that the two trades are equally to be learned by the same degree of application. Therefore, for God's sake, let this trade be the principal object of your thoughts; never lose sight of it. Attend minutely to your style, whatever language you speak or write in; seek for the best words, and think of the best turns. Whenever you doubt of the propriety or elegance of any word, search the dictionary or some good author for it, or inquire of somebody, who is master of that language; and, in a little time, propriety and elegance of diction will become so habitual to you, that they will cost you no more trouble. As I have laid this down to be mechanical and attainable by whoever will take the necessary pains, there will be no great vanity in my saying, that I saw the importance of the object so early, and attended to it so young, that it would now cost me more trouble to speak or write ungrammatically, vulgarly, and inelegantly, than ever it did to avoid doing so. The late Lord Bolingbroke, without the least trouble, talked all day long, full as elegantly as he wrote. Why? Not by a peculiar gift from heaven; but, as he has often told me himself, by an early and constant attention to his style. The present Solicitor-General, Murray,—[Created Lord Mansfield in the year 1756.]—has less law than many lawyers, but has more practice than any; merely upon account of his eloquence, of which he has a never-failing stream. I remember so long ago as when I was at Cambridge, whenever I read pieces of eloquence (and indeed they were my chief study) whether ancient or modern, I used to write down the shining passages, and then translate them, as well and as elegantly as ever I could; if Latin or French, into English; if English, into French. This, which I practiced for some years, not only improved and formed my style, but imprinted in my mind and memory the best thoughts of the best authors. The trouble was little, but the advantage I have experienced was great. While you are abroad, you can neither have time nor opportunity to read pieces of English or parliamentary eloquence, as I hope you will carefully do when you return; but, in the meantime, whenever pieces of French eloquence come in your way, such as the speeches of persons received into the Academy, 'orasions funebres', representations of the several parliaments to the King, etc., read them in that view, in that spirit; observe the harmony, the turn and elegance of the style; examine in what you think it might have been better; and consider in what, had you written it yourself; you might have done worse. Compare the different manners of expressing the same thoughts in different authors; and observe how differently the same things appear in different dresses. Vulgar, coarse, and ill-chosen words, will deform and degrade the best thoughts as much as rags and dirt will the best figure. In short, you now know your object; pursue it steadily, and have no digressions that are not relative to, and connected with, the main action. Your success in parliament will effectually remove all OTHER OBJECTIONS; either a foreign or a domestic destination will no longer be refused you, if you make your way to it through Westminster.

I think I may now say, that I am quite recovered from my late illness, strength and spirits excepted, which are not yet restored. Aix-la-Chapelle and Spa will, I believe, answer all my purposes.

I long to hear an account of your reception at Berlin, which I fancy will be a most gracious one. Adieu.

LETTER CXCVI

LONDON, February 15, 1754

MY DEAR FRIEND: I can now with great truth apply your own motto to you, 'Nullum numen abest, si sit Prudentia'. You are sure of being, as early as your age will permit, a member of that House; which is the only road to figure and fortune in this country. Those, indeed, who are bred up to, and distinguish themselves in particular professions, as the army, the navy, and the law, may, by their own merit, raise themselves to a certain degree; but you may observe too, that they never get to the top, without the assistance of parliamentary talents and influence. The means of distinguishing yourself in parliament are, as I told you in my last, much more easily attained than I believe you imagine. Close attendance to the business of the House will soon give you the parliamentary routine; and strict attention to your style will soon make you, not only a speaker, but a good one. The vulgar look upon a man, who is reckoned a fine speaker, as a phenomenon, a supernatural being, and endowed with some peculiar gift of heaven; they stare at him, if he walks in the Park, and cry, THAT IS HE. You will, I am sure, view him in a juster light, and 'nulla formidine'. You will consider him only as a man of good sense, who adorns common thoughts with the graces of elocution, and the elegance of style. The miracle will then cease; and you will be convinced, that with the same application, and attention to the same objects, you may most certainly equal, and perhaps surpass, this prodigy. Sir W———Y———, with not a quarter of your parts, and not a thousandth part of your knowledge, has, by a glibness of tongue simply, raised him successively to the best employments of the kingdom; he has been Lord of the Admiralty, Lord of the Treasury, Secretary at War, and is now Vice-Treasurer of Ireland; and all this with a most sullied, not to say blasted character. Represent the thing to yourself, as it really is, easily attainable, and you will find it so. Have but ambition enough passionately to desire the object, and spirit enough to use the means, and I will be answerable for your success. When I was younger than you are, I resolved within myself that I would in all events be a speaker in parliament, and a good one too, if I could. I consequently never lost sight of that object, and never neglected any of the means that I thought led to it. I succeeded to a certain degree; and, I assure you, with great ease, and without superior talents. Young people are very apt to overrate both men and things, from not being enough acquainted with them. In proportion as you come to know them better, you will value them less. You will find that reason, which always ought to direct mankind, seldom does; but that passions and weaknesses commonly usurp its seat, and rule in its stead. You will find that the ablest have their weak sides too, and are only comparatively able, with regard to the still weaker herd: having fewer weaknesses themselves, they are able to avail themselves of the innumerable ones of the generality of mankind: being more masters of themselves, they become more easily masters of others. They address themselves to their weaknesses, their senses, their passions; never to their reason; and consequently seldom fail of success. But then analyze those great, those governing, and, as the vulgar imagine, those perfect characters, and you will find the great Brutus a thief in Macedonia, the great Cardinal Richelieu a jealous poetaster, and the great Duke of Marlborough a miser. Till you come to know mankind by your own experience, I know no thing, nor no man, that can in the meantime bring you so well acquainted with them as le Duc de la Rochefoucault: his little book of "Maxims," which I would advise you to look into, for some moments at least, every day of your life, is, I fear, too like, and too exact a picture of human nature.

I own, it seems to degrade it; but yet my experience does not convince me that it degrades it unjustly.

Now, to bring all this home to my first point. All these considerations should not only invite you to attempt to make a figure in parliament, but encourage you to hope that you shall succeed. To govern mankind, one must not overrate them: and to please an audience, as a speaker, one must not overvalue it. When I first came into the House of Commons, I respected that assembly as a venerable one; and felt a certain awe upon me, but, upon better acquaintance, that awe soon vanished; and I discovered, that, of the five hundred and sixty, not above thirty could understand reason, and that all the rest were 'peuple'; that those thirty only required plain common sense, dressed up in good language; and that all the others only required flowing and harmonious periods, whether they conveyed any meaning or not; having ears to hear, but not sense enough to judge. These considerations made me speak with little concern the first time, with less the second, and with none at all the third. I gave myself no further trouble about anything, except my elocution, and my style; presuming, without much vanity, that I had common sense sufficient not to talk nonsense. Fix these three truths strongly in your mind: First, that it is absolutely necessary for you to speak in parliament; secondly, that it only requires a little human attention, and no supernatural gifts; and, thirdly, that you have all the reason in the world to think that you shall speak well. When we meet, this shall be the principal subject of our conversations; and, if you will follow my advice, I will answer for your success.

Now from great things to little ones; the transition is to me easy, because nothing seems little to me that can be of any use to you. I hope you take great care of your mouth and teeth, and that you clean them well every morning with a sponge and tepid water, with a few drops of arquebusade water dropped into it; besides washing your mouth carefully after every meal, I do insist upon your never using those sticks, or any hard substance whatsoever, which always rub away the gums, and destroy the varnish of the teeth. I speak this from woeful experience; for my negligence of my teeth, when I was younger than you are, made them bad; and afterward, my desire to have them look better, made me use sticks, irons, etc., which totally destroyed them; so that I have not now above six or seven left. I lost one this morning, which suggested this advice to you.

I have received the tremendous wild boar, which your still more tremendous arm slew in the immense deserts of the Palatinate; but have not yet tasted of it, as it is hitherto above my low regimen. The late King of Prussia, whenever he killed any number of wild boars, used to oblige the Jews to buy them, at a high price, though they could eat none of them; so they defrayed the expense of his hunting. His son has juster rules of government, as the Code Frederick plainly shows.

I hope, that, by this time, you are as well 'ancre' at Berlin as you was at Munich; but, if not, you are sure of being so at Dresden. Adieu.

LETTER CXCVII

LONDON, February 26, 1754.

MY DEAR FRIEND: I have received your letters of the 4th, from Munich, and of the 11th from Ratisbon; but I have not received that of the 31st January, to which you refer in the former. It is to this negligence and uncertainty of the post, that you owe your accidents between Munich and Ratisbon: for, had you received my letters regularly, you would have received one from me before you left Munich, in which I advised you to stay, since you were so well there. But, at all events, you were in the wrong to set out from Munich in such weather and such roads; since you could never imagine that I had set my heart so much upon your going to Berlin, as to venture your being buried in the snow for it. Upon the whole, considering all you are very well off. You do very well, in my mind, to return to Munich, or at least to keep within the circle of Munich, Ratisbon, and Manheim, till the weather and the roads are good: stay at each or any of those places as long as ever you please; for I am extremely indifferent about your going to Berlin.

As to our meeting, I will tell you my plan, and you may form your own accordingly. I propose setting out from hence the last week in April, then drinking the Aix-la-Chapelle waters for a week, and from thence being at Spa about the 15th of May, where I shall stay two months at most, and then return straight to England. As I both hope and believe that there will be no mortal at Spa during my residence there, the fashionable season not beginning till the middle of July, I would by no means have you come there at first, to be locked up with me and some few Capucins, for two months, in that miserable hole; but I would advise you to stay where you like best, till about the first week in July, and then to come and pick me up at Spa, or meet me upon the road at Liege or Brussels. As for the intermediate time, should you be weary of Manheim and Munich, you may, if you please, go to Dresden, to Sir Charles Williams, who will be there before that time; or you may come for a month or six weeks to The Hague; or, in short, go or stay wherever you like best. So

LETTERS TO HIS SON, COMPLETE

much for your motions.

As you have sent for all the letters directed to you at Berlin, you will receive from thence volumes of mine, among which you will easily perceive that some were calculated for a supposed perusal previous to your opening them. I will not repeat anything contained in them, excepting that I desire you will send me a warm and cordial letter of thanks for Mr. Eliot; who has, in the most friendly manner imaginable, fixed you at his own borough of Liskeard, where you will be elected jointly with him, without the least opposition or difficulty. I will forward that letter to him into Cornwall, where he now is.

Now that you are to be soon a man of business, I heartily wish that you would immediately begin to be a man of method; nothing contributing more to facilitate and dispatch business, than method and order. Have order and method in your accounts, in your reading, in the allotment of your time; in short, in everything. You cannot conceive how much time you will save by it, nor how much better everything you do will be done. The Duke of Marlborough did by no means spend, but he slatterned himself into that immense debt, which is not yet near paid off. The hurry and confusion of the Duke of Newcastle do not proceed from his business, but from his want of method in it. Sir Robert Walpole, who had ten times the business to do, was never seen in a hurry, because he always did it with method. The head of a man who has business, and no method nor order, is properly that 'rudis indigestaque moles quam dixere chaos'. As you must be conscious that you are extremely negligent and slatternly, I hope you will resolve not to be so for the future. Prevail with yourself, only to observe good method and order for one fortnight; and I will venture to assure you that you will never neglect them afterward, you will find such conveniency and advantage arising from them. Method is the great advantage that lawyers have over other people, in speaking in parliament; for, as they must necessarily observe it in their pleadings in the courts of justice, it becomes habitual to them everywhere else. Without making you a compliment, I can tell you with pleasure, that order, method, and more activity of mind, are all that you want, to make, some day or other, a considerable figure in business. You have more useful knowledge, more discernment of characters, and much more discretion, than is common at your age; much more, I am sure, than I had at that age. Experience you cannot yet have, and therefore trust in the meantime to mine. I am an old traveler; am well acquainted with all the bye as well as the great roads; I cannot misguide you from ignorance, and you are very sure I shall not from design.

I can assure you, that you will have no opportunity of subscribing yourself my Excellency's, etc. Retirement and quiet were my choice some years ago, while I had all my senses, and health and spirits enough to carry on business; but now that I have lost my hearing, and that I find my constitution declining daily, they are become my necessary and only refuge. I know myself (no common piece of knowledge, let me tell you), I know what I can, what I cannot, and consequently what I ought to do. I ought not, and therefore will not, return to business when I am much less fit for it than I was when I quitted it. Still less will I go to Ireland, where, from my deafness and infirmities, I must necessarily make a different figure from that which I once made there. My pride would be too much mortified by that difference. The two important senses of seeing and hearing should not only be good, but quick, in business; and the business of a Lord-lieutenant of Ireland (if he will do it himself) requires both those senses in the highest perfection. It was the Duke of Dorset's not doing the business himself, but giving it up to favorites, that has occasioned all this confusion in Ireland; and it was my doing the whole myself, without either Favorite, Minister, or Mistress, that made my administration so smooth and quiet. I remember, when I named the late Mr. Liddel for my Secretary, everybody was much surprised at it; and some of my friends represented to me, that he was no man of business, but only a very genteel, pretty young fellow; I assured them, and with truth, that that was the very reason why I chose him; for that I was resolved to do all the business myself, and without even the suspicion of having a minister; which the Lord-lieutenant's Secretary, if he is a man of business, is always supposed, and commonly with reason, to be. Moreover, I look upon myself now to be emeritus in business, in which I have been near forty years together; I give it up to you: apply yourself to it, as I have done, for forty years, and then I consent to your leaving it for a philosophical retirement among your friends and your books. Statesmen and beauties are very rarely sensible of the gradations of their decay; and, too often sanguinely hoping to shine on in their meridian, often set with contempt and ridicule. I retired in time, 'uti conviva satur'; or, as Pope says still better, ERE TITTERING YOUTH SHALL SHOVE YOU FROM THE STAGE.

EARL OF PHILIP DORMER STANHOPE CHESTERFIELD

My only remaining ambition is to be the counsellor and minister of your rising ambition. Let me see my own youth revived in you; let me be your Mentor, and, with your parts and knowledge, I promise you, you shall go far. You must bring, on your part, activity and attention; and I will point out to you the proper objects for them. I own I fear but one thing for you, and that is what one has generally the least reason to fear from one of your age; I mean your laziness; which, if you indulge, will make you stagnate in a contemptible obscurity all your life. It will hinder you from doing anything that will deserve to be written, or from writing anything that may deserve to be read; and yet one or other of those two objects should be at least aimed at by every rational being.

I look upon indolence as a sort of SUICIDE; for the man is effectually destroyed, though the appetites of the brute may survive. Business by no means forbids pleasures; on the contrary, they reciprocally season each other; and I will venture to affirm, that no man enjoys either in perfection, that does not join both. They whet the desire for each other. Use yourself, therefore, in time to be alert and diligent in your little concerns; never procrastinate, never put off till to-morrow what you can do to-day; and never do two things at a time; pursue your object, be it what it will, steadily and indefatigably; and let any difficulties (if surmountable) rather animate than slacken your endeavors. Perseverance has surprising effects.

I wish you would use yourself to translate, every day, only three or four lines, from any book, in any language, into the correctest and most elegant English that you can think of; you cannot imagine how it will insensibly form your style, and give you an habitual elegance; it would not take you up a quarter of an hour in a day. This letter is so long, that it will hardly leave you that quarter of an hour, the day you receive it. So good-night.

LETTER CXCVIII

LONDON, March 8, 1754

MY DEAR FRIEND: A great and unexpected event has lately happened in our ministerial world. Mr. Pelham died last Monday of a fever and mortification, occasioned by a general corruption of his whole mass of blood, which had broke out into sores in his back. I regret him as an old acquaintance, a pretty near relation, and a private man, with whom I have lived many years in a social and friendly way. He meant well to the public; and was incorrupt in a post where corruption is commonly contagious. If he was no shining, enterprising minister, he was a safe one, which I like better. Very shining ministers, like the sun, are apt to scorch when they shine the brightest: in our constitution, I prefer the milder light of a less glaring minister. His successor is not yet, at least publicly, 'designatus'. You will easily suppose that many are very willing, and very few able, to fill that post. Various persons are talked of, by different people, for it, according as their interest prompts them to wish, or their ignorance to conjecture. Mr. Fox is the most talked of; he is strongly supported by the Duke of Cumberland. Mr. Legge, the Solicitor-General, and Dr. Lee, are likewise all spoken of, upon the foot of the Duke of Newcastle's, and the Chancellor's interest. Should it be any one of the last three, I think no great alterations will ensue; but should Mr. Fox prevail, it would, in my opinion, soon produce changes by no means favorable to the Duke of Newcastle. In the meantime, the wild conjectures of volunteer politicians, and the ridiculous importance which, upon these occasions, blockheads always endeavor to give themselves, by grave looks, significant shrugs, and insignificant whispers, are very entertaining to a bystander, as, thank God, I now am. One KNOWS SOMETHING, but is not yet at liberty to tell it; another has heard something from a very good hand; a third congratulates himself upon a certain degree of intimacy, which he has long had with everyone of the candidates, though perhaps he has never spoken twice to anyone of them. In short, in these sort of intervals, vanity, interest, and absurdity, always display themselves in the most ridiculous light. One who has been so long behind the scenes as I have is much more diverted with the entertainment, than those can be who only see it from the pit and boxes. I know the whole machinery of the interior, and can laugh the better at the silly wonder and wild conjectures of the uninformed spectators. This accident, I think, cannot in the least affect your election, which is finally settled with your friend Mr. Eliot. For, let who will prevail, I presume, he will consider me enough, not to overturn an arrangement of that sort, in which he cannot possibly be personally interested. So pray go on with your parliamentary preparations. Have that object always in your view, and pursue it with attention.

I take it for granted that your late residence in Germany has made you as perfect and correct in German, as you were before in French, at least it is worth your while to be so; because it is worth every man's while to be perfectly master of whatever language he may ever have occasion to speak. A man is not himself, in a language which he does not thoroughly possess; his thoughts are degraded, when inelegantly or imperfectly expressed; he is cramped and confined, and consequently can never appear to advantage. Examine and analyze those thoughts that strike you the most, either in conversation or in books; and you will find that they owe at least half their merit to the turn and expression of them. There is nothing truer than that old saying, 'Nihil dictum quod non prins dictum'. It is only the manner of saying or writing it that makes it appear new. Convince yourself that manner is almost everything, in everything; and study it accordingly.

I am this moment informed, and I believe truly, that Mr. Fox—[Henry Fox, created Lord Holland, Baron of Foxley, in the year 1763]—is to succeed Mr. Pelham as First Commissioner of the Treasury and Chancellor of the Exchequer; and your friend, Mr. Yorke, of The Hague, to succeed Mr. Fox as Secretary at War. I am not sorry for this promotion of Mr. Fox, as I have always been upon civil terms with him, and found him ready to do me any little services. He is frank and gentleman-like in his manner: and, to a certain degree, I really believe will be your friend upon my account; if you can afterward make him yours, upon your own, 'tan mieux'. I have nothing more to say now but Adieu.

LETTER CXCIX

LONDON, March 15, 1754

MY DEAR FRIEND: We are here in the midst of a second winter; the cold is more severe, and the snow deeper, than they were in the first. I presume, your weather in Germany is not much more gentle and, therefore, I hope that you are quietly and warmly fixed at some good town: and will not risk a second burial in the snow, after your late fortunate resurrection out of it. Your letters, I suppose, have not been able to make their way through the ice; for I have received none from you since that of the 12th of February, from Ratisbon. I am the more uneasy at this state of ignorance, because I fear that you may have found some subsequent inconveniences from your overturn, which you might not be aware of at first.

EARL OF PHILIP DORMER STANHOPE CHESTERFIELD

The curtain of the political theatre was partly drawn up the day before yesterday, and exhibited a scene which the public in general did not expect; the Duke of Newcastle was declared First Lord Commissioner of the Treasury, Mr. Fox Secretary of State in his room, and Mr. Henry Legge Chancellor of the Exchequer: The employments of Treasurer of the Navy, and Secretary at War, supposed to be vacant by the promotion of Mr. Fox and Mr. Legge, were to be kept 'in petto' till the dissolution of this parliament, which will probably be next week, to avoid the expense and trouble of unnecessary re-elections; but it was generally supposed that Colonel Yorke, of The Hague, was to succeed Mr. Fox; and George Greenville, Mr. Legge. This scheme, had it taken place, you are, I believe aware, was more a temporary expedient, for securing the elections of the new parliament, and forming it, at its first meeting, to the interests and the inclinations of the Duke of Newcastle and the Chancellor, than a plan of administration either intended or wished to be permanent. This scheme was disturbed yesterday: Mr. Fox, who had sullenly accepted the seals the day before, more sullenly refused them yesterday. His object was to be First Commissioner of the Treasury, and Chancellor of the Exchequer, and consequently to have a share in the election of the new parliament, and a much greater in the management of it when chosen. This necessary consequence of his view defeated it; and the Duke of Newcastle and the Chancellor chose to kick him upstairs into the Secretaryship of State, rather than trust him with either the election or the management of the new parliament. In this, considering their respective situations, they certainly acted wisely; but whether Mr. Fox has done so, or not, in refusing the seals, is a point which I cannot determine. If he is, as I presume he is, animated with revenge, and I believe would not be over scrupulous in the means of gratifying it, I should have thought he could have done it better, as Secretary of State, with constant admission into the closet, than as a private man at the head of an opposition. But I see all these things at too great a distance to be able to judge soundly of them. The true springs and motives of political measures are confined within a very narrow circle, and known to a very few; the good reasons alleged are seldom the true ones: The public commonly judges, or rather guesses, wrong, and I am now one of that public. I therefore recommend to you a prudent Pyrrhonism in all matters of state, until you become one of the wheels of them yourself, and consequently acquainted with the general motion, at least, of the others; for as to all the minute and secret springs, that contribute more or less to the whole machine, no man living ever knows them all, not even he who has the principal direction of it. As in the human body, there are innumerable little vessels and glands that have a good deal to do, and yet escape the knowledge of the most skillful anatomist; he will know more, indeed, than those who only see the exterior of our bodies, but he will never know all. This bustle, and these changes at court, far from having disturbed the quiet and security of your election, have, if possible, rather confirmed them; for the Duke of Newcastle (I must do him justice) has, in, the kindest manner imaginable to you, wrote a letter to Mr. Eliot, to recommend to him the utmost care of your election.

Though the plan of administration is thus unsettled, mine, for my travels this summer, is finally settled; and I now communicate it to you that you may form your own upon it. I propose being at Spa on the 10th or 12th of May, and staying there till the 10th of July. As there will be no mortal there during my stay, it would be both unpleasant and unprofitable to you to be shut up tete-a-fete with me the whole time; I should therefore think it best for you not to come to me there till the last week in June. In the meantime, I suppose, that by the middle of April, you will think that you have had enough of Manheim, Munich, or Ratisbon, and that district. Where would you choose to go then? For I leave you absolutely your choice. Would you go to Dresden for a month or six weeks? That is a good deal out of your way, and I am not sure that Sir Charles will be there by that time. Or would you rather take Bonn in your way, and pass the time till we meet at The Hague? From Manheim you may have a great many good letters of recommendation to the court of Bonn; which court, and it's Elector, in one light or another, are worth your seeing.

From thence, your journey to The Hague will be but a short one; and you would arrive there at that season of the year when The Hague is, in my mind, the most agreeable, smiling scene in Europe; and from The Hague you would have but three very easy days journey to me at Spa. Do as you like; for, as I told you before, 'Ella e assolutamente padrone'. But lest you should answer that you desire to be determined by me, I will eventually tell you my opinion. I am rather inclined to the latter plan; I mean that of your coming to Bonn, staying there according as you like it, and then passing the remainder of your time, that is May and June, at The Hague. Our connection and transactions with the Republic of the United Provinces are such, that you cannot be too well acquainted with that constitution, and with those people. You have established good acquaintances there, and you have been 'fetoie' round by the foreign ministers; so that you will be there 'en pais connu'. Moreover, you have not seen the Stadtholder, the 'Gouvernante', nor the court there, which 'a bon compte' should be seen. Upon the whole, then, you cannot, in my opinion, pass the months of May and June more agreeably, or more usefully, than at The Hague. But, however, if you have any other, plan that you like better, pursue it: Only let me know what you intend to do, and I shall most cheerfully agree to it.

The parliament will be dissolved in about ten days, and the writs for the election of the new one issued out immediately afterward; so that, by the end of next month, you may depend upon being 'Membre de la chambre basse'; a title that sounds high in foreign countries, and perhaps higher than it deserves. I hope you will add a better title to it in your own, I mean that of a good speaker in parliament: you have, I am sure, all, the materials necessary for it, if you will but put them together and adorn them. I spoke in parliament the first month I was in it, and a month before I was of age; and from the day I was elected, till the day that I spoke. I am sure I thought nor dreamed of nothing but speaking. The first time, to say the truth, I spoke very indifferently as to the matter; but it passed tolerably, in favor of the spirit with which I uttered it, and the words in which I had dressed it. I improved by degrees, till at last it did tolerably well. The House, it must be owned, is always extremely indulgent to the two or three first attempts of a young speaker; and if they find any degree of common sense in what he says, they make great allowances for his inexperience, and for the concern which they suppose him to be under. I experienced that indulgence; for had I not been a young member, I should certainly have been, as I own I deserved, reprimanded by the House for some strong and indiscreet things that I said. Adieu! It is indeed high time.

LETTER CC

LONDON, March 26, 1754

MY DEAR FRIEND: Yesterday I received your letter of the 15th from Manheim, where I find you have been received in the usual gracious manner; which I hope you return in a GRACEFUL one. As this is a season of great devotion and solemnity in all Catholic countries, pray inform yourself of, and constantly attend to, all their silly and pompous church ceremonies; one ought to know them. I am very glad that you wrote the letter to Lord————, which, in every different case that can possibly be supposed, was, I am sure, both a decent and a prudent step. You will find it very difficult, whenever we meet, to convince me that you could have any good reasons for not doing it; for I will, for argument's sake, suppose, what I cannot in reality believe, that he has both said and done the worst he could, of and by you; What then? How will you help yourself? Are you in a situation to hurt him? Certainly not; but he certainly is in a situation to hurt you. Would you show a sullen, pouting, impotent resentment? I hope not; leave that silly, unavailing sort of resentment to women, and men like them, who are always guided by humor, never by reason and prudence. That pettish, pouting conduct is a great deal too young, and implies too little knowledge of the world, for one who has seen so much of it as you have. Let this be one invariable rule of your conduct,—Never to show the least symptom of resentment which you cannot to a certain degree gratify; but always to smile, where you cannot strike. There would be no living in courts, nor indeed in the world if one could not conceal, and even dissemble, the just causes of resentment, which one meets with every day in active and busy life. Whoever cannot master his humor enough, 'pour faire bonne mine a mauvais jeu', should leave the world, and retire to some hermitage, in an unfrequented desert. By showing an unavailing and sullen resentment, you authorize the resentment of those who can hurt you and whom you cannot hurt; and give them that very pretense, which perhaps they wished for, of breaking with, and injuring you; whereas the contrary behavior would lay them under, the restraints of decency at least; and either shackle or expose their malice. Besides, captiousness, sullenness, and pouting are most exceedingly illiberal and vulgar. 'Un honnete homme ne les connoit point'.

I am extremely glad to hear that you are soon to have Voltaire at Manheim: immediately upon his arrival, pray make him a thousand compliments from me. I admire him most exceedingly; and, whether as an epic, dramatic, or lyric poet, or prose-writer, I think I justly apply to him the 'Nil molitur inepte'. I long to read his own correct edition of 'Les Annales de l'Empire', of which the 'Abrege Chronologique de l'Histoire Universelle', which I have read, is, I suppose, a stolen and imperfect part; however, imperfect as it is, it has explained to me that chaos of history, of seven hundred years more clearly than any other book had done before. You judge very rightly that I love 'le style le r et fleuri'. I do, and so does everybody who has any parts and taste. It should, I confess, be more or less 'fleuri', according to the subject; but at the same time I assert that there is no subject that may not properly, and which ought not to be adorned, by a certain elegance and beauty of style. What can be more adorned than Cicero's Philosophical Works? What more than Plato's? It is their eloquence only that has preserved and transmitted them down to us through so many centuries; for the philosophy of them is wretched, and the reasoning part miserable. But eloquence will always please, and has always pleased. Study it therefore; make it the object of your thoughts and attention. Use yourself to relate elegantly; that is a good step toward speaking well in parliament. Take some political subject, turn it in your thoughts, consider what may be said both for and against it, then put those arguments into writing, in the most correct and elegant English you can. For instance, a standing army, a place bill, etc.; as to the former, consider, on one side, the dangers arising to a free country from a great standing military force; on the other side, consider the necessity of a force to repel force with. Examine whether a standing army, though in itself an evil, may not, from circumstances, become a necessary evil, and preventive of greater dangers. As to the latter, consider, how far places may bias and warp the conduct of men, from the service of their country, into an unwarrantable complaisance to the court; and, on the other hand, consider whether they can be supposed to have that effect upon the conduct of people of probity and property, who are more solidly interested in the permanent good of their country, than they can be in an uncertain and precarious employment. Seek for, and answer in your own mind, all the arguments that can be urged on either side, and write them down in an elegant style. This will prepare you for debating, and give you an habitual eloquence; for I would not give a farthing for a mere holiday eloquence, displayed once or twice in a session, in a set declamation, but I want an every-day, ready, and habitual eloquence, to adorn extempore and debating speeches; to make business not only clear but agreeable, and to please even those whom you cannot inform, and who do not desire to be informed. All this you may acquire, and make habitual to you, with as little trouble as it cost you to dance a minuet as well as you do. You now dance it mechanically and well without thinking of it.

I am surprised that you found but one letter for me at Manheim, for you ought to have found four or five; there are as many lying for you at your banker's at Berlin, which I wish you had, because I always endeavored to put something into them, which, I hope, may be of use to you.

When we meet at Spa, next July, we must have a great many serious conversations; in which I will pour out all my experience of the world, and which, I hope, you will trust to, more than to your own young notions of men and things. You will, in time, discover most of them to have been erroneous; and, if you follow them long, you will perceive your error too late; but if you will be led by a guide, who, you are sure, does not mean to mislead you, you will unite two things, seldom united, in the same person; the vivacity and spirit of youth, with the caution and experience of age.

Last Saturday, Sir Thomas Robinson, who had been the King's Minister at Vienna, was declared Secretary of State for the southern department, Lord Holderness having taken the northern. Sir Thomas accepted it unwillingly, and, as I hear, with a promise that he shall not keep it long. Both his health and spirits are bad, two very disqualifying circumstances for that employment; yours, I hope, will enable you, some time or other, to go through with it. In all events, aim at it, and if you fail or fall, let it at least be said of you, 'Magnis tamen excidit ausis'. Adieu.

LETTERS TO HIS SON, COMPLETE

LETTER CCI

LONDON, April 5, 1754

MY DEAR FRIEND: I received yesterday your letter of the 20th March, from Manheim, with the inclosed for Mr. Eliot; it was a very proper one, and I have forwarded it to him by Mr. Harte, who sets out for Cornwall tomorrow morning.

I am very glad that you use yourself to translations; and I do not care of what, provided you study the correctness and elegance of your style. The "Life of Sextus Quintus" is the best book of the innumerable books written by Gregorio Leti, whom the Italians, very justly, call 'Leti caca libro'. But I would rather that you chose some pieces of oratory for your translations, whether ancient or modern, Latin or French, which would give you a more oratorical train of thoughts and turn of expression. In your letter to me you make use of two words, which though true and correct English, are, however, from long disuse, become inelegant, and seem now to be stiff, formal, and in some degree scriptural; the first is the word NAMELY, which you introduce thus, YOU INFORM ME OF A VERY AGREEABLE PIECE OF NEWS, namely, THAT MY ELECTION IS SECURED. Instead of NAMELY, I would always use WHICH IS, or THAT IS, that my-election is secured. The other word is, MINE OWN INCLINATIONS: this is certainly correct before a subsequent word that begins with a vowel; but it is too correct, and is now disused as too formal, notwithstanding the hiatus occasioned by MY OWN. Every language has its peculiarities; they are established by usage, and whether right or wrong, they must be complied with. I could instance many very absurd ones in different languages; but so authorized by the 'jus et norma loquendi', that they must be submitted to. NAMELY, and TO WIT, are very good words in themselves, and contribute to clearness more than the relatives which we now substitute in their room; but, however, they cannot be used, except in a sermon or some very grave and formal compositions. It is with language as with manners they are both established by the usage of people of fashion; it must be imitated, it must be complied with. Singularity is only pardonable in old age and retirement; I may now be as singular as I please, but you may not. We will, when we meet, discuss these and many other points, provided you will give me attention and credit; without both which it is to no purpose to advise either you or anybody else.

I want to know your determination, where you intend to (if I may use that expression) WHILE away your time till the last week in June, when we are to meet at Spa; I continue rather in the opinion which I mentioned to you formerly, in favor of The Hague; but however, I have not the least objection to Dresden, or to any other place that you may like better. If you prefer the Dutch scheme, you take Treves and Coblentz in your way, as also Dusseldorp: all which places I think you have not yet seen. At Manheim you may certainly get good letters of recommendation to the courts of the two Electors of Treves and Cologne, whom you are yet unacquainted with; and I should wish you to know them all; for, as I have often told you, 'olim haec meminisse juvabit'. There is an utility in having seen what other people have seen, and there is a justifiable pride in having seen what others have not seen. In the former case, you are equal to others; in the latter, superior. As your stay abroad will not now be very long, pray, while it lasts, see everything and everybody you can, and see them well, with care and attention. It is not to be conceived of what advantage it is to anybody to have seen more things, people, and countries, than other people in general have; it gives them a credit, makes them referred to, and they become the objects of the attention of the company. They are not out in any part of polite conversation; they are acquainted with all the places, customs, courts, and families that are likely to be mentioned; they are, as Monsieur de Maupertuis justly observes, 'de tous les pays, comme les savans, sont de tous les tems'. You have, fortunately, both those advantages: the only remaining point is 'de savoir les faire valoir', for without that one may as well not have them. Remember that very true maxim of La Bruyere's, 'Qu'on ne vaut dans se monde que ce qu'on veut valoir'. The knowledge of the world will teach you to what degree you ought to show 'que vous valez'. One must by no means, on one hand, be indifferent about it; as, on the other, one must not display it with affectation, and in an overbearing manner, but, of the two, it is better to show too much than too little. Adieu.

LETTER CCII

BATH, November 27, 1754

MY DEAR FRIEND: I heartily congratulate you upon the loss of your political maidenhead, of which I have received from others a very good account. I hear that you were stopped for some time in your career; but recovered breath, and finished it very well. I am not surprised, nor indeed concerned, at your accident; for I remember the dreadful feeling of that situation in myself; and as it must require a most uncommon share of impudence to be unconcerned upon such an occasion, I am not sure that I am not rather glad you stopped. You must therefore now think of hardening yourself by degrees, by using yourself insensibly to the sound of your own voice, and to the act (trifling as it seems) of rising up and sitting down. Nothing will contribute so much to this as committee work of elections at night, and of private bills in the morning. There, asking short questions, moving for witnesses to be called in, and all that kind of small ware, will soon fit you to set up for yourself. I am told that you are much mortified at your accident, but without reason; pray, let it rather be a spur than a curb to you. Persevere, and, depend upon it, it will do well at last. When I say persevere, I do not mean that you should speak every day, nor in every debate. Moreover, I would not advise you to speak again upon public matters for some time, perhaps a month or two; but I mean, never lose view of that great object; pursue it with discretion, but pursue it always. 'Pelotez en attendant partie'. You know I have always told you that speaking in public was but a knack, which those who apply to the most will succeed in the best. Two old members, very good judges, have sent me compliments upon this occasion; and have assured me that they plainly find it will do; though they perceived, from that natural confusion you were in, that you neither said all, nor perhaps what you intended. Upon the whole, you have set out very well, and have sufficient encouragement to go on. Attend; therefore, assiduously, and observe carefully all that passes in the House; for it is only knowledge and experience that can make a debater. But if you still want comfort, Mrs.————I hope, will administer it to you; for, in my opinion she may, if she will, be very comfortable; and with women, as with speaking in parliament, perseverance will most certainly prevail sooner or later.

What little I have played for here, I have won; but that is very far from the considerable sum which you heard of. I play every evening, from seven till ten, at a crown whist party, merely to save my eyes from reading or writing for three hours by candle-light. I propose being in town the week after next, and hope to carry back with me much more health than I brought down here. Good-night.

[Mr. Stanhope being returned to England, and seeing his father almost every day, is the occasion of an interruption of two years in their correspondence.]

1756-1758

LETTER CCIII

BATH, November 15, 1756

MY DEAR FRIEND: I received yours yesterday morning together with the Prussian, papers, which I have read with great attention. If courts could blush, those of Vienna and Dresden ought, to have their falsehoods so publicly, and so undeniably exposed. The former will, I presume, next year, employ an hundred thousand men, to answer the accusation; and if the Empress of the two Russias is pleased to argue in the same cogent manner, their logic will be too strong for all the King of Prussia's rhetoric. I well remember the treaty so often referred to in those pieces, between the two Empresses, in 1746. The King was strongly pressed by the Empress Queen to accede to it. Wassenaer communicated it to me for that purpose. I asked him if there were no secret articles; suspecting that there were some, because the ostensible treaty was a mere harmless, defensive one. He assured me that there were none. Upon which I told him, that as the King had already defensive alliances with those two Empresses, I did not see of what use his accession to this treaty, if merely a defensive one, could be, either to himself or the other contracting parties; but that, however, if it was only desired as an indication of the King's good will, I would give him an act by which his Majesty should accede to that treaty, as far, but no further, as at present he stood engaged to the respective Empresses by the defensive alliances subsisting with each. This offer by no means satisfied him; which was a plain proof of the secret articles now brought to light, and into which the court of Vienna hoped to draw us. I told Wassenaer so, and after that I heard no more of his invitation.

I am still bewildered in the changes at Court, of which I find that all the particulars are not yet fixed. Who would have thought, a year ago, that Mr. Fox, the Chancellor, and the Duke of Newcastle, should all three have quitted together? Nor can I yet account for it; explain it to me if you can. I cannot see, neither, what the Duke of Devonshire and Fox, whom I looked upon as intimately united, can have quarreled about, with relation to the Treasury; inform me, if you know. I never doubted of the prudent versatility of your Vicar of Bray: But I am surprised at O'Brien Windham's going out of the Treasury, where I should have thought that the interest of his brother-in-law, George Grenville, would have kept him.

Having found myself rather worse, these two or three last days, I was obliged to take some ipecacuanha last night; and, what you will think odd, for a vomit, I brought it all up again in about an hour, to my great satisfaction and emolument, which is seldom the case in restitutions.

You did well to go to the Duke of Newcastle, who, I suppose, will have no more levees; however, go from time to time, and leave your name at his door, for you have obligations to him. Adieu.

LETTER CCIV

BATH, December 14, 1756.

MY DEAR FRIEND: What can I say to you from this place, where EVERY DAY IS STILL BUT AS THE FIRST, though by no means so agreeably passed, as Anthony describes his to have been? The same nothings succeed one another every day with me, as, regularly and uniformly as the hours of the day. You will think this tiresome, and so it is; but how can I help it? Cut off from society by my deafness, and dispirited by my ill health, where could I be better? You will say, perhaps, where could you be worse? Only in prison, or the galleys, I confess. However, I see a period to my stay here; and I have fixed, in my own mind, a time for my return to London; not invited there by either politics or pleasures, to both which I am equally a stranger, but merely to be at home; which, after all, according to the vulgar saying, is home, be it ever so homely.

The political settlement, as it is called, is, I find, by no means settled; Mr. Fox, who took this place in his way to his brother's, where he intended to pass a month, was stopped short by an express, which he received from his connection, to come to town immediately; and accordingly he set out from hence very early, two days ago. I had a very long conversation with him, in which he was, seemingly at least, very frank and communicative; but still I own myself in the dark. In those matters, as in most others, half knowledge (and mine is at most that) is more apt to lead one into error, than to carry one to truth; and our own vanity contributes to the seduction. Our conjectures pass upon us for truths; we will know what we do not know, and often, what we cannot know: so mortifying to our pride is the bare suspicion of ignorance!

It has been reported here that the Empress of Russia is dying; this would be a fortunate event indeed for the King of Prussia, and necessarily produce the neutrality and inaction, at least, of that great power; which would be a heavy weight taken out of the opposite scale to the King of Prussia. The 'Augustissima' must, in that case, do all herself; for though France will, no doubt, promise largely, it will, I believe, perform but scantily; as it desires no better than that the different powers of Germany should tear one another to pieces.

I hope you frequent all the courts: a man should make his face familiar there. Long habit produces favor insensibly; and acquaintance often does more than friendship, in that climate where 'les beaux sentimens' are not the natural growth.

Adieu! I am going to the ball, to save my eyes from reading, and my mind from thinking.

LETTER CCV

BATH, January 12, 1757

MY DEAR FRIEND: I waited quietly, to see when either your leisure, or your inclinations, would allow you to honor me with a letter; and at last I received one this morning, very near a fortnight after you went from hence. You will say, that you had no news to write me; and that probably may be true; but, without news, one has always something to say to those with whom one desires to have anything to do.

Your observation is very just with regard to the King of Prussia, whom the most august House of Austria would most unquestionably have poisoned a century or two ago. But now that 'terras Astraea reliquit', kings and princes die of natural deaths; even war is pusillanimously carried on in this degenerate age; quarter is given; towns are taken, and the people spared: even in a storm, a woman can hardly hope for the benefit of a rape. Whereas (such was the humanity of former days) prisoners were killed by thousands in cold blood, and the generous victors spared neither man, woman, nor child. Heroic actions of this kind were performed at the taking of Magdebourg. The King of Prussia is certainly now in a situation that must soon decide his fate, and make him Caesar or nothing. Notwithstanding the march of the Russians, his great danger, in my mind, lies westward. I have no great notions of Apraxin's abilities, and I believe many a Prussian colonel would out-general him. But Brown, Piccolomini, Lucchese, and many other veteran officers in the Austrian troops, are respectable enemies.

Mr. Pitt seems to me to have almost as many enemies to encounter as his Prussian Majesty. The late Ministry, and the Duke's party, will, I presume, unite against him and his Tory friends; and then quarrel among themselves again. His best, if not his only chance of supporting himself would be, if he had credit enough in the city, to hinder the advancing of the money to any administration but his own; and I have met with some people here who think that he has.

I have put off my journey from hence for a week, but no longer. I find I still gain some strength and some flesh here, and therefore I will not cut while the run is for me.

By a letter which I received this morning from Lady Allen, I observe that you are extremely well with her; and it is well for you to be so, for she is an excellent and warm puff.

'A propos' (an expression which is commonly used to introduce whatever is unrelative to it) you should apply to some of Lord Holderness's people, for the perusal of Mr. Cope's letters. It would not be refused you; and the sooner you have them the better. I do not mean them as models for your manner of writing, but as outlines of the matter you are to write upon.

If you have not read Hume's "Essays" read them; they are four very small volumes; I have just finished, and am extremely pleased with them. He thinks impartially, deep, often new; and, in my mind, commonly just.
Adieu.

LETTER CCVI

BLACKHEATH, September 17, 1757

MY DEAR FRIEND: Lord Holderness has been so kind as to communicate to me all the letters which he has received from you hitherto, dated the 15th, 19th, 23d, and 26th August; and also a draught of that which he wrote to you the 9th instant. I am very well pleased with all your letters; and, what is better, I can tell you that the King is so too; and he said, but three days ago, to Monsieur Munchausen, HE (meaning you) SETS OUT VERY WELL, AND I LIKE HIS LETTERS; PROVIDED THAT, LIKE MOST OF MY ENGLISH MINISTERS ABROAD, HE DOES NOT GROW IDLE HEREAFTER. So that here is both praise to flatter, and a hint to warn you. What Lord Holderness recommends to you, being by the King's order, intimates also a degree of approbation; for the BLACKER INK, AND THE LARGER CHARACTER, show, that his Majesty, whose eyes are grown weaker, intends to read all your letters himself. Therefore, pray do not neglect to get the blackest ink you can; and to make your secretary enlarge his hand, though 'd'ailleurs' it is a very good one.

Had I been to wish an advantageous situation for you, and a good debut in it, I could not have wished you either better than both have hitherto proved. The rest will depend entirely upon yourself; and I own I begin to have much better hopes than I had; for I know, by my own experience, that the more one works, the more willing one is to work. We are all, more or less, 'des animaux d'habitude'. I remember very well, that when I was in business, I wrote four or five hours together every day, more willingly than I should now half an hour; and this is most certain, that when a man has applied himself to business half the day, the other half, goes off the more cheerfully and agreeably. This I found so sensibly, when I was at The Hague, that I never tasted company so well nor was so good company myself, as at the suppers of my post days. I take Hamburg now to be 'le centre du refuge Allemand'. If you have any Hanover 'refugies' among them, pray take care to be particularly attentive to them. How do you like your house? Is it a convenient one? Have the 'Casserolles' been employed in it yet? You will find 'les petits soupers fins' less expensive, and turn to better account, than large dinners for great companies.

I hope you have written to the Duke of Newcastle; I take it for granted that you have to all your brother ministers of the northern department. For God's sake be diligent, alert, active, and indefatigable in your business. You want nothing but labor and industry to be, one day, whatever you please, in your own way.

We think and talk of nothing here but Brest, which is universally supposed to be the object of our great expedition. A great and important object it is. I suppose the affair must be brusque, or it will not do. If we succeed, it will make France put some water to its wine. As for my own private opinion, I own I rather wish than hope success. However, should our expedition fail, 'Magnis tamen excidit ausis', and that will be better than our late languid manner of making war.

To mention a person to you whom I am very indifferent about, I mean myself, I vegetate still just as I did when we parted; but I think I begin to be sensible of the autumn of the year; as well as of the autumn of my own life. I feel an internal awkwardness, which, in about three weeks, I shall carry with me to the Bath, where I hope to get rid of it, as I did last year. The best cordial I could take, would be to hear, from time to time, of your industry and diligence; for in that case I should consequently hear of your success. Remember your own motto, 'Nullum numen abest si sit prudentia'. Nothing is truer. Yours.

LETTER CCVII

BLACKHEATH, September 23, 1757

MY DEAR FRIEND: I received but the day before yesterday your letter of the 3d, from the headquarters at Selsingen; and, by the way, it is but the second that I have received from you since your arrival at Hamburg. Whatever was the cause of your going to the army, I approve of the effect; for I would have you, as much as possible, see everything that is to be seen. That is the true useful knowledge, which informs and improves us when we are young, and amuses us and others when we are old; 'Olim haec meminisse juvabit'. I could wish that you would (but I know you will not) enter in a book, a short note only, of whatever you see or hear, that is very remarkable: I do not mean a German ALBUM stuffed with people's names, and Latin sentences; but I mean such a book, as, if you do not keep now, thirty years hence you would give a great deal of money to have kept. 'A propos de bottes', for I am told he always wears his; was his Royal Highness very gracious to you, or not? I have my doubts about it. The neutrality which he has concluded with Marechal de Richelieu, will prevent that bloody battle which you expected; but what the King of Prussia will say to it is another point. He was our only ally; at present, probably we have not one in the world. If the King of Prussia can get at Monsieur de Soubize's, and the Imperial army, before other troops have joined them, I think he will beat them but what then? He has three hundred thousand men to encounter afterward. He must submit; but he may say with truth, 'Si Pergama dextra defendi potuissent'. The late action between the Prussians and Russians has only thinned the human species, without giving either party a victory; which is plain by each party's claiming it. Upon my word, our species will pay very dear for the quarrels and ambition of a few, and those by no means the most valuable part of it. If the many were wiser than they are, the few must be quieter, and would perhaps be juster and better than they are.

Hamburg, I find, swarms with Grafs, Graffins, Fursts, and Furstins, Hocheits, and Durchlaugticheits. I am glad of it, for you must necessarily be in the midst of them; and I am still more glad, that, being in the midst of them, you must necessarily be under some constraint of ceremony; a thing which you do not love, but which is, however, very useful.

I desired you in my last, and I repeat it again in this, to give me an account of your private and domestic life.

How do you pass your evenings? Have they, at Hamburg, what are called at Paris 'des Maisons', where one goes without ceremony, sups or not, as one pleases? Are you adopted in any society? Have you any rational brother ministers, and which? What sort of things are your operas? In the tender, I doubt they do not excel;

for 'mein lieber schatz', and the other tendernesses of the Teutonic language, would, in my mind, sound but indifferently, set to soft music; for the bravura parts, I have a great opinion of them; and 'das, der donner dich erschlage', must no doubt, make a tremendously fine piece of 'recitativo', when uttered by an angry hero, to the rumble of a whole orchestra, including drums, trumpets, and French horns. Tell me your whole allotment of the day, in which I hope four hours, at least, are sacred to writing; the others cannot be better employed than in LIBERAL pleasures. In short, give me a full account of yourself, in your un-ministerial character, your incognito, without your 'fiocchi'. I love to see those, in whom I interest myself, in their undress, rather than in gala; I know them better so. I recommend to you, 'etiam atque etiam', method and order in everything you undertake. Do you observe it in your accounts? If you do not, you will be a beggar, though you were to receive the appointments of a Spanish Ambassador extraordinary, which are a thousand pistoles a month; and in your ministerial business, if you have no regular and stated hours for such and such parts of it, you will be in the hurry and confusion of the Duke of N——-, doing everything by halves, and nothing well, nor soon. I suppose you 'have been feasted through the Corps diplomatique at Hamburg, excepting Monsieur Champeaux; with whom, however, I hope you live 'poliment et galamment', at all third places.

Lord Loudon is much blamed here for his 'retraite des dix milles', for it is said that he had above that number, and might consequently have acted offensively, instead of retreating; especially as his retreat was contrary to the unanimous opinion (as it is now said) of the council of war. In our Ministry, I suppose, things go pretty quietly, for the D. of N. has not plagued me these two months. When his Royal Highness comes over, which I take it for granted he will do very soon, the great push will, I presume, be made at his Grace and Mr. Pitt; but without effect if they agree, as it is visibly their interest to do; and, in that case, their parliamentary strength will support them against all attacks. You may remember, I said at first, that the popularity would soon be on the side of those who opposed the popular Militia Bill; and now it appears so with a vengeance, in almost every county in England, by the tumults and insurrections of the people, who swear that they will not be enlisted. That silly scheme must therefore be dropped, as quietly as may be. Now that I have told you all that I know, and almost all that I think, I wish you a good supper and a good-night.

LETTER CCVIII

BLACKHEATH, September 30, 1757

MY DEAR FRIEND: I have so little to do, that I am surprised how I can find time to write to you so often. Do not stare at the seeming paradox; for it is an undoubted truth, that the less one has to do, the less time one finds to do it in. One yawns, one procrastinates, one can do it when one will, and therefore one seldom does it at all; whereas those who have a great deal of business, must (to use a vulgar expression) buckle to it; and then they always find time enough to do it in. I hope your own experience has by this time convinced you of this truth.

I received your last of the 8th. It is now quite over with a very great man, who will still be a very great man, though a very unfortunate one. He has qualities of the mind that put him above the reach of these misfortunes; and if reduced, as perhaps he may, to the 'marche' of Brandenburg, he will always find in himself the comfort, and with all the world the credit, of a philosopher, a legislator, a patron, and a professor of arts and sciences. He will only lose the fame of a conqueror; a cruel fame, that arises from the destruction of the human species. Could it be any satisfaction to him to know, I could tell him, that he is at this time the most popular man in this kingdom; the whole nation being enraged at that neutrality which hastens and completes his ruin. Between you and me, the King was not less enraged at it himself, when he saw the terms of it; and it affected his health more than all that had happened before. Indeed it seems to me a voluntary concession of the very worst that could have happened in the worst event. We now begin to think that our great and secret expedition is intended for Martinico and St. Domingo; if that be true, and we succeed in the attempt, we shall recover, and the French lose, one of the most valuable branches of commerce—I mean sugar. The French now supply all the foreign markets in Europe with that commodity; we only supply ourselves with it. This would make us some amends for our ill luck, or ill conduct in North America; where Lord Loudon, with twelve thousand men, thought himself no match for the French with but seven; and Admiral Holborne, with seventeen ships of the line, declined attacking the French, because they had eighteen, and a greater weight of METAL, according to the new sea-phrase, which was unknown to Blake. I hear that letters have been sent to both with very severe reprimands. I am told, and I believe it is true, that we are negotiating with the Corsican, I will not say rebels, but asserters of their natural rights; to receive them, and whatever form of government they think fit to establish, under our protection, upon condition of their delivering up to us Port Ajaccio; which may be made so strong and so good a one, as to be a full equivalent for the loss of Port Mahon. This is, in my mind, a very good scheme; for though the Corsicans are a parcel of cruel and perfidious rascals, they will in this case be tied down to us by their own interest and their own danger; a solid security with knaves, though none with fools. His Royal Highness the Duke is hourly expected here: his arrival will make some bustle; for I believe it is certain that he is resolved to make a push at the Duke of N., Pitt and Co.; but it will be ineffectual, if they continue to agree, as, to my CERTAIN KNOWLEDGE, they do at present. This parliament is theirs, 'caetera quis nescit'?

Now that I have told you all that I know or have heard, of public matters, let us talk of private ones that more nearly and immediately concern us. Admit me to your fire-side, in your little room; and as you would converse with me there, write to me for the future from thence. Are you completely 'nippe' yet? Have you formed what the world calls connections? that is, a certain number of acquaintances whom, from accident or choice, you frequent more than others: Have you either fine or well-bred women there? 'Y a-t-il quelque bon ton'? All fat and fair, I presume; too proud and too cold to make advances, but, at the same time, too well-bred and too warm to reject them, when made by 'un honnete homme avec des manieres'.

Mr.———is to be married, in about a month, to Miss———. I am very glad of it; for, as he will never be a man of the world, but will always lead a domestic and retired life, she seems to have been made on purpose for him. Her natural turn is as grave and domestic as his; and she seems to have been kept by her aunts 'a la grace', instead of being raised in a hot bed, as most young ladies are of late. If, three weeks hence, you write him a short compliment of congratulation upon the occasion, he, his mother, and 'tutti quanti', would be extremely pleased with it. Those attentions are always kindly taken, and cost one nothing but pen, ink, and paper. I consider them as draughts upon good-breeding, where the exchange is always greatly in favor of the drawer. 'A propos' of exchange; I hope you have, with the help of your secretary, made yourself correctly master of all that sort of knowledge—Course of Exchange, 'Agie, Banco, Reiche-Thalers', down to 'Marien Groschen'. It is very little trouble to learn it; it is often of great use to know it. Good-night, and God bless you!

EARL OF PHILIP DORMER STANHOPE CHESTERFIELD

LETTER CCIX

BLACKHEATH, October 10, 1757

MY DEAR FRIEND: It is not without some difficulty that I snatch this moment of leisure from my extreme idleness, to inform you of the present lamentable and astonishing state of affairs here, which you would know but imperfectly from the public papers, and but partially from your private correspondents. 'Or sus' then— Our in vincible Armada, which cost at least half a million, sailed, as you know, some weeks ago; the object kept an inviolable secret: conjectures various, and expectations great. Brest was perhaps to be taken; but Martinico and St. Domingo, at least. When lo! the important island of Aix was taken without the least resistance, seven hundred men made prisoners, and some pieces of cannon carried off. From thence we sailed toward Rochfort, which it seems was our main object; and consequently one should have supposed that we had pilots on board who knew all the soundings and landing places there and thereabouts: but no; for General M———t asked the Admiral if he could land him and the troops near Rochfort? The Admiral said, with great ease. To which the General replied, but can you take us on board again? To which the Admiral answered, that, like all naval operations, will depend upon the wind. If so, said the General, I'll e'en go home again. A Council of War was immediately called, where it was unanimously resolved, that it was ADVISABLE to return; accordingly they are returned. As the expectations of the whole nation had been raised to the highest pitch, the universal disappointment and indignation have arisen in proportion; and I question whether the ferment of men's minds was ever greater. Suspicions, you may be sure, are various and endless, but the most prevailing one is, that the tail of the Hanover neutrality, like that of a comet, extended itself to Rochfort. What encourages this suspicion is, that a French man of war went unmolested through our whole fleet, as it lay near Rochfort. Haddock's whole story is revived; Michel's representations are combined with other circumstances; and the whole together makes up a mass of discontent, resentment, and even fury, greater than perhaps was ever known in this country before. These are the facts, draw your own conclusions from them; for my part, I am lost in astonishment and conjectures, and do not know where to fix. My experience has shown me, that many things which seem extremely probable are not true: and many which seem highly improbable are true; so that I will conclude this article, as Josephus does almost every article of his history, with saying, BUT OF THIS EVERY MAN WILL BELIEVE AS HE THINKS PROPER. What a disgraceful year will this be in the annals of this country! May its good genius, if ever it appears again, tear out those sheets, thus stained and blotted by our ignominy!

Our domestic affairs are, as far as I know anything of them, in the same situation as when I wrote to you last; but they will begin to be in motion upon the approach of the session, and upon the return of the Duke, whose arrival is most impatiently expected by the mob of London; though not to strew flowers in his way.

I leave this place next Saturday, and London the Saturday following, to be the next day at Bath. Adieu.

LETTER CCX

LONDON, October 17, 1757.

MY DEAR FRIEND: Your last, of the 30th past, was a very good letter; and I will believe half of what you assure me, that you returned to the Landgrave's civilities. I cannot possibly go farther than half, knowing that you are not lavish of your words, especially in that species of eloquence called the adulatory. Do not use too much discretion in profiting of the Landgrave's naturalization of you; but go pretty often and feed with him. Choose the company of your superiors, whenever you can have it; that is the right and true pride. The mistaken and silly pride is, to PRIMER among inferiors.

Hear, O Israel! and wonder. On Sunday morning last, the Duke gave up his commission of Captain General and his regiment of guards. You will ask me why? I cannot tell you, but I will tell you the causes assigned; which, perhaps, are none of them the true ones. It is said that the King reproached him with having exceeded his powers in making the Hanover Convention, which his R. H. absolutely denied, and threw up thereupon. This is certain, that he appeared at the drawing-room at Kensington, last Sunday, after having quitted, and went straight to Windsor; where, his people say, that he intends to reside quietly, and amuse himself as a private man. But I conjecture that matters will soon be made up again, and that he will resume his employments. You will easily imagine the speculations this event has occasioned in the public; I shall neither trouble you nor myself with relating them; nor would this sheet of paper, or even a quire more, contain them. Some refine enough to suspect that it is a concerted quarrel, to justify SOMEBODY TO SOMEBODY, with regard to the Convention; but I do not believe it.

His R. H.'s people load the Hanover Ministers, and more particularly our friend Munchausen here, with the whole blame; but with what degree of truth I know not. This only is certain, that the whole negotiation of that affair was broached and carried on by the Hanover Ministers and Monsieur Stemberg at Vienna, absolutely unknown to the English Ministers, till it was executed. This affair combined (for people will combine it) with the astonishing return of our great armament, not only 're infecta', but even 'intentata', makes such a jumble of reflections, conjectures, and refinements, that one is weary of hearing them. Our Tacituses and Machiavels go deep, suspect the worst, and, perhaps, as they often do, overshoot the mark. For my own part, I fairly confess that I am bewildered, and have not certain 'postulata' enough, not only to found any opinion, but even to form conjectures upon: and this is the language which I think you should hold to all who speak to you, as to be sure all will, upon that subject. Plead, as you truly may, your own ignorance; and say, that it is impossible to judge of those nice points, at such a distance, and without knowing all circumstances, which you cannot be supposed to do. And as to the Duke's resignation; you should, in my opinion, say, that perhaps there might be a little too much vivacity in the case, but that, upon the whole, you make no doubt of the thing's being soon set right again; as, in truth, I dare say it will. Upon these delicate occasions, you must practice the ministerial shrugs and 'persiflage'; for silent gesticulations, which you would be most inclined to, would not be sufficient: something must be said, but that something, when analyzed, must amount to nothing. As for instance, 'Il est vrai qu'on s'y perd, mais que voulez-vous que je vous dise?—il y a bien du pour et du contre; un petit Resident ne voit gueres le fond du sac.—Il faut attendre.—Those sort of expletives are of infinite use; and nine people in ten think they mean something. But to the Landgrave of Hesse I think you would do well to say, in seeming confidence, that you have good reason to believe that the principal objection of his Majesty to the convention was that his Highness's interests, and the affair of his troops, were not sufficiently considered in it. To the Prussian Minister assert boldly that you know 'de science certaine', that the principal object of his Majesty's and his British Ministry's intention is not only to perform all their present engagements with his Master, but to take new and stronger ones for his support; for this is true—AT LEAST AT PRESENT.

You did very well in inviting Comte Bothmar to dine with you. You see how minutely I am informed of your proceedings, though not from yourself. Adieu.

I go to Bath next Saturday; but direct your letters, as usual, to London.

EARL OF PHILIP DORMER STANHOPE CHESTERFIELD

LETTER CCXI

BATH, October 26, 1757.

MY DEAR FRIEND: I arrived here safe, but far from sound, last Sunday. I have consequently drunk these waters but three days, and yet I find myself something better for them. The night before I left London, I was for some hours at Newcastle House, where the letters, which came that morning, lay upon the table: and his Grace singled out yours with great approbation, and, at the same time, assured me of his Majesty's approbation, too. To these two approbations I truly add my own, which, 'sans vanite', may perhaps be near as good as the other two. In that letter you venture 'vos petits raisonnemens' very properly, and then as properly make an excuse for doing so. Go on so, with diligence, and you will be, what I began to despair of your ever being, SOMEBODY. I am persuaded, if you would own the truth, that you feel yourself now much better satisfied with yourself than you were while you did nothing.

Application to business, attended with approbation and success, flatters and animates the mind: which, in idleness and inaction, stagnates and putrefies. I could wish that every rational man would, every night when he goes to bed, ask himself this question, What have I done to-day? Have I done anything that can be of use to myself or others? Have I employed my time, or have I squandered it? Have I lived out the day, or have I dozed it away in sloth and laziness? A thinking being must be pleased or confounded, according as he can answer himself these questions. I observe that you are in the secret of what is intended, and what Munchausen is gone to Stade to prepare; a bold and dangerous experiment in my mind, and which may probably end in a second volume to the "History of the Palatinate," in the last century. His Serene Highness of Brunswick has, in my mind, played a prudent and saving game; and I am apt to believe that the other Serene Highness, at Hamburg, is more likely to follow his example than to embark in the great scheme.

I see no signs of the Duke's resuming his employments; but on the contrary I am assured that his Majesty is coolly determined to do as well as he can without him. The Duke of Devonshire and Fox have worked hard to make up matters in the closet, but to no purpose. People's self-love is very apt to make them think themselves more necessary than they are: and I shrewdly suspect, that his Royal Highness has been the dupe of that sentiment, and was taken at his word when he least suspected it; like my predecessor, Lord Harrington, who when he went into the closet to resign the seals, had them not about him: so sure he thought himself of being pressed to keep them.

The whole talk of London, of this place, and of every place in the whole kingdom, is of our great, expensive, and yet fruitless expedition; I have seen an officer who was there, a very sensible and observing man: who told me that had we attempted Rochfort, the day after we took the island of Aix, our success had been infallible; but that, after we had sauntered (God knows why) eight or ten days in the island, he thinks the attempt would have been impracticable, because the French had in that time got together all the troops in that neighborhood, to a very considerable number. In short, there must have been some secret in that whole affair that has not yet transpired; and I cannot help suspecting that it came from Stade. WE had not been successful there; and perhaps WE were not desirous that an expedition, in which WE had neither been concerned nor consulted, should prove so; M——t was OUR creature, and a word to the wise will sometimes go a great way. M——t is to have a public trial, from which the public expects great discoveries—Not I.

Do you visit Soltikow, the Russian Minister, whose house, I am told, is the great scene of pleasures at Hamburg? His mistress, I take for granted, is by this time dead, and he wears some other body's shackles. Her death comes with regard to the King of Prussia, 'comme la moutarde apres diner'. I am curious to see what tyrant will succeed her, not by divine, but by military right; for, barbarous as they are now, and still more barbarous as they have been formerly, they have had very little regard to the more barbarous notion of divine, indefeasible, hereditary right.

The Praetorian bands, that is, the guards, I presume, have been engaged in the interests of the Imperial Prince; but still I think that little John of Archangel will be heard upon this occasion, unless prevented by a quieting draught of hemlock or nightshade; for I suppose they are not arrived to the politer and genteeler poisons of Acqua Tufana,—[Acqua Tufana, a Neapolitan slow poison, resembling clear water, and invented by a woman at Naples, of the name of Tufana.]—sugar-plums, etc.

Lord Halifax has accepted his old employment, with the honorary addition of the Cabinet Council. And so we heartily wish you a goodnight.

LETTER CCXII

BATH, November 4, 1757

MY DEAR FRIEND: The Sons of Britain, like those of Noah, must cover their parent's shame as well as they can; for to retrieve its honor is now too late. One would really think that our ministers and generals were all as drunk as the Patriarch was. However, in your situation, you must not be Cham; but spread your cloak over our disgrace, as far as it will go. M——t calls aloud for a public trial; and in that, and that only, the public agree with him. There will certainly be one, but of what kind is not yet fixed. Some are for a parliamentary inquiry, others for a martial one; neither will, in my opinion, discover the true secret; for a secret there most unquestionably is. Why we stayed six whole days in the island of Aix, mortal cannot imagine; which time the French employed, as it was obvious they would, in assembling their troops in the neighborhood of Rochfort, and making our attempt then really impracticable. The day after we had taken the island of Aix, your friend, Colonel Wolf, publicly offered to do the business with five hundred men and three ships only. In all these complicated political machines there are so many wheels, that it is always difficult, and sometimes impossible, to guess which of them gives direction to the whole. Mr. Pitt is convinced that the principal wheels, or, if you will, the spoke in his wheel, came from Stade. This is certain, at least that M——t was the man of confidence with that person. Whatever be the truth of the case, there is, to be sure, hitherto an 'hiatus valde deflendus'.

The meeting of the parliament will certainly be very numerous, were it only from curiosity: but the majority on the side of the Court will, I dare say, be a great one. The people of the late Captain-general, however inclined to oppose, will be obliged to concur. Their commissions, which they have no desire to lose, will make them tractable; for those gentlemen, though all men of honor, are of Sosia's mind, 'que le vrai Amphitrion est celui ou l'on dine'. The Tories and the city have engaged to support Pitt; the Whigs, the Duke of Newcastle; the independent and the impartial, as you well know, are not worth mentioning. It is said that the Duke intends to bring the affair of his Convention into parliament, for his own justification; I can hardly believe it; as I cannot conceive that transactions so merely electoral can be proper objects of inquiry or deliberation for a British parliament; and, therefore, should such a motion be made, I presume it will be immediately quashed. By the commission lately given to Sir John Ligonier, of General and Commander-in-chief of all his Majesty's forces in Great Britain, the door seems to be not only shut, but bolted, against his Royal Highness's return; and I have good reason to be convinced that that breach is irreparable. The reports of changes in the Ministry, I am pretty sure, are idle and groundless. The Duke of Newcastle and Mr. Pitt really agree very well; not, I presume, from any sentimental tenderness for each other, but from a sense that it is their mutual interest: and, as the late Captain-general's party is now out of the question, I do not see what should produce the least change.

The visit made lately to Berlin was, I dare say, neither a friendly nor an inoffensive one. The Austrians always leave behind them pretty lasting monuments of their visits, or rather visitations: not so much, I believe, from their thirst of glory, as from their hunger of prey.

This winter, I take for granted, must produce a piece of some kind or another; a bad one for us, no doubt, and yet perhaps better than we should get the year after. I suppose the King of Prussia is negotiating with France, and endeavoring by those means to get out of the scrape with the loss only of Silesia, and perhaps Halberstadt, by way of indemnification to Saxony; and, considering all circumstances, he would be well off upon those terms. But then how is Sweden to be satisfied? Will the Russians restore Memel? Will France have been at all this expense 'gratis'? Must there be no acquisition for them in Flanders? I dare say they have stipulated something of that sort for themselves, by the additional and secret treaty, which I know they made, last May, with the Queen of Hungary. Must we give up whatever the French please to desire in America, besides the cession of Minorca in perpetuity? I fear we must, or else raise twelve millions more next year, to as little purpose as we did this, and have consequently a worse peace afterward. I turn my eyes away, as much as I can, from this miserable prospect; but, as a citizen and member of society, it recurs to my imagination, notwithstanding all my endeavors to banish it from my thoughts. I can do myself nor my country no good; but I feel the wretched situation of both; the state of the latter makes me better bear that of the former; and, when I am called away from my station here, I shall think it rather (as Cicero says of Crassus) 'mors donata quam vita erepta'.

I have often desired, but in vain, the favor of being admitted into your private apartment at, Hamburg, and of being informed of your private life there. Your mornings, I hope and believe, are employed in business; but give me an account of the remainder of the day, which I suppose is, and ought to be, appropriated to amusements and pleasures. In what houses are you domestic? Who are so in yours? In short, let me in, and do not be denied to me.

Here I am, as usual, seeing few people, and hearing fewer; drinking the waters regularly to a minute, and am something the better for them. I read a great deal, and vary occasionally my dead company. I converse with grave folios in the morning, while my head is clearest and my attention strongest: I take up less severe quartos after dinner; and at night I choose the mixed company and amusing chit-chat of octavos and duodecimos. 'Ye tire parti de tout ce gue je puis'; that is my philosophy; and I mitigate, as much as I can, my physical ills by diverting my attention to other objects.

Here is a report that Admiral Holborne's fleet is destroyed, in a manner, by a storm: I hope it is not true, in the full extent of the report; but I believe it has suffered. This would fill up the measure of our misfortunes.

LETTERS TO HIS SON, COMPLETE

Adieu.

LETTER CCXIII

BATH, November 20, 1757

MY DEAR FRIEND: I write to you now, because I love to write to you; and hope that my letters are welcome to you; for otherwise I have very little to inform you of. The King of Prussia's late victory you are better informed, of than we are here. It has given infinite joy to the unthinking public, who are not aware that it comes too late in the year and too late in the war, to be attended with any very great consequences. There are six or seven thousand of the human species less than there were a month ago, and that seems to me to be all. However, I am glad of it, upon account of the pleasure and the glory which it gives the King of Prussia, to whom I wish well as a man, more than as a king. And surely he is so great a man, that had he lived seventeen or eighteen hundred years ago, and his life been transmitted to us in a language that we could not very well understand—I mean either Greek or Latin—we should have talked of him as we do now of your Alexanders, your Caesars, and others; with whom, I believe, we have but a very slight acquaintance. 'Au reste', I do not see that his affairs are much mended by this victory. The same combination of the great Powers of Europe against him still subsists, and must at last prevail. I believe the French army will melt away, as is usual, in Germany; but this army is extremely diminished by battles, fatigues, and desertion: and he will find great difficulties in recruiting it from his own already exhausted dominions. He must therefore, and to be sure will, negotiate privately with the French, and get better terms that way than he could any other.

The report of the three general officers, the Duke of Marlborough, Lord George Sackville, and General Waldegrave, was laid before the King last Saturday, after their having sat four days upon M———t's affair: nobody yet knows what it is; but it is generally believed that M———t will be brought to a court-martial. That you may not mistake this matter, as MOST people here do, I must explain to you, that this examination before the three above-mentioned general officers, was by no means a trial; but only a previous inquiry into his conduct, to see whether there was, or was not, cause to bring him to a regular trial before a court-martial. The case is exactly parallel to that of a grand jury; who, upon a previous and general examination, find, or do not find, a bill to bring the matter before the petty jury; where the fact is finally tried. For my own part, my opinion is fixed upon that affair: I am convinced that the expedition was to be defeated; and nothing that can appear before a court-martial can make me alter that opinion. I have been too long acquainted with human nature to have great regard for human testimony; and a very great degree of probability, supported by various concurrent circumstances, conspiring in one point, will have much greater weight with me, than human testimony upon oath, or even upon honor; both which I have frequently seen considerably warped by private views.

The parliament, which now stands prorogued to the first of next month, it is thought will be put off for some time longer, till we know in what light to lay before it the state of our alliance with Prussia, since the conclusion of the Hanover neutrality; which, if it did not quite break it, made at least a great flaw in it.

EARL OF PHILIP DORMER STANHOPE CHESTERFIELD

The birth-day was neither fine nor crowded; and no wonder, since the King was that day seventy-five. The old Court and the young one are much better together since the Duke's retirement; and the King has presented the Prince of Wales with a service of plate.

I am still UNWELL, though I drink these waters very regularly. I will stay here at least six weeks longer; where I am much quieter than I should be allowed to be in town. When things are in such a miserable situation as they are at present, I desire neither to be concerned nor consulted, still less quoted. Adieu!

LETTER CCXIV

BATH, November 26, 1757

MY DEAR FRIEND: I received by the last mail your short account of the King of Prussia's victory; which victory, contrary to custom, turns out more complete than it was at first reported to be. This appears by an intercepted letter from Monsieur de St. Germain to Monsieur d'Affry, at The Hague, in which he tells him, 'Cette arme est entierement fondue', and lays the blame, very strongly, upon Monsieur de Soubize. But, be it greater or be it less, I am glad of it; because the King of Prussia (whom I honor and almost adore) I am sure is. Though 'd'ailleurs', between you and me, 'ou est-ce que cela mene'? To nothing, while that formidable union of three great Powers of Europe subsists against him, could that be any way broken, something might be done; without which nothing can. I take it for granted that the King of Prussia will do all he can to detach France. Why should not we, on our part, try to detach Russia? At least, in our present distress, 'omnia tentanda', and sometimes a lucky and unexpected hit turns up. This thought came into my head this morning; and I give it to you, not as a very probable scheme, but as a possible one, and consequently worth trying. The year of the Russian subsidies (nominally paid by the Court of Vienna, but really by France) is near expired. The former probably cannot, and perhaps the latter will not, renew them. The Court of Petersburg is beggarly, profuse, greedy, and by no means scrupulous. Why should not we step in there, and out-bid them? If we could, we buy a great army at once; which would give an entire new turn to the affairs of that part of the world at least. And if we bid handsomely, I do not believe the 'bonne foi' of that Court would stand in the way. Both our Court and our parliament would, I am very sure, give a very great sum, and very cheerfully, for this purpose. In the next place, Why should not you wriggle yourself, if possible, into so great a scheme? You are, no doubt, much acquainted with the Russian Resident, Soltikow; Why should you not sound him, as entirely from yourself, upon this subject? You may ask him, What, does your Court intend to go on next year in the pay of France, to destroy the liberties of all Europe, and throw universal monarchy into the hands of that already great and always ambitious Power? I know you think, or at least call yourselves, the allies of the Empress Queen; but is it not plain that she will be, in the first place, and you in the next, the dupes of France? At this very time you are doing the work of France and Sweden: and that for some miserable subsidies, much inferior to those which I am sure you might have, in a better cause, and more consistent with the true interest of Russia. Though not empowered, I know the manner of thinking of my own Court so well upon this subject, that I will venture to promise you much better terms than those you have now, without the least apprehensions of being disavowed. Should he listen to this, and what more may occur to you to say upon this subject, and ask you, 'En ecrirai je d ma cour? Answer him, 'Ecrivez, ecrivex, Monsieur hardiment'. Je prendrai tout cela sur moi'. Should this happen, as perhaps, and as I heartily wish it may, then write an exact relation of it to your own Court. Tell them that you thought the measure of such great importance, that you could not help taking this little step toward bringing it about; but that you mentioned it only as from yourself, and that you have not in the least committed them by it. If Soltikow lends himself in any degree to this, insinuate that, in the present situation of affairs, and particularly of the King's Electoral dominions, you are very sure that his Majesty would have 'une reconnoissance sans bornes' for ALL those by whose means so desirable a revival of an old and long friendship should be brought about. You will perhaps tell me that, without doubt, Mr. Keith's instructions are to the same effect: but I will answer you, that you can, IF YOU PLEASE, do it better than Mr. Keith; and in the next place that, be all that as it will, it must be very advantageous to you at home, to show that you have at least a contriving head, and an alertness in business.

I had a letter by the last post, from the Duke of Newcastle, in which he congratulates me, in his own name and in Lord Hardwicke's, upon the approbation which your dispatches give, not only to them two, but to OTHERS. This success, so early, should encourage your diligence and rouse your ambition if you have any; you may go a great way, if you desire it, having so much time before you.

I send you here inclosed the copy of the Report of the three general officers, appointed to examine previously into the conduct of General M——t; it is ill written, and ill spelled, but no matter; you will decipher it. You will observe, by the tenor of it, that it points strongly to a court-martial; which, no doubt, will soon be held upon him. I presume there will be no shooting in the final sentence; but I do suppose there will be breaking, etc.

I have had some severe returns of my old complaints last week, and am still unwell; I cannot help it.

A friend of yours arrived here three days ago; she seems to me to be a serviceable strong-bodied bay mare, with black mane and tail; you easily guess who I mean. She is come with mamma, and without 'caro sposo'.

Adieu! my head will not let me go on longer.

LETTER CCXV

BATH, December 31, 1757

MY DEAR FRIEND: I have this moment received your letter of the 18th, with the inclosed papers. I cannot help observing that, till then, you never acknowledged the receipt of any one of my letters.

I can easily conceive that party spirit, among your brother ministers at Hamburg, runs as high as you represent it, because I can easily believe the errors of the human mind; but at the same time I must observe, that such a spirit is the spirit of little minds and subaltern ministers, who think to atone by zeal for their want of merit and importance. The political differences of the several courts should never influence the personal behavior of their several ministers toward one another. There is a certain 'procede noble et galant', which should always be observed among the ministers of powers even at war with each other, which will always turn out to the advantage of the ablest, who will in those conversations find, or make, opportunities of throwing out, or of receiving useful hints. When I was last at The Hague, we were at war with both France and Spain; so that I could neither visit, nor be visited by, the Ministers of those two Crowns; but we met every day, or dined at third places, where we embraced as personal friends, and trifled, at the same time, upon our being political enemies; and by this sort of badinage I discovered some things which I wanted to know. There is not a more prudent maxim than to live with one's enemies as if they may one day become one's friends; as it commonly happens, sooner or later, in the vicissitudes of political affairs.

To your question, which is a rational and prudent one, Whether I was authorized to give you the hints concerning Russia by any people in power here, I will tell you that I was not: but, as I had pressed them to try what might be done with Russia, and got Mr. Keith to be dispatched there some months sooner than otherwise, I dare say he would, with the proper instructions for that purpose. I wished that, by the hints I gave you, you might have got the start of him, and the merit, at least, of having 'entame' that matter with Soltikow. What you have to do with him now, when you meet with him at any third place, or at his own house (where you are at liberty to go, while Russia has a Minister in London, and we a Minister at Petersburg), is, in my opinion, to say to him, in an easy cheerful manner, 'He bien, Monsieur, je me flatte que nous serons bientot amis publics, aussi bien qu'amis personels'. To which he will probably ask, Why, or how? You will reply, Because you know that Mr. Keith is gone to his Court with instructions, which you think must necessarily be agreeable there. And throw out to him that nothing but a change of their present system can save Livonia to Russia; for that he cannot suppose that, when the Swedes shall have recovered Pomerania they will long leave Russia in quiet possession of Livonia.

If he is so much a Frenchman as you say, he will make you some weak answers to this; but, as you will have the better of the argument on your side, you may remind him of the old and almost uninterrupted connection between France and Sweden, the inveterate enemy of Russia. Many other arguments will naturally occur to you in such a conversation, if you have it. In this case, there is a piece of ministerial art, which is sometimes of use; and that is, to sow jealousies among one's enemies, by a seeming preference shown to some one of them. Monsieur Hecht's reveries are reveries indeed. How should his Master have made the GOLDEN ARRANGEMENTS which he talks of, and which are to be forged into shackles for General Fermor? The Prussian finances are not in a condition now to make such expensive arrangements. But I think you may tell Monsieur Hecht, in confidence, that you hope the instructions with which you know that Mr. Keith is gone to Petersburg, may have some effect upon the measures of that Court.

I would advise you to live with that same Monsieur Hecht in all the confidence, familiarity, and connection, which prudence will allow. I mean it with regard to the King of Prussia himself, by whom I could wish you to be known and esteemed as much as possible. It may be of use to you some day or other. If man, courage, conduct, constancy, can get the better of all the difficulties which the King of Prussia has to struggle with, he will rise superior to them. But still, while his alliance subsists against him, I dread 'les gros escadrons'. His last victory, of the 5th, was certainly the completest that has been heard of these many years. I heartily wish the Prince of Brunswick just such a one over Monsieur de Richelieu's army; and that he may take my old acquaintance the Marechal, and send him over here to polish and perfume us.

I heartily wish you, in the plain, home-spun style, a great number of happy new years, well employed in forming both your mind and your manners, to be useful and agreeable to yourself, your country, and your friends! That these wishes are sincere, your secretary's brother will, by the time of your receiving this, have remitted you a proof, from Yours.

LETTER CCXVI

LONDON, February 8, 1758.

MY DEAR FRIEND: I received by the same post your two letters of the 13th and 17th past; and yesterday that of the 27th, with the Russian manifesto inclosed, in which her Imperial Majesty of all the Russias has been pleased to give every reason, except the true one, for the march of her troops against the King of Prussia. The true one, I take it to be, that she has just received a very great sum of money from France, or the Empress queen, or both, for that purpose. 'Point d'argent, point de Russe', is now become a maxim. Whatever may be the motive of their march, the effects must be bad; and, according to my speculations, those troops will replace the French in Hanover and Lower Saxony; and the French will go and join the Austrian army. You ask me if I still despond? Not so much as I did after the battle of Colen: the battles of Rosbach and Lissa were drams to me, and gave me some momentary spirts: but though I do not absolutely despair, I own I greatly distrust. I readily allow the King of Prussia to be 'nec pluribus impar'; but still, when the 'plures' amount to a certain degree of plurality, courage and abilities must yield at last. Michel here assures me that he does not mind the Russians; but, as I have it from the gentleman's own mouth, I do not believe him. We shall very soon send a squadron to the Baltic to entertain the Swedes; which I believe will put an end to their operations in Pomerania; so that I have no great apprehensions from that quarter; but Russia, I confess, sticks in my stomach.

Everything goes smoothly in parliament; the King of Prussia has united all our parties in his support; and the Tories have declared that they will give Mr. Pitt unlimited credit for this session; there has not been one single division yet upon public points, and I believe will not. Our American expedition is preparing to go soon; the dis position of that affair seems to me a little extraordinary. Abercrombie is to be the sedantary, and not the acting commander; Amherst, Lord Howe, and Wolfe, are to be the acting, and I hope the active officers. I wish they may agree. Amherst, who is the oldest officer, is under the influence of the same great person who influenced Mordaunt, so much to honor and advantage of this country. This is most certain, that we have force enough in America to eat up the French alive in Canada, Quebec, and Louisburg, if we have but skill and spirit enough to exert it properly; but of that I am modest enough to doubt.

When you come to the egotism, which I have long desired you to come to with me, you need make no excuses for it. The egotism is as proper and as satisfactory to one's friends, as it is impertinent and misplaced with strangers. I desire to see you in your every-day clothes, by your fireside, in your pleasures; in short, in your private life; but I have not yet been able to obtain this. Whenever you condescend to do it, as you promise, stick to truth; for I am not so uninformed of Hamburg as perhaps you may think.

As for myself, I am very UNWELL, and very weary of being so; and with little hopes, at my age, of ever being otherwise. I often wish for the end of the wretched remnant of my life; and that wish is a rational one; but then the innate principle of self-preservation, wisely implanted in our natures for obvious purposes, opposes that wish, and makes us endeavor to spin out our thread as long as we can, however decayed and rotten it may be; and, in defiance of common sense, we seek on for that chymic gold, which beggars us when old.

Whatever your amusements, or pleasures, may be at Hamburg, I dare say you taste them more sensibly than ever you did in your life, now that you have business enough to whet your appetite to them. Business, one-half of the day, is the best preparation for the pleasures of the other half. I hope, and believe, that it will be with you as it was with an apothecary whom I knew at Twickenham. A considerable estate fell to him by an unexpected accident; upon which he thought it decent to leave off his business; accordingly he generously gave up his shop and his stock to his head man, set up his coach, and resolved to live like a gentleman; but, in less than a month, the man, used to business, found, that living like a gentleman was dying of ennui; upon which he bought his shop and stock, resumed his trade, and lived very happily, after he had something to do. Adieu.

LETTER CCXVII

LONDON, February 24, 1758

MY DEAR FRIEND: I received yesterday your letter of the 2d instant, with the inclosed; which I return you, that there may be no chasm in your papers. I had heard before of Burrish's death, and had taken some steps thereupon; but I very soon dropped that affair, for ninety-nine good reasons; the first of which was, that nonody is to go in his room, and that, had he lived, he was to have been recalled from Munich. But another reason, more flattering for you, was, that you could not be spared from Hamburg. Upon the whole, I am not sorry for it, as the place where you are now is the great entrepot of business; and, when it ceases to be so, you will necessarily go to some of the courts in the neighborhood (Berlin, I hope and believe), which will be a much more desirable situation than to rush at Munich, where we can never have any business beyond a subsidy. Do but go on, and exert yourself were you are, and better things will soon follow.

Surely the inaction of our army at Hanover continues too long. We expected wonders from it some time ago, and yet nothing is attempted. The French will soon receive reinforcements, and then be too strong for us; whereas they are now most certainly greatly weakened by desertion, sickness, and deaths. Does the King of Prussia send a body of men to our army or not? or has the march of the Russians cut him out work for all his troops? I am afraid it has. If one body of Russians joins the Austrian army in Moravia, and another body the Swedes in Pomerania, he will have his hands very full, too full, I fear. The French say they will have an army of 180,000 men in Germany this year; the Empress Queen will have 150,000; if the Russians have but 40,000, what can resist such a force? The King of Prussia may say, indeed, with more justice than ever any one person could before him, 'Moi. Medea superest'.

You promised the some egotism; but I have received none yet. Do you frequent the Landgrave? 'Hantex vous les grands de la terre'? What are the connections of the evening? All this, and a great deal more of this kind, let me know in your next.

The House of Commons is still very unanimous. There was a little popular squib let off this week, in a motion of Sir John Glynne's, seconded by Sir John Philips, for annual parliaments. It was a very cold scent, and put an end to by a division of 190 to 70.

Good-night. Work hard, that you may divert yourself well.

LETTER CCXVIII

LONDON, March 4, 1758.

MY DEAR FRIEND: I should have been much more surprised at the contents of your letter of the 17th past, if I had not happened to have seen Sir C. W., about three or four hours before I received it. I thought he talked in an extraordinary manner; he engaged that the King of Prussia should be master of Vienna in the month of May; and he told me that you were very much in love with his daughter. Your letter explained all this to me; and next day, Lord and Lady E——gave me innumerable instances of his frenzy, with which I shall not trouble you. What inflamed it the more (if it did not entirely occasion it) was a great quantity of cantharides, which, it seems, he had taken at Hamburgh, to recommend himself, I suppose, to Mademoiselle John. He was let blood four times on board the ship, and has been let blood four times since his arrival here; but still the inflammation continues very high. He is now under the care of his brothers, who do not let him go abroad. They have written to this same Mademoiselle John, to prevent if they can, her coming to England, and told her the case; which, when she hears she must be as mad as he is, if she takes the journey. By the way, she must be 'une dame aventuriere', to receive a note for 10,000 roubles from a man whom she had known but three days! to take a contract of marriage, knowing he was married already; and to engage herself to follow him to England. I suppose this is not the first adventure of the sort which she has had.

After the news we received yesterday, that the French had evacuated Hanover, all but Hamel, we daily expect much better. We pursue them, we cut them off 'en detail', and at last we destroy their whole army. I wish it may happen; and, moreover, I think it not impossible.

My head is much out of order, and only allows me to wish you good-night.

LETTER CCXIX

LONDON, March 22, 1758

MY DEAR FRIEND: I have now your letter of the 8th lying before me, with the favorable account of our progress in Lower Saxony, and reasonable prospect of more decisive success. I confess I did not expect this, when my friend Munchausen took his leave of me, to go to Stade, and break the neutrality; I thought it at least a dangerous, but rather a desperate undertaking; whereas, hitherto, it has proved a very fortunate one. I look upon the French army as 'fondue'; and, what with desertion, deaths, and epidemical distempers, I dare say not a third of it will ever return to France. The great object is now, what the Russians can or will do; and whether the King of Prussia can hinder their junction with the Austrians, by beating either, before they join. I will trust him for doing all that can be done.

Sir C. W. is still in confinement, and, I fear, will always be so, for he seems 'cum ratione insanire'; the physicians have collected all he has said and done that indicated an alienation of mind, and have laid it before him in writing; he has answered it in writing too, and justifies himself in the most plausible arguments than can possibly be urged. He tells his brother, and the few who are allowed to see him, that they are such narrow and contracted minds themselves, that they take those for mad who have a great and generous way of thinking; as, for instance, when he determined to send his daughter over to you in a fortnight, to be married, without any previous agreement or settlements, it was because he had long known you, and loved you as a man of sense and honor; and therefore would not treat with you as with an attorney. That as for Mademoiselle John, he knew her merit and her circumstances; and asks, whether it is a sign of madness to have a due regard for the one, and a just compassion for the other. I will not tire you with enumerating any more instances of the poor man's frenzy; but conclude this subject with pitying him, and poor human nature, which holds its reason by so precarious a tenure. The lady, who you tell me is set out, 'en sera pour la seine et les fraix du voyage', for her note is worth no more than her contract. By the way, she must be a kind of 'aventuriere', to engage so easily in such an adventure with a man whom she had not known above a week, and whose 'debut' of 10,000 roubles showed him not to be in his right senses.

You will probably have seen General Yorke, by this time, in his way to Berlin or Breslau, or wherever the King of Prussia may be. As he keeps his commission to the States General, I presume he is not to stay long with his Prussian Majesty; but, however, while he is there, take care to write to him very constantly, and to give all the information you can. His father, Lord Hardwicke, is your great puff: he commends your office letters, exceedingly. I would have the Berlin commission your object, in good time; never lose view of it. Do all you can to recommend yourself to the King of Prussia on your side of the water, and to smooth your way for that commission on this; by the turn which things have taken of late, it must always be the most important of all foreign commissions from hence.

I have no news to send you, as things here are extremely quiet; so, good-night.

LETTER CCXX

LETTERS TO HIS SON, COMPLETE

LONDON, April 25, 1758.

DEAR FRIEND: I am now two letters in your debt, which I think is the first time that ever I was so, in the long course of our correspondence. But, besides that my head has been very much out of order of late, writing is by no means that easy thing that it was to me formerly. I find by experience, that the mind and the body are more than married, for they are most intimately united; and when the one suffers, the other sympathizes. 'Non sum qualis eram': neither my memory nor my invention are now what they formerly were. It is in a great measure my own fault; I cannot accuse Nature, for I abused her; and it is reasonable I should suffer for it.

I do not like the return of the impression upon your lungs; but the rigor of the cold may probably have brought it upon you, and your lungs not in fault. Take care to live very cool, and let your diet be rather low.

We have had a second winter here, more severe than the first, at least it seemed so, from a premature summer that we had, for a fortnight, in March; which brought everything forward, only to be destroyed. I have experienced it at Blackheath, where the promise of fruit was a most flattering one, and all nipped in the bud by frost and snow, in April. I shall not have a single peach or apricot.

I have nothing to tell you from hence concerning public affairs, but what you read in the newspapers. This only is extraordinary: that last week, in the House of Commons, above ten millions were granted, and the whole Hanover army taken into British pay, with but one single negative, which was Mr. Viner's.

Mr. Pitt gains ground in the closet, and yet does not lose it in the public. That is new.

Monsieur Kniphausen has dined with me; he is one of the prettiest fellows I have seen; he has, with a great deal of life and fire, 'les manieres d'un honnete homme, et le ton de la Parfaitement bonne compagnie'. You like him yourself; try to be like him: it is in your power.

I hear that Mr. Mitchel is to be recalled, notwithstanding the King of Prussia's instances to keep him. But why, is a secret that I cannot penetrate.

You will not fail to offer the Landgrave, and the Princess of Hesse (who I find are going home), to be their agent and commissioner at Hamburg.

I cannot comprehend the present state of Russia, nor the motions of their armies. They change their generals once a week; sometimes they march with rapidity, and now they lie quiet behind the Vistula. We have a thousand stories here of the interior of that government, none of which I believe. Some say, that the Great Duke will be set aside.

Woronzoff is said to be entirely a Frenchman, and that Monsieur de l'Hopital governs both him and the court. Sir C. W. is said, by his indiscretions, to have caused the disgrace of Bestuchef, which seems not impossible.

In short, everything of every kind is said, because, I believe, very little is truly known. 'A propos' of Sir C. W.; he is out of confinement, and gone to his house in the country for the whole summer. They say he is now very cool and well. I have seen his Circe, at her window in Pall-Mall; she is painted, powdered, curled, and patched, and looks 'l'aventure'. She has been offered, by Sir C. W———'s friends, L500 in full of all demands, but will not accept of it. 'La comtesse veut plaider', and I fancy 'faire autre chose si elle peut. Jubeo to bene valere.

LETTER CCXXI

BLACKHEATH, May 18, O. S. 1758.

MY DEAR FRIEND: I have your letter of the 9th now before me, and condole with you upon the present solitude and inaction of Hamburg. You are now shrunk from the dignity and importance of a consummate minister, to be but, as it were, a common man. But this has, at one time or another, been the case of most great men; who have not always had equal opportunities of exerting their talents. The greatest must submit to the capriciousness of fortune; though they can, better than others, improve the favorable moments. For instance, who could have thought, two years ago, that you would have been the Atlas of the Northern Pole; but the Good Genius of the North ordered it so; and now that you have set that part of the globe right, you return to 'otium cum dignitate'. But to be serious: now that you cannot have much office business to do, I could tell you what to do, that would employ you, I should think, both usefully and agreeably. I mean, that you should write short memoirs of that busy scene, in which you have been enough concerned, since your arrival at Hamburg, to be able to put together authentic facts and anecdotes. I do not know whether you will give yourself the trouble to do it or not; but I do know, that if you will, 'olim hcec meminisse juvabit'. I would have them short, but correct as to facts and dates.

I have told Alt, in the strongest manner, your lamentations for the loss of the House of Cassel, 'et il en fera rapport a son Serenissime Maitre'. When you are quite idle (as probably you may be, some time this summer), why should you not ask leave to make a tour to Cassel for a week? which would certainly be granted you from hence, and which would be looked upon as a 'bon procede' at Cassel.

The King of Prussia is probably, by this time, at the gates of Vienna, making the Queen of Hungary really do what Monsieur de Bellisle only threatened; sign a peace upon the ramparts of her capital. If she is obstinate, and will not, she must fly either to Presburg or to Inspruck, and Vienna must fall. But I think he will offer her reasonable conditions enough for herself; and I suppose, that, in that case, Caunitz will be reasonable enough to advise her to accept of them. What turn would the war take then? Would the French and Russians carry it on without her? The King of Prussia, and the Prince of Brunswick, would soon sweep them out of Germany. By this time, too, I believe, the French are entertained in America with the loss of Cape Breton; and, in consequence of that, Quebec; for we have a force there equal to both those undertakings, and officers there, now, that will execute what Lord L———never would so much as attempt. His appointments were too considerable to let him do anything that might possibly put an end to the war. Lord Howe, upon seeing plainly that he was resolved to do nothing, had asked leave to return, as well as Lord Charles Hay.

We have a great expedition preparing, and which will soon be ready to sail from the Isle of Wight; fifteen thousand good troops, eighty battering cannons, besides mortars, and every other thing in abundance, fit for either battle or siege. Lord Anson desired, and is appointed, to command the fleet employed upon this expedition; a proof that it is not a trifling one. Conjectures concerning its destination are infinite; and the most ignorant are, as usual, the boldest conjecturers. If I form any conjectures, I keep them to myself, not to be disproved by the event; but, in truth, I form none: I might have known, but would not.

Everything seems to tend to a peace next winter: our success in America, which is hardly doubtful, and the King of Prussia's in Germany, which is as little so, will make France (already sick of the expense of the war) very tractable for a peace. I heartily wish it: for though people's heads are half turned with the King of Prussia's success, and will be quite turned, if we have any in America, or at sea, a moderate peace will suit us better than this immoderate war of twelve millions a year.

Domestic affairs go just as they did; the Duke of Newcastle and Mr. Pitt jog on like man and wife; that is, seldom agreeing, often quarreling; but by mutual interest, upon the whole, not parting. The latter, I am told, gains ground in the closet; though he still keeps his strength in the House, and his popularity in the public; or, perhaps, because of that.

Do you hold your resolution of visiting your dominions of Bremen and Lubeck this summer? If you do, pray take the trouble of informing yourself correctly of the several constitutions and customs of those places, and of the present state of the federal union of the Hanseatic towns: it will do you no harm, nor cost you much trouble; and it is so much clear gain on the side of useful knowledge.

I am now settled at Blackheath for the summer; where unseasonable frost and snow, and hot and parching east winds, have destroyed all my fruit, and almost my fruit-trees. I vegetate myself little better than they do; I crawl about on foot and on horseback; read a great deal, and write a little; and am very much yours.

LETTER CCXXII

BLACKHEATH, May 30, 1758.

MY DEAR FRIEND: I have no letter from you to answer, so this goes to you unprovoked. But 'a propos' of letters; you have had great honor done you, in a letter from a fair and royal hand, no less than that of her Royal Highness the Princess of Cassel; she has written your panegyric to her sister, Princess Amelia, who sent me a compliment upon it. This has likewise done you no harm with the King, who said gracious things upon that occasion. I suppose you had for her Royal Highness those attentions which I wish to God you would have, in due proportions, for everybody. You see, by this instance, the effects of them; they are always repaid with interest. I am more confirmed by this in thinking, that, if you can conveniently, you should ask leave to go for a week to Cassel, to return your thanks for all favors received.

I cannot expound to myself the conduct of the Russians. There must be a trick in their not marching with more expedition. They have either had a sop from the King of Prussia, or they want an animating dram from France and Austria. The King of Prussia's conduct always explains itself by the events; and, within a very few days, we must certainly hear of some very great stroke from that quarter. I think I never in my life remember a period of time so big with great events as the present: within two months the fate of the House of Austria will probably be decided: within the same space of time, we shall certainly hear of the taking of Cape Breton, and of our army's proceeding to Quebec within a few days we shall know the good or ill success of our great expedition; for it is sailed; and it cannot be long before we shall hear something of the Prince of Brunswick's operations, from whom I also expect good things. If all these things turn out, as there is good reason to believe they will, we may once, in our turn, dictate a reasonable peace to France, who now pays seventy per cent insurance upon its trade, and seven per cent for all the money raised for the service of the year.

Comte Bothmar has got the small-pox, and of a bad kind. Kniphausen diverts himself much here; he sees all places and all people, and is ubiquity itself. Mitchel, who was much threatened, stays at last at Berlin, at the earnest request of the King of Prussia. Lady is safely delivered of a son, to the great joy of that noble family. The expression, of a woman's having brought her husband a son, seems to be a proper and cautious one; for it is never said from whence.

I was going to ask you how you passed your time now at Hamburg, since it is no longer the seat of strangers and of business; but I will not, because I know it is to no purpose. You have sworn not to tell me.

Sir William Stanhope told me that you promised to send him some Old Hock from Hamburg, and so you did not. If you meet with any superlatively good, and not else, pray send over a 'foudre' of it, and write to him. I shall have a share in it. But unless you find some, either at Hamburg or at Bremen, uncommonly and almost miraculously good, do not send any. Dixi. Yours.

LETTER CCXXIII

BLACKHEATH, June 13, 1758.

MY DEAR FRIEND: The secret is out: St. Malo is the devoted place. Our troops began to land at the Bay of Cancale the 5th, without any opposition. We have no further accounts yet, but expect some every moment. By the plan of it, which I have seen, it is by no means a weak place; and I fear there will be many hats to be disposed of, before it is taken. There are in the port above thirty privateers; about sixteen of their own, and about as many taken from us. 237

Now for Africa, where we have had great success. The French have been driven out of all their forts and settlements upon the Gum coast, and upon the river Senegal. They had been many years in possession of them, and by them annoyed our African trade exceedingly; which, by the way, 'toute proportion gardee', is the most lucrative trade we have. The present booty is likewise very considerable, in gold dust, and gum Seneca; which is very valuable, by being a very necessary commodity, for all our stained and printed linens.

Now for America. The least sanguine people here expect, the latter end of this month or the beginning of the next, to have the account of the taking of Cape Breton, and of all the forts with hard names in North America.

Captain Clive has long since settled Asia to our satisfaction; so that three parts of the world look very favorable for us. Europe, I submit to the care of the King of Prussia and Prince Ferdinand of Brunswick; and I think they will give a good account of it. France is out of luck, and out of courage; and will, I hope, be enough out of spirits to submit to a reasonable peace. By reasonable, I mean what all people call reasonable in their own case; an advantageous one for us.

I have set all right with Munchausen; who would not own that he was at all offended, and said, as you do, that his daughter did not stay long enough, nor appear enough at Hamburg, for you possibly to know that she was there. But people are always ashamed to own the little weaknesses of self-love, which, however, all people feel more or less. The excuse, I saw, pleased.

I will send you your quadrille tables by the first opportunity, consigned to the care of Mr. Mathias here. 'Felices faustaeque sint! May you win upon them, when you play with men; and when you play with women, either win or know why you lose.

Miss————marries Mr.————-next week. WHO PROFFERS LOVE, PROFFERS DEATH, says Weller to a dwarf: in my opinion, the conclusion must instantly choak the little lady. Admiral marries Lady; there the danger, if danger is, will be on the other side. The lady has wanted a man so long, that she now compounds for half a one. Half a loaf—

I have been worse since my last letter; but am now, I think, recovering; 'tant va la cruche a l'eau';—and I have been there very often.

Good-night. I am faithfully and truly yours.

LETTER CCXXIV

BLACKHEATH, June 27, 1758.

MY DEAR FRIEND: You either have received already, or will very soon receive, a little case from Amsterdam, directed to you at Hamburg. It is for Princess Ameba, the King of Prussia's sister, and contains some books which she desired Sir Charles Hotham to procure her from England, so long ago as when he was at Berlin: he sent for them immediately; but, by I do not know what puzzle, they were recommended to the care of Mr. Selwyn, at Paris, who took such care of them, that he kept them near three years in his warehouse, and has at last sent them to Amsterdam, from whence they are sent to you. If the books are good for anything, they must be considerably improved, by having seen so much of the world; but, as I believe they are English books, perhaps they may, like English travelers, have seen nobody, but the several bankers to whom they were consigned: be that as it will, I think you had best deliver them to Monsieur Hecht, the Prussian Minister at Hamburg, to forward to her Royal Highness, with a respectful compliment from you, which you will, no doubt, turn in the best manner, and 'selon le bon ton de la parfaitement bonne compagnie'.

You have already seen, in the papers, all the particulars of our St. Malo's expedition, so I say no more of that; only that Mr. Pitt's friends exult in the destruction of three French ships of war, and one hundred and thirty privateers and trading ships; and affirm that it stopped the march of threescore thousand men, who were going to join the Comte de Clermont's army. On the other hand, Mr. Fox and company call it breaking windows with guineas; and apply the fable of the Mountain and the Mouse. The next object of our fleet was to be the bombarding of Granville, which is the great 'entrepot' of their Newfoundland fishery, and will be a considerable loss to them in that branch of their trade. These, you will perhaps say, are no great matters, and I say so too; but, at least, they are signs of life, which we had not given them for many years before; and will show the French, by our invading them, that we do not fear their invading us. Were those invasions, in fishing-boats from Dunkirk, so terrible as they were artfully represented to be, the French would have had an opportunity of executing them, while our fleet, and such a considerable part of our army, were employed upon their coast. BUT MY LORD LIGONIER DOES NOT WANT AN ARMY AT HOME.

The parliament is prorogued by a most gracious speech neither by nor from his Majesty, who was TOO ILL to go to the House; the Lords and Gentlemen are, consequently, most of them, gone to their several counties, to do (to be sure) all the good that is recommended to them in the speech. London, I am told, is now very empty, for I cannot say so from knowledge. I vegetate wholly here. I walk and read a great deal, ride and scribble a little, according as my lead allows, or my spirits prompt; to write anything tolerable, the mind must be in a natural, proper disposition; provocatives, in that case, as well as in another, will only produce miserable, abortive performances.

Now that you have (as I suppose) full leisure enough, I wish you would give yourself the trouble, or rather pleasure, to do what I hinted to you some time ago; that is, to write short memoirs of those affairs which have either gone through your hands, or that have come to your certain knowledge, from the inglorious battle of Hastenbeck, to the still more scandalous Treaty of Neutrality. Connect, at least, if it be by ever so short notes, the pieces and letters which you must necessarily have in your hands, and throw in the authentic anecdotes that you have probably heard. You will be glad when you have done it: and the reviving past ideas, in some order and method, will be an infinite comfort to you hereafter. I have a thousand times regretted not having done so; it is at present too late for me to begin; this is the right time for you, and your life is likely to be a busy one. Would young men avail themselves of the advice and experience of their old friends, they would find the utility in their youth, and the comfort of it in their more advanced age; but they seldom consider that, and you, less than anybody I ever knew. May you soon grow wiser! Adieu.

LETTER CCXXV

BLACKHEATH, June 30, 1758.

MY DEAR FRIEND: This letter follows my last very close; but I received yours of the 15th in the short interval. You did very well not to buy any Rhenish, at the exorbitant price you mention, without further directions; for both my brother and I think the money better than the wine, be the wine ever so good. We will content our selves with our stock in hand of humble Rhenish, of about three shillings a-bottle. However, 'pour la rarity du fait, I will lay out twelve ducats', for twelve bottles of the wine of 1665, by way of an eventual cordial, if you can obtain a 'senatus consultum' for it. I am in no hurry for it, so send it me only when you can conveniently; well packed up 's'entend'.

You will, I dare say, have leave to go to Cassel; and if you do go, you will perhaps think it reasonable, that I, who was the adviser of the journey, should pay the expense of it. I think so too; and therefore, if you go, I will remit the L100 which you have calculated it at. You will find the House of Cassel the house of gladness; for Hanau is already, or must be soon, delivered of its French guests.

The Prince of Brunswick's victory is, by all the skillful, thought a 'chef d'oeuvre', worthy of Turenne, Conde, or the most illustrious human butchers. The French behaved better than at Rosbach, especially the Carabiniers Royaux, who could not be 'entames'. I wish the siege of Olmutz well over, and a victory after it; and that, with good news from America, which I think there is no reason to doubt of, must procure us a good peace at the end of the year. The Prince of Prussia's death is no public misfortune: there was a jealousy and alienation between the King and him, which could never have been made up between the possessor of the crown and the next heir to it. He will make something of his nephew, 's'il est du bois don't on en fait'. He is young enough to forgive, and to be forgiven, the possession and the expectative, at least for some years.

Adieu! I am UNWELL, but affectionately yours.

LETTER CCXXVI

BLACKHEATH, July 18, 1758.

MY DEAR FRIEND: Yesterday I received your letter of the 4th; and my last will have informed you that I had received your former, concerning the Rhenish, about which I gave you instructions. If 'vinum Mosellanum est omni tempore sanum', as the Chapter of Treves asserts, what must this 'vinum Rhenanum' be, from its superior strength and age? It must be the universal panacea.

Captain Howe is to sail forthwith somewhere or another, with about 8,000 land forces on board him; and what is much more, Edward the White Prince. It is yet a secret where they are going; but I think it is no secret, that what 16,000 men and a great fleet could not do, will not be done by 8,000 men and a much smaller fleet. About 8,500 horse, foot, and dragoons, are embarking, as fast as they can, for Embden, to reinforce Prince Ferdinand's army; late and few, to be sure, but still better than never, and none. The operations in Moravia go on slowly, and Olmutz seems to be a tough piece of work; I own I begin to be in pain for the King of Prussia; for the Russians now march in earnest, and Marechal Dann's army is certainly superior in number to his. God send him a good delivery!

You have a Danish army now in your neighborhood, and they say a very fine one; I presume you will go to see it, and, if you do, I would advise you to go when the Danish Monarch comes to review it himself; 'pour prendre langue de ce Seigneur'. The rulers of the earth are all worth knowing; they suggest moral reflections: and the respect that one naturally has for God's vicegerents here on earth, is greatly increased by acquaintance with them.

Your card-tables are gone, and they inclose some suits of clothes, and some of these clothes inclose a letter.

Your friend Lady————is gone into the country with her Lord, to negotiate, coolly and at leisure, their intended separation. My Lady insists upon my Lord's dismissing the————, as ruinous to his fortune; my Lord insists, in his turn, upon my Lady's dismissing Lord—————; my Lady replies, that that is unreasonable, since Lord creates no expense to the family, but rather the contrary. My Lord confesses that there is some weight in this argument: but then pleads sentiment: my Lady says, a fiddlestick for sentiment, after having been married so long. How this matter will end, is in the womb of time, 'nam fuit ante Helenam'.

You did very well to write a congratulatory letter to Prince Ferdinand; such attentions are always right, and always repaid in some way or other.

I am glad you have connected your negotiations and anecdotes; and, I hope, not with your usual laconism. Adieu! Yours.

LETTERS TO HIS SON, COMPLETE

BLACKHEATH, August 1, 1758

MY DEAR FRIEND: I think the Court of Cassel is more likely to make you a second visit at Hamburg, than you are to return theirs at Cassel; and therefore, till that matter is clearer, I shall not mention it to Lord Holderness.

By the King of Prussia's disappointment in Moravia, by the approach of the Russians, and the intended march of Monsieur de Soubize to Hanover, the waters seem to me to be as much troubled as ever. 'Je vois tres noir actuellement'; I see swarms of Austrians, French, Imperialists, Swedes, and Russians, in all near four hundred thousand men, surrounding the King of Prussia and Prince Ferdinand, who have about a third of that number. Hitherto they have only buzzed, but now I fear they will sting.

The immediate danger of this country is being drowned; for it has not ceased raining these three months, and withal is extremely cold. This neither agrees with me in itself, nor in its consequences; for it hinders me from taking my necessary exercise, and makes me very unwell. As my head is always the part offending, and is so at present, I will not do, like many writers, write without a head; so adieu.

LETTER CCXXVIII

BLACKHEATH, August 29, 1758.

MY DEAR FRIEND: Your secretary's last letter brought me the good news that the fever had left you, and I will believe that it has: but a postscript to it, of only two lines, under your own hand, would have convinced me more effectually of your recovery. An intermitting fever, in the intervals of the paroxysms, would surely have allowed you to have written a few lines with your own hand, to tell me how you were; and till I receive a letter (as short as you please) from you yourself, I shall doubt of the exact truth of any other accounts.

I send you no news, because I have none; Cape Breton, Cherbourg, etc., are now old stories; we expect a new one soon from Commodore Howe, but from whence we know not. From Germany we hope for good news: I confess I do not, I only wish it. The King of Prussia is marched to fight the Russians, and I believe will beat them, if they stand; but what then? What shall he do next, with the three hundred and fourscore thousand men now actually at work upon him? He will do all that man can do, but at last 'il faut succomber'.

Remember to think yourself less well than you are, in order to be quite so; be very regular, rather longer than you need; and then there will be no danger of a relapse. God bless you.

LETTER CCXXIX

BLACKHEATH, September 5, 1758

MY DEAR FRIEND: I received, with great pleasure, your letter of the 22d August; for, by not having a line from you in your secretary's two letters, I suspect that you were worse than he cared to tell me; and so far I was in the right, that your fever was more malignant than intermitting ones generally are, which seldom confines people to their bed, or at most, only the days of the paroxysms. Now that, thank God, you are well again, though weak, do not be in too much haste to be better and stronger: leave that to nature, which, at your age, will restore both your health and strength as soon as she should. Live cool for a time, and rather low, instead of taking what they call heartening things: Your manner of making presents is noble, 'et sent la grandeur d'ame d'un preux Chevalier'. You depreciate their value to prevent any returns; for it is impossible that a wine which has counted so many Syndicks, that can only be delivered by a 'senatus consultum', and is the PANACEA Of the North, should be sold for a ducat a bottle. The 'sylphium' of the Romans, which was stored up in the public magazines, and only distributed by order of the magistrate, I dare say, cost more; so that I am convinced, your present is much more valuable than you would make it.

Here I am interrupted, by receiving your letter of the 25th past. I am glad that you are able to undertake your journey to Bremen: the motion, the air, the new scene, the everything, will do you good, provided you manage yourself discreetly.

Your bill for fifty pounds shall certainly be accepted and paid; but, as in conscience I think fifty pounds is too little, for seeing a live Landgrave, and especially at Bremen, which this whole nation knows to be a very dear place, I shall, with your leave, add fifty more to it. By the way, when you see the Princess Royal of Cassel, be sure to tell her how sensible you are of the favorable and too partial testimony, which you know she wrote of you to Princess Amelia.

The King of Prussia has had the victory, which you in some measure foretold; and as he has taken 'la caisse militaire', I presume 'Messieurs les Russes sont hors de combat pour cette campagne'; for 'point d'argent, point de Suisse', is not truer of the laudable Helvetic body, than 'point d'argent, point de Russe', is of the savages of the Two Russias, not even excepting the Autocratrice of them both. Serbelloni, I believe, stands next in his Prussian Majesty's list to be beaten; that is, if he will stand; as the Prince de Soubize does in Prince Ferdinand's, upon the same condition. If both these things happen, which is by no means improbable, we may hope for a tolerable peace this winter; for, 'au bout du compte', the King of Prussia cannot hold out another year; and therefore he should make the best of these favorable events, by way negotiation.

I think I have written a great deal, with an actual giddiness of head upon me. So adieu.

I am glad you have received my letter of the Ides of July.

LETTER CCXXX

BLACKHEATH, September 8, 1758.

MY DEAR FRIEND: This letter shall be short, being only an explanatory note upon my last; for I am not learned enough, nor yet dull enough, to make my comment much longer than my text. I told you then, in my former letter, that, with your leave (which I will suppose granted), I would add fifty pounds to your draught for that sum; now, lest you should misunderstand this, and wait for the remittance of that additional fifty from hence, know then my meaning was, that you should likewise draw upon me for it when you please; which I presume, will be more convenient to you.

Let the pedants, whose business it is to believe lies, or the poets, whose trade it is to invent them, match the King of Prussia With a hero in ancient or modern story, if they can. He disgraces history, and makes one give some credit to romances. Calprenede's Juba does not now seem so absurd as formerly.

I have been extremely ill this whole summer; but am now something better. However, I perceive, 'que l'esprit et le corps baissent'; the former is the last thing that anybody will tell me; or own when I tell it them; but I know it is true. Adieu.

LETTER CCXXXI

BLACKHEATH, September 22, 1758

MY DEAR FRIEND: I have received no letter from you since you left Hamburg; I presume that you are perfectly recovered, but it might not have been improper to have told me so. I am very far from being recovered; on the contrary, I am worse and worse, weaker and weaker every day; for which reason I shall leave this place next Monday, and set out for Bath a few days afterward. I should not take all this trouble merely to prolong the fag end of a life, from which I can expect no pleasure, and others no utility; but the cure, or at least the mitigation, of those physical ills which make that life a load while it does last, is worth any trouble and attention.

We are come off but scurvily from our second attempt upon St. Malo; it is our last for this season; and, in my mind, should be our last forever, unless we were to send so great a sea and land force as to give us a moral certainty of taking some place of great importance, such as Brest, Rochefort, or Toulon.

Monsieur Munchausen embarked yesterday, as he said, for Prince Ferdinand's army; but as it is not generally thought that his military skill can be of any great use to that prince, people conjecture that his business must be of a very different nature, and suspect separate negotiations, neutralities, and what not. Kniphausen does not relish it in the least, and is by no means satisfied with the reasons that have been given him for it. Before he can arrive there, I reckon that something decisive will have passed in Saxony; if to the disadvantage of the King of Prussia, he is crushed; but if, on the contrary, he should get a complete victory (and he does not get half victories) over the Austrians, the winter may probably produce him and us a reasonable peace. I look upon Russia as 'hors de combat' for some time; France is certainly sick of the war; under an unambitious King, and an incapable Ministry, if there is one at all: and, unassisted by those two powers, the Empress Queen had better be quiet. Were any other man in the situation of the King of Prussia, I should not hesitate to pronounce him ruined; but he is such a prodigy of a man, that I will only say, I fear he will be ruined. It is by this time decided.

Your Cassel court at Bremen is, I doubt, not very splendid; money must be wanting: but, however, I dare say their table is always good, for the Landgrave is a gourmand; and as you are domestic there, you may be so too, and recruit your loss of flesh from your fever: but do not recruit too fast. Adieu.

LETTER CCXXXII

LONDON, September 26, 1758

MY DEAR FRIEND: I am sorry to find that you had a return of your fever; but to say the truth, you in some measure deserved it, for not carrying Dr. Middleton's bark and prescription with you. I foresaw that you would think yourself cured too soon, and gave you warning of it; but BYGONES are BYGONES, as Chartres, when he was dying, said of his sins; let us look forward. You did very prudently to return to Hamburg, to good bark, and, I hope, a good physician. Make all sure there before you stir from thence, notwithstanding the requests or commands of all the princesses in Europe: I mean a month at least, taking the bark even to supererogation, that is, some time longer than Dr. Middleton requires; for, I presume, you are got over your childishness about tastes, and are sensible that your health deserves more attention than your palate. When you shall be thus re-established, I approve of your returning to Bremen; and indeed you cannot well avoid it, both with regard to your promise, and to the distinction with which you have been received by the Cassel family.

Now to the other part of your letter. Lord Holdernesse has been extremely civil to you, in sending you, all under his own hand, such obliging offers of his service. The hint is plain, that he will (in case you desire it) procure you leave to come home for some time; so that the single question is, whether you should desire it or not, NOW. It will be two months before you can possibly undertake the journey, whether by sea or by land,

and either way it would be a troublesome and dangerous one for a convalescent in the rigor of the month of November; you could drink no mineral waters here in that season, nor are any mineral waters proper in your case, being all of them heating, except Seltzer's; then, what would do you more harm than all medicines could do you good, would be the pestilential vapors of the House of Commons, in long and crowded days, of which there will probably be many this session; where your attendance, if here, will necessarily be required. I compare St. Stephen's Chapel, upon those days, to 'la Grotta del Cane'.

Whatever may be the fate of the war now, negotiations will certainly be stirring all the winter, and of those, the northern ones, you are sensible, are not the least important; in these, if at Hamburg, you will probably have your share, and perhaps a meritorious one. Upon the whole, therefore, I would advise you to write a very civil letter to Lord Holdernesse; and to tell him that though you cannot hope to be of any use to his Majesty's affairs anywhere, yet, in the present unsettled state of the North, it is possible that unforeseen accidents may throw in your way to be of some little service, and that you would not willingly be out of the way of those accidents; but that you shall be most extremely obliged to his Lordship, if he will procure you his Majesty's gracious permission to return for a few months in the spring, when probably affairs will be more settled one way or another. When things tend nearer to a settlement, and that Germany, from the want of money or men, or both, breathes peace more than war, I shall solicit Burrish's commission for you, which is one of the most agreeable ones in his Majesty's gift; and I shall by no means despair of success. Now I have given you my opinion upon this affair, which does not make a difference of above three months, or four at most, I would not be understood to mean to force your own, if it should happen to be different from mine; but mine, I think, is more both for your health and your interest. However, do as you please: may you in this, and everything else, do for the best! So God bless you!

LETTER CCXXXIII

BATH, October 18, 1758.

MY DEAR FRIEND: I received by the same post your two letters of the 29th past, and of the 3d instant.

The last tells me that you are perfectly recovered; and your resolution of going to Bremen in three or four days proves it; for surely you would not undertake that journey a second time, and at this season of the year, without feeling your health solidly restored; however, in all events, I hope you have taken a provision of good bark with you. I think your attention to her Royal Highness may be of use to you here; and indeed all attentions, to all sorts, of people, are always repaid in some way or other; though real obligations are not. For instance, Lord Titchfield, who has been with you at Hamburg, has written an account to the Duke and Duchess of Portland, who are here, of the civilities you showed him, with which he is much pleased, and they delighted. At this rate, if you do not take care, you will get the unmanly reputation of a well-bred man; and your countryman, John Trott, will disown you.

I have received, and tasted of your present; which is a 'tres grand vin', but more cordial to the stomach than pleasant to the palate. I keep it as a physic, only to take occasionally, in little disorders of my stomach; and in those cases, I believe it is wholsomer than stronger cordials.

I have been now here a fortnight; and though I am rather better than when I came, I am still far from well.

My head is giddier than becomes a head of my age; and my stomach has not recovered its retentive faculty. Leaning forward, particularly to write, does not at present agree with, Yours.

LETTER CCXXXIV

BATH, October 28, 1758.

MY DEAR FRIEND: Your letter has quieted my alarms; for I find by it, that you are as well recovered as you could be in so short a time. It is your business now to keep yourself well by scrupulously following Dr. Middleton's directions. He seems to be a rational and knowing man. Soap and steel are, unquestionably, the proper medicines for your case; but as they are alteratives, you must take them for a very long time, six months at least; and then drink chalybeate waters. I am fully persuaded, that this was your original complaint in Carniola, which those ignorant physicians called, in their jargon, 'Arthritis vaga', and treated as such. But now that the true cause of your illness is discovered, I flatter myself that, with time and patience on your part, you will be radically cured; but, I repeat it again, it must be by a long and uninterrupted course of those alterative medicines above mentioned. They have no taste; but if they had a bad one, I will not now suppose you such a child, as to let the frowardness of your palate interfere in the least with the recovery or enjoyment of health. The latter deserves the utmost attention of the most rational man; the former is the only proper object of the care of a dainty, frivolous woman.

The run of luck, which some time ago we were in, seems now to be turned against us. Oberg is completely routed; his Prussian Majesty was surprised (which I am surprised at), and had rather the worst of it. I am in some pain for Prince Ferdinand, as I take it for granted that the detachment from Marechal de Contade's army, which enabled Prince Soubize to beat Oberg, will immediately return to the grand army, and then it will be infinitely superior.

Nor do I see where Prince Ferdinand can take his winter quarters, unless he retires to Hanover; and that I do not take to be at present the land of Canaan. Our second expedition to St. Malo I cannot call so much an unlucky, as an ill-conducted one; as was also Abercrombie's affair in America. 'Mais il n'y a pas de petite perte qui revient souvent': and all these accidents put together make a considerable sum total.

I have found so little good by these waters, that I do not intend to stay here above a week longer; and then remove my crazy body to London, which is the most convenient place either to live or die in.

I cannot expect active health anywhere; you may, with common care and prudence, effect it everywhere; and God grant that you may have it! Adieu.

LETTER CCXXXV

LONDON, November 21, 1758.

MY DEAR FRIEND: You did well to think of Prince Ferdinand's ribband, which I confess I did not; and I am glad to find you thinking so far beforehand. It would be a pretty commission, and I will 'accingere me' to procure it to you. The only competition I fear, is that of General Yorke, in case Prince Ferdinand should pass any time with his brother at The Hague, which is not unlikely, since he cannot go to Brunswick to his eldest brother, upon account of their simulated quarrel.

I fear the piece is at an end with the King of Prussia, and he may say 'ilicet'; I am sure he may personally say 'plaudite'. Warm work is expected this session of parliament, about continent and no continent; some think Mr. Pitt too continent, others too little so; but a little time, as the newspapers most prudently and truly observe, will clear up these matters.

The King has been ill; but his illness is terminated in a good fit of the gout, with which he is still confined. It was generally thought that he would have died, and for a very good reason; for the oldest lion in the Tower, much about the King's age, died a fortnight ago. This extravagancy, I can assure you, was believed by many above peuple. So wild and capricious is the human mind!

Take care of your health as much as you can; for, To BE, or NOT To BE, is a question of much less importance, in my mind, than to be or not to be well. Adieu.

LETTER CCXXXVI

EARL OF PHILIP DORMER STANHOPE CHESTERFIELD

LONDON, December 15, 1758.

MY DEAR FRIEND: It is a great while since I heard from you, but I hope that good, not ill health, has been the occasion of this silence: I will suppose you have been, or are still at Bremen, and engrossed by your Hessian friends.

Prince Ferdinand of Brunswick is most certainly to have the Garter, and I think I have secured you the honor of putting it on. When I say SECURED, I mean it in the sense in which that word should always be understood at courts, and that is, INSECURELY; I have a promise, but that is not 'caution bourgeoise'. In all events, do not mention it to any mortal, because there is always a degree of ridicule that attends a disappointment, though often very unjustly, if the expectation was reasonably grounded; however, it is certainly most prudent not to communicate, prematurely, one's hopes or one's fears. I cannot tell you when Prince Ferdinand will have it; though there are so many candidates for the other two vacant Garters, that I believe he will have his soon, and by himself; the others must wait till a third, or rather a fourth vacancy. Lord Rockingham and Lord Holdernesse are secure. Lord Temple pushes strongly, but, I believe, is not secure. This commission for dubbing a knight, and so distinguished a one, will be a very agreeable and creditable one for you, 'et il faut vous en acquitter galamment'. In the days of ancient chivalry, people were very nice who they would be knighted by and, if I do not mistake, Francis the First would only be knighted by the Chevalier Bayard, 'qui etoit preux Chevalier et sans reproche'; and no doubt but it will be recorded, 'dans les archives de la Maison de Brunswick', that Prince Ferdinand received the honor of knighthood from your hands.

The estimates for the expenses of the year 1759 are made up; I have seen them; and what do you think they amount to? No less than twelve millions three hundred thousand pounds: a most incredible sum, and yet already subscribed, and even more offered! The unanimity in the House of Commons, in voting such a sum, and such forces, both by sea and land, is not the less astonishing. This is Mr. Pitt's doing, AND IT IS MARVELOUS IN OUR EYES.

The King of Prussia has nothing more to do this year; and, the next, he must begin where he has left off. I wish he would employ this winter in concluding a separate peace with the Elector of Saxony; which would give him more elbowroom to act against France and the Queen of Hungary, and put an end at once to the proceedings of the Diet, and the army of the empire; for then no estate of the empire would be invaded by a co-estate, and France, the faithful and disinterested guarantee of the Treaty of Westphalia, would have no pretense to continue its armies there. I should think that his Polish Majesty, and his Governor, Comte Bruhl, must be pretty weary of being fugitives in Poland, where they are hated, and of being ravaged in Saxony. This reverie of mine, I hope will be tried, and I wish it may succeed. Good-night, and God bless you!

1759-1765

LETTER CCXXXVII

LETTERS TO HIS SON, COMPLETE

LONDON, New-year's Day, 1759

MY DEAR FRIEND: 'Molti e felici', and I have done upon that subject, one truth being fair, upon the most lying day in the whole year.

I have now before me your last letter of the 21st December, which I am glad to find is a bill of health: but, however, do not presume too much upon it, but obey and honor your physician, "that thy days may be long in the land."

Since my last, I have heard nothing more concerning the ribband; but I take it for granted it will be disposed of soon. By the way, upon reflection, I am not sure that anybody but a knight can, according to form, be employed to make a knight. I remember that Sir Clement Cotterel was sent to Holland, to dub the late Prince of Orange, only because he was a knight himself; and I know that the proxies of knights, who cannot attend their own installations, must always be knights. This did not occur to me before, and perhaps will not to the person who was to recommend you: I am sure I will not stir it; and I only mention it now, that you may be in all events prepared for the disappointment, if it should happen.

G——is exceedingly flattered with your account, that three thousand of his countrymen; all as little as himself, should be thought a sufficient guard upon three-and-twenty thousand of all the nations in Europe; not that he thinks himself, by any means, a little man, for when he would describe a tall handsome man, he raises himself up at least half an inch to represent him.

The private news from Hamburg is, that his Majesty's Resident there is woundily in love with Madame————; if this be true, God send him, rather than her, a good DELIVERY! She must be 'etrennee' at this season, and therefore I think you should be so too: so draw upon me as soon as you please, for one hundred pounds.

Here is nothing new, except the unanimity with which the parliament gives away a dozen of millions sterling; and the unanimity of the public is as great in approving of it, which has stifled the usual political and polemical argumentations.

Cardinal Bernis's disgrace is as sudden, and hitherto as little understood, as his elevation was. I have seen his poems, printed at Paris, not by a friend, I dare say; and to judge by them, I humbly conceive his Eminency is a p——y. I will say nothing of that excellent headpiece that made him and unmade him in the same month, except O KING, LIVE FOREVER.

Good-night to you, whoever you pass it with.

LETTER CCXXXVIII

LONDON, February 2, 1759

MY DEAR FRIEND: I am now (what I have very seldom been) two letters in your debt: the reason was, that my head, like many other heads, has frequently taken a wrong turn; in which case, writing is painful to me, and therefore cannot be very pleasant to my readers.

I wish you would (while you have so good an opportunity as you have at Hamburg) make yourself perfectly master of that dull but very useful knowledge, the course of exchange, and the causes of its almost perpetual variations; the value and relation of different coins, the specie, the banco, usances, agio, and a thousand other particulars. You may with ease learn, and you will be very glad when you have learned them; for, in your business, that sort of knowledge will often prove necessary.

I hear nothing more of Prince Ferdinand's garter: that he will have one is very certain; but when, I believe, is very uncertain; all the other postulants wanting to be dubbed at the same time, which cannot be, as there is not ribband enough for them.

If the Russians move in time, and in earnest, there will be an end of our hopes and of our armies in Germany: three such mill-stones as Russia, France, and Austria, must, sooner or later, in the course of the year, grind his Prussian Majesty down to a mere MARGRAVE of Brandenburg. But I have always some hopes of a change under a 'Gunarchy'—[Derived from the Greek word 'Iuvn' a woman, and means female government]—where whim and humor commonly prevail, reason very seldom, and then only by a lucky mistake.

I expect the incomparable fair one of Hamburg, that prodigy of beauty, and paragon of good sense, who has enslaved your mind, and inflamed your heart. If she is as well 'etrennee' as you say she shall, you will be soon out of her chains; for I have, by long experience, found women to be like Telephus's spear, if one end kills, the other cures.

There never was so quiet, nor so silent a session of parliament as the present; Mr. Pitt declares only what he would have them do, and they do it 'nemine contradicente', Mr. Viner only expected.

Duchess Hamilton is to be married, to-morrow, to Colonel Campbell, the son of General Campbell, who will some day or other be Duke of Argyle, and have the estate. She refused the Duke of B———r for him.

Here is a report, but I believe a very groundless one, that your old acquaintance, the fair Madame C———e, is run away from her husband, with a jeweler, that 'etrennes' her, and is come over here; but I dare say it is some mistake, or perhaps a lie. Adieu! God bless you!

LETTER CCXXXIX

LONDON, February 27, 1759

MY DEAR FRIEND: In your last letter, of the 7th, you accuse me, most unjustly, of being in arrears in my correspondence; whereas, if our epistolary accounts were fairly liquidated, I believe you would be brought in considerably debtor. I do not see how any of my letters to you can miscarry, unless your office-packet miscarries too, for I always send them to the office. Moreover, I might have a justifiable excuse for writing to you seldomer than usual, for to be sure there never was a period of time, in the middle of a winter, and the parliament sitting, that supplied so little matter for a letter. Near twelve millions have been granted this year, not only 'nemine contradicente', but, 'nemine quicquid dicente'. The proper officers bring in the estimates; it is taken for granted that they are necessary and frugal; the members go to dinner; and leave Mr. West and Mr. Martin to do the rest.

I presume you have seen the little poem of the "Country Lass," by Soame Jenyns, for it was in the "Chronicle"; as was also an answer to it, from the "Monitor." They are neither of them bad performances; the first is the neatest, and the plan of the second has the most invention. I send you none of those 'pieces volantes' in my letters, because they are all printed in one or other of the newspapers, particularly in the "Chronicles"; and I suppose that you and others have all those papers among you at Hamburg; in which case it would be only putting you to the unnecessary expense of double postage.

I find you are sanguine about the King of Prussia this year; I allow his army will be what you say; but what will that be 'vis-a-vis' French, Austrians, Imperialists, Swedes, and Russians, who must amount to more than double that number? Were the inequality less, I would allow for the King of Prussia's being so much 'ipse agmen' as pretty nearly to balance the account. In war, numbers are generally my omens; and, I confess, that in Germany they seem not happy ones this year. In America. I think, we are sure of success, and great success; but how we shall be able to strike a balance, as they call it, between good success there, and ill success upon the continent, so as to come at a peace; is more than I can discover.

Lady Chesterfield makes you her compliments, and thanks you for your offer; but declines troubling you, being discouraged by the ill success of Madame Munchausen's and Miss Chetwynd's commissions, the former for beef, and the latter for gloves; neither of which have yet been executed, to the dissatisfaction of both. Adieu.

LETTER CCXL

LONDON, March 16, 1759

MY DEAR FRIEND: I have now your letter of the 20th past lying before me, by which you despond, in my opinion too soon, of dubbing your Prince; for he most certainly will have the Garter; and he will as probably have it before the campaign opens, as after. His campaign must, I doubt, at best be a defensive one; and he will show great skill in making it such; for according to my calculation, his enemies will be at least double his number. Their troops, indeed, may perhaps be worse than his; but then their number will make up that defect, as it will enable them to undertake different operations at the same time. I cannot think that the King of Denmark will take a part in the present war; which he cannot do without great possible danger; and he is well paid by France for his neutrality; is safe, let what will turn out; and, in the meantime, carries on his commerce with great advantage and security; so that that consideration will not retard your visit to your own country, whenever you have leave to return, and that your own ARRANGEMENTS will allow you. A short absence animates a tender passion, 'et l'on ne recule que pour mieux sauter', especially in the summer months; so that I would advise you to begin your journey in May, and continue your absence from the dear object of your vows till after the dog-days, when love is said to be unwholesome. We have been disappointed at Martinico; I wish we may not be so at Guadaloupe, though we are landed there; for many difficulties must be got over before we can be in possession of the whole island. A pro pos de bottes; you make use of two Spanish words, very properly, in your letter; were I you, I would learn the Spanish language, if there were a Spaniard at Hamburg who could teach me; and then you would be master of all the European languages that are useful; and, in my mind, it is very convenient, if not necessary, for a public man to understand them all, and not to be obliged to have recourse to an interpreter for those papers that chance or business may throw in his way. I learned Spanish when I was older than you; convinced by experience that, in everything possible, it was better to trust to one's self than to any other body whatsoever. Interpreters, as well as relaters, are often unfaithful, and still oftener incorrect, puzzling, and blundering. In short, let it be your maxim through life to know all you can know, yourself; and never to trust implicitly to the informations of others. This rule has been of infinite service to me in the course of my life.

I am rather better than I was; which I owe not to my physicians, but to an ass and a cow, who nourish me, between them, very plentifully and wholesomely; in the morning the ass is my nurse, at night the cow; and I have just now, bought a milch-goat, which is to graze, and nurse me at Blackheath. I do not know what may come of this latter, and I am not without apprehensions that it may make a satyr of me; but, should I find that obscene disposition growing upon me, I will check it in time, for fear of endangering my life and character by rapes. And so we heartily bid you farewell.

LETTER CCXLI

LETTERS TO HIS SON, COMPLETE

LONDON, March 30, 1759

MY DEAR FRIEND: I do not like these frequent, however short, returns of your illness; for I doubt they imply either want of skill in your physician, or want of care in his patient. Rhubarb, soap, and chalybeate medicines and waters, are almost always specifics for obstructions of the liver; but then a very exact regimen is necessary, and that for a long continuance. Acids are good for you, but you do not love them; and sweet things are bad for you, and you do love them. There is another thing very bad for you, and I fear you love it too much. When I was in Holland, I had a slow fever that hung upon me a great while; I consulted Boerhaave, who prescribed me what I suppose was proper, for it cured me; but he added, by way of postscript to his prescription, 'Venus rarius colatur'; which I observed, and perhaps that made the medicines more effectual.

I doubt we shall be mutually disappointed in our hopes of seeing one another this spring, as I believe you will find, by a letter which you will receive at the same time with this, from Lord Holderness; but as Lord Holderness will not tell you all, I will, between you and me, supply that defect. I must do him the justice to say that he has acted in the most kind and friendly manner possible to us both. When the King read your letter, in which you desired leave to return, for the sake of drinking the Tunbridge waters, he said, "If he wants steel waters, those of Pyrmont are better than Tunbridge, and he can have them very fresh at Hamburg. I would rather he had asked me to come last autumn, and had passed the winter here; for if he returns now, I shall have nobody in those quarters to inform me of what passes; and yet it will be a very busy and important scene." Lord Holderness, who found that it would not be liked, resolved to push it no further; and replied, he was very sure that when you knew his Majesty had the least objection to your return at this time, you would think of it no longer; and he owned that he (Lord Holderness) had given you encouragement for this application last year, then thinking and hoping that there would be little occasion for your presence at Hamburg this year. Lord Holderness will only tell you, in his letter, that, as he had some reason to believe his moving this matter would be disagreeable to the King, he resolved, for your sake, not to mention it. You must answer his letter upon that footing simply, and thank him for this mark of his friendship, for he has really acted as your friend. I make no doubt of your having willing leave to return in autumn, for the whole winter. In the meantime, make the best of your 'sejour' where you are; drink the Pyrmont waters, and no wine but Rhenish, which, in your case is the only proper one for you.

Next week Mr. Harte will send you his "Gustavus Adolphus," in two quartos; it will contain many new particulars of the life of that real hero, as he has had abundant and authentic materials, which have never yet appeared. It will, upon the whole, be a very curious and valuable history; though, between you and me, I could have wished that he had been more correct and elegant in his style. You will find it dedicated to one of your acquaintance, who was forced to prune the luxuriant praises bestowed upon him, and yet has left enough of all conscience to satisfy a reasonable man. Harte has been very much out of order these last three or four months, but is not the less intent upon sowing his lucerne, of which he had six crops last year, to his infinite joy, and, as he says, profit. As a gardener, I shall probably have as much joy, though not quite so much profit, by thirty or forty shillings; for there is the greatest promise of fruit this year at 'Blackheath, that ever I saw in my life. Vertumnus and Pomona have been very propitious to me: as for Priapus, that tremendous garden god, as I no longer invoke him, I cannot expect his protection from the birds and the thieves.

Adieu! I will conclude like a pedant, 'Levius fit patientia quicquid corrigere est nefas.'

LETTER CCXLII

LONDON, April 16, 1759

MY DEAR FRIEND: With humble submission to you, I still say that if Prince Ferdinand can make a defensive campaign this year, he will have done a great deal, considering the great inequality of numbers. The little advantages of taking a regiment or two prisoners, or cutting another to pieces, are but trifling articles in the great account; they are only the pence, the pounds are yet to come; and I take it for granted, that neither the French, nor the Court of Vienna, will have 'le dementi' of their main object, which is unquestionably Hanover; for that is the 'summa summarum'; and they will certainly take care to draw a force together for this purpose, too great for any that Prince Ferdinand has, or can have, to oppose them. In short, mark the end on't, 'j'en augure mal'. If France, Austria, the Empire, Russia, and Sweden, are not, at long run, too hard for the two Electors of Hanover and Brandenburg, there must be some invisible power, some tutelar deities, that miraculously interpose in favor of the latter.

You encourage me to accept all the powers that goats, asses, and bulls, can give me, by engaging for my not making an ill use of them; but I own, I cannot help distrusting myself a little, or rather human nature; for it is an old and very true observation, that there are misers of money, but none of power; and the non-use of the one, and the abuse of the other, increase in proportion to their quantity.

I am very sorry to tell you that Harte's "Gustavus Adolphus" does not take at all, and consequently sells very little: it is certainly informing, and full of good matter; but it is as certain too, that the style is execrable: where the devil he picked it up, I cannot conceive, for it is a bad style, of a new and singular kind; it is full of Latinisms, Gallicisms, Germanisms, and all isms but Anglicisms; in some places pompous, in others vulgar and low. Surely, before the end of the world, people, and you in particular, will discover that the MANNER, in everything, is at least as important as the matter; and that the latter never can please, without a good degree of elegance in the former. This holds true in everything in life: in writing, conversing, business, the help of the Graces is absolutely necessary; and whoever vainly thinks himself above them, will find he is mistaken when it will be too late to court them, for they will not come to strangers of an advanced age. There is an history lately come out, of the "Reign of Mary Queen of Scots" and her son (no matter by whom) King James, written by one Robertson, a Scotchman, which for clearness, purity, and dignity of style, I will not scruple to compare with the best historians extant, not excepting Davila, Guicciardini, and perhaps Livy. Its success has consequently been great, and a second edition is already published and bought up. I take it for granted, that it is to be had, or at least borrowed, at Hamburg, or I would send it to you.

I hope you drink the Pyrmont waters every morning. The health of the mind depends so much upon the health of the body, that the latter deserves the utmost attention, independently of the senses. God send you a very great share of both! Adieu.

LETTER CCXLIII

LONDON, April 27, 1759

MY DEAR FRIEND: I have received your two letters of the 10th and 13th, by the last mail; and I will begin my answer to them, by observing to you that a wise man, without being a Stoic, considers, in all misfortunes that befall him, their best as well as their worst side; and everything has a better and a worse side. I have strictly observed that rule for many years, and have found by experience that some comfort is to be extracted, under most moral ills, by considering them in every light, instead of dwelling, as people are too apt to do, upon the gloomy side of the object. Thank God, the disappointment that you so pathetically groan under, is not a calamity which admits of no consolation. Let us simplify it, and see what it amounts to. You are pleased with the expectation of coming here next month, to see those who would have been pleased with seeing you. That, from very natural causes, cannot be, and you must pass this summer at Hamburg, and next winter in England, instead of passing this summer in England, and next winter at Hamburg. Now, estimating things fairly, is not the change rather to your advantage? Is not the summer more eligible, both for health and pleasure, than the winter, in that northern frozen zone? And will not the winter in England supply you with more pleasures than the summer, in an empty capital, could have done? So far then it appears, that you are rather a gainer by your misfortune.

The TOUR too, which you propose making to Lubeck, Altena, etc., will both amuse and inform you; for, at your age, one cannot see too many different places and people; since at the age you are now of, I take it for granted that you will not see them superficially, as you did when you first went abroad.

This whole matter then, summed up, amounts to no more than this—that you will be here next winter, instead of this summer. Do not think that all I have said is the consolation only of an old philosophical fellow, almost insensible of pleasure or pain, offered to a young fellow who has quick sensations of both. No, it is the rational philosophy taught me by experience and knowledge of the world, and which I have practiced above thirty years.

I always made the best of the best, and never made bad worse by fretting; this enabled me to go through the various scenes of life in which I have been an actor, with more pleasure and less pain than most people. You will say, perhaps, one cannot change one's nature; and that if a person is born of a very sensible, gloomy temper, and apt to see things in the worst light, they cannot help it, nor new-make themselves. I will admit it, to a certain degree; and but to a certain degree; for though we cannot totally change our nature, we may in a great measure correct it, by reflection and philosophy; and some philosophy is a very necessary companion in this world, where, even to the most fortunate, the chances are greatly against happiness.

I am not old enough, nor tenacious enough, to pretend not to understand the main purport of your last letter; and to show you that I do, you may draw upon me for two hundred pounds, which, I hope, will more than clear you.

Good-night: 'aquam memento rebus in arduis servare mentem': Be neither transported nor depressed by the accidents of life.

LETTER CCXLIV

BLACKHEATH, May 16, 1759

MY DEAR FRIEND: Your secretary's last letter of the 4th, which I received yesterday, has quieted my fears a good deal, but has not entirely dissipated them. YOUR FEVER STILL CONTINUES, he says, THOUGH IN A LESS DEGREE. Is it a continued fever, or an intermitting one? If the former, no wonder that you are weak, and that your head aches. If the latter, why has not the bark, in substance and large doses, been administered? for if it had, it must have stopped it by this time. Next post, I hope, will set me quite at ease.

Surely you have not been so regular as you ought, either in your medicines or in your general regimen, otherwise this fever would not have returned; for the Doctor calls it, YOUR FEVER RETURNED, as if you had an exclusive patent for it. You have now had illnesses enough, to know the value of health, and to make you implicitly follow the prescriptions of your physician in medicines, and the rules of your own common sense in diet; in which, I can assure you, from my own experience, that quantity is often worse than quality; and I would rather eat half a pound of bacon at a meal, than two pounds of any the most wholesome food.

I have been settled here near a week, to my great satisfaction; 'c'est ma place', and I know it, which is not given to everybody. Cut off from social life by my deafness, as well as other physical ills, and being at best but the ghost of my former self, I walk here in silence and solitude as becomes a ghost: with this only difference, that I walk by day, whereas, you know, to be sure, that other ghosts only appear by night. My health, however, is better than it was last year, thanks to my almost total milk diet. This enables me to vary my solitary amusements, and alternately to scribble as well as read, which I could not do last year. Thus I saunter away the remainder, be it more or less, of an agitated and active life, now reduced (and I am not sure that I am a loser by the change) to so quiet and serene a one, that it may properly be called still life.

The French whisper in confidence, in order that it may be the more known and the more credited, that they intend to invade us this year, in no less than three places; that is England, Scotland, and Ireland. Some of our great men, like the devils, believe and tremble; others, and one little one whom I know, laugh at it; and, in general, it seems to be but a poor, instead of a formidable scarecrow. While somebody was at the head of a moderate army, and wanted (I know why) to be at the head of a great one, intended invasions were made an article of political faith; and the belief of them was required, as in the Church the belief of some absurdities, and even impossibilities, is required upon pain of heresy, excommunication, and consequently damnation, if they tend to the power and interest of the heads of the Church. But now that there is a general toleration, and that the best subjects, as well as the best Christians, may believe what their reasons find their consciences suggest, it is generally and rationally supposed the French will threaten and not strike, since we are so well prepared, both by armies and fleets, to receive and, I may add, to destroy them. Adieu! God bless you.

LETTER CCXLV

BLACKHEATH, June 15, 1759

MY DEAR FRIEND: Your letter of the 5th, which I received yesterday, gave me great satisfaction, being all in your own hand; though it contains great, and I fear just complaints of your ill state of health. You do very well to change the air; and I hope that change will do well by you. I would therefore have you write after the 20th of August, to Lord Holderness, to beg of him to obtain his Majesty's leave for you to return to England for two or three months, upon account of your health. Two or three months is an indefinite time, which may afterward insensibly stretched to what length one pleases; leave that to me. In the meantime, you may be taking your measures with the best economy.

The day before yesterday, an express arrived from Guadaloupe which brought an account of our being in possession of the whole island. And I make no manner of doubt but that, in about two months, we shall have as good news from Crown-point, Quebec, etc. Our affairs in Germany, I fear, will not be equally prosperous; for I have very little hopes for the King of Prussia or Prince Ferdinand. God bless you.

LETTER CCXLVI

BLACKHEATH, June 25, 1759

MY DEAR FRIEND: The two last mails have brought me no letter from you or your secretary. I will take this as a sign that you are better; but, however, if you thought that I cared to know, you should have cared to have written. Here the weather has been very fine for a fortnight together, a longer term than in this climate we are used to hold fine weather by. I hope it is so, too, at Hamburg, or at least at the villa to which you are gone; but pray do not let it be your 'villa viciosa', as those retirements are often called, and too often prove; though, by the way, the original name was 'villa vezzosa'; and by wags miscalled 'viciosa'.

I have a most gloomy prospect of affairs in Germany; the French are already in possession of Cassel, and of the learned part of Hanover, that is Gottingen; where I presume they will not stop 'pour l'amour des belles lettres', but rather go on to the capital, and study them upon the coin. My old acquaintance, Monsieur Richelieu, made a great progress there in metallic learning and inscriptions. If Prince Ferdinand ventures a battle to prevent it, I dread the consequences; the odds are too great against him. The King of Prussia is still in a worse situation; for he has the Hydra to encounter; and though he may cut off a head or two, there will still be enough left to devour him at last. I have, as you know, long foretold the now approaching catastrophe; but I was Cassandra. Our affairs in the new world have a much more pleasing aspect; Guadaloupe is a great acquisition, and Quebec, which I make no doubt of, will still be greater. But must all these advantages, purchased at the price of so much English blood and treasure, be at last sacrificed as a peace-offering? God knows what consequences such a measure may produce; the germ of discontent is already great, upon the bare supposition of the case; but should it be realized, it will grow to a harvest of disaffection.

EARL OF PHILIP DORMER STANHOPE CHESTERFIELD

You are now, to be sure, taking the previous necessary measures for your return here in the autumn and I think you may disband your whole family, excepting your secretary, your butler, who takes care of your plate, wine, etc., one or at most two, maid servants, and your valet de chambre and one footman, whom you will bring over with you. But give no mortal, either there or here, reason to think that you are not to return to Hamburg again. If you are asked about it, say, like Lockhart, that you are 'le serviteur des Evenemens'; for your present appointments will do you no hurt here, till you have some better destination. At that season of the year, I believe it will be better for you to come by sea than by land, but that you will be best able to judge of from the then circumstances of your part in the world.

Your old friend Stevens is dead of the consumption that has long been undermining him. God bless you, and send you health.

[Another two year lapse in the letters. D.W.] LETTER CCXLVII

BATH, February 26, 1761.

MY DEAR FRIEND: I am very glad to hear that your election is finally settled, and to say the truth, not sorry that Mr.———has been compelled to do, 'de mauvaise grace', that which he might have done at first in a friendly and handsome manner. However, take no notice of what is passed, and live with him as you used to do before; for, in the intercourse of the world, it is often necessary to seem ignorant of what one knows, and to have forgotten what one remembers.

I have just now finished Coleman's play, and like it very well; it is well conducted, and the characters are well preserved. I own, I expected from the author more dialogue wit; but, as I know that he is a most scrupulous classic, I believe he did not dare to put in half so much wit as he could have done, because Terence had not a single grain; and it would have been 'crimen laesae antiquitatis'. God bless you!

LETTER CCXLVIII

BATH, November 21, 1761.

MY DEAR FRIEND: I have this moment received your letter of the 19th. If I find any alterations by drinking these waters, now six days, it is rather for the better; but, in six days more, I think I shall find with more certainty what humor they are in with me; if kind, I will profit of, but not abuse their kindness; all things have their bounds, 'quos ultra citrave nequit consistere rectum'; and I will endeavor to nick that point.

The Queen's jointure is larger than, from SOME REASONS, I expected it would be, though not greater than the very last precedent authorized. The case of the late Lord Wilmington was, I fancy, remembered.

I have now good reason to believe that Spain will declare war to us, that is, that it will very soon, if it has not already, avowedly assist France, in case the war continues. This will be a great triumph to Mr. Pitt, and fully justify his plan of beginning with Spain first, and having the first blow, which is often half the battle.

Here is a great deal of company, and what is commonly called good company, that is, great quality. I trouble them very little, except at the pump, where my business calls me; for what is company to a deaf man, or a deaf man to company?

Lady Brown, whom I have seen, and who, by the way, has got the gout in her eye, inquired very tenderly after you. And so I elegantly rest, Yours, till death.

LETTER CCXLIX

BATH, December 6, 1761.

MY DEAR FRIEND: I have been in your debt some time, which, you know, I am not very apt to be: but it was really for want of specie to pay. The present state of my invention does not enable me to coin; and you would have had as little pleasure in reading, as I should have in writing 'le coglionerie' of this place; besides, that I am very little mingled in them. I do not know whether I shall be able to follow, your advice, and cut a winner; for, at present, I have neither won nor lost a single shilling. I will play on this week only; and if I have a good run, I will carry it off with me; if a bad one, the loss can hardly amount to anything considerable in seven days, for I hope to see you in town to-morrow sevennight.

I had a dismal letter from Harte, last week; he tells me that he is at nurse with a sister in Berkshire; that he has got a confirmed jaundice, besides twenty other distempers. The true cause of these complaints I take to be the same that so greatly disordered, and had nearly destroyed the most august House of Austria, about one hundred and thirty years ago; I mean Gustavus Adolphus; who neither answered his expectations in point of profit nor reputation, and that merely by his own fault, in not writing it in the vulgar tongue; for as to facts I will maintain that it is one of the best histories extant.

'Au revoir', as Sir Fopling says, and God bless you!

LETTER CCL

BATH, November 2, 1762.

MY DEAR FRIEND: I arrived here, as I proposed, last Sunday; but as ill as I feared I should be when I saw you. Head, stomach, and limbs, all out of order.

I have yet seen nobody but Villettes, who is settled here for good, as it is called. What consequences has the Duke of Devonshire's resignation had? He has considerable connections and relations; but whether any of them are resigned enough to resign with him, is another matter. There will be, to be sure, as many, and as absurd reports, as there are in the law books; I do not desire to know either; but inform me of what facts come to your knowledge, and of such reports only as you believe are grounded. And so God bless you!

LETTER CCLI

BATH, November 13, 1762.

MY DEAR FRIEND: I have received your letter, and believe that your preliminaries are very near the mark; and, upon that supposition, I think we have made a tolerable good bargain with Spain; at least full as good as I expected, and almost as good as I wished, though I do not believe that we have got ALL Florida; but if we have St. Augustin, I suppose that, by the figure of 'pars pro toto', will be called all Florida. We have by no means made so good a bargain with France; for, in truth, what do we get by it, except Canada, with a very proper boundary of the river Mississippi! and that is all. As for the restrictions upon the French fishery in Newfoundland, they are very well 'per la predica', and for the Commissary whom we shall employ: for he will have a good salary from hence, to see that those restrictions are complied with; and the French will double that salary, that he may allow them all to be broken through. It is plain to me, that the French fishery will be exactly what it was before the war.

The three Leeward islands, which the French yield to us, are not, all together, worth half so much as that of St. Lucia, which we give up to them. Senegal is not worth one quarter of Goree. The restrictions of the French in the East Indies are as absurd and impracticable as those of Newfoundland; and you will live to see the French trade to the East Indies, just as they did before the war. But after all I have said, the articles are as good as I expected with France, when I considered that no one single person who carried on this negotiation on our parts was ever concerned or consulted in any negotiation before. Upon the whole, then, the acquisition of Canada has cost us fourscore millions sterling. I am convinced we might have kept Guadaloupe, if our negotiators had known how to have gone about it.

His most faithful Majesty of Portugal is the best off of anybody in this, transaction, for he saves his kingdom by it, and has not laid out one moidore in defense of it. Spain, thank God, in some measure, 'paye les pots cassis'; for, besides St. Augustin, logwood, etc., it has lost at least four millions sterling, in money, ships, etc.

Harte is here, who tells me he has been at this place these three years, excepting some few excursions to his sister; he looks ill, and laments that he has frequent fits of the yellow jaundice. He complains of his not having heard from you these four years; you should write to him. These waters have done me a great deal of good, though I drink but two-thirds of a pint in the whole day, which is less than the soberest of my countrymen drink of claret at every meal.

I should naturally think, as you do, that this session will be a stormy one, that is, if Mr. Pitt takes an active part; but if he is pleased, as the Ministers say, there is no other AEolus to blow a storm. The Dukes of Cumberland, Newcastle, and Devonshire, have no better troops to attack with than the militia; but Pitt alone is ipse agmen. God bless you!

LETTER CCLII

BATH, November 27, 1762.

MY DEAR FRIEND: I received your letter this morning, and return you the ball 'a la volee'. The King's speech is a very prudent one; and as I suppose that the addresses in answer to it were, as usual, in almost the same words, my Lord Mayor might very well call them innocent. As his Majesty expatiates so much upon the great ACHIEVEMENTS of the war, I cannot help hoping that, when the preliminaries shall be laid before Parliament IN DUE TIME, which, I suppose, means after the respective ratifications of all the contracting parties, that some untalked of and unexpected advantage will break out in our treaty with France; St. Lucia, at least. I see in the newspapers an article which I by no means like, in our treaty with Spain; which is, that we shall be at liberty to cut logwood in the Bay of Campeachy, BUT BY PAYING FOR IT. Who does not see that this condition may, and probably will, amount to a prohibition, by the price which the Spaniards may set it at? It was our undoubted right, and confirmed to us by former treaties, before the war, to cut logwood gratis; but this new stipulation (if true) gives us a privilege something like a reprieve to a criminal, with a 'non obstante' to be hanged.

I now drink so little water, that it can neither do me good nor hurt; but as I bathe but twice a-week, that operation, which does my rheumatic carcass good, will keep me here some time longer than you had allowed.

Harte is going to publish a new edition of his "Gustavus," in octavo; which, he tells me, he has altered, and which, I could tell him, he should translate into English, or it will not sell better than the former; for, while the world endures, style and manner will be regarded, at least as much as matter. And so, 'Diem vous aye dans sa sainte garde'!

LETTER CCLIII

BATH, December 13, 1762.

MY DEAR FRIEND: I received your letter this morning, with the inclosed preliminaries, which we have had here these three days; and I return them, since you intend to keep them, which is more than I believe the French will. I am very glad to find that the French are to restore all the conquests they made upon us in the East Indies during this war; and I cannot doubt but they will likewise restore to us all the cod that they shall take within less than three leagues of our coasts in North America (a distance easily measured, especially at sea), according to the spirit, though not the letter of the treaty. I am informed that the strong opposition to the peace will be in the House of Lords, though I cannot well conceive it; nor can I make out above six or seven, who will be against it upon a division, unless (which I cannot suppose) some of the Bishops should vote on the side of their maker. God bless you.

LETTER CCLIV

BATH, December 13, 1762.

MY DEAR FRIEND: Yesterday I received your letter, which gave me a very clear account of the debate in your House. It is impossible for a human creature to speak well for three hours and a half; I question even if Belial, who, according to Milton, was the orator of the fallen angels, ever spoke so long at a time.

There must have been, a trick in Charles Townshend's speaking for the Preliminaries; for he is infinitely above having an opinion. Lord Egremont must be ill, or have thoughts of going into some other place;

perhaps into Lord Granville's, who they say is dying: when he dies, the ablest head in England dies too, take it for all in all.

I shall be in town, barring accidents, this day sevennight, by dinnertime; when I have ordered a haricot, to which you will be very welcome, about four o'clock. 'En attendant Dieu vous aye dans sa sainte garde'!

LETTER CCLV

BLACKHEATH, June 14, 1763

MY DEAR FRIEND: I received, by the last mail, your letter of the 4th, from The Hague; so far so good.

You arrived 'sonica' at The Hague, for our Ambassador's entertainment; I find he has been very civil to you. You are in the right to stop for two or three days at Hanau, and make your court to the lady of that place. — [Her Royal Highness Princess Mary of England, Landgravine of Hesse.] —Your Excellency makes a figure already in the newspapers; and let them, and others, excellency you as much as they please, but pray suffer not your own servants to do it.

Nothing new of any kind has happened here since you went; so I will wish you a good-night, and hope God will bless you.

LETTER CCLVI

BLACKHEATH, July 14, 1763

MY DEAR FRIEND: Yesterday I received your letter from Ratisbon, where I am glad that you are arrived safe. You are, I find, over head and ears engaged in ceremony and etiquette. You must not yield in anything essential, where your public character may suffer; but I advise you, at the same time, to distinguish carefully what may, and what may not affect it, and to despise some German 'minutiae'; such as one step lower or higher upon the stairs, a bow more or less, and such sort of trifles.

By what I see in Cressener's letter to you, the cheapness of wine compensates the quantity, as the cheapness of servants compensates the number that you must make use of.

Write to your mother often, if it be but three words, to prove your existence; for, when she does not hear from you, she knows to a demonstration that you are dead, if not buried.

The inclosed is a letter of the utmost consequence, which I was desired to forward, with care and speed, to the most Serene LOUIS.

My head is not well to-day. So God bless you!

LETTER CCLVII

BLACKHEATH, August 1, 1763.

MY DEAR FRIEND: I hope that by this time you are pretty well settled at Ratisbon, at least as to the important points of the ceremonial; so that you may know, to precision, to whom you must give, and from whom you must require the 'seine Excellentz'. Those formalities are, no doubt, ridiculous enough in themselves; but yet they are necessary for manners, and sometimes for business; and both would suffer by laying them quite aside.

I have lately had an attack of a new complaint, which I have long suspected that I had in my body, 'in actu primo', as the pedants call it, but which I never felt in 'actu secundo' till last week, and that is a fit of the stone or gravel. It was, thank God, but a slight one; but it was 'dans toutes les formes'; for it was preceded by a pain in my loins, which I at first took for some remains of my rheumatism; but was soon convinced of my mistake, by making water much blacker than coffee, with a prodigious sediment of gravel. I am now perfectly easy again, and have no more indications of this complaint.

God keep you from that and deafness! Other complaints are the common, and almost the inevitable lot of human nature, but admit of some mitigation. God bless you!

LETTER CCLVIII

BLACKHEATH, August 22, 1763

MY DEAR FRIEND: You will, by this post, hear from others that Lord Egremont died two days ago of an apoplexy; which, from his figure, and the constant plethora he lived in, was reasonably to be expected. You will ask me, who is to be Secretary in his room: To which I answer, that I do not know. I should guess Lord Sandwich, to be succeeded in the Admiralty by Charles Townshend; unless the Duke of Bedford, who seems to have taken to himself the department of Europe, should have a mind to it. This event may perhaps produce others; but, till this happened, everything was in a state of inaction, and absolutely nothing was done. Before the next session, this chaos must necessarily take some form, either by a new jumble of its own atoms, or by mixing them with the more efficient ones of the opposition.

I see by the newspapers, as well as by your letter, that the difficulties still exist about your ceremonial at Ratisbon; should they, from pride and folly, prove insuperable, and obstruct your real business, there is one expedient which may perhaps remove difficulties, and which I have often known practiced; but which I believe our people know here nothing of; it is, to have the character of MINISTER only in your ostensible title, and that of envoy extraordinary in your pocket, to produce occasionally, especially if you should be sent to any of the Electors in your neighborhood; or else, in any transactions that you may have, in which your title of envoy extraordinary may create great difficulties, to have a reversal given you, declaring that the temporary suspension of that character, 'ne donnera pas la moindre atteinte ni a vos droits, ni a vos pretensions'. As for the rest, divert yourself as well as you can, and eat and drink as little as you can. And so God bless you!

LETTER CCLIX

BLACKHEATH, September 1, 1763

MY DEAR FRIEND: Great news! The King sent for Mr. Pitt last Saturday, and the conference lasted a full hour; on the Monday following another conference, which lasted much longer; and yesterday a third, longer than either. You take for granted, that the treaty was concluded and ratified; no such matter, for this last conference broke it entirely off; and Mr. Pitt and Lord Temple went yesterday evening to their respective country houses. Would you know what it broke off upon, you must ask the newsmongers, and the coffee-houses; who, I dare say, know it all very minutely; but I, who am not apt to know anything that I do not know, honestly and humbly confess, that I cannot tell you; probably one party asked too much, and the other would grant too little. However, the King's dignity was not, in my mind, much consulted by their making him sole plenipotentiary of a treaty, which they were not in all events determined to conclude. It ought surely to have been begun by some inferior agent, and his Majesty should only have appeared in rejecting or ratifying it. Louis XIV. never sat down before a town in person, that was not sure to be taken.

However, 'ce qui est differe n'est pas perdu'; for this matter must be taken up again, and concluded before the meeting of the parliament, and probably upon more disadvantageous terms to the present Ministers, who have tacitly admitted, by this negotiation, what their enemies have loudly proclaimed, that they are not able to carry on affairs. So much 'de re politica'.

I have at last done the best office that can be done to most married people; that is, I have fixed the separation between my brother and his wife; and the definitive treaty of peace will be proclaimed in about a fortnight; for the only solid and lasting peace, between a man and his wife, is, doubtless, a separation. God bless you!

LETTER CCLX

BLACKHEATH, September 30, 1763

MY DEAR FRIEND: You will have known, long before this, from the office, that the departments are not cast as you wished; for Lord Halifax, as senior, had of course his choice, and chose the southern, upon account of the colonies. The Ministry, such as it is, is now settled 'en attendant mieux'; but, in, my opinion cannot, as they are, meet the parliament.

The only, and all the efficient people they have, are in the House of Lords: for since Mr. Pitt has firmly engaged Charles Townshend to him, there is not a man of the court side, in the House of Commons, who has either abilities or words enough to call a coach. Lord B——is certainly playing 'un dessous de cartes', and I suspect that it is with Mr. Pitt; but what that 'dessous' is, I do not know, though all the coffeehouses do most exactly.

The present inaction, I believe, gives you leisure enough for 'ennui', but it gives you time enough too for better things; I mean reading useful books; and, what is still more useful, conversing with yourself some part of every day. Lord Shaftesbury recommends self-conversation to all authors; and I would recommend it to all men; they would be the better for it. Some people have not time, and fewer have inclination, to enter into that conversation; nay, very many dread it, and fly to the most trifling dissipations, in order to avoid it; but, if a man would allot half an hour every night for this self-conversation, and recapitulate with himself whatever he has done, right or wrong, in the course of the day, he would be both the better and the wiser for it. My deafness gives me more than a sufficient time for self-conversation; and I have found great advantages from it. My brother and Lady Stanhope are at last finally parted. I was the negotiator between them; and had so much trouble in it, that I would much rather negotiate the most difficult point of the 'jus publicum Sacri

Romani Imperii' with the whole Diet of Ratisbon, than negotiate any point with any woman. If my brother had had some of those self-conversations, which I recommend, he would not, I believe, at past sixty, with a crazy, battered constitution, and deaf into the bargain, have married a young girl, just turned of twenty, full of health, and consequently of desires. But who takes warning by the fate of others? This, perhaps, proceeds from a negligence of selfconversation. God bless you.

LETTER CCLXI

BLACKHEATH, October 17, 1763

MY DEAR FRIEND: The last mail brought me your letter of the 2d instant, as the former had brought me that of the 25th past. I did suppose that you would be sent over, for the first day of the session; as I never knew a stricter muster, and no furloughs allowed. I am very sorry for it, for the reasons you hint at; but, however, you did very prudently, in doing, 'de bonne grace', what you could not help doing; and let that be your rule in every thing for the rest of your life. Avoid disagreeable things as much as by dexterity you can; but when they are unavoidable, do them with seeming willingness and alacrity. Though this journey is ill-timed for you in many respects, yet, in point of FINANCES, you will be a gainer by it upon the whole; for, depend upon it, they will keep you here till the very last day of the session: and I suppose you have sold your horses, and dismissed some of your servants. Though they seem to apprehend the first day of the session so much, in my opinion their danger will be much greater in the course of it.

When you are at Paris, you will of course wait upon Lord Hertford, and desire him to present you to the King; at the same time make my compliments to him, and thank him for the very obliging message he left at my house in town; and tell him, that, had I received it in time from thence, I would have come to town on purpose to have returned it in person. If there are any new little books at Paris, pray bring them me. I have already Voltaire's 'Zelis dans le Bain', his 'Droit du Seigneur', and 'Olympie'. Do not forget to call once at Madame Monconseil's, and as often as you please at Madame du Pin's. Au revoir.

LETTER CCLXII

BATH, November 24, 1763

MY DEAR FRIEND: I arrived here, as you suppose in your letter, last Sunday; but after the worst day's journey I ever had in my life: it snowed and froze that whole morning, and in the evening it rained and thawed, which made the roads so slippery, that I was six hours coming post from the Devizes, which is but eighteen miles from hence; so that, but for the name of coming post, I might as well have walked on foot. I have not yet quite got over my last violent attack, and am weak and flimsy.

I have now drank the waters but three days; so that, without a miracle, I cannot yet expect much alteration, and I do not in the least expect a miracle. If they proved 'les eaux de Jouvence' to me, that would be a miracle indeed; but, as the late Pope Lambertini said, 'Fra noi, gli miracoli sono passati girt un pezzo'.

I have seen Harte, who inquired much after you: he is dejected and dispirited, and thinks himself much worse than he is, though he has really a tendency to the jaundice. I have yet seen nobody else, nor do I know who here is to be seen; for I have not yet exhibited myself to public view, except at the pump, which, at the time I go to it, is the most private place in Bath.

After all the fears and hopes, occasioned severally by the meeting of the parliament, in my opinion, it will prove a very easy session. Mr. Wilkes is universally given up; and if the ministers themselves do not wantonly raise difficulties, I think they will meet with none. A majority of two hundred is a great anodyne. Adieu! God bless you!

LETTER CCLXIII

BATH, December 3, 1763.

MY DEAR FRIEND: Last post brought me your letter of the 29th past. I suppose C——-T——-let off his speech upon the Princess's portion, chiefly to show that he was of the opposition; for otherwise, the point was not debatable, unless as to the quantum, against which something might be said; for the late Princess of Orange (who was the eldest daughter of a king) had no more, and her two sisters but half, if I am not mistaken.

It is a great mercy that Mr. Wilkes, the intrepid defender of our rights and liberties, is out of danger, and may live to fight and write again in support of them; and it is no less a mercy, that God hath raised up the Earl of S———to vindicate and promote true religion and morality. These two blessings will justly make an epoch in the annals of this country.

I have delivered your message to Harte, who waits with impatience for your letter. He is very happy now in having free access to all Lord Craven's papers, which, he says, give him great lights into the 'bellum tricenale'; the old Lord Craven having been the professed and valorous knight-errant, and perhaps something more, to the Queen of Bohemia; at least, like Sir Peter Pride, he had the honor of spending great part of his estate in her royal cause:

I am by no means right yet; I am very weak and flimsy still; but the doctor assures me that strength and spirits will return; if they do, 'lucro apponam', I will make the best of them; if they do not, I will not make their want still worse by grieving and regretting them. I have lived long enough, and observed enough, to estimate most things at their intrinsic, and not their imaginary value; and, at seventy, I find nothing much worth either desiring or fearing. But these reflections, which suit with seventy, would be greatly premature at two-and-thirty. So make the best of your time; enjoy the present hour, but 'memor ultimae'. God bless you!

LETTER CCLXIV

BATH, December 18, 1763

MY DEAR FRIEND: I received your letter this morning, in which you reproach me with not having written to you this week. The reason was, that I did not know what to write. There is that sameness in my life here, that EVERY DAY IS STILL BUT AS THE FIRST. I see very few people; and, in the literal sense of the word, I hear nothing.

Mr. L———and Mr. C———I hold to be two very ingenious men; and your image of the two men ruined, one by losing his law-suit, and the other by carrying it, is a very just one. To be sure, they felt in themselves uncommon talents for business and speaking, which were to reimburse them.

Harte has a great poetical work to publish, before it be long; he has shown me some parts of it. He had entitled it "Emblems," but I persuaded him to alter that name for two reasons; the first was, because they were not emblems, but fables; the second was, that if they had been emblems, Quarles had degraded and vilified that name to such a degree, that it is impossible to make use of it after him; so they are to be called fables, though moral tales would, in my mind, be the properest name. If you ask me what I think of those I have seen, I must say, that 'sunt plura bona, quaedam mediocria, et quaedam———'

Your report of future changes, I cannot think is wholly groundless; for it still runs strongly in my head, that the mine we talked of will be sprung, at or before the end of the session.

I have got a little more strength, but not quite the strength of Hercules; so that I will not undertake, like him, fifty deflorations in one night; for I really believe that I could not compass them. So good-night, and God bless you!

LETTER CCLXV

BATH, December 24, 1763.

DEAR FRIEND: I confess I was a good deal surprised at your pressing me so strongly to influence Parson Rosenhagen, when you well know the resolution I had made several years ago, and which I have scrupulously observed ever since, not to concern myself, directly or indirectly, in any party political contest whatsoever. Let parties go to loggerheads as much and as long as they please; I will neither endeavor to part them, nor take the part of either; for I know them all too well. But you say, that Lord Sandwich has been remarkably civil, and kind to you. I am very glad of it, and he can by no means impute to you my obstinacy, folly, or philosophy, call it what you please: you may with great truth assure him, that you did all you could to obey his commands.

I am sorry to find that you are out of order, but I hope it is only a cold; should it be anything more, pray consult Dr. Maty, who did you so much good in your last illness, when the great medicinal Mattadores did you rather harm. I have found a Monsieur Diafoirus here, Dr. Moisy, who has really done me a great deal of good; and I am sure I wanted it a great deal when I came here first. I have recovered some strength, and a little more will give me as much as I can make use of.

Lady Brown, whom I saw yesterday, makes you many compliments; and I wish you a merry Christmas, and a good-night. Adieu!

LETTER CCLXVI

BATH, December 31, 1763

MY DEAR FRIEND: Gravenkop wrote me word, by the last post, that you were laid up with the gout: but I much question it, that is, whether it is the gout or not. Your last illness, before you went abroad, was pronounced the gout, by the skillful, and proved at last a mere rheumatism. Take care that the same mistake is not made this year; and that by giving you strong and hot medicines to throw out the gout, they do not inflame the rheumatism, if it be one.

Mr. Wilkes has imitated some of the great men of antiquity, by going into voluntary exile: it was his only way of defeating both his creditors and his prosecutors. Whatever his friends, if he has any, give out of his returning soon, I will answer for it, that it will be a long time before that soon comes.

I have been much out of order these four days of a violent cold which I do not know how I got, and which obliged me to suspend drinking the waters: but it is now so much better, that I propose resuming them for this week, and paying my court to you in town on Monday or Tuesday seven-night: but this is 'sub spe rati' only. God bless you!

LETTER CCLXVII

BLACKHEATH, July 20, 1764.

MY DEAR FRIEND: I have this moment received your letter of the 3d from Prague, but I never received that which you mention from Ratisbon; this made me think you in such rapid motion, that I did not know where to take aim. I now suppose that you are arrived, though not yet settled, at Dresden; your audiences and formalities are, to be sure, over, and that is great ease of mind to you.

I have no political events to acquaint you with; the summer is not the season for them, they ripen only in winter; great ones are expected immediately before the meeting of parliament, but that, you know, is always the language of fears and hopes. However, I rather believe that there will be something patched up between the INS and the OUTS.

The whole subject of conversation, at present, is the death and will of Lord Bath: he has left above twelve hundred thousand pounds in land and money; four hundred thousand pounds in cash, stocks, and mortgages; his own estate, in land, was improved to fifteen thousand pounds a-year, and the Bradford estate, which he———is as much; both which, at only five-and twenty years' purchase, amount to eight hundred thousand pounds; and all this he has left to his brother, General Pulteney, and in his own disposal, though he never loved him. The legacies he has left are trifling; for, in truth, he cared for nobody: the words GIVE and BEQUEATH were too shocking for him to repeat, and so he left all in one word to his brother. The public, which was long the dupe of his simulation and dissimulation, begins to explain upon him; and draws such a picture of him as I gave you long ago.

Your late secretary has been with me three or four times; he wants something or another, and it seems all one to him what, whether civil or military; in plain English, he wants bread. He has knocked at the doors of some of the ministers, but to no purpose. I wish with all my heart that I could help him: I told him fairly that I could not, but advised him to find some channel to Lord B———, which, though a Scotchman, he told me he could not. He brought a packet of letters from the office to you, which I made him seal up; and keep it for you, as I suppose it makes up the series of your Ratisbon letters.

As for me, I am just what I was when you left me, that is, nobody. Old age steals upon me insensibly. I grow weak and decrepit, but do not suffer, and so I am content.

Forbes brought me four books of yours, two of which were Bielefeldt's "Letters," in which, to my knowledge, there are many notorious lies.

Make my compliments to Comte Einsiedel, whom I love and honor much; and so good-night to 'seine Excellentz'.

Now our correspondence may be more regular, and I expect a letter from you every fortnight. I will be regular on my part: but write oftener to your mother, if it be but three lines.

LETTER CCLXVIII

BLACKHEATH, July 27, 1764

MY DEAR FRIEND: I received, two days ago, your letter of the 11th from Dresden, where I am very glad that, you are safely arrived at last. The prices of the necessaries of life are monstrous there; and I do not conceive how the poor natives subsist at all, after having been so long and so often plundered by their own as well as by other sovereigns.

As for procuring you either the title or the appointments of Plenipotentiary, I could as soon procure them from the Turkish as from the English Ministry; and, in truth, I believe they have it not to give.

Now to come to your civil list, if one may compare small things with great: I think I have found out a better refreshment for it than you propose; for to-morrow I shall send to your cashier, Mr. Larpent, five hundred pounds at once, for your use, which, I presume, is better than by quarterly payments; and I am very apt to think that next midsummer day, he will have the same sum, and for the same use, consigned to him.

It is reported here, and I believe not without some foundation, that the queen of Hungary has acceded to the

Family Compact between France and Spain: if so, I am sure it behooves us to form in time a counter alliance, of at least equal strength; which I could easily point out, but which, I fear, is not thought of here.

The rage of marrying is very prevalent; so that there will be probably a great crop of cuckolds next winter, who are at present only 'cocus en herbs'. It will contribute to population, and so far must be allowed to be a public benefit. Lord G———, Mr. B————, and Mr. D————, are, in this respect, very meritorious; for they have all married handsome women, without one shilling fortune. Lord must indeed take some pains to arrive at that dignity: but I dare say he will bring it about, by the help of some young Scotch or Irish officer. Good-night, and God bless you!

LETTER CCLXIX

BLACKHEATH, September 3, 1764.

DEAR FRIEND: I have received your letter of the 13th past. I see that your complete arrangement approaches, and you need not be in a hurry to give entertainments, since so few others do.

Comte Flemming is the man in the world the best calculated to retrieve the Saxon finances, which have been all this century squandered and lavished with the most absurd profusion: he has certainly abilities, and I believe integrity; I dare answer for him, that the gentleness and flexibility of his temper will not prevail with him to yield to the importunities of craving and petulant applications. I see in him another Sully; and therefore I wish he were at the head of our finances.

France and Spain both insult us, and we take it too tamely; for this is, in my opinion, the time for us to talk high to them. France, I am persuaded, will not quarrel with us till it has got a navy at least equal to ours, which cannot be these three or four years at soonest; and then, indeed, I believe we shall hear of something or other; therefore, this is the moment for us to speak loud; and we shall be feared, if we do not show that we fear.

Here is no domestic news of changes and chances in the political world; which, like oysters, are only in season in the R months, when the parliament sits. I think there will be some then, but of what kind, God knows.

I have received a book for you, and one for myself, from Harte. It is upon agriculture, and will surprise you, as I confess it did me. This work is not only in English, but good and elegant English; he has even scattered graces upon his subject; and in prose, has come very near Virgil's "Georgics" in verse. I have written to him, to congratulate his happy transformation. As soon as I can find an opportunity, I will send you your copy.

EARL OF PHILIP DORMER STANHOPE CHESTERFIELD

You (though no Agricola) will read it with pleasure.

I know Mackenzie, whom you mention. 'C'est une delie; sed cave'.

Make mine and Lady Chesterfield's compliments to Comte et Comtesse Flemming; and so, 'Dieu vous aye en sa sainte garde'!

LETTER CCLXX

BLACKHEATH, September 14, 1764

MY DEAR FRIEND: Yesterday I received your letter of the 30th past, by which I find that you had not then got mine, which I sent you the day after I had received your former; you have had no great loss of it; for, as I told you in my last, this inactive season of the year supplies no materials for a letter; the winter may, and probably will, produce an abundant crop, but of what grain I neither know, guess, nor care. I take it for granted, that Lord B———'surnagera encore', but by the assistance of what bladders or cork-waistcoats God only knows. The death of poor Mr. Legge, the epileptic fits of the Duke of Devonshire, for which he is gone to Aix-la-Chapelle, and the advanced age of the Duke of Newcastle, seem to facilitate an accommodation, if Mr. Pitt and Lord Bute are inclined to it.

You ask me what I think of the death of poor Iwan, and of the person who ordered it. You may remember that I often said, she would murder or marry him, or probably both; she has chosen the safest alternative; and has now completed her character of femme forte, above scruples and hesitation. If Machiavel were alive, she would probably be his heroine, as Caesar Borgia was his hero. Women are all so far Machiavelians, that they are never either good or bad by halves; their passions are too strong, and their reason too weak, to do anything with moderation. She will, perhaps, meet, before it is long, with some Scythian as free from prejudices as herself. If there is one Oliver Cromwell in the three regiments of guards, he will probably, for the sake of his dear country, depose and murder her; for that is one and the same thing in Russia.

You seem now to have settled, and 'bien nippe' at Dresden. Four sedentary footmen, and one running one, 'font equipage leste'. The German ones will give you, 'seine Excellentz'; and the French ones, if you have any, Monseigneur.

My own health varies, as usual, but never deviates into good. God bless you, and send you better!

LETTER CCLXXI

BLACKHEATH, October 4, 1764.

MY DEAR FRIEND: I have now your last letter, of the 16th past, lying before me, and I gave your inclosed to Grevenkop, which has put him into a violent bustle to execute your commissions, as well and as cheap as possible. I refer him to his own letter. He tells you true as to Comtesse Cosel's diamonds, which certainly nobody will buy here, unsight unseen, as they call it; so many minutiae concurring to increase or lessen the value of a diamond. Your Cheshire cheese, your Burton ale and beer, I charge myself with, and they shall be sent you as soon as possible. Upon this occasion I will give you a piece of advice, which by experience I know to be useful. In all commissions, whether from men or women, 'point de galanterie', bring them in your account, and be paid to the uttermost farthing; but if you would show them 'une galanterie', let your present be of something that is not in your commission, otherwise you will be the 'Commissionaire banal' of all the women of Saxony. 'A propos', Who is your Comtesse de Cosel? Is she daughter, or grand-daughter, of the famous Madame de Cosel, in King Augustus's time? Is she young or old, ugly or handsome?

I do not wonder that people are wonderfully surprised at our tameness and forbearance, with regard to France and Spain. Spain, indeed, has lately agreed to our cutting log wood, according to the treaty, and sent strict orders to their governor to allow it; but you will observe too, that there is not one word of reparation for the losses we lately sustained there. But France is not even so tractable; it will pay but half the money due, upon a liquidated account, for the maintenance of their prisoners. Our request, to have the Comte d'Estaing recalled and censured, they have absolutely rejected, though, by the laws of war, he might be hanged for having twice broke his parole. This does not do France honor: however, I think we shall be quiet, and that at the only time, perhaps this century, when we might, with safety, be otherwise: but this is nothing new, nor the first time, by many, when national honor and interest have been sacrificed to private. It has always been so: and one may say, upon this occasion, what Horace says upon another, 'Nam fuit ante Helenam'.

I have seen 'les Contes de Guillaume Vade', and like most of them so little, that I can hardly think them Voltaire's, but rather the scraps that have fallen from his table, and been worked up by inferior workmen, under his name. I have not seen the other book you mention, the 'Dictionnaire Portatif'. It is not yet come over.

I shall next week go to take my winter quarters in London, the weather here being very cold and damp, and not proper for an old, shattered, and cold carcass, like mine. In November I will go to the Bath, to careen myself for the winter, and to shift the scene. Good-night.

LETTER CCLXXII

LONDON, October 19, 1764.

MY DEAR FRIEND: Yesterday morning Mr.———came to me, from Lord Halifax, to ask me whether I thought you would approve of vacating your seat in parliament, during the remainder of it, upon a valuable consideration, meaning MONEY. My answer was, that I really did not know your disposition upon that subject: but that I knew you would be very willing, in general, to accommodate them, so far as lay in your power: that your election, to my knowledge, had cost you two thousand pounds; that this parliament had not sat above half its time; and that, for my part, I approved of the measure well enough, provided you had an equitable equivalent. I take it for granted that you will have a letter from———, by this post, to that effect, so that you must consider what you will do. What I advise is this: Give them a good deal of 'Galbanum' in the first part of your letter. 'Le Galbanum ne coute rien'; and then say that you are willing to do as they please; but that you hope an equitable consideration will be had to the two thousand pounds, which your seat cost you in the present parliament, of which not above half the term is expired. Moreover, that you take the liberty to remind them, that your being sent from Ratisbon, last session, when you were just settled there, put you to the expense of three or four hundred pounds, for which you were allowed nothing; and that, therefore, you hope they will not think one thousand pounds too much, considering all these circumstances: but that, in all events, you will do whatever they desire. Upon the whole, I think this proposal advantageous to you, as you probably will not make use of your seat this parliament; and, further, as it will secure you from another unpaid journey from Dresden, in case they meet, or fear to meet, with difficulties in any ensuing session of the present parliament. Whatever one must do, one should do 'de bonne grace'. 'Dixi'. God bless you!

LETTER CCLXXIII

BATH, November 10, 1764.

MY DEAR FRIEND: I am much concerned at the account you gave me of yourself, in your last letter. There is, to be sure, at such a town as Dresden, at least some one very skillful physician, whom I hope you have consulted; and I would have you acquaint him with all your several attacks of this nature, from your great one at Laubach, to your late one at Dresden: tell him, too, that in your last illness in England, the physicians mistook your case, and treated it as the gout, till Maty came, who treated it as a rheumatism, and cured you. In my own opinion, you have never had the gout, but always the rheumatism; which, to my knowledge, is as painful as the gout can possibly be, and should be treated in a quite different way; that is, by cooling medicines and regimen, instead of those inflammatory cordials which they always administer where they suppose the gout, to keep it, as they say, out of the stomach.

I have been here now just a week; but have hitherto drank so little of the water, that I can neither speak well nor ill of it. The number of people in this place is infinite; but very few whom I know. Harte seems settled here for life. He is not well, that is certain; but not so ill neither as he thinks himself, or at least would be thought.

I long for your answer to my last letter, containing a certain proposal, which, by this time, I suppose has been made you, and which, in the main, I approve of your accepting.

God bless you, my dear friend! and send you better health! Adieu.

LETTER CCLXXIV

LONDON, February 26, 1765

MY DEAR FRIEND: Your last letter, of the 5th, gave me as much pleasure as your former had given me uneasiness; and Larpent's acknowledgment of his negligence frees you from those suspicions, which I own I did entertain, and which I believe every one would, in the same concurrence of circumstances, have entertained. So much for that.

You may depend upon what I promised you, before midsummer next, at farthest, and AT LEAST.

All I can say of the affair between you, of the Corps Diplomatique, and the Saxon Ministers, is, 'que voila bien du bruit pour une omelette au lard'. It will most certainly be soon made up; and in that negotiation show yourself as moderate and healing as your instructions from hence will allow, especially to Comte de Flemming. The King of Prussia, I believe, has a mind to insult him personally, as an old enemy, or else to quarrel with Saxony, that dares not quarrel with him; but some of the Corps Diplomatique here assure me it is only a pretense to recall his envoy, and to send, when matters shall be made up, a little secretary there, 'a moins de fraix', as he does now to Paris and London.

Comte Bruhl is much in fashion here; I like him mightily; he has very much 'le ton de la bonne campagnie'. Poor Schrader died last Saturday, without the least pain or sickness. God bless you!

LETTER CCLXXV

LONDON, April 22, 1765

MY DEAR FRIEND: The day before yesterday I received your letter of the 3d instant. I find that your important affair of the ceremonial is adjusted at last, as I foresaw it would be. Such minutiae are often laid hold on as a pretense, for powers who have a mind to quarrel; but are never tenaciously insisted upon where there is neither interest nor inclination to break. Comte Flemming, though a hot, is a wise man; and I was sure would not break, both with England and Hanover, upon so trifling a point, especially during a minority. 'A propos' of a minority; the King is to come to the House to-morrow, to recommend a bill to settle a Regency, in case of his demise while his successor is a minor. Upon the King's late illness, which was no trifling one, the whole nation cried out aloud for such a bill, for reasons which will readily occur to you, who know situations, persons, and characters here. I do not know the particulars of this intended bill; but I wish it may be copied exactly from that which was passed in the late King's time, when the present King was a minor. I am sure there cannot be a better.

You inquire about Monsieur de Guerchy's affair; and I will give you as succinct an account as I can of so extraordinary and perplexed a transaction: but without giving you my own opinion of it by the common post. You know what passed at first between Mr. de Guerchy and Monsieur d'Eon, in which both our Ministers and Monsieur de Guerchy, from utter inexperience in business, puzzled themselves into disagreeable difficulties. About three or four months ago, Monsieur du Vergy published in a brochure, a parcel of letters, from himself to the Duc de Choiseul; in which he positively asserts that Monsieur de Guerchy prevailed with him (Vergy) to come over into England to assassinate d'Eon; the words are, as well as I remember, 'que ce n'etoit pas pour se servir de sa plume, mais de son epee, qu'on le demandoit en Angleterre'. This accusation of assassination, you may imagine, shocked Monsieur de Guerchy, who complained bitterly to our Ministers; and they both puzzled on for some time, without doing anything, because they did not know what to do. At last du Vergy, about two months ago, applied himself to the Grand Jury of Middlesex, and made oath that Mr. de Guerchy had hired him (du Vergy) to assassinate d'Eon. Upon this deposition, the Grand jury found a bill of intended murder against Monsieur de Guerchy; which bill, however, never came to the Petty Jury. The King granted a 'noli prosequi' in favor of Monsieur de Guerchy; and the Attorney-General is actually prosecuting du Vergy. Whether the King can grant a 'noli prosequi' in a criminal case, and whether 'le droit des gens' extends to criminal cases, are two points which employ our domestic politicians, and the whole Corps Diplomatique. 'Enfin', to use a very coarse and vulgar saying, 'il y a de la merde au bout du baton, quelque part'.

I see and hear these storms from shore, 'suave mari magno', etc. I enjoy my own security and tranquillity, together with better health than I had reason to expect at my age, and with my constitution: however, I feel a gradual decay, though a gentle one; and I think that I shall not tumble, but slide gently to the bottom of the hill of life. When that will be, I neither know nor care, for I am very weary. God bless you!

Mallet died two days ago, of a diarrhoea, which he had carried with him to France, and brought back again hither.

LETTER CCLXXVI

BLACKHEATH, July 2, 1765

MY DEAR FRIEND: I have this moment received your letter of the 22d past; and I delayed answering your former in daily, or rather hourly expectation of informing you of the birth of a new Ministry; but in vain; for, after a thousand conferences, all things remain still in the state which I described to you in my last. Lord S. has, I believe, given you a pretty true account of the present state of things; but my Lord is much mistaken, I am persuaded, when he says that THE KING HAS THOUGHT PROPER TO RE-ESTABLISH HIS OLD SERVANTS IN THE MANAGEMENT OF HIS AFFAIRS; for he shows them all the public dislike possible; and, at his levee, hardly speaks to any of them; but speaks by the hour to anybody else. Conferences, in the meantime, go on, of which it is easy to guess the main subject, but impossible, for me at least, to know the particulars; but this I will venture to prophesy, that the whole will soon centre in Mr. Pitt.

You seem not to know the character of the Queen: here it is. She is a good woman, a good wife, a tender mother; and an unmeddling Queen. The King loves her as a woman; but, I verily believe, has never yet spoke one word to her about business. I have now told you all that I know of these affairs; which, I believe, is as much as anybody else knows, who is not in the secret. In the meantime, you easily guess that surmises, conjectures, and reports are infinite; and if, as they say, truth is but one, one million at least of these reports must be false; for they differ exceedingly.

You have lost an honest servant by the death of poor Louis; I would advise you to take a clever young Saxon in his room, of whose character you may get authentic testimonies, instead of sending for one to France, whose character you can only know from far.

When I hear more, I will write more; till when, God bless you!

LETTER CCLXXVII

BLACKHEATH, July 15, 1765

MY DEAR FRIEND: I told you in my last, that you should hear from me again, as soon as I had anything more to write; and now I have too much to write, therefore will refer you to the "Gazette," and the office letters, for all that has been done; and advise you to suspend your opinion, as I do, about all that is to be done. Many more changes are talked of, but so idly, and variously, that I give credit to none of them. There has been pretty clean sweeping already; and I do not remember, in my time, to have seen so much at once, as an entire new Board of Treasury, and two new Secretaries of State, 'cum multis aliis', etc.

Here is a new political arch almost built, but of materials of so different a nature, and without a key-stone, that it does not, in my opinion, indicate either strength or duration. It will certainly require repairs, and a key-stone next winter; and that key-stone will, and must necessarily be, Mr. Pitt. It is true he might have been that keystone now; and would have accepted it, but not without Lord Temple's consent, and Lord Temple positively refused. There was evidently some trick in this, but what is past my conjecturing. 'Davus sum, non OEdipus'.

There is a manifest interregnum in the Treasury; for I do suppose that Lord Rockingham and Mr. Dowdeswell will not think proper to be very active. General Conway, who is your Secretary, has certainly parts at least equal to his business, to which, I dare say, he will apply. The same may be said, I believe, of the Duke of Grafton; and indeed there is no magic requisite for the executive part of those employments. The ministerial part is another thing; they must scramble with their fellow-servants, for power and favor, as well as they can. Foreign affairs are not so much as mentioned, and, I verily believe, not thought of. But surely some counterbalance would be necessary to the Family compact; and, if not soon contracted, will be too late. God bless you!

LETTER CCLXXVIII

BLACKHEATH, August 17, 1765

MY DEAR FRIEND: You are now two letters in my debt; and I fear the gout has been the cause of your contracting that debt. When you are not able to write yourself, let your Secretary send me two or three lines to acquaint me how you are.

You have now seen by the London "Gazette," what changes have really been made at court; but, at the same time, I believe you have seen that there must be more, before a Ministry can be settled; what those will be, God knows. Were I to conjecture, I should say that the whole will centre, before it is long, in Mr. Pitt and Co., the present being an heterogeneous jumble of youth and caducity, which cannot be efficient.

Charles Townshend calls the present a Lutestring Ministry; fit only for the summer. The next session will be not only a warm, but a violent one, as you will easily judge; if you look over the names of the INS and of the OUTS.

I feel this beginning of the autumn, which is already very cold: the leaves are withered, fall apace, and seem to intimate that I must follow them; which I shall do without reluctance, being extremely weary of this silly world. God bless you, both in it and after it!

LETTER CCLXXIX

BLACKHEATH, August 25, 1765

MY DEAR FRIEND: I received but four days ago your letter of the 2d instant. I find by it that you are well, for you are in good spirits. Your notion of the new birth or regeneration of the Ministry is a very just one; and that they have not yet the true seal of the covenant is, I dare say, very true; at least it is not in the possession of either of the Secretaries of State, who have only the King's seal; nor do I believe (whatever his Grace may imagine) that it is even in the possession of the Lord Privy Seal. I own I am lost, in considering the present situation of affairs; different conjectures present themselves to my mind, but none that it can rest upon. The next session must necessarily clear up matters a good deal; for I believe it will be the warmest and most acrimonious one that has been known, since that of the Excise. The late Ministry, THE PRESENT OPPOSITION, are determined to attack Lord B———-publicly in parliament, and reduce the late Opposition, THE PRESENT MINISTRY, to protect him publicly, in consequence of their supposed treaty with him. 'En attendant mieux', the paper war is carried on with much fury and scurrility on all sides, to the great entertainment of such lazy and impartial people as myself: I do not know whether you have the "Daily Advertiser," and the "Public Advertiser," in which all political letters are inserted, and some very well-written ones on both sides; but I know that they amuse me, 'tant bien que mal', for an hour or two every morning. Lord T———is the supposed author of the pamphlet you mention; but I think it is above him. Perhaps his brother C———T———, who is by no means satisfied with the present arrangement, may have assisted him privately. As to this latter, there was a good ridiculous paragraph in the newspapers two or three days ago. WE HEAR THAT THE RIGHT HONORABLE MR. C———-T———IS INDISPOSED AT HIS HOUSE IN OXFORDSHIRE, OF A PAIN IN HIS SIDE; BUT IT IS NOT SAID IN WHICH SIDE.

I do not find that the Duke of York has yet visited you; if he should, it may be expensive, 'mais on trouvera moyen'. As for the lady, if you should be very sharp set for some English flesh, she has it amply in her power to supply you if she pleases. Pray tell me in your next, what you think of, and how you like, Prince Henry of Prussia. God bless you!

LETTER CCLXXX

MY DEAR FRIEND: Your great character of Prince Henry, which I take to be a very just one, lowers the King of Prussia's a great deal; and probably that is the cause of their being so ill together. But the King of

Prussia, with his good parts, should reflect upon that trite and true maxim, 'Qui invidet minor', or Mr. de la Rouchefoucault's, 'Que l'envie est la plus basse de toutes les passions, puisqu'on avoue bien des crimes, mais que personae n'avoue l'envie'. I thank God, I never was sensible of that dark and vile passion, except that formerly I have sometimes envied a successful rival with a fine woman. But now that cause is ceased, and consequently the effects.

What shall I, or rather what can I tell you of the political world here? The late Ministers accuse the present with having done nothing, the present accuse the late ones with having done much worse than nothing. Their writers abuse one another most scurrilously, but sometimes with wit. I look upon this to be 'peloter en attendant partie', till battle begins in St., Stephen's Chapel. How that will end, I protest I cannot conjecture; any farther than this, that if Mr. Pitt does not come into the assistance of the present ministers, they will have much to do to stand their ground. C——-T————will play booty; and who else have they? Nobody but C———-, who has only good sense, but not the necessary talents nor experience, 'AEre ciere viros martemque accendere cantu'. I never remember, in all my time, to have seen so problematical a state of affairs, and a man would be much puzzled which side to bet on.

Your guest, Miss C————, is another problem which I cannot solve. She no more wanted the waters of Carlsbadt than you did. Is it to show the Duke of Kingston that he cannot live without her? a dangerous experiment! which may possibly convince him that he can. There is a trick no doubt in it; but what, I neither know nor care; you did very well to show her civilities, 'cela ne gute jamais rien'. I will go to my waters, that is, the Bath waters, in three weeks or a month, more for the sake of bathing than of drinking. The hot bath always promotes my perspiration, which is sluggish, and supples my stiff rheumatic limbs. 'D'ailleurs', I am at present as well, and better than I could reasonably expect to be, 'annu septuagesimo primo'. May you be so as long, 'y mas'! God bless you!

LETTER CCLXXXI

LONDON, October 25, 1765

MY DEAR FRIEND: I received your letter of the 10th 'sonica'; for I set out for Bath to-morrow morning.

If the use of those waters does me no good, the shifting the scene for some time will at least amuse me a little; and at my age, and with my infirmities, 'il faut faire de tout bois feche'. Some variety is as necessary for the mind as some medicines are for the body.

Here is a total stagnation of politics, which, I suppose, will continue till the parliament sits to do business, and that will not be till about the middle of January; for the meeting on the 17th December is only for the sake of some new writs. The late ministers threaten the present ones; but the latter do not seem in the least afraid of the former, and for a very good reason, which is, that they have the distribution of the loaves and fishes. I believe it is very certain that Mr. Pitt will never come into this, or any other administration: he is absolutely a cripple all the year, and in violent pain at least half of it. Such physical ills are great checks to two of the strongest passions to which human nature is liable, love and ambition. Though I cannot persuade myself that the present ministry can be long lived, I can as little imagine who or what can succeed them, 'telle est la-disette de sujets papables'. The Duke of swears that he will have Lord personally attacked in both Houses; but I do not see how, without endangering himself at the same time.

Miss C————is safely arrived here, and her Duke is fonder of her than ever. It was a dangerous experiment that she tried, in leaving him so long; but it seems she knew her man.

I pity you for the inundation of your good countrymen, which overwhelms you; 'je sais ce qu'en vaut l'aune. It is, besides, expensive, but, as I look upon the expense to be the least evil of the two, I will see if a New-Year's gift will not make it up.

As I am now upon the wing, I will only add, God bless you!

LETTER CCLXXXII

BATH, November 28, 1765

MY DEAR FRIEND: I have this moment received your letter of the 10th. I have now been here a month, bathing and drinking the waters, for complaints much of the same kind as yours, I mean pains in my legs, hips, and arms: whether gouty or rheumatic, God knows; but, I believe, both, that fight without a decision in favor of either, and have absolutely reduced me to the miserable situation of the Sphinx's riddle, to walk upon three legs; that is, with the assistance of my stick, to walk, or rather hobble, very indifferently. I wish it were a declared gout, which is the distemper of a gentleman; whereas the rheumatism is the distemper of a hackney-coachman or chairman, who is obliged to be out in all weathers and at all hours.

I think you will do very right to ask leave, and I dare say you will easily get it, to go to the baths in Suabia; that is, supposing that you have consulted some skillful physician, if such a one there be, either at Dresden or at Leipsic, about the nature of your distemper, and the nature of those baths; but, 'suos quisque patimur manes'. We have but a bad bargain, God knows, of this life, and patience is the only way not to make bad worse. Mr. Pitt keeps his bed here, with a very real gout, and not a political one, as is often suspected.

Here has been a congress of most of the 'ex Ministres'. If they have raised a battery, as I suppose they have, it is a masked one, for nothing has transpired; only they confess that they intend a most vigorous attack. 'D'ailleurs', there seems to be a total suspension of all business, till the meeting of the parliament, and then

'Signa canant'. I am very glad that at this time you are out of it: and for reasons that I need not mention: you would certainly have been sent for over, and, as before, not paid for your journey.

Poor Harte is very ill, and condemned to the Hot well at Bristol. He is a better poet than philosopher: for all this illness and melancholy proceeds originally from the ill success of his "Gustavus Adolphus." He is grown extremely devout, which I am very glad of, because that is always a comfort to the afflicted.

I cannot present Mr. Larpent with my New-Year's gift, till I come to town, which will be before Christmas at farthest; till when, God bless you! Adieu.

LETTER CCLXXXIII

LONDON, December 27, 1765.

MY DEAR FRIEND: I arrived here from Bath last Monday, rather, but not much better, than when I went over there. My rheumatic pains, in my legs and hips, plague me still, and I must never expect to be quite free from them.

You have, to be sure, had from the office an account of what the parliament did, or rather did not do, the day of their meeting; and the same point will be the great object at their next meeting; I mean the affair of our American Colonies, relatively to the late imposed Stamp-duty, which our Colonists absolutely refuse to pay. The Administration are for some indulgence and forbearance to those froward children of their mother country; the Opposition are for taking vigorous, as they call them, but I call them violent measures; not less than 'les dragonnades'; and to have the tax collected by the troops we have there. For my part, I never saw a froward child mended by whipping; and I would not have the mother country become a stepmother. Our trade to America brings in, 'communibus annis', two millions a year; and the Stamp-duty is estimated at but one hundred thousand pounds a year; which I would by no means bring into the stock of the Exchequer, at the loss or even the risk of a million a year to the national stock.

I do not tell you of the Garter given away yesterday, because the newspapers will; but, I must observe, that the Prince of Brunswick's riband is a mark of great distinction to that family; which I believe, is the first (except our own Royal Family) that has ever had two blue ribands at a time; but it must be owned they deserve them.

One hears of nothing now in town, but the separation of men and their wives. Will Finch, the Ex-vice Chamberlain, Lord Warwick, and your friend Lord Bolingbroke. I wonder at none of them for parting; but I wonder at many for still living together; for in this country it is certain that marriage is not well understood.

I have this day sent Mr. Larpent two hundred pounds for your Christmas-box, of which I suppose he will inform you by this post. Make this Christmas as merry a one as you can; for 'pour le peu du bon tems qui nous reste, rien nest si funeste, qu'un noir chagrin'. For the new years—God send you many, and happy ones! Adieu.

1766-1771

LETTER CCLXXXIV

LONDON, February 11, 1766

MY DEAR FRIEND: I received two days ago your letter of the 25th past; and your former, which you mention in it, but ten days ago; this may easily be accounted for from the badness of the weather, and consequently of the roads. I hardly remember so severe a win ter; it has occasioned many illnesses here. I am sure it pinched my crazy carcass so much that, about three weeks ago, I was obliged to be let blood twice in four days, which I found afterward was very necessary, by the relief it gave to my head and to the rheumatic pains in my limbs; and from the execrable kind of blood which I lost.

Perhaps you expect from me a particular account of the present state of affairs here; but if you do you will be disappointed; for no man living (and I still less than anyone) knows what it is; it varies, not only daily, but hourly.

Most people think, and I among the rest, that the date of the present Ministers is pretty near out; but how soon we are to have a new style, God knows. This, however, is certain, that the Ministers had a contested election in the House of Commons, and got it but by eleven votes; too small a majority to carry anything; the next day they lost a question in the House of Lords, by three. The question in the House of Lords was, to enforce the execution of the Stamp-act in the colonies 'vi et armis'. What conclusions you will draw from these premises, I do not know; but I protest I draw none; but only stare at the present undecipherable state of affairs, which, in fifty years' experience, I have never seen anything like. The Stamp-act has proved a most pernicious measure; for, whether it is repealed or not, which is still very doubtful, it has given such terror to the Americans, that our trade with them will not be, for some years, what it used to be; and great numbers of our manufacturers at home will be turned a starving for want of that employment which our very profitable trade to America found them: and hunger is always the cause of tumults and sedition.

As you have escaped a fit of the gout in this severe cold weather, it is to be hoped you may be entirely free from it, till next winter at least.

P. S. Lord having parted with his wife, now, keeps another w——e, at a great expense. I fear he is totally undone.

LETTER CCLXXXV

LONDON, March 17, 1766.

MY DEAR FRIEND: You wrong me in thinking me in your debt; for I never receive a letter of yours, but I answer it by the next post, or the next but one, at furthest: but I can easily conceive that my two last letters to you may have been drowned or frozen in their way; for portents and prodigies of frost, snow, and inundations, have been so frequent this winter, that they have almost lost their names.

You tell me that you are going to the baths of BADEN; but that puzzles me a little, so I recommend this letter to the care of Mr. Larpent, to forward to you; for Baden I take to be the general German word for baths, and the particular ones are distinguished by some epithet, as Weissbaden, Carlsbaden, etc. I hope they are not cold baths, which I have a very ill opinion of, in all arthritic or rheumatic cases; and your case I take to be a compound of both, but rather more of the latter.

You will probably wonder that I tell you nothing of public matters; upon which I shall be as secret as Hotspur's gentle Kate, who would not tell what she did not know; but what is singular, nobody seems to know any more of them than I do. People gape, stare, conjecture, and refine. Changes of the Ministry, or in the Ministry at least, are daily reported and foretold, but of what kind, God only knows. It is also very doubtful whether Mr. Pitt will come into the Administration or not; the two present Secretaries are extremely desirous that he should; but the others think of the horse that called the man to its assistance. I will say nothing to you about American affairs, because I have not pens, ink, or paper enough to give you an intelligible account of them. They have been the subjects of warm and acrimonious debates, both in the Lords and Commons, and in all companies.

The repeal of the Stamp-act is at last carried through. I am glad of it, and gave my proxy for it, because I saw many more inconveniences from the enforcing than from the repealing it.

Colonel Browne was with me the other day, and assured me that he left you very well. He said he saw you at Spa, but I did not remember him; though I remember his two brothers, the Colonel and the ravisher, very well. Your Saxon colonel has the brogue exceedingly. Present my respects to Count Flemming; I am very sorry for the Countess's illness; she was a most well-bred woman.

You would hardly think that I gave a dinner to the Prince of Brunswick, your old acquaintance. I glad it is over; but I could not avoid it. 'Il m'avait tabli de politesses'. God bless you!

LETTER CCLXXXVI

BLACKHEATH, June 13, 1766.

MY DEAR FRIEND: I received yesterday your letter of the 30th past. I waited with impatience for it, not having received one from you in six weeks; nor your mother neither, who began to be very sure that you were dead, if not buried. You should write to her once a week, or at least once a-fortnight; for women make no allowance either for business or laziness; whereas I can, by experience, make allowances for both: however, I wish you would generally write to me once a fortnight.

Last week I paid my midsummer offering, of five hundred pounds, to Mr. Larpent, for your use, as I suppose he has informed you. I am punctual, you must allow.

What account shall I give you of ministerial affairs here? I protest I do not know: your own description of them is as exact a one as any I, who am upon the place, can give you. It is a total dislocation and 'derangement'; consequently a total inefficiency. When the Duke of Grafton quitted the seals, he gave that very reason for it, in a speech in the House of Lords: he declared, "that he had no objection to the persons or the measures of the present Ministers; but that he thought they wanted strength and efficiency to carry on proper measures with success; and that he knew but one man MEANING, AS YOU WILL EASILY SUPPOSE, MR. PITT who could give them strength and solidity; that, under this person, he should be willing to serve in any capacity, not only as a General Officer, but as a pioneer; and would take up a spade and a mattock." When he quitted the seals, they were offered first to Lord Egmont, then to Lord Hardwicke; who both declined them, probably for the same reasons that made the Duke of Grafton resign them; but after their going a-begging for some time, the Duke of———-begged them, and has them 'faute de mieux'. Lord Mountstuart was never thought of for Vienna, where Lord Stormont returns in three months; the former is going to be married to one of the Miss Windsors, a great fortune. To tell you the speculations, the reasonings, and the conjectures, either of the uninformed, or even of the best-informed public, upon the present wonderful situation of affairs, would take up much more time and paper than either you or I can afford, though we have neither of us a great deal of business at present.

I am in as good health as I could reasonably expect, at my age, and with my shattered carcass; that is, from the waist upward; but downward it is not the same: for my limbs retain that stiffness and debility of my long rheumatism; I cannot walk half an hour at a time. As the autumn, and still more as the winter approaches, take care to keep yourself very warm, especially your legs and feet.

Lady Chesterfield sends you her compliments, and triumphs in the success of her plaster. God bless you!

LETTER CCLXXXVII

BLACKHEATH, July 11, 1766.

MY DEAR FRIEND: You are a happy mortal, to have your time thus employed between the great and the fair; I hope you do the honors of your country to the latter. The Emperor, by your account, seems to be very well for an emperor; who, by being above the other monarchs in Europe, may justly be supposed to have had a proportionably worse education. I find, by your account of him, that he has been trained up to homicide, the only science in which princes are ever instructed; and with good reason, as their greatness and glory singly depend upon the numbers of their fellow-creatures which their ambition exterminates. If a sovereign should, by great accident, deviate into moderation, justice, and clemency, what a contemptible figure would he make in the catalogue of princes! I have always owned a great regard for King Log. From the interview at Torgaw, between the two monarchs, they will be either a great deal better or worse together; but I think rather the latter; for our namesake, Philip de Co mines, observes, that he never knew any good come from l'abouchement des Rois. The King of Prussia will exert all his perspicacity to analyze his Imperial Majesty; and I would bet upon the one head of his black eagle, against the two heads of the Austrian eagle; though two heads are said, proverbially, to be better than one. I wish I had the direction of both the monarchs, and they should, together with some of their allies, take Lorraine and Alsace from France. You will call me 'l'Abbe de St. Pierre'; but I only say what I wish; whereas he thought everything that he wished practicable.

Now to come home. Here are great bustles at Court, and a great change of persons is certainly very near. You will ask me, perhaps, who is to be out, and who is to be in? To which I answer, I do not know. My conjecture is that, be the new settlement what it will, Mr. Pitt will be at the head of it. If he is, I presume, 'qu'il aura mis de l'eau dans son vin par rapport a Mylord B———; when that shall come to be known, as known it certainly will soon be, he may bid adieu to his popularity. A minister, as minister, is very apt to be the object of public dislike; and a favorite, as favorite, still more so. If any event of this kind happens, which (if it happens at all) I conjecture will be some time next week, you shall hear further from me.

I will follow your advice, and be as well as I can next winter, though I know I shall never be free from my flying rheumatic pains, as long as I live; but whether that will be more or less, is extremely indifferent to me; in either case, God bless you!

LETTER CCLXXXVIII

BLACKHEATH, August 1, 1766.

MY DEAR FRIEND: The curtain was at last drawn up, the day before yesterday, and discovered the new actors, together with some of the old ones. I do not name them to you, because to-morrow's Gazette will do it full as well as I could. Mr. Pitt, who had carte blanche given him, named everyone of them: but what would you think he named himself for? Lord Privy Seal; and (what will astonish you, as it does every mortal here) Earl of Chatham. The joke here is, that he has had A FALL UP STAIRS, and has done himself so much hurt, that he will never be able to stand upon his leg's again. Everybody is puzzled how to account for this step; though it would not be the first time that great abilities have been duped by low cunning. But be it what it will, he is now certainly only Earl of Chatham; and no longer Mr. Pitt, in any respect whatever. Such an event, I believe, was never read nor heard of. To withdraw, in the fullness of his power and in the utmost gratification of his ambition, from the House of Commons (which procured him his power, and which could alone insure it to him), and to go into that hospital of incurables, the House of Lords, is a measure so unaccountable, that nothing but proof positive could have made me believe it: but true it is. Hans Stanley is to go Ambassador to Russia; and my nephew, Ellis, to Spain, decorated with the red riband. Lord Shelburne is your Secretary of State, which I suppose he has notified to you this post, by a circular letter. Charles Townshend has now the sole management of the House of Commons; but how long he will be content to be only Lord Chatham's vicegerent there, is a question which I will not pretend to decide. There is one very bad sign for Lord Chatham, in his new dignity; which is, that all his enemies, without exception, rejoice at it; and all his friends are stupefied and dumbfounded. If I mistake not much, he will, in the course of a year, enjoy perfect 'otium cum dignitate'. Enough of politics.

Is the fair, or at least the fat, Miss C―――with you still? It must be confessed that she knows the arts of courts, to be so received at Dresden, and so connived at in Leicester-fields.

There never was so wet a summer as this has been, in the memory of man; we have not had one single day, since March, without some rain; but most days a great deal. I hope that does not affect your health, as great cold does; for, with all these inundations, it has not been cold. God bless you!

LETTER CCLXXXIX

BLACKHEATH, August 14, 1766.

MY DEAR FRIEND: I received yesterday your letter of the 30th past, and I find by it that it crossed mine upon the road, where they had no time to take notice of one another.

The newspapers have informed you, before now, of the changes actually made; more will probably follow, but what, I am sure, I cannot tell you; and I believe nobody can, not even those who are to make them: they will, I suppose, be occasional, as people behave themselves. The causes and consequences of Mr. Pitt's quarrel now appear in print, in a pamphlet published by Lord T———; and in a refutation of it, not by Mr. Pitt himself, I believe, but by some friend of his, and under his sanction. The former is very scurrilous and scandalous, and betrays private conversation. My Lord says, that in his last conference, he thought he had as good a right to nominate the new Ministry as Mr. Pitt, and consequently named Lord G———, Lord L———, etc., for Cabinet Council employments; which Mr. Pitt not consenting to, Lord T———-broke up the conference, and in his wrath went to Stowe; where I presume he may remain undisturbed a great while, since Mr. Pitt will neither be willing nor able to send for him again. The pamphlet, on the part of Mr. Pitt, gives an account of his whole political life; and, in that respect, is tedious to those who were acquainted with it before; but, at the latter end, there is an article that expresses such supreme contempt of Lord T———-, and in so pretty a manner, that I suspect it to be Mr. Pitt's own: you shall judge yourself, for I here transcribe the article: "But this I will be bold to say, that had he (Lord T———-) not fastened himself into Mr. Pitt's train, and acquired thereby such an interest in that great man, he might have crept out of life with as little notice as he crept in; and gone off with no other degree of credit, than that of adding a single unit to the bills of mortality" I wish I could send you all the pamphlets and half-sheets that swarm here upon this occasion; but that is impossible; for every week would make a ship's cargo. It is certain, that Mr. Pitt has, by his dignity of Earl, lost the greatest part of his popularity, especially in the city; and I believe the Opposition will be very strong, and perhaps prevail, next session, in the House of Commons; there being now nobody there who can have the authority and ascendant over them that Pitt had.

People tell me here, as young Harvey told you at Dresden, that I look very well; but those are words of course, which everyone says to everybody. So far is true, that I am better than at my age, and with my broken constitution, I could have expected to be. God bless you!

LETTER CCXC

BLACKHEATH, September 12, 1766.

MY DEAR FRIEND: I have this moment received your letter of the 27th past. I was in hopes that your course of waters this year at Baden would have given you a longer reprieve from your painful complaint. If I do not mistake, you carried over with you some of Dr. Monsey's powders. Have you taken any of them, and have they done you any good? I know they did me a great deal. I, who pretend to some skill in physic, advise a cool regimen, and cooling medicines.

I do not wonder, that you do wonder, at Lord C———-'s conduct. If he was not outwitted into his peerage by Lord B———, his accepting it is utterly inexplicable. The instruments he has chosen for the great office, I believe, will never fit the same case. It was cruel to put such a boy as Lord G—-over the head of old Ligonier; and if I had been the former, I would have refused that commission, during the life of that honest and brave old general. All this to quiet the Duke of R——to a resignation, and to make Lord B—— Lieutenant of Ireland, where, I will venture to prophesy, that he will not do. Ligonier was much pressed to give up his regiment of guards, but would by no means do it; and declared that the King might break him if he pleased, but that he would certainly not break himself.

I have no political events to inform you of; they will not be ripe till the meeting of the parliament. Immediately upon the receipt of this letter, write me one, to acquaint me how you are.

God bless you; and, particularly, may He send you health, for that is the greatest blessing!

LETTER CCXCI

BLACKHEATH, September 30, 1766.

MY DEAR FRIEND: I received, yesterday, with great pleasure, your letter of the 18th, by which I consider this last ugly bout as over; and, to prevent its return, I greatly approve of your plan for the south of France, where I recommend for your principal residence, Pezenas Toulouse, or Bordeaux; but do not be persuaded to go to Aix en Provence, which, by experience, I know to be at once the hottest and the coldest place in the world, from the ardor of the Provencal sun, and the sharpness of the Alpine winds. I also earnestly recommend to you, for your complaint upon your breast, to take, twice a-day, asses' or (what is better mares' milk), and that for these six months at least. Mingle turnips, as much as you can, with your diet.

I have written, as you desired, to Mr. Secretary Conway; but I will answer for it that there will be no difficulty to obtain the leave you ask.

There is no new event in the political world since my last; so God bless you!

LETTER CCXCII

LONDON, October 29, 7766.

MY DEAR FRIEND: The last mail brought me your letter of the 17th. I am glad to hear that your breast is so much better. You will find both asses' and mares' milk enough in the south of France, where it was much drank when I was there. Guy Patin recommends to a patient to have no doctor but a horse, and no apothecary but an ass. As for your pains and weakness in your limbs, 'je vous en offre autant'; I have never been free from them since my last rheumatism. I use my legs as much as I can, and you should do so too, for disuse makes them worse. I cannot now use them long at a time, because of the weakness of old age; but I contrive to get, by different snatches, at least two hours' walking every day, either in my garden or within doors, as the weather permits. I set out to-morrow for Bath, in hopes of half repairs, for Medea's kettle could not give me whole ones; the timbers of my wretched vessel are too much decayed to be fitted out again for use. I shall see poor Harte there, who, I am told, is in a miserable way, between some real and some imaginary distempers.

I send you no political news, for one reason, among others, which is that I know none. Great expectations are raised of this session, which meets the 11th of next month; but of what kind nobody knows, and consequently everybody conjectures variously. Lord Chatham comes to town to-morrow from Bath, where he has been to refit himself for the winter campaign; he has hitherto but an indifferent set of aides-decamp; and where he will find better, I do not know. Charles Townshend and he are already upon ill terms. 'Enfin je n'y vois goutte'; and so God bless you!

LETTER CCXCIII

BATH, November 15, 1766.

MY DEAR FRIEND: I have this moment received your letter of the 5th instant from Basle. I am very glad to find that your breast is relieved, though perhaps at the expense of your legs: for, if the humor be either gouty or rheumatic, it had better be in your legs than anywhere else. I have consulted Moisy, the great physician of this place, upon it; who says, that at this distance he dares not prescribe anything, as there may be such different causes for your complaint, which must be well weighed by a physician upon the spot; that is, in short, that he knows nothing of the matter. I will therefore tell you my own case, in 1732, which may be something parallel to yours. I had that year been dangerously ill of a fever in Holland; and when I was recovered of it, the febrific humor fell into my legs, and swelled them to that degree, and chiefly in the evening, that it was as painful to me as it was shocking to others. I came to England with them in this condition; and consulted Mead, Broxholme, and Arbuthnot, who none of them did me the least good; but, on the contrary, increased the swelling, by applying poultices and emollients. In this condition I remained near six months, till finding that the doctors could do me no good, I resolved to consult Palmer, the most eminent surgeon of St. Thomas's Hospital. He immediately told me that the physicians had pursued a very wrong method, as the swelling of my legs proceeded only from a relaxation and weakness of the cutaneous vessels; and he must apply strengtheners instead of emollients. Accordingly, he ordered me to put my legs up to the knees every morning in brine from the salters, as hot as I could bear it; the brine must have had meat salted in it. I did so; and after having thus pickled my legs for about three weeks, the complaint absolutely ceased, and I have never had the least swelling in them since. After what I have said, I must caution you not to use the same remedy rashly, and without the most skillful advice you can find, where you are; for if your swelling proceeds from a gouty, or rheumatic humor, there may be great danger in applying so powerful an astringent, and perhaps REPELLANT as brine. So go piano, and not without the best advice, upon a view of the parts.

I shall direct all my letters to you 'Chez Monsieur Sarraxin', who by his trade is, I suppose, 'sedentaire' at Basle, while it is not sure that you will be at any one place in the south of France. Do you know that he is a descendant of the French poet Sarrazin?

Poor Harte, whom I frequently go to see here, out of compassion, is in a most miserable way; he has had a stroke of the palsy, which has deprived him of the use of his right leg, affected his speech a good deal, and perhaps his head a little. Such are the intermediate tributes that we are forced to pay, in some shape or other, to our wretched nature, till we pay the last great one of all. May you pay this very late, and as few intermediate tributes as possible; and so 'jubeo te bene valere'. God bless you!

LETTER CCXCIV

BATH, December 9, 1766.

MY DEAR FRIEND: I received, two days ago, your letter of the 26th past. I am very glad that you begin to feel the good effects of the climate where you are; I know it saved my life, in 1741, when both the skillful and the unskillful gave me over. In that ramble I stayed three or four days at Nimes, where there are more remains of antiquity, I believe, than in any town in Europe, Italy excepted. What is falsely called 'la maison quarree', is, in my mind, the finest piece of architecture that I ever saw; and the amphitheater the clumsiest and the ugliest: if it were in England, everybody would swear it had been built by Sir John Vanbrugh.

This place is now, just what you have seen it formerly; here is a great crowd of trifling and unknown people, whom I seldom frequent, in the public rooms; so that I may pass my time 'tres uniment', in taking the air in my post-chaise every morning, and in reading of evenings. And 'a propos' of the latter, I shall point out a book, which I believe will give you some pleasure; at least it gave me a great deal. I never read it before. It is 'Reflexions sur la Poesie et la Peinture, par l'Abbee de Bos', in two octavo volumes; and is, I suppose, to be had at every great town in France. The criticisms and the reflections are just and lively.

It may be you expect some political news from me: but I can tell you that you will have none, for no mortal can comprehend the present state of affairs. Eight or nine people of some consequence have resigned their employments; upon which Lord C———made overtures to the Duke of B———and his people; but they could by no means agree, and his Grace went, the next day, full of wrath, to Woburn, so that negotiation is entirely at an end. People wait to see who Lord C———will take in, for some he must have; even HE cannot be alone, 'contra mundum'. Such a state of affairs, to be sure, was never seen before, in this or in any other country. When this Ministry shall be settled, it will be the sixth Ministry in six years' time.

Poor Harte is here, and in a most miserable condition; those who wish him the best, as I do, must wish him dead. God bless you!

LETTER CCXCV

LONDON, February 13, 1767.

MY DEAR FRIEND: It is so long since I have had a letter from you, that I am alarmed about your health; and fear that the southern parts of France have not done so well by you as they did by me in the year 1741, when they snatched me from the jaws of death. Let me know, upon the receipt of this letter, how you are, and where you are.

I have no news to send you from hence; for everything seems suspended, both in the court and in the parliament, till Lord Chatham's return from the Bath, where he has been laid up this month, by a severe fit of the gout; and, at present, he has the sole apparent power. In what little business has hitherto been done in the House of Commons, Charles Townshend has given himself more ministerial airs than Lord Chatham will, I believe, approve of. However, since Lord Chatham has thought fit to withdraw himself from that House, he cannot well do without Charles' abilities to manage it as his deputy.

I do not send you an account of weddings, births, and burials, as I take it for granted that you know them all from the English printed papers; some of which, I presume, are sent after you. Your old acquaintance, Lord Essex, is to be married this week to Harriet Bladen, who has L20,000 down, besides the reasonable expectation of as much at the death of her father. My kinsman, Lord Strathmore, is to be married in a fortnight, to Miss Bowes, the greatest heiress perhaps in Europe. In short, the matrimonial frenzy seems to rage at present, and is epidemical. The men marry for money, and I believe you guess what the women marry for. God bless you, and send you health!

LETTER CCXCVI

LONDON, March 3, 1767

MY DEAR FRIEND: Yesterday I received two letters at once from you, both dated Montpellier; one of the 29th of last December, and the other the 12th of February: but I cannot conceive what became of my letters to you; for, I assure you, that I answered all yours the next post after I received them; and, about ten days ago, I wrote you a volunteer, because you had been so long silent, and I was afraid that you were not well; but your letter of the 12th of February has removed all my fears upon that score. The same climate that has restored your health so far will probably, in a little more time, restore your strength too; though you must not expect it to be quite what it was before your late painful complaints. At least I find that, since my late great rheumatism, I cannot walk above half an hour at a time, which I do not place singly to the account of my years, but chiefly to the great shock given then to my limbs. 'D'ailleurs' I am pretty well for my age and shattered constitution.

As I told you in my last, I must tell you again in this, that I have no news to send. Lord Chatham, at last, came to town yesterday, full of gout, and is not able to stir hand or foot. During his absence, Charles Townshend has talked of him, and at him, in such a manner, that henceforward they must be either much worse or much better together than ever they were in their lives. On Friday last, Mr. Dowdeswell and Mr. Grenville moved to have one shilling in the pound of the land tax taken off; which was opposed by the Court; but the Court lost it by eighteen. The Opposition triumph much upon this victory; though, I think, without reason; for it is plain that all the landed gentlemen bribed themselves with this shilling in the pound.

The Duke of Buccleugh is very soon to be married to Lady Betty Montague. Lord Essex was married yesterday, to Harriet Bladen; and Lord Strathmore, last week, to Miss Bowes; both couples went directly from the church to consummation in the country, from an unnecessary fear that they should not be tired of each other if they stayed in town. And now 'dixi'; God bless you!

You are in the right to go to see the assembly of the states of, Languedoc, though they are but the shadow of the original Etats, while there was some liberty subsisting in France.

LETTER CCXCVII

LONDON, April 6, 1767.

MY DEAR FRIEND: Yesterday I received your letter from Nimes, by which I find that several of our letters have reciprocally miscarried. This may probably have the same fate; however, if it reaches Monsieur Sarrazin, I presume he will know where to take his aim at you; for I find you are in motion, and with a polarity to Dresden. I am very glad to find by it, that your meridional journey has perfectly recovered you, as to your general state of health; for as to your legs and thighs, you must never expect that they will be restored to their original strength and activity, after so many rheumatic attacks as you have had. I know that my limbs, besides the natural debility of old age, have never recovered the severe attack of rheumatism that plagued me five or six years ago. I cannot now walk above half an hour at a time and even that in a hobbling kind of way.

I can give you no account of our political world, which is in a situation that I never saw in my whole life. Lord Chatham has been so ill, these last two months, that he has not been able (some say not willing) to do or hear of any business, and for his 'sous Ministres', they either cannot, or dare not, do any, without his directions; so everything is now at a stand. This situation, I think, cannot last much longer, and if Lord Chatham should either quit his post, or the world, neither of which is very improbable, I conjecture, that which is called the Rockingham Connection stands the fairest for the Ministry. But this is merely my conjecture, for I have neither 'data' nor 'postulata' enough to reason upon.

When you get to Dresden, which I hope you will not do till next month, our correspondence will be more regular. God bless you!

LETTER CCXCVIII

LONDON, May 5, 1767,

MY DEAR FRIEND: By your letter of the 25th past, from Basle, I presume this will find you at Dresden, and accordingly I direct to you there. When you write me word that you are at Dresden, I will return you an answer, with something better than the answer itself.

If you complain of the weather, north of Besancon, what would you say to the weather that we have had here for these last two months, uninterruptedly? Snow often, northeast wind constantly, and extreme cold. I write this by the side of a good fire; and at this moment it snows very hard. All my promised fruit at Blackheath is quite destroyed; and, what is worse, many of my trees.

I cannot help thinking that the King of Poland, the Empress of Russia, and the King of Prussia, 's'entendent comme larrons en foire', though the former must not appear in it upon account of the stupidity, ignorance, and bigotry of his Poles. I have a great opinion of the cogency of the controversial arguments of the Russian troops, in favor of the Dissidents: I am sure I wish them success; for I would have all intoleration intolerated in its turn. We shall soon see more clearly into this matter; for I do not think that the Autocratrice of all the Russias will be trifled with by the Sarmatians.

What do you think of the late extraordinary event in Spain? Could you have ever imagined that those ignorant Goths would have dared to banish the Jesuits? There must have been some very grave and important reasons for so extraordinary a measure: but what they were I do not pretend to guess; and perhaps I shall never know, though all the coffeehouses here do.

Things are here in exactly the same situation, in which they were when I wrote to you last. Lord Chatham is still ill, and only goes abroad for an hour in a day, to take the air, in his coach. The King has, to my certain knowledge, sent him repeated messages, desiring him not to be concerned at his confinement, for that he is resolved to support him, 'pour et contre tous'. God bless you!

LETTER CCXCIX

LONDON, June 1, 1767.

MY DEAR FRIEND: I received yesterday your letter of the 20th past, from Dresden, where I am glad to find that you are arrived safe and sound. This has been everywhere an 'annus mirabilis' for bad weather, and it continues here still. Everybody has fires, and their winter clothes, as at Christmas. The town is extremely sickly; and sudden deaths have been very frequent.

I do not know what to say to you upon public matters; things remain in 'statu quo', and nothing is done. Great changes are talked of, and, I believe, will happen soon, perhaps next week; but who is to be changed, for whom, I do not know, though everybody else does. I am apt to think that it will be a mosaic Ministry, made up 'de pieces rapportees' from different connections.

Last Friday I sent your subsidy to Mr. Larpent, who, I suppose, has given you notice of it. I believe it will come very seasonably, as all places, both foreign and domestic, are so far in arrears. They talk of paying you all up to Christmas. The King's inferior servants are almost starving.

I suppose you have already heard, at Dresden, that Count Bruhl is either actually married, or very soon to be so, to Lady Egremont. She has, together with her salary as Lady of the Bed-chamber, L2,500 a year, besides ten thousand pounds in money left her, at her own disposal, by Lord Egremont. All this will sound great 'en ecus d'Allemagne'. I am glad of it, for he is a very pretty man. God bless you!

I easily conceive why Orloff influences the Empress of all the Russias; but I cannot see why the King of Prussia should be influenced by that motive.

LETTER CCC

BLACKHEATH, JULY 2, 1767.

MY DEAR FRIEND: Though I have had no letter from you since my last, and though I have no political news to inform you of, I write this to acquaint you with a piece of Greenwich news, which I believe you will be very glad of; I am sure I am. Know then that your friend Miss――-was happily married, three days ago, to Mr.――――-, an Irish gentleman, and a member of that parliament, with an estate of above L2,000 a-year. He settles upon her L600 jointure, and in case they have no children, L1,500. He happened to be by chance in her company one day here, and was at once shot dead by her charms; but as dead men sometimes walk, he walked to her the next morning, and tendered her his person and his fortune; both which, taking the one with the other, she very prudently accepted, for his person is sixty years old.

Ministerial affairs are still in the same ridiculous and doubtful situation as when I wrote to you last. Lord Chatham will neither hear of, nor do any business, but lives at Hampstead, and rides about the heath. His gout is said to be fallen upon his nerves. Your provincial secretary, Conway, quits this week, and returns to the army, for which he languished. Two Lords are talked of to succeed him; Lord Egmont and Lord Hillsborough: I rather hope the latter. Lord Northington certainly quits this week; but nobody guesses who is to succeed him as President. A thousand other changes are talked of, which I neither believe nor reject.

Poor Harte is in a most miserable condition: He has lost one side of himself, and in a great measure his speech; notwithstanding which, he is going to publish his DIVINE POEMS, as he calls them. I am sorry for it, as he had not time to correct them before this stroke, nor abilities to do it since. God bless you!

LETTER CCCI

BLACKHEATH, July 9, 1767.

MY DEAR FRIEND: I have received yours of the 21st past, with the inclosed proposal from the French 'refugies, for a subscription toward building them 'un temple'. I have shown it to the very few people I see, but without the least success. They told me (and with too much truth) that while such numbers of poor were literally starving here from the dearness of all provisions, they could not think of sending their money into another country, for a building which they reckoned useless. In truth, I never knew such misery as is here now; and it affects both the hearts and the purses of those who have either; for my own part, I never gave to a building in my life; which I reckon is only giving to masons and carpenters, and the treasurer of the undertaking.

Contrary to the expectations of all mankind here, everything still continues in 'statu quo'. General Conway has been desired by the King to keep the seals till he has found a successor for him, and the Lord President the same. Lord Chatham is relapsed, and worse than ever: he sees nobody, and nobody sees him: it is said that a bungling physician has checked his gout, and thrown it upon his nerves; which is the worst distemper that a minister or a lover can have, as it debilitates the mind of the former and the body of the latter. Here is at present an interregnum. We must soon see what order will be produced from this chaos.

The Electorate, I believe, will find the want of Comte Flemming; for he certainly had abilities, and was as sturdy and inexorable as a Minister at the head of the finances ought always to be. When you see Comtesse Flemming, which I suppose cannot be for some time, pray make her Lady Chesterfield's and my compliments of condolence.

You say that Dresden is very sickly; I am sure London is at least as sickly now, for there reigns an epidemical distemper, called by the genteel name of 'l'influenza'. It is a little fever, of which scarcely anybody dies; and it generally goes off with a little looseness. I have escaped it, I believe, by being here. God keep you from all distempers, and bless you!

LETTER CCCII

LONDON, October 30, 1767.

MY DEAR FRIEND: I have now left Blackheath, till the next summer, if I live till then; and am just able to write, which is all I can say, for I am extremely weak, and have in a great measure lost the use of my legs; I hope they will recover both flesh and strength, for at present they have neither. I go to the Bath next week, in hopes of half repairs at most; for those waters, I am sure, will not prove Medea's kettle, nor 'les eaux de Jouvence' to me; however, I shall do as good courtiers do, and get what I can, if I cannot get what I will. I send you no politics, for here are neither politics nor ministers; Lord Chatham is quiet at Pynsent, in Somersetshire, and his former subalterns do nothing, so that nothing is done. Whatever places or preferments are disposed of, come evidently from Lord————, who affects to be invisible; and who, like a woodcock, thinks that if his head is but hid, he is not seen at all.

General Pulteney is at last dead, last week, worth above thirteen hundred thousand pounds. He has left all his landed estate, which is eight and twenty thousand pounds a-year, including the Bradford estate, which his brother had from that ancient family, to a cousin-german. He has left two hundred thousand pounds, in the funds, to Lord Darlington, who was his next nearest relation; and at least twenty thousand pounds in various legacies. If riches alone could make people happy, the last two proprietors of this immense wealth ought to have been so, but they never were.

God bless you, and send you good health, which is better than all the riches of the world!

EARL OF PHILIP DORMER STANHOPE CHESTERFIELD

LETTER CCCIII

LONDON, November 3, 1767.

MY DEAR FRIEND: Your last letter brought me but a scurvy account of your health. For the headaches you complain of, I will venture to prescribe a remedy, which, by experience, I found a specific, when I was extremely plagued with them. It is either to chew ten grains of rhubarb every night going to bed: or, what I think rather better, to take, immediately before dinner, a couple of rhubarb pills, of five grains each; by which means it mixes with the aliments, and will, by degrees, keep your body gently open. I do it to this day, and find great good by it. As you seem to dread the approach of a German winter, I would advise you to write to General Conway, for leave of absence for the three rigorous winter months, which I dare say will not be refused. If you choose a worse climate, you may come to London; but if you choose a better and a warmer, you may go to Nice en Provence, where Sir William Stanhope is gone to pass his winter, who, I am sure, will be extremely glad of your company there.

I go to the Bath next Saturday. 'Utinam de frustra'. God bless you!

LETTER CCCIV

BATH, September 19, 1767.

MY DEAR FRIEND: Yesterday I received your letter of the 29th past, and am very glad to find that you are well enough to think that you may perhaps stand the winter at Dresden; but if you do, pray take care to keep both your body and your limbs exceedingly warm.

As to my own health, it is, in general, as good as I could expect it, at my age; I have a good stomach, a good digestion, and sleep well; but find that I shall never recover the free use of my legs, which are now full as weak as when I first came hither.

You ask me questions concerning Lord C———, which neither I, nor, I believe, anybody but himself can answer; however, I will tell you all that I do know, and all that I guess, concerning him. This time twelvemonth he was here, and in good health and spirits, except now and then some little twinges of the gout. We saw one another four or five times, at our respective houses; but for these last eight months, he has been absolutely invisible to his most intimate friends, 'les sous Ministres': he would receive no letters, nor so much as open any packet about business.

His physician, Dr.———, as I am told, had, very ignorantly, checked a coming fit of the gout, and scattered it about his body; and it fell particularly upon his nerves, so that he continues exceedingly vaporish; and would neither see nor speak to anybody while he was here. I sent him my compliments, and asked leave to wait upon him; but he sent me word that he was too ill to see anybody whatsoever. I met him frequently taking the air in his post-chaise, and he looked very well. He set out from hence for London last Tuesday; but what to do, whether to resume, or finally to resign the Administration, God knows; conjectures are various. In one of our conversations here, this time twelvemonth, I desired him to secure you a seat in the new parliament; he assured me that he would, and, I am convinced, very sincerely; he said even that he would make it his own affair; and desired that I would give myself no more trouble about it. Since that, I have heard no more of it; which made me look out for some venal borough and I spoke to a borough-jobber, and offered five-and-twenty hundred pounds for a secure seat in parliament; but he laughed at my offer, and said that there was no such thing as a borough to be had now, for that the rich East and West Indians had secured them all, at the rate of three thousand pounds at least; but many at four thousand, and two or three that he knew, at five thousand. This, I confess, has vexed me a good deal; and made me the more impatient to know whether Lord C——had done anything in it; which I shall know when I go to town, as I propose to do in about a fortnight; and as soon as I know it you shall. To tell you truly what I think—I doubt, from all this NERVOUS DISORDER that Lord C———is hors de combat, as a Minister; but do not ever hint this to anybody. God bless you!

LETTER CC

BATH, December 27, 1767. 'En nova progenies'!

MY DEAR FRIEND: The outlines of a new Ministry are now declared, but they are not yet quite filled up; it was formed by the Duke of Bedford. Lord Gower is made President of the Council, Lord Sandwich, Postmaster, Lord Hillsborough, Secretary of State for America only, Mr. Rigby, Vice-treasurer of Ireland. General Canway is to keep the seals a fortnight longer, and then to surrender them to Lord Weymouth. It is very uncertain whether the Duke of Grafton is to continue at the head of the Treasury or not; but, in my private opinion, George Grenville will very soon be there. Lord Chatham seems to be out of the question, and is at his repurchased house at Hayes, where he will not see a mortal. It is yet uncertain whether Lord Shelburne is to keep his place; if not, Lord Sandwich they say is to succeed him. All the Rockingham people are absolutely excluded. Many more changes must necessarily be, but no more are yet declared. It seems to be a resolution taken by somebody that Ministers are to be annual.

Sir George Macartney is next week to be married to Lady Jane Stuart, Lord Bute's second daughter.

I never knew it so cold in my life as it is now, and with a very deep snow; by which, if it continues, I may be snow-bound here for God knows how long, though I proposed leaving this place the latter end of the week.

Poor Harte is very ill here; he mentions you often, and with great affection. God bless you!

When I know more you shall.

LETTER CCCVI

LONDON, January 29, 1768.

MY DEAR FRIEND: Two days ago I received your letter of the 8th. I wish you had gone a month or six weeks sooner to Basle, that you might have escaped the excessive cold of the most severe winter that I believe was ever known. It congealed both my body and my mind, and scarcely left me the power of thinking. A great many here, both in town and country, have perished by the frost, and been lost in the snow.

You have heard, no doubt, of the changes at Court, by which you have got a new provincial, Lord Weymouth; who has certainly good parts, and, as I am informed, speaks very well in the House of Lords; but I believe he has no application. Lord Chatham is at his house at Hayes; but sees no mortal. Some say that he has a fit of the gout, which would probably do him good; but many think that his worst complaint is in his head, which I am afraid is too true. Were he well, I am sure he would realize the promise he made me concerning you; but, however, in that uncertainty, I am looking out for any chance borough; and if I can find one, I promise you I will bid like a chapman for it, as I should be very sorry that you were not in the next parliament. I do not see any probability of any vacancy in a foreign commission in a better climate; Mr. Hamilton at Naples, Sir Horace Mann at Florence, and George Pitt at Turin, do not seem likely to make one. And as for changing your foreign department for a domestic one, it would not be in my power to procure you one; and you would become 'd'eveque munier', and gain nothing in point of climate, by changing a bad one for another full as bad, if not worse; and a worse I believe is not than ours. I have always had better health abroad than at home; and if the tattered remnant of my wretched life were worth my care, I would have been in the south of France long ago. I continue very lame and weak, and despair of ever recovering any strength in my legs. I care very little about it. At my age every man must have his share of physical ills of one kind or another; and mine, thank God, are not very painful. God bless you!

LETTER CCCVII

LONDON, March 12, 1768.

MY DEAR FRIEND: The day after I received your letter of the 21st past, I wrote to Lord Weymouth, as you desired; and I send you his answer inclosed, from which (though I have not heard from him since) I take it for granted, and so may you, that his silence signifies his Majesty's consent to your request. Your complicated complaints give me great uneasiness, and the more, as I am convinced that the Montpellier physicians have mistaken a material part of your case; as indeed all the physicians here did, except Dr. Maty. In my opinion, you have no gout, but a very scorbutic and rheumatic habit of body, which should be treated in a very different manner from the gout; and, as I pretend to be a very good quack at least, I would prescribe to you a strict milk diet, with the seeds, such as rice, sago, barley, millet, etc., for the three summer months at least, and without ever tasting wine. If climate signifies anything (in which, by the way, I have very little faith), you are, in my mind, in the finest climate in the world; neither too hot nor too cold, and always clear; you are with the gayest people living; be gay with them, and do not wear out your eyes with reading at home. 'L'ennui' is the English distemper: and a very bad one it is, as I find by every day's experience; for my deafness deprives me of the only rational pleasure that I can have at my age, which is society; so that I read my eyes out every day, that I may not hang myself.

You will not be in this parliament, at least not at the beginning of it. I relied too much upon Lord C――'s promise above a year ago at Bath. He desired that I would leave it to him; that he would make it his own affair, and give it in charge to the Duke of G――, whose province it was to make the parliamentary arrangement. This I depended upon, and I think with reason; but, since that, Lord C has neither seen nor spoken to anybody, and has been in the oddest way in the world. I have sent to the D――of G――, to know if L――C――had either spoken or sent to him about it; but he assured me that he had done neither; that all was full, or rather running over, at present; but that, if he could crowd you in upon a vacancy, he would do it with great pleasure. I am extremely sorry for this accident; for I am of a very different opinion from you, about being in parliament, as no man can be of consequence in this country, who is not in it; and, though one may not speak like a Lord Mansfield or a Lord Chatham, one may make a very good figure in a second rank. 'Locus est et pluribus umbris'. I do not pretend to give you any account of the present state of this country, or Ministry, not knowing nor guessing it myself.

God bless you, and send you health, which is the first and greatest of all blessings!

LETTER CCCVIII

LONDON, March 15, 1768.

MY DEAR FRIEND: This letter is supplemental to my last. This morning Lord Weymouth very civilly sent Mr. Wood, his first 'commis', to tell me that the King very willingly gave you leave of absence from your post for a year, for the recovery of your health; but then added, that as the Court of Vienna was tampering with that of Saxony, which it seems our Court is desirous to 'contrequarrer', it might be necessary to have in the interim a 'Charge d'Affaires' at Dresden, with a defalcation out of your appointments of forty shillings a-day, till your return, if I would agree to it. I told him that I consented to both the proposals, upon condition that at your return you should have the character and the pay of Plenipotentiary added to your present character and pay; and that I would completely make up to you the defalcation of the forty shillings a-day. He positively engaged for it: and added, that he knew that it would be willingly agreed to. Thus I think I have made a good bargain for you, though but an indifferent one for myself: but that is what I never minded in my life. You may, therefore, depend upon receiving from me the full of this defalcation, when and how you please, independently of your usual annual refreshment, which I will pay to Monsieur Larpent, whenever you desire it. In the meantime, 'Cura ut valeas'.

The person whom Mr. Wood intimated to me would be the 'Charge d'Affaires' during your absence, is one Mr. Keith, the son of that Mr. Keith who was formerly Minister in Russia.

LETTER CCCIX

LONDON, April 12, 1768.

MY DEAR FRIEND: I received, yesterday, your letter of the 1st; in which you do not mention the state of your health, which I desire you will do for the future.

I believe you have guessed the true reason of Mr. Keith's mission; but by a whisper that I have since heard, Keith is rather inclined to go to Turin, as 'Charge d'Affaires'. I forgot to tell you, in my last, that I was almost positively assured that the instant you return to Dresden, Keith should decamp. I am persuaded that they will keep their words with me, as there is no one reason in the world why they should not. I will send your annual to Mr. Larpent, in a fortnight, and pay the forty shillings a-day quarterly, if there should be occasion; for, in my own private opinion, there will be no 'Charge d'Affaires' sent. I agree with you, that 'point d'argent, point d'Allemand', as was used to be said, and not without more reason, of the Swiss; but, as we have neither the inclination nor I fear the power to give subsidies, the Court of Vienna can give good things that cost them nothing, as archbishoprics, bishoprics, besides corrupting their ministers and favorite with places.

Elections here have been carried to a degree of frenzy hitherto unheard of; that for the town of Northampton has cost the contending parties at least thirty thousand pounds a side, and——————-has sold his borough of————-, to two members, for nine thousand pounds. As soon as Wilkes had lost his election for the city, he set up for the county of Middlesex, and carried it hollow, as the jockeys say. Here were great mobs and riots upon that occasion, and most of the windows in town broke, that had no lights for WILKES AND LIBERTY, who were thought to be inseparable. He will appear, the 10th of this month, in the Court of King's Bench, to receive his sentence; and then great riots are again expected, and probably will happen. God bless you!

LETTER CCCX

BATH, October 17, 1768.

MY DEAR FRIEND. Your last two letters, to myself and Grevenkop, have alarmed me extremely; but I comfort myself a little, by hoping that you, like all people who suffer, think yourself worse than you are. A dropsy never comes so suddenly; and I flatter myself, that it is only that gouty or rheumatic humor, which has plagued you so long, that has occasioned the temporary swelling of your legs. Above forty years ago, after a violent fever, my legs swelled as much as you describe yours to be; I immediately thought that I had a dropsy; but the Faculty assured me, that my complaint was only the effect of my fever, and would soon be cured; and they said true. Pray let your amanuensis, whoever he may be, write an account regularly once a-week, either to Grevenkop or myself, for that is the same thing, of the state of your health.

I sent you, in four successive letters, as much of the Duchess of Somerset's snuff as a letter could well convey to you. Have you received all or any of them? and have they done you any good? Though, in your present condition, you cannot go into company, I hope that you have some acquaintances that come and sit with you; for if originally it was not good for man to be alone, it is much worse for a sick man to be so; he thinks too much of his distemper, and magnifies it. Some men of learning among the ecclesiastics, I dare say, would be glad to sit with you; and you could give them as good as they brought.

Poor Harte, who is here still, is in a most miserable condition: he has entirely lost the use of his left side, and can hardly speak intelligibly. I was with him yesterday. He inquired after you with great affection, and was in the utmost concern when I showed him your letter.

My own health is as it has been ever since I was here last year. I am neither well nor ill, but UNWELL. I have in a manner lost the use of my legs; for though I can make a shift to crawl upon even ground for a quarter of an hour, I cannot go up or down stairs, unless supported by a servant. God bless you and grant you a speedy recovery!

NOTE.—This is the last of the letters of Lord Chesterfield to his son, Mr. Philip Stanhope, who died in November, 1768. The unexpected and distressing intelligence was announced by the lady to whom Mr. Stanhope had been married for several years, unknown to his father. On learning that the widow had two sons, the issue of this marriage, Lord Chesterfield took upon himself the maintenance of his

grandchildren. The letters which follow show how happily the writer

adapted himself to the trying situation.

Made in the USA
San Bernardino, CA
27 May 2018